DICTIONARY
OF
AMERICAN
MILITARY
BIOGRAPHY

DICTIONARY
OF
AMERICAN
MILITARY
BIOGRAPHY

Volume II
H–P

ROGER J. SPILLER
Editor
JOSEPH G. DAWSON III
Associate Editor
T. HARRY WILLIAMS
Consulting Editor

Greenwood Press
Westport, Connecticut • London, England

Library of Congress Cataloging in Publication Data

Main entry under title:

Dictionary of American military biography.

  Includes index.
  Contents: v. 1. Creighton W. Abrams—Leslie R.
Groves—v. 2. Henry W. Halleck—Israel Putnam—
v. 3. John A. Quitman—Elmo R. Zumwalt, Jr.
  1. United States—Armed Forces—Biography. 2. United
States—Biography. I. Spiller, Roger J. II. Dawson,
Joseph G., 1945-
U52.D53   1984   355'.0092'2 [B]   83-12674
ISBN 0-313-21433-6 (lib. bdg. : set)
ISBN 0-313-24161-9 (lib. bdg. : v. 1)
ISBN 0-313-24162-7 (lib. bdg. : v. 2)
ISBN 0-313-24399-9 (lib. bdg. : v. 3)

Library of Congress Catalog Card Number: 83-12674
ISBN 0-313-21433-6 (lib. bdg. : set)

First published in 1984

Greenwood Press
A division of Congressional Information Service, Inc.
88 Post Road West, Westport, Connecticut 06881

Printed in the United States of America

10 9 8 7 6 5 4 3 2 1

Contents

H

HALLECK, Henry Wager (b. Westernville, N.Y., January 16, 1815; d. Louisville, Ky., January 9, 1872), Army officer and military intellectual. Halleck served as general in chief and chief of staff of the Union armies during the Civil War.

Born in Oneida County of generally prosperous, old New York farming families, Halleck disliked farming and to escape it ran away to live with his maternal grandfather, Henry Wager. Wager, a friend of Frederic William Steuben* (Baron von), adopted the boy and financed his schooling at Hudson Academy. Halleck went on to Union College, where he was elected to Phi Beta Kappa and received the A.B. degree in 1837, two years after he left the college for West Point. In 1839 Halleck was graduated from the Military Academy third in a class of thirty-one and was commissioned second lieutenant in the Corps of Engineers. As the favorite student of Dennis Hart Mahan,* Halleck had taught classes while still a cadet and after graduation was appointed assistant professor of engineering. The next year he became an assistant to the Board of Engineers for Atlantic Coast Defences, contributing a *Report on the Means of National Defence* (28th Congress, 2d Session, *Senate Executive Document No. 85*). Following this acquaintance with the overall planning of coastal fortifications, Halleck did practical work on the defenses of New York Harbor, where he served from 1840 to 1844. He toured European fortifications, returning to resume his work at New York in 1845.

Halleck united to his growing mastery of military engineering a broad study of European literature on military policy, strategy, and tactics. While still a first lieutenant—he was commissioned in that rank on January 1, 1845—he was invited to deliver a series of lectures on military topics before the Lowell Institute of Boston late in 1845. In 1846 the lectures were published as *Elements of Military Art and Science; or, Course of Instruction in Strategy, Fortification, Tactics of Battles, &c.* This book, which was to appear in 1862 in a third edition with comments on the Mexican and Crimean Wars during the Civil War, would alone assure Halleck a major place in the history of American military thought.

It was the first comprehensive study of the military art by an American author, encompassing in addition to the subjects enumerated in the title a moral apology for war, logistics, military education, and American military policy, all approached from a historical perspective. Although Halleck disclaimed originality and critics have sometimes dismissed the book as a mere paraphrase of Antoine Henri Jomini, the work surpasses its author's modest assessment. Halleck's *Elements of Military Art and Science* is an early flowering of the professional and intellectual approach to officership nourished by the West Point of Sylvanus Thayer* and Dennis Hart Mahan.

After the outbreak of the war with Mexico, Halleck left New York for Monterey, California. He occupied the six-month sailing trip translating Jomini's *Vie politique et militaire de Napoléon*; the translation was published in four volumes in 1864. Halleck and his fellow passengers, including Lieutenant William Tecumseh Sherman,* reached California too late to participate in the conquest of the territory. Halleck prepared defensive works against counterattacks as far south as the Mexican west coast port of Mazatlán, and he was sufficiently involved in the backwash of the fighting to win a brevet as captain. His meritorious service included administrative achievements as secretary of state to the military government of California. Halleck also participated in the 1849 convention that drew up the constitution under which California was admitted to statehood. Following various staff postings in California, Halleck in 1853 returned to his first expertise to plan and construct Pacific Coast fortifications. He was commissioned captain on July 1, 1853.

Halleck had begun reading law early in his military career, and his involvement in creating civil government in California stimulated his interest in the law. A legal career in the new state, where he was an influential figure, obviously offered more encouraging prospects for advancement than the peacetime Army. In 1849 he helped found the San Francisco law firm of Halleck, Peachy and Billings, and on August 1, 1854, he resigned his commission to give full time to the firm. On April 10, 1855, he married Elizabeth Hamilton, grand-daughter of Alexander Hamilton. A scholar as well as a practitioner in the law as in the Army, Halleck established a major reputation as a jurist with his synthesis, *International Law, or Rules Regulating the Intercourse of States in Peace and War* (1861; new edition 1908).

It testifies to the eminence of "Old Brains" Halleck as a citizen as well as a soldier that President Abraham Lincoln* appointed him on August 19, 1861, as one of the few full major generals of the Regular Army at the beginning of the Civil War. Two months later, on November 18, Halleck succeeded John Charles Frémont* in command of the Department of the Missouri, with headquarters at St. Louis and encompassing Illinois, Iowa, Minnesota, Wisconsin, Missouri, and Arkansas, as well as Kentucky west of the Cumberland River. The administrative capacity that Halleck had displayed in California served well to restore good order to the command which Frémont had left in an administrative shambles. Halleck probably arrived too late to be successful in restoring a larger kind of law, order, and loyalty to the Union in Missouri. He received partially merited credit, however, for the successes of his subordinate Ulysses Simpson Grant* at Forts Henry and Donelson. In March 1862 the credit became tangible with the extension of his command, as the Department of the Mississippi, to include in addition to his old department the Department of Kansas to the west and the area eastward as far as a north-south line through Knoxville, Tennessee. Halleck coordinated the movement of the armies under Grant and Don Carlos Buell* in the offensive that led to the Battle of Shiloh. Halleck then took personal command of these armies, and another under John Pope,* for the campaign to complete the conquest of western Tennessee down to the Memphis and Charleston Railroad by taking Corinth, Mississippi. Corinth fell to Halleck on June 10, 1862.

The cautious pace that characterized the drive against Corinth after Halleck took the field might have raised doubts about "Old Brains' " vigor and resolution in the face of direct responsibility for combat. Nevertheless, Union victories in Halleck's department so exceeded progress elsewhere that on July 11, 1862, Lincoln appointed Halleck general in chief of the armies of the United States. Halleck chose to make this command mainly one for the exercise of his administrative talents, rather than a strategic headquarters. He coordinated communications between the widespread Union armies and the War Department, and served as a useful liaison between President Lincoln and Secretary of War Edwin McMasters Stanton* on the one hand and the generals in the field on the other. Knowing at first hand both the military and the political worlds, he could better make the wishes and anxieties of each understandable to the other. But Halleck did not produce the coherent direction of the war for which Lincoln had hoped. Whenever possible, he avoided responsibility for decisions that might involve risks.

Coherent strategic direction awaited Halleck's supercession by Grant on March 9, 1864. Because Grant desired to campaign with the Army of the Potomac while also commanding the overall war effort, he retained Halleck in Washington in the new post of chief of staff of the Army to continue serving as coordinator of communications. This post of administration without pressing responsibility was altogether appropriate to both the strengths and the weaknesses Halleck had demonstrated throughout the war, as well as to his scholarly knowledge of military procedures.

After Robert Edward Lee* surrendered in April 1865, Grant transferred Halleck to another appropriate post, command of the Military Division of the James with charge over the initial reconstruction of Virginia. Halleck offended Sherman and to some degree Grant by his brusque intervention from Richmond to overrule Sherman's initially generous surrender terms to Joseph Eggleston Johnston.* In August Halleck was shifted to the less sensitive Division of the Pacific, where he remained far from the turmoil of Reconstruction for four years. In July 1869 he returned east to head the Division of the South. By this time, the vindictiveness toward the South that had influenced Halleck's quarrel with Sherman had cooled, and Halleck was inclined to believe that using military force in the South simply stirred up resentments creating an occasion for yet more application of force. Halleck died in 1872 with the issues of Reconstruction still unresolved.

An unprepossessing, paunchy, rather pop-eyed man without personal warmth, Halleck had few friends and could readily emerge from the Civil War a scapegoat for all sorts of things that went wrong during the nearly two years when he commanded the Union armies or even in his year as chief of staff. His reputation as a Civil War military commander is probably lower than it ought to be. Despite his shying away from responsibility, certain strategic achievements stand to his credit. He helped conceive the Henry-Donelson Campaign and generally encouraged Grant throughout it, Grant's later testimony to the contrary notwithstanding. The larger conception of moving up the Tennessee River as an avenue toward breaking the Confederacy's best lateral line of communication, the Memphis and Charleston Railroad, was to a major degree Halleck's. He displayed moral courage when he first assumed the office of general in chief by deciding promptly to withdraw George Brinton McClellan's* army from the Virginia Peninsula, on the ground that nothing more could be expected from it there; this decision meant accepting at least the appearance of a severe setback at the outset of Halleck's command. Despite the tendency of his writings toward a conservative, limited style of war, Halleck contributed to the design of campaigns led by Sherman and Philip Henry Sheridan* in Georgia, the Carolinas, and the Shenandoah Valley to destroy Confederate economic resources and morale, reaching for decisive objectives beyond the enemy armies.

Meanwhile, Halleck's administrative accomplishments remained consistently impressive, though it is misleading to interpret him as a forerunner of the twentieth-century Army chiefs of staff. His offices and his conduct of them were different from the chief professional post as designed by Elihu Root.* The Civil War command system among Stanton, Grant, and Halleck functioned not as a model of military organization in a democracy but as a triumph of individuals over illogical organization charts.

Halleck was not always as generous and adaptable as when he stepped down from command of the armies to be chief of staff under Grant. His pettiness toward Sherman had been foreshadowed by his jealous efforts to slow Grant's rise to prominence during and just after the Shiloh Campaign. His moral qualities did not consistently equal his military brain. But in the scholarly products of his brain, he left enduring monuments. His *Elements of Military Art and Science* makes Halleck, along with Dennis Hart Mahan, one of the two founders of American professional military scholarship and thought.

BIBLIOGRAPHY

Ambrose, Stephen E. *Halleck: Lincoln's Chief of Staff.* Baton Rouge: Louisiana State University Press, 1960.
Grant, Ulysses S. *Personal Memoirs of U. S. Grant.* 2 vols. New York: Webster, 1885.
Thomas, Benjamin P., and Harold M. Hyman. *Stanton: The Life and Times of Lincoln's Secretary of War.* New York: Alfred A. Knopf, 1962.

Weigley, Russell F. *Towards an American Army: Military Thought from Washington to Marshall*. New York: Columbia University Press, 1962.
Williams, Kenneth P. *Lincoln Finds a General: A Military Study of the Civil War*. 5 vols. New York: Macmillan Company, 1950–1959.

RUSSELL F. WEIGLEY

HALSEY, William Frederick, Jr. (b. Elizabeth, N.J., October 30, 1882; d. Fishers Island, N.Y., August 16, 1959), naval officer. Halsey was a fleet commander in the Pacific during World War II.

William F. Halsey, Jr., came from a long line of seafarers. Halsey's father, a Naval Academy man, class of 1873, retired from the service with the rank of captain. Young Halsey entered the Academy in 1900, stood in the middle of his class academically, and played football on an often defeated Navy team. Following graduation in 1904, Ensign Halsey served in the battleship *Kansas* when it steamed around the world as part of President Theodore Roosevelt's* Great White Fleet. In December 1909 he married Frances Cooke Grandy.

Soon after the United States entered World War I, Commander Halsey joined the American Destroyer Force based at Queenstown, Ireland, commanding the *Benham* and then the *Shaw*. For his services during the war, Halsey was awarded the Navy Cross. After World War I, Halsey held various assignments, including stints at the Naval War College at Newport, Rhode Island, and the Army War College in Washington, D.C., spending most of his sea time on destroyers.

Subsequently, Halsey's career was oriented toward aircraft carriers. After training at Pensacola and qualifying as a pilot in the spring of 1935 at the age of fifty-two, he commanded the carrier *Saratoga*. He then became commandant of the Pensacola Naval Air Station and later, alternately commanded both U.S. Navy carrier divisions. In the spring of 1940, the Navy Department designated Halsey as commander, Aircraft Battle Force, with the rank of vice admiral, commanding all the carriers of the Pacific Fleet.

On December 7, 1941, Halsey with his force, including the *Enterprise*, three cruisers, and nine destroyers, was 150 miles west of Oahu when the Japanese struck Pearl Harbor. Refueling at Pearl Harbor, the *Enterprise* sortied before dawn on December 9 with orders to hunt down enemy submarines. Meanwhile, Admiral Chester William Nimitz* had relieved Admiral Husband Edward Kimmel* as commander in chief, Pacific Fleet. In late January 1942 Nimitz decided to send a carrier force, commanded by Halsey, to strike the Japanese bases in the Marshall Islands. Although the results proved meager, the carrier force gained valuable combat experience. After leading his campaign against the heart of the Japanese defenses in the Central Pacific, Halsey was suddenly acclaimed the nation's first naval hero of the war.

Soon after returning to Pearl Harbor, Halsey's force was ordered to carry the B-25 bombers of Colonel James Harold Doolittle* across the Pacific to within striking range of Tokyo. Doolittle and his men delivered their blow on April

18, 1942, causing little damage, but the news that Tokyo had actually been bombed lifted American morale.

Halsey fell ill in May 1942, and, much to his disgust, he was unable to command the American forces against the Japanese in the Battle of Midway. Instead, Raymond Ames Spruance* served as commander. Fully recovered in early fall, Halsey became commander of the South Pacific Force in mid-October 1942.

Although the U.S. Marines had landed on Guadalcanal in August, the Japanese Navy still commanded the sea in the southern Solomon Islands. Halsey infused the American forces in the South Pacific with new confidence, and after several battles, his ships became more adept at night fighting and destroying enemy planes. Simultaneously, Marine and Army units on Guadalcanal began consistently defeating the enemy. The Japanese evacuated Guadalcanal on February 9, 1943.

As a part of the push toward the Philippines, three naval actions in the Solomons during July 1943 won control of surrounding waters, and on August 5, 1943, the XIV Corps captured Munda Field in New Georgia. The essence of Halsey's strategy had been to bypass the principal Japanese strongpoints, including Rabaul, sealing them off with sea and air power, leaving their garrisons stranded, while the Allies constructed new air and naval bases in some less strongly defended spots several hundred miles nearer to Japan. Subsequently, on November 5 and 11 carrier-based planes pounded Rabaul, and, day by day, bombers based on Bougainville continued the work of wearing away the enemy air forces. By March 25, 1944, Rabaul was neutralized. The war in the South Pacific had ended.

After conferring with naval brass in Pearl Harbor, San Francisco, and Washington, Halsey and his Third Fleet steamed out of Pearl Harbor on August 24, 1944, to cooperate with the forces under General Douglas MacArthur* and Admiral Thomas Cassin Kinkaid* in the invasion of the Philippines. On October 20 American forces sloshed ashore on Leyte Island. In response, the Japanese high command decided to commit the entire Imperial Fleet to defeat American naval forces at Leyte and isolate MacArthur. Japan divided its fleet into three separate units. The Southern Force of battleships and cruisers was to maneuver through Surigao Strait, break into Leyte Gulf at daybreak on October 25, and rendezvous with the powerful Center Force, which was to move through San Bernardino Strait and come around Samar from the north. The Japanese Northern Force, built around four carriers, was to lure Halsey's Task Force 38, the American carrier force, northward, away from Leyte Gulf.

As the battle was joined, Kinkaid deployed almost every battleship, cruiser, and destroyer to catch the Southern Force as it came through Surigao Strait in the early hours of October 25. The high-caliber fire of the American unit sank several enemy ships and sent the rest of the Southern Force fleeing. Japan's massive Center Force had been damaged and delayed by American aircraft in the Sibuyan Sea on October 24. Halsey overestimated the damage that his bombers had inflicted. After his search planes discovered the Northern Force of carriers coming down from Japan, Halsey chose to move his force north and sink the carriers, not even leaving a destroyer to guard San Bernardino Strait.

The Center Force left the strait unopposed and approached the northern entrance of Leyte Gulf undetected. Off the island of Samar the Japanese attacked Kinkaid's escort carriers. The ensuing battle was perhaps the most gallant action in naval history, and the bloodiest. As the Japanese had no air support, the Americans were able to defeat a fleet that had more than ten times their firepower.

Up north in the battle off Cape Engano, Halsey's planes sank all four enemy carriers. The battle for Leyte Gulf on October 25, 1944, left the U.S. Navy in command of Philippine waters. Never again could the Japanese fleet mount an effective offensive. However, Halsey was severely criticized for dividing his forces and leaving Leyte beachhead open to enemy naval attack. Controversy has continued to surround Halsey's handling of his force at Leyte Gulf.

In the last months of the war, Halsey's forces launched strikes over other Philippine islands, Formosa, Okinawa, and Japanese installations on the China coast. In the summer of 1945 Halsey's Third Fleet conducted air raids against Tokyo and nearby naval installations. In August 1945 American bombers dropped atomic bombs on Hiroshima and Nagasaki with devastating effect. Japan's leaders, recognizing that their country faced certain destruction, surrendered unconditionally on August 14. The official surrender took place on September 2 on board Halsey's flagship, *Missouri*, anchored in Tokyo Bay.

In November 1945 at San Pedro, California, Halsey hauled down his four star flag and turned over command of his fleet to Rear Admiral Howard Kingman. A month later Halsey was promoted to five star rank, fleet admiral of the U.S. Navy.

After retiring in 1947, Halsey refought the Battle of Leyte Gulf with his critics, managed the University of Virginia's Development Fund, and made goodwill tours to South America and Australia.

Halsey was a risk-taker who welcomed hazardous missions. For years before World War II he had been an apostle of naval air power, touting its importance, its effectiveness, its flexibility. He argued that airplanes could bring the battleground into "streets and gardens far removed from the scene of a formalized surface engagement." In the kind of war that the vast expanses of the Pacific dictated, strong, fast carrier forces were indispensable since they could strike at long range. Halsey displayed a shrewd confidence in the extremely mobile fast carrier task force, appraising it as a force that could gain command of the air at a required time and place to establish the conditions necessary for amphibious operations.

To this day students of naval history have refought the Battle of Leyte Gulf. Was Halsey right in steaming off to destroy enemy carriers, or did he leave Admiral Kinkaid in the lurch? Halsey insisted that his decision to move north was correct. If the Center Force did steam through San Bernardino Strait, it could at best, Halsey believed, "merely hit and run."

Admiral Halsey was not one of the Navy's intellectuals. His official reports are couched in the commonplace. His speeches, private correspondence, and reports reveal that he often thought in clichés and that his vocabulary was narrow. Despite his shortcomings, he had the knack of appointing extremely intelligent officers to his staff upon whom he relied for decision-making. Only on rare occasions did he overrule them.

"Another of Halsey's traits," remembered a staff member, "was the fierceness with which he defended his staff, even his men. He gave them credit for the victories won, he blamed himself for the losses."

"Halsey possessed to a magnificent degree," said a naval commander, "the intuition that let him know just how to get the best out of his people under any conditions."

"Admiral Halsey's strongest point," wrote another staff officer, "was his superb leadership. While always the true professional and exacting professional performances from all his subordinates, he had a charismatic effect on them which was like being touched by a magic wand. Anyone so touched was determined to excel."

Admiral Raymond Spruance described Halsey as "a grand man to be with," a "splendid seaman," able to "smack them [the enemy] hard every time he gets a chance."

Halsey may well have been America's most colorful and most famous admiral.

BIBLIOGRAPHY

Halsey, William F., and J. Bryan III. *Admiral Halsey's Story*. New York: McGraw-Hill, 1947.
Merrill, James M. *A Sailor's Admiral: A Biography of William F. Halsey*. New York: Thomas Y. Crowell, 1976.
Morison, Samuel E. *History of United States Naval Operations in World War II*. 15 vols. Boston: Atlantic, Little, Brown, 1947–1962.
Potter, E. B., ed. *Sea Power: A Naval History*. Englewood Cliffs, N.J.: Prentice-Hall, 1960.

JAMES M. MERRILL

HAMMOND, William Alexander (b. Annapolis, Md., August 28, 1828; d. Washington, D.C., January 5, 1900), Army surgeon general. Hammond is considered one of the pioneers of American neurology and an expert in military medical administration.

Hammond's early education was in the Harrisburg, Pennsylvania, area where his family moved in 1832. At the age of sixteen he began the study of medicine, attended the Medical Department of the University of the City of New York, and was graduated in 1848. He spent the next year at Pennsylvania Hospital in Philadelphia.

In June 1849 Hammond was appointed an assistant surgeon in the Army. He accompanied troops to New Mexico, where he engaged in field operations for three years. To recuperate from this service, he took a leave of absence and traveled to Europe using his time to study and observe medical practices and hospitals. Upon his return to the United States, he devoted his spare time to the study of his own physiology and physiological chemistry which resulted in several papers, one of which earned him the American Medical Association Prize in 1857. His writings garnered him professional recognition outside of the Army and led to offers to teach in medical schools.

Hammond was stationed at West Point and then transferred to Fort Meade, Florida, joining troops campaigning against the Seminoles. His next post was Fort Riley, Kansas, where he campaigned against the Sioux. His last station was Fort Mackinac, Michigan, where he resigned his commission in October 1860 to accept the Chair of Anatomy and Physiology at the University of Maryland in Baltimore.

At the outbreak of the Civil War, Hammond resigned his professorship and applied for a commission in the Army. Accepted as an assistant surgeon, he was assigned the task of organizing hospitals in Hagerstown, Frederick, and Baltimore, Maryland, and was then transferred to Wheeling, West Virginia, as medical inspector of camps and hospitals. His skill as an organizer and administrator was revealed during this period. When Surgeon General Clement Finley was forced to resign by Secretary of War Edwin McMasters Stanton,* the U.S. Sanitary Commission began a search for someone who could reorganize the poorly administered Medical Department. They were so impressed with Hammond's reputation in medical circles and his administrative ability that they actively lobbied to have President Abraham Lincoln* appoint him Army surgeon general. Lincoln agreed and appointed Hammond in the spring of 1862.

Hammond did not disappoint the members of the commission. The change in the department was immediate; its efficiency and morale showed marked improvement. He redesigned the military hospital, creating a ''pavilion'' type which resulted in a substantially lower mortality rate. He established the Army Medical Museum and laid the groundwork for the *Medical and Surgical History of the War of the Rebellion.* By establishing permanent boards of examination, he improved the quality of surgeons and he enforced rigid standards of excellence. He revised the supply table several times and enforced a strict accountability, made available a liberal supply of medical books and journals, established a new and complete system of hospital reports, commissioned volumes on gunshot wounds, camp diseases, and administration, and wrote a comprehensive volume on military hygiene himself. Hammond systematized the employment of female nurses and established medical laboratories to obtain high-quality medicines at modest cost. He supported Jonathan Letterman,* who reorganized the medical system in the Army of the Potomac, and encouraged other Union armies to adopt Letterman's methods. He tried to attain autonomy for the Medical Department in the construction of hospitals and the transportation of supplies.

Because of a personality conflict with Stanton, however, many of Hammond's ideas for the improvement of medical service were postponed, including the creation of a permanent Medical Department enlisted force, an ambulance corps, an army medical school, a separate Army medical library, and a permanent general hospital in Washington. Hammond's assertive personality clashed with Stanton's peremptory character, and in August 1863 Hammond was relieved of his duties. A year later a court-martial dismissed him from the Army. In 1878 Congress approved a bill to have the president investigate the verdict and either confirm it or set it aside. Hammond was cleared and placed on the retired list as a brigadier general.

Hammond's court-martial exhausted him physically and financially, but the same qualities that made him a great surgeon general served him well in building a practice and reputation in neurology, a field in which he was self-taught. Within ten years of his dismissal he had become one of the foremost specialists in America. He was appointed a lecturer on neurology successively at the College of Physicians and Surgeons, the Bellevue Hospital Medical College, and the University of the City of New York. Seeing a need for postgraduate medical education, he assisted in founding the New York Post-Graduate Medical School and Hospital. During his career he also edited six professional journals. Hammond's practice became enormous and lucrative, and he returned to Washington in 1888, establishing a practice and a sanitarium.

Hammond's medical achievements alone would mark him as a man of prominence, but he was also famous in areas outside of medicine. His romantic novels placed him as one of the period's most talented authors in this genre. He was an enthusiastic naturalist, collecting specimens of the flora, fauna, geology, and native culture at each post where he was stationed. Like so many other surgeons, Hammond became an able amateur ornithologist, "Hammond's flycatcher" being named for him. His search for knowledge bordered on the compulsive, and he was indefatigable in its pursuit.

Hammond was recognized more as a leader in physiology and neurology than as a brilliant chief of the Army Medical Department. His great intelligence, unstinting devotion to the soldier, powerful drive, and the ability to see the whole rather than the parts made him one of the best surgeons general, however. His drive and constant refusal to compromise or to go through channels when a direct route was quicker proved to be his downfall. Although serving for only a brief time, he faced and solved the problems of changing an ultraconservative, tradition-bound department to meet the unprecedented challenges of war, overcoming obstacles that would have defeated lesser men. His policies and actions, both those carried out and those proposed, set the tone of the operation of the U.S. Army Medical Department for the remainder of the Civil War.

BIBLIOGRAPHY

Adams, George W. *Doctors in Blue: The Medical History of the Union Army in the Civil War*. New York: Henry Schuman, 1952.

Kelly, Howard Atwood, ed. *A Cyclopedia of American Medical Biography*. Vol. 1. Philadelphia: W. B. Saunders Company, 1912.

*A Memorial Meeting on February 23, 1900, in Honor of the Late Surgeon-General,
   William A. Hammond, M.D.* New York: New York Post-Graduate Medical School
   and Hospital, 1900.
Pilcher, James Evelyn. *The Surgeon Generals of the Army of the United States of America.*
   Carlisle, Pa.: Association of Military Surgeons, 1905.

DWIGHT OLAND

HAMPTON, Wade (b. Halifax county, Va., c. 1751, d. Columbia, S.C.,
February 4, 1835), major general, War of 1812.

Wade Hampton, the third son of a Virginia frontiersman, acquired only the
rudiments of a formal education in his youth. Like many another frontier youngsters he was brought up to labor in the fields. Hampton's father, a "flax-breaker"
by trade, gradually drifted south from Virginia, settling finally in Spartanburg,
South Carolina, in 1774. Two years later he, his wife, a son, and a grandson
were killed by Cherokee Indians. Five other sons survived, however, and all of
them later served as American officers in the Revolution.

Wade Hampton was a latecomer to the patriot cause. He still declared himself
a loyal subject of the Crown in September 1780, but six months later, and for
reasons best known to himself, he had a change of heart. Joining the command
of General Thomas Sumter on April 2, 1780, Hampton was commissioned
colonel of cavalry. In this capacity he served creditably, if not brilliantly, for
the remainder of the war, rendering his greatest service at the Battle of Eutaw
Springs in September 1781.

Acumen as a military leader, as later events would prove, was not Hampton's
forte. His skills lay in quite another direction: making money. And in this field
he acknowledged few peers. Resourceful, energetic, imaginative, farsighted—
and not overly scrupulous—Hampton pursued and amassed wealth with fanatical
zeal. Indeed, he acquired land and slaves on such a colossal scale that his fortune
became the touchstone for several generations of lesser Southern grandees. Profiting equally from shrewd marriages—three over the course of eighteen years,
all to socially well-connected women—and even shrewder investments—he figured prominently in several Yazoo Land Company speculations. By the time of
his death, Hampton was reputedly the wealthiest planter in America. His domains
included several plantations in South Carolina, as well as sugar plantations on
the lower Mississippi.

Hampton also prospered in the political realm, albeit not as spectacularly.
From 1782 to 1794 he served in a variety of local and statewide posts: member
of the state legislature, justice of the peace for Richland county, sheriff of Camden
District, and, as a decided anti-Federalist, member of the convention that ratified
the Constitution. Nominally a Democrat but not ill-disposed towards some Federalist measures, Hampton served twice in the national House of Representatives
(1795–1797, 1803–1805), failing of reelection after both terms. In 1801 he was
a presidential elector on the Jefferson-Burr ticket.

With war threatening, Hampton reentered the Army in October 1808 at the rank of colonel. Promoted to brigadier general the following February, Hampton succeeded General James Wilkinson* as commander of the New Orleans garrison in December 1809. Appalled by the wretched condition of the Army, he alerted Washington, an act that not only prompted a congressional investigation into the mortality rates of the Army in Louisiana, but also earned Hampton Wilkinson's undying enmity.

Hampton remained in Louisiana until May 1812, when he assumed command of the fortifications at Norfolk. Advanced to the rank of major general on March 2, 1813, he took command of the Army on Lake Champlain in July. A few days later Wilkinson was appointed district commander, thus becoming Hampton's immediate superior. Hampton agreed to serve under Wilkinson only on the condition that his be treated as a separate command, with orders directly from the War Department. The loathing the two men entertained for one another, not to mention their equally mutual incompetence, virtually guaranteed the failure of the ensuing campaign.

Theoretically, the four thousand-man force that Hampton led from Plattsburgh to the Canadian border on September 19, 1813, formed the eastern wing of a concerted two-pronged assault on Montreal. Actually, Hampton operated alone. The other American force under Wilkinson started its descent of the St. Lawrence late, moved slowly, and was severely trounced at Chrysler's Farm on November 11. By that time Hampton's campaign had also ended.

After a long march—he swung forty miles westward after encountering drought conditions to his north—and almost a month's inactivity at his base at Four Corners on the Chateaugay River, Hampton finally met the enemy fifteen miles north of his base on October 26. The following skirmish, the so-called Battle of Chateaugay, was Hampton's first and last engagement of the war. A small but strongly positioned force of Canadian militia made a shambles of Hampton's battle plan. Believing himself outnumbered, out of forage, and in total ignorance of Wilkinson's whereabouts, Hampton immediately fell back on Four Corners. Ignoring Wilkinson's preemptory orders to join forces with him, he retired to Plattsburgh on November 11, 1813.

A disgusted Hampton tendered his resignation on November 1, 1813; it was accepted the following May. His last service to the Army was presiding over the court-martial of General William Hull.* After the war Hampton devoted himself exclusively to planting.

With good reason Wade Hampton is a sixth magnitude star in the galaxy of American military luminaries. With all the faults of a typical Southern planter baron—pride, sensitivity, irritability, harshness, and (some said) an overfondness for alcohol—he lacked compensating virtues as a soldier. A spirit of subordination was foreign to him, as was aggressiveness. His habit of meticulous preparation and glacial movement cloaked a basic indecisiveness in his nature. Moreover, Hampton was green. Although he had exhibited commendable pluck at Eutaw Springs during the Revolution, holding up the left wing of a swiftly crumbling line, he had garnered little military experience beyond administration since then. Hampton owed his rapid rise during the War of 1812 to his friends in the capital, President James Madison not least among them. In short, Hampton was a "political" general: his military prominence was in no way attributable to either ability or experience.

For all his failings, Hampton possessed a soul of honor. He recognized Wilkinson for what he was: an unprincipled scoundrel and a contemptible opportunist. Nonetheless, he accepted his duty and agreed to submit to Wilkinson should their commands ever be joined. He realized the value of training, and he imposed a rigorous regimen on the raw militia force committed to his care in 1813.

His ineptness aside, Hampton was more a victim of circumstances than anything else. The Montreal Campaign was the creature of John Armstrong, Jr.,* a secretary of war who also fancied himself a field general. He and Wilkinson, after much time-wasting discussion and without consulting Hampton, had formulated strategy. Instead of attending to coordinating the movements of the two armies as he had led Hampton to believe he would, Armstrong returned to Washington. Undertaken as a Canadian winter set in, with forces too meager and ill-prepared to achieve its objective, and commanded by generals who despised each other, the campaign was foredoomed to fail, a fact that escaped none of the leaders involved. Intent on avoiding blame for the predictable fiasco, Armstrong, having set the campaign in motion, abandoned it to its fate. On October 25, one week after ordering Hampton north and before either army had met the enemy, the secretary directed the erection of winter quarters for the troops.

Given the incapacity of his chief subordinates—another of his liabilities—and his ignorance of the terrain, Hampton's battle plan at Chateaugay, which called for simultaneous frontal and flanking attacks, was far too ambitious. It would have mattered little, however, had he won the engagement. A thousand of his New York militia had refused to cross into Canada, and his supplies were almost depleted. Wilkinson's force, buffeted by severe weather, had as yet to embark on its own inglorious march. Its commander, however, determined to exert his own authority, ordered Hampton to join forces with him and to bring three months' supplies for the entire army (approximately thirteen thousand men). Realizing the futility of the venture, Hampton made the only sensible decision and withdrew to Plattsburgh.

Understandably, Wade Hampton has few defenders among historians, but few of his contemporaries save Wilkinson (and after Hampton's death, Armstrong too) faulted him. It was clear then, as it should be now, that Hampton had been placed by the vagaries of a politicized command system into a position far beyond his capabilities, let alone his control. Palpably unfit though he was, Hampton was but a tile in a larger mosaic of incompetence.

BIBLIOGRAPHY

Adams, Henry. *A History of the United States During the Administrations of Jefferson and Madison.* Vol. 7. New York: Charles Scribner's Sons, 1911.

Cauthen, Charles E., ed. *Family Letters of the Three Wade Hamptons 1782–1901.* Columbia: University of South Carolina Press, 1953.

Hitsman, J. Mackay. *The Incredible War of 1812*. Toronto: University of Toronto Press, 1965.

Horsman, Reginald. *The War of 1812*. New York: Alfred A. Knopf, 1969.

Jacobs, James Ripley. *Tarnished Warrior: Major General James Wilkinson*. New York: Macmillan, 1938.

Lucas, C. P. *The Canadian War of 1812*. Oxford: Clarendon Press, 1906.

Mahone, John K. *The War of 1812*. Gainesville: University of Florida Press, 1972.

Shreve, Royal O. *The Finished Scoundrel, General James Wilkinson*. Indianapolis: Bobbs-Merrill Company, 1933.

                                                            THOMAS E. SCHOTT

HANCOCK, Winfield Scott (b. Montgomery Square, Pa., February 14, 1824; d. Governor's Island, N.Y., February 9, 1886), Army officer. Hancock was among the most successful Union corps commanders of the Civil War.

Named for General Winfield Scott,* one of America's greatest soldiers, Winfield Scott Hancock won an appointment to the U.S. Military Academy in 1840 and was graduated eighteenth of twenty-five. After service at Fort Towson, Indian Territory, Lieutenant Hancock joined Scott's Mexican Expedition and distinguished himself under fire at Churubusco and Molino del Rey. Thereafter Hancock performed staff duties efficiently at several posts.

In May 1859 Hancock was named quartermaster at Los Angeles. A nonvoting Democrat sympathetic to states' rights and friendly with Southern officers, Hancock nonetheless protected Federal property in southern California. After returning to Washington, D.C., in September 1861, he was appointed brigadier general of volunteers.

Hancock was patient with volunteer troops, yet managed to instill professional pride which they displayed in the Peninsula Campaign. On May 5, 1862, Hancock turned the Confederate left at Williamsburg and routed the enemy. George Brinton McClellan* exulted that "Hancock was superb today," and the adjective stuck. On September 17, 1862, during the Battle of Antietam, McClellan assigned Hancock to command the highly regarded 1st Division, II Corps.

At Fredericksburg (December 13, 1862), the three brigades of Hancock's division made a courageous but futile frontal attack on the Confederate left, entrenched behind the stone fence on Marye's Heights. Of 5,006 men Hancock led into action, 2,064 were killed or wounded. At Chancellorsville (May 1863) Hancock's division held down the left and protected the Federal line of retreat when Joseph Hooker* found that the enemy had crushed his right wing. On June 9, 1863, President Abraham Lincoln* named Hancock to command the II Corps.

More than any other officer, Hancock deserves credit for the Union victory at Gettysburg. Acting on instructions from George Gordon Meade,* Hancock took command at the front late in the afternoon of July 1, 1863. Hancock surveyed the chaotic aftermath of the Union retreat to the hills south of Gettysburg and decided that a successful fight could be made there. He moved troops to better positions, encouraged demoralized officers, and impressed all observers with his energy and coolness. On July 2 Hancock led the II Corps in a splendid defense of the Federal left center. They repulsed Confederate assaults and protected their adjacent center and right at critical moments. The next day was the culmination of the Civil War's greatest battle. During a severe Confederate bombardment, Hancock reassured his men by riding along the crest of Cemetery Ridge and insisting that the Union artillery reply. Hancock watched as "Pickett's Charge" (led by George Edward Pickett*) aimed at the left of the II Corps, faltered before reaching his lines. As the enemy began to withdraw, Hancock was struck by a Minie ball which lodged near his right thighbone. Seldom, if ever, has an American soldier had three such brilliant days in a row. Gettysburg was the zenith of Hancock's career and earned him a place among his country's military heroes.

Ironically, the wound probably cost Hancock even greater fame. The bullet was removed but a painful abscess remained. Hancock lost energy, gained weight due to idleness, and henceforward had to command from an ambulance, which detracted from the magnetism of his presence and limited his ability to see what lay around him.

In March 1864, after Ulysses Simpson Grant* was given command of the Union armies, Hancock resumed command of the II Corps. At the Battle of the Wilderness (May 6) Hancock's right drove Ambrose Powell Hill* one and a half miles. Hancock believed that if John Gibbon* had led his division in an assault on the Confederate right, the enemy would have collapsed, but James Longstreet* launched a counterattack and prevented a sweeping Federal victory. On May 12 Hancock emptied the Salient at Spotsylvania despite fierce Confederate resistance. At Cold Harbor on June 3, 1864, Hancock and the II Corps took the heaviest losses (3,510 men) in the saddest day of the Army of the Potomac. Hancock's men, having reconnoitered Confederate fortifications, wrote their names on slips of paper and pinned them to their blouses so that their remains could be identified.

Then Hancock's corps led the Army of the Potomac southward across the James River. Grant and Meade failed to make clear Hancock's responsibility to assist "Baldy" Smith's corps in the capture of Petersburg. Consequently, Hancock deferred to Smith's inaction on June 15, 1864, and thus helped squander the chance for a great strategic victory. As if to accentuate Hancock's growing ineffectiveness, the II Corps was routed on August 25, 1864, at Reams' Station, losing seven hundred killed and wounded, and seventeen hundred prisoners. Staff officers later wrote that Hancock never recovered from the humiliation at Reams' Station, but shortly thereafter the II Corps repulsed a Confederate attack on the Boydton Road. Illness and infirmity compelled Hancock to leave the II Corps on November 26, 1864.

Hancock held a variety of postwar commands. Appointed major general in the Regular Army and sent to command the Department of the Missouri, Hancock in 1867 attempted to pacify the Southern Cheyennes and Kiowas. In September 1867 President Andrew Johnson selected Hancock to replace General Philip Henry Sheridan* as commanding officer of the Fifth Military District (Texas and Louisiana). Hancock did not want this controversial assignment, but his beliefs in states' rights and quick constitutional restoration pleased the foes of military Reconstruction. Hancock's General Orders No. 40, proclaiming reliance on civilian governance in the Fifth District, thrilled Southern conservatives and enraged Republicans. Grant overruled several of Hancock's decisions, complied with his request to be relieved, and assigned him to the Department of Dakota, which represented virtual exile for a senior officer. In 1872 Hancock assumed command of the Division of the Atlantic and resided at Governor's Island until his death.

Although Hancock supported Lincoln in 1864, he was a life-long Democrat. In 1880 the Democratic presidential nomination went to Hancock on the second ballot. Following the prevalent custom, Hancock did not campaign but blundered on a sensitive topic ("the Tariff question is a local question") and thus may have contributed to his narrow loss in the popular vote to Republican James A. Garfield.

Winfield Scott Hancock had one of the most distinguished careers of nineteenth-century American military leaders. Possessing neither the strategic grasp of Grant and Robert Edward Lee* nor the martial fire of Sheridan and Thomas Jonathan ("Stonewall") Jackson,* Hancock nonetheless should be counted among the small number of outstanding combat leaders. Although his contributions at Gettysburg alone ensured his reputation, in addition, Hancock embodied certain traits that are instructive to leaders of a nation that has long relied on citizen-soldiers.

Hancock was a professional soldier whose services in the prewar Regular Army earned him a solid reputation among his peers. When forced to train and lead volunteer troops in the Civil War, many professional soldiers failed to adjust to the new circumstances. Hancock not only established himself as a fairminded disciplinarian and drillmaster, but he was also as comfortable personally with volunteers as with regulars. His staff always contained a majority of volunteer officers whose judgments he accepted and trusted. Though never fawning or emotional, volunteers who served under Hancock liked and respected him.

Hancock also was a Democrat in a military establishment where Republican values and officers eventually were dominant. Hancock made no secret of his allegiance to the party of Andrew Jackson,* states' rights, and general conservatism on social and economic issues. Yet the interests of the Union came first, as demonstrated by Hancock's loyalty when McClellan was relieved in November 1862. Hancock's politics briefly endangered his career only in 1867–1868 when he aligned himself with Andrew Johnson and against Grant. That incident permanently alienated Hancock from Grant. But William Tecumseh Sherman,* who commanded the Army during most of Hancock's postwar career, respected Hancock and protected him. Sheridan never personally warmed to Hancock and disagreed with him on political matters; nonetheless, "Little Phil" admired Hancock's record in battle and maintained a correct, formal relationship with him.

Finally, Hancock never had an independent command at a critical moment in the war. Nonetheless, as Grant stated in his *Memoirs*, Hancock stood above all subordinate Union officers in talent and record. He contributed significantly to Union victory by fighting as a member of a team, the Army of the Potomac. In the Civil War, an independent command carried with it a measure of prestige and esteem, but Hancock's reputation depended not on administrative title but on the performance of duty. On that basis he earned and deserved the sobriquet "Hancock the Superb."

BIBLIOGRAPHY

Coddington, Edwin B. *The Gettysburg Campaign: A Study in Command*. New York: Charles Scribner's Sons, 1968.

Hancock, Almira Russell. *Reminiscences of Winfield Scott Hancock by His Wife*. New York: Charles L. Webster and Company, 1887.

Tucker, Glenn. *Hancock the Superb*. Indianapolis, Ind.: Bobbs-Merrill Company, 1960.

———. *High Tide at Gettysburg*. Indianapolis, Ind.: Bobbs-Merrill Company, 1958.

Walker, Francis A. *General Hancock*. ("Great Commanders," edited by James Grant Wilson.) New York: D. Appleton and Company, 1894.

MICHAEL WHALON

HARBORD, James Guthrie (b. Bloomington, Ill., March 21, 1866; d. Rye, N.Y., August 20, 1947), Army officer; World War I commander; corporation executive.

James G. Harbord, the eldest child and only son of George Washington Harbord and Effie Critton (Gault) Harbord, was born in Bloomington, Illinois, on March 21, 1866. His paternal ancestors settled in Illinois in 1823, having moved from Virginia to Kentucky in the late eighteenth century. His father was a farmer of modest means and had served in the Union cavalry in the Civil War. His mother's forebears had migrated to Ohio from Maryland and Pennsylvania. In 1870 the Harbord family moved to Pettis County, Missouri, and eight years later moved on to Lyon County, Kansas, where young James grew up on the family farm. He attended Kansas State Agricultural College where he studied telegraphy and typewriting and developed an interest in a military career. Subsequent to his graduation in 1886, young Harbord unsuccessfully sought to obtain an appointment to West Point and taught school for two years in Butler County, Kansas, and at the college in Manhattan, Kansas.

On January 10, 1889, Harbord enlisted as a private soldier in Company A, 4th U.S. Infantry Regiment. In his brief two and one-half years of enlisted service in Washington Territory and Idaho, he rose rapidly to the rank of quartermaster sergeant. Having placed first in the examination for appointment from the ranks in 1891, Harbord was commissioned a second lieutenant in the 5th U.S. Cavalry on July 31 of that year. In 1895 he graduated from the Infantry and Cavalry School at Fort Leavenworth and also received an honorary M.S. degree from his alma mater. Between May 24 and October 24, 1898, he served as a major in the 2d U.S. Volunteer Cavalry ("Torrey's Terrors"), but the regiment, unlike the more famous "Rough Riders," did not see active service in the field. Promoted to first lieutenant in the Regular Army on July 1, 1898,

Harbord was transferred to the 10th U.S. Cavalry where in the fall of 1899 he met and began a life-long association with John Joseph Pershing.*

Following service on the staff of Major General Leonard Wood* (then military governor of Cuba), administrative duty in Washington, and promotion to captain in the 11th U.S. Cavalry on February 2, 1901, Harbord was posted to the Philippine Islands in 1902. On August 18, 1903, he was appointed assistant chief of the Philippine Constabulary with rank equivalent to that of colonel. For the next ten and one-half years, he served the insular government in that capacity and displayed high competence in duties of great authority and responsibility.

On January 1, 1914, Harbord was reassigned to the 1st U.S. Cavalry. He was promoted to major on December 10, 1914, and was a student at the Army War College in April 1917 when the United States entered World War I. As an indication of the esteem he had garnered in twenty-eight years of active service, Harbord was selected by Theodore Roosevelt* as one of the three brigade commanders in the volunteer division which the ex-president proposed to raise for the war in Europe.

Roosevelt's scheme fell through, however, and on May 15, 1917, Harbord was picked by his old friend, John J. Pershing, to serve as chief of staff of the American Expeditionary Force (AEF). He was promoted to lieutenant colonel and accompanied Pershing and the embryonic staff of the AEF to France aboard the SS *Baltic* in May 1917. During the next year, Harbord played a key role in helping Pershing to select and organize the staff and to prepare the AEF for its entrance into combat as an independent force. On August 5, 1917, he was promoted to brigadier general, National Army. During the period from May 1917 to May 1918, Harbord displayed an unusual talent for organizing and focusing the efforts of the staff responsible for coordinating America's greatest military undertaking up to that time.

On May 6, 1918, Pershing reassigned Harbord to command the 4th Marine Brigade of the AEF's 2d Infantry Division. Harbord led the Marines in the Verdun sector and in their great defensive battle in Belleau Wood (June 6–25, 1918) which blunted the third German offensive toward Paris and which convinced the French high command of the fighting spirit of American troops. On June 26, 1918, Harbord was promoted to major general, National Army, and in mid-July he was placed in command of the 2d Division, only three days before its participation in the Allied counteroffensive Battle of Soissons (July 18–19, 1918).

Harbord's personal hopes for higher combat command were dashed in late July 1918 when Pershing named him to command the AEF Services of Supply. Faced with growing problems in the proper organization and operation of his logistical resources and wishing to preempt a plan by Army Chief of Staff Peyton Conway March* designed to establish a support command in France co-equal in authority with the commander in chief, AEF, Pershing asked his old friend and loyal subordinate to assume the herculean task. Despite his own disappointment, Harbord quickly and efficiently applied himself to the organization and operation of the large and diverse organization responsible for the support of two million American soldiers three thousand miles from their base. In the remaining three and one-half months of the war, Harbord successfully molded the vast material resources and more than half a million men of the SOS into the most efficient military supply organization in Europe.

After the war's end, Harbord was promoted to brigadier general in the Regular Army on November 30, 1918. On May 25, 1919, he again assumed the duties of the chief of staff, AEF, for a short while before being sent by President Woodrow Wilson as chief of the military mission to Armenia for the purpose of investigating the political, social, and economic conditions in that troubled area and making a recommendation regarding a possible U.S. mandate. Harbord's report favored the proposed mandate, but Congress subsequently rejected it.

On September 8, 1919, Harbord was promoted to major general, Regular Army, and in November of that year he returned to the United States to assume command of the 2d Division at Camp Travis, Texas. In July 1921 Pershing became chief of staff of the Army, and Harbord was named as his deputy. Harbord bore much of the administrative load of the office of the chief of staff and was responsible in large part for carrying out a major reorganization of the War Department General Staff, reorganizing it along the lines of that developed in the AEF during the war. Also in 1921, Harbord represented the U.S. Army in the Washington Conference on the Limitation of Armaments. After nearly thirty-four years of active service, he retired on December 29, 1922.

On January 1, 1923, Owen D. Young, Radio Corporation of America (RCA) chairman of the board, named Harbord president of the growing young corporation. Chosen primarily for his value as a spokesman of unassailable patriotism and for his contacts in government, Harbord presided over RCA's period of spectacular growth and the development of radio's tremendous influence on American and world society. He served as RCA president from 1923 until 1930 when he became chairman of the board. He retired as honorary chairman of the board and director in July 1947.

Harbord also served on the boards of several other corporations and public service organizations, and was active in Republican politics. President of the National Republican Club in 1931, he was among the nominees for vice-president at the 1932 Republican Convention. Throughout his life he remained a close friend and advisor of John J. Pershing. He was promoted to lieutenant general on the retired list on July 9, 1942. Married twice, to Emma Yeatman Ovenshine on January 21, 1899, and after her death in 1937 to Mrs. Ann Lee Brown, the daughter of Fitzhugh Lee,* on December 31, 1938, Harbord had no children. He died at his home in Rye, New York, on August 20, 1947, and was buried at Arlington National Cemetery.

In his maturity, James G. Harbord was a large, balding man of stern visage, impressive appearance, and forceful personality. Personally energetic and a demanding taskmaster, he gained not so much the love as the respect of his subordinates. Frank and decisive in all his dealings, he could also be a loyal and selfless subordinate as he demonstrated with Pershing. In later life, Harbord proved something of an opinionated chauvinist.

Like many of his contemporaries, Harbord saw himself first and foremost as a combat commander, despite the fact that his greatest strength and contribution lay in his service in administrative capacities. As commander of the Marine Brigade and of the 2d Infantry Division in World War I, Harbord was an adequate but not a brilliant combat commander and tactician. Indeed, his handling of the 2d Division in the Soissons counteroffensive has been criticized as confused and lacking in firm control. Whatever his skill as a tactical commander, Harbord's ability as an organizer and administrator is certain. In progressively more challenging and difficult positions as assistant chief of the Philippine Constabulary, chief of staff of the AEF, commander of the Services of Supply, and deputy chief of staff of the U.S. Army, Harbord repeatedly demonstrated his ability to manage large and complex organizations in an efficient and forceful manner.

His ability to bring order and focus out of the chaos of the Services of Supply in less than four months in 1918 was especially striking. Probably no larger or more difficult task has faced a single officer in the nation's military history. Harbord's achievement is all the more admirable when one considers that, unlike his counterparts in the other Allied armies, he had no special logistical expertise or experience beyond that gained as a regimental quartermaster sergeant almost thirty years before and that gained incidentally during his tenure as AEF chief of staff.

With the Army's responsibilities growing in size, complexity, and scope subsequent to the Spanish-American War, the Army adopted many management techniques first developed in the American business community. The introduction of "scientific" management principles and procedures in the first decade of the twentieth century was followed in the second decade by the actual induction into uniform of corporate executives to manage the logistical support of the Army in World War I, both in the bureaus in Washington and in France. The thirst of the American Army for "scientific" management has scarcely been quenched even today.

General Harbord's post-retirement career as a top executive of a major business corporation began a counterflow of talent and management skills from the Army to private industry, and it highlights the similarity of the experience required to manage big business to that needed to direct a modern army. Harbord was the first of a long line of retired general officers whose demonstrated ability to manage the complex and demanding conduct of war has been utilized subsequently to satisfy the needs of American industry. Although many deny the compatibility of the two endeavors and the desirability of governing one by the techniques of the other, such has been a major aspect of American life since the turn of the century.

BIBLIOGRAPHY

Barnouw, Erik. *A Tower in Babel: A History of Broadcasting in the United States*. Vol. 1: to 1933. New York: Oxford University Press, 1966.
Davies, Charles G. *A Journal of the Great War*. 2 vols. Boston and New York: Houghton Mifflin Company, 1921.

Hagood, Johnson. *The Services of Supply: A Memoir of the Great War*. Boston and New York: Houghton Mifflin Company, 1927.
Harbord, James G. *The American Army in France, 1917–19*. Boston: Little, Brown and Company, 1936.
———. *Leaves from a War Diary*. New York: Dodd, Mead and Company, 1931.
Pershing, John J. *My Experiences in the World War*. 2 vols. New York: Frederick A. Stokes, 1931.

CHARLES R. SHRADER

HARDEE, William Joseph (b. Little Satilla Neck, Ga., October 12, 1815; d. Wytheville, Va., November 6, 1873), Army officer, Confederate general. Hardee's *Rifle and Light Infantry Tactics* was the primary tactical manual of the Civil War.

William J. Hardee was born into a family of Georgia cotton planters. His grandfather was a Revolutionary War officer, and his father commanded a battalion of Georgia cavalry during the War of 1812. Hardee attended West Point and graduated in 1838 near the middle of his class. He was assigned as a lieutenant to the 2d Dragoons and served with this unit during the Second Seminole War. He studied at the Royal Cavalry School at Saumur, France, and returned to his regiment in 1842. Hardee was promoted to captain two years later.

On the eve of the Mexican War, Hardee was stationed with Zachary Taylor's* command along the disputed Texas border. Hardee was captured on April 25, 1846, with a detachment from Company C of the 2d Dragoons at the Carricitos ranch, north of the Rio Grande. President James K. Polk learned of this skirmish on May 9 and the next day drafted his war message, which contended that Mexico had "shed American blood upon American soil." Hardee was criticized for surrendering at the Carricitos ranch, but a court of inquiry upheld his conduct and his official report of the action. Hardee won two brevets during the Mexican War and later fought against the Comanches in Texas.

Hardee's career was advanced by some of the decisions made in the 1850s by Secretary of War Jefferson Davis.* When the 1st and 2d Cavalry were created in 1855, Hardee became major of the 2d Cavalry. In the same year Hardee served on a cavalry equipment board and promoted what came to be called the "Hardee hat," the high-crowned black hat later made famous by the Iron Brigade. When the rifle replaced the musket, Davis called on Hardee to prepare a tactical manual for the new shoulder arms. The result was Hardee's *Rifle and Light Infantry Tactics*, which replaced Winfield Scott's* *Infantry-Tactics*. Scott's manual had been published in several editions, but it had never been revised. Hardee's *Tactics* attempted to compensate attacking infantry for the greater firepower of defenders armed with rifles. The most important change made by the new manual was an increase in the step rates at which attacking infantry advanced. Hardee's *Tactics* also provided for more rapid deployments from column to line, introduced changes in skirmisher tactics, and made other, minor changes. From 1856 to 1860 Hardee was commander of cadets at West Point, where he introduced the new rifle tactics.

After Georgia seceded, Hardee resigned from the U.S. service and was eventually promoted to the highest ranks of the Confederate Army. He was appointed colonel in March 1861 and promoted to brigadier general in June. During the summer of 1861 Hardee organized troops in Arkansas. In the fall he was transferred to Kentucky and promoted to major general. Hardee became a lieutenant general on October 11, 1862. He served in the western theater throughout the Civil War as a corps commander and on brief occasions as temporary commander of the Army of the Tennessee.

Hardee trained and led his troops well, and they won a reputation for dependable fighting on many Western battlefields. At Shiloh in April 1862, Hardee's corps formed the first line of the Confederate attack. It had been in the field as a unit longer than the other two Southern corps at Shiloh. Pierre Gustave Toutant Beauregard* later called Hardee's corps "the best trained in field service" of the Confederate corps at Shiloh. In this battle Hardee was slightly wounded in the arm, his only wound of the war. The first Confederate infantry fighting at Perryville was done by some of Hardee's troops. When the advance units of Don Carlos Buell's* army approached some springs of water near Perryville, the springs were defended by St. John R. Liddell's brigade of Hardee's command. Hardee's units later participated in the main Confederate attacks of the battle. On the first day at Murfreesboro, December 31, 1862, Hardee's corps opened the battle with an attack against the Union right flank. Hardee broke in the Federal right and drove it back almost three miles, until his troops were fought out and could advance no further. At Chattanooga in November 1863, units of Hardee's corps fought in defense of both Lookout Mountain and Missionary Ridge.

Hardee played a prominent role in several important battles during the Atlanta Campaign. He fought successfully against William Tecumseh Sherman's* attacks on Kennesaw Mountain, but he was not successful during the Confederate offensives around Atlanta. At Peach Tree Creek on July 20, 1864, John Bell Hood* ordered Hardee to attack down the Federal left flank. Hardee's attack was late, and, because the Union flank was refused in a curved line, Hardee failed to locate the flank and attack it as Hood expected. In the Battle of Atlanta on July 22, the attack by Hardee's corps resulted in the death of a Union Army commander, James Birdseye McPherson,* and inflicted great losses on the Federals. But Hardee's corps also suffered heavy casualties, and the assault failed to drive Sherman away from Atlanta. Hardee's official report characterized the battle as "one of the most desperate and bloody of the war." The defeat of the two Confederate corps under Hardee at Jonesboro was immediately followed by Sherman's capture of Atlanta.

After the Atlanta Campaign, Jefferson Davis assigned Hardee to command the Department of South Carolina, Georgia, and Florida. Hardee faced the hopeless task of preventing Sherman's March to the Sea. Confronted by Sherman's overwhelming numbers, Hardee could not save either Savannah or Charleston. After fighting a delaying action against Sherman's advance on March 16, 1865, at Averasboro, North Carolina, Hardee joined Joseph Eggleston Johnston's* command three days later at Bentonville. Hardee was late getting to the Bentonville battlefield, but on his arrival he attacked vigorously and fought well. On the evening of March 21, Hardee personally led a charge against Joseph A. Mower's division and saved Johnston's line of retreat from Bentonville. Hardee's son was mortally wounded in this assault. Hardee's corps retreated from Bentonville with Johnston's other units. In the last days of the Western war, Hardee was left in temporary command of the Army of the Tennessee, while Johnston conferred with Davis at Greensboro and negotiated the surrender to Sherman at Durham Station.

For nine months after the war, Hardee supervised two cotton plantations near Demopolis, Alabama. He then moved to Selma, where he made several business investments. He was president of the Selma and Meridian Railroad in the late 1860s. While returning to Alabama from a trip to West Virginia, Hardee died of illness in November 1873.

Hardee is best remembered for the *Tactics* associated with his name. This work brought him to national attention and became the primary tactical manual in both armies in 1861. In his biography of Hardee, Nathaniel C. Hughes, Jr., praised Hardee's *Tactics* and argued that Hardee did not simply translate the manual from French but also added important contributions to it. The adoption of the rifle made a new tactical manual necessary, and Hardee's manual did introduce significant changes. But Hardee's rifle tactics were as much close order tactics as the musket tactics they replaced. Hardee's manual formed ranks at the same close distance as Scott's *Infantry-Tactics*, aligned the ranks by having the men touch elbows, and was similar to Scott's work in other details. The changes that were introduced in Hardee's manual proved inadequate to compensate Civil War attackers in assaults against defenders armed with rifles and protected by entrenchments. By the end of the Civil War, the need for a new tactical manual was evident.

The Atlanta Campaign was the most controversial in Hardee's career. In his official report of the campaign, in correspondence, and in his memoirs, John B. Hood criticized Hardee's generalship during the Atlanta Campaign. Hood blamed Hardee for the Confederate failure at Peach Tree Creek, where, he complained in his memoirs, Hardee's troops "did nothing more than skirmish with the enemy." Hood was equally critical of Hardee's performance in the Battle of Atlanta. Hood wrote in his memoirs: "It had rested in [Hardee's] power to rout McPherson's Army by simply moving a little further to the right, and attacking in rear and flank instead of assaulting an entrenched flank." In his official report on the Atlanta Campaign, Hood virtually blamed the fall of Atlanta on Hardee's defeat at Jonesboro. Hardee made errors of judgment during the fighting around Atlanta, and he did not fight as well as he had earlier in the war. Hardee and the other Confederate leaders fought at Atlanta under difficult circumstances. As soon as Hood assumed command of the Army of the Tennessee, he took the tactical offensive against Sherman's superior numbers and artillery. The Confederates often assaulted against defenders massed in entrenched positions. The

444	HARKINS, PAUL DONAL

Army of the Tennessee was inadequately supplied, and Southern morale was low. It was under these circumstances that Hood's aggressive tactics failed, and he became critical of Hardee.

Hardee was a capable subordinate commander, but he was neither an outstanding tactician nor a successful independent commander. He was a dependable officer, and his troops had the reputation of being well drilled and disciplined. His corps was a reliable unit, often called on to open a battle. Hardee was not, however, a brilliant leader or an innovative tactician. His greatest tactical success was the attack against the Union right at Murfreesboro, but even this attack was not a decisive one. Although he sometimes served as temporary commander of the Army of the Tennessee, Hardee showed little enthusiasm for army command. He held an independent command in only two engagements: Jonesboro, a defeat, and Averasboro, a small action fought in the last weeks of the war.

BIBLIOGRAPHY

Hardee, William J. *Rifle and Light Infantry Tactics.* 2 vols. Philadelphia: Lippincott, Grambo, and Company, 1855.

Hood, John B. *Advance and Retreat.* Bloomington: Indiana University Press, 1959.

Hughes, Nathaniel C., Jr. *General William J. Hardee, Old Reliable.* Baton Rouge: Louisiana State University Press, 1965.

Johnson, Robert U., and Clarence C. Buel, eds. *Battles and Leaders of the Civil War.* 4 vols. New York: Thomas Yoseloff, 1956.

U.S. War Department. *The War of the Rebellion: A Compilation of the Official Records of the Union and Confederate Armies.* Series 1, vols. 10, 16, 20, 31, 38, 44, 47. Washington, D.C.: U.S. Government Printing Office, 1884–1895.

PERRY JAMIESON

HARKINS, Paul Donal (b. Boston, Mass., May 15, 1904; d. Dallas, Tex., August 21, 1984), Army officer, World War II, Korea, Vietnam.

The son of a journalist and drama critic and the self-styled maverick of his family, Paul Donal Harkins attended the prestigious Boston Latin School but fared poorly, dropping out at the age of fourteen and never graduating. A love of horses attracted him into the National Guard, through which he later secured an appointment to the U.S. Military Academy, graduating in the upper half of his class in 1929. A cavalryman, he was stationed in various posts in the United States before the beginning of World War II and advanced to the rank of captain.

Harkins served with distinction as a staff officer in the North African and European theaters. He was deputy chief of staff for the I Armored Corps in North Africa from 1941 to 1943 and held a similar position with the Seventh Army, in which capacity he helped plan the invasion of Italy. During the final year of the European conflict, he was deputy chief of staff for the Third Army and became a favorite and protegé of its famous commander George Smith Patton, Jr.* The two men shared a love for the cavalry and polo, and although Harkins' tact and circumspection contrasted sharply with the tough demeanor of his boss, he earned Patton's respect and the sobriquet "Ramrod" for his drive and determination in carrying out orders. After Patton's death in 1945, Harkins helped his widow edit Patton's wartime papers, subsequently published under the title *War As I Knew It*.

From 1946 to 1951 Harkins served as assistant commandant and then as commandant of cadets at West Point. Under the superintendency of Maxwell Davenport Taylor,* with whom he formed a close, career-long association, Harkins helped to institute major changes, including curriculum reform, deemphasis on hazing, and transfer to the cadets of greater responsibility for training and discipline. His interest in educating young leaders at West Point inspired him to compile a basic manual of tactics, leadership, and protocol entitled *The Army Officers Guide*; it was written in collaboration with his brother, the novelist Philip Harkins, and published in 1951.

As in World War II, Harkins served in the Korean conflict primarily in staff positions. From 1951 to 1953 he was in Washington as assistant chief and then chief of staff of the plans division in the Office of the Assistant Chief of Staff. When Taylor assumed command of the Eighth Army in Korea in 1953, Harkins, now a brigadier general, joined him as chief of staff and later commanded the 45th and 24th Infantry Divisions. Remaining in Korea for a little more than a year, he assisted Taylor with such post-armistice problems as reorganizing American forces, training Korean troops, and implementing a special program employing U.S. Army resources and manpower to assist with the economic reconstruction of war-torn South Korea.

Returning from Korea in 1954, Harkins did additional staff work in Washington. He was promoted to lieutenant general in 1957 and given command of NATO land forces in Southeastern Europe. In 1960 he was named deputy commander and chief of staff of U.S. Army Forces, Pacific.

Harkins closed a career marked by quiet competence in second-echelon positions with a major command in Vietnam where he became a central figure in sustained and stormy controversy. His friendship with Maxwell Taylor, John F. Kennedy's personal military advisor, and his reputation as an efficient administrator and a man of tact and sound judgment, led to his appointment in January 1962 as head of the newly formed U.S. Military Assistance Command, Vietnam. The reorganization of what had been a small military advisory group into a full-fledged command and Harkins' promotion to general symbolized the commitment of the Kennedy administration, through drastically increased American aid, to provide the embattled government of Ngo Dinh Diem the means to defeat the Vietcong insurgency. In Saigon, Harkins was responsible for equipping and training the South Vietnamese Army and, in coordination with the Diem government, for planning military operations. He administered an aid program that soon exceeded $1.5 million per day and an American advisory team that by the end of 1962 numbered more than eleven thousand officers and men. His faith in conventional warfare, his unqualified optimism, and his unrelenting support for Diem brought him into bitter conflict with the American press corps in Saigon, with civilians in Vietnam and in Washington, and with some of his own officers. Recalled to Washington in 1964, he served briefly as military advisor to President Lyndon B. Johnson and retired in August after thirty-five years in the Army.

Harkins was the first American to assume a command position in Vietnam and the first victim of a war that would become a graveyard of American military reputations. Despite his lengthy service in the Army, he was not well prepared for the challenge he faced. He had no first-hand knowledge of Vietnam and no experience with the type of warfare being waged there. The problems were enormous. The Vietcong controlled much of the countryside and had put together a tightly organized and highly effective guerrilla army. The South Vietnamese Army (ARVN) was large in numbers but short on morale, experience, and training, and had demonstrated no capacity to deal with a determined enemy. The Diem government, a narrow family oligarchy, had displayed little political or military sagacity. It firmly resisted pressures for reform and brooked little interference from its American advisors. By the time Harkins arrived in Saigon, a total collapse seemed possible, if not likely.

Harkins presided over a vigorous South Vietnamese counteroffensive in 1962. Buoyed by drastically increased American aid and by a huge increase in the number of American advisors, ARVN launched a series of clear and bold operations against Vietcong strongholds. Relying heavily on American helicopters for mobility and on the vast destructive capacity of American firepower, the reinvigorated South Vietnamese Army scored a number of major victories and for the first time since the war began seemed to gain the military initiative.

The successes of 1962 proved illusory. The Vietcong quickly adapted to ARVN's aggressive tactics, regaining the upper hand in 1963 and inflicting heavy losses on attacking units. ARVN's will to fight declined proportionately. Military operations were not effectively coordinated with political programs, so that success on the battlefield was rarely translated into political gain. Harkins came under heavy fire from civilians in Washington and Saigon and from some of his own officers for his emphasis on conventional warfare at the expense of counterinsurgency tactics and political methods, and for the use of massive firepower and napalm which, critics said, turned the villagers against a government that desperately needed to win their support.

Harkins' optimistic reporting from Saigon added fuel to the fire. By early 1963 many of Kennedy's advisors were deeply troubled by developments in Vietnam, but Harkins remained sublimely confident, rashly predicting in April that the war might be over by the end of the year. In fairness to Harkins, it should be emphasized that he came to Vietnam at a time of rampant defeatism, and his optimism was at least partly calculated to combat a mood which itself could be fatal. He depended to a large degree on information provided by the Diem government which only later was proven to be grossly distorted. Harkins' optimism nevertheless persisted long after there was good reason to be skeptical, producing bitter conflict with the American press corps and within his own command. In his zeal to demonstrate progress, moreover, he vigorously rebutted and even attempted to suppress contrary reports. His overoptimistic reporting eventually caused Washington to question his credibility.

Harkins' unstinting support for Diem provided the immediate reason for his recall. An upheaval among South Vietnam's Buddhists in 1963 posed a new and ominous threat to a government already in serious danger. Unable or unwilling to conciliate the Buddhists, Diem attempted to put down the uprising by force. Many Americans concluded that the war could not be won as long as Diem remained in power, and they were therefore receptive when a group of ARVN generals apprised them of plans for a coup. From the outset, Harkins vigorously opposed the overthrow of Diem. He was not uncritical of the South Vietnamese leader, but he had established a close working relationship with him, and, like many Americans, he saw no real alternative. He also felt, as he informed Washington, that it was "incongruous" after nine years of supporting Diem to "get him down, kick him around and get rid of him." Harkins' firm support of Diem placed him at odds with the American ambassador, Henry Cabot Lodge, Jr., who was committed to a change of government. Convinced that Harkins was undermining the coup forces, Lodge refused to keep him informed of plans and even cut him off from cable traffic with Washington. Once the coup of November 1963 had succeeded, Lodge pressed for Harkins' removal on the grounds that the junta that had replaced Diem would not trust him. By this time, Harkins' optimistic assessments of military progress had been proven mistaken, and the Johnson administration decided to replace him.

Harkins has frequently—and unfairly—been made a scapegoat for America's failure in Vietnam during the Kennedy years. The conventional tactics he employed adapted poorly to a guerrilla war, to be sure, but it cannot be demonstrated that the approaches advocated by his critics would have worked. Harkins erred badly in his appraisal of the war, but the mistake was repeated by his successors, none of whom ever developed an effective yardstick for measuring military progress. That the United States could have prevailed with Diem seems at best doubtful, but the political disarray that followed the coup underscored the validity of Harkins' warnings about the lack of alternatives. Harkins' failure in Vietnam reflects more the intractability of problems for which the United States never found solutions and the difficulties of applying the American military experience in an alien environment than his own personal deficiencies. After his retirement in 1964, Harkins lived quietly in Dallas, refusing to participate in the controversy that raged throughout the war and persisted after its end.

BIBLIOGRAPHY

Halberstam, David. *The Best and the Brightest.* New York: Random House, 1972.
Hilsman, Roger. *To Move a Nation: The Politics of Foreign Policy in the Administration of John F. Kennedy.* New York: Doubleday and Company, 1964.
The Pentagon Papers: The Senator Gravel Edition. Vol. 2. Boston: Beacon Press, 1971.
Taylor, Maxwell D. *Swords and Ploughshares.* New York: W. W. Norton and Company, 1972.

GEORGE C. HERRING

HARMAR, Josiah (b. Philadelphia, Pa., November 10, 1753; d. Philadelphia, Pa., August 20, 1813), Continental Army officer; commander of the American military establishment, 1784–1791; adjutant general of Pennsylvania, 1793–1799.

Josiah Harmar's family enjoyed modest respect and affluence in late eighteenth-century Philadelphia. He attended the Quaker school of Robert Proud where he received the typical education of minor gentlemen in the classic subjects.

After the American Revolution began in earnest in 1775, Harmar secured appointment as captain commanding the D Company of the newly formed 1st Pennsylvania Battalion, which was destined to join the Continental Congress' newly adopted army in New England. Barely into his twenties, Harmar served with distinction in the arduous 1776 campaign under Brigadier General Benedict Arnold* in Canada and upper New York. Late in the same year Harmar won appointment as major of the newly designated 3d Pennsylvania Regiment. He served in that capacity with Brigadier General Thomas Conway's* brigade until further promoted in June 1777 to the vacant lieutenant-colonelcy in the 6th Pennsylvania Regiment. In the extended absence of its colonel, Harmar virtually commanded this regiment for the next three years with George Washington's* main army in New Jersey and Pennsylvania. He led the regiment, as part of Conway's and then Brigadier General Anthony Wayne's* brigades, through the winter at Valley Forge, in the important battles of Brandywine, Germantown, Monmouth, and Stony Point, and in numerous smaller actions. Harmar finally received his own regiment in August 1780 when he was appointed lieutenant colonel commandant of the 7th Pennsylvania Regiment. He retained his command until the Pennsylvania Line mutinied in January 1781. In the resulting consolidation of the Pennsylvania regiments into three provisional battalions, Harmar was transferred to the rolls of the 3d Pennsylvania Regiment. This administrative move was necessitated by the disbandment of his own regiment (the 7th) and his superiors' desire to keep a proven officer on active duty. Harmar accompanied the provisional Pennsylvania battalions south in 1781 to participate in the Virginia campaigns and later in 1782–1783 under Major General Nathanael Greene* in the last South Carolina Campaign. He resigned from the Army in its November 1783 dissolution with the brevet rank of colonel.

Harmar emerged from the Revolution with a brilliant reputation, having served throughout the war under several distinguished leaders in most of the important campaigns and theaters. In the fashion of eighteenth-century gentlemen, he took advantage of the valuable contacts he had made with influential persons during his service. Very soon after returning to Pennsylvania in late 1783, he became personal secretary to Thomas Mifflin, a fellow Pennsylvanian and a former major general who was at the time the president of the Continental Congress. Mifflin shortly dispatched Harmar to England to carry a copy of the ratified treaty of peace to the British government.

While Harmar was absent, the Continental Congress disbanded the last units of the Continental Army in June 1784 and replaced them with a new regiment formed for one year from militia contingents from four states. Because Harmar's own state of Pennsylvania supplied the largest contingent of the new seven hundred man regiment, Congress allowed that state to appoint the lieutenant colonel commanding the unit, as well as several other officers. Harmar's patron, Mifflin, induced the Pennsylvania Assembly to reserve the commander's appointment for Harmar, pending his return from England.

On August 12, 1784, Harmar, then only thirty-one, accepted command of the United States' new military establishment. Because many experienced former officers would have welcomed the security and prestige of the position, the appointment was generally considered a plum. While the newly recruited Pennsylvania companies of his regiment marched west to Fort Pitt during October 1784, Harmar remained in Philadelphia to marry Sarah Jenkins. He and his bride left soon thereafter to join his regiment.

Harmar's responsibilities on the Ohio frontier were wide ranging, frequently difficult, and occasionally onerous or dangerous—in his regiment's early years even its existence was often tenuous. For at least the first two years, Harmar had to appeal to state authorities as well as the Continental Congress for support. As subsequent resolutions by the Continental Congress perpetuated Harmar's regiment and lengthened the enlistment term to three years, it gradually lost its ties to the states that had provided the original militia contingents. By 1786 Harmar dealt exclusively with Henry Knox,* the Congress' secretary at war.

Between 1784 and 1789 Harmar gradually extended his regiment's efforts to police the frontier by building forts at successive intervals along the Ohio River. He was executing Secretary Knox's policy of simultaneously extending an American military presence in the Northwest Territory and negotiating treaties with its Indian population. Harmar's men guarded various treaty commissions and surveying parties, patrolled between the forts, evicted squatters from Indian lands on the north side of the Ohio, and fought occasional bands of marauding Indians. Congress recognized Harmar's service in July 1787 by awarding him the brevet rank of brigadier general.

By 1789 the pressure of white settlement along the Ohio frontier had generated Indian resistance to alarming proportions. In response to the threat in the Ohio region, Harmar and the territorial governor, Arthur St. Clair,* developed a proposal to the newly installed federal government for a punitive expedition against the villages of the hostile Indians. Under continuing pressure from many quarters, President George Washington and Knox approved the proposal in June 1790 and ordered Harmar to mount an expedition that year. To reinforce Harmar's efforts, Congress had earlier authorized an expansion of Harmar's regular force as well as the raising of an additional force of militia levies.

For the rest of the summer Harmar struggled to organize his force for the coming expedition. The Kentucky and Pennsylvania militia levies assembled reluctantly, most of them without necessary campaign equipment and many without weapons. Their poor discipline was a constant source of aggravation to Harmar and his regulars.

At the end of September, when his whole force left Fort Washington (Cincinnati) and moved northward toward the Ohio Indian villages, it comprised 320 regular troops and about 1,100 militia. Moving and camping his predominantly infantry force in the ponderous conventional fashion of the day, Harmar reached the Maumee villages (Fort Wayne, Indiana) in mid-October, only after their Indian populations had fled. He remained in the area of these villages several days to destroy houses and crops. On October 19 and again on October 21 Harmar sent out reconnoitering detachments that both fell into ambushes and suffered demoralizing losses. The breakdown of morale and the onset of frost, which began to ruin pack animal forage, persuaded Harmar to turn back on October 23, beginning what amounted to a retreat that ended only on November 3 when his force reached Fort Washington.

Harmar immediately discharged the militia and composed his reports. By his own reckoning he claimed to have killed about two hundred Indians and destroyed 184 Indian cabins and about twenty thousand bushels of corn and other vegetables. Harmar's own casualties numbered 75 regulars killed, 3 wounded, and 108 militia killed, 28 wounded.

The public perception of the expedition, as well as that of most of its participants, was of a failure. The Indians had not been cowed; on the contrary, they were only enraged at the destruction of their towns and were encouraged to further depredations out of revenge and contempt for the government's demonstrated military inadequacy.

Harmar continued to command the one-regiment army until he was relegated to a subordinate position on March 4, 1791, by congressional legislation that established an additional regiment. Stung by persistent criticism and encouraged by his friends, Harmar requested a court of inquiry that finally sat in September 1791, while Arthur St. Clair* was preparing his own expedition against the Indians. The court's findings exonerated Harmar, but the damage to his reputation had already been done. He resigned his federal commission on January 1, 1792, and returned to Pennsylvania, where he served as adjutant general from 1793 to 1799.

Harmar is most often remembered for what history legitimately calls his defeat. In military terms, he failed to accomplish his mission and incurred what were probably unnecessary losses in the process. In the longer perspective, Harmar was merely among the first in a line of victims of circumstance, sharing the company of other unfortunates such as Admiral Husband Edward Kimmel* and/or Major General Lloyd Ralston Fredendall.*

To be sure, Harmar faced daunting problems in organizing the support for his expedition. He nevertheless enjoyed relative success in that regard; his men had sufficient arms and rations throughout the expedition. The matter of the abysmal discipline of his militia and the ineptitude of their officers has been raised in his defense, but Harmar had dealt with this sort of force before on the Ohio frontier as well as during the Revolution, especially in the South. Whatever problems the militia posed, Harmar knew he would have to control them to succeed, but he discovered too late that he could not. Another consideration raised in his defense is the inadequate time left to Harmar to train his force, and the pressure exerted by the government to get his expedition moving once it was assembled. Harmar himself is to be blamed for much of that pressure, or at least his failure to resist it, because he and St. Clair had urged the expedition on the government in the first place.

In all fairness to Harmar, his essentially conventional tactics were not at fault, as some historians have argued. The same tactics served Wayne quite well four years later.

Harmar was an exemplary officer for all but the very last of his career, and his stewardship of the nation's infant military establishment in its first six years was a worthy one. For a variety of reasons, not the least of which may have been a lassitude inflicted upon him by long, static years on the frontier before 1790, his former vigor had atrophied, and he had neither the personal capacity to understand nor the physical means to cope with the realities of campaigning against the hostile Indians of the Northwest in 1790.

BIBLIOGRAPHY

Butterfield, Consul W., ed. *Journal of Capt. Jonathan Heart, with the Dickinson Harmar Correspondence of 1784–5*. Albany, N.Y.: Joel Munsell's Sons, 1885.

Jacobs, James Ripley. *The Beginning of the U.S. Army, 1783–1812*. Princeton, N.J.: Princeton University Press, 1947.

Kohn, Richard H. *Eagle and Sword: The Federalists and the Creation of the Military Establishment in America, 1783–1802*. New York: Free Press, 1975.

Meek, Basil. "General Harmar's Expedition." *Ohio Archeological and Historical Quarterly* 20, no. 1 (January 1911): 74–108.

Trussell, John B.B., Jr. *The Pennsylvania Line: Regimental Organization and Operations, 1776–1783*. Harrisburg: Pennsylvania Historical and Museum Commission, 1977.

DAVID CARRAWAY

HARRISON, William Henry (b. Charles City County, Va., February 9, 1773; d. Washington, D.C., April 4, 1841), frontier general. Harrison is best remembered for his victory at Tippecanoe.

Harrison was born into a leading family of the Virginia gentry; his father was a signer of the Declaration of Independence who marked this younger son for a professional career. In 1791 the youth entered the Regular Army as an ensign, ultimately rising to captain during service in the Northwest Territory that included a period as aide de camp to General Anthony Wayne* and distinction at the Battle of Fallen Timbers. Marriage in 1795 to a daughter of the prominent Cincinnati politician and land speculator John Cleves Symmes awakened Harrison's political ambitions. He resigned his commission three years later, becoming successively secretary and congressional delegate for the Northwest Territory. President John Adams then named him in 1800 to the first of five terms as governor of the Indiana Territory.

Harrison's widely varied duties as governor included conduct of Indian affairs and command of the militia. Initially unimportant, these became of increasing significance as Western Indian relations deteriorated rapidly after 1805 in the face of such factors as settler expansion, tribal disintegration, and British intrigue. By 1811 an emerging Indian confederation under the Shawnee Prophet, Elskwatawa, and his brother, Tecumseh,* became the focus of concern. Harrison sought to deal with this by marching a mixed force of regulars and militia up the Wabash River from Vincennes to the Prophet's town, near the mouth of the Tippecanoe River. Encamped a short distance from there, Harrison's small army repulsed a series of tenacious pre-dawn attacks on November 7. Harrison held the field and later destroyed the town, but the casualty list totaled approximately a fifth of his force. Continued Indian resistance rendered the victory inconclusive. These hostilities were soon caught up in the larger War of 1812, in which Harrison aspired to play a leading role. Invoking wide political connections and family ties, he soon obtained general's commissions in both the Kentucky militia and the Regular Army, and with them command of the Northwestern Army after William Hull's* surrender at Detroit. From August 1812 until October 1813 Harrison undertook a seesaw series of campaigns for control of the American and Canadian lands and forts at the western end of Lake Erie. Opposing him was a poorly coordinated Indian and British alliance, whose chief advantage lay in their naval control of the upper Great Lakes.

To counter the hostile tribes, who were aggressively raiding the Western frontier, Harrison launched several punitive expeditions designed to destroy their towns and crops. To attack the British, whose limited Canadian resources would ultimately cast them in a defensive role when control of the lakes changed hands, Harrison simultaneously began to construct and provision a series of fortified camps across Ohio that would permit him to operate beyond the terrain obstacle of the Black Swamp of the Maumee River.

He soon encountered difficulty converting the numerically large population of the Western country into military units. Few civilians would enlist as regulars, and government policy often discouraged calls for poorly trained short-term volunteers. Thus, Harrison was often placed on the defensive, particularly after his divided army's advanced left wing under General James Winchester was defeated and captured at the River Raisin, Michigan Territory, on January 22, 1813. Forced to endure two subsequent sieges of his main camp at Fort Meigs near the mouth of the Maumee on May 1–9 and July 21–28, Harrison was further weakened when Colonel William Dudley's regiment of General Green Clay's relief force was captured on May 5 while attempting to lite the first siege.

Accordingly, it was not until the autumn of 1813, following both Oliver Hazard Perry's* naval victory near Put-in-Bay on September 10 and the arrival of additional Kentucky volunteers under Governor Isaac Shelby,* that Harrison possessed the combination of men, supplies, and mobility to recepture Detroit and push into Upper Canada (Ontario). Vigorous pursuit then overtook the retreating British defenders, under Henry Proctor, and their Indian auxiliaries, under Tecumseh, along the Thames River near Moravian Town on October 5. There the allied force was destroyed in an engagement highlighted by an unorthodox charge by mounted riflemen against the British regulars, and by a savage melee between the tribesmen and Colonel Richard Johnson's regiment, in which Tecumseh was slain.

Sharp differences with Secretary of War John Armstrong, Jr.,* later a bitter political critic, caused Harrison to resign his commission in early 1814. He soon moved to the North Bend, Ohio, estate of his father-in-law, and returned to a political career that included subsequent service as congressman, senator, and ambassador to Columbia. In the 1830s his military reputation and his flexible approach to issues made him an increasingly popular Whig presidential contender. He ultimately unseated incumbent Martin Van Buren in the "log cabin and hard cider" campaign of 1840, only to die in office shortly after his inauguration.

Harrison's extreme flexibility in matters of party doctrine and belief deservedly earned him the reputation of a trimmer and caused most of his contemporaries to judge him for his personal qualities rather than his issue positions. All agreed he was a likeable man, but not all felt he was a good commander. As a general he was praised most for his driving energy and for the blend of patrician dignity and frontier openness that endeared him to so many volunteers. Supporters saluted his extreme attention to both logistics and security, contending his resulting losses in time and mobility were preconditions to the victories of Tippecanoe and the Thames. Critics, on the other hand, enjoyed attributing the high casualties of his campaigns to the ample response time that those methodical movements gave his enemies. More seriously, he was questioned for his ability to support or control men who were not within his personal presence, a charge to which the defeats of Winchester and Dudley lent credence.

Such personal evaluations reflect the realization that Harrison was not a highly original military thinker. Instead he was a good imitator who based his campaigns primarily upon lessons learned while serving his apprenticeship under Wayne in the 1790s. Harrison saw the Indian tribes, with their irregular warfare, as the key obstacle to American penetration of the West. The thinly spread British were important chiefly for their cynical manipulation of the tribesmen. Each Indian and British war was a prelude to further negotiations for expansion. Western campaigns involved the destruction of the Indians' agrarian economy as much as did any victory in battle. Surprise was the Indians' best weapon, and thus the danger most to be guarded against. Harrison admired the popular and accurate western rifle but argued that the key to victory lay in logistics, superior numbers, and the shock advantages that regulars enjoyed over irregulars. Competent and unimaginative, Harrison was normally the most predictable of generals. His one great innovation, the charge of mounted volunteers at the Thames, succeeded in large part because it was so unexpected from him.

In his later political career, Harrison concentrated upon military issues but dealt largely with such routine matters as pensions and appropriations. His own difficulties recruiting regulars and his victories while in command of volunteers combined to make him a continued, if unsuccessful, champion of new and more rigorous militia laws that would retain the vitality of an institution upon which he placed his greatest rhetorical emphasis.

Harrison's modern reputation owes much to the attention focused upon his later election to the presidency, and his election in turn owed much to the symbolic values that his exploits served in the newly nationalistic American republic of the nineteenth century. In their search for appropriate self-images, many Americans became enamored of a concept often called "middle land-scape." This pictured the nation balanced between the primitive, intuitive savagery of the Indian wilderness, where nature controlled man, and the sophisticated, rational civilization of cosmopolitan Europe, where man controlled nature. Many Americans visualized themselves as living in a middle rural environment where man and nature lived in harmony, drawing upon the best of both extremes while rejecting the undesirable elements of each. Voters responded favorably to leaders who appeared to reflect this condition, which the "Farmer of North Bend" certainly did after he led armies of middle Americans to victory over both savage Indian and civilized British forces. Later images, not actual events, made "Old Tippecanoe" a heroic military figure.

BIBLIOGRAPHY

Cleaves, Freeman. *Old Tippecanoe, William Henry Harrison and His Time*. New York: Charles Scribner's Sons, 1939.
Esarey, Logan, ed. *Governors Messages and Letters, Messages and Letters of William Henry Harrison*. 2 vols. Indianapolis: Indiana Historical Commission, 1922.
Gilpin, Alec R. *The War of 1812 in the Old Northwest*. East Lansing: Michigan State University Press, 1958.
Goebel, Dorothy Burne. *William Henry Harrison, A Political Biography*. Indianapolis: Historical Bureau of the Indiana Library and Historical Department, 1926.
Green, James A. *William Henry Harrison, His Life and Times*. Richmond, Va.: Garrett and Massie, 1941.
Gunderson, Robert Gray. *The Log-Cabin Campaign*. Lexington: University of Kentucky Press, 1957.
McAfee, Robert Breckenridge. *History of the Late War in the Western Country*. Lexington, Ky.: Worsley and Smith, 1816. Reprint: *March of America Facsimile Series*, Number 54. Ann Arbor, Mich.: University Microfilms, 1966.

GEORGE W. GEIB

HART, Thomas Charles (b. Davison, Mich., June 12, 1877; d. Sharon, Conn., July 4, 1971), naval officer. Hart commanded the U.S. Asiatic Fleet at the start of World War II.

In 1897 Thomas Hart was graduated thirteenth in a class of forty-seven from the Naval Academy. Aboard the messenger boat *Vixen*, Passed Midshipman Hart met Theodore Roosevelt* and observed the battle off Santiago in 1898. After two years of sailing in the *Hartford*, the Civil War flagship of Admiral David Glasgow Farragut,* Hart was posted to Annapolis. Aside from other duties, he co-authored *Ordnance and Gunnery* (1903) which was a standard work for several years. Sea duty followed this tour ashore, in the battleship *Missouri* (1904–1905) and, with the rank of lieutenant, as commander of the destroyer *Lawrence* (1905–1907).

Subsequently, Hart's career pointed toward ordnance, especially the development and use of torpedoes. He ran the Division of Maintenance and Repair at Newport, Rhode Island, where he tested torpedoes (1911–1914). Hart commanded the 3d Submarine Division of the Pacific Torpedo Flotilla at Pearl Harbor (1916–1917). During World War I, he commanded four K-boats (submarines) in a cruise to the Azores, acted as liaison to British submariners, and served as special advisor on submarine matters to Admiral William S. Benson, the first chief of naval operations.

After the Great War, Hart worked on the Submarine Design Board with Chester William Nimitz.* Later, Captain Hart commanded the Third Submarine Flotilla and took his U-boats from the East Coast to Pearl Harbor. He attended the Naval War College and the Army War College (1922–1924). In 1925 he got a prize assignment, command of the thirty-three-thousand-ton battleship *Mississippi.*

Then it was back to torpedoes and submarines. From 1927 to 1929 at the Newport Torpedo Station, Hart supervised the manufacture and testing of the Mark VI magnetic exploder, a device that later evidenced significant deficiencies. In 1929 he was promoted to rear admiral and commanded submarines in the Pacific. Next he became commanding officer, Submarine Force, based at New London, Connecticut. During 1930–1931, the U.S. government significantly reduced the number of American submarines, well below the tonnage allowed by the London Naval Conference of 1930.

In 1931 Hart was designated superintendent of the U.S. Naval Academy. He introduced more courses in the humanities, attempting to tone down what he perceived as the "trade school" image of Annapolis. In 1932 Hart got in a squabble with Army Chief of Staff Douglas MacArthur* over reinstituting the popular Army-Navy football game, which had been discontinued in 1927.

Leaving the Academy in 1934, Hart commanded Cruiser Division 6 of the Scouting Force for two years and operated off both the East and West coasts. He was then posted to a seat on the General Board of the Navy. (The General Board was an advisory body to the secretary of the Navy, and considered matters of strategy and tactics as well as ship and weapons development. The first chairman was George Dewey.*) Hart served as chairman of the board from December 1936 to June 1939. During this time the General Board approved the designs for submarines that would be fleet mainstays during World War II. Hart expected that his next command would be his last before his retirement in 1941, and he wanted to become commander in chief, U.S. Fleet. Instead, he was made commander of the Asiatic Fleet.

The Asiatic Fleet was small and scattered in China and the Philippines. Hart was not sympathetic to Japan's expansionistic aims in China, where fighting had been underway since the Japanese invasion in 1937. Hart had many problems in his new command. Fleet training and drill needed improvement, and he saw to that. Concerned with the vulnerability of Manila, Hart asked for reinforcements and planned to withdraw the river gunboats and Marines to the Philippines. The British and Dutch wanted Hart to make advance commitments of joint naval action, but the admiral could not provide such promises. Finally, General MacArthur was uncooperative. At first, MacArthur was in charge of the Philippine armed forces, and later, of U.S. Army ground and air units in the islands.

Hart outranked MacArthur, but the general tried to dominate arrangements to defend the Philippines and the two officers regularly disagreed on what military steps to take in preparation for war.

Despite being notified of the Japanese attack on Pearl Harbor, the Army Air Force units in the Philippines were caught on the ground on December 8, 1941. The Japanese gained air superiority over the islands, thus threatening the U.S. Navy in Philippine waters. Hart reckoned that the fall of the islands was only a matter of time. Leaving his submarines based on Manila, Hart sent most of his surface ships to join the Dutch and British in the East Indies. On December 26, two days after MacArthur left for Australia, Hart left Manila for Java in the submarine *Shark*.

Hart became naval commander of ABDA, the American, British, Dutch, and Australian forces. He held this position until February 1942 when, ostensibly for reasons of health, he left the post and returned to the United States. Hart fulfilled a variety of administrative duties during the next three years (including service on the General Board) and conducted an investigation of the Pearl Harbor disaster.

Retiring in February 1945, Hart accepted the appointment by Connecticut's Republican governor to fill one of the state's U.S. Senate seats left vacant by the death of the incumbent. Hart left the Senate in November 1946. He lived in quiet retirement until his death in 1971.

"Tough Tommy" Hart, well known among his peers as a strict disciplinarian, was a good choice as commander of the Asiatic Fleet in 1939. (He did so well that he was kept on past retirement in mid-1941.) Hart anticipated reinforcements and made plans for the defense of the Philippines. The reinforcements were forthcoming and brought his command up to three cruisers, thirteen destroyers, twenty-nine submarines, thirty-two PBYs (patrol bombers), six patrol-torpedo (PT) boats, seven river gunboats, and a smattering of lesser vessels. Hart had no Navy dive bombers, torpedo planes, or fighter planes. In contrast, the U.S. Pacific Fleet, based on Pearl Harbor, had nine battleships, three aircraft carriers, twenty cruisers, fifty destroyers, thirty-three submarines, and many aircraft as well as auxiliaries. In other words, Hart's fleet was greatly outnumbered by Japanese naval and air forces and was an inviting target. It was no wonder that observers figured a Japanese attack to open hostilities in the Pacific would come against the Philippines.

Hart realized that his forces in China were exposed and weak, and brought them back to the Philippines. The 4th Marine Regiment was a welcome addition to the islands' defense. Hart's sailors laid mines in Subic and Manila bays. PBYs made daily patrols. Under direct orders from President Franklin Roosevelt, an unusual surface patrol, led by the chartered boat *Lanikai*, was launched toward Indochina. Nevertheless, defense of the Philippines rested in large part on the Army Air Force under the overall command of Douglas MacArthur.

MacArthur and Hart were personal and professional opposites. Hart was realistic, taciturn, and felt the pressure that Japan's naval and air forces could exert against his fleet. MacArthur was overly optimistic, verbose, and did not expect Japan to launch an attack against U.S. forces in the islands until the spring of 1942. The Army Air units were a significant part of MacArthur's military strength, but the general and his chief of staff, General Richard K. Sutherland, seldom consulted with General Lewis Hyde Brereton,* senior Army Air Force officer in Manila. MacArthur's failure to react swiftly to the news of the Japanese attack on Pearl Harbor by either ordering a strike on Japan's airfields on Formosa or relocating his Army Air units to safer bases on the island of Mindoro resulted in the catastrophe of having nearly half of his planes destroyed on the ground by strong Japanese air attacks.

As a consequence of these attacks, Hart's ships were quite vulnerable, and his decision to concentrate them with British and Dutch ships was logical. MacArthur, on the other hand, insinuated that Hart lacked nerve, and he virtually accused Hart and the Navy of failing to support the Army. Indeed, Hart believed that it would be a mistake to try to hold the Philippines without air cover, and thus he did not favor bringing the large convoy, led by the cruiser *Pensacola*, to the Philippines. He thought that the *Pensacola* convoy and other reinforcements should be used to build up Allied forces in Australia. Of course, MacArthur disagreed and wanted all ships and supplies rushed to the islands. Meantime, Hart had concluded that his submarines could inflict serious damage on Japanese ships bringing invaders to the Philippines. Because of the malfunctioning of the Mark VI magnetic exploder, which Hart had helped to develop and test, U.S. submarines were ineffective.

Relations and communications between the Army and the Navy in the Philippines, and between MacArthur and Hart in particular, provided glaring examples of poor coordination, interservice rivalry, and pigheaded antagonisms. Thus, chances for unified defense of the Philippines were crippled. Hart bears some of the responsibility, but the burden of the blame for these conditions must fall on MacArthur.

Upon leaving the Philippines, Hart found the ABDA command structure in disarray. America had the largest number of ships in the Allied fleet, making it logical that an American be named naval commander, but that officer did not have to be Hart. Dutch Admiral Conrad Helfrich knew the waters and, with help from diplomatic and military friends, energetically pressed his case for the command. Hart did not help matters by often referring to his own advanced age (sixty-four) and his poor health (he was actually quite fit, but the strain of the weeks prior to war had taken a toll on his stamina). After only a month with ABDA, on February 15 Hart was relieved from command and replaced by Helfrich. Most of the Allied fleet was subsequently lost in the Battle of the Java Sea, February 27, 1942.

Hart's command of the Asiatic Fleet was overshadowed by the grandeur of MacArthur. Hart's name slipped into obscurity. In contrast, the name of Admiral Husband Edward Kimmel,* who commanded the Pacific Fleet based on Pearl Harbor in December 1941, has remained in the forefront of discussions of the naval war in the Pacific.

BIBLIOGRAPHY

James, D. Clayton. *The Years of MacArthur, 1941–1945*. Boston: Houghton Mifflin Company, 1975.

Leutze, James R. *Bargaining for Supremacy: Anglo-American Naval Collaboration, 1941–1947*. Chapel Hill: University of North Carolina Press, 1977.

————. *A Different Kind of Victory: A Biography of Admiral Thomas C. Hart*. Annapolis, Md.: Naval Institute Press, 1981.

Morton, Louis B. *The Fall of the Philippines. The U.S. Army in World War II: The War in the Pacific*. Washington, D.C.: Office of the Chief of Military History, 1953.

Tolley, Kemp. *Cruise of the Lanikai*. Annapolis, Md.: Naval Institute Press, 1973.

JOSEPH G. DAWSON III

HAUPT, Herman (b. Philadelphia, Pa., March 26, 1817; d. New York City, N.Y., December 14, 1905), civil engineer. Haupt pioneered the use of railroads for military purposes during the Civil War.

A third-generation American of Palatinate German ancestry, Haupt was raised in a Philadelphia mercantile family that had fallen on hard times. Thanks to a Pennsylvania congressman of remote family connection, Haupt won an appointment to West Point and journeyed up the Hudson in 1831 to become reputedly the youngest cadet ever to attend the Academy. Four years later he was graduated thirty-first out of fifty-six cadets in his class and was commissioned a brevet second lieutenant in the 3d Regiment of Infantry. After only one month he resigned his commission to take a job as a draftsman. The depression of 1839, however, brought to an abrupt halt all the local internal improvement projects on which Haupt had been working.

To support his growing family, Haupt opened a private school in Gettysburg and began his investigations into bridge design that led him in 1851 to publish his important work, *General Theory of Bridge Construction*, which for decades was the standard text on the subject at West Point and other engineering schools. Construction of the Pennsylvania Railroad drew Haupt into that corporation's orbit. He rose quickly through the ranks to become, when the road was opened in 1849, its first superintendent of transportation. Haupt served in that capacity until 1852 when he left to assume a position as chief engineer on the Southern Railroad of Mississippi. The next year he was back in the Keystone State as chief engineer of the Pennsylvania Railroad. Haupt finished the main line from Philadelphia to Pittsburgh, amassed a moderate fortune from rail-related private investments, and after serving a year on the road's board, resigned in 1856.

For the next six years Haupt engaged in a titanic, but ultimately futile, struggle to drive a railway tunnel four and one-half miles through Massachusetts' unyielding Hoosac Mountain. Insufficient capital, unreliable partners, primitive technology, and labyrinthine state politics all combined to deal him the first major setback of his career. In 1862 the state legislature relieved Haupt of his contract, leaving him deeply in debt.

Haupt did not have long to fret over his predicament, however, for he was immediately called to Washington to lend his desperately needed talents to the

Union cause. By the end of the first year of the Civil War, military authorities had begun to appreciate the value of railroads, and Haupt was one of the many civilian experts brought into the Army to keep the vital rail lines in operation. He was appointed a colonel, attached to the staff of General Irvin McDowell,* and charged with rebuilding rail facilities to support McDowell's projected advance on Richmond. Using a hastily assembled untrained labor force, in a mere twenty days Haupt completed his assignment, which included his famous bridge over Potomac Creek described by an amazed President Abraham Lincoln* as containing only "beanpoles and cornstalks." Although McDowell's advance was canceled, Haupt stayed on to organize and drill a railroad transportation corps that later performed yeoman duty at the Second Battle of Bull Run, Fredericksburg, and Gettysburg. Haupt's outstanding performance in behalf of the losing cause at Bull Run earned him a promotion to brigadier general. By mid-1863 his corps was a model of efficiency, and, although Haupt served a series of losing commanders, not one blamed his defeat on Haupt's slowness in moving or supplying his troops. Under pressure from the governor of Massachusetts, however, Secretary of War Edwin McMasters Stanton* forced Haupt, who had refused to sign his commissions so that he would be free to petition the Bay State's legislature to recover his tunnel investment, either to sign his commission or quit. Haupt chose to quit, which prompted him to remark that he was the only man "ever guilty of the crime of refusing to be made a general."

The following seven years were the nadir of Haupt's career as he vainly sought redress for his Hoosac losses. Beginning in 1870, however, he became successively chief engineer of Tom Scott's Shenandoah Valley Railroad, general manager of the Pennsylvania Railroad's Southern interests, designer and chief engineer of the world's first long distance crude oil pipeline, and finally general manager of the transcontinental Northern Pacific Railroad. Throughout the postwar period, Haupt also worked as a consulting engineer on enterprises as varied as electrical transmission apparatus, steam heating schemes, Mississippi River flood control, and a process for condensing milk. He often invested his own money in these ventures but never recouped his huge Hoosac losses and worked right up until the last day of his life.

Haupt's fame stems from his unremitting activities in behalf of the Union cause from April 1862 through September of the following year. During those dark days he brought his indomitable energy and practical nature to Washington in exchange for only his expenses, as he never drew a salary or pension from the government. He organized and trained a corps to build, repair, and operate railways in the shortest possible time for military use. Adopting the self-assumed title of "Chief of Construction and Transportation, U.S. Military Railroads" (although his jurisdiction never extended beyond the areas occupied by the Army of the Potomac and his appointment conflicted with General Daniel C. McCallum's authority), Haupt proved the feasibility of rail transportation for highly mobile field armies. Exploiting his quasi-official status, he cut through bureaucratic snarls to bring organization out of the chaos he found on the military railroads.

The secret to Haupt's success with the wartime railroads was his ability to create a workable transportation corps composed whenever possible of experienced civilian railroadmen and as free from political and military interference as the situation would allow, and then to delegate his authority, allowing his subordinates the greatest possible leeway. Within a year Haupt could ignore most of the actual details of the construction work; instead, he focused his attention on anticipating his commanders' future needs and tinkering with technical improvements that would reduce the time required to bring wrecked railways back into operation. He originated the idea for the prefabricated truss bridges that were carried along in supply trains; Confederates quipped that General William Tecumseh Sherman* had railroaders—Haupt's former assistants—who also carried tunnels with them. Moreover, Haupt realized that to deprive the South of its rail links was to cripple its war effort. To that end he designed, had manufactured, and distributed to Union troops several simple portable devices that enabled raiders to bend rails out of shape and destroy bridges.

Haupt built well and effectively. In one twenty-four hour period during the Second Battle of Bull Run, his transportation corps moved fifteen thousand men along with their supplies, forage, and ammunition on a dilapidated single track railroad. By noon of July 5, after the Battle of Gettysburg, his men had rebuilt all the destroyed rail lines and the first trainload of badly needed supplies steamed into that desolated town.

With all his efficiency, Haupt had become dispensable. As he delegated more authority to his subordinates, they could, following his precedents, do what he had done earlier and with their increased manpower and equipment, and with more able commanders, do it more quickly. It was greatly to Haupt's credit when his former aides successfully supported Sherman's devastating campaign through Georgia. Railroads, as tools of war, had by then definitely come of age, and Haupt deserves a major share of the credit for his revolution in warfare. His contributions were recognized when the United States entered World War I in 1917. Railway and government authorities, facing a massive transport breakdown that brutal winter, drew on Haupt's Civil War experiences to organize the domestic railroads for the fight to make the world safe for democracy.

BIBLIOGRAPHY

Haupt, Herman. *Reminiscences of General Herman Haupt.* Milwaukee: Wright and Joys Company, 1901.

Lord, Francis A. *Lincoln's Railroad Man: Herman Haupt.* Rutherford, N.J.: Fairleigh Dickinson University Press, 1969.

Turner, George E. *Victory Rode the Rails: The Strategic Place of Railroads in the Civil War.* Indianapolis, Ind.: Bobbs-Merrill Company, 1953.

Ward, James A. *That Man Haupt: A Biography of Herman Haupt*. Baton Rouge: Louisiana State University Press, 1973.

Weber, Thomas. *The Northern Railroads in the Civil War*. New York: King's Crown Press, Columbia University, 1952.

JAMES A. WARD

HENDERSON, Archibald (b. Colchester, Fairfax County, Va., January 21, 1783; d. Washington, D.C., January 6, 1859), Marine Corps officer. Henderson is considered the father of the United States Marine Corps.

Archibald Henderson was one of the ten children of Alexander Henderson and Sarah Moore. After leaving the hands of his governess, he attended academies at Bladensburg and Frederick, Maryland, and studied French under a private tutor. In 1802 he worked at the Ante Eatum (Antietam) Iron Works in Maryland.

He was appointed a second lieutenant in the Marine Corps on June 4, 1806, and was promoted to first lieutenant on March 3, 1807. His first command was that of the Marine guard in the sloop *Wasp* on a cruise to Europe, April-October 1807. Henderson was then assigned to settle the accounts of the guard on the frigate *Constitution* at New York on December 1, 1807. Transferred to Washington, D.C., he was appointed adjutant of the Corps in January 1809 but resigned this post in May of the same year to take command of the Marines at Charleston, South Carolina, and St. Marys, Georgia, where he served through March 1811. His promotion to captain was effective April 1, 1811. Between October 1811 and March 1812 he commanded the Marines in the frigate *President*. From September 1812 through September 8, 1813, Henderson commanded the Marines at the Charlestown (Boston) Navy Yard.

Henderson was assigned to the command of the Marines in the *Constitution* late in the War of 1812. He participated in the engagement with HBM *Cyane* (32-guns) and HBM *Levant* (20-guns), when these ships were defeated and captured on February 20, 1815. Returning to shore duty after the War of 1812, he assumed command of the Marine Barracks at Portsmouth, New Hampshire, for the next three years. Recognition for his services came in February 1816, when Congress voted medals for the officers of the *Constitution* for her capture of *Cyane* and *Levant* and again in April when he received the brevet rank of major, backdated to August 1814.

In 1817, in a surprising and daring action, Henderson filed charges against the commandant of the Corps, Lieutenant Colonel Franklin Wharton. Henderson charged Wharton with neglect of duty and with conduct unbecoming an officer and gentleman. Wharton was acquitted, but his death the next year left his post vacant. Henderson was called to headquarters upon Wharton's death as acting commandant, serving from September 16, 1818, until March 3, 1819.

Brevet Major Anthony Gale, as senior officer, was promoted to commandant. Henderson, after a furlough lasting eight months, assumed command of the Marines at New Orleans. Gale's tenure as commandant was brief and stormy, culminating in his being "cashiered" effective October 16, 1820. Henderson was again called to headquarters to act as commandant of the Corps. On January 2, 1821, he was appointed lieutenant colonel commanding and commandant, officially to date from October 17, 1820.

Despite a proposal by President Andrew Jackson* to eliminate the Marine Corps, Congress passed the act of June 30, 1834, clarifying the position of the Marine Corps and confirming its separate existence by placing it under the secretary of the Navy, but it gave the president authority to order the Marines to serve with the Army. The Corps was enlarged, and the rank of the commandant was raised to colonel. Accordingly, Henderson was promoted to colonel.

The shortage of Army troops to fight the Creek and Seminole Indians led to an assuaging offer by Henderson to President Jackson of a regiment of Marines under his personal command. Jackson accepted the offer readily. Henderson assembled and organized the regiment, and moved it south in less than two weeks. Henderson served as acting brigade commander early in 1837 and at the Battle of Hatchee-Lustee. He was ordered to return to Washington on May 23, 1837, and resumed command of the Corps at headquarters on June 20, 1837. In 1843 the U.S. Senate approved his promotion to brevet brigadier general to rank from January 27, 1837, "for gallant and meritorious services while in command of the Marines in Alabama, Florida, and Tennessee, during the campaign against the Indians."

During the War with Mexico (1846–1848), the commandant again offered the services of his Marines to the Army. Once more his offer was accepted, but the Army made but little use of the Marines until the final days of the campaign for Mexico City. Their contribution has been perpetuated in the opening line of the Marines' Hymn ("From the Halls of Montezuma to the shores of Tripoli...").

On January 6, 1859, just fifteen days before his seventy-sixth birthday, Archibald Henderson died peacefully and unexpectedly in the Commandant's House at the Washington Marine Barracks. He was followed in death thirteen days later by his wife, Anne Maria Cazenove. They had been married on October 16, 1823, and were survived by six of their nine children.

Henderson commanded the Marine Corps for more than thirty-eight years and set a record for any officer before or since of fifty-two years, seven months, and two days of active service.

Henderson took command at a time of low morale following the cuts in the size of the Corps under the Peace Establishment Act of 1817 and the effect of the court-martial and dismissal of his predecessor. To combat this situation, Henderson saw to it that new officers received training and indoctrination at headquarters before being assigned to a station or ship, discipline was firm, and unsatisfactory officers were asked to resign or brought before a court-martial. The new commandant defended his Marines against illegal or discriminatory actions on the part of others, but he insisted upon internal discipline which was strict but fair. During his thirty-eight years as commandant, Henderson personally and frequently inspected every shore station as well as many of the ships' detachments. He insisted on strict economy in the expenditure of government funds and worked continuously to establish the Corps as a separate and distinct organization, yet one that was highly supportive of the Navy. Naval officers frequently expressed their appreciation of the Marine Corps, and Henderson utilized this support when the Corps was forced to justify and defend its very existence against political pressures.

Henderson developed the beginnings of the doctrine of amphibious warfare far in advance of other military thinkers of his day. He maintained at least a skeletonized battalion at Corps headquarters in Washington which served not only as a training unit for new officers and enlisted recruits, but also as a force in readiness for any contingency. He advocated artillery training for Marines and prophetically advised in 1853 that "Artillery drill, especially that of Light Artillery, would be highly beneficial in case of landing a force in a foreign country." Along this line, he recommended that the military education for Marine officers include a course of study in landing operations and in engineering.

Henderson was politically astute and maintained good relations with members of the federal government, the other armed services, and the general public. He built what amounted to a highly effective public relations program by making his officers, men, and the Marine Band available in support of public activities.

Under Henderson, the small Corps repeatedly demonstrated its efficiency, discipline, and usefulness. Marines served in the ships and at the shore stations of the Navy, helping the Navy "show the flag" around the world. Furthermore, the Corps conducted punitive actions against hostile native populations and fought alongside Army soldiers in Georgia, Florida, and Mexico. In addition, Marines assisted in handling domestic emergencies and disturbances. For example, Commandant Henderson, at age seventy-four, took an active personal part in restoring order in Washington, D.C., on the occasion of the "Plug Ugly" election rioting on June 1, 1857. During his long term as commandant, Henderson established the place of the Corps within the American military system.

BIBLIOGRAPHY

Donnelly, Ralph W. "Archibald Henderson—Marine." *Virginia Cavalcade* 20 (Winter 1971): 39–47.
Lewis, Charles L. *Famous American Marines.* Boston: L. C. Page and Company, 1950.
Pierce, Philip N., and Frank O. Hough. *The Compact History of the United States Marine Corps.* New York: Hawthorne, 1960.
Schoun, Karl. *U.S. Marine Corps Biographical Dictionary.* New York: Franklin Watts, 1963.

                                              RALPH W. DONNELLY

HERSHEY, Lewis Blain (b. Steuben County, Ind., September 12, 1893; d. Angola, Ind., May 20, 1977), Army officer, mobilizer of manpower, director of the military draft.

When the bugler at Arlington National Cemetery blew taps for the interment of General Lewis B. Hershey, a remarkable career of fifty-three years of public service ended. The life began in 1893 on a farm in rural northeast Indiana. The son of Latta Freleigh and Rosetta Richardson Hershey, Lewis descended from the Hersche family which migrated from Appenzell, Switzerland, to Pennsylvania in 1709. His mother died in 1898, even as Hershey entered a one-room school house. His 1910 graduating class at Fremont High contained less than a dozen students. The same year, seeking an escape from farming, he spent the summer obtaining teacher certification from Tri-State College. After one year teaching elementary school, he reentered Tri-State, supported himself by working as deputy sheriff, and played varsity basketball. By 1914 he had earned three different bachelor degrees: science, arts, and pedagogy. From 1914 to 1916 he served as principal at Flint High School.

After enlisting in the Indiana National Guard in February 1911, he won election to first lieutenant in 1916, just as his unit was federalized for duty along the Mexican border. After a few months of fighting mosquitoes, thirst, and boredom, his entire outfit returned home and was mustered out.

America's entry into World War I cut short Hershey's attempts to obtain a graduate degree in education from Indiana University. He served as first lieutenant in Battery "C," 137th Field Artillery. During training at Camp Shelby, Mississippi, he married Ellen Dygert, his childhood sweetheart from Angola. In October 1917, newly promoted to captain, Hershey accompanied his unit to Europe. Missing combat, he volunteered for extended duty and for eleven months worked at Brest, France, supervising troop embarkation. Upon return to the United States in September 1919, he applied for and received a Regular Army commission as captain on July 1, 1920.

The next sixteen years were spent moving from one Army post to another and raising a family that soon included four children. Promotion proved elusive. In November 1927 at Fort Bliss, Texas, a fellow polo player hit Hershey with a mallet and permanently blinded his left eye. Despite this handicap, he attended the Command and General Staff School in August 1931 and the Army War College in August 1933.

Following duty at Fort Shafter in Hawaii and promotion to major in July 1935, he obtained his most important assignment. In September 1936 he reported to the General Staff of the War Department for duty as secretary of the Joint Army and Navy Selective Service Committee, a group planning for wartime mobilization. Out of this planning came the Selective Training and Service Act, passed in September 1940. As one of the most knowledgeable men on the draft, Hershey became deputy director. In July 1941 President Franklin D. Roosevelt appointed Hershey to the directorship, which he retained until February 1970.

During World War II the system performed well, and some thirteen million men were drafted. Hershey's reputation and rank climbed: lieutenant colonel in August 1940; brigadier general in October 1940; major general in April 1942. He found men for the armed forces, established a system of deferments, administered an alternate duty program for conscientious objectors, and aided in the reemployment of returning veterans.

After the war President Harry S. Truman at first refused Hershey's suggestion that the draft be made a permanent part of the national defense system. Truman sought congressional support for a program of universal military training (UMT). In March 1947 the Selective Service law expired, but Hershey simply assumed a new title as director of the Office of Selective Service Records, committed to continued planning for mobilization. When Congress rejected Truman's call for UMT, and when voluntary recruitment proved inadequate to staff the armed forces, the Selective Service System was reborn in July 1948 as a temporary expedient. Hershey continued as director. The expedient expanded dramatically and smoothly when the Korean War began in June 1950.

After the armistice in Korea, the Army reduced its calls on the draft. Hershey now began a program of liberal deferments to channel manpower into areas of national interest. The scientific and educational establishments provided guidelines to Selective Service in creating deferments for college students.

By the 1960s Hershey faced another shift in priorities. Inductions expanded, and deferments had to be limited to meet the increasing demands of the Vietnam War. After a decade of liberal deferments, such a reversal provoked protest as the draft made itself felt in middle-class America. As the draft expanded, so did disillusionment with the conflict in Vietnam. Hershey and the draft soon became symbols of an oppressive government, which in the eyes of protestors, was fighting an immoral war in Asia. Following President Lyndon Johnson's urging, Hershey recommended that draft boards revoke deferments from protestors.

Suddenly, Hershey became an issue in the 1968 election. Democratic hopeful Hubert Humphrey threatened to fire the general. The victorious Richard Nixon considered Hershey a political liability because of his age and his resistance to change. Hershey opposed attempts to remove the autonomy of local boards and had little enthusiasm for employing computers. In February 1970 Nixon promoted Hershey to the rank of four star general and named him presidential advisor on manpower. Ousted from Selective Service, Hershey had little influence. The Army retired him in April 1973.

Hershey's importance for American history rests upon his directorship of the Selective Service System, a career that spanned from World War II to Vietnam, from total war to limited war, from Cold War to Detente. During this period he worked under six different presidents. Within the limits imposed by Congress and the president, he shaped the draft apparatus to fit his own Jeffersonian ideology. Theoretically, policy came from Washington, supervision from state headquarters, and action from local boards—"a little group of neighbors." Hershey referred to his system as "creative federalism." In fact, Hershey exercised huge influence over the operations by his personal contacts and through his interpretation of the law and regulations.

The system, which at times numbered over sixty thousand volunteers and several thousand employees, provided the manpower essential for American defense from 1940 through 1973. Over 14.6 million Americans found new homes in the armed forces after receiving greetings from Hershey. For better or worse, Hershey played a major role in the durability of this apparently unpopular institution. In lean years he kept the agency alive by lobbying Congress and the public. He soon became the leading authority on manpower mobilization.

His career abounded in paradoxes. He was a four star general who never fought in combat and an extraordinary politician who never ran for office. Hershey's durability and influence rested on a variety of talents. He knew more about the problems of manpower mobilization than anyone. Although he was a military man, he thought as a civilian. His sense of political reality and public relations remained keen until the 1960s. He functioned effectively in both the military and civilian world. The thousands of prominent citizens who worked as volunteers in the system gave him unstinting loyalty and provided a formidable lobby. A life-long Republican, Hershey never engaged in partisan politics. He dealt astutely with Congress. His Jeffersonianism, with its emphasis on decentralization and on local control, appealed to many congressmen.

Even in the late 1960s, he had enough support in Congress to prevent radical surgery on the draft system. Possessing great personal charm and a homespun humor, he enjoyed the respect of friends and enemies. Unlike J. Edgar Hoover, with whom he was often compared, Hershey left Selective Service after thirty years with his integrity intact.

BIBLIOGRAPHY

Davis, James W., Jr., and Kenneth M. Dolbeare. *Little Group of Neighbors: The Selective Service System*. Chicago: Markham Publishing Company, 1968.

Flynn, George Q. *The Mess in Washington: Manpower Mobilization in World War II*. Westport, Conn.: Greenwood Press, 1979.

Gerhardt, James M. *The Draft and Public Policy: Issues in Military Manpower Procurement, 1945–1970*. Columbus: Ohio State University Press, 1971.

Marmion, Harry A. *Selective Service: Conflict and Compromise*. New York: John Wiley and Sons, 1968.

Seiverling, R. E. *Lewis B. Hershey: A Pictorial and Documentary Biography*, 1969.

Wamsley, Gary L. *Selective Service and a Changing America: A Study of Organizational-Environmental Relationships*. Columbus, Ohio: Charles E. Merrill Publishing Company, 1969.

GEORGE Q. FLYNN

HEWITT, Henry Kent (b. Hackensack, N.J., February 11, 1887; d. Middlebury, Vt., September 15, 1972), naval officer. Hewitt specialized in amphibious operations in the Mediterranean during World War II.

Educated in local schools, Kent Hewitt had no particular desire to make the Navy his career, but in response to a newspaper notice decided to take the competitive examination for congressional appointment to the Naval Academy. He did well on the exam, received an appointment, and, after passing the Academy's own entrance exam, entered Annapolis with the class of 1907. Among his classmates who achieved flag rank was Raymond Ames Spruance.*

The reserved Hewitt apparently did not participate much in extracurricular activities at the Academy, but he did rank high academically (finishing in the upper one-third of his class) and was graduated in September 1906, almost a year ahead of time. The purpose of the accelerated schedule was to provide sufficient junior officers for the rapidly expanding Navy. He thus left Annapolis as a passed midshipman and served more than three years in the battleship *Missouri*, during the world cruise of the Great White Fleet (1907–1909), initially under the command of Admiral Robley Dunglison Evans.* Over the next several years he held billets in the battleship *Connecticut*, the destroyer *Flusser* (commanded for a time by William Frederick Halsey, Jr.*), and the *Florida*, a battleship of the dreadnought class. Despite the routine nature of the billets he held, Hewitt was not one to complain. Married in 1913 to Floride Hunt of San Francisco, Hewitt next served a three-year tour as an instructor in the Department of Mathematics at the Naval Academy.

World War I brought Hewitt a promotion to temporary lieutenant commander and assignment to command the new destroyer *Cummings* based on Brest, France. His ship was employed in the escort of convoys and in patrolling for enemy submarines.

After the war Hewitt rejoined the faculty of the Naval Academy, this time in the Department of Electrical Engineering and Physics. Following the completion of his tour there in 1921, Hewitt resumed work in naval gunnery; he had had extensive experience in it during his early service in battleships. While doing a stint as gunnery officer in the *Pennsylvania*, Hewitt was able to secure dramatic improvement in the ship's previously poor record in target practices and thereby earned the important assignment as head of the Gunnery Section of the Division of Fleet Training in the Office of Naval Operations. Subsequently, he became gunnery officer and tactical officer on the staff of the commander, Battle Fleet. Based in the Pacific since 1921, the Battle Fleet, composed of the more modern battleships and appropriate supporting craft, provided the bulk of the Navy's striking power. A commander since 1922, Hewitt was due for another shore billet following his tour with the Battle Fleet and in 1928 was ordered to the senior course at the Naval War College. Upon completing the course, he remained at Newport to serve two more years on the staff of the War College.

During the 1930s Hewitt's career continued to move steadily ahead. In 1931 he received command of a squadron of destroyers. Promoted to captain the following year, he saw more staff duty—as operations officer of the recently organized Battle Force of the Pacific Fleet—and then returned for his third tour at the Naval Academy to head the Department of Mathematics. After nearly three years at Annapolis, Hewitt received his first major command, the heavy cruiser *Indianapolis* in which President Franklin D. Roosevelt journeyed to the Pan-American Conference at Buenos Aires in November 1936. Hewitt captained the *Indianapolis* for little more than a year before being designated chief of staff to the commander, Cruisers, Scouting Force. Between 1938 and 1940 Hewitt commanded the U.S. Naval Ammunition Depot, Puget Sound.

With the attainment of flag rank, Hewitt assumed command of a division of light cruisers in the Pacific Fleet. Ordered to the Atlantic in June 1941, Hewitt remained in charge of his cruiser division and in addition was named commander, Cruisers, Atlantic Fleet by virtue of seniority. The Lend Lease policy had recently been implemented, and tensions between America and Germany were worsening as the two nations moved toward what by the fall of 1941 became an undeclared war in the Atlantic. Hewitt led task groups that carried out patrols, looking for German submarines and surface raiders and escorted troop convoys. During the first months of American belligerency, Hewitt continued to conduct similar operations. In the spring of 1942, however, he entered a new phase of his career when he was appointed head of the newly created Amphibious Force of the Atlantic Fleet. It was charged with training crews for the large number of landing craft then under construction and with providing training in amphibious warfare for fleet units and assigned Army troops.

The success with which Hewitt exercised this command led directly to his involvement in the first major amphibious undertaking of the war against Germany—Operation TORCH—the invasion of French North Africa. In it Hewitt commanded the Western Naval Task Force comprised of transports, amphibious landing craft, and covering units. Operating directly from bases in the United States, Hewitt's task force was to land American troops near Casablanca in November 1942. Forecasts of threatening weather raised the difficult question of proceeding to alternate, and less desirable, landing sites, but Hewitt relied on the more favorable predictions of his own meteorologist and ordered the landings to proceed as planned. Despite some spirited opposition from the French forces responsible to Marshal Philippe Petain's Vichy government, the operation was conducted successfully and some thirty-five thousand troops commanded by General George Smith Patton, Jr.,* were landed along the Moroccan coast. In a campaign lasting several months, Patton's troops combined with other forces landed near Algerian ports and General Bernard Montgomery's British Eighth Army advancing westward from Egypt to seize undisputed control of North Africa from the Axis.

Promoted to vice admiral soon after the Moroccan landings, Hewitt was relieved as commander of the amphibious force and named to command the newly established U.S. Eighth Fleet operating in northwest African waters. Hewitt's main responsibilities would continue to be in amphibious warfare. He set up his headquarters in Algiers under the Supreme Allied Command of General Dwight David Eisenhower* and the naval leadership of admiral of the fleet, Sir Andrew Cunningham, Royal Navy. Plans to invade the strategically located island of Sicily had to be formulated. The landings were scheduled for July 1943. A task force under Hewitt's direction put Patton's Seventh Army ashore on Sicily's south coast. With the conclusion of the operation, Hewitt next commanded two more major amphibious assaults in the Mediterranean: in September the landings at Salerno, Italy, and the following year, in August 1944, Operation ANVIL-DRAGOON in which American and French troops were landed in southern France. Involving almost nine hundred ships of different classifications from battleship and carrier to minesweeper and landing craft, ANVIL-DRAGOON was the largest amphibious operation Hewitt commanded.

Although his involvement in Mediterranean operations and planning kept Hewitt from participating in the Normandy invasion (ANVIL-DRAGOON was originally planned to take place simultaneously with it), by any assessment he was one of the foremost practitioners of amphibious warfare in the Mediterranean and European Theaters of War. Of all the operations he commanded, only the one at Salerno was put in serious jeopardy, and that because of difficulties encountered after the troops had been landed. An exponent of pre-invasion bombardment, a tactic to which the Army did not consent until after the near disaster at Salerno, Hewitt also believed in shore-to-shore operations in locales like the Mediterranean where distances between embarkation ports and beachheads were not excessive. Where such conditions prevailed, Army personnel would be carried in the invasion craft themselves rather than transfer to them from transports.

Like other American naval leaders who flew their flags in the Atlantic and Mediterranean, Hewitt did not win a great deal of recognition among the American people, but those who knew him best appreciated his contributions to amphibious warfare. For instance, General Eisenhower characterized Hewitt's potentially troublesome relationship with his immediate superior, Sir Andrew Cunningham, as one of "mutual respect and confidence." And Samuel Eliot Morison,* in discussing Hewitt's qualifications for command in the invasion of Sicily, had this to say of him: "In amphibious experience he was surpassed by none and equaled by few."

With the war against Germany drawing to a conclusion in early 1945, Hewitt was given an assignment he did not particularly relish: conducting still another in a series of Pearl Harbor investigations. Although he had previously commanded a division of cruisers under Admiral Husband Edward Kimmel,* the ill-fated officer who commanded the Pacific Fleet on December 7, 1941, Hewitt had been serving in the Atlantic at that time. He conducted a careful investigation, reviewing evidence gathered in the earlier inquiries and questioning more than two dozen witnesses about Pearl Harbor. Hewitt had great respect for Kimmel's abilities and for the steps he had taken to ready the Pacific Fleet for war and was not as harsh toward him as the earlier Roberts report had been, but he concluded that Kimmel had been remiss in not ordering more extensive reconnaissance measures in view of the deteriorating situation in the Pacific in the last months of 1941.

After the war Hewitt served for a year as commander of the Twelfth Fleet (U.S. Naval Forces in Europe), spent a year as consultant at the Naval War College, and did his final tour of duty as liaison officer between the chief of naval operations and the Military Staff Committee of the Security Council of the United Nations. The committee was charged with formulating plans for the raising and deployment of U.N. peacekeeping forces in the event they should some day be needed.

Transferred to the retired list in 1949, Hewitt, unlike many of his service contemporaries, eschewed both business and public office. He preferred to enjoy the tranquility of retirement in a large hillside home in Orwell, Vermont.

BIBLIOGRAPHY

Clagett, John. "Admiral H. Kent Hewitt, U.S. Navy: High Command." *Naval War College Review* 28 (Fall 1975): 60–86.

Hewitt, H. Kent. "Executing Operation ANVIL-DRAGOON." United States Naval Institute *Proceedings* 78 (August 1954): 897–911.

Melosi, Martin V. *The Shadow of Pearl Harbor: Political Controversy over the Surprise Attack, 1941–1946*. College Station: Texas A&M University Press, 1977.

Morison, Samuel E. *History of United States Naval Operations in World War II*. 15 vols. Boston: Atlantic, Little, Brown and Company, 1947–1962.

LLOYD J. GRAYBAR

HILL, Ambrose Powell (b. Culpeper County, Va., November 9, 1825; d. near Petersburg, Va., April 2, 1865), Army officer. Hill was a Confederate division and corps commander during the Civil War.

Ambrose Powell Hill was born into the family of a prosperous Virginia merchant and politician. In his youth, he engaged in many outdoor activities and became an excellent horseman. He also developed an intense admiration for the exploits of Napoleon. He received his early education at a neighborhood school and then attended Simms' Academy (Black Hill Seminary) before being accepted at the U.S. Military Academy at West Point, New York, in 1842. Because of illness and deficiencies in chemistry and philosophy, he had to repeat his third year, graduating fifteenth in a class of thirty-eight in 1847. Commissioned second lieutenant, 1st Artillery, as of August 26, 1847, he hastened to join his regiment in Mexico.

Arriving during the final stages of the Mexican War, Hill participated in some of the engagements leading to the capture of Mexico City. After the war, he was stationed briefly at Fort McHenry, Maryland. His regiment was next ordered to Florida to participate in unsuccessful campaigns against the Seminole Indians (1850–1851, 1853–1855). He was promoted to first lieutenant in 1851. Hill contracted yellow fever in 1855, and after recuperating, transferred to the U.S. Coast Survey office in Washington, D.C., serving from November 23 until obtaining a leave of absence on October 26, 1860.

Hill opposed slavery on moral grounds, but he was such a firm supporter of states' rights on the eve of the Civil War that he felt obliged to support his native state. Consequently, he resigned from the U.S. Army as of March 1, 1861, and was commissioned colonel, Virginia Volunteers, as of May 9, commanding the 13th Virginia Infantry. After brief service in western Virginia, he was present at the First Battle of Manassas (Bull Run), but his regiment was not engaged. Hill was appointed brigadier general as of February 26, 1862, and placed in command of the 1st Brigade, 2d Division, commanded by Major General James Longstreet.* Hill fought his brigade well at Williamsburg, Virginia, on May 5, but it suffered 326 casualties, which were more than any other Confederate brigade engaged that day.

Promoted to major general as of May 26, Hill was assigned to command a newly constituted division near Richmond which he named the Light Division.

Presumably, Hill meant the name to imply a force organized for rapid movement, and the name caught the imagination of the Southern press (which he also may have intended). Hill opened the Battle of the Seven Days at Mechanicsville, Virginia, on June 26, attacked first at Gaines' Mill the following day, and participated in the attack on Union lines at Frazier's Farm on June 30. His division suffered heavy losses during these fights.

Because of friction that developed between Hill and Longstreet, General Robert Edward Lee* sent Hill to reinforce Lieutenant General Thomas Jonathan ("Stonewall") Jackson* in the Shenandoah Valley. Hill, however, became involved in a bitter dispute with Jackson too. Yet, he was invaluable to Jackson during the battles of Cedar Mountain and Second Manassas. During the Maryland Campaign, Hill received the surrender of the Union garrison at Harper's Ferry on September 14. He saved the Army of Northern Virginia from disaster at the Battle of Antietam by making a forced march from Harper's Ferry on September 17 to arrive on the field just as the Confederate lines were collapsing.

Returning to action with Lee's army on December 13, Hill fought in the battle of Fredericksburg, where a gap between his units allowed the only Union penetration of Confederate lines. At the Battle of Chancellorsville, Hill participated in the flanking movement that smashed the Union lines. He assumed command of the II Army Corps when Jackson was mortally wounded, only to be severely wounded himself shortly thereafter. For his skill as a division commander, Hill was promoted to lieutenant general as of May 23, 1863, and was given command of the III Army Corps of the newly reorganized Army of Northern Virginia.

As a corps commander, Hill committed Confederate forces to battle at Gettysburg without orders or a clear understanding of the situation, suffering heavy casualties on July 1. He made some gains on the first day of the battle, but his attacks on July 2 were poorly organized and uncoordinated, and, as a result, unsuccessful. On the third day of the battle, most of his troops were placed under Longstreet's command for the unsuccessful assault on Cemetery Ridge. On October 14, Hill launched another poorly organized and uncoordinated attack on Union positions at Bristoe Station, Virginia, resulting in heavy Confederate losses without any positive results.

Hill's corps was heavily engaged during the Battle of the Wilderness, May 6–7, 1864, and his line was collapsing when saved by reinforcements from Longstreet. He then took a leave of absence due to illness, returning on May 21 to participate marginally in the battles of North Anna and Cold Harbor. After Union forces crossed to the south side of the James River, Hill's corps was involved in the defense of Petersburg during the final months of the war. He was killed by Union soldiers near Petersburg on April 2, 1865, trying to rejoin his troops after the Confederate line had been shattered.

Hill's reputation as a soldier is based on his performance as a division commander. His Light Division was extremely well trained and effective on the battlefield. He could move his troops with astonishing speed and was an aggressive officer with a good sense of timing, but often at heavy cost in casualties.

His finest hour as a commander was the forced march of his division from Harper's Ferry to Antietam on September 17. Without his timely arrival, Lee's army would have been destroyed on that bloody day. His inability to get along with Jackson and Longstreet somewhat limited his effectiveness, but as a division commander, he was without peer, and Lee described him in May 1863 as "the best soldier of his grade with me."

While Hill was a first-class division commander, his performance as a corps commander was uneven at best. At both Gettysburg and Bristoe Station, Hill's unplanned and poorly organized attacks came at heavy cost to the Army of Northern Virginia. During the Battle of the Wilderness, his corps was nearly overwhelmed, and his effectiveness as a commander deteriorated thereafter. He was plagued by constant illnesses. Self-doubt and failure deeply affected his performance, and the evidence suggests that his illnesses were psychosomatic. Ambrose Powell Hill can best be described as a brilliant division commander who was promoted beyond his ability.

BIBLIOGRAPHY

Freeman, Douglas Southall. *Lee's Lieutenants: A Study in Command*. 3 vols. New York: Charles Scribner's Sons, 1942–1944.
Hassler, William Woods. *A. P. Hill: Lee's Forgotten General*. Richmond: Garrett and Massie, 1957.
Schenck, Martin. *Up Came Hill: The Story of the Light Division and Its Leaders*. Harrisburg, Pa.: Stackpole Company, 1958.

DAVID L. WILSON

HINES, John Leonard (b. White Sulphur Springs, Greenbrier County, W. Va., May 21, 1868; d. Washington, D.C., October 13, 1968), Army officer, general and chief of staff of the Army.

John Hines was the first born of seven children of Edward and Mary Leonard Hines, both Irish emigrants. His early education was provided in the typical one-room school in the mountains of West Virginia. His formal education began in 1875 at a small private school near Athens, West Virginia, where he aspired to become a teacher and remained until 1887. That year he was appointed to the U.S. Military Academy. Hines graduated in 1891, with a standing of forty-eighth in a class of sixty-five, receiving a commission in the infantry. His first assignments took him west to serve at various Indian agencies.

In the spring of 1898, with the outbreak of the Spanish-American War, Hines volunteered for combat. Prior to departure to Cuba, Lieutenant Hines held the distinction of commandeering a troop train for Teddy Roosevelt's* "Rough Riders." He landed with his regiment in Cuba and served in the Santiago Campaign of June-July 1898. He participated in the Battle of San Juan Hill and earned a War Department citation for gallantry in action against Spanish forces as well as later receiving one of the Army's highest decorations, the Silver Star.

Upon his return to the United States, Hines married Harriet Schofield (Rita) Wherry in Columbus, Ohio, on December 19, 1898. She was one of the daughters of Colonel, later Brigadier General, William M. Wherry, who was a Civil War veteran, recipient of the Medal of Honor, and Hines' former commanding officer. The Hines had two children, a daughter Alice in 1900, and a son John, Jr., in 1905.

After serving one year in Cuba, Hines then proceeded to the Philippines for the first of three tours there. Promoted to captain, he participated in the Philippine Insurrection, winning a commendation. He later participated in the subjugation of the Moros.

Completing a series of minor assignments, he was promoted to major and given battalion command. In 1916 he rode with General John Joseph Pershing* on the Punitive Expedition into Mexico in pursuit of Pancho Villa. Major Hines served as adjutant of the expedition. From this close, initial contact with General Pershing, a warm relationship developed. Promoted to lieutenant colonel, Hines was selected by General Pershing for the first group of officers in May 1917 to form the staff of what became GHQ, the headquarters of the American Expeditionary Force.

World War I marked the apex of Hines' battle experience. Receiving an accelerated promotion to colonel, he was assigned to command the 16th Infantry. Having successfully trained the 16th, he was nominated and promoted to brigadier general and given command of the 1st Brigade of the 1st Division. As such, he participated in the Battle of Soissons and in the Second Battle of the Marne, July 1918. For "extraordinary heroism in action," he was awarded the Distinguished Service Cross.

His effectiveness as a battle leader led to further promotion. In August 1918 Hines was promoted to major general and was assigned to command the 4th Infantry Division. He led the division during the American operations at St. Mihiel and in the Meuse-Argonne. His final achievement came at the close of the war when he received command of the III Corps which he led during the occupation of the Rhineland. General Hines holds the unique distinction of being the only American officer to command successively in battle, during World War I, a regiment, brigade, division, and an army corps. At that time only one other American military figure had held that distinction—Thomas Jonathan ("Stonewall") Jackson.*

During the immediate postwar years, General Hines served in a series of divisional commands among the Army's dwindling forces. In September 1924 he attained the crowning point of his military career. Upon General Pershing's recommendation, he was appointed to succeed Pershing as chief of staff of the Army.

As chief of staff, Hines was confronted with severe problems incidental to a peacetime military establishment. He strove to curtail further reductions in appropriations as well as manpower. He worked to improve the various Army schools. He advocated an aggressive training program and interservice cooperation through a series of high command exercises known as the Grand Joint Army-Navy Maneuvers. Perhaps his most controversial problem, one of internal Army strife, was the court-martial of William ("Billy") Mitchell.*

He departed the Office of Chief of Staff in 1926, requesting and receiving a field command. In 1930 he returned to the scene of earlier military experiences—the Philippines. He succeeded General Douglas MacArthur* as commanding general of the Philippine Department and held that position until April 1932, when he was relieved. Completing his last assignment, General Hines retired from active service on May 31, 1932, at the age of sixty-four. His early retirement was spent in his native West Virginia.

At the outbreak of World War II Hines applied for active duty. This request was tactfully refused as he had passed his seventy-third birthday. As his health declined, he was admitted to Walter Reed Army Hospital where, on October 13, 1968, at one hundred years of age, John Leonard Hines died. Before his death, he was the oldest living graduate of West Point.

Hines' contribution to American military history is twofold: first, his exceptional ability to lead men in battle; and second, his capability as an administrator. In battle he was a natural leader, professionally competent, an organizer, and, like Pershing, a strict disciplinarian. Troops under his command in battle were never engaged in a losing fight or defeat.

As chief of staff of the Army, General Hines idealized the stewardship principle. His ability was based upon long experience and attention to detail in handling a massive amount of administrative work. His tirelessness was unending, and perseverance was stamped into his character.

He was caretaker of the smallest fighting force in the world (1926) in relation to population, wealth, and area. He worked under the most difficult of impositions; yet he never wavered in his support of the Army.

In physical stature Hines was tall and lean, with a square jaw and a close-clipped moustache. Bodily, he was strong and tough; yet he appealed to children. He enjoyed dancing, horseback riding, and athletic competition. He also enjoyed congenial company, good cigars, and, occasionally, whiskey. He was a silent man, often for long periods; yet he spoke forcefully when he needed to.

Hines lived his entire life under the tenets of the Military Academy—Duty, Honor, Country. From subordinates he expected two things, obedience and loyalty, both of which he possessed and considered virtues.

While he was progressive, at the same time he was imbued in Army tradition. His forty-one years of military service spanned one world war and combat service in four other campaigns as well as numerous administrative posts. John Leonard Hines was a professionally knowledgeable officer and leader dedicated to the service of the Army and the nation. In the final appraisal, only a most versatile soldier of ability and skill could have performed the job Hines did.

BIBLIOGRAPHY

Bolte, Charles L. "John Leonard Hines." *Assembly* 29 (Spring 1970).
Comstock, Jim. *The West Virginia Heritage Encyclopedia*. Vol. 2. Richwood, W. Va.: 1976.
Peake, Louis A. "Major General John L. Hines: Chief of Staff and the Army, 1924–1926." M.A. Thesis, Marshall University, 1976.

————. "West Virginia's Best Known General Since 'Stonewall Jackson': John L. Hines." *West Virginia History* 3 (April 1977).

U.S. Army. Office of the Adjutant General. "Statement of the Military Service of *John Leonard Hines*." Washington, D.C., 1966.

LOUIS A. PEAKE

HITCHCOCK, Ethan Allen (b. Vergennes, Vt., May 18, 1798; d. Sparta, Ga., August 5, 1870), Army officer. Hitchcock was known as "The Pen of the Army" by his contemporaries.

Ethan Allen Hitchcock was born into an old and venerable family in Vermont; his father was a prosperous lawyer whose ancestors had settled in New England in the seventeenth century, and his mother was the daughter of Ethan Allen,* a general in the Revolutionary War. Hitchcock was offered and accepted an appointment to West Point in 1814, largely because of the reputation and memory of his illustrious grandfather. Hitchcock was graduated and commissioned in 1817; as rank rolls were not maintained at that time, his academic position in his class cannot be determined. While he enjoyed his military and professional training at West Point, his real interest was more of an academic and scholarly nature. At the Point and throughout his fifty years in the Army, he read the classics, theology, and philosophy with the voracity and the respect of the professional academician. During the later stages of his career, he found time to publish several works on various aspects of theology and philosophy.

Hitchcock's first tour of duty paralleled that of other career junior officers of his day. Between 1817 and 1823 he served on garrison duty at Fort Bowyer in Mobile, Alabama, and in a similar capacity at Baton Rouge, Louisiana. He also was assigned to recruiting duty at various posts in the latter months of 1823.

From 1824 until 1827, Lieutenant Hitchcock held the position of assistant professor of military tactics at West Point. Because of a quarrel with Superintendent Major Sylvanus Thayer* over a rather minor administrative matter, he was relieved of this duty. Protests to the secretary of war and to President John Quincy Adams were of no avail, and Hitchcock was exiled to further garrison duty in Wisconsin.

Returning to West Point in 1829, Captain Hitchcock was appointed to the position of commandant of cadets. In the three years he served in this capacity, Hitchcock turned out such officers as Joseph Eggleston Johnston,* Jefferson Davis,* and Robert Edward Lee.* Once more however, the outspoken Hitchcock ran afoul of his superiors. In 1833 President Andrew Jackson* attacked the alleged elitism of West Point and of its professional officer-instructor corps. Hitchcock went directly to the president and explained his duties as he understood them, but Jackson was not only unimpressed by his arguments, he also held up Hitchcock's promotion to major.

Leaving West Point in 1833, Captain Hitchcock was assigned to General Edmund Pendleton Gaines* as adjutant general; under Gaines' command, he saw service in the Seminole wars of the late 1830s. Hitchcock fully believed that this conflict was unnecessary and that it was the direct result of unfair and treacherous U.S. policies toward the Indians; particularly, he argued that the attitudes and conduct of Andrew Jackson made this bloody war inevitable.

From 1837 to 1842, Hitchcock served as *de facto* superintendent of Indian affairs. In this capacity, he worked tirelessly to halt the widespread corruption and fraud of the War Department and other federal agencies that dealt with Indians. When he was recalled from this duty in 1843 in order to assist in the final disposition of the continuing Seminole Wars, he had reached the rank of lieutenant colonel.

As early as 1836 while serving on the Texas border, Hitchcock had been convinced that the United States' desire for the annexation of that newly created republic was not prompted by an American concern for the liberty of the Texans. Rather, he believed that U.S. interest in the acquisition of Texas was the result of naked land hunger and expansionism. Similarly, while serving in 1844 with General Gaines on the Louisiana-Texas border, he repeatedly stated that the United States' Mexican policy would lead inevitably to war. Such a war, he believed, would be both unnecessary and immoral. Moreover, he correctly perceived that the annexation of Texas would lead ultimately to the dissolution of the Union.

After the Mexican War erupted in 1846, Hitchcock served as commandant of the U.S. Army garrison at Corpus Christi, Texas. The next year found Major Hitchcock being transferred from the command of General Zachary Taylor* to the forces under General Winfield Scott.* He served Scott until 1848 as inspector general. After seeing action at Cerro Gordo and Vera Cruz in Mexico, he was brevetted colonel.

With the cessation of hostilities in 1848, Hitchcock toured Europe for two years, and then, once again, the outspoken Hitchcock became entangled with politics and personalities in the Army. After being brevetted brigadier general in 1851 and serving three years as commanding general of the Department of the Pacific, he was relieved of duty in 1854 by Secretary of War Jefferson Davis. Hitchcock had been a close personal friend of Winfield Scott; Davis, a Democrat, purged most of the friends of Scott, the former Whig presidential candidate. Because of this personal and political enmity with Davis and President Franklin Pierce (who had defeated Scott in 1852), Hitchcock resigned from the Army in 1855 after forty-one years of active service.

Believing his days in the Army to be over, Hitchcock returned to private life and to his growing collection of books. After the firing on Fort Sumter in April 1861, however, his Army friends urged that he return to active duty. Accordingly, Hitchcock came out of retirement and was appointed major general of volunteers in early 1862. Because of the alleged ineptitude of General George Brinton McClellan,* Hitchcock was offered command of the Army of the Potomac by President Abraham Lincoln* in March 1862; because of advancing age and deteriorating health, however, the old general refused this extraordinary opportunity and instead accepted a post as military advisor to President Lincoln and Secretary of War Edwin McMasters Stanton.* He served in this capacity for the duration of the Civil War; during the last two years of the war, he also held a presidential appointment as commissioner for the exchange of prisoners.

In the spring of 1866 Hitchcock was seriously injured in the streets of Washington, D.C., by a runaway horse. Due to his disabilities and age, he was mustered out of the Army on October 1, 1867. Three years later, he died of natural causes, and his body was enterred in the cemetery at West Point.

While Ethan Allen Hitchcock served in the military from the waning days of the War of 1812 to the end of the Civil War, he was never known as a battlefield commander. Although he saw considerable service on the frontier, in the early Indian wars, and experienced combat in the Mexican War, his reputation was not forged in battle. Nevertheless, his ability as a professional officer was never challenged; he was a stern and rigid disciplinarian who reputedly had the best drilled, most highly trained regiments in the pre-Civil War Army. His real talent was as an administrator. Serving first as a training officer at West Point, later as *de facto* superintendent of Indian affairs, and finally as presidential military advisor and commissioner for the exchange of prisoners during the Civil War, Hitchcock was a model administrator who knew how to run an army. Rarely in the foreground, he was a most capable manager; while other, more flamboyant generals led their troops to glory in the field, Hitchcock quietly saw that the Army ran smoothly, efficiently, and effectively.

Hitchcock was a leading soldier-scholar of his era. Not only did he serve with two generations of military men from the early days with Generals William Worth and Gideon Johnson Pillow* to the times of Generals Scott and Taylor, but he was also closely associated with such Civil War leaders as McClellan and Ulysses Simpson Grant.* He was personally acquainted with the leading politicians and literary figures of his day. He dined with Daniel Webster and Henry Clay; he argued furiously with two presidents: by correspondence with John Quincy Adams and in person with Andrew Jackson. He also maintained friendships with Ralph Waldo Emerson, Nathaniel Hawthorne, and Washington Irving, as well as with lesser nonmilitary intellectuals.

A bookish man who delighted in the study and writing of history, philosophy, and theology, he was both a moralist and a humanitarian. Hitchcock's attempts to improve the lot of the Indians, his opposition to the jingoists whose foreign politics eventually led to war with Mexico, and his efforts in behalf of prisoners of war attest to his great concern for others and to his sense of intellectual independence and moral duty.

BIBLIOGRAPHY

Ambrose, Stephen E. *Duty, Honor, Country: A History of West Point*. Baltimore: Johns Hopkins University Press, 1966.

Croffut, W. A., ed. *Fifty Years in Camp and Field: Diary of Major-General Ethan Allen Hitchcock, U.S.A.* New York: G. P. Putnam's Sons, 1909.

Weigley, Russell F. *History of the U.S. Army*. New York: Macmillan Company, 1967.

Williams, Kenneth P. *Lincoln Finds a General.* Vol. 3. New York: Macmillan Company, 1952.
Williams, T. Harry. *Lincoln and His Generals.* New York: Alfred A. Knopf, 1952.

                                              WILLIAM TEAGUE

HOBBY, Oveta Culp (Killeen, Tex., January 19, 1905), government official, newspaper owner, publisher, director of broadcasting and TV stations, philanthropist. Mrs. Hobby is best known as the first director of both the Women's Army Auxiliary Corps and the Women's Army Corps.

Born Oveta Culp, the second child in a large family, she was christened with the unlikely name of Oveta, a romantic American Indian name meaning "forget," which hardly predicted her future personality and accomplishments. From early childhood, she was the close companion of her father, Isaac W. Culp, a lawyer and horsebreeder. She got her first exposure to law by reading the *Congressional Record* to him. At fourteen, as his confidante and assistant, she accompanied him to the state legislature in Austin and returned with him each time he was reelected.

Oveta Culp was precocious and serious. Practical observation was more stimulating to her than formal education, and after one year at the Mary Hardin Baylor College she left school and returned to Austin to work with her father in the legislature. She obtained a position codifying the state's banking laws, an undertaking that had a lasting effect on her philosophy, which retains a strong conservative strain. At twenty-one, she was appointed the first woman legislative parliamentarian of the Texas legislature. She served in that capacity from 1926 to 1931, and again in 1939 and 1941. Her book, *Mr. Chairman*, written in 1936 for high school students, demonstrated her clear thinking, simple logical deductions, and concise presentation of facts—innate attributes that were to be manifested throughout her official and private careers.

In 1931 Oveta Culp married William Pettus Hobby, a widower, former governor of Texas, twenty-seven years her senior. He was then president and later became owner and publisher of *The Houston Post*. Two children were born of this marriage, William, Jr., in 1932, and Jessica, in 1935. She was able to combine family and professional life and by 1938 was elected executive vice-president of *The Post*.

In 1941, when she was still in her thirties, Hobby had already achieved recognition in three distinct fields: legal, parliamentary, and journalistic. Her background and experience took her to Washington as chief, Women's Interest Section, Bureau of Public Affairs in the War Department (1941–1942). Early in 1942, General George Catlett Marshall,* chief of staff, asked her to study plans for establishing a Women's Army Auxiliary Corps. On May 16, 1942, the WAAC was officially authorized by Congress, and Hobby was made director with the rank of colonel.

Her leadership of the Women's Army Auxiliary Corps from its inception in 1942 to its integration into the armed forces in 1943 as the Women's Army Corps (WAC), and then on to the end of World War II, received worldwide recognition. More than 140,000 volunteer officers and enlisted women had made significant contributions to the success of the Allied forces.

At the beginning of the program, working under the dual pressures of time and politics in the context of a national emergency, with a miniscule staff, a few civilian volunteers, and one experienced military officer, Colonel Hobby organized the WAAC. She established procedures for recruiting and training a women's officer corps that, in its turn, would be prepared to recruit, train, and administer a volunteer auxiliary to the U.S. Army, with an authorized strength of twenty-five thousand (later increased to one hundred and fifty thousand) officers and enlisted personnel. The women were to replace men, thereby releasing them for combat duty.

The task was not easy. Fighting for ''serious recognition for serious'' women during the national crisis, Hobby won the respect and admiration of critics and unbelievers in civilian, military, and legislative circles. In 1943, in spite of enormous difficulties and initial misunderstandings, the Women's Army Auxiliary Corps (WAAC) became the Women's Army Corps (WAC), an integral part of the Army. Hobby continued to hold the rank of colonel, although her command status ended and her new status as advisor began.

She was determined that established Army discipline and traditions should remain unchanged, but she fought for, and the Corps earned, its full recognition, which provided all the rights and services authorized for their male counterparts in all ranks. She stood firmly in her demand that members should be volunteers. She insisted that no gratuitous appointments to the officer corps be made; she established a policy that only mentally and physically qualified candidates could attend Officers' Candidate School (OCS); and she insisted that only upon successful completion of the program would commissions be granted. (General Marshall had to intervene to keep Colonel Hobby from attending WAAC OCS herself.)

Hobby believed there should be no distinction in evaluating the conscripted man and the volunteer woman. Were they not both serving their country? Did not the woman serve under a definite, defined line of duties, subject to prescribed discipline? A much discussed and publicized stand taken by Colonel Hobby was that concerning PWOP—''pregnant without permission.'' She argued that the girl alone should not be condemned and thus receive a dishonorable discharge, while the man went unpunished. She won for the WAC honorable discharge with all necessary medical treatment.

In July 1945 Colonel Hobby resigned because of poor health and returned to Texas, rejoining her husband in ownership and operation of *The Houston Post*. It was the end of a period. She had completed her mission to organize the WAC.

Oveta Hobby had been a life-long Democrat, but in 1948 she supported Republican Thomas E. Dewey for the presidency. In 1952 she became a director of Democrats for Dwight David Eisenhower* and played an active role in Texas in his election. Recalling Hobby's leadership of the WAC, the newly elected president appointed her head of the Federal Security Agency. That office was expanded to form the new Department of Health, Education and Welfare (HEW), and Hobby was appointed secretary on April 11, 1953, the only woman in the cabinet.

Hobby's extraordinary tact and ability to deal with all levels of government and before Congress were essential to the success of the new department and fully justified the confidence the president had expressed in her abilities. During her tenure the Clinical Center of the National Institute of Health was founded, social security was extended to farm and domestic workers and to the self-employed, veterans' benefits were enhanced, and manufacturers were licensed to produce in quantity the Dr. Jonas Salk vaccine against paralytic poliomyelitis.

In 1955, because of the declining health of her husband, now seventy-seven, she resigned her cabinet post and returned to Houston.

Oveta Culp Hobby will be remembered primarily for her leadership as the first director of the WAAC and the WAC. Her appointment in 1942 by General Marshall was made with a definite purpose. It was to establish a volunteer corps of women to operate as an auxiliary to the Army until such time as "we could evaluate its worth to the military." This was a pioneer project, without historic precedent or even basic guidelines, but experience showed its value. By the end of World War II 140,000 had served in the WAAC or WAC, and members of the Corps had been stationed throughout the continental United States and in all theaters of operations abroad. Requests for WACs exceeded 600,000—far more than could have been provided.

The leadership, the dedication, the devotion to duty, and the vision Hobby exemplified and exercised quieted the laughter and derision that first greeted the undertaking. The early uneasy adjustment by both the male military and the women volunteers slowly improved through a common bond of purpose, mutual respect, and hard work. General Marshall once commented that when difficulties arose Colonel Hobby would often say, "Give me my sword." She had a refreshing and redeeming sense of humor, and could employ it as a weapon as adroitly as her cool judgment and unswerving purpose in pursuit of her objectives. Her success and that of the Women's Army Corps reflected her high standard in every field of endeavor.

In 1944, in recognition of her service to the United States and the WAC, she received the nation's highest military award for meritorious service—the Distinguished Service Medal—the first WAC to do so. Later, in 1978, the Association of the U.S. Army gave her its highest award, the George Catlett Marshall Medal for Public Service. The presentation noted that "Oveta Culp Hobby, citizen and patriot, had given of herself unstintingly and answered every call to service with dedication, courage and integrity."

The recipient of many honors and awards for her civic and cultural contributions to state and nation, she directs the vast Hobby enterprises with the same foresight, political acumen, serene dignity, and confident assurance she has shown throughout her life.

BIBLIOGRAPHY

Congressional Record, March 9, 1943. House Committee on Military Affairs Hearings, "To Establish the Women's Army Corps for Service in the Army of the United States," S. 495. Washington, D.C.: U.S. Government Printing Office, 1943.

Miles, Rufus E. *The Department of Health, Education and Welfare*. New York: Praeger, 1974 (The Praeger Library of U.S. Government Departments and Agencies, no. 39).

Roosevelt, Eleanor, and Lauren A. Hickok. *Ladies of Courage*. New York: G. P. Putnam's Sons, 1954, pp. 33, 221–30, 232–47.

Treadwell, Mattie E. *The Women's Army Corps*. United States Army in World War II, Special Studies. Washington, D.C.: U.S. Department of the Army, 1954.

U.S. Congress. *Hearings Before the Committee on Finance, U.S. Senate, 1st Session*, January 19, 1953. "Confirmation, Oveta Culp Hobby, Federal Security Administrator-Designate." Washington, D.C.: U.S. Government Printing Office, 1953, pp. 23–28.

U.S. Department of Health, Education and Welfare. *A Common Thread of Service: An Historical Guide to HEW*. Washington, D.C.: U.S. Government Printing Office.

JANE D. CONNELLY

HODGES, Courtney Hicks (b. Perry, Ga., January 5, 1887; d. San Antonio, Tex., January 16, 1966), World War II commanding general of the U.S. First Army in Europe.

The son of a small-town newspaper publisher, Courtney Hodges entered West Point in 1904 but was dismissed after his first year, having failed in geometry. Overcoming parental reluctance, he enlisted in the infantry in 1906 and three years later gained a commission through competitive examination. In World War I Hodges commanded a battalion in the 5th Infantry Division, earning a Distinguished Service Cross for seizing and holding a key bridgehead across the Meuse River. Because of a "hump" of wartime officers granted regular commissions, Hodges remained a permanent major from 1920 to 1934. Nevertheless, the interwar period was for him one of significant professional development. Besides attending the usual General Staff and War College courses, Hodges graduated from the Field Artillery School at Fort Sill and taught infantry tactics at Langley Field, experiences that made him keenly aware of the vital role of artillery and tactical air support in ground warfare. From 1929 to 1933 he was stationed at Fort Benning, where he won the friendship of Omar Nelson Bradley* and the confidence of George Catlett Marshall,* then assistant commandant of the Infantry School.

As the Army's chief of staff in 1940, Marshall promoted Hodges to brigadier general and commandant of the Infantry School. Early in 1941 he brought Hodges to the War Department as the major general in charge of its Infantry Bureau. Following the massive departmental reorganization of March 1942, Hodges headed briefly the Army's new Replacement and School Command. Regarded professionally as a leading expert on infantry training, equipment, weapons, and tactics, in each of the foregoing assignments Hodges significantly influenced the preparation of the American citizen-army for overseas ground combat.

From mid-1942 to the end of 1943 Hodges successively commanded the X Corps and Third Army, both of which were training organizations. As commander of a field army he advanced to lieutenant general. For the invasion of Europe, however, he relinquished the Third Army to George Smith Patton, Jr.,* a proven master of exploitation and pursuit. Still highly esteemed by both Marshall and Bradley (to be the senior American ground commander in the invasion), Hodges went to England early in 1944 as deputy head of Bradley's First Army. Once the Third Army had followed the First into the Normandy battle, Bradley would supervise both formations from a new command echelon: the 12th Army Group. Hodges would replace Bradley at the First Army.

Hodges took over as planned on August 1, 1944, directing the First Army on a swift drive across France to the German border. During the autumn months his troops fought a series of costly, inconclusive battles of attrition along the Siegfried Line in the Aachen and Huertgen Forest region. Just before Christmas of 1944, an unforeseen German offensive erupted from the Ardennes Forest, rolling back the First Army's right wing. Absorbing the main weight of the massive German attack, Hodges counterattacked on January 3, 1945. During much of the Battle of the Bulge, his First Army was directed by Field Marshal Sir Bernard L. Montgomery's 21st Army Group. Returning on January 17, 1945, to Bradley's control, Hodges' command battled into the Rhineland. In March at Remagen it seized a vital bridge across the Rhine. The First Army, together with the Ninth to its left, then encircled more than three hundred thousand German troops in the Ruhr Valley and drove into the heart of Germany. Less celebrated than Patton's Third, Hodges' was nevertheless the first Allied army to pass the German border, breach the Siegfried Line, capture an important German city, cross the Rhine, and make contact with the westward-moving Soviet Army at the Elbe River.

Promoted to full general in April 1945, Hodges was reassigned with First Army headquarters to General Douglas MacArthur's* Pacific command. Had the war lasted until March 1946, the First would have been one of two American armies assaulting Honshu in the Japanese home islands. After the Japanese surrender, the First resumed its peacetime role as an area-defense and training-army headquarters at Governor's Island in New York Harbor. From there Hodges retired early in 1949 to San Antonio, Texas, where he died seventeen years later.

At forty-one Hodges had married Mrs. Mildred Lee Buchner, a widow who, like her new husband, was an expert shot. The general was renowned throughout his long career as a trap shooter and big-game hunter.

Asked once to compare his own First Army with Patton's Third, Courtney Hodges responded by saying, "We were a zonal army. We just slugged.... Some people [like Patton] just naturally attract attention, and all my friends tell me I look more like a school teacher than a general." Hodges remained a comparatively obscure figure during and after the war, despite heading a command with a peak strength over half that of the Union Army in the Civil War. Although Hodges was the subject of several wartime magazine feature articles, after 1945 he did not bother to justify his record by publishing his memoirs. By V-E Day few American generals had more battleline experience than Hodges, nor had any Allied army on the Western Front fought harder or more successfully than the First. Yet he had no nickname. Even the sober, methodical Bradley was celebrated widely as "the GI's General," whereas of Hodges the *New York Times* could say only that "most of the troops under him would be at a loss to describe him or even give you his full name."

Up to a point, Hodges' reticence commended him to his superiors, who understandably became weary of Patton's childish posturing and Montgomery's overweening vanity. According to General Dwight David Eisenhower,* the Allied supreme commander, Hodges was "sturdy and steady." Without knowing Hodges well, Eisenhower nevertheless accepted him as a prospective Army commander in December 1943, after Marshall had praised the Georgian as being "exactly [the] same class of man as Bradley.... [Hodges is]...quiet [and] self-effacing." After the war Bradley described his friend Hodges as "a military technician whose faultless techniques made him one of the most skilled craftsmen of my entire command." Charles B. MacDonald, one of the Army's official historians, refers to Hodges as an Army commander "of the first rank," although MacDonald is severely critical of Hodges' handling of the Battle of the Huertgen Forest. To clear the dense forest First Army troops struggled for many weeks. So rugged was the Huertgen that it denied to the Americans effective exploitation of their air and artillery superiority. Hodges, who normally did not visit subordinate headquarters below the divisional level, failed to see the atrocious conditions with which his men had to contend. Moreover, neither he nor any other Allied senior commander was quick to grasp the overriding strategic importance of certain dams controlling the floodwaters of the Roer River. Pinching out the dams ought to have been the First Army's principal objective from the beginning of the Siegfried Line Campaign. Even after losing the Huertgen Forest, the Germans continued to cling to the Roer Reservoirs.

In December 1944 all of the Allied commanders and their intelligence officers were painfully surprised by the German Ardennes counteroffensive. From Adolph Rosengarten, a liaison officer, Hodges had received frequent briefings on German wireless communications intercepted and deciphered by ULTRA, but even this priceless source failed to betray the planned German attack. Then, when the First Army came under the direction of the 21st Army Group, Montgomery was apparently put off by Hodges' lack of outward charisma. The field marshal considered changing Army commanders, but was dissuaded by Eisenhower, who pointed out that "Hodges is the quiet...type and does not appear as aggressive as he really is. Unless he becomes exhausted he will always wage a good fight." Caught between Montgomery, who wished to make tactical withdrawals in order to build up his reserves, and his subordinate commanders, who insisted on launching immediate counterattacks, Hodges somehow fought his share of the Battle of the Bulge with considerable skill. Eisenhower did not at once realize how effectively Hodges had performed, however. On a confidential evaluation he ranked Hodges below several American generals with comparable responsibilities and experience, and even behind two First Army corps commanders. By the end of March 1945 Eisenhower had come to understand the magnitude of Hodges' achievements, hailing the First Army commander as "the spearhead and the scintillating star" of the climactic thrusts across the Rhine.

Throughout his active command of the First Army, Hodges worked harmoniously with the efficient staff he had inherited from Bradley. He and his headquarters officers kept close track of all the Army's units down to the platoon level. In contrast, Patton's Third Army plotted nothing lower than regiments. At times Hodges' subordinate commanders chafed under his tight leash. Hodges neither overawed his corps and divisional commanders with the egocentric, but magnetic, personality of a Patton, nor won their affection with the warmth of a Bradley. It was widely known that Hodges invariably entrusted the First Army's most important missions to Joseph Lawton Collins'* VII Corps, an understandable preference in view of Collins' exceptional abilities.

In short, Hodges directed the First Army after the fashion of a business executive: objective, detached, and personally colorless—and quick to scrutinize statements of profit and loss. Whatever his personality shortcomings, as commander of the First Army the trim, silver-haired, mild-mannered general with the close-cropped mustache and plastic cigarette-holder oversaw a remarkably successful military organization. Near the end of the war Eisenhower concluded that "by and large" he would find it "difficult to choose" the best of his several exceptionally capable Army commanders. Unlike Patton, Hodges would have been well satisfied by his chief's fairminded assessment.

BIBLIOGRAPHY

Bradley, Omar N. *A Soldier's Story*. New York: Henry Holt, 1951.
Eisenhower, Dwight D. *The Papers of Dwight David Eisenhower*. Edited by Alfred D. Chandler, et al. Vols. 3 and 4. Baltimore: Johns Hopkins University Press, 1970–.
Hill, Gladwin. "For Hodges History Repeats." *New York Times Magazine* (March 25, 1945): 8, 34–35.
MacDonald, Charles B. *The Siegfried Line Campaign*. Washington, D.C.: U.S. Government Printing Office, 1963.
———. *The Mighty Endeavor: American Armed Forces in the European Theater in World War II*. New York: Oxford University Press, 1969.
Murray, Patrick. "Courtney Hodges." *American History Illustrated* (January 1973): 12–25.

                                                                RICHARD G. STONE, JR.

HOOD, John Bell (b. Owingsville, Ky., June 1, 1831; d. New Orleans, August 30, 1879), Army officer. John Hood is best known as the commander of the Texas Brigade during the Civil War.

Born to a well-to-do Kentucky family, John Hood enjoyed an unbridled childhood until entering West Point in 1849. The Spartan simplicity of the Military Academy clashed with young Hood's spirit; he was almost dismissed for excessive demerits. Not caring much about academics, John Hood was graduated forty-fourth in a class of fifty-five in 1853. Hood's graduation order of merit gained him a first assignment with the 4th Infantry Regiment in California. For the next fifteen months Hood's most exciting task was surviving on a lieutenant's pay in Gold Rush country. His next duty station, however, gave him much more valuable experience. Posted to the 2d Cavalry Regiment, commanded by Colonel Albert Sidney Johnston* and Lieutenant Colonel Robert Edward Lee,* Hood worked very closely with both men, gaining their respect for his personal courage and aggressiveness in fighting the Comanches.

Unlike Lee, Hood never hesitated when it came time to choose between the Union or the Confederacy. He resigned from the U.S. Army in April, 1861 and, because his native Kentucky stayed with the Union, adopted Texas as his new home. Accepting a Confederate commission, Hood first commanded the cavalry forces in the Virginia Peninsula.

Hood's association with the cavalry soon ended when President Jefferson Davis* appointed him the commander of the 4th Texas Regiment. This unit had arrived in Virginia without a qualified commander, and Davis, who desired to have native sons leading state units, gave the adopted Hood his chance. The new commander spent the next few months establishing a rapport with the rowdy Texans by always explaining why training and discipline were necessary and by developing a deep sense of unit pride. Davis recognized Hood's talent with the frontiersmen and in March 1862 gave the young colonel command of the entire Texas Brigade. In their first fight two months later, the Texans established a reputation for steadiness under fire. At Eltham Landing in May 1862, Hood's unit repulsed a Federal attempt to turn the Confederate position. Performing like veterans, the Texans demonstrated the value of Hood's training and discipline.

In the remaining months of 1862 Hood and his troops performed gallantly. Robert E. Lee called Hood one of his most promising officers, while the Texas Brigade became the South's shock troops—always being placed where the hardest fighting was about to occur. At Gaines' Mill, in June, Hood led his soldiers in a decisive frontal assault against the entrenched Union infantry and artillery forces, breaching the Northern lines and routing the blueclad troops. Although not requiring a great deal of tactical brilliance, Hood's assault was highly praised by Lee, who described it as one of the most courageous acts he had ever witnessed.

Hood and his brigade again proved their mettle at Antietam. Positioned on Lee's left flank, Hood's unit prevented the Confederates' early defeat by repelling the attacks of two Union corps, thereby buying the required time for Lee to feed his reserves into the battle. The Texas Brigade was shattered, but Lee, praising Hood for his stubborn defense and audacious counterattack, promoted him to major general and gave him command of the division which included his Texans.

The next summer, Lee again marched north, this time to Gettysburg. Receiving the assignment of taking Little Round Top, Hood, after pleading unsuccessfully to be sent further south and around the Federal left, led a frontal assault—the tactic for which he had become so famous. This time not even Hood's inspiration could move his men up that hill. Suffering a terrible arm wound, Hood left the field and missed the remainder of this disastrous battle.

After less than ten weeks of medical care, Hood rejoined the division, his now paralyzed arm strapped to his body. Once again luck abandoned the young general; in September 1863 he lost a leg at Chickamauga leading a charge against the Union center. Convalescing in Richmond, Hood became the darling of Confederate society. Having suffered grievous losses, the South needed heroes to bolster morale, and the adopted Texan gallantly accepted his new role. Gaining political support by serving as an advisor to President Davis, Hood soon gained command of a corps in the Army of the Tennessee under Joseph Eggleston Johnston,* who was defending Atlanta. Promoted to lieutenant general, the aggressive Hood was soon at odds with Johnston, the master of the defense. Hood believed that Johnston, by his constant retreat, had given up excellent opportunities to strike at the Federal army under William Tecumseh Sherman* and had thereby lost men and territory without gaining any benefits. President Davis agreed and gave command of the army to Hood.

With Sherman's army slowly closing on Atlanta, the offensively minded Hood made two audacious attacks that achieved initial surprise. Failing to coordinate his forces, however, Hood could not achieve decisive results and did not check Sherman's advance. Threatened with the envelopment of his entire force inside Atlanta by Sherman's southward moving troops, Hood evacuated the city and attempted a desperate gamble. He intended to march north and, by cutting Sherman's supply lines from Nashville, force a Union withdrawal from Atlanta.

Slipping away from Sherman's troops, Hood, who had to be strapped on his horse, began the bold attack on the Federal supply lines. After an initial effort to catch the elusive Confederates, Sherman cut himself off from his supply base and headed for the sea. The job of stopping Hood fell to General George Henry Thomas.* Failing again to coordinate and control his corps commanders, Hood was unable to strike at the scattered Union forces and allowed them to fall back on Franklin, Tennessee, where they entrenched. After a futile frontal assault in which the Army of the Tennessee suffered tremendous casualties, Hood marched his force to Nashville, hoping for a miracle. There General Thomas, using a series of flanking movements, crushed the last remaining troops in the Army of the Tennessee. Hood asked to be relieved after this defeat. He learned of Lee's surrender on his way back to Texas to recruit another army.

John Bell Hood spent his remaining fourteen years in New Orleans. Failing at a variety of business endeavors, he struggled hard to support his wife and eleven children. When yellow fever swept New Orleans in 1879, it claimed the gallant Hood.

Hood's finest quality was his ability to lead men in combat. The shot and shell which made other men apprehensive never seemed to affect him. His coolness under fire was legendary and became an inspiration to all around him. The chief beneficiary of this leadership was the Texas Brigade—a group of rowdy frontiersmen to whom the word discipline meant absolutely nothing. Hood was able to harness their spirit and match it to his own. By explaining the reasons for training and discipline, he gained their respect and trust. In the crucible of combat this respect was soon transformed into genuine mutual admiration. Hood and the Texas Brigade became the same, with the unit acquiring his personality—courageous, aggressive, and possessing an indomitable will to fight. Their performance earned them the title ''Grenadier Guards of the Army of Northern Virginia'' and Hood the reputation as one of the bravest men in the Confederacy. John Bell Hood never commanded the Texas Brigade; he led it.

This form of leadership, absolutely vital at the brigade and division level, was of less value when Hood became a corps and later an army commander. Too far removed from the troops to exert his charisma, Hood lacked the capability to command the entire Army of the Tennessee. His failure to coordinate among his corps cost him victories outside Atlanta and Nashville. At a time when the South needed a brilliant strategist, all Hood could offer was a well-worn tactician. His greatest flaw lay in his utter dependence on the unimaginative frontal assault. Determined to let courage and will instead of maneuver decide the issue, he weakened his army before Atlanta and then destroyed it at Franklin and Nashville.

Hood's career mirrored the major problem that plagued the Confederacy as the war dragged on. The qualities for brigade and division command were not always the same as those required for higher command. John Bell Hood was a fighter, not a strategist; but when the battle flags were unfurled and the drums began to beat, there was no better assault force than Hood and his Texas Brigade.

BIBLIOGRAPHY

Dyer, John P. *The Gallant Hood*. New York: Bobbs-Merrill Company, 1950.
Freemen, Douglas Southall. *Lee's Lieutenants*. New York: Charles Scribner's Sons, 1943.
Hood, John B. *Advance and Retreat*. Bloomington: Indiana University Press, 1959.
O'Conner, Richard. *Hood: Cavalier General*. New York: Prentice-Hall, 1949.
Simpson, Harold B. *Hood's Texas Brigade: Lee's Grenadier Guard*. Waco, Tex.: Texian Press, 1970.

ROBERT E. WOLFF

HOOKER, Joseph (b. Hadley, Mass., November 13, 1814; d. Garden City, N.Y., October 31, 1879), Army officer. Hooker was commander of the Union Army of the Potomac at Chancellorsville during the Civil War.

The grandson of a captain in the American Revolution, Joseph Hooker received his early education at the Hopkins Academy in Hadley, Massachusetts. He was graduated twenty-ninth out of fifty in the West Point class of 1837. Following service in the Second Seminole War and along the Canadian border, he returned to the Military Academy as adjutant.

In the War with Mexico, Hooker participated heroically in the campaigns of both Zachary Taylor* and Winfield Scott,* winning three brevets for meritorious conduct at Monterrey, the National Bridge, and Chapultepec. His record was marred, however, when, at a court of inquiry, he testified unwisely and inaccurately on behalf of schemer Gideon Johnson Pillow* against Scott, thereby incurring Scott's permanent enmity.

Restless and ambitious, and faced with slow promotions after the Mexican War, Hooker resigned from the Army in 1853 and farmed without conspicuous success near Sonoma, California. He was later superintendent of military roads in Oregon in 1858–1859 and a colonel of California militia in 1859–1861. While on the West Coast, he gained the hostility of Henry Wager Halleck* that would follow him in the Civil War.

When Fort Sumter was bombarded by the Confederates in mid-April 1861, Hooker offered his services to the Union. When no high commission was tendered him, he journeyed to Washington, D.C., and was a civilian observer at the First Battle of Bull Run in July. He finally secured an interview with President Abraham Lincoln,* during which he proclaimed that he was a better general than any the Federals had at Bull Run. Lincoln apparently liked his self-assurance and named him a brigadier general of volunteers. He commanded successively a brigade and division in the Army of the Potomac that George Brinton McClellan* was organizing near Washington.

Hooker was at this time a fine figure of an officer—tall, robust, and of soldierly bearing. He had a florid complexion, a great shock of graying hair, and penetrating blue eyes. Immensely self-confident, he could savagely denounce superiors as well as subordinates, although he was well liked by most of the men in the ranks and the officers under him. Possessed with lion-hearted courage, he was exhilarated by personally experiencing mortal combat in the field. While preeminently the officer of action and dash, he could ably plan military operations and, up to a point, execute them dexterously. Hooker played a prominent part in the Battle of Williamsburg on the Peninsula, May 5, 1862, as well as in several of the heavier engagements of the Seven Days' Battle in late June. His combativeness won for him the sobriquet "Fighting Joe," although the actual words resulted from a journalistic error and he was never proud of the nickname.

At South Mountain on September 14, 1862, in command of the I Corps, Hooker played a leading role in driving the Southerners from Turner's Gap, thereby helping significantly to force Robert Edward Lee* and his Army of Northern Virginia back into a cramped defensive position along the Antietam Creek near Sharpsburg, Maryland. In the Battle of Antietam, on September 17, while impetuously leading his troops forward early in the day on the northern end of the field, he was wounded in the foot and borne from the field. In the Fredericksburg Campaign of Ambrose Everett Burnside* in December, Hooker commanded a grand division of two corps. While his spirited attacks against the stonewall were abortive, Hooker's advice to Burnside to desist from such suicidal assaults was sound and should have been heeded.

When Burnside was relieved of his command, Hooker was named commander of the Army of the Potomac in January 1863, although Lincoln felt impelled to write him a remarkable letter. In it, the president said, accurately and bluntly, "...you have taken counsel of your ambition....I have heard...of your recently saying that both the army and the Government needed a dictator. Of course, it was not for this, but in spite of it, that I have given you the command. Only those generals who gain successes can set up dictators. What I now ask of you is military success, and I will risk the dictatorship.'' Hooker was profoundly moved by the letter.

Hooker's stewardship of the Army of the Potomac began auspiciously in the winter of early 1863 when he capably instituted a number of needed administrative reforms. He then turned toward planning a campaign against the Confederate Army still ensconced at Fredericksburg. Fighting Joe would have some one hundred and thirty-two thousand men compared to Lee's sixty-two thousand. The Federal commander would dispatch his cavalry to operate on the enemy's line of communications between Fredericksburg and Richmond while Hooker, leaving John Sedgwick with some forty thousand men opposite Lee, would move the bulk of the national army up the north bank and cross the Rappahannock and Rapidan rivers and come in from the west against Lee's rear at Fredericksburg. It was a brilliant and feasible plan. But Hooker damaged his good reputation as head of the army by his loud and bombastic overconfidence.

The campaign began well enough in late April 1863, despite the ineffectiveness of the Federal cavalry, when, in a masterfully executed maneuver, Hooker crossed the rivers and reached Chancellorsville, just ten miles to the west of Lee's army, still in position at Fredericksburg facing Sedgwick. On the morning of May 1 Hooker pushed his large force eastward, the advance elements of it emerging from the tangled Wilderness onto open ground, where the superior Union artillery could play to good effect. But Hooker was astonished to see Lee, now apprised of the Federal threat, actually moving westward to confront him, the Confederate chieftain leaving Jubal Early* with some ten thousand men to contain Sedgwick at Fredericksburg. Losing his nerve, and uncharacteristically refusing to fight offensively, Hooker, against the advice of all of his top generals, recoiled back into the Wilderness and deployed his army in a defensive arc about the crossroads at Chancellorsville. This enabled Lee to send Thomas Jonathan (''Stonewall'') Jackson* on the latter's famous turning movement and flank attack of May 2 against Hooker's exposed right (west) wing, which was shattered by Jackson's sledgehammer blow and sent reeling backward. But nightfall and the mortal wounding of Jackson halted the Confederate advance.

The next day in a resumption of the fighting, Hooker was injured but would not relinquish command, and he still insisted that the army fight passively on the defensive. After Sedgwick had driven Early away from Fredericksburg, Sedgwick was bettered by Lee at the Battle of Salem Church and forced to the north side of the river via Banks Ford. Near Chancellorsville, Hooker's lines were forced back slowly, the Union commander refusing to use two of his best corps which had remained unengaged. Despite the recommendation of a majority of his corps commanders to stay and fight it out, the demoralized Hooker retreated back to his starting point opposite Fredericksburg after having lost some 17,287 men at Chancellorsville, as against Lee's 12,463. With Lee launching his second invasion of the North in June 1863, Hooker maneuvered his army well in the early stages of the Gettysburg Campaign; but, having incurred the loss of confidence of Lincoln, Secretary of War Edwin McMasters Stanton,* and General in Chief Halleck, he was replaced in command of the Army of the Potomac by George Gordon Meade.*

After the battle at Gettysburg, Hooker was later given command of the newly formed XX Corps, made up of the remnants of the XI and XII Corps, and he again showed his high ability as a corps commander under Ulysses Simpson Grant* at the fighting around Chattanooga—especially at Lookout Mountain— in late 1863 and with the armies under William Tecumseh Sherman* in Sherman's advance upon Atlanta in the spring and summer of 1864. But Hooker resigned his command when a junior officer—Oliver Otis Howard*—was given command of one of Sherman's armies instead of himself.

From September 28, 1864, to July 5, 1865, Hooker headed the Northern Department; from July 8, 1865, to August 6, 1866, the Department of the East; and from August 23, 1866, to June 1, 1867, the Department of the Lakes. He had been married in 1865 to Olivia Groesbeck. Owing to partial paralysis stemming from his old Chancellorsville injury, he retired from the Army as a major general on October 15, 1868.

Except for exceptionally meritorious service rendered in the Mexican War, Joseph Hooker's career up to the Civil War was largely an unrewarding one. Possessing self-confidence, high physical courage, audacity, and administrative abilities of a high order, Hooker was fatally flawed by his lack of self-control, mercurial temperament, and sharp tongue. Even more serious were his lack of subordination and his talk of a military dictatorship.

But Hooker was graced with real military talents, and, up through the level of corps or grand division (wing) commander, he was one of the ablest of all Civil War generals. He was incapable of sustained mental concentration, however, and he lacked the intellect and character to command a great army, as shown at Chancellorsville. This operation was masterfully planned and, in its initial stages, brilliantly executed. Hooker, however, could not make war on the map or successfully command troops that he could not actually see with his own eyes, nor could he improvise adequately. Even after Stonewall Jackson's successful flank attack, Hooker would still have been master of the situation had he counterattacked with his thirty-seven thousand fresh troops. That he refused to do so shows that Lee had regained the initiative and had reasserted the moral ascendancy over Fighting Joe.

Hooker had started out the Chancellorsville Campaign determined to remain on the strategic and tactical offensive. He was convinced that Lee would have to retreat, and he was astounded and stunned into mental paralysis when Lee daringly refused to withdraw and instead turned upon the Federals. The Union commander acknowledged in his official report that he "could not get his men in position" to employ all of them in the combat. Some argue that Hooker, said to have been "a three-bottle man," suddenly stopped his drinking and that this helped cause his loss of nerve at the climax of the operations at Chancellorsville.

When he resumed his habit, he again performed excellently as a corps commander under Grant and Sherman.

Some historians believe that Lincoln should never have named Hooker to the army command in the first place and that the president's own remarkable letter to the general contains within it ample reasons why so reckless a person as one who talked of a dictatorship should never have been entrusted with a position of such great military responsibility.

BIBLIOGRAPHY

Bigelow, John, Jr. *The Campaign of Chancellorsville: A Strategic and Tactical Study.* New Haven, Conn.: Yale University Press, 1910.
Dodge, Theodore A. *The Campaign of Chancellorsville.* Boston: J. R. Osgood, 1881.
Hassler, Warren W., Jr. *Commanders of the Army of the Potomac.* Baton Rouge: Louisiana State University Press, 1962.
Hebert, Walter H. *Fighting Joe Hooker.* Indianapolis: Bobbs-Merrill Company, 1944.
Williams, T. Harry. *Lincoln and His Generals.* New York: Alfred A. Knopf, 1952.

WARREN W. HASSLER, JR.

HOPKINS, Esek (b. Providence, R.I., April 26, 1718; d. Scituate, R.I., February 26, 1802), naval officer. Hopkins commanded the U.S. Fleet during the American Revolution.

Esek Hopkins was one of nine children born to William and Ruth Wilkinson Hopkins. The family lived in modern-day Scituate, Rhode Island. Esek's grandfather, Thomas Hopkins (along with Roger Williams), was one of the founders of the town of Providence.

After his father's death in 1738, Esek, "a stout, tall and handsome young man," left the family farm and went to sea. He rose quickly to command and became a well-known New England mariner. In 1741 he married Desire Burroughs and shortly thereafter moved to Newport, Rhode Island. In 1748 they returned to Providence where he kept his home for the remainder of his life. The Hopkins had ten children. During the French and Indian War (1754–1763), Hopkins commanded a privateer. His ventures were successful and it was perhaps with some of his prize money that he purchased his two hundred acre farm. Hopkins came from a politically active family. His older brother Stephen was elected governor, and Esek himself served as a representative in the Rhode Island Assembly. Despite his political and family obligations, Hopkins continued going to sea. He made several long voyages to Africa and the East Indies as well as shorter ones to the West Indies. Sometime in the early 1770s Hopkins "swallowed the anchor" and settled down on his farm with his wife and family. Events in the spring and summer of 1775, however, wrecked any hopes that he might have had for a peaceful retirement.

In the aftermath of the battles at Lexington and Concord, royal authority collapsed in Rhode Island. Fearful that their coast was undefended and open to British attack, the Rhode Island Assembly made plans for defense. Hopkins' sea experience and political connections made him a logical choice to lead the colony's forces, and on October 4, 1775, he was commissioned state commander in chief with the rank of brigadier general.

While Hopkins was laboring to protect Rhode Island, in Philadelphia representatives from all the colonies were meeting in a Continental Congress. In June they had created an American army, and now in the fall they were making preparations to launch a navy. The New England delegates were the most vocal supporters of a navy, including one of the representatives from Rhode Island, Esek's brother Stephen. After considerable debate, Congress authorized the Naval Committee (later known as the Marine Committee) to charter and arm eight merchantmen to sail as Continental warships. To command this squadron Congress selected Esek Hopkins, bestowing on him the title commander in chief.

It took Hopkins several weeks to prepare the ships and recruit seamen, but by February 1776 he was ready to sail. The squadron set sail from Philadelphia, down Delaware Bay, past the Capes, and into the Atlantic. Their course was due south. Hopkins' orders were to sail along the Virginia and Carolina coasts to "search out and attack, take or destroy all the Naval force of our Enemies that you may find there." For his own reasons Hopkins disobeyed his orders. He bypassed the American coast and struck out for Nassau on the island of New Providence in the Bahamas. Virtually undefended, the islands fell easily to Hopkins. After taking the fort at Nassau, he had his sailors load a considerable amount of munitions and a number of captured cannon on his ships. This ordnance eventually reached the American Army. He left Nassau bound north on March 17, 1776.

Off Block Island the American squadron fell in with the British frigate *Glasgow*. In the running battle that followed, Hopkins' ill-trained sailors and lubberly merchantmen proved no match for *Glasgow*'s well-disciplined crew. Although she was outgunned and outnumbered, the *Glasgow* managed to damage the Americans and escape. The engagement was an embarrassment for Hopkins.

Shortly after the squadron was safely back in Rhode Island, Hopkins and two of his officers, Dudley Saltonstall and Abraham Whipple, were ordered to appear before Congress to answer complaints about their conduct. After considerable delay, Hopkins finally appeared before an unfriendly Congress in August. The debate over his conduct lasted two days and aroused considerable passion. Those most angry with him were the representatives from the South whose coasts he had bypassed and had left to be harassed by British warships. He was defended by William Ellery, a Rhode Island delegate, and by John Adams. It was to no avail. On August 16 Congress voted to censure him.

Hopkins returned to Rhode Island and made efforts to get his ships to sea again. Disease, desertion, and competition for men and supplies from privateers complicated matters. Adding to the commander in chief's woes, in December 1776 the British occupied Newport. Entering or leaving Providence would now be extremely hazardous. Delays in distribution of prize money and wages caused discontent among the American sailors in Providence. In February 1777 ten of his officers presented their complaints against Hopkins to Congress. Chief among their allegations was that Hopkins had publicly ridiculed Congress. After considering the charges, on May 14, 1777, Congress suspended Hopkins from command. He remained in limbo until January 2, 1778, when he was officially dismissed from the service.

Esek Hopkins spent the remainder of his life in Rhode Island. He served again as a representative in the Assembly as well as collector of imports and trustee of Rhode Island College (later Brown University). He died in 1802 at the age of eighty-four.

Esek Hopkins had the misfortune of being given an impossible task and then was blamed for not accomplishing it. In trying to create a navy, Congress was building a preposterous structure on a pitiful foundation. It would have taken a naval officer of vast experience and wisdom to have accomplished the task. Hopkins was neither experienced nor wise.

His decision to bypass Virginia and the Carolinas might have been strategically sound, but it was political folly. Southerners in the Congress had always viewed the Navy as a New England scheme to make money building ships and capturing prizes. Hopkins' conduct reinforced that prejudice. Furthermore, Hopkins appears not to have been particularly adept at handling his men or maintaining good relations with local merchants. He was an irascible sort.

Hopkins was a good seaman, but his failures as an administrator and naval officer eventually caused his downfall. Southern congressmen suspicious of New England's motives were not likely to tolerate the mistakes of a Yankee commander in chief.

BIBLIOGRAPHY

Allen, Gardner W. *The Naval History of the American Revolution*. 2 vols. Boston: Houghton Mifflin Company, 1913.

Field, Edward. *Esek Hopkins: Commander-in-Chief of the Continental Navy*. Providence, R.I.: Preston and Rounds Company, 1898.

Fowler, William M., Jr. *Rebels Under Sail: The American Navy During the Revolution*. New York: Charles Scribner's Sons, 1976.

Morgan, William J. *Captains to the Northward: The New England Captains in the Continental Navy*. Barre, Maine: Barre Gazette, 1959.

WILLIAM M. FOWLER, JR.

HOWARD, Oliver Otis (b. Leeds, Maine, November 8, 1830; d. Burlington, Vt., October 26, 1909), Army officer. Howard was a corps commander in the U.S. Army during the Civil War and commissioner of the Bureau of Refugees, Freedmen and Abandoned Lands (Freedmen's Bureau).

A descendant of a family that had arrived in New England in 1634, young Otis Howard early developed the characteristics of sobriety, perseverance, and piety that would later earn him the sobriquet "Christian soldier." After six months of intense study at North Yarmouth Academy near Portland, Maine, Howard entered Bowdoin College in 1846. Upon completing his studies in 1850, he went to West Point. Graduating fourth in a class of forty-six, Howard, still uncertain about his future, decided to stay in the Army.

Howard served as an ordnance officer in Maine and Florida and fell into the languid routine of peacetime military service. He married Elizabeth Waite in 1855, and by 1857, the young couple had two children. Howard became an instructor in mathematics at West Point, a post well suited to his intellectual interests and personality. After several years of tortuous self-examination, Howard became an Episcopalian and considered studying for the ministry. The outbreak of the Civil War, however, dashed these dreams.

Howard became a colonel (3d Maine Volunteer Infantry Regiment), but his military experience, connections with James G. Blaine, other Maine politicians, and his own ability would bring rapid promotions. Howard's regiment arrived in Virginia in July 1861, and he received a brigade command in the army of General Irvin McDowell.* At the First Battle of Bull Run, Howard's soldiers joined the fighting late in the day but could make no headway against well-entrenched Confederates and had to withdraw from the field with the rest of McDowell's units. Shortly after the battle, Howard was promoted to the rank of brigadier general. At the Battle of Fair Oaks on June 1, 1862, Howard was wounded twice in the right arm, forcing an amputation halfway between the elbow and shoulder. Howard recuperated back in Maine, and returned to the field with the Army of Virginia under General John Pope* shortly before the Second Battle of Bull Run. Howard's brigade was in hard fighting at the Battle of Antietam, and when General John Sedgewick was wounded, Howard took over command of the 2d Division, II Corps. Howard's men suffered heavy losses at the Battle of Fredericksburg in attacking the strong Confederate positions above the town. In November Howard was promoted to major general, and in March 1863 he received command of the XI Corps, which consisted largely of Germans, many of whom resented the departure of their popular commander, Franz Sigel.

At Chancellorsville, Howard's corps was on the extreme left of the Union line. Convinced that the Confederates were retreating, Howard failed to secure his lines against attack from the west. Suddenly, toward dusk on May 2, 1863, the soldiers of Thomas Jonathan ("Stonewall") Jackson* came charging through the thick underbrush of the area known as the Wilderness. Brigade after brigade dissolved under the assault, but Howard gathered the remnants of his forces and slowed the enemy advance. His negligence had hurt the Union side badly, but it was the loss of nerve by General Joseph Hooker* that decided the battle.

Howard arrived at Gettysburg on July 1 and found a battle already in progress. Once again his corps of Germans had to retreat before Confederate attacks, but he did manage to regroup his men and hold on to a vital position on Cemetery Hill. Howard remained a controversial general, and he was soon transferred to the west under the command of William Tecumseh Sherman.* Profiting from his earlier mistakes, Howard became a skilled field general in the final year of the war. Still, his overall record was checkered at best. His promotion of prayer meetings and temperance had, as often as not, offended the less pious and sober men under his command, and his performance in battle had been mediocre.

In May 1865 President Andrew Johnson appointed Howard commissioner of the newly created Freedmen's Bureau. Howard's military rank along with his sincere concern for the plight of Southern blacks made him particularly qualified for this post. Howard sought to ease the transition from slavery to freedom, encourage the blacks in productive labor, and liquidate the role of the federal government as soon as possible. He generally appointed Army officers with whom he was personally acquainted as assistant commissioners, but personnel problems plagued the Freedmen's Bureau throughout its existence (1865–1872).

Howard dutifully administered the issuance of rations to the destitute as well as providing them medical assistance. He favored distributing confiscated and abandoned lands to the blacks, but President Johnson overturned this policy. In the full belief that the former rebels meant to restore slavery, Howard encouraged the signing of labor contracts and provided for a minimal protection of black rights in the Bureau courts. After the passage of the Reconstruction Acts, Howard advised his subordinates to avoid political activity, but he openly favored black suffrage. Howard likewise devoted great attention to the problems of Negro education and was instrumental in the founding of his namesake institution, Howard University, in Washington, D.C.

During his Bureau years, Howard was an active member of the First Congregational Church in Washington and became embroiled in a heated controversy over his advocacy of blacks for membership. Howard's enemies charged that he had profited from his position in the Freedmen's Bureau, but in 1874 a military court of inquiry fully exonerated him of any wrongdoing.

The last years of Howard's career were anticlimactic. Ironically, Howard, who was deeply concerned over the welfare of Indians, ended up chasing them through Idaho, Wyoming, and Montana during the tragic Nez Perce War of 1877. He served briefly as the superintendent at West Point and retired in 1894.

Howard's performance as commissioner of the Freedmen's Bureau remains controversial. The Dunning school of Reconstruction historians generally castigated him as a misguided, if not corrupt, visionary who never understood the necessity for keeping the blacks in a subordinate status. Beginning in the 1950s, revisionist scholars refurbished Howard's reputation by portraying him as an idealist sincerely devoted to the interests of the freedmen. John A. Carpenter capped this trend by writing a biography, which, while recognizing Howard's faults, portrayed him in a favorable light. More recently, William McFeely branded Howard a "Yankee stepfather," that is, a conservative and often vacillating administrator who failed as a spokesman and defender of Southern blacks.

Each of these interpretations contains an element of truth. Howard's inordinate pride and self-righteousness often offended his colleagues, and his administrative methods were frequently lax. Yet few could doubt Howard's genuine devotion to emancipation or his Christian commitment to a more just society. That the Bureau failed to achieve its major goals of guiding, educating, and improving the lot of the newly freed slaves was not so much a result of Howard's flawed character as it was indicative of the spirit of the age. McFeely unfairly applies twentieth-century values to Howard's work, weighs the general in his own peculiar balance, and naturally finds him wanting. But by the standards of his own time, Howard was certainly a radical on the race question: he favored black suffrage, advocated distributing land to the freedmen, and scoffed at the phony issue of amalgamation. In the end Howard, like so many other figures of the period, seems to have been doomed to tragic failure. Certainly, Army officers were not ideal instruments for reforming Southern society, but the refusal of the white South to accept any real changes in race relations made Howard's task a Herculean one. Howard and his Bureau were a godsend for many Southern blacks in the years immediately following the Civil War, and this limited success would serve as an epitaph to Howard's long life.

BIBLIOGRAPHY

Bentley, George R. *A History of the Freedmen's Bureau.* Philadelphia: University of Pennsylvania Press, 1955.

Carpenter, John A. *Sword and Olive Branch: Oliver Otis Howard.* Pittsburgh: University of Pittsburgh Press, 1964.

Howard, Oliver Otis. *Autobiography of Oliver Otis Howard.* 2 vols. New York: Baker and Taylor, 1907.

McFeely, William S. *Yankee Stepfather: General O. O. Howard and the Freedmen.* New Haven, Conn.: Yale University Press, 1968.

GEORGE C. RABLE

HULL, Isaac (b. Derby, Conn., March 9, 1773; d. Philadelphia, Pa., February 13, 1843), naval officer. Hull is best known for his victory in the *Constitution* over the *Guerriere* in the War of 1812.

Isaac Hull was the second of seven sons of Joseph and Sarah Bennett Hull. He apparently began going to sea as a teenager in his father's ships trading to the West Indies and then moved to Boston where he worked his way up to command of his first vessel in 1794. His merchant career did not prosper, and after two successive captures by French privateers he applied for a commission in the Navy. His application was fostered by his uncle, William Hull, and in 1798 Isaac Hull was commissioned a lieutenant and assigned as fourth in the 44-gun frigate *Constitution* under Samuel Nicholson.

Hull made two cruises under Nicholson, and by the time Nicholson was replaced by Silas Talbot he had risen to first lieutenant of the frigate. Under Talbot, in May 1800, he got his first opportunity for glory as leader of a cutting-out expedition in Puerto Plata, Santo Domingo, an achievement of which he was always proud, even though the prize had to be surrendered because Puerto Plata was technically a neutral harbor. When the Quasi-War ended, Hull was retained on the Peace Establishment as the Navy's second-ranking lieutenant. He nearly resigned, however, when he was made executive of the 28-gun frigate *Adams* under a junior captain, Hugh G. Campbell. Second thoughts and his own distaste for the merchant service kept him in the Navy, and in 1803 he received his first command, the 12-gun schooner *Enterprize*. In *Enterprize*, and from 1803 to 1806 in the 18-gun brig *Argus*, Hull was one of the most active junior commanders in the Mediterranean in the successive squadrons of Richard V.

Morris, Edward Preble,* and Samuel Barron. Promoted to master commandant in 1804, he led the naval support force for William Eaton's expedition to "the shores of Tripoli" and capture of the city of Derna.

After his promotion to captain and return to the United States in 1806, Hull was in charge of building gunboats in Connecticut and Rhode Island until the *Chesapeake* crisis of 1807. He then went to Norfolk to sit on the court of inquiry which recommended the court-martial of James Barron and his officers, and he subsequently commanded the gunboat flotilla in Chesapeake Bay. In 1809 Hull was given command of the 36-gun frigate *Chesapeake*. He took the frigate to Boston where he remained until 1810 when he transferred to the 44-gun frigate *President*. This command was brief because Commodore John Rodgers,* the senior officer afloat, was dissatisfied with his frigate, *Constitution*, as too slow, and demanded an exchange. Hull, after assuming command of the *Constitution*, worked hard at improving her sailing. She was somewhat better by 1811, when she carried Joel Barlow to France as U.S. minister, but after her return in February 1812 she had to be hove out and recoppered at Washington. This was barely completed and she was still in the Potomac when the United States declared war on Great Britain in June 1812.

In July Hull sailed for New York to join Rodgers' squadron, but the *Constitution* was pursued off the New Jersey coast by the British fleet under Commodore P.B.V. Broke. Her narrow escape after a three-day chase was credited to Hull's ever-renowned seamanship. Blocked from entering New York, Hull went to Boston, whence he sailed again on August 2 without receiving orders from the Navy Department—luckily for him, since the orders on the way instructed him to surrender the *Constitution* to William Bainbridge,* his senior, and to take command of the 38-gun frigate *Constellation*. Cruising to the northward, the *Constitution* on August 19 met the British frigate *Guerriere* (38-guns) and in half an hour reduced her to a dismasted wreck; the *Constitution* took small damage and only fourteen casualties herself. Hull's victory, the first of the war, made him a national hero. He was feted from Boston to Washington, made a romantic marriage in January 1813 to Ann McCurdy Hart, a Connecticut belle, and spent the remaining war years at Portsmouth, New Hampshire, commanding the Navy Yard where one of the first American line-of-battle ships was being built. This ship, the 74-gun *Washington*, was not quite complete when the war ended.

In 1815 Hull somewhat reluctantly accepted appointment to the first Board of Navy Commissioners, but a few months in Washington convinced him that he was not cut out for that kind of post. He asked for and received command of the Charlestown (Boston) Navy Yard, where he remained until 1823, but not without controversy. William Bainbridge, on his return from the Mediterranean in late 1815, claimed the right to resume command of the Charlestown Yard, beginning a three-year struggle which Hull won but leaving Bainbridge angry and vengeful. He incited junior officers to gossip and quarrel with Hull, leading ultimately to a series of bitter trials in 1822. The controversy took on political overtones, as Federalists and Republicans arrayed themselves on the sides of the accusers or of Hull.

Hull was glad to go to sea again as commodore of the Pacific Squadron from 1824 to 1827. He was present at the final acts of the Peruvian and Chilean struggle for independence, movements for which he felt great sympathy. From 1829 to 1835 he had an uneventful tour as commandant of the Washington Navy Yard. After two years spent in Europe for his wife's health, and service on a board to revise the tables of allowances, he assumed command in October 1838 of the Mediterranean Squadron with his flag in the 84-gun ship-of-the-line *Ohio*. But this last cruise was a bitter one, for the lieutenants of the *Ohio* objected to their rooms on the orlop deck which, although ordered by the Navy commissioners as an experiment, they blamed on the presence in the ship of Mrs. Hull and her sister. After much unpleasantness, Hull sent several of these men home and was humiliated when they were ordered back by Secretary of the Navy James K. Paulding. Hull suffered two apoplectic strokes in 1840–1841, but he saw his cruise to the end in the face of a war scare with Great Britain over the Maine boundary question. After returning to the United States in 1841 he traveled a while for his health, and in the winter of 1842 settled in Philadelphia, where he died on February 13, 1843.

Isaac Hull's life was the epitome of a nineteenth-century naval life. Unsuccessful in his early merchant career, he never seriously considered any life but the Navy, which he served with devotion for forty-five years. This devotion was at times unrequited. Before the War of 1812, Hull was a minor figure, widely regarded within the Navy as an outstanding seaman but lacking the family connections and personal drive that might have made him a leader of the officers. He never liked to "make waves" in personal relationships; a condescending comment by William Bainbridge that "Hull is as fat and good-natured as ever" suggests the ambivalence with which some of his fellows regarded him. At the outbreak of war, Hull stood ninth on the list of captains, and it was only because several of his seniors were absent on merchant voyages in 1810–1811 that he had been given command of the *Constitution*.

The War of 1812 changed this situation dramatically. His brilliant actions catapulted Hull into the public eye, making him the first hero of the war. Naval men had to take him seriously from then on, but the result for Hull was not always happy, because fellow officers, including Bainbridge, thenceforward saw him as a rival for fame and leadership. Their hostility kept Hull from being as influential in the postwar Navy as his reputation might have warranted. His wife's social ambitions also drew him into more exalted circles than his ever-precarious finances allowed, making his later years ones of constant anxiety over money.

John Rodgers, in making recommendations for the Board of Navy Commissioners in 1814, gave a sketch of Hull which is very apt: "he is ... a man of most amiable disposition, and although he does not pretend to much science is however an excellent seaman." Hull's schooling was almost entirely acquired through practice, and as a seaman he was unexcelled, a fact that everyone granted. He was, moreover, known as a friend to sailors: there was a near-mutiny in the *Constitution* in September 1812, when he resigned the command to the martinet Bainbridge. Young officers regarded him in his later years as "a captain of the old school," and by the 1840s he seemed to some of them a species of ancient monument. His passing in 1843 marked the end of an era, of "iron men in wooden ships," the era of sail power, smoothbore cannon, and of naval education by experience and example, an era he personified.

BIBLIOGRAPHY

Forester, C. S. *The Age of Fighting Sail.* Garden City, N.Y.: Doubleday, 1956.

Grant, Bruce. *Isaac Hull, Captain of Old Ironsides.* New York: Pellegrini and Cudahy, 1947.

Guttridge, Leonard F., and Jay D. Smith. *The Commodores: U.S. Navy in the Age of Sail.* New York: Harper and Row, 1969.

McKee, Linda. "By Heaven, That Ship Is Ours," *American Heritage* 16 (December 1964): 4–11, 94–98.

———. "*Constitution* Versus *Guerriere.*" U.S. Naval Institute *Proceedings* 88 (August 1962): 72-79.

LINDA M. MALONEY

HULL, William (b. Derby, Conn., June 24, 1753; d. Newton, Mass., November 29, 1825), Army officer in the Revolution and War of 1812.

William Hull was born into a respected family at Derby, Connecticut, on June 24, 1753. At fifteen he entered Yale and left it with a degree four years later. Soon thereafter he enrolled in the school of law founded by Tapping Reeve at Litchfield, Connecticut, one of the earliest colleges for the study of law in America. He was admitted to the bar in 1775, but hardly had he begun practice than the folk at Derby elected him captain of a militia company formed to oppose the British. This began Hull's military career at age twenty-two.

He and his company were integrated into a Connecticut regiment which was active against the British Army in Boston. They assisted in preparing Dorchester Heights for the emplacement of the cannon being dragged from Ticonderoga. Once these guns were in place, the British position in Boston became untenable. After the enemy evacuated Boston, Hull's troops moved northward and so were not present as George Washington fought for Long Island and Manhattan. But when the Americans were forced to leave Manhattan, Washington called back the Connecticut troops, and with him, they took part in the Battle of White Plains in September 1776. After that, Hull was sent with his regiment to the Highlands of the Hudson, the key to the eastern theater.

Because the fortunes of the new United States were at low ebb in December, Washington planned a surprise attack upon Trenton. Hull took part in the Trenton-Princeton Campaign with courage and competence. Shortly afterward a chance to become major opened in the 8th Massachusetts Regiment, and Hull, willing to transfer to Massachusetts troops, took it. As a major he traveled northward beyond the Highlands, and so he was engaged in the campaign against General

John Burgoyne's invasion from Canada in 1777. Once more he was in dangerous action and performed well.

Late in 1777 the men of the 8th Massachusetts prepared comfortable winter quarters for themselves, only to receive orders from General Washington to come southward again. After some protest the units did as they were ordered, and so instead of spending a comfortable winter, they froze and starved with the main American army at Valley Forge where it was quartered to keep close to the British force cozily settled in Philadelphia. Harsh though the winter was, Major Hull gained much. He was sent out with detachments to harass British foraging parties, and in this activity he picked up a good deal about the conduct of irregular warfare. The balance of the time he acquired the skills of conventional war from Baron Frederic William von Steuben.*

When the British finally abandoned Philadelphia in June 1778, Hull commanded the 8th Massachusetts in the attacks made on the foe as he withdrew toward the coast. Many men on both sides died from the heat, but once more Hull came through with honor.

After the Battle of Monmouth Court House in June 1778, the 8th Massachusetts returned to the Highlands and late in the year prepared to settle into winter quarters at Poughkeepsie. Then, as in the winter of Valley Forge, they were summoned to come south to contain the enemy army in New York City. This time the men refused to fall out to make the grueling march, but Hull and his officers entered the huts and prodded them out. The ringleaders were punished, but not by execution, and the troops did as told. Hovering on the flanks of the British force, Hull put into practice the scouting and marauding tactics he had learned at Valley Forge. He rose at one o'clock each morning, whatever the season, and rode twenty miles on an average during the remaining hours of darkness, inspecting pickets and conferring with a network of civilian spies.

Before long Hull and his associates were back at West Point in the Highlands. There they were selected to be among the troops which Anthony Wayne* led against Stony Point. This audacious action began at midnight on July 16, 1779. Because the attack was to be made in silence using only the bayonet, Wayne ordered the officers to kill any man who attempted to load his firearm. One of Hull's officers ran a man through for that offense. The attack was successful, Hull and his men carried out their assignment, and for this Hull was promoted to lieutenant colonel.

During all of 1780 William Hull assisted Steuben as inspector of the Army. General Washington at this time invited Hull to join his staff, but after careful deliberation, and entreaties from Steuben, Hull remained with the inspector general. At the start of the year 1781, the American Army was strung along the Hudson River from Manhattan northward to the Highlands, and Hull, in command of selected volunteer units, actively harassed British parties who got outside their fortifications. Especially hazardous was an attack on Morrisania, close by New York City on January 22, 1781. Withdrawing after a successful attack on that place, Hull's men were sorely pressed by a superior force in pursuit. By previous agreement between Hull and Colonel Moses Hazen, Hazen placed his men behind stone walls on both sides of the road. As soon as Hull had passed through, they rose up and poured fire into the British pursuers from both sides. This ended the pursuit.

Six years had passed in which Hull had served without leave, so he asked to be away for the balance of the winter. When this request was granted he went to Boston and married. Of course, when the campaigning season opened again, he was there with the American forces. The French allies were increasingly active in the cause, and Hull was thrown in a good deal with the Compte de Rochambeau and the Duc de Lauzun. Earlier he had been associated with the Marquis de Lafayette* for whom he had a strong affection. Unfortunately, however, the French marched south with Washington to end up at Yorktown, but Hull's regiment was one of twenty left to guard the Highlands.

Yorktown ended the conventional fighting, and the Army had no more campaigning to do. Not until November 25, 1783, did the British leave New York City and General Washington enter it. Hull's troops were Washington's escort. Hull was present, too, when the general took his leave of the army in New York and started for Mount Vernon.

With hostilities ended, Congress cut the Army to one regiment of infantry and a corps of artillery. Most of the officer corps was sent away, owed a great deal of backpay, but Hull was chosen to be second-in-command of the infantry regiment. While still commissioned, he was sent to Quebec to arrange with the authorities there for the transfer of the western posts under the terms of the treaty of peace. Since the government in England had decided not to give up those places, the authorities in Canada stalled, and Hull was forced to return without success. Next, the remaining regiment was discharged in favor of a new arrangement, whereupon he became, for the first time in a decade, a civilian.

Hull commenced the practice of law in Newton, Massachusetts, but spent much of his time on public affairs. For example, when Shays' Rebellion occurred in 1786, he slipped back into a military posture for a short time and commanded one wing of the army of forty-four hundred militiamen which was assembled under Benjamin Lincoln* to suppress Daniel Shays* insurrectionists. He was a member of the Society of Cincinnati, and as such went to Congress in 1792 to ask compensation for the officers who had suffered severely because of the depreciation of the currency in which they had been paid. Next, in January 1793 he was designated a commissioner to go to Upper Canada and try to find a way to ease American-Indian relations. The United States widely believed that the government in Canada was inciting the Indians against them. Although this was not true, and the British officials tried to demonstrate that it was not, Hull's mission did not ease tensions on the Western frontier. In 1798 Hull became a judge of the Massachusetts Court of Common Pleas. For a time too he was a senator in the state's legislature. In addition, he was first brigadier and then major general commanding the 3d Division of Massachusetts militia. His official tasks in Massachusetts came to an end when President Thomas Jefferson appointed him governor of the newly created Territory of Michigan in 1805.

The record narrated so far is plainly that of an efficient field grade officer and a brave man. Unfortunately, the few persons who recognize William Hull's name do not remember him for this part of the record. Rather, he became notorious for the part he played in the second war with England.

Late in 1811, when trouble loomed with England, Hull informed the government that he was available for military command and that, although fifty-eight years old, he was strong and well. Accordingly, the administration offered him command, but he turned it down. Later, when assured that he could continue as governor of Michigan Territory, he accepted the appointment. At this time he was in Washington where as early as March 1812 he began to make preparations, but his commission as brigadier general did not come through until April 8, 1812. His orders were to gather most of his force from the Ohio militia and then to advance to Detroit, where he was to await further orders. At first Hull moved with surprising speed. On the way from Washington to Ohio, he averaged fifty-six miles a day, and once in the state he expedited arrangements efficiently. When his column started, it had literally to cut a road from Urbana in Ohio for two hundred miles through wilderness to Detroit. The rate of advance averaged 9.5 miles a day.

Once close to the foe, Hull seemed to grow too cautious. He claimed that he did not expect to be called on to invade Canada, especially with citizen-soldiers who did not have to cross an international boundary if they did not want to. Moreover, he knew that his line of communications was in constant danger as long as the British controlled Lake Erie and had the support of Tecumseh,* the Shawnee chief, who controlled many Indians. Finally, he had put his papers on a lake vessel bound for Detroit, before he knew that war was declared, and the British had captured them and so knew his plans. General Hull felt aggrieved that the government had made no effort to be sure that he knew at once when war was declared, with the result that the British were aware of it many days before he was.

Hull's army, around twenty-five hundred in strength, reached Detroit on July 5. Next, his subordinates persuaded him to cross the Detroit River into Canada and to occupy Sandwich, which was hardly defended on July 12. That was as far into Canada as Hull advanced. Down the Detroit River from him lay Amherstburg, a major British naval base, and Fort Malden which defended the town, but Hull never believed, right or wrong, that he had enough strength to capture these places. He was not disposed to take chances. Sure enough, as he had expected, Tecumseh interdicted his line of communications, cutting off supplies and intelligence from Ohio. He sent out two expeditions to clear the route, but both were thrown back. Meanwhile, Mackinac, two hundred miles or so to the north, had fallen to the British, a transfer that Hull expected would bring down on him a legion of warriors from the northern tribes. Now concerned for the very safety of his force, Hull pulled back to Detroit on August 8. The Ohio colonels claimed that he did this contrary to the judgment of the other officers and the wishes of the Army. The general wanted to retreat farther southward, but the Ohio officers told him that if he did so his army would dissolve.

It was Hull's misfortune to be opposed by as daring an officer as existed in

America. This was Major General Isaac Brock, British commander in Upper Canada. Brock, benefiting from British control of the lake, reached the Detroit area from the eastern side of the Ontario Peninsula in record time. Next he followed Hull's army across the Detroit River, and on August 15, although he did not have the strength to back it up, he demanded that Hull surrender. He used every device to alarm his opponent. One was the swarm of Indians with him, and he hinted that if it was necessary to assault the American works, he might not afterwards be able to restrain them. He also planted some cannon on the Canadian side to fire into the fort and lobbed some shots that caused casualties. There were, of course, women and children with the Americans, and Hull brooded over what might happen to them. In the end Hull concluded that his army was trapped and outnumbered. He surrendered it on August 16, 1812.

A shock ran all across the United States when the news of the surrender spread. President James Madison, who had been traveling home to Virginia, turned around and went back to the capital. Hull was carried off to Canada as a prisoner, but when he returned to the United States on parole, he was arrested and held for court-martial on three charges: treason, cowardice, and neglect of duty and bad conduct. But his trial did not take place until the spring of 1814. It was presided over by Major General Henry Dearborn* whose failure to produce a diversion at the eastern side of the Ontario Peninsula had contributed to Hull's surrender. On March 26 the court gave its verdict: not guilty of charges one and two, but guilty of the third charge. The court imposed a sentence of death but recommended clemency because of Hull's noble record in the Revolution. President Madison suspended the sentence and Hull lived the last eleven years of his life on a farm, inherited from his wife's family, outside Newton, Massachusetts. He bore his disgrace with dignity, but he spent much of his time trying to prove that the failure of his campaign was not solely his fault. He was still so occupied when he died on November 29, 1825.

William Hull is the only general officer in American military history who was ever sentenced to be executed for a military failure. He personifies the American need for a scapegoat when things go badly. He was a victim of the tendency of the United States to jump into war without careful plans and with no preparation. Hull was certainly neither a traitor nor a coward. Moreover, much of what caused him to fail was beyond his own control. He contended in his own defense that his line of communications was too vulnerable, through no fault of his. He was probably correct. He complained of the militia, and justly, for it was a defensive system, not adapted to offensive warfare. He argued that his orders were restrictive, which they were, but a more aggressive officer would have stretched them. He claimed that he was outnumbered two to one, whereas General Brock said the ratio was exactly the reverse. But in the light of latter-day scholarship Hull seems to have been correct. From the very start of the campaign, he had argued that the United States must gain control of Lake Erie, but this was never done when it would have helped Hull. Finally, the diversion at the far end of the Peninsula, which he had a right to expect, never took place. In all these points he was correct; still, it remains true that if he had shown one-quarter of Brock's audacity, the outcome would have been different.

The Madison administration can be faulted for picking Hull for this command. He was fifty-nine and had naturally slowed down from revolutionary days; yet the record of those days was what got him the appointment. Moreover, Hull had never had an independent command of a force any larger than a regiment during the Revolution. His record was that of a good officer of field, not general grade. It could not show what he could do when he alone had to make the decisions. If we consider the officers with experience who were available, the gamble the government took in appointing Hull was not an irrational one; it just did not happen to work out well.

BIBLIOGRAPHY

Campbell, Marie Hull. *Revolutionary Services and Civil Life of General William Hull*. New York: Appleton, 1848.
Clark, James Freeman. *History of the Campaign of 1812 and the Surrender of the Post of Detroit*. New York: Appleton, 1848.
Hull, William. *Memoirs of the Campaign of the Northwest Army*. Boston, 1824.
Mahon, John K. *The War of 1812*. Gainesville: University of Florida Press, 1972.
The Trial of Brigadier General William Hull. Boston: Printed for Russell Cutler and Company, 1814.

JOHN K. MAHON

HUMPHREYS, Joshua (b. Haverford, Pa., June 17, 1751; d. Haverford, Pa., January 12, 1838), naval constructor and shipbuilder. Considered by some as America's most important naval architect of the late eighteenth century, Humphreys was primarily responsible for designing the "Humphreys frigates."

Son of a Quaker farmer who captained a privateer in the Seven Years' War, Joshua Humphreys grew to manhood on the Philadelphia docks. At age fourteen, Humphreys was apprenticed to James Penrose, a Philadelphia ship's carpenter. Before the young man completed the apprenticeship, Master Penrose died in 1771. Six years of Penrose's training left Humphreys deficient in some technical skills; for example, his draftsmanship was only adequate. Nevertheless, twenty-year-old Humphreys assumed the master's mantle and began his own shipbuilding business. In 1774 Humphreys entered into partnership with his older cousin, John Wharton, a ship chandler and an astute entrepreneur who had political connections. The combination of "Wharton & Humphreys" was a mutually beneficial enterprise. Thus, by the beginning of the American Revolution in 1775, Humphreys was a shipbuilder of repute in Philadelphia.

The self-styled Continental Congress, meeting in Philadelphia, aimed to put warships under the revolutionary banner. John Wharton was on close terms with Robert Morris, Pennsylvania's delegate on the Congress' Marine Committee. The committee naturally turned to Wharton and Humphreys and commissioned the firm to refit merchantmen as war vessels. Some of the vessels Humphreys converted sailed in the squadron commanded by Esek Hopkins.* The Marine Committee next asked Wharton and Humphreys to submit designs for new warships—three classes of frigates, to carry 24, 28, or 32 guns. Humphreys patterned the 24-gun model after his father's privateer, but he may have had assistance on the designs of the 28s and 32s. Whoever drafted the designs, Humphreys submitted them to the Marine Committee, which approved the plans. Humphreys took charge of building one of the frigates, the *Randolph* (32 guns), which later sailed under Nicholas Biddle.*

Humphreys made additional contributions to the American cause. At the request of the Marine Committee in 1777 he produced, probably with some assistance, a design for a 74-gun ship-of-the-line. Once again his design was approved. But the commission to build a 74-gun ship was given to a company in Portsmouth, New Hampshire, and the final appearance of the ship, *America*, differed significantly from Humphreys' plans. Meanwhile, working at the request of Congress, Humphreys built the sloop-of-war *Saratoga* (18 guns) and the packet *Mercury*.

Following the Revolution, Congress ordered the ships of the Continental Navy to be sold, and between 1785 and 1797 America had no navy. American commercial ships were vulnerable to attack. Operating out of harbors along the Barbary Coast in the Mediterranean, pirates in powerful frigates captured American ships and held merchant seamen for ransom. On May 24, 1794, Congress passed the Navy Act, calling for the United States to acquire or build six frigates (three of 44-guns and three of 36-guns) that would deal with the Barbary pirates.

The design of these warships had been under consideration for several months before Congress passed the Naval Act. Secretary of War Henry Knox* consulted with many men, among them former naval officers and knowledgeable merchants and shipbuilders, including Wharton and Humphreys. Following these consultations, Knox decided that the proposed American frigates "would be superior to any European frigate of the usual dimension; that if assailed by numbers they would always be able to lead ahead; that they would never be obliged to go into action but on their own terms, except in a calm; and that in heavier weather they would be capable of engaging doubledecked ships." A super-frigate was what the secretary of war had in mind.

Knox called for designs of frigates to be submitted for approval. He accepted the plans offered by Joshua Humphreys, after they had been criticized and amended by several consultants, including Josiah Fox, a young English-educated naval architect. Humphreys' designs incorporated all of the features Knox had wanted, and therefore they were referred to as the "Humphreys frigates."

To achieve the broadest political support for the new American Navy, the six frigates would be built in six shipyards in six states, using woods, construction materials, equipment, and workers from across the nation. Six shipbuilders were hired, one for each frigate. Knox gave Humphreys the responsibility for the 44-gun to be built in Philadelphia and appointed him naval constructor with an annual stipend of $2,000.

Humphreys worked for the federal government as a naval constructor from 1794 to 1801. In addition to building one of the frigates, Humphreys made repairs on other ships and converted merchantmen for use as naval vessels. In

1798 Congress passed legislation creating the Navy Department. Secretary of the Navy Benjamin Stoddert* directed Humphreys to conduct a survey of the Atlantic Coast and then to recommend the best sites for government naval yards. In 1799 Humphreys was commissioned to draft a design for a 74-gun ship-of-the-line, but the ship was never built. During his tenure as naval contractor, he made several suggestions to the Navy Department regarding changes and improvements in equipments, but these innovations were not adopted. After leaving federal employ, Humphreys was hired in 1806 to select the land, layout a plan, and begin construction on the Philadelphia Navy Yard. He worked at his profitable ship repair business until his death in 1838.

Joshua Humphreys was an innovative naval architect and brilliant ship-builder—at least that is the well-accepted view put forward by historians such as Fletcher Pratt and Marion Brewington. In contrast, Howard Chapelle advanced a different thesis, based on extensive research into eighteenth-century documents and ships' plans.

Chapelle concluded that Humphreys was *not* a great naval architect in either 1775 or 1794. According to Chapelle, Wharton's political connections and the fact that Humphreys was located in the capital of Philadelphia had more to do with their firm obtaining naval contracts in the 1770s and 1790s than any brilliance on Humphreys' part. Furthermore, Chapelle showed that Humphreys' drafting abilities were weak; he had to have a skilled assistant do most of his ship design work. Moreover, Chapelle argued that Humphreys' contributions to the design and production of the so-called Humphreys frigates had been overrated. Chapelle's key conclusions were that (1) American planners had reached a consensus on the type of ships needed before the designs were rendered, and (2) several persons—particularly the brilliant thirty-year-old Josiah Fox—amended the initial proposals offered by Humphreys to such an extent that the final result must be considered a group effort.

Certainly by 1794, Humphreys was in an excellent position: his company was located in the seat of government; his cousin John Wharton had contacts in federal circles; and Humphreys himself possessed a good reputation and twenty-three years of experience in shipbuilding. He may not have been America's leading naval architect in 1775, but he probably was among a select number in 1794. Furthermore, Humphreys knew well the criticisms of American ships used during the Revolution: some were too small—did not carry enough guns—for their class; others were too narrow and failed to handle well in heavy weather. In view of the fact that the Barbary corsairs used a variety of ships, some carrying forty or more guns, the need was evident for America to have 44-gun frigates.

Thus, Humphreys made his drafts for the super-frigate with the assistance of his excellent draftsman William Doughty, an employee of Wharton and Humphreys. The designer gave the 44-gun frigates an extra sharpness to enable them to sail close into the wind; extra length (175 feet, longer by twenty feet than an average British frigate and by thirteen feet than an average Frenchman of the same class); extra beam (forty-four feet) by a foot or two over their European counterparts; a flush spar deck on which guns could be placed to create a more powerful broadside; the capability to carry main batteries of 24-pounder cannon, when most European frigates carried 18-pounders; and extra trussing intended to give the ships greater internal strength. Humphreys expected that ships made from his design would be very durable and very fast. He was right.

Of course, several individuals (including the ships' captains, who gave personal advice on their frigates during construction) had roles in the frigates' final design and building, but the contributions of Josiah Fox remain controversial. Some contemporaries—and at times Fox himself—claimed that the Englishman deserved most of the credit for the "Humphreys frigates," and thus that phrase was a misnomer. Although both men were given official commendations for their work on the frigates, Fox's claim does not appear valid. In 1794 Fox was a traditional ship designer. He thought that frigates built according to Humphreys' design would be too long (even the 36s, upgraded to 38s, measured 163' × 40'), too heavy, too slow, and too weak structurally to carry the number of cannon Humphreys proposed. Fox and others criticized the stern's rake and the bow's sharpness. (Some critics seemed to think that the frigates borrowed too much from the French razées, slower, larger ships that had their top decks cut down.) Fox's recommended alterations, some of which Knox accepted, detracted from the frigates' revolutionary design. Humphreys and Doughty made the basic drafts; Fox and Doughty produced the plans used by the six builders. Moreover, Fox failed to use the unusual features from the Humphreys frigates for the ships he designed. For example, Fox drafted the plan of the 38-gun frigate *Philadelphia* (which sailed under William Bainbridge*) along traditional English lines (measuring 157' × 39'). Fox also designed the small frigate *John Adams* (measuring 127' × 33' and carrying 28 guns). Both of these vessels contrasted significantly with Humphreys' plans and offered no innovations or improvements. Some years later, however, Fox moved more toward Humphreys' design when, as a naval constructor himself (1804–1809), he drafted and built the rakish sloops *Hornet* and *Wasp* (18 guns each).

Politics dictated that construction take place in six cities. Humphreys supervised the building of the *United States* in Philadelphia; at Boston, George Claghorne, who had an excellent reputation, took charge of the *Constitution*, which later sailed under Isaac Hull*; Constructor David Stodder laid down the *Constellation* (38 guns) for Captain Thomas Truxton* at Baltimore. The second three ships were the *President* (44 guns) built by William Doughty at New York; the *Congress* (38 guns) laid down by James Hackett at Portsmouth; and the *Chesapeake* (38 guns) built by Fox at Norfolk. The first three frigates came down the ways in 1797. The others were not completed until 1799 and 1800. Subsequently, the six ships formed the nucleus of the American Navy in the War of 1812.

Chapelle acknowledges that the design of the Humphreys frigates "influenced American frigates to the end of the sailing ship period." Humphreys' distinctive hull design put his stamp on the ships. They were stable firing platforms, fast sailors, and mounted a surprising number of cannon. In their day they were the best ships of their class.

BIBLIOGRAPHY

Brewington, Marion V. "The Design of Our First Frigates." *American Neptune* 7, (1948).
Chapelle, Howard I. *The History of the American Sailing Navy: The Ships and Their Development.* New York: W. W. Norton, 1949.
Potter, E. B., ed. *Sea Power: A Naval History.* Englewood Cliffs, N.J.: Prentice-Hall, 1960.
Pratt, Fletcher. *The Navy: A History.* Garden City, N.Y.: Garden City Publishing Company, 1941.

JOSEPH G. DAWSON III

I

INGERSOLL, Royal Eason (b. Georgetown, D.C., June 20, 1883; d. Bethesda, Md., May 20, 1976), naval officer. Ingersoll commanded the Atlantic Fleet and Western Sea Frontier in World War II.

Royal Eason Ingersoll liked to date his entry into the Navy from the time he was "carried into the Naval Academy in the arms of [his] nurse" when his father, then Lieutenant and later Rear Admiral Royal Rodney Ingersoll, became an instructor there in the fall of 1883. His mother was Cynthia Eason of La Porte, Indiana, where he attended public schools during his father's long deployments at sea. He also attended private schools in Annapolis along with William Frederick Halsey, Jr.,* and made practice cruises with the Academy midshipmen. Ingersoll won a competition for the appointment from Indiana's Thirteenth Congressional District and entered the Academy in May 1901 along with Chester William Nimitz.* He graduated with distinction in 1905, standing fourth in a class of 114.

Ingersoll's first tour after graduation was in the old battleship *Missouri*, with Halsey as a roommate and Lieutenant (later Admiral) Thomas Charles Hart* as a senior shipmate. Then as a boat officer he ferried delegates to the Russo-Japanese Peace Conference around Portsmouth Harbor and served in the gunboat *Marietta*, the transport *Hancock*, and (until felled by appendicitis after six days) the presidential yacht *Mayflower*. Ingersoll made part of the world cruise of the Great White Fleet in its flagship *Connecticut*. Commissioned ensign in 1907 and lieutenant (both grades) in 1910, he married Louise Van Harlingen, a La Porte friend, in 1910. He soon taught seamanship and English at the Academy, and in 1913 he went to the protected cruiser *Saratoga*, flagship of the Asiatic Fleet, at the height of the Chinese revolution. He held various staff jobs, including fleet engineer and flag secretary, before going to another Asiatic Fleet ship, the protected cruiser *Cincinnati*, as her executive officer.

In 1916 Ingersoll came home to head, as a lieutenant commander (and temporary commander after February 1918), the communications office at Navy

Department headquarters. In Paris he organized communications for the American delegation to the Peace Conference. After successive tours as the executive officer in the battleships *Connecticut* and *Arizona*, he received the permanent rank of commander in 1921 and took over the Japanese espionage desk at the Office of Naval Intelligence in Washington for three years. There he worked with projects that helped with the subsequent cryptographic breakthrough known as MAGIC. In 1924 he missed the chance for a destroyer as his first command; offered the choice of a transport, a cargo ship, or the converted yacht *Nokomis*, he chose the *Nokomis* and hydrographic survey duty in the Caribbean.

In July 1926 Ingersoll began the full-year course at the Naval War College in international law, strategy and tactics, problem-solving, and situation estimates, after which the college president, Admiral William V. Pratt, brought him onto the staff for a year. Then Pratt became commander, Battle Fleet, and took Ingersoll, a captain since June 1927, as his assistant chief of staff. When Pratt became commander in chief, U.S. Fleet, in 1929, Ingersoll accompanied him. In 1930 Pratt became chief of naval operations (CNO) and took Ingersoll to head the Fleet Training Division. Pratt gave high priority to the post-World War revision of tactical and war instructions, and this task consumed Ingersoll's time until 1933.

In May 1933 Ingersoll took command of the heavy cruiser *Augusta*, flagship of the Scouting Force and based in the Pacific; in October he went to Mare Island Navy Yard to supervise the fitting out and commissioning of the new heavy cruiser *San Francisco*, which he commanded until June 1935. There followed three years as director of war plans in the CNO's office, where Ingersoll worked extensively with "Plan Orange" and served also as a technical advisor at the London Naval Conference of 1935–1936. As of July 1, 1937, he was thirty-fifth on the list of 271 captains, sixteen numbers below Husband Edward Kimmel,* ten below Halsey, and two above Nimitz; he was the most junior of the seven captains on the current promotion list for rear admiral, a rank that took effect on May 1, 1938. Flag rank brought him command of Cruiser Division Six in the Pacific, and in the summer he became assistant to the CNO, Admiral Harold Raynsford Stark.*

Stark, calculating potential wartime assignments in the autumn of 1941, expected to leave Ernest Joseph King* in command of the Atlantic Fleet, send Nimitz to the Asiatic Fleet in place of Hart, and give Ingersoll the Pacific command, leaving Kimmel with the superior post of commander in chief, U.S. Fleet. Pearl Harbor changed things. Kimmel lost both his positions, King went to Washington as Fleet commander in chief, and Secretary William Franklin Knox* picked Nimitz for the Pacific Fleet. Hart kept the Asiatic Fleet, a command approaching closer to oblivion with every passing day. Stark finally agreed to give up his chief deputy, and thus, with the temporary rank of vice admiral, Ingersoll became commander in chief, Atlantic Fleet, on December 30, 1941. On July 1, 1942, he received the rank of admiral, also a temporary wartime commission. He gave up the flagship *Augusta* to patrol and escort duty and shifted to the ancient frigate *Constellation*, permanently moored at Newport, thus becoming the only American admiral to fight a war from a commissioned flagship nearly 150 years old. Later, in the converted yacht *Vixen*, he could move up and down the coast to visit ports.

In November 1944 Ingersoll went to San Francisco to command the Western Sea Frontier, which embraced all installations in the ten Western states. Unquestioned control over all aspects of mobilization, logistics, training, and manpower for the final assault on Japan required the additional titles of deputy commander in chief, U.S. Fleet, and deputy CNO. "I was like Pooh Bah in The Mikado," he recalled. "If I couldn't accomplish what I wanted under one head, I could accomplish it under another." On April 10, 1946, he gave up all active duty, and on August 1, 1946, he retired with the permanent rank of admiral to date from July 1, 1942. For the duration of the war after mid-1942, Ingersoll was the fourth ranking officer on the active list (other than recalled retirees), Stark, King, and Nimitz being senior in the grade of admiral. The five star rank of fleet admiral, created in December 1944 and limited to four officers, went immediately to William Daniel Leahy,* who had been recalled from retirement in 1942 to chair the Joint Chiefs of Staff, King, and Nimitz; the fourth slot remained vacant until December 1945 when Halsey was promoted over Stark and Ingersoll. At the time of his death, Ingersoll was the senior officer on the Navy retired list.

During his forty-year career, Royal Eason Ingersoll experienced most of the major events of naval history. Three contributions deserve special evaluation. First, Ingersoll performed well a vital function of the commanding officer: teaching juniors. Ensigns and lieutenants who served under him in *San Francisco*, and themselves retired as captains and admirals, still recall him as fair and effective. When observing junior officers on watch, he did not publicly berate them for errors but instead made mental notes, let the junior bail himself out of trouble, went to his cabin, rang up on the bridge phone, and began an even-tempered conversation with "Well, now, that little maneuver didn't work very well, did it?" The same skills underlay his work on instructions and manuals at the Fleet Training Division. As commander in chief, Atlantic Fleet, he was responsible for preparing thousands of men and hundreds of new ships for combat in one of the largest, most complex, and most demanding wartime training programs ever undertaken.

A second contribution was Ingersoll's extremely keen ability at staff work, particularly operations and planning. His work in naval intelligence and war plans kept him versed in major issues of international relations, and by Pearl Harbor, because highly placed admirals valued his work, he had reached the highest policymaking and executive levels of the Navy.

Ingersoll's third contribution was his command of the Atlantic Fleet and later of the Western Sea Frontier. The Atlantic Fleet position involved staggering responsibilities and often insufficient resources to carry them out. The Atlantic

Fleet's principal early tasks of protecting shipping in the North Atlantic and controlling ocean approaches to the Western Hemisphere were well underway upon Ingersoll's arrival. While the battle of the Atlantic against surface raiders and submarines raged from Greenland to Brazil, and Ingersoll had to respond to subordinates, "I wish I could give you a few more destroyers but the 'musts' keep us living from hand to mouth to satisfy demands," the Atantic Fleet had to train and prepare ships built in East Coast yards but scheduled for the Pacific. In addition, Ingersoll had to train, transport, land, and supply the amphibious forces of the Western Task Force in the North African landings of November 1942. The 1943 invasion of Sicily occasioned similar duties, and the responsibilities of the twelve months prior to Normandy dwarfed anything that had gone before. At a press conference on June 6, 1944, Admiral King introduced Ingersoll and praised him for never saying he could not do the job. "He has gone ahead and done it—just how, I don't quite understand."

Although Ingersoll was a fleet commander, his duties were administrative rather than combat. Nor did his personality and style match those of a Halsey. Unassuming, modest, and even a bit shy, the pipe-smoking, stamp-collecting Ingersoll did his job quietly, with the aid of a remarkably small staff, a famous little black notebook full of facts and figures, and a keen intellect. Among his American decorations was one for World War II service, of which he characteristically said, "I always regarded that decoration as the 'croix de chair' for commanding an LMD—a large mahogany desk."

BIBLIOGRAPHY

Administrative History of the U.S. Atlantic Fleet in World War II: Vol. 1. *Commander-in-Chief, U.S. Atlantic Fleet*. 2 vols. Washington, D.C.: U.S. Naval History Division, 1946.
Administrative History of Western Sea Frontier During World War II. 7 vols. Washington, D.C.: U.S. Naval History Division, 1946.
Furlong, William Rea, ed. *Class of 1905, United States Naval Academy*. Annapolis, Md.: U.S. Naval Academy, 1930.
Ingersoll, Royal E. "The Reminiscences of Admiral Royal E. Ingersoll." Oral History Research Project, Columbia University, 1965.
Morison, Samuel E. *History of U.S. Naval Operations in World War II*. 15 vols. Boston: Atlantic, Little, Brown and Company, 1947–1962.

JAMES E. SEFTON

ISHERWOOD, Benjamin Franklin (b. New York City, N.Y., October 6, 1822; d. New York City, N.Y., June 19, 1915), chief of the Bureau of Steam Engineering during the Civil War. Isherwood is considered the leading marine engineer of the middle nineteenth century.

Isherwood was the son of Benjamin, a New York physician, and his wife Eliza Hicks Isherwood. His father died soon after his birth, and he was brought up by his mother. In 1831 he entered Albany Academy, then at the peak of its scientific reputation, and studied under Joseph Henry, who remained a friend

for the rest of his life. Isherwood was expelled in 1836 for unspecified misconduct. He secured a position as draftsman with the Utica and Schenectady Railroad
and later transferred to the civil engineering department. After the completion
of the railroad, he worked on the Croton Aqueduct and on the Erie Railroad.
Later, Isherwood joined the Treasury Department as an engineer for the construction of lighthouses.

Subsequently, Isherwood took a job with the Novelty Iron Works in New
York to gain the practical experience necessary for appointment to the newly
organized Engineer Corps of the Navy. On May 23, 1844, he received his warrant
as a first assistant engineer. Later that year he reported to the Pensacola Navy
Yard, serving both as yard engineer and the engineering officer of the small yard
steamer *General Taylor*. Upon his return to Washington late the following year,
he was tested by an examining board of engineers who reduced him in grade to
second assistant engineer. On January 26, 1846, four days after the demotion
took effect, Isherwood received orders to the screw sloop *Princeton*. During the
Mexican War, he participated in the blockade of Mexican ports, bombardment
of Vera Cruz, and amphibious operations of the Home Squadron in the *Princeton*
and the smaller steamer *Spitfire*. Isherwood rose again to first assistant engineer
in July 1847. The following month he returned home and after a leave was
reassigned to lighthouse duty. During 1848 he married a widow, Mrs. Anna
Hansine Munster Ragsdale. On August 13, 1849 (later backdated to October 31,
1848), he received his commission as chief engineer.

In December 1850 Isherwood was recalled for special duty in the Office of
the Engineer-in-Chief Charles B. Stuart to salvage the badly designed propeller
and rudder of the screw sloop *San Jacinto*. He then resumed his work with the
Light House Service, superintending the construction of a lighthouse at Sankaty
Head on Nantucket. He was recalled to devise a new engine for the gunboat
Allegheny. The design, while ingenious, proved to be too weak for her old hull
which caused Isherwood to design his later engines with exceptionally heavy
and durable parts.

During the 1850s Isherwood returned to sea as chief engineer of the *San
Jacinto* in the Far East (1854–1858). On the cruise he contracted dysentery which
would plague him several times in later life. Following his return from the Orient,
Isherwood received an extended leave. He used it, in part, to design the engines
and supervise the construction of a pair of gunboats for Russia in New York.
Isherwood had co-authored his first professional paper in 1842 and published
several others during the 1850s. At the end of the decade, he produced the two
volumes of *Engineering Precedents for Steam Machinery* (New York, 1858–
1859), which contained material he had collected over the past twelve years.

Upon returning to active duty, Isherwood served on a pair of engineering
boards. One studied the feasibility of converting the sailing vessels to steam,
but concluded that only ships-of-the-line offered any potential as steam warships.
The second met in 1860–1861 on board the gunboat *Michigan* and conducted

pioneering studies which proved that increasing the expansion of steam beyond a point produces a loss rather than a gain in efficiency.

On March 26, 1861, Isherwood became the engineer in chief of the Navy and embarked upon the most important and controversial five years of his life. Shortly after taking office, he went to Norfolk to expedite the repairs to the engines of the screw frigate *Merrimack* so that she might be moved out of danger. Threatening Confederate forces were nearby. Isherwood had the vessel ready to depart when Commodore Charles McCauley canceled her sailing and ordered her scuttling.

After his return to Washington, Isherwood worked sixeen-hour days, promoted the well-being of the Engineer Corps, and presided over the wartime expansion of the Corps and the steam Navy. He designed the engines for forty-six side-wheel and seventy-nine screw steamers, and prevailed upon the Navy Department to order twenty-three screw gunboats on plans similar to the pair he previously had superintended for Russia. Eleven of these "Ninety-Day" gunboats were in service before the end of 1861. In addition, Isherwood designed engines for a dozen large, double-ended gunboats intended for operations in Southern bays and rivers, as well as ten screw sloops for blockade duty. He intentionally designed the machinery for strength, since he recognized that the conditions of service and the hastily recruited engineers would subject them to great stress. The machinery's reliability proved his wisdom. Isherwood's many activities and successful designs drew antagonism from a wide range of opponents who were seldom mollified by Isherwood's cold, dispassionate personality. The antagonism caused a delay of nearly a year in Isherwood's confirmation as chief of the newly formed Bureau of Steam Engineering. (When finally confirmed on March 10, 1863, he received the rank of commodore which made him the senior staff officer in the Navy.)

Isherwood's masterpiece was the set of engines designed for a group of extremely large, fast commerce-raiding cruisers. Their huge, horizontal back-acting, geared engines drove them at unheard of speeds. One, the *Wampanoag*, raced 17.5 knots into the teeth of a gale during her trials, almost five knots faster than her sistership *Madawaska* whose engines had come from the drawing board of John Ericsson.* Despite their success, the big cruisers saw little service because their engines consumed enormous quantities of coal; they carried too few supplies for peacetime cruising; and their hulls were too narrow to support their masts adequately.

During the war Isherwood found that no navy yard was equipped to manufacture marine engines and most civilian plants disliked Navy contracts because they demanded high quality and precise specifications. Whenever possible during the war and immediately afterwards, he purchased the tools to allow the Navy to build its own engines. This involved him in a bitter conflict, largely political, involving charges of mismanagement which shortened his tenure as bureau chief. Removed from office through the efforts of Admiral David Dixon Porter* after Ulysses Simpson Grant* became president, Isherwood was exiled to California at the Mare Island Navy Yard. He used his year there to conduct a series of experiments on the efficiency of propellers which formed the theoretical basis of propeller design for the next quarter-century.

In 1871 Isherwood returned to New York and served as president of a series of experimental boards. In 1881 he served with John Rodgers* on the First Naval Advisory Board, which developed the initial recommendations for a new steel-hulled Navy. It is an interesting commentary on Isherwood's inherent conservatism that he supported the use of iron rather than steel as the building material because of its known qualities. He unsuccessfully argued for the construction of fast commerce raiders similar to the *Wampanoag* as well as large, deep-water ironclads. Possibly because of his outspoken independence, Isherwood was not included among the members of the Second Naval Advisory Board, which met in 1882. He retired on October 6, 1884.

Following retirement, Isherwood often contributed articles to the *Journal of the American Society of Naval Engineers* after its appearance in 1889. The American Society of Mechanical Engineers named him an honorary member in 1894. Although an invalid after 1910, Isherwood continued his professional writing for another four years.

Isherwood was a superbly trained engineer, although he lacked extensive formal education. His experiments with the *Michigan* are considered the prototype of modern experimental engineering studies, and his engine designs placed him at the head of the profession in the 1860s. His experiments overthrew long-established theories and helped point the way to high-pressure, multi-expansion engines. Isherwood published the *Michigan* studies in *Experimental Researches in Steam Engineering* (2 vols., Philadelphia, 1863–1865), along with reports of other experiments in which he had participated. The volumes long served as an engineering text and were translated into six languages.

Isherwood was a cold perfectionist, so dedicated to his work that he easily earned the enmity of lesser men. Nevertheless, when he died in 1915 he was recognized and revered as one of the leading figures in the engineering profession.

BIBLIOGRAPHY

Bennett, Frank M. *The Steam Navy of the United States*. Pittsburgh, Pa.: Warren and Company, 1896.
Dyson, George W. "Benjamin Franklin Isherwood." *United States Naval Institute Proceedings* 67 (August 1941): 1138–46.
Sloan, Edward William III. *Benjamin Franklin Isherwood, Naval Engineer*. Annapolis, Md.: Naval Institute Press, 1965.

K. JACK BAUER

IZARD, George (b. Richmond, England, October 21, 1776; d. Little Rock, Arkansas Territory, November 22, 1828), soldier and territorial governor of Arkansas. Izard is usually remembered for his controversial handling of the Niagara Campaign during the War of 1812.

George Izard was born in Richmond, England, while his father was on a diplomatic mission for the American colonies. His family was one of the wealthiest and most important in South Carolina. Although his father returned to America in 1780, George did not set foot on American soil until 1783. He was enrolled in school in Charleston and later in Philadelphia, finishing his education in England, Germany, and France. In 1794, while he was attending the *Ecole du Genie* in Metz, he was commissioned a second lieutenant in the U.S. Army Artillery. Upon his return to the United States in 1797, he was ordered to Charleston to take command of Castle Pinckney. Izard was promoted to captain in 1799 and appointed aide to Major General Alexander Hamilton. When the Army was reduced in size in 1803 and he was sent back to the artillery, he resigned his commission and returned to private life in South Carolina. He returned to the Army in 1812 as a colonel in the artillery and was promoted to brigadier general in March 1813 and placed in charge of the defense of New York City, which was then thought to be threatened by a British attack.

Until his promotion to major general on January 21, 1814, Izard had been constantly shifted from place to place, never having the trained troops or supplies that he needed for the type of operations he felt he was capable of conducting. He blamed the secretary of war, John Armstrong, Jr.,* for most of the problems he encountered and was convinced Armstrong was incompetent. Izard finally got his opportunity when Generals Wade Hampton* and James Wilkinson* were forced to resign in 1814 and he became the senior officer on the Canadian border with command of about four thousand regulars. In early September, the secretary of war ordered Izard to move his command toward Sackets Harbor, one of the most important American positions on the border. On September 10, 1814, as he was about to take up a position at Sackets Harbor, he received an urgent dispatch from Major General Jacob Jennings Brown,* requesting his support at Fort Erie. Izard marched four hundred miles through rough terrain in bad weather and camped two miles north of Fort Erie on the night of October 10–11. Since he was the senior officer, Izard took command of the combined force which numbered approximately eight thousand regulars and militia. At Brown's urging, Izard took the offensive against the British commander, General Gordon Drummond, who had been forced to withdraw north of the Chippewa River after failing to take Fort Erie. Fielding fifty-five hundred regulars augmented by eight hundred militia, Izard had an excellent opportunity to destroy Drummond's depleted force of twenty-five hundred before winter. On October 13, Izard moved his forces against Drummond's position on the Chippewa in an effort to draw the British into an attack. A series of skirmishes resulted during which the British suffered severe losses while the American Army only lost twelve men killed and fifty-four wounded.

When Drummond retreated to Fort George and Burlington Heights, Izard decided that it was too dangerous to continue the attack and retreated to Buffalo where he went into winter quarters. He also decided to abandon Fort Erie and ordered it blown up on November 5, 1814. Both Armstrong and Brown com-

plained about his handling of the campaign; Izard, sensitive to criticism, recommended that Brown replace him because he was better qualified to lead militia.
On December 18, 1814, he sent his resignation to the War Department but it
was refused. Nevertheless, his military career was over. Izard remained in Buffalo and did nothing, allowing the initiative to pass to the British. The war ended
before they were able to begin operations against Sackets Harbor in 1815. General
Izard published his correspondence with the War Department in 1816 but did
not attempt to defend his decisions.

After the war, Izard returned to Philadelphia and became an active member
of the American Philosophical Society. When his old friend James Monroe was
elected president, Izard was appointed governor of the Arkansas Territory on
March 4, 1825. His administration was fairly successful, especially in the area
of his main responsibility, Indian policy. The governor's only problems seem
to have come from his dictatorial manner toward the Legislative Council, which
he once ordered home after the completion of their business in the interest of
public economy. Izard remained governor until his death in 1828.

George Izard was one of the few trained soldiers on the American side during
the War of 1812 and should have had a successful military career. He was
impressive in appearance, and his manners showed that he was used to command.
He was affable and seldom had altercations with any of his fellow officers, a
trait that was rare in the Army that included Winfield Scott,* Edmund Pendleton
Gaines,* and Andrew Jackson.* His performance in the War of 1812 was mediocre at best, but since he was shifted from place to place and never really had
a firm grip on the situation, it would have been hard to expect more. His major
problem seemed to be his inability to inspire and lead militia. Izard evidently
recognized this deficiency when he recommended that Jacob Brown replace him
in 1814. Historians are still divided in their estimation of Izard's decision to go
into winter quarters in November 1814. It was the safest course of action in the
short run. However, if the war had not ended when it did, it could have caused
a shift in the balance of power on the U.S.-Canadian border and could have led
to disastrous consequences. Certainly, it would have meant the siege of Sackets
Harbor and possibly its loss to the British.

BIBLIOGRAPHY

Adams, Henry. *History of the United States During the Administration of James Madison.*
     Vols. 7 and 8. New York: Albert and Charles Boni, 1930.
Cruikshank, Ernest A. *Documentary History of the Campaigns upon the Niagara Frontier
     in 1813 and 1814.* 9 vols. Welland, Ontario: Lundy's Lane Historical Society,
     n.d.
Mahon, John K. *The War of 1812.* Gainesville: University of Florida Press, 1972.

                                                              JACK W. THACKER

J

JACKSON, Andrew (b. Waxhaw, S.C., March 15, 1767; d. Nashville, Tenn., June 8, 1845), lawyer, politician (U.S. representative, senator, and president), judge, major general. Jackson was the first person to give his name to an era of American history.

Andrew Jackson was the youngest of three sons of Scotch-Irish immigrants. His father died shortly before Andrew's birth. Both of his brothers and his mother died during the Revolutionary War. Jackson himself, as a fourteen-year-old captured partisan, was slashed with a sabre on his hand and forehead when he refused to polish a British officer's boots.

After studying law, Jackson went to Nashville in 1788 and quickly became successful. In 1796 he was elected U.S. representative. Appointed to the Senate in 1797, Jackson resigned the next year to accept a judgeship on the Tennessee Supreme Court. He was elected major general of the Tennessee militia in 1802. Jackson took his military duties seriously. He studied a translation of French Army regulations and applied the principles he learned to his men.

When war with England came in June 1812, Jackson offered the services of his command. The government accepted but did not call him to active duty because President James Madison disliked Jackson and had no intention of using the Tennessean if he could help it.

By the autumn, however, the administration was contemplating an attack on east Florida, so Jackson was commissioned a major general of U.S. volunteers and ordered to New Orleans where the Tennesseans would be under the overall command of one of Jackson's old enemies, General James Wilkinson.* When Jackson reached Natchez, he was told to halt. Fuming over the delay, Jackson was astounded to get a letter from the secretary of war in March 1813 which informed him that the expedition was canceled and that he and his men were dismissed.

Realizing that his men probably would join Wilkinson, Jackson decided to lead them personally back to their homes in Tennessee. On this return march,

Jackson's strength in adversity revealed itself clearly for the first time. Noting it, his men nicknamed him, affectionately, "Old Hickory."

Back in Tennessee, Jackson became involved in a brawl with Thomas and Jesse Benton. Jackson was shot in the shoulder and gravely wounded. While recovering, he heard that the Creeks had killed over four hundred people at Fort Mims. Forcing himself out of his sick bed, Jackson ordered volunteers to assemble.

The general moved rapidly to the upper Coosa River, where he built his main base. Two successful battles were fought in November 1813, but they did not break Creek power. Jackson's men became rebellious when vital supplies failed to arrive and disputes erupted over terms of enlistment. Jackson prevented mutiny, but the sullen mood remained.

In February reinforcements began arriving, including the welcome addition of a regular infantry regiment which Jackson knew could be used against refractory militia. By March 1814 Old Hickory had approximately five thousand men and was ready to hit the Indians decisively at one of their fortified camps at the Horseshoe Bend of the Tallapoosa River. This battle, fought on March 27, broke the power of the Creek Nation forever.

To show its gratitude, the government on May 28 appointed Jackson major general in the U.S. Army and assigned him to command the Seventh Military District in the South. On August 9, 1814, he concluded the Treaty of Fort Jackson with the Creeks by which they ceded twenty-three million acres of land.

He then raced to Mobile and defended it in September against a small British force. Jackson pursued the British to Spanish Pensacola and captured the town on November 7. Jackson was planning to attack the British in a nearby fort when they blew it up and departed. Fearing another attack on Mobile, Jackson hurried back. Waiting there, he decided that New Orleans was the target. He arrived there on December 2.

Despite Jackson's energetic preparations for various possible British lines of advance, one bayou south of the city was not blocked. The British discovered this open waterway and were within seven miles of the city by December 23. Jackson was shocked but immediately ordered a night attack. After a confused engagement, Jackson withdrew.

Jackson prepared a defensive position along the Rodriguez Canal. The line ran from the levee over to a cypress swamp. Jackson also had a battery of heavy guns on the west bank to prevent a flanking attack.

When a show of force on December 28 and an artillery duel on January 1 failed to dislodge the Americans, the British commander, Lieutenant General Sir Edward Pakenham, decided to make a massive frontal assault on January 8. As a prelude, one of his four brigades was to cross the river and capture the American guns on the west bank, thus outflanking Jackson's position. When this was delayed, Pakenham ordered the main attack to begin anyway at dawn. The American artillery made a shambles of the advancing British columns. Within a half hour it was over. Pakenham was dead, and his army had suffered almost two thousand casualties, against six killed and seven wounded on the American side.

In the meantime, the British attack on the west bank had succeeded, but Pakenham's successor was so sickened by the destruction of the main force that he decided to retreat and so ordered the troops back to the east bank. In early March word arrived finally that the war had been concluded by the Treaty of Ghent on December 24, 1814.

Jackson returned to Nashville in April, the greatest hero of the war. The army was reorganized into two divisions, a southern and northern, each commanded by a major general. Jackson was given command of the southern division with headquarters at the "Hermitage," his home in Nashville.

In November 1817 the Seminoles in Spanish Florida were provoked into attacking an American troop boat on the Apalachicola River. The next month, Secretary of War John Caldwell Calhoun* ordered Jackson to chastise them, and the First Seminole War had begun.

Jackson invaded in March 1818. He captured the Spanish town of St. Marks, then headed east toward a large Seminole village on the Suwannee River. On the way, he destroyed all Indian villages in his path. He burned his objective and then went back to St. Marks, where he ordered the execution of two British subjects he had captured. He was convinced they were inciting the Indians; he was half right. Jackson next moved west to Pensacola which he captured on May 24.

During this whirlwind campaign, Jackson had completely demoralized the Indians by destroying their homes and executing several of their prominent leaders. By the end of May, the Hero was returning home, again the center of controversy and admiration. Spain protested Jackson's actions violently, but it did see that it could not hold Florida and ceded the area to the United States.

In 1821 Congress reduced the size of the Army. One of the two major generals, Jackson or Jacob Jennings Brown,* would have to be demoted, but both were powerful men with influential friends. By persuading Jackson to take the governorship of Florida and thus to quit the Army, President James Monroe avoided an embarrassing dilemma. Jackson was appointed governor in March and resigned his Army commission on June 1, 1821. He resigned the governorship in October to return to Nashville where some friends were already beginning to use his military fame to push him for president.

Unsuccessful in 1824, Jackson was elected president in 1828. During his two terms, he created the modern presidency through his use of executive power with the veto and his misguided but powerful attack on the Bank of the United States. During the Nullification Crisis with South Carolina, Jackson threatened to take to the field again, as commander in chief, before the controversy was resolved. He retired to the "Hermitage" in 1837.

Jackson did not contribute anything new to the art or science of war, but he did give the American people confidence and pride in themselves. He was an amateur soldier, but like George Washington,* another amateur, he had enormous battlefield presence. It is noteworthy that a third amateur soldier-president, Theodore Roosevelt,* admired Jackson immensely.

Jackson was capable of error. It was his fault, ultimately, that the bayou south of New Orleans was not obstructed as he had ordered. He erred in failing to realize until too late the crucial importance of the American position on the west bank of the Mississippi. Under different circumstances, this could have cost him the Battle of New Orleans.

Jackson also had an unfortunate tendency to overreact; his execution of errant militiamen during the War of 1812 and the execution of the two Britons during the Seminole War are good examples. A related shortcoming was his habit of taking everything that went wrong as a personal attack on him. For instance, the Madison administration canceled the invasion of Florida by Jackson's Tennesseans in 1813 because of congressional opposition, but Jackson believed it to be the machinations of evil men out to destroy him. Similarly, a public feud which Jackson had with the War Department during the first months of Monroe's presidency grew out of bureaucratic blundering, not, as he supposed, as a conscious effort to undermine his authority.

His shortcomings were more than compensated by his achievements. His defeat of the Creeks at Horseshoe Bend may not have shown brilliant generalship, but the battle was carefully planned and boldly executed. His next effort, the rapid march from Mobile to Pensacola and back in the autumn of 1814, was truly inspired. Capture of Pensacola made success at New Orleans more certain. Furthermore, if Jackson made mistakes at New Orleans, he did many things right. His concept of a flexible defense until the British revealed their intentions, his daring night attack once they had done so, his ability to get a motley crew to work together effectively at the Rodriguez Canal, and his refusal to pursue the British after January 8—all had the hallmark of professionalism. His lightning thrusts during the First Seminole War were faultless in a strictly military sense. He also had a professional's appreciation of the importance of a regular source of supply and ensured he had such during the Seminole Campaign.

Indeed, even though Jackson gained entree to the military through the militia, his actions and attitudes always were more like those of a regular than a militia general. James Parton was wrong when he described Jackson as being wholly ignorant of the art of war. He studied military writings and tried to instill professional precepts in his Tennesseans. He was a rigid disciplinarian who never tried to court popularity with his men. He valued regular troops in his command principally as a check against mutiny by his militiamen. He was contemptuous of the New York militia who justified their refusal to invade Canada in 1812 on constitutional grounds. He insisted that his own militiamen would not be allowed such scruples over an invasion of Florida.

Along with this undeniable military talent, Jackson also had his share of good luck. As Robert Remini has observed, much of Jackson's success in the War of 1812 was "a matter of his being in the right place at the right time," but every successful general needs good fortune occasionally.

Ultimately, what made Andrew Jackson the most famous and successful general of his generation—more than talent and luck—was his iron resolution to succeed no matter what the odds or price. His will kept his army together after the aborted invasion of Florida in 1813; his will kept an army in the field during the nadir of the Creek War; his will stiffened the resolve of the Louisianans to do their utmost to resist British invasion.

His fortitude is even more remarkable when one realizes that during his campaigns in 1813–1815, he was a very sick man. When he took the field he was still enfeebled from his wound in the Benton fight. To this was soon added dysentery which kept him dangerously weak through the New Orleans Campaign. There were times when only his unconquerable spirit kept him in action.

The ferocity of his nature, his determination to avoid defeat at all costs, is illustrated also in his comments on the defeat of a man he admired—Napoleon Bonaparte. Jackson said that the emperor should have done what he would have done, burned Paris to the ground rather than let it fall to the enemy. There are indications that Jackson would have done this if necessary at New Orleans. In his faults (overreacting and taking everything personally) and his virtues (rapidity of movement and a resolve never to be defeated), Jackson resembles General George Smith Patton, Jr.,* more than any other American general.

BIBLIOGRAPHY

Coles, Harry L. *The War of 1812*. Chicago: University of Chicago Press, 1965.
James, Marquis. *Andrew Jackson: The Border Captain*. Indianapolis, Ind.: Bobbs-Merrill, 1933.
Mahon, John K. *The War of 1812*. Gainesville: University of Florida Press, 1972.
Parton, James. *General Jackson*. New York: Appleton, 1897.
Reilly, Robin. *The British at the Gates: The New Orleans Campaign in the War of 1812*. New York: G. P. Putnam's Sons, 1974.
Remini, Robert. *Andrew Jackson: And the Course of American Empire, 1767–1821*. New York: Harper and Row, 1977.
Ward, John W. *Andrew Jackson: Symbol for an Age*. New York: Oxford University Press, 1955.

JOHN M. WERNER

JACKSON, Thomas Jonathan (b. Clarksburg, Va., January 21, 1824; d. Guiney's Station, Va., May 10, 1863), Army officer. "Stonewall" Jackson was commander of the 2d Corps, Army of Northern Virginia, during the American Civil War.

Thomas Jackson's Scot-Irish father, Jonathan, brought his son into a mountain world characterized by poor-land poverty. Thomas was the second son and third of four children. Following the death of his parents, Thomas lived with his uncle Cummins Jackson. As a young man, Thomas worked in various capacities, including a term as constable, and battled a tendency toward bad health. In the spring of 1842 he obtained an appointment to the U.S. Military Academy at West Point.

Jackson struggled as a student, his deficiencies making the stiff course of study at West Point seem insurmountable at times. His classmates and instructors thought him "slow," and his awkwardness and insecurity produced demerits. But the fragile-looking, wiry frame hosted a soul of steel, and gradually his dogged determination won admirers, friends, and respect. In 1846 he was graduated seventeenth in a class of fifty-nine, among them George Brinton McClellan* and Ambrose Powell Hill.*

War began with Mexico in 1846, and Jackson distinguished himself at Vera Cruz, Cerro Gordo, and Chapultepec. By war's end he had become a brevet major.

In February 1851 Jackson received an inquiry from the superintendent of the Virginia Military Institute (VMI) at Lexington, who wished to know Jackson's interest in an appointment as professor of natural and experimental philosophy. At the time Jackson was involved in an argument with his post commander (Major W. H. French at Fort Meade, Florida) over a technical point of command. Consequently, Jackson applied for the professorship, was selected to fill it, and resigned from the Army in February 1852. When Jackson reported as a teacher at VMI, he was twenty-seven years of age, frail, and already considered eccentric. Jackson's skills as a teacher were limited, but he worked diligently. The cadets played practical jokes on him, and some of them tried to get him dismissed. But the superintendent admired Jackson and successfully defended his professor.

Jackson's social life in Lexington was at first limited to the austere military opportunities at the campus, but eventually they broadened to include an active and devoted relationship with the Presbyterian church. Becoming a famed keeper of the Sabbath, he dutifully attended church meetings, even if he slept through them; and he insisted on taking his turn in oral prayer, although his inarticulateness made these experiences painful for him, for his auditors, and, some said, for the Lord. Church activity brought Jackson increased social invitations. Miss Elinor Junkin, daughter of a Presbyterian minister, set her cap for Major Jackson, and they were wed in August 1853. Their brief time together ended with her death on October 22, 1854, evidently from complications arising from her pregnancy. Jackson despaired at Ellie's death, but he was wed again in July 1857, to Mary Ann Morrison, another daughter of a Presbyterian minister. For the remainder of the 1850s Jackson continued to teach at VMI. In 1859 he commanded the cadet corps which attended the hanging of abolitionist leader John Brown.

When Virginia seceded in April 1861, Jackson received a commission as a colonel of infantry and in June was promoted to brigadier general. He drilled his troops to high efficiency and moved under the command of Joseph Eggleston Johnston* to the field at Manassas Junction (Bull Run), where the first major battle of the Civil War occurred. At a critical moment in the battle, General Bernard Bee rallied his own troops by shouting, "There is Jackson standing like a stone wall." The name stuck. Jackson received promotion to major general in October and in November assumed command in the Shenandoah Valley, a part of the Department of Northern Virginia.

The battles in the spring of 1862 brought Jackson lasting fame. Johnston evacuated Manassas in early March, forcing Jackson to abandon Winchester. He thus began the famous Shenandoah Valley Campaign, rated by many historians as one of the most remarkable in military history. Marching up the Valley, Jackson attacked General James Shields at Winchester on March 23. Shields' superior numbers prevailed, and the Union forces turned back the Confederates. But strategically, Jackson's bold attack proved to be a success, alarming the Federal high command, which shifted troops intended to assist General George Brinton McClellan* in his attack on Richmond. From mid-April until mid-May Jackson operated under the supervision of General Robert Edward Lee* because Johnston was before Richmond facing McClellan. Lee allowed Jackson to remain in the Valley and act independently instead of ordering him to reinforce Johnston. Moving up and down the Valley, Jackson attacked various Federal units, which altogether numbered more than sixty thousand men; but with the Federals separated into parts, Jackson's force of seventeen thousand matched them in action after action, always alarming the Union command that he might break out of the Valley and attack Washington, which seemed ill-defended with so many soldiers engaged in the Richmond Campaign. Thus, actions against Generals N. P. Banks at Front Royal, May 23–25, John Charles Frémont* at Cross Keys on June 8, and James Shields the next day held thousands of Federal troops in the Valley which McClellan required, at least for his own confidence, miles to the east.

Owing to a wound he received in the defense of Richmond, Johnston was replaced by Lee, who thereafter commanded Jackson's troops. Lee brought Jackson to the Richmond area to help relieve the capitol in the Seven Days' Campaign. In action at White Oak Swamp, on unfamiliar grounds, and without the aid of his usual cartographer, Jedediah Hotchkiss, Jackson's actions lacked sharpness.

In July Lee and Jackson advanced on the base of General John Pope* at Manassas Junction. Jackson's men covered fifty-one miles in only two days, engaged the enemy, and then joined other Confederate forces for the Second Battle of Manassas, pushing Pope's army nearly to Washington's defenses. This rapid marching gave Jackson's command a new name: the foot cavalry. These actions made Jackson a Southern hero. Now thirty-eight years of age, his eccentricities, such as holding his arm in the air to improve circulation, became endearing instead of amusing.

In the fall of 1862 Jackson moved into Maryland with Lee, and one of his divisions, under A. P. Hill, helped to stop a desperate Union attack in the Battle at Sharpsburg (Antietam). Later that year, at Fredericksburg, Jackson's men fought well beside those of James Longstreet* to repulse the crossing of the Rappahannock River by General Ambrose Everett Burnside.* In the spring Lee and Jackson faced the Federals, now commanded by Joseph Hooker,* at Chancellorsville. Lee employed a plan he and Jackson had used before; Jackson marched rapidly to flank Hooker, and together a two-pronged and coordinated attack caught the Union Army in a vice. The fighting went well at first, but at nightfall (May 2, 1863), while on reconnaissance, Jackson was wounded by men of his own command who mistook his staff for Union cavalrymen. He was taken to Guiney's Station, suffered the amputation of his left arm, and on May 10, died of pneumonia and complications from the wounds. "I know not how to replace him," said Robert E. Lee, and "I have lost my good right arm." As Jedediah Hotchkiss observed: "I was in no great battle subsequent to Jackson's death in which I did not see the opportunity which, in my opinion, he would have seized, and have routed our opponents."

Jackson's significance to the Confederate military cause rests on a broad base. First, he seemed always at his best in independent command. Actually, he worked well *with* his commanders, Johnston and especially Lee, and they needed only to give him an outline of intended actions. He could be relied upon to fill in the details of the action, and, always keeping his own counsel, execute the plan with swiftness and skill. Early in the war Jackson's secretive nature led many to think him a glory-seeker or at least uncooperative. In time it became his trademark and worked remarkably well as long as he had Lee, and Lee had him, in a kind of partnered command in which each understood the other's role. Lee could never rely on Jackson's successors this way, and thereafter his army became more of a single unit, and also less successful.

Second, Jackson's significant Valley Campaign in the spring of 1862, more than any other factor, spared Richmond's capture. The Army of the Potomac drew almost within the city's limits, but McClellan's own fearful character, much affected by the absence of the extra soldiers he expected to have with him but who instead had been detained in the Valley to oppose Jackson, doomed his campaign to fail. Meanwhile, Jackson handled his small Valley army brilliantly in what became a classic military campaign.

Third, Jackson's acceptance of his own limitations, and the ability to assemble and coordinate a brilliant staff, made him a successful general. With Colonel A. S. Pendleton as assistant adjutant general and coordinator, and others including Captain Jedediah Hotchkiss, his cartographer, to draw upon, Jackson used his staff to greatest advantage by assigning each man his duty and granting him autonomy to perform it. For example, Jackson would draw his mapmaker aside and in complete secrecy order him to select a route to a camp or rendezvous. Jackson had no real facility for grasping the lay of the land, routes, or directions, but Hotchkiss did and the commander used his engineer's skills. He also used Pendleton's skills at organization in the same way. The other staff members performed well, and when the troops arrived at Hotchkiss' chosen spot, everything was usually in readiness.

Fourth, Jackson's keeping of his own council is something of a miracle. Coupled with his loyalty to and confidence in Lee, this made him the ideal subordinate commander. In this role he had no peer in the American Civil War, and it qualified him for this final significance: Jackson became one of the great heroes of the Confederacy. His death martyred him, and his loss was enormous. Soldiers who followed Jackson blindly moved more cautiously behind Richard Stoddert Ewell* or later successors. Duty remained, and the Confederates performed it, but like Hotchkiss and Lee, they always missed Jackson.

BIBLIOGRAPHY

Chambers, Lenoir. *Stonewall Jackson.* 2 vols. New York: Morrow and Company, 1959.
Douglas, Henry Kyd. *I Rode with Stonewall.* Chapel Hill: University of North Carolina Press, 1940.
Henderson, G.F.R. *Stonewall Jackson and the American Civil War.* New York: Longmans, Green, 1898.
McDonald, Archie P. *Make Me a Map of the Valley: The Civil War Journal of Stonewall Jackson's Cartographer.* Dallas: Southern Methodist University Press, 1973.
Vandiver, Frank E. *Mighty Stonewall.* New York: McGraw-Hill, 1957.

ARCHIE P. McDONALD

JOHNSON, Hugh Samuel (b. Fort Scott, Kans., August 5, 1882; d. Washington, D.C., April 15, 1942), Army officer; military mobilizer.

Hugh S. Johnson was the son of a struggling Western lawyer who repeatedly moved his family in search of better fortune. In 1893 the family moved to the Cherokee Strip in Oklahoma Territory, where Hugh's father finally prospered as postmaster for the town of Alva and as a rancher. Johnson received his early education in the public schools of Wichita, Kansas, and Alva and attended Oklahoma Northwestern Normal School. In 1899 he was appointed to the U.S. Military Academy. He graduated in 1903, receiving his commission in the cavalry.

For the next eleven years Johnson served at frontier posts, from the Mexican border to the Philippines. Service with the cavalry accentuated the dual nature of his personality. Outwardly, he was hard-bitten and tempestuous. Beneath this gruff exterior, however, he was sentimental and viewed the world with a romantic eye. In his leisure hours Johnson pursued his literary interests and published more than thirty potboiling short stories about frontier and military life in popular magazines; he also published two juveniles, *Williams of West Point* and *Williams on Service.* In 1914 the judge advocate general, Brigadier General Enoch H. Crowder, picked Johnson to attend the University of California Law School to prepare for appointment to the Army's legal office. Two years later Johnson (now a captain) was acting judge advocate for Brigadier General John Joseph Pershing's* punitive expedition to Mexico. Impressed with his legal acumen, Crowder brought Johnson to Washington, D.C., in October 1916 to brief cases to be argued before the Supreme Court.

World War I marked the turning point in Johnson's career. In 1917 he assisted in the planning and administration of the selective draft; in 1918 he helped regiment industry and reorganize the Army supply system. His wartime performance earned him an enviable reputation as a military mobilizer and rapid promotion.

In April 1918, at the age of thirty-five, Johnson became the Army's youngest brigadier general since the Civil War. Nevertheless, Johnson was disillusioned at the war's end. His dream of seeing combat in France had been thwarted. Facing the prospect of reduced rank in the postwar Army, he resigned his commission in February 1919 and sought new worlds to conquer in business.

Wartime contacts with business leaders provided Johnson with the pick of several lucrative jobs in private industry. He accepted an offer from close friend George N. Peek to be an executive with the Moline Plow Company. It was an inopportune choice, for a farm slump forced a painful liquidation of the company in 1924. In the meantime, Johnson worked with Peek to develop the seminal ideas of the McNary-Haugen Bill that dominated the congressional debate over federal aid to agriculture during the 1920s. In 1925 Johnson reorganized the remnants of Moline Plow as a new company, and in the fall of 1927 he became an economic advisor and speech writer for financier Bernard M. Baruch. During the next five years he investigated the investment potential of numerous firms for Baruch and also served in a management position with Lea Fabrics.

In the summer of 1932 Johnson joined Franklin D. Roosevelt's presidential campaign team as a speech writer, and during the heady "Hundred Days" that followed Roosevelt's inauguration in March 1933, he drafted key sections of the National Industrial Recovery Act. Roosevelt found Johnson's vigor and enthusiasm for the bill irresistible. Ignoring warnings from Baruch that Johnson was "not a number-one man," Roosevelt in June 1933 named him head of the National Recovery Administration (NRA). Johnson carried out the assignment with "demonic energy." Invoking the war spirit of 1917, he directed the formulation of fair-trade codes for hundreds of industries and used the "Blue Eagle" emblem to enlist millions of Americans in his army of Depression fighters. In the process, he shouldered aside the rest of the recovery program, made himself the personification of the New Deal, and momentarily united the nation in the hope that the Depression could be surmounted. Baruch's warning, however, proved prophetic. Too anxious to make things happen quickly, Johnson overextended himself. His previously controlled faults, in particular excesses of scorn, language, and drink, came to the forefront, and he openly feuded with NRA associates and countless businessmen, labor leaders, cabinet officers, and senators. Johnson's truculence persuaded Roosevelt that his usefulness was at an end, and in October 1934, Johnson, at the president's request, resigned his position with NRA.

Johnson's interest in public affairs continued, and in 1935 he briefly served as Works Progress administrator in New York City. Most of his time, however, was devoted to his new career as a lecturer, syndicated columnist for the Scripps-Howard newspaper chain, and radio broadcaster. Initially, Johnson supported Roosevelt and the New Deal. But by 1937 he was castigating the administration's "radical" tendencies, and in 1940 he helped generate the boom for Wendell L. Willkie as the Republican presidential candidate. Johnson also sharply attacked Roosevelt's foreign politics and charged that the president was "Hell-Bent for

War.'' Johnson's vitriolic criticism so angered Roosevelt that in the spring of 1941 he rejected Johnson's application for renewal of his reserve commission as brigadier general. It was a crushing blow for Johnson, who had always thought that the Army should be above politics. He died of pneumonia the following April.

Johnson's place in American military history rests on his role in the manpower and supply programs during World War I. In the spring of 1917 Crowder was entrusted with the task of implementing the selective draft. It was a difficult assignment, for the Civil War draft, America's only precedent for conscripting large numbers of men, had bred widespread resentment and reinforced the nation's traditional commitment to volunteerism. In carrying out his assignment Crowder relied heavily on Johnson. Crowder's ideas and direction gave form to the draft. But Johnson, more than anyone else, translated these into policy. He helped to write the Selective Service law and penned the original plan for executing the draft, the plan for registering the millions of potential draftees, the final regulations for selecting men, and the rationale for the famous ''work or fight'' order. Each marked a major step in the development of the draft, and collectively they helped insure a fair and effective system.

In March 1918, Johnson moved over to the War Department General Staff to assist in the reinvigoration of the languishing Army supply program. The supply bureaus were competing with each other and other government supply agencies for new materials and transportation and manufacturing facilities. Insisting that the military must procure as it saw fit, they steadfastly resisted the efforts of businessmen to utilize the War Industries Board (WIB) to insure a rational distribution of war contracts. Many feared that the Army's haphazard procurement would doom the war effort. Unlike most Army officers, who believed that the WIB was attempting to usurp legitimate military domain, Johnson recognized that in an age of total war the Army must cooperate with the WIB. Only in this manner could supply be synchronized with demand. As director of purchase and supply and as a member of the WIB, Johnson prodded the bureaus to provide the WIB with meaningful requirements statements and to procure exclusively through its auspices. In addition, he developed a mechanism whereby the functional organization of the Army supply system could ''head in'' with the WIB's commodity organization. Finally, under the watchful eye of Major General George Washington Goethals,* director of purchase, storage, and traffic, he restructured the Army supply system to eliminate interbureau competition. Largely as a result of Johnson's efforts, the military and industrial sectors were integrated for the first time to put American industry behind a massive military program.

During the interwar period, Johnson fervently advocated ongoing planning for manpower and industrial mobilization. Unfortunately, he died before he could see how many of the mobilization methods he had helped pioneer in 1917–1918 would be put to even greater use during World War II.

BIBLIOGRAPHY

Johnson, Hugh S. *The Blue Eagle from Egg to Earth*. Reprint ed. New York: Greenwood Press, 1968.
Ohl, John Kennedy. "General Hugh S. Johnson and the War Industries Board." *Military Review* 55 (May 1975): 35–48.
————. "Hugh S. Johnson and the Draft, 1917–1918." *Prologue; The Journal of the National Archives* 8 (Summer 1976): 85–96.
————. "Tales Told by a New Dealer." *Montana; The Magazine of Western History* 25 (Autumn 1975): 66–77.
————. "The Wartime Career of General Hugh S. Johnson." Unpublished Ph.D. dissertation, University of Cincinnati, 1971.

                                                                    JOHN KENNEDY OHL

JOHNSON, Richard Mentor (b. Beargrass Station [now Louisville], Ky., 1780; d. Frankfort, Ky., November 19, 1850), Kentucky militia leader in the War of 1812 and the ninth vice-president of the United States.

Johnson's parents, Robert and Jemima Suggett Johnson, had arrived from Virginia shortly before Richard's birth. The family soon thereafter moved to Bryan's Station, a small settlement just north of Lexington. Although frontier Kentucky offered little in the way of formal schooling, Richard managed on his own to study Latin and prepare for the law curriculum at Lexington's Transylvania University, the first college west of the Alleghenies. In 1802 he was admitted to the Kentucky bar, winning election two years later to the state legislature. In 1807 he began his first of six consecutive terms as a Jeffersonian-Republican member of the U.S. House of Representatives.

When the 12th Congress convened in December 1811, Johnson emerged as a leading War Hawk, declaring enthusiastically that hostilities against Great Britain had in fact begun already with the recently fought Battle of Tippecanoe in the Indiana Territory. Johnson shared fully the confidence of other Kentucky lawyer-and-country-gentleman political leaders that the established American militia system was equal to the conquest of Canada. In Congress he opposed increases in naval appropriations, proclaiming in January 1812 that when "a nation puts forth her strength upon the ocean, the interior of the country will be neglected and oppressed with contributions." Like Isaac Shelby,* Kentucky's governor from August 1812, Johnson vigorously seconded the claim of Governor William Henry Harrison* of Indiana to wartime command over the Old Northwest.

Serving as an aide to Harrison during the 1812 congressional recess, Johnson also raised and led a battalion of Kentucky-militia mounted volunteers. Without previous military experience, he nevertheless possessed innate gifts as a leader and tactician, talents which he enhanced by diligent study of the military manuals of the day. Back in Washington for the 1812–1813 congressional session, Johnson successfully petitioned Secretary of War John Armstrong, Jr.,* for authorization to raise a regiment of a thousand mounted Kentuckians for four to six months of active duty. In the summer of 1813 Johnson's men became highly proficient cavalrymen during a series of northwestern raids covering more than seven hundred miles and eroding Indian confidence in the ability of the British to retain their effective control over the Great Lakes region.

Following a brief interval for resting and remounting his regiment, Johnson rejoined Harrison's army, which had now been augmented with thirty-five hundred mounted Kentucky militiamen mustered by Governor Shelby in the hope of striking a climactic strategic blow in the Old Northwest. Most of Harrison's force, less horses, was ferried to Malden in Upper Canada by Oliver Hazard Perry's* American squadron, which had won naval control of Lake Erie on September 10. Johnson's troopers, however, made their way into Canada by proceeding on horseback west of the lake, then through Detroit. Linking up with Harrison, Johnson hotly pursued Tecumseh's* Indians and General Henry Proctor's British troops, forcing them on October 5, 1813, to make a stand beside the River Thames at a point some fifty-five miles east of Detroit. Insisting that the enemy must not be allowed to escape, Johnson besought Harrison's approval for an immediate mounted charge, arguing that his Kentucky frontiersmen could gallop and fight in the densest of terrains. Under Lieutenant Colonel James Johnson, Richard's older brother and second-in-command, the 1st Battalion burst through the British line next to the Thames, then wheeled about to make prisoners of most of the stunned redcoats. In the meantime Richard Johnson personally directed his 2d Battalion, reinforced by other Kentucky militiamen, in a desperate hand-to-hand struggle to dislodge Tecumseh's braves from a strong position shielded by a swamp. Wounded several times, Johnson shot and killed an Indian chief said to be Tecumseh himself. It was impossible, however, to identify Tecumseh's body or to verify the circumstances of his death, although Johnson never contradicted those who credited him with being the Indian's slayer. Largely attributable to the courage and innovative methods of Johnson's command, as well as to the special militia muster called by Governor Shelby, the Battle of the Thames won for the United States confirmation of its sovereignty over the Old Northwest some three decades after claim to that territory had first been staked out in the Treaty of Paris.

For the remainder of his life Richard M. Johnson pursued his political career. Elected to the U.S. Senate in 1819, he became a spokesman for education and against imprisonment for debt. After the elimination of Henry Clay from the 1824 presidential race, Johnson joined political forces with Andrew Jackson.* He returned to the House after being denied reelection to the Senate in 1829. In 1836 Jackson rewarded the Kentuckian's political loyalty and personal friendship by designating him as Martin Van Buren's vice-presidential running mate. The nomination was especially unpopular in Virginia because life-long bachelor Johnson had violated the racial taboos of his era, having openly acknowledged and educated his two daughters by Julia Chinn, a mulatto slave inherited from his father. The defection of Virginia's electors denied Johnson an Electoral College majority, thus making him the only vice-president to be elected in the

Senate. His oratorical powers increasingly impaired by age and alcohol, Johnson retired from public life in 1841, only to be elected once again in 1850 to the Kentucky legislature. He died just two weeks after taking his seat.

Johnson was politically a Jacksonian, but his career was also reminiscent of that of William Henry Harrison. He won popularity and high public office largely because of his gallant participation in military campaigns to extend the frontiers of the new republic. Possibly to his own detriment, Johnson loyally backed Jackson in opposition to the second Bank of the United States and to federally funded internal improvements. Johnson's support of Jackson's policies often went against his own preferences and those of his constituents. Few students now question Johnson's sincere devotion to political equality for the common man, but none now attributes any special significance to his congressional or vice-presidential service.

The irony of Johnson's life was that he spent most of it in politics, where he was a colorful but comparatively inconsequential figure. The total length of his military service was little more than a year, with only a few consecutive months at a time of active duty. Yet in that short time Johnson displayed an exceptional aptitude for leadership in combat. Blessed with personal magnetism and experienced as a speaker on the political stump, Johnson had little difficulty in attracting short-term volunteers to his standard in 1812—or even in 1813, after American defeats in the Northwest had dampened Kentucky's previous enthusiasm for the war. Strictly a militiaman—not a professional soldier—Johnson nevertheless subjected his men to strict discipline and put them through rigorous tactical training. It was based upon a well-thought-out combat doctrine emphasizing mobility, firepower, and shock, and exploiting his Kentuckians' traditional affinity for mounted service and their ability to gallop and fire from horseback or on foot in the most rugged of terrain. Even though Johnson's strategic horizons failed to reach beyond the Old Northwest, his battlefield methods were well suited to the campaigns in which he fought. In many respects Johnson's combat-worthy mounted militiamen anticipated the best of the Civil War volunteers, fighting men who blended the patriotic ardor of citizens with the discipline of soldiers.

BIBLIOGRAPHY

Bolt, Robert. "Vice President Richard Johnson." *Register of the Kentucky Historical Society* 75 (July 1977): 191–203.
Mayo, Bernard. "The Man Who Killed Tecumseh." *American Mercury* 39 (April 1930): 446–53.
Meyer, Leland W. *The Life and Times of Colonel Richard M. Johnson.* New York: 1932.
Padgett, James A., ed. "The Letters of Colonel Richard M. Johnson." *Register of the Kentucky Historical Society* (1940–1942).

Pratt, Fletcher. *Eleven Generals*. New York: William Sloan Associates, 1949.
Tucker, Glenn. *Tecumseh: Vision of Glory*. Indianapolis: Bobbs-Merrill Company, 1956.

RICHARD G. STONE, JR.

JOHNSON, Sir William (b. County Meath, Ireland, 1715; d. Johnson Hall [near the present Johnstown], N.Y., July 11, 1774), Indian superintendent, victor at the Battle of Lake George, September 8, 1755. Johnson, more than any other provincial leader, was responsible for rallying Iroquois support for the British cause during the last two colonial wars.

Born in Ireland, William Johnson migrated in about 1737 to the province of New York, where he settled in the valley of the Mohawk River. There he quickly became involved in the Indian trade and the acquisition of land. Purchasing some land on the north side of the river, he established his residence at Mount Johnson. Later, he removed a short distance upriver to a place that became known as Fort Johnson. In 1763 he constructed Johnson Hall, a commodious home nine miles from his previous residence, and there he spent the last years of his very active life. It is not certain that Johnson ever was legally married, although he did live successively with two women who presided over his household and provided him with children. The first was a runaway servant named Catherine Weisenberg; the second was a Mohawk Indian named Molly Brant, sister of Joseph Brant* of Revolutionary War fame.

As an Indian trader Johnson was quite unusual. Somehow he managed to win the confidence and even the affection of the Iroquois tribes known as the Six Nations, whose homeland was strategically located in upper New York athwart both the British and the French routes of access to the West. This gave him great influence on the course of Indian-white relations until the very moment of his death in 1774. During King George's War, in 1745, Johnson was successful in preventing the Six Nations from shifting their support away from the British. The following year Governor Henry Clinton made Johnson colonel and principal agent in the affairs of those tribes. Because of his activity in trade and diplomacy, the Indians came to call Johnson Warraghiyagey ("doer of great things"). Johnson also gained prominence in provincial civil government. In 1750 he became a member of the governor's council, a post he held for the remainder of his life. As a councilor he was involved in the intercolonial conference of 1754, known as the Albany Congress, which attempted to deal with the problems of Indian relations and colonial disunity in the face of the impending crisis with New France.

When General Edward Braddock* came to Virginia in 1755 with the assignment of rolling back the French advance into the Ohio Valley, he appointed Johnson superintendent of the Six Nations and allied tribes. At that time Johnson was one of those provincial leaders who believed that Niagara rather than Fort Duquesne at the Forks of the Ohio should be Braddock's primary target, but the British general felt obligated to proceed first against the Forks, which led to his downfall and death. Like many prominent colonial civilians, Johnson had acquired a commission in the provincial militia, but that hardly prepared him for his appointment in 1755 as commander of the intercolonial army that was to assemble at Albany, at the same time as Braddock's advance, with the mission of capturing the French fort at Crown Point on Lake Champlain. Johnson's temporary commission as major general came from New York and the New England colonies, whose contingents comprised his army of more than three thousand provincial troops and Indians. Soon Johnson became enmeshed in an unfortunate quarrel with Governor William Shirley* of Massachusetts, commander of the army being assembled, also at Albany, for the purpose of taking the French fort at Niagara. In due course, the two armies went their separate ways.

Johnson was in the process of constructing a fortified base at the south end of Lake George (so named by him in honor of the king) when he was attacked on September 8, 1755, by a strong force of French and Indians under the command of Baron Dieskau. Firing from behind makeshift breastworks, Johnson's provincials poured a hot fire into the advancing enemy, driving them off with heavy losses. The baron, critically wounded, became a prisoner and was treated with admirable magnanimity by Johnson, who himself had received a lesser wound. Following, as it did, Braddock's disastrous defeat, the Battle of Lake George raised the sunken spirits of the American colonists, with Johnson as the hero of the moment. But casualties and disease undermined the spirit of the provincial army at Lake George, so that Johnson found it impossible to advance farther toward Crown Point and eventually had to terminate the mission. Nevertheless, the Crown showed its gratitude by awarding him a baronetcy, while Parliament voted him £5,000. In addition, early in 1756 Johnson received a royal appointment as sole superintendent of the northern Indians, in recognition of the extraordinary influence he wielded among those tribes in a time when Anglo-Indian relations were a crucial factor in the struggle with France.

As the war continued, regular forces came to dominate the campaigning, while provincial officers such as Johnson were relegated to subordinate roles. In 1756, learning that the enemy was threatening Fort Bull at the western end of the Mohawk portage, Johnson led a relief force to the scene only to find the fort destroyed and the attackers gone. When General James Abercromby attempted to capture Ticonderoga in July 1758, Johnson showed up at the head of 395 armed Indians in support, but his participation in the battle apparently was limited to relatively ineffective long-range sniping. The following year Johnson was second-in-command to General John Prideaux in the expedition against Niagara. After Prideaux was accidentally killed during the siege, the New Yorker assumed command and conducted the siege to a successful conclusion, which further enhanced his military reputation. In 1760 Johnson, commanding a contingent of Indians, accompanied General Jeffery Amherst's* expedition down the St. Lawrence River against Montreal. His greatest contribution in this climactic campaign of the war was in neutralizing the Canadian Indians along the way.

British victory in the Great War for the Empire deepened the apprehensions and resentments of the Western tribes. Johnson headed a delegation sent to Detroit by Amherst in the summer of 1761 to confer with Indian leaders there, a mission he carried out with skill and apparent success. But the underlying problems had not been solved, as evidenced by Pontiac's* Uprising in 1763. Johnson soon became active in the difficult process of pacifying the Western tribes. In 1764 he accompanied Colonel John Bradstreet to Niagara, where he conferred with leaders from various tribes. Two years later, after British military power had regained its dominance, Johnson met with Pontiac himself at Oswego in July 1766, at which time a general agreement for peace was reached.

In the fall of 1768 Johnson negotiated with the Six Nations the Treaty of Fort Stanwix, by which the Iroquois abandoned their claims to any territory east and south of a line drawn from the vicinity of Fort Stanwix generally southwesterly to Fort Pitt at the Forks of the Ohio and thence down the Ohio River as far as the mouth of the Tennessee. This, along with other cessions by the Southern tribes, opened vast extents of land to British development. After the outbreak of Lord Dunmore's War in 1774, Johnson held a conference with Iroquois leaders at Johnson Hall in an attempt to forestall their active involvement. He became ill while immersed in the negotiations and expired on July 11, 1774.

Sir William Johnson was an amateur at war, an occasional commander, who never gave evidence of any unusual military talent, although he undoubtedly was personally courageous. His life exemplifies frontier initiative and opportunism. Arriving in the Mohawk Valley at a time when that important avenue to the West was beginning to develop as an area of great opportunity, Johnson began his brilliant economic, social, and political rise which was to continue until his fame as an Indian agent and military commander was known throughout the colonies and in England. Johnson's greatest importance to the British cause in North America was as a liaison with the strategically located Six Nations of the Iroquois Confederacy, whose continuing support of the British during the last two colonial wars was a major factor in the ultimate defeat of the French.

BIBLIOGRAPHY

Flexner, James T. *Mohawk Baronet: Sir William Johnson of New York.* New York: Harper, 1959.

Gipson, Lawrence Henry. *The Great War for the Empire: The Years of Defeat, 1754– 1757* [The British Empire Before the American Revolution, Vol. 6]. New York: Alfred A. Knopf, 1946.

———. *The Great War for the Empire: The Victorious Years, 1758–1760* [The British Empire Before the American Revolution, Vol. 7]. New York: Alfred A. Knopf, 1949.

Hamilton, Milton W. *Sir William Johnson: Colonial American, 1715–1763.* Port Washington, N.Y.: Kennikat Press, 1976.

Pound, Arthur, in collaboration with Richard E. Day. *Johnson of the Mohawks: A Biography of Sir William Johnson, Irish Immigrant, Mohawk War Chief, American*

Soldier, Empire Builder. New York: Macmillan Company, 1930.
Sullivan, James, and Alexander C. Flick, eds. *The Papers of Sir William Johnson*. 13 vols. Albany: University of the State of New York, 1921–1962.

DOUGLAS EDWARD LEACH

JOHNSTON, Albert Sidney (b. Washington, Ky., February 2, 1803; d. Shiloh, Tenn., April 6, 1862), Army officer. Johnston was a general in the service of three republics.

Albert Sidney Johnston was descended from New Englanders, but he was Southern by birth and association, and he died defending the South against the land of his ancestors. After two years of schooling at Transylvania University in Lexington, Kentucky, Johnston in 1822 accepted an appointment to the U.S. Military Academy. He was graduated in 1826, standing eighth in his class and having served his senior year in the most prestigious assignment in the Corps of Cadets, that of adjutant of the Corps.

Johnston had an unusually versatile military career. In 1832 he participated in the Black Hawk War as adjutant to the commanding general. Two years later he resigned his commission, and after another two years he went to the infant Republic of Texas, where he soon became the ranking general of the army and later the secretary of war. In the Mexican War he was elected colonel of a regiment of volunteers from his adopted state, Texas, and after the expiration of their enlistments he distinguished himself as a staff officer in the Battle of Monterey. In 1849 President Zachary Taylor* appointed him to the rank of major in the U.S. Army as paymaster of troops on the Texas frontier.

After a long drudgery as paymaster, Johnston in 1855 received a promotion to the rank of colonel in command of the newly formed 2d Cavalry Regiment. More than a dozen officers in that organization would one day be Union or Confederate generals in the Civil War. Among these, in addition to Johnston, were such outstanding figures as Robert Edward Lee,* William Joseph Hardee,* and George Henry Thomas.*

In 1857 Johnston was ordered to lead the military expedition against the so-called Mormon Rebellion in Utah. This duty brought him another promotion, to brevet brigadier general, and paved the way to his being appointed in 1860 to command the Department of the Pacific. He was in this position when the seven states of the lower South seceded from the Union.

Johnston's strongest loyalties lay with Texas; when it left the Union he resigned his commission, though he opposed secession in principle. In June 1861 he joined a company of other Southerners who marched cross-country from California to offer their services to the Confederacy. "It seems like fate," he was quoted as saying, "that Texas has made me a Rebel twice." By now Johnston had the reputation, along with Robert E. Lee, of having been one of the foremost active officers in the U.S. Army. Moreover, Johnston was a close personal friend of Confederate President Jefferson Davis,* who immediately appointed him to command the western theater of Confederate operations, with the rank of general, second in seniority only to the elderly Confederate Adjutant General Samuel Cooper.

Johnston's line of defense stretched from the Appalachians on the eastern flank to Indian Territory on the western flank. He made his headquarters at Bowling Green, Kentucky. He was at great disadvantage in numbers and arms, and in naval power on the rivers that threaded his front, the Mississippi, Tennessee, and Cumberland. His first critical test came in February 1862 when Union forces under Brigadier General Ulysses Simpson Grant* attacked and captured Forts Henry and Donelson on the Tennessee and Cumberland rivers, thus breaching the Confederate position. Johnston failed either to concentrate his forces for a determined blow against Grant or to extricate all of them by a prompt abandonment of the forts. Instead, he gave up the Kentucky-Tennessee line but belatedly ordered nearly one-third of his troops into Fort Donelson where most of them were captured. A loud public outcry now arose against him, but Davis supported him and said: "If [Johnston] is not a general...we have no general."

With a Herculean effort Johnston now gathered his scattered forces at the town of Corinth in northern Mississippi, an important rail center. On April 6 he struck Grant's unsuspecting army at Pittsburg Landing (near Shiloh church) on the Tennessee River in Tennessee, seventeen miles from Corinth. The Confederate attack came within an inch of destroying the Union Army. But Johnston was killed early in the afternoon at the climax of the battle. General Pierre Gustave Toutant Beauregard,* second-in-command, took his place and, late in the afternoon, halted the attack until the following morning. That night Grant was heavily reinforced with troops under Don Carlos Buell*; the next day Grant defeated the Confederates and drove them back to Corinth.

Because Johnston died so early in the Civil War, in the first great battle of that conflict, his true promise as a commander must remain in question. His indecisiveness in the loss of Forts Henry and Donelson and his subsequent reticence in contrast to the assertiveness of his brilliant and flamboyant subordinate, Beauregard, have caused many students of the Civil War to rate Johnston mediocre at best. Grant later wrote that Johnston was bold in design but vacillating and faltering in execution. T. Harry Williams, the preeminent biographer of Beauregard, expressed doubt that Johnston was capable of exercising high command effectively. J.F.C. Fuller, a British analyst of Civil War military leadership, dismissed Johnston as a "brave but stupid" man.

Yet in the Shiloh Campaign Johnston succeeded in achieving what Napoleon said was one of the most difficult feats in warfare, that of turning a general retreat into an advance. Johnston clearly outdid Grant in bringing together the wings of his army under Grant's very eyes and in staging against him one of the most remarkable surprise assaults in military history. Johnston stood above Beauregard also when at the last moment—Carl von Clausewitz's "moment of truth"—Johnston ordered the attack to proceed over the objection of his unnerved second-in-command.

Finally, although the effect of Johnston's death on the outcome at Shiloh is a point of endless controversy and cannot be determined with certainty, without question he demonstrated in a superb manner a number of the most important qualities of battlefield command. These included presence of mind in the heat of combat, steadfastness in pressing the attack toward its objective, and charisma in arousing his troops to an utmost effort. Weighing everything, one may reasonably suppose Johnston would have been an outstanding source of strength to the Confederacy if he had lived to develop his talents fully.

BIBLIOGRAPHY

Connelly, Thomas H. *Army of the Heartland: The Army of Tennessee, 1861–1862*. Baton Rouge: Louisiana State University Press, 1967.
McDonough, James Lee. *Shiloh: In Hell Before Night*. Knoxville: University of Tennessee Press, 1977.
Roland, Charles P. *Albert Sidney Johnston: Soldier of Three Republics*. Austin: University of Texas Press, 1964.
Sword, Wiley. *Shiloh: Bloody April*. New York: Morrow, 1974.
Williams, T. Harry. *P.G.T. Beauregard: Napoleon in Gray*. Baton Rouge: Louisiana State University Press, 1954.

CHARLES P. ROLAND

JOHNSTON, Joseph Eggleston (b. "Cherry Grove," Prince Edward County, Va., February 3, 1807; d. Washington, D.C., March 21, 1891), Army officer. Johnston held various Confederate commands during the Civil War.

Johnston was of Scottish descent, and his father, Peter Johnston, had served in the Revolution under Henry ("Light-Horse" Harry) Lee.* Johnston's boyhood was spent near Abington, where he received his early education at the Abington Academy. In 1825 he enrolled at West Point, graduating in 1829, ranking thirteenth in a class of forty-six.

Resigning from the Army after eight years as a second lieutenant of artillery, having served on the Black Hawk Expedition and in the Seminole War, Johnston became a civil engineer in Florida. In 1837, he returned to the Army as a first lieutenant of topographical engineers. On July 10, 1845, Johnston married Lydia McLane, of Maryland.

Promoted to captain in 1846, he fought in the Mexican War, and was wounded twice at Cerro Gordo and three times at Chapultepec. After the war Johnston was chief of topographical engineers in Texas and served as lieutenant colonel of the 1st Cavalry from 1855 to 1860 on the frontier. In 1860 he was promoted to brigadier general and became quartermaster general of the U.S. Army.

When Virginia seceded from the Union, Johnston immediately resigned his commission and became first a major general in Virginia's state troops, and later a brigadier general in the Confederate service.

Johnston played a major role at the Battle of Manassas (Bull Run), July 21, 1861. Slipping away from a superior Union force in the Shenandoah Valley, Johnston rapidly moved his troops to join the army of General Pierre Gustave

Toutant Beauregard* at Manassas. As the ranking officer, Johnston approved Beauregard's plans for the battle, but the engagement began with a Federal assault on the Rebel left which almost carried the Union to victory. Johnston was then at the right of the line, where the Confederates intended to launch an attack. At once he rode to the sound of the guns, arriving in time to help rally the first companies that had been driven back by the enemy onslaught. He then left the Henry Hill, hastened to a vantage point at Portici, about a mile to the southeast where he could see a good portion of the field, and assumed overall direction of the Confederate effort. Johnston exerted a dominant influence on the battle, calling up regiments and brigades, dispatching them to those sections of the front where they were most needed, and finally driving the enemy back in a rout. Although widely complimented for his role at Bull Run, Johnston received far less publicity than the more colorful and dramatic Beauregard, who, ironically, seemed not to have had a clear understanding of the general battle situation at the time decisive action was required.

Johnston next saw major action in the spring of 1862, when a Union army moved to Fortress Monroe. He transferred the bulk of his army east of Richmond to the peninsula between the James and York rivers, recommending that it be concentrated near the Confederate capital. President Jefferson Davis,* concurring with the advice of General Robert Edward Lee,* directed that the Confederates should not retreat. Nevertheless, Johnston eventually fell back to defenses on the outskirts of Richmond. Moving up the peninsula, General George Brinton McClellan* split his army, with three corps on the northeast bank of the Chickahominy River and two corps on the south side. Grasping this opportunity, Johnston attacked the Federals south of the stream on May 31, in the Battle of Fair Oaks (Seven Pines). The Confederate attack, planned for dawn, did not get underway until after noon, and then in disorganized fashion. Johnston was never in the area of the main attacking force but was twice wounded. His plan had been good, and because some results were achieved, Johnston's reputation was further enhanced. Because of his wounds, however, Lee replaced him as the Army's commander.

By November 1862 Johnston had sufficiently recovered to report for duty, and he was assigned to command all the territory between the Appalachians and the Mississippi River. His authority was vague, with department heads reporting directly to Richmond rather than to Johnston. Realizing that he was not in good favor with Davis, Johnston suspected he had been given a nominal command with little power and heavy responsibilities to make him look bad. Therefore, Johnston asked to be relieved. Davis refused to comply with the request. But Johnston would not have been without power, if he had been more willing to accept responsibility and take action. For example, in the aftermath of the Battle of Stones River, when the Rebel high command reeked with dissension, Johnston stood by General Braxton Bragg* even when Davis finally ordered him to replace that general.

Another crisis occurred when General Ulysses Simpson Grant* crossed into

Mississippi to attack Vicksburg. General John Pemberton requested reinforcements, and Johnston instructed him to unite all forces against Grant. Still suffering from his wound received at Seven Pines, Johnston was not in good physical condition, which may explain why he took no further action until ordered by Davis to assume command in Mississippi. Arriving at Jackson, Johnston found that Grant was between him and Pemberton, and ordered Pemberton to advance upon Grant's rear. Although he replied affirmatively, Pemberton did nothing for hours. Responding to a second order, Pemberton again indicated that he would act, but once more did nothing, until it was too late. Grant drove Pemberton back at Champion's Hill and the Big Black River. Johnston ordered him to pull out of the Vicksburg defenses immediately before Grant trapped him in the river fortress. Once more Pemberton disobeyed and was soon completely invested by Grant's army. Perhaps even more enigmatic than Pemberton's behavior was Johnston's failure to relieve that incompetent commander and either assume command himself or substitute some other general who would obey orders.

In December 1863 Johnston was assigned to command the Army of the Tennessee, then before Chattanooga. He was reinforced to a strength of about sixty-two thousand but refused to attack on the ground of insufficient forces. In early May 1864 the Federals advanced, one hundred thousand strong, led by General William Tecumseh Sherman.*

Johnston hoped that the Union Army would attack his strong defensive position in north Georgia, but Sherman marched around the Confederate Army, forcing it to retreat. Johnston dropped back skillfully, and again Sherman threatened to envelop his position, thus forcing another Confederate withdrawal. The Fabian policy created a tide of protest from Richmond and much of the Southern populace. With Sherman advancing on a broad front, Johnston concentrated around Cassville, hoping to fall upon an isolated enemy flank. Planning to personally lead an attack, he boosted his soldiers' morale, but the assault did not materialize and Johnston became embroiled in controversy with one of his major subordinates, General John Bell Hood.* Whatever the reason, Johnston withdrew from Cassville without fighting a pitched battle. On July 17, in front of Atlanta, he was relieved from command, on the ground that he had failed to stop the advance of the enemy. Hood succeeded him and soon lost a major part of the army in unsuccessful attacks.

Reassigned to the Army of the Tennessee on February 23, 1865, Johnston signed an armistice with Sherman in North Carolina on April 18, surrendering on April 26.

After the war Johnston engaged in the insurance business. He also served one term in the U.S. Congress, after which he settled in Washington, D.C., and was appointed a federal railroad commissioner. Johnston also developed a close friendship with General Sherman. He died of pneumonia, contracted while standing hatless in the winter rain at Sherman's funeral.

Johnston was fifty-four years old and in his prime when the Civil War began. His prewar record seemed to promise a highly successful service with the Confederacy. The small, slight general, distinctively marked by a goatee projecting from a slender face, was conscious of his reputation, perhaps to a fault. He never fully measured up to expectations, although there are several positive factors when his military service is evaluated.

Johnston enjoys the enviable distinction of having never lost a battle. Undoubtedly, he possessed outstanding tactical ability and a talent for grasping an overall battle situation. Furthermore, he had the ability to inspire the soldiers he led. His strategic sense is a moot point; and because his best fighting, as well as most of his fighting, was done from a defensive stance, he appears cautious to a fault. The circumstances never seemed satisfactory to Johnston for an offensive movement.

In spite of outstanding ability, the general was frequently unwilling to shoulder responsibility for major decisions, tended to despondency and depression, did not enjoy a good relationship with President Davis (in fact, his contentious personality earned him many enemies), and too often refused to communicate with Richmond and explain his plans and actions. His failure to communicate was especially detrimental in the north Georgia Campaign.

The only important attack Johnston launched was at Seven Pines, which was badly managed. In all his other campaigns he avoided the offensive. The lack of aggressiveness may have reflected a basic personality trait, or perhaps the general felt great pressure to protect the reputation he had built before the war. Whatever the reason, an unwillingness to risk offensive warfare relegates Johnston to the stature of a second-rank commander.

BIBLIOGRAPHY

Connelly, Thomas L. *Autumn of Glory*. Baton Rouge: Louisiana State University Press, 1971.
Davis, William C. *Battle at Bull Run*. New York: Doubleday, 1977.
Govan, Gilbert E., and James W. Livingood. *A Different Valor: The Story of General Joseph E. Johnston*. New York: Bobbs-Merrill, 1956.
Horn, Stanley F. *The Army of Tennessee*. Indianapolis, Ind.: Bobbs-Merrill, 1941.
Johnston, Joseph E. *Narrative of Military Operations*. New York: D. Appleton and Company, 1874.

JAMES LEE McDONOUGH

JONES, John Paul (b. Kirkbean Parish, Scotland, July 6, 1747; d. Paris, France, July 18, 1792), naval officer. Jones is considered the father of the American Navy.

The fifth child of John Paul, gardener at "Arbigland," John Paul, as he was known then, received only a rudimentary education before being apprenticed to a Whitehaven shipowner. When his master went bankrupt, John Paul received his release from apprenticeship and signed on a slaver for two voyages before returning to the merchant service. By age twenty-one he had become a ship-master, and by age twenty-five he formed a partnership with a merchant-planter in Tobago. In 1773 John Paul's crew mutinied, and he was forced to kill the ringleader in self-defense. Friends in Tobago advised him to "retire incognito to the continent of America" until a court of admiralty could be formed to hear his case. Jones took their advice, fled to Virginia, and adopted a new surname as a precaution.

At the outbreak of the American Revolution, Jones was commissioned the senior lieutenant in the Continental Navy (December 7, 1775). He refused to accept command of the 12-gun sloop *Providence*, choosing instead to serve aboard the 30-gun frigate *Alfred* in the hope that he could expand his knowledge of ship handling and fleet maneuvering. In this capacity he took part in the New Providence raid and the squadron's engagement with HMS *Glasgow* (20 guns). In the shuffling of positions which followed that skirmish, Jones was posted to command the *Providence* (May 10, 1776).

With this, his first independent command, Jones took sixteen prizes and de-stroyed local fishing fleets in Nova Scotia. Promoted in rank to captain (October 10, 1776) and transferred to command of the *Alfred*, he led a second successful cruise to the Grand Banks, taking seven prizes.

Upon return to port, Jones learned that he had been placed eighteenth on the seniority list established by Congress and that he had again been assigned to the *Providence*. Incensed, he wrote letters of complaint charging in one that several men placed senior to him were "altogether illiterate and utterly ignorant of marine affairs." Jones was partly vindicated in 1777 when he was posted to command the 18-gun sloop-of-war *Ranger* then under construction, and was subsequently ordered to Europe with the promise of command of a frigate under construction in Holland.

When he arrived in France and found that the promised ship had been trans-ferred to France, Jones sought and obtained from the American commissioners discretionary orders that allowed him to set sail for the Irish Sea in April 1778. Within a month Jones took two merchantmen as prizes and destroyed several others; descended on Whitehaven where he spiked the fort's guns and set fire to the colliers in the harbor; landed at St. Mary's Isle in an attempt to capture the earl of Selkirk, whom Jones hoped to exchange for American seamen held in British prisons; and captured the British sloop-of-war *Drake* (20 guns).

Upon his return to France, plans were laid for future assaults on the British coast in which Jones would command some naval forces and the Marquis de Lafayette* an army. When these plans aborted, Jones settled on a cruise around the British Isles in an old East Indiaman, the *Duc de Duras*, which he renamed the *Bonhomme Richard* in honor of his patron, Benjamin Franklin.

On August 14, 1778, he put to sea from L'Orient with five naval vessels and two privateers and proceeded clockwise around the British Isles, taking seventeen prizes before reaching Scotland's east coast. Jones' control of his subordinates was tenuous at best; the two privateers deserted him, and the captains of the remaining ships refused to support his proposed landing at Leith. Jones next proposed a raid to destroy the Newcastle-on-Tyne coal yards, but again his subordinates refused to follow him.

On September 23, a fleet of forty-one sail was intercepted off Flamborough Head, and after hours of maneuvering there ensued one of the hottest naval engagements of the Age of Sail. Both the 42-gun *Richard* and HMS *Serapis* (44 guns) opened fire almost simultaneously, two of the *Richard*'s largest guns burst, and quickly it became clear that Jones' only hope of victory lay in boarding the more powerful ship. After his attempt at boarding was repulsed, the ships jockeyed for position and finally became entangled. For two hours the *Serapis* poured deadly cannon fire into the *Richard*'s topsides while the seamen and French marines of the *Richard* swept the enemy's deck with small arms and swivels. At 10:00 P.M. a grenade ignited powder charges on the *Serapis* killing a score of men. Becoming desperate, Captain Richard Pearson of the *Serapis* ordered his men to board the *Richard*. When they were thrown back, he sought to continue the battle, but within a half hour his mainmast began trembling and, seeing no hope of victory, he surrendered. Both commanders lost almost half their crews; Jones also lost the *Richard* which sank two days later.

Subsequently, Jones went to Paris where he was accorded a hero's reception, was entertained lavishly, and was presented with a gold-hilted sword by Louis XVI. In June 1779 he planned to return to America, but he was outmaneuvered for command of the frigate *Alliance* and was forced to remain in France until December when he took command of the *Ariel*, a French ship on loan, to carry war supplies to America.

Upon Jones' arrival in Philadelphia, Congress considered a public investigation of his involvement "relative to the detention of the clothing and arms belonging to these United States, in France," but then decided that the Board of Admiralty should examine the captain privately on the matter. He skillfully answered the board's questions in such a way as to give a detailed account of his triumphs and to lay blame for any delays on others. Governmental restraint soon turned to acclaim as France's ambassador decorated Jones with the *Ordre du Merite Militaire* (which brought with it the title chevalier), and Congress voted "that the thanks of the United States in Congress assembled, be given to Captain John Paul Jones, for the zeal, prudence and intrepidity with which he has supported the honor of the American flag." More importantly, Congress voted unanimously to appoint him to command the 74-gun *America*, the Continental Navy's only ship-of-the-line, then building at Portsmouth. After a frustrating year spent in grappling with problems of obtaining supplies and skilled workmen, Jones was able to get the ship launched only to see it turned over to France. Unable to procure another command, he sought and was given permission to join a French fleet for a cruise to the Caribbean in order to view at first hand the handling of a large fleet.

After the war, the chevalier, as he was known in France, cast about for future employment. He considered several commercial ventures, invested in a few, and sought service in the French Navy. When there was no response to his overtures, Jones traveled to the United States where he defended his financial accounts presented to Congress and tried unsuccessfully to obtain promotion to rear admiral. In 1788 he left America for the last time and traveled to Denmark, where he unsuccessfully pressed claims for prize money due him there.

In mid-April Jones received and accepted Catherine the Great's formal offer of a command in the Russian Imperial Navy. Attracted to Russian service chiefly by the promise of adventure and the opportunity to gain experience in commanding a fleet, Jones left for St. Petersburg where he tarried only briefly before reporting to the Black Sea to take command of a squadron of sailing ships under the direction of Prince Potemkin, commander in chief of all forces in the region. Although plagued by jealous rivals, Jones took a leading part in defeating the Turkish fleet in the Liman Campaign of June 1789. There followed four months of political intrigue and bickering over credit for the victory. Jones emerged the loser, and in November he received orders to report to St. Petersburg under the pretense of reassignment to the Baltic fleet. For several months he languished in the capital, devoting much of his time to compiling a ''Narrative of the Campaign of the Liman'' and to answering the attacks of his enemies. In April 1790 a trumped-up scandal linking Jones to a young girl ended any chance for a recall to command and led to his decision to leave Russia.

Jones returned to Paris (May 1790) to live out his final days writing letters to friends in America and to Catherine in hope of being restored to command. Short of funds, he sought and received a commission from the American government naming him ''commissioner with full powers to negotiate with the Dey of Algiers concerning the ransom of American citizens in captivity.'' Jones' health had been in decline since his winter journey to Russia four years before, and the broken sailor died before receiving news of his new position. He was almost alone during his last days. Gouverneur Morris, America's minister to France, accepted his will, listing considerable assets, but he ordered that Jones be buried cheaply in order to minimize any personal financial responsibility. When informed of Morris' intentions, the French National Assembly assumed charge of the funeral arrangements and dispatched a detachment of grenadiers to take part in the ceremonies. Jones was buried in the Protestant cemetery outside the city gates of Paris where he lay until 1905 when his remains were transferred to the Naval Academy in Annapolis, Maryland.

Jones' reputation rests on his exploits of 1778 and 1779 which brought the war home to the British people and strengthened American morale at a time when the war appeared to be deadlocked. Jones generated strong feelings in others. As an individual he was always jealous and vain. A man of strong opinions, he resented anyone not up to his standard who was in a position to control his affairs. Robert Morris, Benjamin Franklin, and Thomas Jefferson respected his abilities, but none could be called his close friend. He often quarreled with subordinates and others with whom he had to work. That he was a man of talent cannot be denied, nor can his patriotism be questioned. His disappointments in terms of recognition and command rivalled those of Benedict Arnold,* but his reaction differed sharply. His courage under fire and his solicitude for his men's welfare brought him their respect, but his violent temper cost him their affection.

Jones was continually guided by a high sense of professionalism which led him to seek opportunities to further his own education and to write extensively on naval matters. His plans for the administration of the Navy, his design for an academy to train officers, and his treatises on tactics and strategy show him to have been a man of vision.

Jones never fully adjusted to peacetime. His success as a diplomat was no compensation for his failure to obtain a suitable command and for his disappointment in Russian service. His prophetic plans for American naval power were rejected in his time. His legacy rests not so much on what he did but on how he did it. As the inscription on his tomb asserts: "He gave our navy its earliest traditions of heroism and victory."

BIBLIOGRAPHY

De Koven, Mrs. Reginald. *The Life and Letters of John Paul Jones.* 2 vols. New York: Charles Scribner's Sons, 1913.

Golder, F. A. *John Paul Jones in Russia.* Garden City, N.Y.: Doubleday, Page and Company, 1927.

Lorenz, Lincoln. *John Paul Jones, Fighter for Freedom and Glory.* Annapolis, Md.: Naval Institute Press, 1943.

Morison, Samuel Eliot. *John Paul Jones: A Sailor's Biography.* Boston: Little, Brown and Company, 1959.

Walsh, John E. *Night on Fire: The First Complete Account of John Paul Jones's Greatest Battle.* New York: McGraw-Hill, 1978.

JAMES C. BRADFORD

JOSEPH, Chief (b. Wallowa, Ore., ca. 1840; d. Nespelem, Wash., September 21, 1904), Nez Perce Indian Chief.

Joseph's father, Tu-eka-kas (Old Joseph), was a chief of the Nez Perce tribe, one of the larger and more powerful tribes in the American Northwest. Young Joseph, or Hin-mah-too-yah-lat-kekht (Thunder Traveling to Loftier Heights), spent his early days following the same pursuits as other youth of his tribe. The Nez Perce wintered in small, independent settlements along the Snake River and its tributaries in present-day southeastern Washington, northcentral Idaho, and northwestern Oregon. Not agriculturists, the tribesmen taught their young men to fish, especially salmon, and to gather food and hunt game, including buffalo, which caused their range to extend over hundreds of square miles.

Probably Joseph's life would have been almost wholly taken up with sustaining life through a subsistence economy had not the white man's coming intervened. The expedition of Meriwether Lewis* and William Clark* straggled into Nez Perce country in Idaho seeking a route through the Bitterroot Mountains to the

Columbia River. These explorers were aided by the tribe, and on their return journey from the Pacific in 1807, they tarried in the tribal villages for several weeks waiting out severe weather. The cordial relations established at this initial contact between the Nez Perce and white men extended nearly to the hostilities in 1877.

Chief Tu-eka-kas was among the first of his tribe to embrace Christianity. Converted in 1839, he abetted the spread of the white man's religion, and in 1845 he offered his eldest son, aged five, to the Reverend Henry Spaulding for baptism and christening as "Joseph." For two years Joseph and his brother, Ollokot, attended Spaulding's day school located on Lapwai Creek in western Idaho. The boys gained a scant knowledge of English before their only formal education was permanently interrupted by the troublesome times that began with the massacre of Spaulding's fellow missionary, Dr. Marcus Whitman, in Oregon by Cayuse Indians in 1847.

The former good relations between Anglo-American and Nez Perce grew increasingly strained during the next thirty years as Joseph attained his manhood. Absorbed along with traditional tribal life and beliefs was the awareness of the encroachments of the white man. He watched as his father and other Nez Perce chiefs tried to maintain an aloof, friendly neutrality during the Jakima Indian War of 1856–1858, the declaration in 1859 of Oregon statehood (which encompassed Joseph's birthplace and homeland), and the Gold Rush of 1861 at Colville, Washington, which increased pressure on the tribe to cede additional lands from a reservation accepted only grudgingly in 1855.

Tu-eka-kas and Joseph held their band of Nez Perce in the Wallowa Valley and refused to move onto the designated reserve farther north. After 1871, following his father's death, Joseph continued to defy all attempts to force his people to leave the Wallowa or to have his homeland declared a reservation, a suggestion made by the federal government in 1876. He did agree to parley with General Oliver Otis Howard* at Fort Lapwai in May 1877. Although fighting nearly broke out during the discussions, Joseph was one of those who counseled forbearance and acceptance of the government's superior force.

Having agreed to vacate the Wallowa, Joseph returned there, gathered his band and its possessions, including large numbers of horses, and began the trek north to the reservation. He never arrived. Three young warriors of another band, disgruntled over the state of affairs, killed some white settlers and the Nez Perce found themselves faced with suspicion and hostility. Reluctantly, Joseph joined four other Nez Perce bands in organizing a flight to Montana where they hoped to find refuge and aid from the Crows.

During the next eleven weeks the Nez Perce fighting men, encumbered with wives, children, and possessions, electrified America by successfully traversing seventeen hundred miles from Oregon through Idaho and Yellowstone Park to the Bear Paw Mountains of northern Montana. They eluded ten separate Army columns, fighting in thirteen battles and skirmishes, most notably at White Bird Canyon (June 15), Clearwater River (July 11), Big Hole (August 9), and the

Bearpaws (September 30–October 6). The exhausted Nez Perce surrendered to Colonel Nelson Appleton Miles* with Chief Joseph offering a memorable epitaph, "From where the sun now stands I will fight no more forever."

Joseph had surrendered on the Army's promise that his people be permitted to return to Oregon. Instead, their horses, saddles, and arms were confiscated, and they were shunted off through Dakota Territory to Fort Leavenworth, Kansas, and finally a tiny reserve in Indian Territory (Oklahoma). After much hardship, the surviving Nez Perce were allowed to go home in 1885, although for Joseph it was a brief visit before being ordered to the Colville Reservation in Washington where he lived out his remaining years.

The Nez Perce' military achievements were impressive. The Volunteer and Regular Army units that faced them were constantly surprised at the Indians' knowledge of tactics and strategy. Fighting defensively, the Nez Perce took superb advantage of the rugged terrain covered during the long retreat. They illustrated a complete familiarity with the use of advance and rearguard movements, skirmish lines, and field fortifications which they combined effectively with their native mobility and maneuverability. Had not the U.S. troops been exceptionally tenacious, the Nez Perce might have reached safety across the Canadian border.

Joseph's reputation as a military genius stemmed from his adversaries' ignorance and his own considerable abilities as a peacetime leader. There were five bands of Nez Perce involved in the 1877 flight. While there was cooperation among the bands, it came from a continuous series of war councils at which Looking Glass and the half-blood Lean Elk (also called Poker Joe) dominated. Nor was Joseph a leader in battle, for his younger brother, Ollokot, proved a much more active warrior. Joseph's primary role during the flight was that of camp guardian and protector of the women, children, and elderly. His surrender speech, which was widely publicized, and his dignified and judicious behavior after the war made him the symbol of the heroic Nez Perce defiance.

BIBLIOGRAPHY

Bed, Merrill D. *"I Will Fight No More Forever"*: *Chief Joseph and the Nez Perce War*. Seattle: University of Washington Press, 1963.

Brown, Mark H. *The Flight of the Nez Perce*. New York: G. P. Putnam's Sons, 1967.

Howard, Helen Addison. *Saga of Chief Joseph*. Lincoln: University of Nebraska Press, 1965.

Josephy, Alvin M., Jr. *The Nez Perce Indians and the Opening of the Northwest*. New Haven, Conn.: Yale University Press, 1965.

TERRY P. WILSON

K

KEARNY, Stephen Watts (b. Newark, N.J., August 30, 1794; d. St. Louis, Mo., October 31, 1848), frontier Army commander, conqueror of New Mexico, governor of California.

The youngest of fifteen children born to Philip and Susanna Watts Kearny, Stephen was descended from a well-known New Jersey family which despite its name had very little Irish blood. His father was a lawyer and landowner, while his mother was related to many of the leading New York landed families. After common school education in Newark, young Kearny entered Columbia College in 1808. He attended for at least two years but did not graduate. His activities between 1810 and 1812 are not known, although he became an ensign in the New York militia on April 24, 1810.

Following the outbreak of the War of 1812, he applied for a commission in the Regular Army. He was named a first lieutenant on March 12, 1812, and was assigned to the newly organized 13th Infantry in July. The regiment marched to the Niagara frontier where on October 13 Kearny played a major role in the Battle of Queenston Heights. He was wounded and taken prisoner but paroled early in 1813. Although advanced to captain on April 1, 1813, he apparently did not receive his commission until 1817. Meanwhile, Kearny served with his regiment at Sackets Harbor and at Plattsburgh. He transferred to the 2d Infantry during the reorganization of the Army after the War of 1812. In 1819 he took part in the massive movement of troops from Plattsburgh to Council Bluffs on the Missouri River to join Colonel Henry Atkinson's* Yellowstone Expedition. For Kearny this started nearly thirty years of Western service. In 1820 he helped explore a route from Council Bluffs to the St. Peter's River in Minnesota. Later in that year he moved to Fort Smith, Arkansas, as inspector and paymaster.

Having finally secured his long-delayed commission as captain, Kearny joined the 3d Infantry at Detroit in June 1821. Two years later he received a brevet as major for ten years' service in grade and moved to the 1st Infantry at Baton Rouge, Louisiana. During 1824–1825 he participated in the Second Yellowstone

Expedition up the Missouri River. The following year he brought four companies from Fort Atkinson (near present-day Omaha, Nebraska) to St. Louis to build Jefferson Barracks as the central garrison point for the Middle Plains. During 1827 he served in the Winnebago War. In 1828–1829 as commander of Fort Crawford (Prairie du Chien, Wisconsin), he demonstrated his strong sense of justice and earned local enmity by seizing timber cut by the settlers on Indian lands. Although promoted to major of the 3d Infantry on May 1, 1829, Kearny remained in the area to play a significant role in the negotiations leading up to the Treaty of Prairie du Chien in 1830. The arrangement of the treaty brought him into close contact with General William Clark,* whose stepdaughter Mary Radford he married on September 5, 1830.

The following year Kearny returned to the frontier to rebuild the abandoned Fort Towson on the Texas border as protection for the Choctaw Indians being transferred from the Southeast. After establishing the post, he was detached in 1832 to serve as superintendent of recruiting at New York City. He vacated the recruiting post following his March 4, 1833, appointment as lieutenant colonel of the newly formed 1st Dragoon Regiment at Jefferson Barracks. The following year he participated in Brigadier General Henry Leavenworth's* tragic expedition into the Southern Plains which culminated in the Treaty of Fort Gibson. During the fall of 1834 Kearny led three companies of dragoons from Fort Gibson on the Neosho River to garrison the unfinished Fort Des Moines (present-day Keokuk, Iowa). In 1835 Kearny conducted an expedition into Sioux territory in Minnesota.

Promoted to colonel of his regiment on June 4, 1836, Kearny moved its headquarters to Fort Leavenworth. There he moulded the dragoons into one of the crack units in the Army and wrote his *Carbine Manual, or Rules for the Exercise and Manoeuvers for the U.S. Dragoons* (Washington, D.C.: Globe Office, 1837). In 1837 he led an expedition that laid out a military road from Fort Leavenworth to the Arkansas River, and two years later he interceded to prevent hostilities between the Potowatomies and the Otoes. In 1840 he took a large detachment of dragoons into Cherokee territory to help quiet an incipient civil war, and in 1842 he led five companies to the Texas frontier to dissuade the Indians there from taking part in the renewed Texas-Mexican hostilities. In July 1842 Kearny returned to Jefferson Barracks to assume command of the newly created Third Military District. From there in 1845 he set out on a major expedition along the Oregon Trail to South Pass in Wyoming, returning by way of the Colorado plains and the Santa Fe Trail.

In late May 1846 Kearny received orders to organize an expedition of dragoons and Missouri volunteers to seize Santa Fe. Kearny had his Army of the West in motion by June 30, and on August 18 he led them into the dusty New Mexico town. He put on the stars of a brigadier general and organized the newly won territory. He quickly won over most of the inhabitants by his honesty and even-handedness; promulgated a territorial constitution; and established a civil government. He left Santa Fe on September 25 to accomplish his second objective, the seizure of California and the institution there of an occupation government.

Upon learning of Commodore Robert Field Stockton's* conquest of the province, Kearny sent most of his escort back to Santa Fe and began the extremely difficult overland trek to California. His band arrived there on December 2, following the successful uprising around Los Angeles. Uncertain of the true state of affairs, Kearny requested an escort to Stockton's temporary base at San Diego. At the urging of the commander of the escort and a number of others, including Kit Carson, Kearny decided to attack a nearby detachment of Californians. The ensuing Battle of San Pascual on December 6, 1846, left the Americans in possession of the battlefield but scarcely able to move. They were rescued by a second detachment from San Diego.

Kearny and Stockton clashed almost immediately over command of the attack against Los Angeles which began later in the month. Stockton claimed command because most of the troops were naval. Kearny acquiesced, but once Los Angeles was regained and peace was restored in California he again pressed his claims to control ashore, relying on his orders from the president. Stockton refused to recognize Kearny's authority, basing his claim on prior conquest. Not until Commodore W. Branford Shubrick replaced Stockton in March was the dispute settled in Kearny's favor. With California safely in American hands, Kearny returned home, but before departing he launched a campaign in conjunction with the naval commanders to seize Baja California. By the end of the war, the inhabited portions of the peninsula were under American control.

The explorer John Charles Frémont,* although a Regular Army officer, defied orders from Kearny and sided with Stockton during the dispute over control of the California government. After his return to Fort Leavenworth in August 1847, Kearny preferred charges of insubordination against Frémont. They were upheld in a heated court-martial whose findings caused the explorer to leave the Army. Both during the trial and afterwards, Frémont's father-in-law, Senator Thomas Hart Benton, conducted a campaign to discredit Kearny, which has affected his reputation to the present.

Following his return east, Kearny spent most of the rest of 1847 on the Frémont case. In April 1848 he joined Major General Winfield Scott's* army in Mexico as commander at Vera Cruz. There he contracted such a bad case of yellow fever that he had to be sent to Mexico City for recovery. While in the Mexican capital, he served both as military governor and commander of the 2d Division of the Army. On June 6 he led his men on their march back to the coast. He sailed from Vera Cruz on July 11, landed at New Orleans, and returned to Jefferson Barracks where he assumed command of the Sixth Military District on July 30. He was now very sick from the dysentery which developed out of his yellow fever attack. Kearny died on the last day of October soon after learning that the Senate, over the strong objections of Benton, had confirmed his brevet rank of major general.

One of the best frontier officers prior to the Civil War, Kearny was an able administrator of conquered lands and a brave and sensible field commander. He was a strict disciplinarian and a man of extremely strong character whose even-handed treatment of others earned him great respect, if little love. Kearny's peripatetic career illustrates well the role of the Army on the frontier before the Civil War. Exploration, native diplomacy, and war against Indians, Mexicans, and the elements themselves punctuated his life.

BIBLIOGRAPHY

Bancroft, Hubert Howe. *History of California*. Vol. 5. San Francisco: History Company, 1886.
Bauer, K. Jack. *The Mexican War 1846–1848*. New York: Macmillan Company, 1974.
Beers, Henry Putney. *The Western Military Frontier, 1815–1846*. Philadelphia: n.p., 1935.
Clarke, Dwight L. *Stephen Watts Kearny, Soldier of the West*. Norman: University of Oklahoma Press, 1961.
Kearny, Thomas. "The Mexican War and the Conquest of California." *California Historical Society Quarterly* 8 (September 1929): 251–61.
Smith, Justin H. *The War with Mexico*. 2 vols. New York: Macmillan Company, 1919.

                                                              K. JACK BAUER

KENNEY, George Churchill (b. Yarmouth, Nova Scotia, August 6, 1889; d. Bay Harbor Islands, Fla., August 9, 1977), Army officer, aviator, air commander in World War II.

Although born in Nova Scotia, George Kenney was reared in Brookline, Massachusetts. He entered the Massachusetts Institute of Technology in 1907, studied civil engineering there for three years, but left prior to graduation and took an engineering job with the Quebec Saguenay Railroad. In the next four years he held positions in civil engineering and construction management with several companies, becoming president of the Beaver Contracting and Engineering Corporation in 1916.

Two months after America's entry into World War I, Kenney enlisted as a flight cadet in the Aviation Section of the Army Signal Corps and subsequently earned a commission as a first lieutenant. He was sent to France that autumn where he underwent advanced pilot training, and in early 1918 he was assigned to the 91st Aero Squadron. He flew seventy-five combat missions, mainly in the Toul and Meuse-Argonne sectors, and he shot down two German aircraft. By the time of the Armistice he was a captain, flight commander, and recipient of the Distinguished Service Cross and the Silver Star. He served with the American occupation forces in Germany until mid-1919 when he returned to the United States.

During the ensuing fourteen years he served tours of duty as squadron commander, instructor, inspector, and production engineer at Army airfields in Texas, Ohio, and New York. He also attended and graduated from the Army Air Service Engineering School in 1921, the Army Air Corps Tactical School in 1926, the

Army Command and General Staff School in 1927, and the Army War College in 1933.

Upon graduation from the War College, he remained in Washington for two years on the staff of the Office of the Chief of the Army Air Corps. In 1935–1940 he advanced in rank to major and lieutenant colonel while serving in staff and command assignments at Langley, Mitchell, and Wright fields, as well as at the Infantry School and the American Embassy in Paris. In early 1941 he was promoted to brigadier general and was given command of the Army Air Corps Experimental Division and Engineering School. Elevated to major general in early 1942, he was appointed commanding general of the Fourth Air Force, with headquarters at Riverside, California.

Between the world wars Kenney gained a reputation as an aggressive, industrious, and innovative air officer. As early as the 1920s he was boldly experimenting with combat aircraft engineering and tactics; he allegedly introduced the use of the parachute fragmentation bomb and the wing-mounted machine gun. He was an ardent advocate of air power and of expanded funding for military air research and development. He returned from his brief tour as assistant air attaché in Paris in 1940 strongly convinced that the U.S. Army Air Corps was markedly inferior to the major European air forces in quantity and quality of planes and personnel.

In August 1942 Kenney joined General Douglas MacArthur's* General Headquarters in Brisbane, Australia, as commander of Allied Air Forces, Southwest Pacific Area, a position he retained until the end of the war. For the next year he relied on the Royal Australian Air Force and American Fifth Air Force; after that, Kenney's air operations, steadily moving northward with new ground conquests and new bases, were dominated by American squadrons. He served as commanding general of the Fifth Air Force, his principal strike force, until June 1944 when he relinquished that command to Major General Ennis C. Whitehead, his former deputy. At that time Kenney assumed command of the newly created Far East Air Forces, which ultimately included the American Fifth, Seventh, and Thirteenth air forces. A lieutenant general since late 1942, he was promoted to general in March 1945.

Kenney planned and oversaw Allied air operations in the Southwest Pacific Theater, ranging from strategic bombing raids against oil refineries on Borneo to close-support strikes for nearly sixty amphibious operations on New Guinea, the Solomons, the Bismarcks, the Admiralties, the Moluccas, and the Philippines. Up to March 1944 his Fifth Air Force had flown over 117,000 sorties, ranking second in that category among the eleven numerical combat air forces of the U.S. Army Air Forces. In the spring and summer of 1945 his planes supported the invasion of Okinawa and conducted raids against the Japanese home islands. Among the most notable achievements of his air command were the transport and supply of Australian and American troops in the Papuan Campaign of 1942–1943, the sinking of virtually an entire invasion armada in the Battle of the Bismarck Sea in early 1943, and the airborne invasions of Nadzab, northeast of New Guinea, in late 1943 and of Corregidor, at the entrance of Manila Bay, in early 1945. Kenney became not only one of MacArthur's most valued confidants and strategic advisors but also the most distinguished air commander in the war with Japan, winning numerous American and Allied awards and citations for his bold, brilliant leadership.

After World War II he held the following commands: Pacific Air Command, 1945–1946; Strategic Air Command, 1946–1948; and Air University, 1948–1951. Besides his other duties in 1946, for nine months of that year he was also the senior U.S. representative on the United Nations Military Staff Committee. Retiring in August 1951, he served as president of the National Arthritis and Rheumatism Foundation for the next twelve years. He wrote four books, all relating to the Southwest Pacific war: *General Kenney Reports: A Personal History of the Pacific War* (1949); *The MacArthur I Know* (1951); *The Saga of Pappy Gunn* (1959); and *Dick Bong, Ace of Aces* (1960).

Nicknamed "Little George" by colleagues, Kenney had a stocky build and stood slightly less than five feet-six inches in height. Some of the assets and liabilities of his personal traits are indicated by these typical comments about him made by fellow officers of the Southwest Pacific Command: "extremely colorful," "lots of fun," "pompous but very competent," "a smart and decisive thinker," "always hot to get things done," "arrogant and extremely opinionated," "a buccaneer of the 'go-get-'em' and 'to-hell-with-how-we-do-it' type," "great ability to raise morale," "too optimistic about the capabilities of his air forces," "convinced that without him the war couldn't have been won." Such characteristics also stand out in his own writings, especially *General Kenney Reports*.

Within a few months after he arrived in Brisbane in 1942, Kenney had transformed the Southwest Pacific air organization from a passive, defense-minded, and poorly administered command into one that rapidly wrested control of the skies from the Japanese and engaged in ever-mounting attacks against enemy land and sea targets. Kenney, like MacArthur, was sometimes criticized by Australian commanders and American admirals of the South and Central Pacific Theaters for inadequate attention to interservice and intertheater coordination in planning and operations. Kenney later admitted that during the Pacific conflict he often "threw the book away" and adopted the motto, "Hell, let's try it." Among his most successful innovations against the Japanese were skip-bombing ships and using parachute bombs against small ground targets such as parked aircraft. In view of the Southwest Pacific Theater's lack of carrier aircraft to support its assaults until late in the war, Kenney's air support was indispensable to the success of the Allied offensives from New Guinea to the Philippines. MacArthur maintained that the key to his strategic planning was "pushing my own land-based air cover progressively forward with each advance" and utilizing Kenney's air units "to the maximum extent."

Among Kenney's lesser known abilities was that of selecting high-performance subordinates in air staff and command positions, outstanding of whom was Whitehead. Kenney also demonstrated a broad grasp of strategy and ably argued his theater's needs and interests at various Washington conferences involving representatives of the Pacific commands and strategic planners of the Joint Chiefs of Staff. MacArthur said of him, "Of all the brilliant air commanders of the war, none surpassed him in those three great essentials of combat leadership: aggressive vision, mastery of air tactics and strategy, and the ability to exact the maximum in fighting qualities from both men and equipment." The Joint Chiefs regarded him as one of the most able commanders in the Pacific war. Indeed, Kenney was one of the few MacArthur lieutenants to be entrusted by the Pentagon with positions of high command in the postwar era.

BIBLIOGRAPHY

Craven, Wesley F., and James L. Cate, eds. *The Army Air Forces in World War II. The Pacific: Guadalcanal to Saipan, August 1942 to July 1944*. Chicago: University of Chicago Press, 1950.
———. *The Army Air Forces in World War II. The Pacific: Matterhorn to Nagasaki, June 1944 to August 1945*. Chicago: University of Chicago Press, 1953.
James, D. Clayton. *The Years of MacArthur*. Vol. 2, *1941–1945*. Boston: Houghton Mifflin Company, 1975.
Kenney, George C. *General Kenney Reports: A Personal History of the Pacific War*. New York: Duell, Sloan and Pearce, 1949.
MacArthur, Douglas. *Reminiscences*. New York: McGraw-Hill, 1964.
U.S. Strategic Bombing Survey. *The Fifth Air Force in the War Against Japan*. Washington, D.C.: U.S. Government Printing Office, 1947.

D. CLAYTON JAMES

KENT, Jacob Ford (b. Philadelphia, Pa., September 14, 1835; d. Troy, N.Y., December 22, 1918), Army officer, combat leader. Kent commanded the 1st Division, Fifth Army Corps, in the assault on San Juan Hill during the Santiago Campaign in the Spanish American War.

Born into an old American family, Kent entered the U.S. Military Academy on July 1, 1856, and graduated five years later, number thirty-one in a class of forty-five members. Commissioned a second lieutenant in the 3d Infantry on May 6, 1861, he proceeded to Washington to assist in drilling the newly raised volunteer regiments. He accompanied the 3d Infantry in the Manassas Campaign and was wounded three times and captured at the Battle of First Bull Run. After spending over a year in Libby Prison, he was exchanged and rejoined his regiment in time to participate in the campaign and Battle of Antietam and, subsequently, the march to Falmouth and the bloody defeat at Fredericksburg. By now a first lieutenant in the 3d Infantry, he received a promotion to the temporary rank of lieutenant colonel-staff and was assigned as assistant inspector general of the IX Army Corps. After little more than a month, he transferred to a similar post with the VI Army Corps, commanded by Major General John Sedgwick. Kent remained on the corps staff until shortly before the surrender at Appomattox

Court House, when he became assistant inspector general of the Department of Washington.

During the war, Kent had earned a reputation for professional expertise and bravery under fire; he received successive brevets as major and lieutenant colonel in the Regular Army for heroism in the storming of Marye's Heights in the Chancellorsville Campaign and in the battles around Spotsylvania Court House and a brevet colonelcy in the volunteers for "meritorious services in the field during the campaign before Richmond." In September 1865 the War Department posted him to West Point as assistant instructor of infantry tactics. Four years on the Hudson were followed by almost thirty years of garrison duty in the South and on the frontier with most of the time spent in the little one- and two-company posts that characterized the Indian-fighting army. His only opportunity for work on a larger scale came from 1890 to 1894 when he served as the acting inspector general of the Department of the Columbia.

The hump in promotions caused by the Civil War contributed to the stagnation of Kent's career. Promoted to captain in the 3d Infantry in 1864, he did not receive his majority in the 4th Infantry until 1885. Advancements followed fairly rapidly thereafter. The declaration of war against Spain found him a colonel at Fort Douglas, Utah, commanding the 24th Infantry. His Civil War record earned him a commission of brigadier general of volunteers, and his seniority won him the command of the 1st Infantry Division of the V Army Corps mobilizing at Tampa, Florida.

During the Santiago Campaign, Kent commanded a feint against Cabanas to cover the main landing at Siboney. The 1st Division landed after all the other units had disembarked and saw no action until July 1, 1898, when it and the Cavalry Division captured the outer line of Spanish entrenchments on San Juan and Kettle Hills. In the conference of general officers which the corps commander, Major General William Rufus Shafter,* called on July 2, Kent alone of the division commanders voted to withdraw, explaining that while he was personally opposed all of his brigade commanders favored a retreat. Following the surrender at Santiago, he signed the "round robin" letter urging the withdrawal of the corps before yellow fever destroyed it. Promoted major general of volunteers for his part in the assault on San Juan Hill, Kent received no further employment following his return to the United States. He voluntarily retired on October 15, 1898, eleven days after his elevation to brigadier general in the Regular Army and almost one year earlier than the law required. In 1916 Congress advanced him to major general on the retired list.

Kent's military reputation depends upon what he did and failed to do during a few hours of a hot July day in 1898. His division was a division in name only. It had never maneuvered or trained as a division nor had any of the brigades. Some of the regiments had not operated as units since the Civil War. Kent did nothing to correct these deficiencies, but then neither did Shafter or the other division commanders. Consequently, the actual assault was an affair of company and battalion commanders, with Kent providing no supervision to this phase of the battle. His contribution came during the deployment of the division prior to the attack, a problem complicated for Kent by the fact that he and Brigadier General Samuel S. Sumner, the commander of the Cavalry Division, did not realize that Shafter contemplated an attack by their divisions that day.

Shafter had planned that the 2d Infantry Division under Brigadier General Henry Ware Lawton* would attack El Caney, a detached outpost on the right flank of the V Corps and then advance upon the outer line of Spanish fortifications, anchored on San Juan Hill (actually a ridge), which protected the city of Santiago. When the 2d Division arrived in front of the Spanish lines, the 1st Division on the left and the Cavalry Division in the center would join it in an all-out assault. Unfortunately, Kent's and Sumner's commands became heavily engaged and had to attack prematurely.

The road by which Kent and Sumner were to advance, the only road of which corps headquarters was aware due to faulty reconnaissance, led through thick jungle which retarded off-road movement. It ran perpendicular to the Spanish lines which meant that the Spaniards could fire from the safety of their trenches into the two divisions jammed along the length of the road and hardly avoid hitting someone. Only a few Americans at the head of the column could shoot back. The open ground between the jungle and the ridge was dominated by Spanish fire.

Kent believed that his instructions required him to move his division a few miles closer to the front and bivouac by the side of the road, a maneuver Shafter had ordered on several preceding days. Consequently, Kent rode at the head of his column without attempting any reconnaissance of the terrain until his troops came under fire. He then pushed his way to the front through the Cavalry Division which had preceded his division down the road. Kent decided that the blockhouses on San Juan were the key to the position and hurried back to clear the traffic jam which prevented his men from advancing. He accepted the decision of Lieutenant Colonel John D. Miley of the corps staff to order a corps attack in General Shafter's name. (Shafter was ill and out of contact.) When Lieutenant Colonel George Derby in the Signal Corps balloon, which served as an excellent range marker for the Spaniards, sighted an alternate trail leading off the main road, Kent sent the 71st New York Infantry and his 2d and 3d Brigades less one regiment down the trail. This relieved pressure on the main road and probably made the assault possible, because it allowed the division to deploy much more rapidly.

Unfortunately, the leading battalion of the 71st panicked under fire. Kent and his staff formed a straggler line and urged on the other units. In the confusion the message he sent to Hawkins informing him of what had happened to the 71st failed to arrive. Kent, knowing that Hawkins had planned to flank the blockhouses with the 71st, had ordered the regiment to its deployment area by the shortest possible route—the trail.

Following his intervention on the trail, Kent superintended the positioning of his 2d and 3d Brigades and then returned to Hawkins' front. In the interim Hawkins had decided that his two regiments could no longer endure the heavy Spanish fire in their exposed position and had attacked. His advance acted as a signal for other American units to move forward. It was a great victory, but it cost Kent bitter recriminations from the guardsmen in the 71st who disliked his forthright account of their panic in his official report and from Hawkins who criticized the way Kent had split without his knowledge. Kent did not reply; he let the record speak for him.

Kent never held Shafter's confidence, and after the battle he lost what little support he had enjoyed. Shafter recommended Kent for promotion to major general of volunteers only after the secretary of war queried V Corps headquarters as to why Kent's name had been omitted from an earlier promotion list. After the surrender of the Spanish garrison and before the War Department decided to withdraw the corps to the mainland, Shafter tried to separate Kent from his command and return him to the United States as a "surplus" major general.

Clearly, Kent had lost his sharp professional edge in the years of slow promotion and small responsibilities after the Civil War. His performance as a division commander appears very amateurish compared to modern professional canons, but those canons were only in the process of development at the time Kent headed his division toward San Juan. Once under fire he proved able to make rapid and correct appreciations of a confusing situation and was probably the best division commander in the campaign. His performance was certainly superior to that of any Union Army division commander during the first nine months of the Civil War with the possible exceptions of Ulysses Simpson Grant* at Belmont and George Henry Thomas* at Mill Springs. Kent led his division better than anyone had a right to expect.

BIBLIOGRAPHY

Bonsal, Stephen. *The Fight for Santiago: The Story of the Soldier in the Cuban Campaign from Santiago to the Surrender*. New York: Doubleday and McClure, 1899.

Brown, Charles Henry. *The Correspondent's War: Journalists in the Spanish-American War*. New York: Charles Scribner's Sons, 1967.

Chadwick, French Ensor. *The Relations of the United States to Spain: The Spanish-American War*. New York: Charles Scribner's Sons, 1911.

Miley, John D. *In Cuba with Shafter*. New York: Charles Scribner's Sons, 1899.

Millis, Walter. *The Martial Spirit*. Boston: Literary Guild, 1931.

Post, Charles Johnson. *The Little War of Private Post*. Boston: Little, Brown and Company, 1960.

EDGAR F. RAINES, JR.

KIMMEL, Husband Edward (b. Henderson, Ky., February 26, 1882; d. Groton, Conn., May 14, 1968), naval officer. Kimmel was serving as commander in chief, U.S. Fleet, and commander in chief, Pacific Fleet, at the time of the Japanese attack on Pearl Harbor on December 7, 1941.

Husband Edward Kimmel—the son of Major Marius M. Kimmel, a West

Point graduate—attended Central University in Richmond, Kentucky, before he received an appointment to the U.S. Naval Academy from Kentucky in June 1900. On February 1, 1904, he graduated thirteenth in a class of sixty-two and, after the two years of sea duty then required by law, received his ensign's commission. He joined the new pre-dreadnought battleship *Virginia* in 1906.

Kimmel spent his tours of duty in the years preceding World War I principally in the fields of gunnery and ordnance. After engineering instruction at the Bureau of Ordnance in Washington, he served in the battleships *Georgia, Wisconsin,* and *Louisiana*, in succession, participating in the dramatic round-the-world cruise of the Great White Fleet commanded by Admirals Robley Dunglison Evans* and Charles Sperry. Kimmel then served ashore as assistant to the director of target practices and engineering performances before he returned to sea as ordnance officer in the armored cruiser *California* and later served as fleet gunnery officer for two commanders of the Pacific Fleet.

After a tour as aide to Assistant Secretary of the Navy Franklin D. Roosevelt— an important association in light of the future—Kimmel served a second stint as assistant to the director of target practices and engineering performances at a key time—when the United States entered World War I. He received orders to London in October 1917 and served as an instructor with the Royal Navy, imparting recent developments in gunnery spotting. He also went to sea as a naval observer and witnessed the Battle of Heligoland Bight. Kimmel became gunnery officer on the staff of Rear Admiral Hugh Rodman, who commanded Battleship Division Nine of the Atlantic Fleet, after the arrival of that group of American dreadnoughts in British waters in December 1917. He remained on Rodman's staff into 1919, when he became executive officer in the battleship *Arkansas.*

Subsequently serving as production officer at the Naval Gun Factory in Washington, Kimmel returned to sea in December 1923, journeying to the Asiatic Station where he commanded, in succession, the destroyers *Preble* and *Tracy*, and concurrently served as commander of two destroyer divisions. Coming back to the United States in the spring of 1925, Kimmel attended the Naval War College, where he excelled in strategy and tactics, and completed the senior course in 1926.

As in the earlier phases of his career, Kimmel alternated tours ashore and afloat, in billets of increasing responsibility into the 1930s. As he advanced up the ladder toward flag rank, Kimmel worked, successively, in the policy and liaison division of the office of the Chief of Naval Operations (CNO) at the time of the Nicaraguan intervention in 1927; commanded Destroyer Squadron 12, Battle Force; served as director of ship movements, office of the CNO; commanded the battleship *New York*; served as chief of staff to Vice Admiral T. T. Craven, commander, Battleships, Battle Force; and was budget officer for the Navy Department.

He achieved flag rank in November 1937, while budget officer, and subsequently broke his flag at sea for the first time in the spring of 1938, in the heavy cruiser *San Francisco* as commander, Cruiser Division Seven. Upon the conclusion of Fleet Problem XX in the spring of 1939, Kimmel led Cruiser Division Seven on a good-will voyage around South America. Kimmel was given the concurrent responsibilities of commander of Cruiser Division Nine and commander of Cruisers, Battle Force, shortly before the outbreak of war in Europe in the summer of 1939.

Within a year of Kimmel's assuming command of the Battle Force cruisers, President Franklin D. Roosevelt—hoping to deter the Japanese from further aggressive steps in the Far East—made a move that ultimately affected the admiral's future. After the end of Fleet Problem XXI, the president directed that the Fleet remain in Hawaiian waters, basing on Pearl Harbor, until further notice. The decision irritated the incumbent commander in chief, U.S. Fleet, Admiral James O. Richardson, who, in two ensuing visits to Washington, unsuccessfully attempted to dissuade the president from his course. Roosevelt ultimately relieved Richardson and picked Kimmel to succeed him over the heads of forty-six more senior officers.

Kimmel relieved Richardson on February 1, 1941, and from that time to early December of that pivotal year, he energetically prepared the Pacific Fleet for war. Less than a year later, however, a Japanese carrier task force—the largest, most powerful unit of its kind in the world—steamed in secrecy from the fog-shrouded Kuril Islands and descended, undetected, upon Oahu on December 7, 1941. Japanese planes from six carriers attacked the ships of the Pacific Fleet at Pearl Harbor early that Sunday morning, and, in less than two hours, sank or damaged eighteen ships, including the bulk of American battleship strength in the Pacific.

Removing the Pacific Fleet as a deterrent at the outset gave the Japanese an early victory and assured the success of their southern operation into British, Dutch, and American Far Eastern possessions. Although the Japanese attack of December 7 caught Oahu's defenders unawares, Kimmel soon set in motion the United States' first offensive—an attempt to relieve Wake Island. Unfortunately for that island outpost, defended bravely by Marines, delays and Kimmel's untimely relief prevented a successful conclusion to that effort. Kimmel was relieved on December 17, 1941, by Vice Admiral W. S. Pye, who was in turn relieved by Admiral Chester William Nimitz* on December 31. Wake fell shortly before Christmas. After testifying at the initial inquiries into the Pearl Harbor disaster, Kimmel retired from the Navy, with the rank of rear admiral, on March 1, 1942, to face ensuing inquiries that lasted into 1946.

After a brief civilian career with the engineering consulting firm of Frederick R. Harris, Inc., in 1947, Kimmel retired from public life to Groton, Connecticut. There he lived out the rest of his days fighting relentlessly and ceaselessly to clear his name; during that time he wrote *Admiral Kimmel's Story* (Chicago, 1955), an uncompromising book in which he set forth his account of what happened on Oahu before December 7, 1941.

Husband Edward Kimmel was a career naval officer who spent the better part of his life preparing for high command; he reached the top of the Navy ladder and then plummetted to the bottom, retired in disgrace and deprived of a chance to redeem himself in uniform. He should rightly have been relieved, but he should not have been disgraced. The Pearl Harbor issue is still lively, and partisans of Admiral Kimmel remain quite vociferous in their criticisms of those in Washington on the eve of hostilities in the Pacific. Yet the blame must be leveled equally upon those in Washington who failed to appreciate Kimmel's need for intelligence data available to them but not to him (and evaluating that data imaginatively); and upon Kimmel himself for failing to properly evaluate the information he did possess.

Kimmel had proved, as Admiral Henry Kent Hewitt* pointed out in his inquiry into Pearl Harbor, "indefatigable, energetic, resourceful, and positive" in preparing the Pacific Fleet for war. From the outset, he showed an appreciation of the security of the fleet at anchor in Pearl Harbor, but at the same time maintained—even into the last critical week before the Japanese attack—a rigorous and unbending training schedule for the fleet. The maintenance of that training resulted in the Fleet settling into a predictable routine that made it relatively easy for the Japanese to predict ship movements.

Kimmel allowed himself to become hamstrung by relying upon Washington for prior warning of an impending break in diplomatic relations between the United States and Japan. Such a signal could presage war. Despite the last-minute indecision of Admiral Harold Raynsford Stark,* the CNO, and even without the special intelligence (the "MAGIC" intercepts) that he later claimed were crucial, Kimmel had enough information available to him by December 7, 1941, to indicate a situation of unusual severity. He had the "War Warning" message of November 27; the information of December 3 in which the Japanese were destroying their codes; and the information of December 6 in which outlying bases in the Pacific were instructed to destroy their confidential publications. In addition, the monitoring of Japanese naval radio traffic had revealed two key call sign changes, leading to the "loss" of the Japanese carriers on December 1. Kimmel should have judged more accurately the gravity of the situation confronting him, and of the danger to which Oahu, and specifically Pearl Harbor, was exposed. He could have instituted long-range reconnaissance of areas already recognized as probable routes for a Japanese carrier air strike, and he also could have rotated his fleet's "in-port" periods, producing a less predictable routine for the Japanese to anticipate correctly. However, hindsight obscures the fact that the situation looked different to the men in charge at the time. The prevailing attitude evident among Kimmel, his opposite number, General Walter Campbell Short,* and most high government, naval, and military officials in Washington was that the Japanese would strike first somewhere in the Far East, not at Oahu.

Schools of thought for Kimmel's responsibility for what happened on December 7, 1941, are divided. The Navy Board of Inquiry concluded that Kimmel, on the basis of the information available to him, neither committed any offense nor incurred any blame for the disaster. On the other hand, Admiral Ernest Joseph King* believed that Kimmel's errors were those of omission, not commission, and opined that Kimmel lacked superior judgment necessary for his post.

In the final analysis, then, Kimmel is a tragic figure. He kept his mind almost microscopically focused on the probabilities of Japan's courses of action rather than on his enemy's capabilities. Despite working diligently and energetically to be ready for war when it came, he was not prepared for it when it confronted him on December 7, 1941.

BIBLIOGRAPHY

Lord, Walter. *Day of Infamy*. New York: Henry Holt and Company, 1957.
Melosi, Martin V. *The Shadow of Pearl Harbor: Political Controversy over the Surprise Attack, 1941–1946*. College Station: Texas A&M University Press, 1977.
Millis, Walter. *This Is Pearl!* New York: Morrow and Company, 1947.
Morison, Samuel E. *The Rising Sun in the Pacific*. Vol. 3 of *United States Naval Operations in World War II*. Boston: Little, Brown and Company, 1958.
Prange, Gordon. *At Dawn We Slept: The Untold Story of Pearl Harbor*. New York: McGraw-Hill, 1981.
Wohlstetter, Roberta. *Pearl Harbor: Warning and Decision*. Stanford, Calif.: Stanford University Press, 1962.

ROBERT J. CRESSMAN

KING, Ernest Joseph (b. Lorain, Ohio, November 23, 1878; d. Portsmouth, N.H., June 25, 1956), naval officer. King is noted for being commander in chief, U.S. Fleet, and chief of naval operations, 1941–1945.

Ernest J. King had but one aim in life during his first forty years of naval service: he wanted to become the chief of naval operations (CNO). He sought that goal with zealous ambition and unswerving determination; his aspirations were common knowledge throughout the Navy. His family had been literate, industrious working-class Scots and Englishmen who had emigrated to northern Ohio in the late nineteenth century. Young King had brains and talent, and he was a popular student who graduated as valedictorian of his small high school class. When he decided to attend the Naval Academy, the people of Lorain were proud and delighted.

King excelled at Annapolis, rising to the top leadership position as battalion commander. While still a naval cadet, he saw action in the Spanish-American War. King graduated fourth in the class of 1901. During the fifteen years following graduation he served as often on staffs as on ships, shrewdly seeking enhancing assignments that would most rapidly advance his career. When World War I began, he was a staff officer for Admiral Henry T. Mayo, commander in chief, Atlantic Fleet, the Navy's most influential flag officer. As a Mayo protégé, by war's end King had received a meritorious promotion to captain at the youthful age of thirty-nine, together with a Navy Cross.

After the war the Navy entered an inevitable decline owing to peacetime disarmament, and King was an impatient junior captain with nowhere to go. Despairing of getting a major warship command within a reasonable time, King volunteered in 1922 for the submarine service which he hoped would offer better opportunities. Although he never qualified as a submariner, he nevertheless commanded a submarine division and then the Submarine Base at New London, Connecticut. King achieved recognition in 1925 when he salvaged the submarine *S–51*, which had been sunk off Block Island in Rhode Island Sound.

Naval aviation was a developing branch of the naval service in the late 1920s. Federal law required commanding officers of carriers and air stations to be fliers or aviation observers. Most Navy pilots were too junior for such assignments. To remedy the problem, King was among a number of older surface officers who volunteered for flight training in order to qualify for major aviation commands. At age forty-nine King won his wings and subsequently commanded the carrier *Lexington*, which earned him a promotion to rear admiral in 1932.

Owing to the death of Rear Admiral William A. Moffett in the crash of the dirigible *Akron*, King succeeded to command of the Navy's Bureau of Aeronautics in 1933. Despite the austere appropriations caused by the Depression, King's well-run bureau continued to contribute to the advance of naval aviation. King returned to sea in 1936 to command the Navy's patrol plane squadrons; he maintained high standards of combat readiness and established bases throughout the Pacific. In 1938 he was promoted to vice admiral and took command of all carriers and associated aircraft in the fleet. During his tenure, the carrier forces developed advanced doctrine that became standard practice during World War II. When Admiral William Daniel Leahy* retired as chief of naval operations in 1938, King entertained hopes that he would succeed Leahy. But Harold Raynsford Stark* got the job, and in the summer of 1939 King went to the General Board to pass time until his mandatory retirement in November 1942.

World War II changed everything. King's experience and competence were again in demand, and he returned to sea in early 1941 as commander in chief, Atlantic Fleet. Wearing four stars, he took charge of the unofficial American involvement in the Battle of the Atlantic and personally transported President Franklin D. Roosevelt to the Atlantic Charter Conference at Argentia, Newfoundland. The president and Secretary of the Navy William Franklin Knox* frequently sought his counsel, and King so won their confidence that they elevated him to commander in chief, U.S. Fleet, immediately after the attack on Pearl Harbor. In March 1942 Roosevelt sent Stark to London, and King assumed the title of chief of naval operations as well. Throughout the war King served on both the Joint Chiefs of Staff (JCS) and the Combined Chiefs of Staff as one of the principal shapers of Allied grand strategy. Under King's urging, the Allies decided upon a limited offensive against Japan despite the official policy of "Germany first." King concurrently shaped the U.S. Navy into the most powerful naval force in the history of the world.

After the war King retired in Washington, D.C. Following a stroke in 1947 his health declined, and he died at the Portsmouth Naval Hospital in 1956. He was survived by his wife, Martha Lamkin Egerton, six daughters, and a son.

King had a reputation for outspoken bluntness that went to extremes, owing to his sense of self-righteousness and an undisciplined temper. Tact and discretion too often lost out to emotional excesses, especially in his early years. Together with his intellectual arrogance and lack of humility, King simply considered that he had more brains than anyone else in the Navy and acted accordingly. Older officers often felt intimidated in his presence, and they resented the way King made them feel inferior. King also loved parties, chased women, and drank too much, but he never suffered from hangovers owing to his extraordinary stamina.

King vowed that he would become a flag officer solely through professional merit, so he refused to ingratiate himself either with influential cliques or with Franklin D. Roosevelt, who loved the Navy and could make or break a naval career. Consequently, King avoided Washington duty for thirty-two years—until he was promoted to rear admiral. His hope of becoming CNO was wishful thinking, because in 1938 he was an outcast. He was a stranger to the president, and he had too many enemies after years of feuds, fights, and insults.

Following his 1941 resurrection as commander of the Atlantic Fleet, King became a frequent visitor to the White House and Hyde Park, allowing opportunities for FDR to evaluate King at first hand. The president was perceptive enough to recognize in King the indefatigable strength, the moral courage, and the fighting spirit needed to resurrect the Navy from the defeat and shambles of Pearl Harbor.

But commanding the Navy was not King's sole contribution. King had studied strategy for a lifetime, and he was intellectually superior to his colleagues on the Joint Chiefs of Staff. His only equal on the British Chiefs of Staff was Air Chief Marshal Sir Charles Portal of the Royal Air Force. Roosevelt relied more on King than on any other member of the Joint Chiefs for strategic advice, especially in the first eighteen months of the war. King recognized the danger of ignoring Japan while concentrating upon Germany, for if left undisturbed Japan would have consolidated its conquests and would have become impregnable. The war would have lasted years longer if King had not gotten his way for a limited offensive in the Pacific.

On the negative side, King was too much a single-minded professional warrior, thinking solely about how to defeat the Axis by overwhelming force. Other wartime considerations were secondary: he loathed the press, spurned the Congress, and was indifferent to public opinion, logistics, and industrial mobilization. He was a poor public speaker and was content to let General George Catlett Marshall* serve as the principal spokesman for the armed forces. He resented civilian authority and tangled frequently with Frank Knox and James Vincent Forrestal.* Roosevelt was the only supreme authority to whom King would respectfully defer. Given King's aversion to wartime publicity, the Army Air

Force's public relations program was far superior to that of the Navy. Furthermore, Air Force leaders planned for a postwar reorganization while King rarely thought beyond the Axis surrender. By early 1945 the strategy for ending the war had been well established, and King and his JCS colleagues were rarely consulted in the political considerations that dominated the Big Power conferences at Yalta and Potsdam.

King is remembered as brilliant, ruthless, irascible, cold, and arrogant. There is a legend that he would have preferred to have made only one statement about the war: at the proper time he would simply announce, "We won." Another apocryphal legend is that when summoned by FDR to lead the Navy in December 1941, King remarked, "Whenever they get into trouble, they always call for the sons-of-bitches." Indeed, he was delighted with his reputation for toughness and was pleased when a friend sent him a miniature blowtorch from Tiffany's to use for "shaving." Among his friends, however, he was a man of great warmth, sensitivity, and charitableness. Like most great men, his was a complex and fascinating personality.

BIBLIOGRAPHY

Buell, Thomas B. *Master of Seapower: A Biography of Fleet Admiral Ernest J. King.* Boston: Little, Brown and Company, 1980.
Graybar, Lloyd. "Admiral King's Toughest Battle." *Naval War College Review* 32 (February 1979): 38–45.
King, Ernest J., and Walter M. Whitehill. *Fleet Admiral King: A Naval Record.* New York: Norton, 1952.
Morison, Samuel E. *Two Ocean War: A Short History of the U.S. Navy in the Second World War.* Boston: Little, Brown and Company, 1963.
Reynolds, Clark. "Admiral Ernest J. King and the Strategy for Victory in the Pacific." *Naval War College Review* 28 (Winter 1976): 57–67.

                                                        THOMAS B. BUELL

KINKAID, Thomas Cassin (b. Hanover, N.H., April 3, 1888; d. Washington, D.C., November 17, 1972), naval officer. Kinkaid is known for having led American naval forces against the Aleutian Islands and in the Battle of Leyte Gulf during World War II.

Like many naval officers of his generation, Thomas Cassin Kinkaid was born into a service family. His father, Thomas Wright Kinkaid, a Naval Academy graduate, was an engineering specialist. When his son was born, the elder Kinkaid was on duty at the New Hampshire College of Agricultural and Mechanical Arts. Kinkaid's early life was spent in Alaska and then at a series of duty stations on the East Coast. Upon graduation from high school in the spring of 1904, he sought and obtained a presidential appointment to the Naval Academy. After four undistinguished years, he was graduated in June 1908. His class standing was 136 out of 201.

After graduation, Passed Midshipman Kinkaid served two years in the battleship *Nebraska* and took part in the world cruise of the Great White Fleet, initially

under the command of Admiral Robley Dunglison Evans.* He then transferred
to the battleship *Minnesota* and received his ensign's commission. In 1911 he
married Helen Sherbourne Ross of Philadelphia. During his battleship duty Kinkaid developed a lifetime interest in naval gunnery, and at the conclusion of five
years' sea duty he requested assignment to the ordnance course at the Naval
Postgraduate School in Annapolis.

Completing his postgraduate course in 1916, Lieutenant Kinkaid joined the
new battleship *Pennsylvania* as assistant fire control officer and chief spotter.
Although the United States entered the World War in April 1917, the *Pennsylvania* remained in home waters. In May 1918 Lieutenant Commander Kinkaid
left the *Pennsylvania* and reported to the new battleship *Arizona* as gunnery
officer.

During the 1920s and 1930s Kinkaid held a variety of assignments. After the
war, he spent three years at desk duty in the Washington Navy Yard and then
received orders to join the staff of Rear Admiral M. L. Briston, commander of
an American naval detachment in Turkish waters. In 1924 he returned to the
United States and took command of the destroyer *Isherwood*. This brief but very
successful tour was followed by another two years in the Naval Gun Factory in
the Washington area. In 1927, then a commander, Kinkaid commenced two
years at sea as an aide and fleet gunnery officer on the staff of Admiral H. A.
Wiley, commander in chief, U.S. Fleet. From this service he went to a year's
instruction at the Naval War College. Commander Kinkaid returned to the Navy
Department in 1930 to assume the duties of secretary to the General Board of
the Navy. In 1933 he accepted orders as executive officer of the battleship
Colorado. This duty concluded in 1934, and the commander again returned to
the Navy Department in Washington. Promoted to captain in 1937, Kinkaid took
command of the heavy cruiser *Indianapolis*, flagship of the commander, Scouting
Force, U.S. Fleet. In 1938 Captain Kinkaid began two and a half years' service
in Rome as naval attaché, returning to America in April 1941. He took command
of Destroyer Squadron Eight, Atlantic Fleet, in June 1941. In mid-November,
having been selected for rear admiral, he was ordered to Pearl Harbor to assume
command of Cruiser Division Six.

Rear Admiral Kinkaid arrived at Pearl Harbor five days after the devastating
Japanese attack of December 7. He quickly joined Cruiser Division Six and
accompanied it on an abortive mission to reinforce the Marine garrison on Wake
Island. During the next six months, Kinkaid's cruiser division participated in
task force operations throughout the South Pacific. It supported a carrier strike
against Lae and Salamaua in New Guinea (March 1942) and then fought in the
Battle of the Coral Sea (May 4–8). From the Coral Sea, Kinkaid's cruisers went
to the Midway Island area where they helped repulse Admiral Isoroku Yamamoto's invasion fleet. Kinkaid was awarded the first of four Distinguished Service
Medals he won during World War II for his work in the Battle of the Coral Sea.

Following Midway, Kinkaid assumed control of Task Force 16 with his flag
in the carrier *Enterprise*. He commanded this carrier task force during the invasion

of Guadalcanal (August 7) and then through major carrier engagements in the Battle of the Eastern Solomons (August 24) and the Battle of Santa Cruz Islands (October 26). *Enterprise* was struck repeatedly during bombing attacks in these latter two engagements. With a patched-up flagship, Kinkaid brought Task Force 16 back to the Guadalcanal area to assist in turning back the last major Japanese attempt to storm Guadalcanal in mid-November.

After the battles around Guadalcanal, Kinkaid was transferred to command of the North Pacific Force and Task Force 8 in Alaskan waters. Kinkaid's job was to prevent any further territorial seizures by the Japanese and, in time, to expel them from the Aleutians. On January 12, 1943, Kinkaid's forces seized Amchitka and four months later took Attu. Following the capture of Attu, Kinkaid and Army General Simon B. Buckner laid plans to take Kiska. After two months of preparatory bombardments, a full amphibious assault was launched against Kiska. To the consternation of all involved, the Japanese had evacuated several weeks earlier.

In June 1943 Kinkaid was promoted to vice admiral and assigned to the Southwest Pacific Area. On November 26, 1943, he reported to General Douglas MacArthur* in Brisbane, Australia, becoming commander of naval forces in the Southwest Pacific and commander of the Seventh Fleet. Kinkaid's predecessors had failed to develop satisfactory relations with MacArthur; the Joint Chiefs of Staff hoped that Kinkaid's tact would serve him well in this new duty. Kinkaid's principal mission, and that of the Seventh Fleet, was to provide amphibious lift and beachhead protection to MacArthur's ground forces as they moved against Japanese garrisons on the road back to the Philippines. Before the Leyte landings in October 1944, the largest assault by the Seventh Fleet was a three-pronged attack aimed at Hollandia on April 21, 1944.

On October 20, 1944, the Seventh Fleet, assisted by the Third Fleet under Admiral William Frederick Halsey, Jr.,* landed MacArthur's troops on Leyte in the central Philippines. Five days later, a three-part battle for Leyte Gulf was fought against the Japanese Navy. Kinkaid deployed his battleship force to defend Surigao Strait (the southern access to Leyte Gulf) against an approaching Japanese force of two battleships, a cruiser, and four destroyers. At Kinkaid's orders, Rear Admiral Jesse Barrett Oldendorf* fought a night action in the early hours of October 25 and completely destroyed these Japanese vessels. As this action was closing, a much larger force, consisting of four battleships, six cruisers, and eleven destroyers under Admiral Takeo Kurita, transited San Bernardino Strait (between Samar and Luzon) and approached the entrance to Leyte Gulf by way of the west coast of Samar. While Kinkaid tried to bring a portion of Oldendorf's battleships north to meet this threat, three escort carrier groups, consisting of sixteen carriers and attending destroyers under the command of Rear Admiral Thomas L. Sprague, stood off Kurita's force until it retreated back through San Bernardino Strait. Two American escort carriers had been sunk, along with three destroyers, but the Leyte beachhead had been saved. While the battle off Samar ensued, a third naval action occurred five hundred miles to the north off Cape Engaño. A Japanese carrier task force under Admiral Jisaburo Ozawa, with a few aircraft on board, had approached from Empire waters in order to decoy American forces away from the Leyte area and clear the way for Kurita and Nishimura. Admiral Halsey took the bait and steamed to the attack with most of the Third Fleet, in the process uncovering San Bernardino Strait. Halsey's carrier-battleship task force annihilated Ozawa's task force, sinking four empty carriers plus several cruisers and a handful of destroyers. The three-part battle for Leyte Gulf was clearly an American victory. Heavily damaged and very short of fuel, the Japanese Navy no longer existed as a serious menace to American naval operations.

The landings at Leyte were followed by the invasion of Mindoro (December 15) and finally by the largest amphibious operation of the Seventh Fleet, the assault in Lingayen Gulf on January 9, 1945. Once Manila was secure, MacArthur and Kinkaid moved their headquarters to that port and began planning for the invasion of Japan. The surrender of the Japanese on August 15 terminated these plans.

Between 1946 and 1950 Admiral Kinkaid served as commander, Eastern Sea Frontier, and commander, Reserve Fleet, Atlantic. With headquarters in New York City, most of his duties were largely ceremonial. Finally, at age sixty-two and with forty-two years of service, Admiral Kinkaid retired on May 1, 1950.

After retirement Admiral Kinkaid served six years as a member of the National Security Training Commission and fifteen years as a member of the American Battle Monuments Commission. He died at Bethesda Naval Hospital on November 17, 1972, and was buried with full military honors in Arlington National Cemetery.

Admiral Kinkaid's career was, in many ways, the fulfillment of the epigram "I saw my opportunities and I made the most of them." Certainly, his prewar career provided very few clues to his future greatness, but the expansion of the fleet and the war in the Pacific provided the need for flag officers and the opportunity to prove competence in action. His early success as a cruiser division commander opened the door to the opportunity to lead carrier task forces, even though he was a nonaviator. In cruiser and carrier task force commands, he proved innovative in developing antiaircraft defense measures and in using his air groups boldly to achieve tactical ends. At the end of 1942, when aviation flag officers finally became available, he went to the Aleutians to unsnarl some serious problems in command relations among the Army, Navy, and Army Air Force. His good sense and accommodating personality opened the way to smooth planning and successful operations. From the Aleutians he moved to General MacArthur's Southwest Pacific Area, again to try to improve working relations among the services. Kinkaid won the confidence and respect of MacArthur quite early because his plans worked.

Until the Battle of Leyte Gulf, Kinkaid's amphibious commanders carried the burden of operations; Kinkaid himself merely saw that the planning was accomplished and carefully coordinated with the Army. In that October battle he proved able to sort out the important tasks and let his subordinate commanders carry them out. He also had an immense amount of good luck. Had Admiral Kurita's nerve not failed, Kinkaid might well have been in the position of directing a major engagement while under direct fire. Because he rarely lacked confidence in himself, and he did have excellent subordinate commanders, there is no reason to expect that the ultimate victory would not have lain with the Seventh Fleet. Kinkaid's fourth Distinguished Service Medal citation described him as ''a master of naval warfare''; his enduring reputation rests on that accolade.

BIBLIOGRAPHY

Garfield, Brian. *The Thousand-Mile War: World War II in Alaska and the Aleutians*. New York: Doubleday Company, 1969.

James, D. Clayton. *The Years of MacArthur, 1941–1945*. Boston: Houghton Mifflin Company, 1975.

Morison, Samuel Eliot. *History of the United States Naval Operations in World War II*. 15 vols. Boston: Atlantic, Little, Brown and Company, 1947–1962.

Potter, E. B. *Nimitz*. Annapolis, Md.: Naval Institute Press, 1976.

Stafford, Edward P. *The Big E: The Story of the USS Enterprise*. New York: Random House, 1962.

Woodward, C. Vann. *The Battle for Leyte Gulf*. New York: Macmillan Company, 1947.

GERALD E. WHEELER

KNOX, Henry (b. Boston, Mass., July 25, 1750; d. Thomaston, Maine, October 25, 1806), major general and chief of artillery, Continental Army; secretary of war, 1785–1789, 1789–1794.

Knox was the seventh of ten children (four lived to maturity) of Scotch-Irish immigrants. His father, a shipmaster, died when Knox was twelve years old. Forced to quit the Boston Public Latin School because of economic necessity, Knox was apprenticed to Wharton and Bowles, Booksellers. In 1771 he opened his own London Bookstore in Boston, which became a popular meeting place for British officers. Early siding with the Whig cause, Knox reported military intelligence he overheard in his bookstore to the patriot leaders. Knox himself obtained a textbook knowledge of artillery and military engineering by reading from his large stock of military treatises and books. Knox joined the militia artillery company and upon its reorganization became second-in-command. A hunting accident in 1773 lopped off two small fingers on his left hand, and thereafter he kept his left hand wrapped in a handkerchief.

In June 1774 Knox married Lucy Flucker, the daughter of the provincial royal secretary, Thomas Flucker. The marriage was warm and touching, as the many letters between Henry and Lucy reveal. The ebullient, witty Knox was a genial fat man, topping about 280 pounds; Lucy herself weighed around 240 pounds. Although supposedly having a stentorian voice, Knox did not have the gift of oratory, and at times seemed rambling and even incoherent, if Thomas Jefferson is to be believed.

Knox entered the war as a "voluntary engineer," with civilian status, after having met George Washington* near Cambridge shortly after the new commander in chief had arrived to take command of the Army. Knox was made a colonel in charge of the Continental artillery on November 17, 1775, at which time he began his famous and heroic mission to bring captured cannon and mortars (fifty-nine in all) from Fort Ticonderoga, three hundred miles over the Berkshires to Washington's headquarters at Cambridge. Succeeding brilliantly, Knox delivered the cannon and mortars in January, and they were used in the fortifying of Dorchester Heights which forced the British evacuation of Boston in March 1776. Knox then drew up plans for the defense of southern New England and personally made an inspection tour for that purpose. He was with Washington constantly throughout the war, participating in all of Washington's campaigns. His guns made the difference between defeat and victory, as at Trenton in December 1776. On December 26, 1776, Knox was appointed brigadier general. After the Battle of Princeton, Knox set up an artillery yard at Pluckimin, near Morristown, and thereafter Washington's army always had an arms laboratory, which was moved about to different sites, at a safe distance from the field of operations.

Knox spent much time during 1779–1780 surveying American works along the Hudson and elsewhere. At Yorktown Knox was responsible for laying out the siege works. On March 22, 1782, he was promoted to major general by Congress, retroactive to November 15, 1781. On August 29, 1782, Knox succeeded General William Heath as commander of West Point; he led the victory parade into New York City on November 25, 1781, as the British evacuated the city. On December 23, 1783, Knox succeeded Washington as commander in chief of what was left of the Continental Army, numbering only several hundred troops at West Point. Technically, he was commander in chief until June 20, 1784, when he took leave of the Army.

On March 9, 1785, Knox was appointed secretary of war by the Confederation Congress, and when the Constitution went into effect he was the only top Confederation official carried over on a permanent basis. Washington relied on Knox more than on any other person in the governmental transition. Knox served as secretary of war until December 31, 1794. In his later years as secretary of war, Knox had to contend with Alexander Hamilton's attempts to usurp the duties of his department as well as put up with the ridicule of Thomas Jefferson and his party.

Knox was active during Shays' Rebellion (1786–1787) and made a test of the Confederation government by bringing about a defense of the federal armory at Springfield. Although he got Congress to authorize the raising of some two thousand troops, Knox was able to recruit only a scant hundred or so during the crisis. In 1794, however, Knox let Hamilton take over the show in repressing the Whiskey insurgents.

During his tenure under both the Confederation and the Constitution, Knox was charged with administration of Indian affairs. Efforts were made to lay

Arthur St. Clair's* defeat by the Ohio Indians in 1791 at his door, when in reality he had nothing to do with the ill-timed and ill-advised decisions that led to the catastrophe—only some responsibility in procurement. Knox had much to do with Anthony Wayne's* eventual success against the western Indians.

Knox was a leading participant in the Ohio and Scioto land speculation companies. He also became a large speculator in Maine. He and his family moved to Thomaston, where he built a great mansion, "Montpelier," which gained a reputation for gala entertainment. Knox acquired his Maine lands through his wife. Forming an association for the sale and development of his Maine lands first with William Duer and then with William Bingham, Knox found that because squatters were so numerous and were threatening insurgency, he could realize very little profit from his lands. He lived his last years as a gentleman farmer and experimented with various enterprises, including sawmilling and lime-making. He also became involved with several other speculative operations such as canal building and copper mining.

The only public affair that interrupted Knox's later years—and his last encounter with Hamilton—was President John Adams naming him fourth in command of a proposed army to be employed against the French during the Quasi-War, 1798–1799. Knox refused to serve under Hamilton, who had been his subordinate during the war. The army was not raised, but the matter caused considerable bitterness and to some extent was disruptive of the Federalist party.

Knox, who had been a strong advocate for the Constitution, was a Federalist. Although he usually refrained from direct partisan political involvement, he retained a distant friendship with John Adams, who had been one of his chief backers during the war, although Adams' refusal to appoint Knox's son to a midshipman commission strained the relationship. In 1806 Knox died of what was diagnosed at the time as infection setting in from a chicken bone lodged in his intestines, but what may have been appendicitis.

Henry Knox's importance during the Revolutionary era rests on four of his roles: (1) as organizer and commander of the Artillery Corps during the Revolution; (2) as friend and constant comrade of George Washington—much like Nathanael Greene* during the early years of the war—becoming the commander in chief's alter ego; (3) as incisive observer of events of the Revolution and the early Federal period, always turning out a stream of letters and reports, some of which would be highly influential, as at the time of Shays' Rebellion, the Constitutional Convention (though he was not a member), and the ratifications contest in Massachusetts; and (4) as administrator of the War Department under the Confederation and the Constitution.

Learning from experience, Knox developed substantial expertise in the transportation, mounting, and use of artillery, and won grudging commendation from professionally trained French officers. In the Continental Army he was universally well liked by his fellow officers. He won the respect of his men, and he was an able organizer. There was less disaffection in his artillery regiments than probably any other units in the service.

Knox probably had no more influence on the overall planning of operations than other generals. Some contemporaries and historians have criticised him for attempting to hold an artillery position behind British lines on Manhattan (September 1776) and allegedly persuading Washington to concentrate on taking the Chew house at the Battle of Germantown, supposedly costing valuable time and the battle.

As head of the War Department under the Confederation and the Constitution, Knox, assisted by only a secretary or two, had immense responsibilities. For example, he supervised the commissioners laying out military lands in the Northwest Territory; he was the watchdog of federal arms and military stores; he had to conduct recruitment with little support from Congress; he was responsible for federal Army posts on the frontier; he was in charge of Indian affairs, including treaty making (the Treaty of New York with the Creeks in 1790 was the result of Knox's negotiations and was the first treaty ratified under the Constitution); and he was in charge of naval affairs. In 1785 and again in 1790 Knox presented the first comprehensive plan for the "General Arrangement of the Militia of the United States," calling for universal military training.

Knox's role as secretary at war under the Confederation exemplifies the weakness of that government. As no more than an agent of Congress, although he was charged with implementing the policies of the Congress, he had no independent executive power. As a member of Washington's cabinet, he was very much part of decision-making, especially concerning military and Indian affairs, despite being caught in the middle of the power struggle between Hamilton and Jefferson. Although he acquired a dislike for Hamilton, Knox, also a nationalist, invariably sided with him in Washington's cabinet.

BIBLIOGRAPHY

Brooks, Noah. *Henry Knox: A Soldier of the Revolution.* New York: G. P. Putnam, 1900.

Drake, Francis S. *Life and Correspondence of Henry Knox.* Boston: Samuel G. Drake, 1873.

Freeman, Douglas S. *George Washington.* Vols. 3–7. New York: Charles Scribner's Sons, 1951–1957.

Ward, Harry M. *Department of War, 1781–1795.* Pittsburgh, Pa.: University of Pittsburgh Press, 1962.

HARRY M. WARD

KNOX, William Franklin (b. Boston, Mass., January 1, 1874; d. Washington, D.C., April 28, 1944), Secretary of the Navy, 1940–1944.

Frank Knox was the only son and the eldest of six surviving children born to Boston oyster dealer William Edwin Knox and his wife Sara Barnard Knox. His parents were both Canadians who had come to New England during their childhood. In 1881 the Knoxes moved to Grand Rapids, Michigan, where the father operated a grocery store and the son attended public school. Frank dropped out of high school at the end of his junior year to take a job, but when the economic depression in 1893 left him unemployed he entered Michigan's Alma College. Although he dropped out of college to enlist in the Army at the outbreak of the Spanish-American war, Alma eventually conferred his A.B. degree in 1912 after he completed a special reading program.

When the Spanish-American War was declared in 1898, Knox attempted to enlist in a Michigan militia regiment but, because of a technicality, he was not properly mustered into service. Thus, he had an opportunity to join the Rough Riders (1st U.S. Volunteer Cavalry) and was sworn in as a private by Theodore Roosevelt* himself. In Cuba he fought in the skirmish at Las Guasimas and the battle up the San Juan Hill. Knox was invalided home because of sun stroke and malaria and was honorably discharged in September. Three months later he married Annie Reid, his college sweetheart. They had no children.

Knox's vivid wartime letters home won him a job as a reporter for the *Grand Rapids Herald*, and he started a successful career as a journalist. He and a partner built two newspapers in Sault Ste. Marie, Michigan (1901–1912) and Man- chester, New Hampshire (1913–1944). Knox also served as William Randolph Hearst's general manager in the late 1920s. He reached the pinnacle of his career when he bought the *Chicago Daily News* in 1931 and revived that great paper's sagging fortunes during the depths of the Depression.

Knox's achievements as a newspaper publisher were not matched by similar successes in politics. He managed the winning gubernatorial campaign of Republican Chase Osborn in Michigan in 1910, but after that he was never associated in a personal way with a political victory. He supported Theodore Roosevelt's Progressive party in 1912 and lost. He failed to win the New Hampshire Republican gubernatorial primary in 1924 and ran as the Republican vice-presidential nominee in 1936 with Alfred M. Landon. That ticket was crushingly defeated by Franklin D. Roosevelt.

When the United States declared war on Germany in 1917, Knox was forty-three years old and could have avoided service. Instead, he volunteered in the Army and was commissioned a captain after completing Officers' Training School at Madison Barracks, New York. He embarked for France with the 78th Infantry Division, commanding the 303d Ammunition Train of the division's 153d Field Artillery Brigade. Promoted to major, he led his men through the Battle of St. Mihiel Salient and in the Meuse-Argonne Campaign.

When war broke out in Europe in 1939 he supported his former opponent, Franklin D. Roosevelt, and called for the repeal of the neutrality laws and the buildup of military strength, especially the power of the Navy. Roosevelt took the first halting step toward a coalition cabinet in December 1939 by asking Knox to be Secretary of the Navy. Knox declined then on the grounds that it would take more than one Republican to make such a cabinet. The following spring, after Nazi successes in Denmark, Norway, and the Low Countries created a new sense of emergency, Roosevelt again asked Knox to be Secretary of the Navy. This time Knox accepted and was sworn into office on July 11, 1940.

Knox entered office just as the Navy started the most spectacular growth in its long history. He admitted at once that he knew little about technical, tactical, or strategic matters and had to trust the Chief of Naval Operations Admiral Harold Raynsford Stark,* the Navy's Bureau chiefs, and the staff sections in the Department to provide him with policies and plans that would bring the new Navy into existence. He was served effectively and with integrity by the Navy's officers, and in turn he gave them vigorous, dedicated support before congressional committees, with other government departments, and with the public.

Knox soon surrounded himself with able civilian associates, including James Vincent Forrestal,* who became under secretary. He organized his secretaries and other civilian assistants into a loyal, efficient working team, giving individuals direction and support when necessary but otherwise allowing them freedom to discharge their responsibilities without his interference.

The new secretary believed that he could be most effective by applying his experiences in business administration to the naval establishment. During Knox's first month in office, he introduced the Navy to management engineering by hiring a consultant to advise him on improvements in the functioning of his own office. The first study was followed by many more management surveys, and the reforms that resulted aided efficient administration of the Navy Department as it expanded rapidly to meet the problems brought on by the war. Knox, as a professional journalist, assumed the role of the Navy's chief press agent. He held press conferences often and frequently distressed conservative naval officers with his open and frank news policies.

Before America entered the war, Knox was convinced that the survival of Great Britain was essential to the security of the United States. Therefore, he willingly played a leading part in arranging the destroyers-for-bases exchange with Great Britain in 1940 and was a vigorous advocate of the Lend Lease law in 1941. He gave enthusiastic support to the active role the U.S. Navy played in the Battle of the Atlantic during the summer and fall of 1941.

Knox worked hard to get to know the Navy he headed. During his first year as secretary, he visited bases and naval stations on both coasts, inspected the fleet and Pearl Harbor, and toured Caribbean installations. Wherever he went he urged officers and men to get ready for a fighting war as fast as they could. Usually, he was favorably impressed by what he saw, and he became confident that the Navy was ready to respond effectively whenever war came.

Such a conviction was badly shaken on December 7, 1941. The Japanese attack on Pearl Harbor surprised Knox completely, and he flew at once to Hawaii to inspect the damage and to meet with Admiral Husband Edward Kimmel.*

Soon after Pearl Harbor, Knox brought Admiral Ernest Joseph King* to Washington to be commander in chief, U.S. Fleet (COMINCH). In March 1942, when Admiral Stark left for duty in England, the secretary approved King for the additional post of chief of naval operations (CNO). Knox and King sometimes disagreed with each other over such matters as publicity policy and expanded authority for the CNO-COMINCH. However, their reserve of mutual respect and their friendship, which was not always readily apparent, made them effective partners during their time of service together. Perhaps Knox's most important wartime contribution was the coordination and teamwork he developed between the Navy's service heads, such as King, and the civilian secretaries, such as Forrestal.

Knox's relationship with President Roosevelt was close and cordial during the months before Pearl Harbor. After America's declaration of war, the president counseled frequently with the generals and admirals and spent much less time with the civilian service heads. However, the secretary was so busy he had little time to be vexed over the fact that he was not a member of the White House's inner circle.

As the war progressed, Knox came to believe that his presence in the war zones contributed significantly to the fighting Navy's morale. Accordingly, he traveled to Brazil in 1942 and then to the Pacific. He was bombed by the Japanese while visiting Guadalcanal. In September and October 1943 he journeyed twenty-two thousand miles in twenty-four days, visiting Scotland, England, and North Africa, and watched part of the amphibious assault on Naples from a motor torpedoboat.

An arduous travel schedule and a full round of time-consuming duties in Washington unexpectedly took their toll on Knox's health in 1944, and on April 22 he suffered a mild heart attack without realizing it. Two days later he had a severe heart seizure and died on April 28. He was buried with full military honors in Arlington National Cemetery.

BIBLIOGRAPHY

Beasley, Norman. *Frank Knox, American*. Garden City, N.Y.: Doubleday, Doran and Company, 1936.

Buell, Thomas B. *Master of Seapower: A Biography of Fleet Admiral Ernest J. King*. Boston: Little, Brown and Company, 1980.

Furer, Julius A. *Administration of the Navy Department in World War II*. Washington, D.C.: U.S. Government Printing Office, 1959.

Lobdell, George H. "Frank Knox." In *American Secretaries of the Navy*. Edited by Paolo Coletta. Annapolis, Md.: Naval Institute Press, 1980.

GEORGE H. LOBDELL

KOSCIUSZKO, Tadeusz Andrzej Bonawentura   (b. Mereczowszczyna, Province of Polesie, Poland, February 12, 1746; d. Soleure, Switzerland, October 15, 1817), military engineer; Revolutionary leader.

Tadeusz Kościuszko was the youngest of four children born into a family of Lithuanian-Ruthenian origins who traced their title of nobility to 1509. Of modest means, the family nevertheless was able to send their youngest son to a Jesuit college near Brześć at the age of thirteen. On December 18, 1765, Kościuszko entered the newly established Royal Military School in Warsaw. After completing his studies, he was commissioned in the Polish Army and assigned to the same school as an instructor. Promoted to the rank of captain, he received one of four royal stipends awarded in 1769 for study in France. While abroad he studied military engineering and artillery at Mézières, as well as attending several other schools.

Upon the first Partition of Poland in 1772, the royal subsidy ceased. Though burdened by economic problems, Kościuszko remained in France until 1774. Returning to Poland, he found his family finances in ruins and no chance to advance his career in Poland's limited military establishment. A broken love affair finally provided the impetus that drove him back to France. There he apparently borrowed enough money to take him to North America.

Kościuszko reached Philadelphia in August 1776. He soon found employment as a civilian engineer contracted by the Pennsylvania Committee of Defense to fortify Billingsport on the Delaware River. On August 30 he presented a memorial to the Continental Congress, which rewarded him with a commission as colonel of engineers on October 18. He spent the winter of 1776–1777 planning and beginning the foundations of Fort Mercer on the New Jersey shore of the Delaware River. His work there attracted the attention of General Horatio Gates* who requested that the Pole accompany him as engineering officer when the general took command of the Northern army in March 1777. Upon his arrival in New York, Kościuszko examined and strengthened the fortifications at Fort Ticonderoga. Following the fall of that post to the British, he helped cover the retreat of the American Army and selected the site for Gates' entrenchments near Saratoga. On March 5, 1778, he was assigned to design and construct the fortress at West Point, a mission that occupied his time until June 1780.

In the summer of 1780 General Gates invited Kościuszko to join him as engineering officer for the Southern army. The colonel received permission for the transfer in August but did not arrive until after Gates' defeat at Camden and subsequent removal from command. General Nathanael Greene,* Gates' replacement, assigned Kościuszko to explore the Catawba River during the winter of 1780–1781. During Greene's famous race to the Dan against Lord Charles Cornwallis in 1781, the Pole rendered distinguished service as officer in charge of transportation. The summer of 1782 found Kościuszko near Charleston where he conducted intelligence activities and proved successful as a cavalry leader. In the spring of 1783 he accompanied Greene north where he received a brevet promotion to the rank of brigadier general on October 13, 1783, and became a founding member of the Society of the Cincinnati.

With the conclusion of hostilities in North America, Kościuszko left New York for Europe in July 1784. Upon his arrival in Poland, he settled into retirement on his ancestral estate at Siechnowicze but was called into the service of the Polish Army as a major general (October 1, 1789) following the Diet reforms of 1788. Kościuszko distinguished himself in the campaign against

Russian invasion in 1792 but resigned his commission when King Stanislas Poniatowski ordered a halt to Polish resistance. With a number of other officers he emigrated to Paris where his efforts to secure aid from the French government failed.

In 1794 Kościuszko returned to Warsaw to proclaim a revolution on March 24. As commander in chief of the revolutionary forces and a virtual dictator, he instituted many liberal reforms patterned on his experience in America. He also reformed the Polish Army, including the establishment of peasant units not unlike North American militia units except that they were armed with scythes. As a military commander, Kościuszko won several engagements including a victory over the Russians at Racławice (April 4, 1794) and the successful defense of Warsaw against Russian and Prussian armies under King Frederick William II (July 13–September 6, 1794). Rewarded with the Cross of the *Virtuti Militari* and a promotion to lieutenant general, Kościuszko was finally defeated, wounded, and captured at Maciejowice (October 10, 1794) by the Russians under Fersen.

Released from two years of imprisonment by Czar Paul I, Kościuszko returned to the United States, arriving in Philadelphia to a triumphal welcome in August 1797. In America Kościuszko collected over $12,000 and five hundred acres of land due him for service in the Revolution. He then arranged for Thomas Jefferson to invest and administer these funds in the United States. He left for Europe again in May 1798, intent upon working for the independence of his native land. Three years in Paris, however, failed to elicit a promise of support for Polish independence. In 1800, at the request of General William R. Davie, he wrote a treatise entitled *Manoeuvres of Horse Artillery*, which was later used for instruction in the Military Academy at West Point. For this reason he is sometimes called the father of American artillery.

In 1801 he moved to the estate of Peter Zeltner in Berville, near Fontainbleau, where he lived as a French citizen. With the failure of his dream for an independent Poland, Kościuszko left France to reside at Soleure, Switzerland, in 1815. Following his death there on October 15, 1817, his body was buried in the Wawel Cathedral in Kraków amidst the remains of Poland's monarchs. A great earthen mound was raised to his honor containing soil from all of his battlefields. His heart, however, was buried in Rapperswyl, Switzerland, until such time as Poland might again be free.

Kościuszko's career in the United States was one of success and controversy. His service with Gates in 1777 was particularly distinguished, if often underestimated. His advice to fortify Sugar Loaf Hill (Mount Defiance) overlooking Fort Ticonderoga is often dismissed as having been unrealistic in view of the limited resources available. The fact remains, however, that he correctly anticipated both the weakness of the defenses and the British tactics in forcing their evacuation. During the retreat that followed, according to General James Wilkinson,* Kościuszko directed the successful delaying actions that cost John Burgoyne's army valuable time. Rejoining Gates, Kościuszko then selected and fortified the American position on Bemis Heights. General John Armstrong, Jr.,* reported that Gates, in commenting on his decisive victory at Saratoga, noted that "the great tacticians of the campaign were hills and forests which a young Polish engineer was skillful enough to select for my encampment."

At West Point Kościuszko's work drew favorable comments from nearly all who viewed it, but he was equally well known for his simple life-style which included sharing his rations with starving British prisoners. During the Southern campaigns, however, he was criticized for the failure of his plan during the siege of the British post at Ninety-Six (May 1781). General Henry ("Light-Horse Harry") Lee,* in particular, castigated Kościuszko for his failure to take the elementary precaution of cutting off the garrison's water supply. Whether the garrison possessed wells inside the works is uncertain at this point in history. In Kościuszko's defense it can only be said that an aggressive British commander and the failure to prevent the arrival of British reinforcements were also significant factors in the American repulse.

Kościuszko is sometimes credited with saving the lives of some forty British prisoners during the action at Eutaw Springs, but he was probably not present on that field. General Nathanael Greene, under whom he served in the South, rendered the following opinion of the Pole:

> His zeal for public service seems to be incomparable and in the solution of com-
> plicated problems...there could have been nothing more useful than his opinion,
> his watchfulness and his constant application to the task in hand. In the execution
> of my orders he has always been willing, competent, inaccessible to any temptation
> of pleasure, not fatigued by any labor, intrepid in any danger. He is incomparably
> modest. He has never expressed a desire for anything in his favor, and has never
> omitted any opportunity to commend and reward the services of others.

Perhaps Kościuszko's unique feature was his devoted and unselfish personality. He emancipated the serfs on his own estates and attempted to leave all of his American assets for the emancipation and education of American slaves, although the latter move was foiled by legal technicalities following his death. When his name was proposed for promotion during the Revolution, the Pole wrote to Colonel Troup: "My dear Colonel, if you see that my promotion will make a great many Jealous, tell the General (Gates) that I will not accept of one because I prefer peace more than the greatest Rank in the world." Thomas Jefferson, a close friend with whom Kościuszko corresponded throughout his remaining years, probably left the best eulogy of the Pole when he wrote: "He is as pure a son of liberty as I have ever known, and of that liberty which is to go to all, and not to the few and rich alone."

BIBLIOGRAPHY

Gardner, Monica M. *Kościuszko, a Biography*. New York, Charles Scribner's Sons, 1920.
Haiman, Miecislaus. *Kościuszko in the American Revolution*. New York: Kościuszko Foundation, 1975.

————. *Kościuszko, Leader and Exile*. New York: Polish Institute of Arts and Sciences, 1946.
Korzon, Tadeusz. *Kościuszko, Życiorys z dokumentów wysnuty*. Kraków: 1894.
Skałhowski, Adam M. *Kościuszko w świetle nowszych badań*. Poznań: 1924.
Śreniowska, Krystyna. *Kościuszko, Kształtowanie poglądów na bohatera narodowego 1794–1894*. Warszawa: 1964.

JAMES PULA

KRUEGER, Walter (b. Flatow, Germany, January 26, 1881; d. Valley Forge, Pa., August 20, 1967), Army officer, Sixth Army commander in World War II.

At the age of eight Walter Krueger was brought by his German parents to the American Midwest. When the Spanish-American War began, he left high school in Cincinnati, enlisted as a volunteer, and participated in the Cuban Campaign. In mid-1899 he joined the Regular Army as a private and spent the next four years on Luzon, taking part in many engagements of the Philippine Insurrection and rising through the ranks to second lieutenant.

Except for another tour in the Philippines, 1908–1909, he served in the United States until World War I on assignments as infantry commander, National Guard inspector-instructor, and assistant in the Office of the Chief of the Militia Bureau. He also graduated from the Infantry-Cavalry School and the General Staff College, and in 1909–1912 he was on the faculty of the Army Service School. By 1916 when he was promoted to captain, he had become, in addition, an authority on German infantry, cavalry, and artillery tactics with the publication and widespread use in Army schools of his translations of four German books on those subjects.

In early 1918 he joined the American Expeditionary Force (AEF) in France. After attending the General Staff College at Langres, he served at the front as assistant chief of staff for operations with the 26th Division and later the 84th. That October, with the Meuse-Argonne Campaign underway, he took command of the AEF Tank Corps. His wartime record earned for him the Distinguished Service Cross and the Distinguished Service Medal. After the Armistice he served on the faculty of the Line School at Langres and then became assistant chief of staff for operations of the VI Corps in France and later of the IV Corps in Germany. Having been elevated to the temporary ranks of major and lieutenant colonel in 1918 and colonel in May 1919, he reverted to his permanent rank of captain after his return to the United States in the summer of 1919.

Between the world wars Krueger won increasing respect as a teacher of tactics, staff planner, and troop commander. In a period when promotions were at a slow pace, he rose steadily, becoming a colonel by 1932, brigadier general four years later, major general in 1939, and lieutenant general in May 1941. During the 1920s he graduated from the Army War College, Naval War College, and Army Air Corps Primary Flying School, and he served on the faculty of the Infantry School, Army War College, and Naval War College. His staff assignments included tours of duty with the War Plans Division of the War Department in 1922–1925 and 1934–1938; he headed that division as assistant chief of staff for war plans in 1936–1938. He also gained wide experience in troop command at the regimental level until 1934, then commanding, in order, the 16th Brigade, 2d Division, and VIII Corps in 1938–1940. He was appointed commanding general of the Third Army and the Southern Defense Command in 1941. During the maneuvers in Louisiana that summer, which involved over six hundred thousand troops, he led his Third Army to a brilliant victory over the Second Army.

Upon the request of General Douglas MacArthur,* commander in chief of the Southwest Pacific Area, Krueger was transferred to Australia in February 1943 to command the newly created American Sixth Army. At first he had only two divisions, but by the end of 1943 the Sixth Army comprised eleven divisions besides many smaller units. his initial offensives were in Operation CARTWHEEL, September 1943–February 1944, which secured the Lae-Salamaua area and Huon Peninsula of Northeast New Guinea as well as the western end of New Britain and also the Admiralty Islands. Bypassing Japanese strongholds in a six hundred-mile leap northward along the New Guinea coast in April 1944, Krueger's army seized the Hollandia-Wakde region of Netherlands New Guinea. That summer his forces completed American operations on New Guinea with the capture of Biak, Noemfoor, and Sansapor. The containment and mop-up of bypassed enemy units were relegated to the Australian Army.

Moving north of the Equator in September 1944, Krueger's Sixth Army captured Morotai in the Moluccas and the next month invaded Leyte in the central Philippines. After two months of intense combat that secured much of Leyte, operations there were taken over by Lieutenant General Robert Lawrence Eichelberger's* recently organized Eighth Army. With the invasion of Luzon in January 1945, Krueger's army, now possessing over two hundred eighty thousand troops, engaged General Tomoyuki Yamashita's Japanese army of nearly the same strength in the largest campaign of the Pacific war, including the only major battle for a large city in that conflict—the month-long fight for Manila. With most of Luzon secured by July, control passed to the Eighth Army, which had earlier recaptured much of the Philippines.

Krueger's leadership in over twenty major operations in the Southwest Pacific brought him promotion to general in March 1945 and also numerous American and Allied decorations. He was preparing his army to spearhead Operation OLYMPIC, the invasion of Kyushu scheduled for that autumn, when Japan surrendered in August. Subsequently, he and his army moved to Japan and assumed occupation duties. The Sixth Army was deactivated in early 1946, whereupon he returned to the United States and retired that summer. He wrote *From Down Under to Nippon: The Story of Sixth Army in World War II* (1953).

Krueger's two outstanding contributions to the American military effort in World War II were his widespread influence on officer education and troop training and his command of MacArthur's principal army in the war against

Japan. A high proportion of the junior officers of the American Army before 1941 who became wartime commanders studied under him during his many tours of duty as a teacher in various service schools. He was considerd to be one of the Army's most learned authorities on strategy, tactics, and military history. Moreover, he was generally regarded to rank next to General Lesley James MacNair* in his impact on the training of the soldiers of 1941–1943. A reliable Pentagon spokesman commented in 1943 that virtually every American infantry division then in action "has learned from Krueger, either because it served under his command, or because it got a first-hand knowledge of his methods by opposing him in maneuvers."

Nearly sixty-three years old when he undertook his first offensive in the Southwest Pacific in late 1943, Krueger was of MacArthur's generation, and their paths had crossed professionally numerous times in the past. Although lacking the charisma and striking personal traits of MacArthur or Eichelberger, Krueger possessed the uncommon ability to command effectively large bodies of troops sometimes engaged in combat sectors far apart. In mid-1944, for example, his Sixth Army units were involved in battles at six locations simultaneously spread over a five hundred-mile stretch of the New Guinea coast. In the Luzon Campaign he had under his command more American troops than fought in the operations in North Africa, Sicily, Italy, or South France. Although reluctant to publicize Krueger's achievements during the war, MacArthur belatedly but generously praised him in his memoirs: "I do not believe that the annals of American history have shown his superior as an Army commander. Swift and sure in attack, tenacious and determined in defense, modest and restrained in victory—I do not know what he would have been in defeat, because he was never defeated."

MacArthur failed to add, however, that both he and Eichelberger were severely critical of Krueger's methodical preparations for battle and overcautiousness in advancing that allegedly slowed operations on Biak, Leyte, and Luzon. Privately but with some justification, some of his fellow officers referred to him as "Molasses in January." There were occasions of tension between MacArthur and Krueger when objectives were not secured on schedule, but MacArthur entrusted to him the command responsibility for nearly all of the principal ground operations in his theater from the fall of 1943 onward and chose him to lead the ground forces in what would have been the greatest amphibious assault of World War II—the invasion of Japan. The extraordinarily low American casualty rate in the Southwest Pacific Theater, which MacArthur was not reticent to proclaim, was made possible largely because of the thorough planning and cautious but effective tactics of Krueger, who remains one of the least heralded Army commanders of World War II.

BIBLIOGRAPHY

Cannon, M. Hamlin. *Leyte: The Return to the Philippines. U.S. Army in World War II: The War in the Pacific*. Washington, D.C.: Office of the Chief of Military History, U.S. Department of the Army, 1954.

Eichelberger, Robert L., with Milton Mackaye. *Our Jungle Road to Tokyo*. New York: Viking Press, 1950.

James, D. Clayton. *The Years of MacArthur*. Vol. 2. *1941–1945*. Boston: Houghton Mifflin Company, 1975.

Krueger, Walter. *From Down Under to Nippon: The Story of Sixth Army in World War II*. Washington, D.C.: Combat Forces Press, 1953.

Luvaas, Jay, ed. *Dear Miss Em: General Eichelberger's War in the Pacific, 1942–1945*. Westport, Conn.: Greenwood Press, 1972.

Miller, John, Jr. *Cartwheel: The Reduction of Rabaul. U.S. Army in World War II: The War in the Pacific*. Washington, D.C.: Office of the Chief of Military History, U.S. Department of the Army, 1959.

Smith, Robert R. *The Approach to the Philippines. U.S. Army in World War II: The War in the Pacific*. Washington, D.C.: Office of the Chief of Military History, U.S. Department of the Army, 1953.

———. *Triumph in the Philippines. U.S. Army in World War II: The War in the Pacific*. Washington, D.C.: Office of the Chief of Military History, U.S. Department of the Army, 1963.

U.S. Sixth Army. *The Sixth Army in Action, January 1943–June 1945*. Kyoto, Japan: n.p., 1945.

Willoughby, Charles A., ed. *Reports of General MacArthur*. Vol. 1. *The Campaigns of MacArthur in the Pacific*. Washington, D.C.: U.S. Department of the Army, 1966.

D. CLAYTON JAMES

L

LAFAYETTE, Marquis de Marie Joseph Paul Yves Roch Gilbert du Motier (b. Auvergne, France, September 8, 1757; d. Paris, France, May 20, 1843), military officer, political leader.

A distinguished family, the Lafayettes had great wealth but less social prestige. Lafayette's father was killed in battle with the English before his son's second birthday. Young Lafayette enlisted in the French Army at thirteen and at seventeen was a captain of dragoons. In April 1777, armed with the promise of a high commission, he sailed secretly for America. On July 31 Congress commissioned him a major general, without pay or independent command.

Lafayette served with distinction at the Battle of Brandywine, receiving a superficial wound. On December 1 Congress gave him command of a Virginia division. That winter he shared the privations of Valley Forge, warned Washington of the machinations of Thomas Conway,* and in January was given command of a proposed invasion of Canada, a visionary scheme that never got off the ground.

With news of the French alliance, in the spring of 1778 Lafayette became a hero and a celebrity, the center of attention. Five feet-nine inches tall, with sandy red hair and hazel eyes, a receding forehead and sharp nose, Lafayette made up in vitality, ambition, dash, and verve what he may have lacked in physical beauty. In May, at Barren Hill, he skirmished with the British and avoided defeat by skillful maneuver. At Monmouth, near the end of June, he was deprived of what might have been a brilliant victory by the jealousy and ineptitude of Charles Lee,* but still merited George Washington's praise. That summer he was active in preparation for John Sullivan's* abortive attack on Newport. In October Congress granted him a furlough to return to France.

During a year in France, Lafayette received a hero's welcome, rendered unique and impressive service in his liaison with the king and his ministers, and formulated schemes for French aid to America. "The thought of seeing England humiliated and crushed makes me tremble with joy," he wrote. At the end of

April 1780, he was back in America, eager to rejoin Washington's army and to help prepare for the arrival of French forces. For nearly a year Lafayette served as a frequent intermediary with Rochambeau and sometimes as a trusted emissary to the Congress. With George Washington at West Point when Benedict Arnold's* treason was discovered, Lafayette served on the court that voted the death penalty to Major John André. In the spring of 1781, at the head of twelve hundred New England troops, he marched south to Virginia. For the next six months he marched and countermarched, fought sharp skirmishes while avoiding a probably disastrous all-out engagement, frequently outwitted Cornwallis, cooperated with Anthony Wayne,* and eventually played a major role in bottling up Cornwallis and the final victory at Yorktown. That December he returned to France.

In August 1784 he made a triumphant six-month return to his adopted land. He was entertained by Washington at Mount Vernon and was enthusiastically received wherever he went. In 1824 he returned once more to the United States. Invited by President James Monroe, generously rewarded by Congress, he was given a hero's welcome throughout a year-long tour that Senator Sumner said "belongs to the poetry of history." Never has a visitor to America been accorded such demonstrations of gratitude and affection.

Lafayette's career in his native land deserves more space than is available. As a liberal philosopher, a would-be reformer, and a devotee of republicanism, he was important from 1787 until his death. In the early years of the French Revolution he played a leading role; in the 1820s he was a significant figure. Dreaming of a republic in the mould of his beloved United States, he accepted constitutional monarchy as a step in that direction. In his last great public speech he attacked the reactionary policies of Louis-Philippe whom he had helped to power. Always he was a friend, frequently an important friend, to his second country, the United States. When he was buried, in Picpus Cemetery in Paris, soil from Bunker Hill was spread on his grave.

No one questions Lafayette's psychological contribution to the winning of American independence. In November 1777 Baron Johann de Kalb noted that "No one deserves more than he the esteem which he enjoys here. He is a prodigy for his age, full of courage, spirit, judgment, good manners, feelings of generosity and zeal for the cause of liberty on this continent." Lafayette's zeal for liberty, his unbounded energy, his deference and charm, all contributed to the high esteem in which he was held. He constantly urged his government to send more aid to America, and he became the symbol of that assistance. His courage in battle and his desire to be in the thickest fighting endeared him to the soldier in the ranks.

What of his military skill? his leadership in action? Was this "boy," with little military training and no battle experience, able to make a significant contribution to the American cause? Not yet twenty when he landed on our shores, he was not devoid of military knowledge. Howard H. Peckham noted that "He probably did a great deal of reading . . . in the military field. Otherwise it is impossible to explain the ease with which he exercised a major general's command in the Continental army.'' We know that he was diligent. In December 1777 he wrote his father-in-law, ''I read, I study, I examine, I listen, I think, and out of all that I try to form an idea into which I put as much common sense as I can.''

Central to Lafayette's excellence as a staff officer were his devotion and loyalty to the commander in chief. ''Our General,'' Lafayette wrote only a few months after his arrival, ''is a man truly made for this revolution, which could not succeed without him.'' Peckham believes that few of the American generals were ''more devoted'' to Washington than was Lafayette. Louis Gottschalk gives Lafayette primary credit for destroying the ''cabal'' aimed at replacing Washington.

Lafayette's administrative ability and his concern for the troops under his command cannot be overstressed. Gottschalk wrote, ''Greater credit than he has often received . . . is due to Lafayette for the extraordinary efforts to move impoverished, incompetent, and lethargic commissary agents of Virginia and Maryland to effective measures.'' Peckham wrote, ''Lafayette scrupulously looked after his men, spending his own money when Congress failed to provide them necessities.''

Lafayette's contemporaries respected him as an officer as well as a human being. When Lafayette commanded troops in Virginia, Washington wrote, ''. . . it is my opinion, the command of the troops in that State cannot be in better hands than the Marquis.'' In June 1781 General Nathanael Greene* wrote Jefferson, ''I have the highest opinion of the Marquis's abilities and zeal.''

How may the twentieth century regard his military leadership? At Brandywine, under fire for the first time, Lafayette showed physical courage and desire for action. When the British struck Washington's right flank, Lafayette jumped off his horse, urged the men around him to charge the British, and remained at the front after he was wounded. As Washington's men retreated, near dusk, Lafayette rallied troops at the stone bridge across Chester Creek and helped prevent the retreat from becoming a rout.

Lafayette next saw important action on May 18, 1778, when he made camp on Barren Hill with a reconnaissance force of twenty-two hundred men. He selected an excellent defensive position and posted militia at Whitemarsh to protect two fords. These militia did not retain their post; Howe learned from a deserter of the militia's withdrawal and attacked. Lafayette avoided Sir William Howe's trap, outmaneuvered the older general, and forced the British to withdraw to Philadelphia. Lafayette had made mistakes: posting untrained militia in a key spot, failing to check to make sure they retained their position, and remaining two nights in the same camp. Yet, he had outmaneuvered Howe, and he had inflicted more casualties than he had received.

In February 1781, in command of twelve hundred Continentals, Lafayette successfully defended Richmond. In mid-May Cornwallis, determined to wipe out the patriot bases in Virginia, arrived from North Carolina with seventy-two hundred men. On May 24 Lafayette wrote Washington, "I am . . . determined to scarmish [skirmish], but not engage too far. I am not strong enough even to get beaten."

For several weeks Lafayette maneuvered brilliantly, protecting supply bases and keeping open routes for possible reinforcement. In early June, Anthony Wayne* joined him with nine hundred Continentals; William Campbell came with six hundred mounted riflemen, and Frederick William von Steuben* added four hundred and fifty men. By the end of June Lafayette commanded five thousand. At Green Springs, on July 6, Cornwallis outwitted Wayne. Wayne fought stubbornly; Lafayette came up with the main body of his troops, had two horses shot from under him, and suffered rather heavy casualties.

With the exception of that one engagement, Cornwallis steadily retreated; Lafayette followed. Cornwallis was bottled up, Yorktown was brilliantly planned and fought, and independence was guaranteed. Lafayette merits high praise for his role in the Virginia Campaign. He demonstrated boundless energy, strong determination, a genius for administration and public relations, and superior ability to command and lead.

BIBLIOGRAPHY

Gottschalk, Louis. *Lafayette: A Guide to the Letters, Documents & Manuscripts in the United States.* Ithaca, N.Y.: Cornell University Press, 1975.
————. *Lafayette and the Close of the American Revolution.* Chicago: University of Chicago Press, 1974.
————. *Lafayette Joins the American Army.* Chicago: University of Chicago Press, 1937.
Idzerda, Stanley J., et al. *Lafayette in the Age of the American Revolution; Selected Letters and Papers, 1776–1790.* Ithaca, N.Y.: Cornell University Press, 1977.
Loveland, Anne C. *Emblem of Liberty; The Image of Lafayette in the American Mind.* Baton Rouge, La.: Louisiana State University Press, 1971.

RALPH ADAMS BROWN

LAWRENCE, James (b. Burlington, N.J., October 1, 1781; d. off Halifax, Nova Scotia, June 5, 1813), naval officer. Lawrence enjoyed a short, brilliant career, participating in the Quasi-War with France, the Barbary Wars, and the War of 1812.

John Lawrence, James' father, was mayor of Burlington in 1775, a staunch Loyalist during the American Revolution, and was jailed for his sympathies. While imprisoned, John Lawrence befriended fellow inmate Lieutenant Colonel John G. Simcoe, commander of the Queen's Rangers. After the war, Simcoe became lieutenant governor of Canada and invited the Lawrences to live in Canada, which they did until John Lawrence's death in 1796. Returning to New Jersey, James Lawrence entered grammar school in Burlington to prepare for a career in law, according to his father's wishes, but chose instead to follow the sea. For three months, he studied navigation under a Mr. Griscomb and entered the U.S. Navy on September 4, 1798.

That year also marked the beginning of hostilities between the United States and France. Midshipman Lawrence was ordered to the 26-gun frigate *Ganges* (Captain Richard Dale). On May 23, 1800, Lawrence was transferred to the 36-gun frigate *New York*, under Captain Thomas Robinson, who took Lawrence with him when he assumed command of the 28-gun frigate *Adams*. At the war's end, Lawrence survived the personnel reductions made by the Peace Establishment Act of March 3, 1801, and on September 1, he was reassigned to the frigate *New York*, then laid up at the Washington Navy Yard.

The outbreak of the Barbary Wars necessitated an increase in the number of officers, men, and ships stationed in the Mediterranean. Lawrence reported on board the 12-gun schooner *Enterprise*, under Andrew Sterett, was made acting first lieutenant, and sailed from Baltimore on February 12, 1802. He was promoted to lieutenant on April 6, 1802. Lawrence was one of the men who volunteered to sail under Lieutenant Stephen Decatur* on board the ketch *Intrepid* to burn the frigate *Philadelphia*. The *Philadelphia* had grounded on an uncharted reef and fell into Tripolitan hands on October 31, 1803. She was being refitted for action against the American fleet when Commodore Edward Preble* decided to destroy her. With Lawrence as Decatur's first lieutenant, the crew surprised the Tripolitans, boarded, set fire to the *Philadelphia*, and escaped without a man being killed. For his leadership of this exploit, Decatur was awarded a sword by Congress and made a post-captain, while Lawrence and other officers were rewarded with two months' pay. Lawrence thought this to be a "paltry" sum and declined his share.

Between August 3 and September 3, 1804, Lawrence took part in five attacks on the port of Tripoli, and during the fourth attack, he commanded *Gunboat No. 5*. Later that month, Lawrence was appointed first lieutenant of the 28-gun frigate *John Adams*, under Isaac Chauncey,* which departed the Mediterranean in February 1805. Shortly after his return to the United States, Lawrence was called upon to command *Gunboat No. 6* which had been ordered to the Mediterranean with six other gunboats to oppose the "mosquito fleet" of Tripoli. The Tripolitan War ended on June 5, 1805, with the signing of a peace treaty, but Lawrence remained in command of *No. 6* and did not return to the United States until July 1806, when he put his gunboat out of commission at Baltimore.

During the next six years, Lawrence served as inspector of gunboats at Portland, Maine, was appointed a member of the court-martial trial that tried Captain James Barron for his role in the *Chesapeake-Leopard* affair, served as first lieutenant on board the 44-gun frigate *Constitution*, and was appointed commanding officer of the brigs *Vixen* (12-guns), *Argus* (18 guns), and *Hornet* (20 guns), successively. He received his promotion to master commandant on November 3, 1810. On the domestic side, in 1808 he married Julia Montaudevert, the daughter of a French sea captain, who bore him two children, a son who died in infancy and a daughter, Mary, who married Lieutenant William Preston Griffin of the U.S. Navy.

During the early months of 1812, when pressures for war with Great Britain were increasing, Lawrence's *Hornet* made a rapid passage to Europe carrying diplomatic dispatches to France and Britain. He returned before the declaration of war of June 18, and the *Hornet* was then attached to the squadron of Commodore John Rodgers,* including the 44-gun frigates *President* and *United States*, and the 36-gun frigate *Congress*, and *Argus*. Rodgers sortied from New York on June 21. During the cruise, the *Hornet* took three prizes for the squadron and participated in the chase of the British frigate *Belvidera* (36 guns).

Lawrence's next assignment was to sail in the *Hornet* with the *Constitution*, under Commodore William Bainbridge,* and the 32-gun frigate *Essex*, under David Dixon Porter,* with orders to attack commerce en route to Britain from the West Indies and South America. The *Essex* never joined the squadron, however, and upon reaching Salvador, Brazil, the *Constitution* and *Hornet* went their separate ways. Lawrence tried to provoke an engagement with the British sloop *Bonne Citoyenne* (18 guns), whose captain refused to leave port, much to Lawrence's frustration. He blockaded the port until the arrival of HMS *Montagu* (74 guns) and then sailed northward for the Guianas. On February 24, 1813, Lawrence attacked the British brig *Peacock* (18 guns) off Pernambuco. The *Hornet* was victorious in a brief but devastating engagement that resulted in the surrender of the *Peacock* in fifteen minutes and her sinking shortly afterward. Lawrence was humane in his treatment of his prisoners, and when the news of his battle arrived in the United States, he was hailed as the latest of a new breed of young naval heroes, tenacious in battle and gracious in victory. Lawrence was promoted to captain on March 4, 1813, and despite his preference for the *Hornet* was ordered to command the 36-gun frigate *Chesapeake* at Boston.

Lawrence reported on board the *Chesapeake* in the middle of May, only to discover her crew in a mutinous state due to a dispute with the previous captain over prize money. Almost one-third of the officers and men were new to the ship, though not to the Navy. During late May Lawrence was busy preparing his ship for sea. He had received orders to cruise to the northward toward the Gulf of St. Lawrence where he could intercept supplies and reinforcements for British forces in Canada. By the end of May the *Chesapeake* was ready for sea but not for battle. She was in dire need of a shakedown cruise. During his few weeks on board, Lawrence had exercised the men at General Quarters frequently but the guns had not once been fired.

At dawn on June 1, the British frigate *Shannon* (38 guns), Captain Philip Vere Broke, sailed into Boston Bay near the mouth of the harbor and fired a cannon, offering ship-to-ship combat. Lawrence felt personally provoked and undertook to defend his honor and that of the United States. Within hours the *Chesapeake* was underway, but Lawrence was seemingly unaware of the odds he was facing. Captain Broke had commanded his ship and crew for six years and enjoyed a reputation as an expert in naval gunnery. His crew fought their guns like clockwork and with great accuracy. In the ensuing engagement, the *Chesapeake* followed *Shannon* out to a point eighteen miles east of Boston Light where the *Shannon* waited, sails aback. Lawrence was thereby given the weather gauge, an initial advantage which he immediately relinquished. Rather than rake across the *Shannon*'s stern, Lawrence put down his helm, came alongside, and exchanged broadsides. Broke then had the upper hand, considering *Chesapeake*'s lack of gun drill. Great guns and musketry soon took their effect, wounding Lawrence and damaging *Chesapeake*'s rigging so that she became unmanageable. Lawrence was taken below decks as the fight turned against him. Realizing this, he cried out "Don't give up the ship," urging his officers and crew to resist to the utmost. But British boarding parties soon controlled the decks. A heavy toll in killed and wounded was taken on both sides. The *Shannon* lost thirty-three who died instantly or from their wounds, while the *Chesapeake* suffered sixty-one killed or mortally wounded. Captain Broke received a severe headwound in hand-to-hand fighting and never fully recovered, but Lawrence died on board the *Shannon* en route to Halifax Harbor.

Much has been written on the battle, but it remains clear that Lawrence's hasty decision to accept combat before his ship and crew were ready and his romantic sense of honor led to the undoing of not only the man but also those who sailed with him. His mission, of raiding the Gulf of St. Lawrence, was of greater importance than the possible defeat of a single British frigate. Far more was lost than might have been gained had the *Chesapeake* defeated the *Shannon*.

Despite his defeat, Lawrence's plucky fight has been seen as a stirring example in the annals of the U.S. Navy. His physical courage and nobility of spirit were inspiring to his contemporaries. His death was widely and deeply felt, for he was one of the most popular officers in the Navy and had just reached the peak of his career when he died.

BIBLIOGRAPHY

Knox, Dudley W. *A History of the United States Navy*. New York: G. P. Putnam's Sons, 1936.
Mahan, Alfred Thayer. *Sea Power in Its Relations to the War of 1812*. 2 vols. Boston: Little, Brown and Company, 1905.
Poolman, Kenneth. *Guns Off Cape Ann: The Story of the Shannon and the Chesapeake*. London: Evans Brothers, 1961.
Pullen, Hugh F. *The Shannon and the Chesapeake*. Toronto: McClelland and Stewart, 1970.
Roosevelt, Theodore. *The Naval War of 1812*. New York: G. P. Putnam's Sons, 1882.

                                                                    WILLIAM S. DUDLEY

LAWTON, Henry Ware (b. Manhattan, Ohio, March 17, 1843; d. December 19, 1899), Army officer, commander during the Indian Wars, the Spanish-American and Philippine Wars.

Born near Toledo, Ohio, in the small community of Manhattan, Henry Ware Lawton moved with his family to Fort Wayne, Indiana, when he was only five. Orphaned four years later, he was raised by an uncle and attended the Fort Wayne Methodist Episcopal College.

Four days after South Carolinians attacked Fort Sumter on April 12, 1861,

Lawton, then only eighteen, enlisted in the 9th Indiana Volunteer Infantry. Seeing brief service in what was soon to become West Virginia, Lawton joined the 30th Indiana Infantry later in the year and eventually saw duty in more than twenty battles, including Shiloh, Stone's River, Chickamauga, Atlanta, Franklin, and Nashville. His role in leading a successful charge against the entrenched Confederates at Atlanta won him a Congressional Medal of Honor. In late November 1865 he was mustered out of the service with the brevet rank of lieutenant colonel.

Following the war, Lawton studied law at Harvard but returned to the Army in July 1866 to accept a commission as second lieutenant of the 41st Infantry, a black company. Two years later the 41st was consolidated with the 24th; Lawton remained with the unit until 1871 when he was transferred to the 4th Cavalry, where he was to serve in the Indian Wars for the better part of the next two decades.

It was during his years on the frontier that Lawton played his most publicized, and controversial, role in pursuing Geronimo* and a small but elusive band of Chiricahua Apaches in 1886. Ordered by General Nelson Appleton Miles* to track down the wily Geronimo, Lawton embarked on a rugged campaign that consumed more than four months and covered more than thirteen hundred miles in Arizona, New Mexico, and Mexico. Frequently beginning the day's march at 4:00 A.M., resting between midmorning and late-afternoon, and resuming the chase about suppertime, Lawton operated in the face of extreme heat and frequent storms that often obliterated the Indian trail within hours. Before the campaign was over, Lawton's troops were relegated to the casual attire of battered campaign hats and long underwear, and the 230-pound Lawton lost forty pounds.

Whether Lawton's indefatigible pursuit finally convinced Geronimo to surrender—as Lawton and Miles adamantly contended—or whether Lieutenant Charles B. Gatewood's personal diplomacy was ultimately decisive—as many later historians have concluded—Lawton's actions clearly found favor with Miles. Praising his tenacious captain for doggedly pursuing the Apaches, Miles saw to it that Lawton was promoted in the next few years to lieutenant colonel. This made Lawton, along with Leonard Wood,* the only non-West Pointers so rewarded for service in the Geronimo Campaign.

In the decade prior to the Spanish-American War, Lawton was transferred to the Inspector General's Department. When war broke out in April 1898, Lawton was on an inspection tour of military posts in the eastern part of the United States. Immediately offering his services, he was appointed brigadier general of volunteers and assigned to command the 2d Division, V Army Corps, in the Cuban Campaign.

Arriving in Cuba with William Rufus Shafter's* troops in late May, Lawton was chosen to lead the American advance on the Spanish stronghold of Santiago. Promoted at this time to colonel in the Regular Army, Lawton commanded a portion of the forces that attacked the Spanish outpost at El Caney. Meeting stubborn resistance from a small force of Spanish defenders, Lawton and the nearly seven thousand troops under his command were prevented from following General Shafter's original plans which envisaged Lawton's rapidly routing the Spanish at El Caney and then joining the major American attack at San Juan and Kettle Hills. In the end, Lawton's superior numbers and dogged persistence along with a shortage of Spanish ammunition did bring an American victory but only after a grueling ten-hour battle.

Their ranks badly depleted, Lawton's exhausted troops were forced to march all night in order to strengthen the Americans at San Juan and to join the siege of Santiago. On July 17, the Spanish garrison at Santiago capitulated, with Lawton serving as one of the American commissioners at the surrender ceremonies.

Once the fighting in Cuba had ceased, Lawton was appointed military governor of the Santiago district and promoted to brevet major general. In October 1898 he returned to the United States and assumed command of the IV Army Corps at Huntsville, Alabama. By December, however, he had a new assignment and, within the month, had departed San Francisco for service in the Philippines.

Lawton commanded the 1st Division, VIII Army Corps, in Luzon in 1899 and saw frequent action in the field. In April he took Santa Cruz, a Filipino stronghold. A month later his troops captured San Isidro, another source of insurgent strength. By June he had been given command of the defenses of Manila, and during that same month his regulars were successful in a vigorous campaign in Cavite Province in extending the defensive perimeter of Manila to the south.

Early in October, following the heavy rains of late summer, the American forces prepared to launch a major offensive in central Luzon. The advance was a three-pronged attack with General Arthur MacArthur* marching his troops up the western side of the Luzon plain, Lawton taking his forces up the eastern side, and General Loyd Wheaton positioning his men at the northern end of the plain to prevent large numbers of Filipinos from escaping into the adjacent mountains.

Initially, the main force of thirty-five hundred under Lawton moved northward swiftly and effectively, but eventually—after dispersing Emilio Aguinaldo's insurgents—the advance slowed. The heavy rains were not yet over, and severe transportation problems developed. Turning over his command to General Wheaton on December 16, Lawton returned to Manila to make preparations for yet another offensive, this one in the Marizuina Valley east of Manila, where he hoped to disrupt communications between the northern and southern forces of the insurgents. On December 19, eleven months to the day after he had departed from San Francisco for the archipelago, Lawton was fatally wounded while leading an attack on the city of San Mateo. Shot in the heart, his death was almost instantaneous.

A large and imposing individual who stood over six feet-four inches in height and weighed more than two hundred pounds, Lawton was a ''soldier's soldier'' who excelled in matters of organization and field command. Because of his tenaciousness and persistence, to say nothing of his physical endurance, he was Miles' choice to capture Geronimo, an ambitious assignment which he probably filled as well as anyone could have. Later in Cuba and again in the Philippines, he often resorted to the dogged tactics learned in the American Southwest during the Indian campaigns of the 1880s to defeat his opposition. Critics rarely faulted him, choosing instead to direct their fire to the overall strategy of such superiors as Miles in the Geronimo Campaign and Shafter in Cuba.

Yet for all his aggressiveness on the field of battle, Lawton was sensitive to the political and social dimensions of warfare. In the Philippines at the height of his power, he strongly supported the overall American strategy of basic benevolence toward the Filipinos and urged the development of municipal governments in that archipelago as soon as practicable. It was Lawton who was responsible for the first such native government under American jurisdiction at Baliuag, and, in 1899, he organized municipal governments in Cavite Province generally. To pacify the Philippines, he liked to say, "we should impress the inhabitants with the idea of our good intentions and destroy the idea that we are barbarians." However idealistic and even naive Lawton's ideas in this regard, they exemplified the dichotomy in late nineteenth-century American thinking between wanting to act in a strong and decisive military fashion in the world as a whole and wishing to retain the essence of an anticolonial tradition which was then under heavy attack.

Lawton also symbolized the dedicated soldier ready to sacrifice financial gain for national glory. He died a poor man in 1899, and only a fund of $98,000 raised by general solicitation aided his widow, Mary Craig Lawton, and their four surviving children.

BIBLIOGRAPHY

Faulk, Odie B. *The Geronimo Campaign*. New York: Oxford University Press, 1969.
Gates, John Morgan. *Schoolbooks and Krags: The United States Army in the Philippines, 1898–1902*. Westport, Conn.: Greenwood Press, 1973.
Hagedorn, Hermann. *Leonard Wood: A Biography*. 2 vols. New York: Harper and Brothers Publishers, 1931.
Thrapp, Dan L. *The Conquest of Apacheria*. Norman: University of Oklahoma Press, 1967.
Trask, David F. *The War with Spain in 1898*. New York: Macmillan, 1981.
Utley, Robert M. *Frontier Regulars: The United States Army and the Indian: 1866–1891*. New York: Macmillan Publishing Company, 1973.

JACK L. HAMMERSMITH

LEA, Homer (b. Denver, Colo., November 17, 1876; d. Ocean Park, Calif., November 1, 1912), military adventurer and prophet.

Offspring of a transplanted Southerner who had prospered in Colorado's gold fields, Homer Lea early manifested an affinity for all things military. Lea never relinquished his dreams of leading great armies in combat, even though he was afflicted from birth with a badly curved spine and poor eyesight. In order to prepare himself for command, he read voraciously on the lives and deeds of the great captains of history. Even before he moved with his family to Los Angeles, California, in 1892, Lea had become known among his schoolmates as a brilliant but eccentric young man.

While completing high school, Lea discovered China as the second great force in his life. Fascinated by Chinese culture, he immersed himself in its language, customs, and politics. A frequent visitor to the Chinese section of Los Angeles, Lea gradually gained acceptance there as one of the few Westerners who did not view the Chinese people with condescension. This interest in Chinese affairs continued into his college years, first at Occidental College and then at Stanford University. Ostensibly, Lea studied to be a lawyer since his misshapen body seemingly precluded a military career; yet his dreams of military glory remained undimmed.

Lea's interest in military and Chinese subjects matured during his years at Stanford. China itself was in the midst of turmoil as its young Emperor Kuang-hsu attempted to institute reforms against the wishes of the Regent Empress Dowager Tz'u-hsi. Many Chinese-Americans were sympathetic to the reformist faction in China, and several reformists were among Lea's classmates at Stanford. Lea frequented San Francisco's Chinatown with the young revolutionaries and was eventually inducted into their secret societies. When a bout with smallpox delayed his progress toward graduation, he impulsively decided to leave Stanford and go to China as a fighter for the cause of reform. Disowned by his father for abandoning his education, Lea raised passage money in the Chinese-American community and sailed for Canton in July 1899.

In China Lea contacted forces loyal to the reformer K'ang Yu-wei, whose goal was to free the emperor from the reactionary domination of his aunt, the regent empress dowager. As an American supporter of Chinese political reform, Lea was valuable to K'ang's movement and was enlisted accordingly. The facts of Lea's involvement in the ensuing events are in dispute, but he was apparently only one of many foreigners offered military commissions by the revolutionaries. According to one account, Lea was commissioned a lieutenant general and sent to Shensi Province to organize a band of cutthroats and adventurers into a "division." A similar version has him accompanying the multinational force that relieved the foreign legations at Peking during the Boxer Rebellion of 1900. More plausible, though less romantic, is the statement that he assisted the planners of an abortive uprising in south China in the same year.

Disappointed but not disillusioned, Lea returned to the United States in 1901. There his Los Angeles home became a center for Chinese expatriate factions plotting the overthrow of the Manchu regime. Active in both fund-raising and propagandizing, Lea threw most of his energies into recruiting and training Chinese-American volunteers for service against the Manchus. Aided by several veterans of the U.S. Army, Lea soon controlled a force of respectable size, though of uncertain quality. Gradually, he let his ties with the right-wing faction of K'ang Yu-wei lapse in favor of a close association with Dr. Sun Yat-sen, who eventually appointed the hunchback his military advisor. Dressed in a general's uniform, surrounded by a doting retinue, and immersed in the arcane rituals of secret societies, Lea had finally turned his private fantasies into reality. To a friend he confided his expectation of becoming "the Napoleon of the Far East."

Unable to confine his enthusiasm to the drill field, Lea turned from the sword to the pen. His first literary effort, a novel called *The Vermillion Pencil*, was published in 1908, but its turgid style condemned it to obscurity. A similar fate befell a play, "The Crimson Spider," published in 1909, but the same year also saw publication of Lea's masterwork, *The Valor of Ignorance*. This volume, which brought Lea an international reputation as a military prophet, was applauded by those who saw a "Yellow Peril" threatening America from Asia. In it Lea portrayed an America grown soft and defenseless, a great nation on the verge of defeat due to a "decline in militancy." In strong contrast, a surging, virile Japan was poised to strike for empire in the Pacific. Lea not only predicted a war between Japan and the United States, but described its course in an analysis so detailed it lent credence to the prophecy.

The Valor of Ignorance received mixed reviews in the United States, but its reception in Europe was phenomenal. Lea received invitations to visit both Field Marshal Lord Roberts of Great Britain and Kaiser Wilhelm II of Germany. Although his health, always precarious, had begun to decline precipitously, he sailed for Europe in 1910. He was accompanied by Ethel Powers Lea, formerly his nurse and secretary, now his wife. With her assistance, Lea completed a sequel, *The Day of the Saxon*, which forecast the destruction of the British Empire. When news arrived that the long-awaited revolution had broken out in China, the Leas sailed at once for the Orient. As Sun Yat-sen's military advisor, he was present at the ceremony announcing the overthrow of the Manchu Dynasty. He was preparing a third volume of prophecy, *The Swarming of the Slav*, when he suffered a stroke that left him paralyzed and blind. Returning to the United States in the spring of 1912, he lingered in agony until his death on November 1, just before his thirty-sixth birthday.

Although Lea cherished his brief period of field service in China, its effect on the course of Chinese history was nil. Nor were his efforts at training cadres of overseas Chinese for Sun Yat-sen a major factor in the upheaval of 1911. The ferment that produced the Chinese Revolution was too vast for any one individual to claim credit for the results. Chinese leaders like K'ang Yu-wei and Sun Yat-sen freely used foreigners to further their revolutionary goals, and Homer Lea was only one among many. Had Homer Lea never lived, the Chinese Revolution in all likelihood would have unfolded exactly as it actually did.

Lea's true significance rests upon his reputation as a military prophet. In general, his ideas fit comfortably within the mainstream of American imperialist rhetoric produced in the decades preceding World War I. *The Valor of Ignorance* differs from similar works, however, in its precise delineation of military realities. Solidly based upon his extensive reading of military history, Lea's military predictions received wide circulation in Britain, Germany, Russia, and Japan, nations with a more martial tradition than Lea's own United States. Just as Alfred Thayer Mahan's* works became the gospel of those advocating naval preparedness, Lea's writings performed a similar function for proponents of strong land forces.

Like many successful prophets, Lea died before his prophecies could be validated by events. The accuracy of his specific predictions is occasionally startling and shows his grasp of strategy to have been sound. His more general theses, however, can be twisted to mean almost anything. Lea accurately predicted the fall of the Philippines and the Japanese conquest of the western Pacific. He also correctly forecast the threat posed to Britain by Germany and the inability of the British Navy to protect the Empire east of Suez. Less accurate was his prediction of the invasion of the American West Coast by the Japanese, although for a time in 1942 that prospect seemed all too real to many Americans. His final prediction, that only an Anglo-American alliance could counterbalance the growing power of Russia in the inevitable struggle for world domination, remains untested to this day.

BIBLIOGRAPHY

Hofstadter, Richard. *Social Darwinism in American Thought*. Boston: Beacon Press, 1955.
Kolb, Avery E. "The Bitter Tea of Homer Lea." *Army Combat Forces Journal* 5, No. 12 (July 1955): 17–19.
Lea, Homer. *The Valor of Ignorance*. New York: Harper and Brothers Publishers, 1942 [Original edition, 1909].
O'Connor, Richard. *Pacific Destiny*. Boston: Little, Brown and Company, 1969.
Schiffrin, Harold Z. *Sun Yat-sen: Reluctant Revolutionary*. Boston: Little, Brown and Company, 1980.
Sharman, Lyon. *Sun Yat-sen: His Life and Its Meaning*. New York: John Day Company, 1934.
Sien-chong, Niu. "Two Forgotten American Strategists." *Military Review* 46, No. 11 (November 1966): 53–59.
Wilbur, C. Martin. *Sun Yat-sen: Frustrated Patriot*. New York: Columbia University Press, 1976.

WILLIAM GLENN ROBERTSON

LEAHY, William Daniel (b. Hampton, Iowa, May 6, 1875; d. Bethesda, Md., July 20, 1959), naval officer. Leahy served as chief of staff to Presidents Roosevelt and Truman during World War II and after (1942–1949).

William Daniel Leahy was born into the family of Michael Arthur and Rose (Hamilton) Leahy. His father had led Wisconsin volunteers in the Civil War. Young Leahy attended Ashland High School, Ashland, Wisconsin, and was graduated from that institution in 1892. Soon afterward, he was appointed to the plebe class at the U.S. Naval Academy at Annapolis, Maryland. Following graduation in 1897, ranking an unpretentious thirty-fifth in a class of forty-seven, Passed Midshipman Leahy served two years on board the battleship *Oregon* and participated in the ship's historic sixty-six day fourteen thousand-mile transit from San Francisco, California, to Key West, Florida, via the Strait of Magellan. Leahy received his baptism of fire when the *Oregon* took part in naval operations that resulted in the destruction of Admiral Pascual Cervera's fleet at Santiago de Cuba, during the Spanish-American War.

After serving the obligatory two-year probationary period for Naval Academy graduates, Leahy was commissioned an ensign on July 1, 1899. The young officer was soon dispatched to the Asiatic Station, where the Navy was involved in quelling the Philippine Insurrection and protecting American lives in the Chinese Boxer Rebellion of 1900. Leahy spent the next four years learning the trade of a junior officer in the gunboat *Castine* and supply ship *Glacier*. During this time he achieved his first command as captain of the former Spanish gunboat *Mariveles*.

Having completed the heady experience of active service in the Far East, Leahy returned in 1902 to the more mundane pursuits of the peacetime Navy. However, duty training the prospective crew of the protected cruiser *Tacoma*, then under construction at Mare Island, California, allowed him to court Louise Tennent Harrington of San Francisco. The couple was married on February 3, 1904. (The marriage produced a son, William Harrington Leahy, who eventually reached the rank of rear admiral in the U.S. Navy.) From 1904 to 1911 the aspiring naval officer enhanced his knowledge of ships and men while assigned to the protected cruiser *Boston*, stationed off Panama to watch over construction of the canal, and the armored cruiser *California*, a unit of the Pacific Fleet. Also during this time, he completed a two-year tour instructing cadets as a faculty member of the Department of Physics and Chemistry at the Naval Academy.

After fifteen years of naval service, most of it spent at sea, Leahy was initiated into the realm of staff work. He was appointed fleet ordnance officer of the commander in chief, U.S. Pacific Fleet in 1911. This experience with technical matters was supplemented with greater understanding of naval operations and diplomacy when he assumed the duties of chief of staff to Admiral W.H.H. Southerland, commander of U.S. naval forces in Nicaragua during the American occupation of 1912. After several years as assistant director of gunnery practice and engineering competitions in the Navy Department, and in the Bureau of Navigation, Leahy returned to the Caribbean.

He commanded the despatch gunboat *Dolphin*, operating with other U.S. naval forces in support of the 1916 occupation of Santo Domingo, the Punitive Expedition into Mexico, and the following year as part of the force searching for German supply ships. This command was fortuitous for quite another reason, however. The *Dolphin* was often used to transport high-level U.S. government officials. On several such occasions, Franklin D. Roosevelt, then assistant secretary of the Navy, was a passenger. The cordial relationship established between Roosevelt and Leahy would bear fruit in later years.

With American entry into World War I in the spring of 1917, the Navy directed its full attention to the European conflict. Leahy served as executive officer of the Atlantic Fleet battleship *Nevada* from July 1917 to April of the following year, when he assumed command of the *Princess Matoika*, an expropriated German liner. Leahy handled the dangerous task of transporting troops and supplies to France so professionally that he was awarded the Navy Cross.

After the Great War, Leahy alternated sea duty and shore billets and served in a variety of positions. Upon completing a two and one-half year stint in the Navy Department as director of gunnery exercises and engineering performances, Leahy (by then a captain) commanded the cruiser *St. Louis* in the Mediterranean to ensure the safety of American citizens and interests imperiled by the Greek-Turkish war (1921). Subsequently, he headed the Officer Personnel Division in the Bureau of Navigation (1923–1926). This duty was followed by a sixteen-month tour as commanding officer of the battleship *New Mexico* on the Pacific Coast. Because of his long association with gunnery and related matters, Leahy was appointed chief, Bureau of Ordnance, with the rank of rear admiral in October 1927. The flag officer went back to sea in 1931, commanding the destroyers in both the U.S. Fleet and the Scouting Force. Rear Admiral Leahy then served as the chief, Bureau of Navigation, from 1933 to 1935. Again at sea in 1935, Leahy commanded Battleships, Battle Force in the rank of vice admiral. Only one year later, he was promoted to admiral as commander in chief of the Battle Force.

After almost forty years of naval service, which included hazardous duty in every major sea in which the Navy operated, various staff positions, and command of ships and large naval forces, Admiral Leahy, on January 2, 1937, ascended to the highest command in the Navy, that of chief of naval operations (CNO). He became the only U.S. naval officer ever to have held that command after heading both the Bureau of Ordnance and the Bureau of Navigation. Serving as CNO for two years, Leahy retired from the Navy in August 1939, receiving the Distinguished Service Medal for his outstanding performance.

Even before leaving the Navy, Admiral Leahy was embarked on a new career. Appointed by President Franklin Roosevelt as governor of Puerto Rico in June 1939, Leahy began exercising that office in September. A little more than a year later, the president reassigned him to a diplomatic post of even greater importance. Admiral Leahy assumed the duties of the U.S. ambassador to Vichy France, a regime then desperately trying to balance pro-American sympathy with the reality of German power.

Following American entry into World War II, Leahy was recalled to the United States and, on July 20, 1942, was appointed chief of staff to the commander in chief of the U.S. Army and Navy. He served in this position throughout the war and under both Presidents Roosevelt and Harry Truman, until March 1949. At the same time, Admiral Leahy acted as the senior member of the U.S. Joint Chiefs of Staff and represented the United States on the Allied Combined Chiefs of Staff. In recognition of the importance of his duties and his performance of them, on December 15, 1944, Leahy was promoted to the rank of fleet admiral, held by only three other distinguished officers in the Navy. From 1949 until his death ten years later, Fleet Admiral Leahy completed his memoirs and advised the secretary of the Navy on international and strategic matters.

Fleet Admiral Leahy's significance lies in his exercise of influence as chief military advisor to Presidents Roosevelt and Truman during a time when the United States was engaged in a global war and taking on the mantle of leadership of the Western world. His service to the country, spanning over forty years, as a naval officer and diplomat, important in itself, can be seen as both prelude and preparation for his duty as chief of staff to two presidents and as the senior American member of both the Joint Chiefs of Staff and the Allied Combined Chiefs of Staff.

During his naval career, Admiral Leahy became highly proficient at commanding, organizing, and administering large armed forces in both peace and war. He achieved the billet of CNO along the traditional path in the Navy's surface fleet and in the Washington headquarters. In doing so, he became thoroughly familiar with the mainstream of the American military establishment.

At the same time, Leahy's dealings with foreign leaders and peoples in the Far East, in Europe, and especially in the Caribbean provided him with a sensitivity and understanding of the fine art of diplomacy. Admiral Leahy's performance as ambassador to Vichy France, under the most trying and complicated of circumstances, attested to the expertise he had attained in foreign affairs. He had much to do with preventing more extensive collaboration between the Vichy government and Hitler's Germany, especially with regard to use of the potentially dangerous French fleet.

When Leahy became chief of staff to President Roosevelt in 1942, his past experiences served him well. His training in the international arena and his military knowledge enabled him to provide the president with informed opinion on foreign policy, grand strategy in coalition warfare, armed forces organization, weaponry, and a myriad of related matters. Functioning as the direct conduit between the president and U.S. and Allied military heads, Admiral Leahy was a vital link in the wartime command structure. His ability to reconcile Allied differences was also considerable. In the postwar era, the admiral continued to furnish advice on world affairs and reorganization of the U.S. armed forces. His detractors bemoan a lack of policymaking acumen, his fervent nationalism, and the absence of intellectual breadth. But his basic integrity, unswerving loyalty to superiors, devotion to national service, and lack of political ambition or need for popular acclaim made the admiral ideally suited to the role of presidential advisor.

BIBLIOGRAPHY

Buell, Thomas B. *Master of Seapower: A Biography of Fleet Admiral Ernest J. King.* Boston: Little, Brown and Company, 1980.

Furer, Julius A. *Administration of the Navy Department in World War II.* Washington, D.C.: U.S. Government Printing Office, 1959.

Langer, William L. *Our Vichy Gamble*. New York: Alfred A. Knopf, 1947.
Leahy, William D. *I Was There: The Personal Story of the Chief of Staff to Presidents Roosevelt and Truman*. New York: Whittlesey House, 1950.

EDWARD J. MAROLDA

LEAVENWORTH, Henry (b. New Haven, Conn., December 10, 1783; d. Camp Washita, Indian Territory, July 21, 1834), frontier commander, fort builder, Indian campaigner.

Henry Leavenworth was born into the family of Jesse and Catharine Leavenworth, residents of New Haven, Connecticut. While he was still a boy his parents separated, and Henry went to live with his father in Delhi, New York. He appears to have had at least the usual education of that day because in 1804 he was able to study law and be admitted to the New York State bar.

When war with Britain seemed certain in early 1812, he helped raise a company of volunteers in Delaware County, New York, and was promptly elected as its captain. He accepted a commission as captain of the 25th Infantry, and by August 15, 1813, he had been promoted to major and transferred to the 9th Infantry. Serving under Generals Jacob Jennings Brown* and Winfield Scott* along the New York-Canada border, Leavenworth played a major role in the hard-won American victory at the Battle of Chippewa. There he led the men of the 9th Infantry and 22d Infantry in a charge that helped carry the right and center of the battleline. Less than three weeks later, at the July 20, 1814, Battle of Niagara or Lundy's Lane, he again served with distinction. A year later he was brevetted first lieutenant colonel and then colonel for his actions in those two battles.

In the reduction of the Army following the end of the War of 1812, Leavenworth was transferred to the 2d Infantry in May 1815, and later that year he received a leave of absence to enable him to serve a term in the New York State legislature.

On February 10, 1818, Leavenworth became a lieutenant colonel and was transferred to the 5th Infantry. That unit, along with the 6th Infantry and the Rifle Regiment, had been chosen by the War Department to take part in an ambitious plan to assert American control over new portions of the northwestern frontier. Secretary of War John Caldwell Calhoun* and Army leaders wanted to establish a string of forts throughout the upper Mississippi and Missouri River valleys, and Leavenworth received orders to gather units of the 5th Infantry at Detroit and lead them west. During the spring of 1819 the soldiers moved across the Great Lakes via schooner to Fort Howard on Green Bay. From there they traveled up the Fox River and then down the Wisconsin to Fort Crawford at Prairie du Chien, Wisconsin. On August 8, 1819, Leavenworth led a flotilla of sixteen boats up the Mississippi River. By the end of the month the command reached the juncture of the Mississippi and Minnesota rivers, located a temporary Army post, and Leavenworth returned downstream. In May 1820 he moved the troops to the permanent site for the fort and ordered construction begun on what became Fort Snelling.

As a result of the Army reduction and reorganization of 1821, Leavenworth was transferred to the 6th Infantry. His new assignment brought him to Fort Atkinson, Nebraska, an outpost built just the preceding year. From there he was to deal with the Indian tribes of the upper Missouri Valley. This duty caused the one incident in his Army career that raised a controversy about his decisiveness as a commander.

In early June 1823 William H. Ashley and a party of his trappers stopped at the Arikara Indian Villages in South Dakota to trade while on their way up the Missouri River. Although they appeared friendly, the tribesmen launched a surprise attack against Ashley's party, inflicting twenty-four casualties on the whites and driving them back downstream. When Leavenworth got news of the attack on June 18, 1823, he acted promptly. He ordered six infantry companies to move north to help Ashley's men, and he recruited sixty fur traders to accompany the soldiers. On June 22 they set off up the Missouri by boat. With the traders' help Leavenworth recruited about 750 Sioux warriors to serve against their longtime enemies, the Arikara.

Near evening on August 9, 1823, Leavenworth's little army halted near the Arikara Villages. With the Sioux riding in advance, the soldiers and trappers drove the defenders back inside their palisaded towns. In the morning the soldiers launched an artillery attack, but most of their shot flew harmlessly over the frightened defenders. By late afternoon Leavenworth decided to offer the Arikara a truce. His troops lacked adequate ammunition to do much more fighting, his Sioux allies appeared to have deserted, and he was hundreds of miles from his base of supply and reinforcements. To the disgust of the fur traders, the Arikara seemed to accept Leavenworth's offer of peace, but the talks dragged because the colonel demanded that Ashley's stolen property be returned. While the Army waited for the Indians to gather and return the trade goods, the Indians decided to flee, and on the morning of August 14, 1823, when the soldiers resumed their attack they found that the Arikara had slipped past their sentries the preceding night. After a futile search for the Indians, Leavenworth led his troops back down the Missouri to Fort Atkinson.

For the next decade mostly routine garrison duty and administrative detail occupied Leavenworth's attention. On July 25, 1824, he was brevetted a brigadier general for having served ten years at his brevet rank of colonel. Then in December of that same year he received a promotion to the regular rank of colonel and was assigned to command the 3d Infantry with headquarters at Green Bay, Wisconsin. By 1826 the commanding general of the Army, Jacob Brown,* had decided to build an infantry training school near St. Louis, and Colonel Leavenworth soon became involved in this project. In September he moved most of the 3d Infantry to the construction site where they worked with troops of the 1st Infantry to erect the buildings of Jefferson Barracks throughout the fall and winter months.

The next spring the War Department decided to abandon Fort Atkinson on the Missouri River and to establish a new Army post farther down that stream.

Once again Leavenworth received the assignment, and he took his troops to the site of what became Fort Leavenworth in eastern Kansas. For a time in 1829 he commanded Jefferson Barracks, and in February 1834 he was assigned to command the Left Wing of the Western Department of the Army. This region included the area south of Missouri and west of the Mississippi River. There Leavenworth's chief task was to maintain peace with the Indian tribes of the Southern Plains.

The War Department hoped to use the newly formed dragoons to impress the Southwestern tribesmen with American strength and to persuade them to cease their raids on eastern Indians being moved onto the Plains, pioneers, and Santa Fe traders. By June 1834 Leavenworth and five hundred officers and men of the 1st Dragoons started west from Fort Gibson. This expedition proved disastrous for the troops as they sickened and died in large numbers. While buffalo hunting on June 27, Leavenworth fell off his horse and apparently injured himself seriously. His fellow officers reported that after his fall he never fully recovered his vigor, and just over three weeks later, on July 21, 1834, Henry Leavenworth died at a temporary camp near the mouth of the Washita River.

Leavenworth's contributions to the Army of his day are more difficult to see clearly, for most of his career he held subordinate rather than command positions. Nevertheless, some of his activities do stand out. Certainly, during the War of 1812 he was one of the junior officers who rose to prominence because of a determination to train troops effectively. Through his skill in using his men successfully, Leavenworth came to be recognized as one of the best officers of his day.

His career on the frontier offers other examples of his competence. He moved the 5th Infantry with little difficulty in 1819, and he successfully directed the building of Fort Snelling. He participated in the construction of Jefferson Barracks and of Fort Leavenworth with the 3d Infantry. In 1823 he led troops from Fort Atkinson up the Missouri to punish the Arikara, and in 1834 he led the 1st Dragoons west to seek peace with the tribes of the Southern Plains. Contemporaries recognized Leavenworth as having strongly influenced the ideas of duty, training, and discipline in the early Army. Memorial statements published soon after his death acknowledged his energy, bravery, and good judgment in carrying on his duties.

BIBIOGRAPHY

Agnew, Brad. "The Dodge-Leavenworth Expedition of 1834." *Chronicles of Oklahoma* 53 (Fall 1975): 376–96.

Forsyth, Thomas. "Fort Snelling, Colonel Leavenworth's Expedition to Establish It in 1819." *Minnesota Historical Collections* 2. Minneapolis, Minnesota, 1880.

Hansen, Marcus L. *Old Fort Snelling, 1819–1859*. Iowa City: State Historical Society of Iowa, 1918.

Hunt, Elvid. *History of Fort Leavenworth, 1827–1927*. Fort Leavenworth, Kans.: General Service Schools Press, 1926.

Kimball, Jeffrey. "The Battle of Chippewa: Infantry Tactics in the War of 1812." *Military Affairs* 31 (Winter 1967–1968): 169–86.

Mahon, Bruce E. *Old Fort Crawford and the Frontier*. Iowa City: State Historical Society of Iowa, 1926.

Robinson, Doane, ed. "Official Correspondence of the Leavenworth Expedition of 1823 into South Dakota for the Conquest of the Ree Indians." *South Dakota Historical Collections* 1. Pierre, South Dakota, 1902.

Sunder, John E. *Joshua Pilcher: Fur Trader and Indian Agent*. Norman: University of Oklahoma Press, 1968.

ROGER L. NICHOLS

LEE, Charles (b. Chester, England, January 26, 1731/2; d. Philadelphia, Pa., October 2, 1782), major general in the Continental Army. Modern authorities believe Lee was politically the most radical American general during the early years of the War for Independence.

Many members of Lee's family served in the British Army, and his father, who commanded the 44th Regiment of Foot, decided early in his son's life that the boy would continue this tradition. When Charles was fourteen, Colonel Lee purchased him a commission in the 44th. Charles began his active service in 1748 and, after seven years of garrison duty in Ireland, went with the regiment to North America in 1755.

By the end of the Seven Years' War, Lee had extensive experience as a combat officer. He fought in every major campaign in America from 1755 to 1760, with the single exception of James Wolfe's* conquest of Quebec. In addition, he took part in the defense of Portugal in 1762. He was, by all accounts, a courageous, intelligent officer in the field. On two occasions, his superiors showed their confidence in him by trusting him with important missions. In 1759 Lee was ordered to take fifteen men and search the wilderness between Niagara and Fort Pitt for signs of a French force. In 1762 he led a small force on a surprise raid on a Spanish camp at Villa Velha and destroyed large quantities of munitions and supplies.

Lee analyzed his wartime experiences carefully, reached thoughtful conclusions, and stuck to them in the face of the prevailing wisdom. He felt that the war had amply proven the great effectiveness of light infantry tactics against regular troops, particularly in rugged, sparsely populated countries like America and Portugal. The major reason for their effectiveness was obvious to Lee. An army's logistical systems, so essential to its existence as a fighting force, were peculiarly vulnerable to accident or attack in such areas, and light infantry tactics helped an opposing army take maximum advantage of its opportunities. The difficulties of supplying an army in America had brought home another lesson to Lee: the paramount importance of civilian support. The enthusiastic aid of civilian society could ease logistical burdens considerably and replenish the Army's manpower. Moreover, another advantage of light infantry tactics would appear as recruits entered the service. Since these tactics required less rigorous training and discipline, new recruits could be integrated into the force more quickly. In Lee's opinion, his theories were fully justified by the outcome of the war in America. Unlike most British officers, and despite his own occasional quarrels with civilians over supply contacts and recruiting, Lee believed that Americans' civil and military support had ultimately been crucial to victory. He liked the people and respected them as soldiers. During 1774–1776 these ideas and affections would guide his actions.

Life in England during 1763–1773 frustrated and infuriated Lee. His hot temper, caustic wit, and impolitic fondness for public disputes made for him powerful civilian and military enemies who kept him on half-pay and unpromoted until the general upgrading of the Army in 1772. By that time, he had thoroughly imbibed the principles of the radical, "Real Whig" opposition. Convinced that corrupt ministers had bribed, deceived, and coerced the British people into yielding most of their liberties, certain that that "despicable . . . dolt" George III was no patriot king, Lee decided that America was the last refuge of liberty in the world. Early during the decade of peace, Lee's dissatisfactions and rest-lessness had carried him to Eastern Europe, where he observed the sporadic fighting there and became in 1769 a major general in the Polish Army. In 1773 those same feelings encouraged him to make a business trip to North America to inspect his extensive land grants and to scout the possibility of moving there. He arrived two months before the Boston Tea Party and the beginning of the imperial crisis.

Since Lee had a public reputation as an opponent of the taxation and coercion of the colonies that preceded him to America, and since he had military expe-rience that might prove necessary, prominent patriots like Patrick Henry, George Washington,* and the Adamses received him enthusiastically during 1774. Lee was equally enthused. He warned them that they must stand firm, or their liberties would be lost. He also encouraged them by scoffing at the notion that British regulars, "the refuse of an exhausted nation," could conquer two hundred thou-sand "active, vigorous yeomanry, fired with noble ardor, . . . all armed, all expert in the use of arms." He devised a simplified training manual, and he promised that three months of drill would make the militia able to deal effectively with any invader. By December 1774 he was putting his preaching into practice by drilling patriotic forces in Maryland.

In June 1775, after receiving Congress' assurance that he would be compen-sated for any confiscation of his English property, Lee accepted appointment as major general and resigned his British commission. A summary of his service record for the next year reveals his importance to the American cause. From June until December 1775 Lee commanded the left wing of the army besieging Boston, and he oversaw the training of troops and the construction of entrench-ments. From December through March 1776, Washington and Congress made him responsible for encouraging the civilians and preparing the defenses of Rhode Island and New York City. In February Congress, reasoning that he was the only officer who could "speak and think in French," gave him the Canadian command. Then, on March 1, these orders were rescinded, and he was assigned the command of the Southern Military District. From late March through August, he organized defenses from Virginia to Georgia. In June, he commanded the forces that repelled the British invasion of Charleston, and he earned popular acclaim as "The Palladium of American Liberty."

Lee began this year certain that he could conduct the war better than anyone else; he ended it even more certain. At Boston, he tried to avert further fighting by secretly establishing, in direct contradiction to the orders of the Massachusetts provincial congress, contacts with British officers. He was among the first to advise Congress openly to declare independence. Then, having dispensed political advice, he urged Congress to put all militia under Continental control and to draft regular soldiers out of those units. In Rhode Island, New York, Maryland, and Virginia, he was publicly and harshly critical of what he felt was the local patriots' timidity in handling suspected Tories and their former governors. To his mind, the time for persuasion had passed; lenient measures would only guarantee that a British army would have vital civilian support. On his own authority, and frequently in opposition to the wishes of local committees, Lee harassed Loyalists, forcing them to take oaths, threatening them in some areas with prison and loss of property, and in Virginia actually sequestering men, destroying homes, and forcing families to move away from the coast. In South Carolina, Lee discovered that local patriots had ignorantly sited their defenses and lazily left them uncompleted. The Carolinians also obstinately refused to place their militia under his command, although they did follow his technical advice on finishing the forts and on using their ordnance effectively. Lee praised their bravery but realized that the victory was largely due to the harbor's winds and tides and "a most unaccountable languor and inertness on [the enemy's] part." Charleston confirmed to him again that the political timidity and military ignorance of Congress and local committees drastically weakened the war effort. It also reinforced his determination to disobey or modify the politicians' orders whenever he felt it was necessary.

In August, Congress ordered Lee to return to Washington's army. He rejoined it in New York in mid-October and insisted on an immediate retreat into New Jersey. But Washington, under pressure from Congress, kept troops on Manhattan too long and lost twenty-nine hundred men and large quantities of stores. Furious that his commander had listened to "the cattle" in Congress, Lee concluded that he did not have the sense or courage to resist erroneous advice. As a result of this conclusion, Lee essentially stopped obeying Washington. When ordered to bring his forces across the Delaware quickly, Lee moved slowly and advised Washington to return to New Jersey. The local militia "seemed sanguine," he wrote, and the British lines were overextended and vulnerable. Clearly, Lee thought he could duplicate his triumph at Villa Velha, force the British back toward New York, and "re-conquer the Jerseys." Before he could do that, however, he carelessly dawdled at a tavern in Basking Ridge on December 13, 1776, and a British patrol captured him.

Unquestionably, this turn of events, which Lee blamed on the "rascality" of his guards, demoralized him. Perhaps Sir William Howe's obvious desire to try him for desertion and treason disturbed him too. Even if it did not (and Howe soon realized that a court-martial was probably illegal and certainly unwise), the seeming slowness of Congress and Washington to threaten reprisals must have angered Lee. Such was his emotional state when he reflected on the past eighteen months and concluded that America could not win the war, and would only accomplish the weakening of itself and Britain. He discussed his intellectual reason for reaching this conclusion in a plan for militarily ending the war which he sent to Howe in March 1777. Conquer ports in Maryland, issue a proclamation of pardon, and wait for settlers in Maryland and Pennsylvania to declare their loyalty, he advised Howe. The wait would not, he promised, be long. The Germans in particular had been "the most staunch assertors of the American cause," but they were "so remarkably tenacious of their property and apprehensive of the least injury being done to [it]" that they would choose peace before their land became battlefields. This statement exposes the depths of Lee's disenchantment with the American cause. The American people, he now believed, were not merely poorly led. They suffered also from their own unwillingness to make necessary major sacrifices. They were not virtuous enough to win independence.

Lee acted on this conclusion. In February 1777 he cooperated in efforts to open informal peace negotiations. When Congress refused to send agents, he told Howe that seizing the Chesapeake would end the war with a minimum of bloodshed. For the rest of his captivity, and even for two months after his exchange in April 1778, Lee continued to explore ways of negotiating peace. Lack of success resigned him to fighting on. When he returned to the American lines, he coolly told Congress that the Continental Army was inferior to the British in every respect, including morale, and opined that it should never take the offensive. He was probably skeptical of its defensive capacity as well, for he advised Congress to strengthen the cavalry and convert infantry units into light infantry, changes that would force any commander in the direction of harassment and away from confrontation on the battlefield. In May 1778, when he resumed active duty, he urged Washington to be cautious. When the British retreated toward New York in June, Lee was prominent among those who advised a "partial attack" only if a "general action" could be avoided.

Washington agreed with this advice but then increased the size of the attacking force to the point that Lee felt obliged to assume command of it at Monmouth. Because of difficult terrain, torrid heat, poor communications, and unexpectedly strong resistance, the attack foundered. A disorganized retreat began. Fearful that his troops would be trapped and slaughtered, Lee ordered his officers to withdraw to stronger defensive positions. At this time, Washington arrived on the battlefield. Before he fully grasped the situation, he angrily accused Lee in public of disobeying orders. After the British counterattack was fought off, Lee demanded in insulting terms a court-martial to clear his name. Washington responded with charges of disobedience, "making an unnecessary, disorderly, and shameful retreat," and disrespect to a superior officer.

In retrospect, Lee seems innocent of the first two charges and clearly guilty of the third. At the time, however, abstract questions of guilt or innocence mattered little to the court or Congress. Both bodies felt they had to support Washington's authority, and the only way to do that was to find Lee guilty as charged. He was suspended from the Army for a year. After fruitless appeals to Congress and, through the press, to the public for justice, he indulged himself in vicious attacks on Washington and the American people, who "have always a god of the day, whose infallibility is not to be disputed." He never served again in the Army. Lee died convinced that he had unwittingly helped establish an arbitrary government in America.

As John Shy has noted, Lee's contributions to the American Revolution were substantial but difficult to measure. Without doubt, his energy, example, and experience were valuable in 1775–1776. Without doubt, too, had Lee, not Washington, been the hero of the times that tried men's souls in December 1776, the relationship of the military to civil authorities during the crucial years that followed would have been different. This last thought suggests one significance of his career for military historians. An examination of his acts and plans may well reveal what the War for Independence could have been. Equally important, an examination of the causes and progress of his disillusion and tragedy may well reveal what it was.

BIBLIOGRAPHY

Alden, John R. *General Charles Lee: Traitor or Patriot?* Baton Rouge: Louisiana State
      University, 1951.
Higginbotham, Don. *The War of American Independence.* New York: Macmillan, 1971.
Shy, John. "American Strategy: Charles Lee and the Radical Alternative." In John Shy,
      *A People Numerous and Armed: Reflections on the Military Struggle for American
      Independence.* Oxford: Oxford University Press, 1976, pp. 133–62.
Thayer, Theodore. *The Making of a Scapegoat: Washington and Lee at Monmouth.* Port
      Washington, N.Y.: Kennikat Press, 1976.

                                                                                                    JOHN L. BULLION

LEE, Fitzhugh (b. "Clermont," Fairfax County, Va., November 19, 1835; d. Washington, D.C., April 28, 1905), Army officer. Lee was a Confederate cavalry commander during the Civil War.

Fitzhugh Lee was a grandson of Henry ("Light-Horse Harry") Lee* and a nephew of Robert Edward Lee.* He attended West Point and was graduated in 1856, forty-fifth in his class of forty-nine. During his stay at the Military Academy, Lee was almost dismissed for bad behavior. Receiving his commission in the cavalry, Lee served as an instructor at Carlisle Barracks, Pennsylvania, for two years. He then received orders for active duty in Texas with the 2d Cavalry Regiment under Colonel Albert Sidney Johnston.* With this unit, he participated in several campaigns against the Indians and was severely wounded. In 1860 Lee assumed the duties of assistant instructor of tactics at West Point. On May 21, 1861, he resigned his commission as first lieutenant and joined the Confederate Army.

Accepting a commission as first lieutenant, Lee served initially as assistant adjutant general on the staff of Brigadier General Richard Stoddert Ewell.* In this capacity he participated in the Battle of First Manassas. He received a commission as lieutenant colonel of the 1st Virginia Cavalry Regiment in August 1861. The following March he was promoted to colonel of his regiment. His unit served with Brigadier General James Ewell Brown Stuart* during Stuart's famous ride around the Union Army commanded by General George Brinton McClellan.* For his services in this raid and in the various battles around Richmond, Lee received promotion to brigadier general on July 24, 1862.

Lee led a brigade of cavalry in the Second Manassas Campaign and at South Mountain and Sharpsburg during General Robert E. Lee's invasion of Maryland. The brigade later accompanied Stuart in his Dumfries and Occoquan raids in December 1862. Lee's next action took place at Kelly's Ford on the Rappahannock River in March 1863. There he beat back an attempt to surprise and crush his brigade. Stuart chose Lee to screen troops led by Lieutenant General Thomas Jonathan ("Stonewall") Jackson* in their flank march against the Federal Army under Major General Joseph Hooker* at Chancellorsville in May 1863. During this maneuver, Lee discovered that the Federal XI Corps, commanded by Major General Oliver Otis Howard,* was unsupported. This discovery led to Jackson's successful attack and rout of Howard's troops.

Following his participation in the Gettysburg Campaign, Lee received a promotion to major general to date from August 3, 1863, and he assumed command of a division in the reorganized Cavalry Corps. He distinguished himself at Spotsylvania Court House in May 1864 when his troops held back the enemy long enough to allow the corps under General James Longstreet* to gain control of the strategic crossroads. After Stuart's death at Yellow Tavern, General Robert E. Lee considered appointing his nephew to command of the cavalry but chose instead Major General Wade Hampton.* Fitz Lee served under Hampton at Trevilian Station in June 1864 and contributed to the Confederate victory there over Union cavalry led by Philip Henry Sheridan.*

Lee took his division to the Shenandoah Valley in August 1864 to participate in campaigns with Lieutenant General Jubal Anderson Early.* On September 19, 1864, at the Battle of Winchester, Lee had three horses killed under him and received a severe wound that incapacitated him until early 1865. Lee assumed nominal command of the Cavalry Corps of the Army of Northern Virginia when Hampton left to join General Joseph Eggleston Johnston* in the Carolinas but acted under his uncle's control until late March 1865. During the Battle of Five Forks, Lee was absent in the rear with Major General George Edward Pickett* at a shad-bake. Lee and a portion of his cavalry cut their way through the Federal lines near Appomattox Court House on April 9 but surrendered two days later at Farmville.

After the war, Lee operated a farm in Stafford County, Virginia. He served as governor of Virginia from 1885 to 1890 and ran unsuccessfully for the U.S. Senate in 1893. President Grover Cleveland appointed Lee consul general at Havana, Cuba, in 1896, and he retained that post under President William McKinley.

When the Spanish-American War broke out in 1898, Lee offered his services to the Army and became a major general of volunteers. His command, the VII Corps, was never ordered to active duty in Cuba, however. Lee received an appointment as military governor of Havana and Pinar del Rio Province in early 1899. In March of that year, after a reorganization of the Army, he was given the rank of brigadier general of volunteers. When he retired from the Army in 1901, Lee was commanding the Department of Missouri.

Like Jeb Stuart, Lee was one of the "laughing cavaliers" who enjoyed battle as well as the "pomp and circumstance" of war. For these reasons, he was close to Stuart and one of Stuart's favorites. Lee had the aptitude and experience to be a capable cavalry commander and generally performed competently under the direction of Stuart and Hampton. In none of his battles, however, did he exhibit any particular brilliance. Douglas Southall Freeman praised Lee for his abilities in finding forage for his horses, a noteworthy accomplishment in war-ravaged Virginia.

Lee had a rivalry with Hampton, dating from the Gettysburg Campaign, because he resented the South Carolinian's challenge to the domination of the Cavalry Corps by Virginians. To Lee's credit, he worked well with Hampton when Hampton succeeded to command of the cavalry. Lee's tardiness in joining Hampton's main force at Trevilian Station allowed Federal cavalry under Brigadier General George Armstrong Custer* to overrun Hampton's supply train, but he arrived on the field in time to prevent a greater disaster and helped turn the tide of battle in favor of the Confederates.

In the Second Manassas Campaign, Lee was probably responsible for preventing a much more resounding victory over the Union Army commanded by Major General John Pope.* Fitz Lee's brigade did not join the Army on schedule from an unnecessary side trip, and his absence caused Robert E. Lee to delay Jackson's attack on Pope's rear for two days. The delay enabled Pope to recognize his danger and pull his army behind the Rappahannock River. Fitz Lee's absence from a battle again worked to the detriment of the Confederates at Five Forks. He was overconfident and did not realize the real danger to the Army's flank. Had he been present with his troops, he might have been able to stem the Federal attack and prevent the rout that occurred.

An extensive assessment of Fitzhugh Lee's abilities as a military commander is difficult to make. He had no large or independent command during the Civil War until the conflict was almost over. He exercised no field command during the Spanish-American War, but his appointment as major general of volunteers and military governor of Havana may be seen as symbolic gestures to the South to "bind up the wounds" of the Civil War. Joseph Wheeler,* another former Confederate cavalry officer, actually led U.S. troops in the Cuban Campaign. Together, Lee and Wheeler later produced a book, *Cuba's Struggle Against Spain* (1899).

BIBLIOGRAPHY

Alexander, Edwin Porter. *Military Memoirs of a Confederate*. New York: Charles Scribner's Sons, 1907.

Cooke, John Esten. *Wearing of the Gray*. Bloomington: Indiana University Press, 1959.

Cosmas, Graham A. *An Army for Empire: The United States Army in the Spanish-American War*. Columbia: University of Missouri Press, 1971.

Freeman, Douglas Southall. *Lee's Lieutenants: A Study in Command*. 3 vols. New York: Charles Scribner's Sons, 1945.

Starr, Stephen Z. *The Union Cavalry in the Civil War*. 2 vols. Baton Rouge: Louisiana State University Press, 1979–1981.

ARTHUR W. BERGERON, JR.

LEE, Henry (b. Prince William County, Va., January 29, 1756; d. Cumberland Island, Ga., March 25, 1818), Revolutionary cavalryman popularly known as "Light-Horse Harry." Lee's independent corps provided services essential to the survival of the Continental Army.

Henry Lee knew from an early age that he belonged to a notable family and was expected to play a leading role in colonial society. Before him four generations of Lees prospered in Virginia, taking a place in the ranks of the colony's landed gentry. As his father's eldest son and heir apparent to a bachelor uncle, Henry was destined to be a prominent planter. His preparation for that life included three years of study at Princeton where he graduated in 1773 with a taste for Latin classics and debate. He was planning to read law in England when the War of Independence began.

Lee, like all of his family, supported the American cause, and despite his medium height and slight build, he was eager to serve it as a soldier, an ambition possibly inspired by his father's near neighbor George Washington.* In July 1775 and April 1776 Washington solicited General Charles Lee,* an unrelated Lee whom he met at Mount Vernon on the eve of Lexington, for a position as aide de camp, but without success. Henry Lee's chance to serve came on June 13, 1776, when the Virginia Convention, having decided to raise six cavalry troops of thirty-seven officers and men each for state defense, chose him to be captain of a troop.

The Virginia horse was summoned to join the Continental Army in late 1776, and by February 1777 Lee's troop had arrived at Washington's headquarters in Morristown, New Jersey. Washington soon put the unit on detached duty to scout, forage, and provide security for the Army. So proficient was Lee at these tasks that he continued to act independently through much of the next year, although officially his troop was incorporated with the others from Virginia as the 1st Continental Light Dragoons. He particularly distinguished himself near Valley Forge on January 20, 1778, by coolly repulsing an enemy force bent on destroying his isolated troop.

To give Lee's abilities greater scope, in March 1778 Washington offered to make him an aide de camp, but Lee refused, having learned that he preferred field duty. An assignment more to his liking came on April 7, 1778, when Congress, at Washington's urging, promoted him to major and gave him command of an independent corps consisting of two troops of horse. Lee's new unit performed well, but by 1779 the Northern war had become a "war of posts" around New York City, and infantry were needed to attack enemy fortifications. With Washington's approval Congress on July 13, 1779, made Lee's corps legionary by adding a small detachment of foot to his horse. On August 19 Lee overran an enemy outpost at Paulus Hook, New Jersey, within sight of New York City, carrying off 158 prisoners. "The affair, considered abstractedly," wrote Arthur St. Clair* five days later, "is of very little Moment; but it shews that a Spirit of Enterprize exists amongst us." Congress commemorated the daring raid with a gold medal.

Allowed more infantry in February 1780, Lee's Legion set out that spring to reinforce Continental troops in South Carolina, but Washington recalled the Legion after Charleston surrendered in May. Lee was again ordered south in October to aid the new Southern commander, Nathanael Greene.* Before going Lee was given permission to recruit additional horse and foot, bringing his Legion's authorized strength to 150 cavalry and 150 infantry. On November 6, 1780, he was promoted to lieutenant colonel.

Lee's Legion reached General Greene in South Carolina in January 1781, and after an abortive raid on Georgetown, South Carolina, joined Greene's February retreat north to the Dan River, riding hard to help fend off the vanguard of Cornwallis' pursuing army. Lee soon resumed the offensive, annihilating a Loyalist detachment near Haw River, North Carolina, on February 25. Following the March 15 battle at Guilford Court House, North Carolina, where the Legion fought on the American left flank, Greene evaded Cornwallis to attack British defenses in South Carolina and Georgia, an unorthodox strategy for which Lee later claimed credit. Whether it was his plan or not, Lee excelled at implementing it. Between April 15 and June 5 he took four major enemy outposts. Later in June he assisted Greene at the siege of Ninety Six, South Carolina, and in September played a prominent part in Greene's final battle at Eutaw Springs, South Carolina.

Greene greatly valued Lee's services, but Lee was disappointed that his actions in the South were not more generally acclaimed. Embittered, physically exhausted, and convinced that his talents were unneeded in the quiet days following the Yorktown surrender, which he witnessed as a visitor to Washington's camp, Lee left the Army in February 1782 to marry his cousin Matilda Lee, heiress to the family's Stratford Hall plantation in Westmoreland County, Virginia.

As a civilian Lee served in the Continental Congress during 1785–1788, vigorously defended the U.S. Constitution at the 1788 Virginia Ratifying Convention, and was governor of Virginia during 1791–1794. After his wife died in 1790, however, he began to seek a return to a military career. He was passed over in 1792 for command of a federal expedition against the western Indians and in 1793 was persuaded by Washington that joining the French Revolutionary Army would be madness. Then in August 1794 Washington offered Lee command of the militia army that was to suppress the western Whiskey Insurrection. Despite his June 1793 marriage to Anne Hill Carter and the fact that he was serving as Virginia's governor, he accepted. The task was completed by November without bloodshed.

Lee was commissioned a major general in the U.S. Army during the war scare of 1798 but saw no active duty and closed his public life with a term as a Federalist congressman, 1799–1801. Bankrupted by ill-advised investments, he lived in poverty thereafter. While imprisoned for debt during 1809–1810, he began writing his *Memoirs of the War in the Southern Department of the United States*, which was published in 1812. In July 1812 he visited Baltimore and was severely beaten by a mob for joining in efforts to protect a Federalist newspaper publisher. Broken in health, he sought recovery by living in the West Indies from 1813 to 1818. He died in Georgia at the home of Nathanael Greene's daughter on his way back to Virginia.

In a war where American commanders normally found themselves inferior to the enemy in mobility, discipline, training, and equipment, Henry Lee's presence was always welcomed, for he had shaped a corps that could help offset those disadvantages in a variety of circumstances. Superbly mounted, Lee's cavalry swiftly covered long distances, and over short distances Legion infantry sometimes rode behind the saddles of their cavalry comrades. Lee maintained high standards for the uniforms, weapons, and accoutrements of his men. Most of his recruits were intelligent volunteers, attracted as much by the esprit of Lee's corps as by the American cause. They took readily to military discipline and learned to execute ambitious plans with patience and precise coordination. Lee and his men were thorough professionals who enhanced the effectiveness of other units.

Lee's most important contributions to the Continental Army were not made in battle, however. Often too weak to risk open combat, Washington and Greene gave priority to protecting their armies, confident that the British could not win while an organized American force remained in the field. Lee aided in the success of this strategy in several ways. By regular reconnaissance and contacts with informers, he provided reliable intelligence of enemy movements by land or sea; his patrols hindered both American deserters and enemy raiders; and when food was needed, he expedited the flow of provisions from distant regions. Lee also served a more active strategy, notably in the South but in the North as well. Using his mobility and his own intelligence reports, he surprised neglectful enemy detachments, forced quick surrenders, and departed before the enemy retaliated—tactics that helped erode British strength and morale without unduly endangering lives or the American cause. If others performed functions similar to Lee's, none did so more consistently or ably than he.

Lee owed his success in war to a family tradition that prepared him to lead but more to his own character which well fitted him for independent command. "Henry Lee," wrote an acquaintance during his Princeton days, "is more than strict in his morality, he has a fine genius & is too diligent." Never in doubt when distinguishing right from wrong, he was a very effective disciplinarian, unhesitatingly rewarding good conduct and punishing bad. His quick intelligence made him an imaginative and skillful tactician, while his painstaking attention to detail often saved him from careless errors. Lee's Achilles' heel was an insatiable ambition. The tragedy of his life was not that his talents proved less useful in peace than in war, but that his achievements, honorable as they were, could not secure the perfect fame and glory that he sought.

BIBLIOGRAPHY

Boyd, Thomas. *Light-Horse Harry Lee*. New York: Charles Scribner's Sons, 1931.
Hendrick, Burton J. *The Lees of Virginia: Biography of a Family*. New York: Halcyon House, 1935.
Jones, Charles C., Jr. *Reminiscences of the Last Days, Death and Burial of General Henry Lee*. Albany, N.Y.: Joel Munsell, 1870.
Lee, Henry (1756–1818). *Memoirs of the War in the Southern Department of the United States*. New York: University Publishing Company, 1869.
Lee, Henry, Jr. (1787–1837). *The Campaign of 1781 in the Carolinas with Remarks Historical and Critical on Johnson's Life of Greene*. 1824. Reprint. Chicago: Quadrangle Books, 1962.
Royster, Charles. *Light-Horse Harry Lee and the Legacy of the American Revolution*. New York: Alfred A. Knopf, 1981.

PHILANDER D. CHASE

LEE, Robert Edward (b. Stratford, Westmoreland County, Va., January 19, 1807; d. Lexington, Va., October 12, 1870), Army officer. After serving for more than thirty years in the U.S. Army, Lee commanded the Army of Northern Virginia for the Confederacy during the Civil War.

Robert E. Lee was a man in search of place. He was born, in 1807, into a famous Virginia family. His father, Henry ("Light-Horse Harry") Lee,* a hero of the American Revolution, managed to fritter away both his reputation and the family fortune. This circumstance necessitated that Robert seek his education at West Point, where he was graduated in 1829, second in his class of forty-six. (The number one graduate, Charles Mason of New York, resigned from the Army two years later and did not serve in the Civil War.) In 1831 Lee married Mary Custis, the daughter of another distinguished Virginia family and heiress to "Arlington," a great estate in northern Virginia.

Lee, in keeping with his high rank in his graduating class, spent several years in the engineers. In 1847 he was assigned to the staff of General Winfield Scott* (at Scott's request) in Mexico. Lee did not command troops in Scott's campaign against Mexico City, but he distinguished himself for his military acumen, timely advice regarding terrain, and great personal bravery.

In 1852 Lee was named superintendent at West Point, an office that he distinguished. Lee stressed high academic standards, curriculum reform, and stringent military discipline. With all that, he was almost a father to the young men under his tutelage.

In 1855 Lee was posted as lieutenant colonel to Texas, to serve with the 2d Cavalry Regiment (commanded by Albert Sidney Johnston*). He remained with the 2d Cavalry until 1858 when he took an extended leave to "Arlington," which came under his care (but not ownership) upon the death of his father-in-law. In early 1860 he was dispatched to San Antonio to take command of the Department of Texas. It was the spiritual nadir for Lee, exacerbated by the absence from his family, his despair over his military career, and deep misgivings over the open talk of secession among Southern officers and politicians. Lee opposed disunion, regretted slavery, and wished to serve no flag other than the "Star Spangled Banner." (As if to demonstrate that fact, while on leave at "Arlington" Lee had led the soldiers and Marines who helped to quell John Brown's fanatical raid on Harper's Ferry in 1859.) Yet, as war approached, and in spite of the near-pleading General Scott, Lee resigned from the Army of the United States on April 20, 1861. He could not bring himself to lead that army against the South, and especially Virginia.

The first year of the Civil War was not auspicious for Lee, although he clearly was in the confidence of President Jefferson Davis.* Lee had his opportunity in the late spring of 1862 when he assumed command of the Army of Northern Virginia after Joseph Eggleston Johnston* (his classmate at West Point) was severely wounded at Seven Pines. Lee faced a formidable Union Army under George Brinton McClellan.* To submit to McClellan's siege tactics would, in Lee's mind, end in the capture of Richmond and, in any case, such was against his inclinations. He proposed to take the offensive, encouraged by the success of Thomas Jonathan ("Stonewall") Jackson* in the Shenandoah Valley and the apparent vulnerability of McClellan's right wing, practically isolated north of the Chickahominy River. Thus, on June 26, Lee launched his first campaign, a series of bloody, if inconclusive, battles called the Seven Days. His penchant for the attack emerged, as well as his propensity for holding only a slack rein on subordinates, and his reliance upon the frontal assault, which caused such carnage at Malvern Hill. He did force the intimidated McClellan to withdraw from in front of Richmond, however; this was no insignificant feat, even given McClellan's mishandling of his magnificent army.

In August Lee followed his success on the Peninsula with a strike against John Pope* at Manassas, where he thoroughly befuddled and thrashed that vainglorious incompetent. These victories encouraged Lee to invade Maryland, a decision of great military and political consequence. But he allowed his army to advance in dispersed order, and thus in mid-September, at Sharpsburg, Maryland (on Antietam Creek), with some twenty-five thousand men he faced a force three times that number under the resurrected McClellan. Discretion would have suggested retreat, but Lee stood. After a day's vicious fighting, marked by inept Union leadership and the providential arrival of Confederate reinforcements under Ambrose Powell Hill,* Lee managed to save his army. President Abraham Lincoln,* manifestly disappointed, replaced McClellan with Ambrose Everett Burnside,* who responded with the infamous attack against Lee at Fredericksburg, a fight that left Lee at a moral, if not military, advantage in Virginia.

Lee's next adversary was Joseph Hooker* who concentrated his reorganized army near Chancellorsville. Lee moved the bulk of his army to meet the threat (leaving ten thousand men under Jubal Anderson Early* to guard his rear at Fredericksburg). And at Chancellorsville he effected his greatest victory. Jackson's strike against Hooker's right and rear confused the Union forces and most assuredly demoralized their commander. When Lee turned back to confront John Sedgwick, who had broken through with his corps at Fredericksburg, Hooker remained in position, intimidated by Lee and confused even more by a near concussion from a Confederate shell. During the night of May 5–6, the Army of the Potomac retreated, beaten more by the character of the enemy army and its commander than by military circumstances. It was a brilliant victory for Lee, but costly in casualties and the great individual loss of Jackson, mortally wounded by his own men.

Lee now proposed a more ambitious move, this time into Pennsylvania. An invasion of the North would free Virginia from the immediate threat of the still powerful Union Army and would give Lee access to sorely needed supplies. Moreover, he believed that a battle won on Northern soil would be of considerable political effect. Thus Gettysburg.

The Gettysburg Campaign was not Lee's finest. He did not use his cavalry to best advantage; James Ewell Brown Stuart* blazed his own trail northward, Lee could not know the precise disposition of the Union forces, even after the first contact west of Gettysburg. When Richard Stoddert Ewell* (Jackson's replacement) did not press his apparent advantage on July 1, it was at least partly because Lee had not issued precise orders to him. The inconclusive second day was the responsibility of James Longstreet,* obstinate to the point of insubordination, but also the responsibility of Lee who could not bring himself to press his senior corps commander. The failure of the infamous assault on July 3 (the so-called Pickett's charge, led by George Edward Pickett*) was, as Lee said, his fault. Perhaps it was Malvern Hill revisited; he did not know what else to do. He did once again rescue his army, aided by the inactivity of his opponent, George Gordon Meade,* who appeared to be stymied and did not or could not follow up his advantage after July 3.

The Virginia campaigns of 1864–1865 are often personalized as a duel between Lee and Ulysses Simpson Grant,* with Grant inexorably wearing down the outmanned Lee until the final meeting at Appomattox Court House. Grant made

Lee's army the focus of his campaign, to hold Lee while William Tecumseh Sherman* effected his advance into Georgia. Lee anticipated this tactic and urged a concentration, one that would strengthen him and allow him to make even better use of his geographical ally, the area of trees, briers, and ravines called the Wilderness. The first battles, in early May, had the effect of "fixing" Lee, that is, Grant had made his contact with the Army of Northern Virginia and would not let go. From the Wilderness until the end of the war, Lee was, practically speaking, on the defensive. His often brilliant defensive tactics severely bloodied the enemy, but he lost in terms of men and initiative. Even the old ploy of a threat on Washington failed. When Jubal Early approached the capital in June, Grant had already resolved to move on Petersburg. Lee seemed almost bemused. Perhaps, as J.F.C. Fuller has noted, he may have doubted that Grant was capable of such imagination. Lee could only consolidate at Petersburg and absorb punishment until his army was worn away by casualties and, increasingly, desertions.

In assessing Robert E. Lee, the temptation is to distinguish between the man and the general, a division that is basically artificial and unhistorical. Lee, the man, was by all accounts an admirable figure, possessed of all the virtues of Southern manhood and few of the faults. Some of his virtues—a certain forbearance, even diffidence—led him to slight his duty as a military advisor to his president and on occasion to fail to impress upon his subordinates the need for forceful, coherent action. His undeniable personal courage and devotion to duty led him to expect the same of others; similarly, his devotion to Virginia, the land and the idea, led him to demand much of his soldiers, even when such entailed sacrifices greater than his. His penchant for the audacious offensive made him almost reckless of the cost of lives. Perhaps his early successes, through Chancellorsville, reinforced his low regard for his opponents, "those people" as he patronizingly referred to them. He adopted Winfield Scott's policy of planning the general operation and then leaving the execution to his corps commanders, a failing, if it was such, shared by many generals of the war. As long as he could depend on Stonewall Jackson, his lack of exact orders seemed to make little difference. With Jackson gone, and less bold or less understanding commanders leading his corps, the absence of more precise directives made a considerable difference. Lee knew the efficacy of flanking maneuvers in terms of casualties avoided and strong positions rendered untenable; yet on two notable occasions he ordered assaults on fixed artillery and with disastrous results.

Occasionally, sometimes because of ill-health (as at North Anna), Lee seemed almost bemused, possessed by inertia, when plans did not materialize. Or he attacked, with elan and imagination at Chancellorsville, with a certain fatalism at Gettysburg. His intellect was a curious blend of intuition and reason, vagueness and precision. He appeared to understand the strategic importance of the middle South, yet preoccupied himself with Virginia. That he seldom brought his keen intelligence and imposing personality to bear on broad questions of strategy remains an enigma, unless one accepts his natural preoccupation with his native state, his place.

Lee emerged from the war as the most admired general even after close analysis suggests that others may have been his superior, Grant and Sherman in particular. The profound graciousness of Lee during the negotiations at Appomattox, his heart-rending farewell to his soldiers, and his restrained and decorous postwar career as president of Washington College (renamed Washington and Lee University in 1871) added to his host of admirers and confirmed for them that their admiration was deserved. But the manner in which Lee accepted defeat obscures the extent to which he contributed to that defeat, and that of the commanders of the Civil War; his army absorbed casualties beyond those incurred by his major opponents. The adulation accorded him by his advocates, by fellow officers and historians, remains a monument to the Lee mystique.

BIBLIOGRAPHY

Connelly, Thomas L. *The Marble Man: Robert E. Lee and His Image in American Society.* New York: Alfred A. Knopf, 1977.
Freeman, Douglas Southall. *R. E. Lee: A Biography.* 4 vols. New York: Charles Scribner's Sons, 1936.
Fuller, J.F.C. *Grant and Lee: A Study in Personality and Generalship.* London: Eyre and Spottiswoode, 1933.

JOHN T. HUBBELL

LEE, Samuel Phillips (b. at Sully, Fairfax County, Va., February 13, 1812; d. Silver Spring, Md., June 5, 1897), naval officer. Lee served as commander of the Union's North Atlantic Blockading Squadron for two years during the Civil War.

S. Phillips Lee, born into the sixth generation of one of the oldest and most distinguished families of Virginia, was the eldest son of Francis Lightfoot Lee II and Jane Fitzgerald, daughter of Colonel John Fitzgerald, aide to George Washington* during the Revolution. His paternal grandfather was Richard Henry Lee, signer of the Declaration of July 4, 1776. His atypical (for a Lee) Christian name came from the New England schoolmaster, Samuel Phillips, the founder of Phillips Academy, Andover, Massachusetts, under whom Francis Lightfoot studied in preparation for Harvard.

Orphaned by the death of their mother in 1816 (a tragedy that drove their father into profound melancholy from which he never recovered), young Phillips and his four siblings became the responsibilities of a court-appointed committee. A series of New England tutors provided him with a solid basic education at Sully. In part because of happy associations between John Adams and Richard Henry Lee, President John Quincy Adams gave young Lee an acting midshipman's warrant in November 1825, five months after his third cousin, Robert Edward Lee,* began his military career at the U.S. Military Academy.

Phillips Lee's active naval career began in early 1827, a month before his fifteenth birthday, with orders to Norfolk. His early training in seamanship and navigation followed the old-time pattern, at sea in a series of vessels: in the sloop *Hornet* on the West India Station, and in the frigates *Delaware* and *Java* in the Mediterranean Squadron. Returning home in September 1830, Lee attended the Norfolk naval school before becoming a passed midshipman the following June. He first distinguished himself as sailing master of the frigate *Brandywine* when, in September 1834, her rudder carried away off Cape Horn. His prompt actions saved the ship. He transferred to the sloop *Vincennes*, Captain John H. Aulick, as her sailing master; Commodore Alexander Wadsworth, commanding U.S. naval forces in the Pacific, promoted him to acting lieutenant in the *Vincennes*, at Aulick's recommendation. Lee served in that capacity for the balance of her cruise around the world, reaching Norfolk in June 1836. He was promoted to lieutenant early the next year, three days before his twenty-fifth birthday.

Lee's next sea duty nearly crippled his naval career: he shipped aboard the sloop *Peacock* in the Exploring Expedition commanded by Charles Wilkes* in 1838. Thanks to a series of bitter disagreements between the two, Wilkes relieved Lee in February 1839 and ordered him home. This might have remained a permanent blot on his record, if Wilkes' conduct of the expedition had not come under severe criticism; Wilkes was even tried by court-martial and publicly reprimanded. More important, for Lee's personal happiness, the young lieutenant reached home in the late summer of 1839 to meet and fall in love with Elizabeth, only daughter of the great Jacksonian editor, Francis Preston Blair. After a tormented courtship (the Blairs opposed the union because they thought Lee a fortune-hunting sailor), the couple married on April 27, 1843. This was a felicitous union which, besides the shared joys of a satisfying marriage, provided the young officer with powerful political connections (not always an entirely unmixed blessing).

After duty aboard another *Hornet* in the West Indies Squadron, out of Pensacola, Lee in 1842 joined the Coast Survey, getting his first command, the surveying schooner *Vanderbilt*, off Newport in 1844. After a year of naval duty at Pensacola, Lee began eight years of Coast Survey activity, surveying, *inter alia*, both Chesapeake and Delaware Bays. Given command of the brig *Washington* in late 1846, Lee supervised her refitting at the Philadelphia Navy Yard and took her to join the Home Squadron under Commodores David Conner* and Matthew Calbraith Perry* off Mexico in the summer of 1847. After participating in the second Tobasco Expedition, Lee returned to Coast Survey duty, which he "considered one of the best schools of Naval practice." In 1851 his performance record on the Survey won him command of the brig *Dolphin* on special service making deep-sea soundings in the Atlantic. The U.S. Senate published his *Cruise of the Dolphin* in 1854, which helped toward his promotion to commander in 1855.

Continued hydrographic duty and work on wind and current charts kept him in Washington and at the Naval Observatory until late 1860 when Secretary of the Navy Isaac Toucey gave him command of the sloop *Vandalia* with orders to the East Indies. Lee took her out of New York in December, but at Capetown, where he learned of the outbreak of war, he turned her around and came home, disregarding his orders. He found immediate employment on blockade and took a prize or two before transfer to a new steam sloop, *Oneida*, building in New York in early 1862.

Lee and *Oneida* joined Flag Officer David Glasgow Farragut* in the Mississippi, to play dangerous and significant roles in passing the forts below New Orleans. In *Oneida*, Lee sank one Confederate vessel and saved the crew of a sister ship, *Varuna*, aground and afire. After the fall of New Orleans, Farragut sent Lee upriver with inadequate ground forces under General Thomas Williams. Lee took his squadron all the way to Vicksburg, after raising the Union flag at Baton Rouge and Natchez. Although Lee succeeded in running the Vicksburg batteries, in mid-July the Union forces abandoned efforts to take the Rebel stronghold. At that moment, orders came from Washington directing Lee to report to the Navy Department for a new assignment.

On September 2, 1862, Lee took command of the North Atlantic Blockading Squadron with the rank of acting rear admiral. In that capacity he served the Union well for two years until he was transferred to command the Mississippi Squadron. President Abraham Lincoln* had, in early 1863, promoted him to captain, to date from July 16, 1862. On the Western waters, Lee worked closely with Major General George Henry Thomas* in the Nashville Campaign and was partially successful in efforts to cut off defeated Confederate forces under John Bell Hood.* Lee's ironclads operated as far up the Tennessee as Muscle Shoals, destroying "all visible means of crossing." In the closing months of the war Lee attempted to curb Rebel activities along the multiple rivers of his extensive command. Finally, he had the exacting task of breaking up the Mississippi Squadron at war's end, discharging the crews, and selling off the ships. His long war ended in mid-August 1865.

He had served with distinction on every assignment, in the *Vandalia* on blockade, in the *Oneida* at New Orleans, and in the first Union attacks on Vicksburg, for two long years on blockade and lending close gunboat support to Union armies in North Carolina and Virginia, and in the exhausting business of patrolling the rivers of the West. A short year after the war ended, President Andrew Johnson belatedly promoted Lee to commodore. President Ulysses Simpson Grant* made him a rear admiral in April 1870.

Lee's postwar naval service involved him in a variety of examining boards— of volunteer officers desiring Regular Navy assignment and of the Atlantic coast naval yards, for which he wrote a report in 1869. Besides occasional court-martial duty and a stint as chief of the Signal Service, he had one last sea command: the North Atlantic Squadron until detachment in the late summer of 1872. He retired from the Navy on his sixty-first birthday, February 13, 1873.

During those two years in command of the North Atlantic Blockading Squadron, Lee quite literally put the union blockade on a paying basis, as the steadily lengthening list of prizes taken and ships destroyed attests. His personal rewards were appropriately great: he brought home from the war the biggest sea-bag of prize money in U.S. naval history—which occasioned considerable professional jealousy among his comrades, as well as political animosity among opponents of the Blair family, who were active but conservative supporters of President Lincoln. In the eyes of some Radicals, Phillips Lee was "Old Man Blair's third son," and his removal from blockade command followed hard on the heels of his brother Montgomery Blair's departure from the Post Office Department. Far more significant is the fact that Lee's reorganization of his section of the blockade into three parallel "girdles" of cruisers became the model for other Union squadrons on blockade in the war's last years.

After retirement, Lee undertook management of his father-in-law's farm, "Silver Spring," in Montgomery County, Maryland. After forty-six years in the Navy, he ran the Blair farm as if it had been a ship, even to maintaining a daily log of its operations, from 1873 until his death in 1897.

Rear Admiral S. Phillips Lee earned the epitaph cut on his modest stone in Arlington: "Devoted to duty and just in command." He deserves far more from history than he has so far received.

BIBLIOGRAPHY

Anderson, Bern. *By Sea and by River: The Naval History of the Civil War*. New York: Alfred A. Knopf, 1962.

Jones, Virgil C. *The Civil War at Sea*. 3 vols. New York: Holt, Rinehart, and Winston, 1960–1962.

Reed, Rowena. *Combined Operations in the Civil War*. Annapolis, Md.: Naval Institute Press, 1978.

DUDLEY T. CORNISH

LEE, Stephen Dill (b. Charleston, S.C., September 22, 1833; d. Vicksburg, Miss., May 28, 1908), Army officer. Lee is considered one of the best artillery officers of the Civil War.

Stephen D. Lee was born into a socially prominent Carolina family with strong martial and patriotic attitudes. It was distantly related to the Lees of Virginia, which Stephen considered "quite an honor." He received little formal education during his early years. At the age of eleven he went to a boarding school run by his namesake uncle who previously had been a professional soldier. Lee subsequently secured an appointment to the U.S. Military Academy at West Point, from which he was graduated in 1854, seventeenth in a class of thirty-six.

Thereafter he served, until 1861, with the 4th Artillery, rising to first lieutenant. In Florida during the Third Seminole War (1856–1857), he saw limited action, serving primarily as a staff officer. He acquired a reputation as an organizer, a logistician, a trainer; he was marked as a good disciplinarian, a methodical and quiet man who could elicit confidence and cooperation, but whose retiring personality might somewhat limit his ability to command—a supposition that proved quite false.

In February 1861 Stephen Lee resigned his lieutenant's commission in the U.S. Army and took a commission as captain with South Carolina volunteers. He served for a time as aide de camp to General Pierre Gustave Toutant Beauregard* at Charleston when Southerners shelled Fort Sumter. Subsequently, Lee's principal achievements in battle occurred at Second Bull Run, Chickasaw Bayou, and Nashville.

At Second Bull Run (August 1862), Lee had command of the artillery in the corps commanded by General James B. Longstreet.* The Confederates occupied a line that formed a sharp angle, with Lee's artillery toward the center, about at the vortex, where the guns stood on a commanding ridge, just over a quarter of a mile in length. Lee's gunners delivered so effective an enfilade fire that they halted a massive Union charge and allowed the Confederates to launch a punishing counterattack. The episode is one of the most important in the history of muzzle-loading artillery.

Transferred to the West, Lee saw his next major action in the vicinity of Vicksburg, at Chickasaw Bayou, Mississippi (December 1862). Lee defended Vicksburg initially with twenty-seven hundred men against thirty thousand troops under General William Tecumseh Sherman.* Reinforcements arrived piecemeal during the campaign and brought Lee's forces up to ten thousand. Sherman unleashed a desperate assault. Lee's careful planning and exploitation of terrain advantages produced a "funnel effect," forcing the Federals into an ever smaller area, where they took heavy fire from the well-entrenched Southerners. Vanquished, Sherman's army lost 1,776 to Lee's 207. One of the stunned Federal brigade commanders thought that Chickasaw Bayou was "a repetition of Balaklava."

At the Battle of Nashville (December 1864), Lee's corps stood out as by far the best in the Confederate Army led by General John Bell Hood.* Lee's corps held firm the longest against an inexorable onslaught by Federal forces under General George Henry Thomas.* After the situation became untenable, Lee and his corps provided the only security behind which Hood's routed units could find any protection. Lee sustained a wound but continued to lead his men as they conducted a critical holding action on the Franklin Pike and made it possible for the other Confederate corps to slip to the rear.

After the war ended Lee engaged in many activities aimed at rebuilding Mississippi, thereby becoming, along with John Brown Gordon,* one of the most important leaders of the New South. Lee served in the Mississippi state legislature for one term and was appointed president of Mississippi Agricultural and Mechanical College. Furthermore, Lee helped to establish the Vicksburg National Military Park and led the United Confederate Veterans from 1904 until his death in 1908.

Entering Confederate service as a captain, Stephen Dill Lee rose to lieutenant general by the age of thirty, one of the youngest officers to hold that rank. Moreover, he had to earn every single promotion, not skipping any ranks. He did not attain independent command until 1863, by which time he had fought in both the East and West, including the Seven Days' battles around Richmond, Antietam, and the siege at Vicksburg. Made a prisoner when Vicksburg fell to Ulysses Simpson Grant,* Lee was soon exchanged. Already recognized as an outstanding artillery officer, he took command of Confederate cavalry in Mississippi (August 1863). Subsequently, he fought in engagements around Atlanta and then took over Hood's old infantry corps in the abortive campaign against Nashville. Thus, Lee commanded units of artillery, cavalry, and infantry, and served in both major theaters during the war. He surrendered with General Joseph Eggleston Johnston* in North Carolina.

Lee's contemporaries and Civil War historians have given him high praise. President Jefferson Davis* called Lee ''one of the best all-around soldiers which the war produced.'' Sherman pronounced Lee ''the most enterprising in all of their army.'' In his magisterial *War for the Union*, Allan Nevins called him ''an able chief of artillery.'' In his classic reference work *Generals in Gray*, Ezra Warner observed that Lee's wide and varied experience made him ''one of the most capable corps commanders in the army.'' Stanley Horn concluded that ''he was a first-rate officer.''

Returning to Mississippi, Lee had a long and productive postwar career. Briefly a planter, an insurance executive, and a state legislator, he then settled in as the first president of the state's Agricultural and Mechanical College (later renamed Mississippi State University), which he served commendably for nineteen years. He preached diversification in farming, scientific agricultural techniques, and industrial and mechanical innovations. Admirers bestowed upon him the title of father of industrial education in the South.

Lee's work, as a commission member, in behalf of the Vicksburg National Military Park became a consuming labor of love. He wrote thousands of letters on park business, spend hundreds of hours working on the site, and helped to build a lasting and impressive memorial to the epic struggle for control of the Mississippi River.

Lee also engaged in significant activities with the United Confederate Veterans. A man of complex loyalties and sentiments, he ever revered what he had fought for and yet reconfirmed his attachment for the Union. He helped to build the Southern veterans' organization into one of considerable social potency and longevity. Furthermore, under Lee's guidance, the organization was an effective vehicle for asserting the symbolism of the Lost Cause.

BIBLIOGRAPHY

Bearss, Edwin C. *Decision in Mississippi*. Jackson, Miss.: Mississippi Commission on the War between the States, 1962.
Bettersworth, John K. *People's College: A History of Mississippi State*. Baton Rouge: Louisiana State University Press, 1953.
Hattaway, Herman. *General Stephen Lee*. Jackson: University Press of Mississippi, 1976.

Horn, Stanley. *The Decisive Battle of Nashville*. Baton Rouge: Louisiana State University Press, 1956.

Swanberg, W. A. *First Blood: The Story of Fort Sumter*. New York: Charles Scribner's, 1957.

HERMAN HATTAWAY

LEISLER, Jacob (b. Frankfurt, Germany, 1640; d. New York City, N.Y., May 16, 1691), colonial militia captain. Leisler became acting governor of colonial New York during the political confusion of the Glorious Revolution and led a revolutionary administration ("Leisler's Rebellion") for almost two years.

The son of a Palatine clergyman, Jacob Leisler was a poor soldier employed by the Dutch West India Company when he immigrated to New Amsterdam in 1660. He quickly improved his sagging fortunes by marrying a rich merchant's widow and prospered under English rule. Although many of his wife's relatives were prominent members of New York aristocracy, Leisler remained socially unacceptable. Later, the influential Dutch and English elite would vigorously oppose the democratic tendencies of his brief "rebellious" administration.

As a prosperous merchant, Leisler held a variety of official, if not influential, colonial posts. He was a captain in the militia when he suddenly emerged from obscurity to prominence and power. Leisler's opportunity arrived in early 1689 when the political and religious turmoil of England's Glorious Revolution spilled across the Atlantic. The triumph of the new Protestant monarchs, William and Mary, inspired New Yorkers to rise against the Catholic-influenced Dominion government established by the ousted James II. Lieutenant Governor Francis Nicholson fled to England in the face of domestic disturbances and left behind a political vacuum.

Previously on the periphery of power, Leisler quickly took advantage of the political uncertainty in New York City. Commissioned "captain of the fort" on June 8, 1689, he gained a following particularly among the primarily Dutch populace and took the lead in restoring order. Uncertain of his legal position, Leisler gathered delegates who were generally representative of the towns and encouraged them to form a committee of public safety with himself as head. In December documents granting authority to rule in the name of William and Mary arrived. Although these documents were intended for the departed Nicholson, Leisler interpreted them as the legitimate basis for his regime.

Although popular at first, Leisler gradually dissipated the good-will toward his rule by antagonizing his supporters by his increasingly despotic actions. He imposed heavy taxes, exerted pressure for military recruitment, and reacted harshly against dissenters. As opposition to his rule became more vocal, Leisler became more unreasonable in his response. He jailed those who actively opposed him and intimidated others with his increasingly arbitrary rule by force. The basis of his power rested with the militia, and he sought military success to solidify his position.

Leisler's opportunity came with renewed conflict involving French Canada. Paralleling the outbreak of hostilities in Europe, English-French clashes in the New World began in early 1690. Violently against "papists" of any nationality, Leisler was impatient to strike at the heart of French power to the north. The French raid on Schenectady provided the governor his opportunity to consolidate his political position by initiating the move against New France.

Leisler called an intercolonial conference to convene at New York City on May 1, 1690. Only four colonies accepted the invitation, even though colonies as far south as Maryland were invited. Nevertheless, Leisler prodded the delegates to pledge over 350 soldiers to mount a coordinated, two-pronged attack: over land to Montreal and over water to Quebec. In cooperation with one thousand Iroquois Indians, a force would advance on Montreal while a New England fleet would envelop Quebec by way of the St. Lawrence River. The simultaneous assault was designed to surprise the French and stretch their limited defenses to the breaking point.

Leisler desired to lead the attack on Montreal himself; however, his political position was so tenuous that he dared not leave New York City. He also failed to have his son-in-law, Jacob Milborne, appointed commander and yielded to New England's wish to have Connecticut's Fitz-John Winthrop* lead the expedition. As a result, Leisler's personal influence on the actual conduct of the campaign was minimal. Nevertheless, in a practical sense he staked his reputation on the success of the attack.

Unfortunately for Leisler, the campaign was a disaster. Plagued by poor leadership, disease, supply problems, and just plain bad luck, Winthrop's army never reached the St. Lawrence River. Only seventy Iroquois materialized to support the campaign, and the thirty-two vessel fleet of Sir William Phips* was late sailing from Boston and stalled in front of Quebec. Instead of enjoying the unity of victory, the colonists engaged in an aftermath of bitter recriminations.

The military failure further isolated Leisler and forced him into increasingly repressive military rule to retain power. His aristocratic enemies had been in contact with London urging the early appointment of a new royal governor. Finally, their efforts were rewarded. Major Richard Ingoldesby arrived before the new governor with regular troops in January 1691 and immediately came in conflict with Leisler. Skirmishes occurred, and New York verged on civil war by the time the governor, Henry Sloughter, arrived on March 19. Sloughter was forced to make three requests before Leisler surrendered the fort where he had been besieged by Ingoldesby.

Sloughter arrested Leisler and his aides and charged them with treason. Leisler and Milborne were quickly convicted by a jury packed with their enemies and were executed on May 16. The social and political passions which Leisler evoked, however, took many years to cool. Not even Leisler's formal exoneration several years later was sufficient to calm the turbulent waters stirred up by "Leisler's Rebellion."

The turbulent nature of Leisler's governorship and his abrupt execution should not obscure his positive leadership and strategic vision. He was courageous, he worked hard to provide order to a factionalized colony, he influenced men with his forceful personality, and he displayed remarkable strategic vision. His grasp of what it would require to defeat New France was readily apparent. Leisler's initiative and forceful personality were instrumental in the degree of intercolonial cooperation displayed during the conference of 1690. Leisler's plan involving a pincer operation against Canada established the pattern for later English attacks, culminating with the final French defeat during the French and Indian War.

It is more difficult to assess Leisler's responsibility for the campaign's actual failure. His faith in Jacob Milborne appeared to be misplaced as Milborne was chiefly responsible for the supply problem. However, Leisler cannot be blamed for the disease, lack of Indian support, and hesitant leadership that doomed the expedition. In retrospect, it must be remembered that intercolonial cooperation was a rarity until the Revolutionary War and that Leisler's attempt succeeded remarkably well up to the point of his plan's execution.

Leisler's primary shortcoming was not in his military ability but rather in his political acumen. He early personified the general difficulty that American military figures have experienced when they enter the political arena. The highly factionalized and changeable nature of American society has not responded well to the military man's passion for order and discipline. Leisler's demise can be directly attributed to his failure to recognize the severe limitations on his political actions and to modify his policies accordingly.

BIBLIOGRAPHY

Andrews, Charles M. *The Colonial Period of American History: The Settlements.* New Haven, Conn.: Yale University Press, 1937.
Kammen, Michael. *Colonial New York: A History.* New York: Charles Scribner's Sons, 1975.
Leach, Douglas Edward. *Arms for Empire: A Military History of the British Colonies in North America, 1607–1763.* New York: Macmillan Company, 1973.
Lovejoy, David S. *The Glorious Revolution in America.* New York: Harper and Row, 1972.
Peckham, Howard H. *The Colonial Wars: 1689–1762.* Chicago: University of Chicago Press, 1964.
Reich, Jerome R. *Leisler's Rebellion.* Chicago: University of Chicago Press, 1953.
Rothbard, Murray N. *Conceived in Liberty: A New Land, A New People.* New Rochelle, N.Y.: Arlington House, 1975.

ROGER B. FOSDICK

LEJEUNE, John Archer (b. "Old Hickory" Plantation, Raccourci District, Pointe Coupee Parish, La., January 10, 1867; d. Baltimore, Md., November 20, 1942), Marine Corps officer. Lejeune was commandant of the Corps (1920– 1929) and supervised its modernization.

John Archer Lejeune was the younger of the two children of Ovide and Laura

Archer Turpin Lejeune and grew up in genteel poverty in Reconstruction Louisiana. His father, of Acadian stock and a Confederate officer, had lost all of
his extensive landholdings immediately after the Civil War. Through hard work,
the elder Lejeune bought back his original plantation but was able to retain only
seventy-five acres. John received his primary education from his mother at home.
At age thirteen, Lejeune left Louisiana and attended for a year a boarding school
run by his uncle James Archer near Natchez, Mississippi.

Influenced at a young age by the martial exploits of his father and his own
reading, in September 1881 the young Lejeune entered Louisiana State University
(LSU), which at the time was a combination of military preparatory school and
college. Although he wanted to go to West Point, Lejeune remained at LSU
until 1884, when he accepted an appointment to the Naval Academy, the only
vacancy at a service school open to him. He completed his class work at the
Academy in 1888, becoming a passed midshipman, and shipped on board the
ill-fated cruiser *Vandalia*, which sank off Apia in Samoa during a hurricane in
1889. Surviving the sinking, Lejeune returned to Annapolis in 1890 to take his
final examinations. Ranking sixth in a class of thirty-seven, Lejeune elected to
enter the Marine Corps. He later explained that he arrived at his choice through
a process of elimination; he did not want to be an engineer, and he did not want
to spend the greater part of his life at sea.

In October 1890 Lejeune began his first duty assignment at the Marine Barracks
at Norfolk, Virginia, where he served for a year. Lejeune next was assigned to
the Marine guard in the cruiser *Bennington*. Shortly after Lejeune's arrival, the
Bennington steamed for South American waters to rendezvous with the American
fleet awaiting developments in the crisis with Chile. Once the war scare with
Chile was resolved diplomatically, the *Bennington* departed for Europe. Lejeune
returned to the United States in 1893 and was once more assigned to the Norfolk
Barracks, remaining there for the next four years. In October 1895 he married
Ellie Harrison Murdaugh, a daughter of a local judge. In 1897 Lejeune assumed
command of the Marine guard in the cruiser *Cincinnati*. With the outbreak of
the Spanish-American War in April 1898, the *Cincinnati* participated in the
blockade of Cuba but saw relatively little action.

Following the war and the expanding American responsibilities in the Caribbean and the Pacific, Congress in March 1899 authorized a Marine Corps of
more than six thousand men, nearly double its prewar strength. After several
years of stagnation, the officer corps expanded and promotions, based on seniority, were relatively rapid. A first lieutenant since 1892, Lejeune became a
captain in 1899 and a major in 1903. During this period, Lejeune commanded
the Marine guard in the battleship *Massachusetts* (1899–1900), served as the
recruiting officer in Boston and New York, and commanded the Marine Barracks
at Pensacola, Florida.

In the summer of 1903 Lejeune assumed command of the Marine "floating"
battalion, which was eventually put aboard the transport *Dixie*. Formed to seize
and defend advance bases in support of the fleet, a mission given to the Marine

Corps by the Navy General Board in 1900, the battalion was an early precursor of the modern Marine battalion landing team. While at sea in November, the *Dixie* received orders to land Lejeune's battalion in Panama, which had declared its independence from Colombia. President Theodore Roosevelt,* whose canal treaty had been rejected by the Colombian Senate, seized the opportunity to recognize the new Panamanian government and landed the American Marines to prevent the Colombians from putting down the revolution. Lejeune's battalion remained on the Isthmus until December 1904, when it was relieved by another battalion.

Lejeune commanded the Marine Barracks in Washington (1905–1907) and then joined the Marine brigade in the Philippines, which at the time was considered the Marine Pacific Advance Base Force. Upon his arrival, Lejeune took charge of the Marine Barracks at Cavite and later assumed command of the brigade. During the Japanese war scare in the summer of 1907, the Marines in the Philippines received orders to defend Subic Bay and fortify Grande Island which guarded the entrance to the bay. Although the crisis ended quickly, the exercise provided the Marines with valuable experience in the advance base mission. Returning from the Philippines as a lieutenant colonel in the summer of 1909, Lejeune became the first Marine officer to attend the Army War College (1909–1910), where he received his first formal education since leaving the Naval Academy. After leaving the War College, Lejeune received the coveted post of commander of the Marine Barracks in the New York Navy Yard (1910–1913).

In November 1913 Lejeune assumed command of the Mobile Regiment of the newly formed Advanced Base Brigade which was completing its plans for participation in the Atlantic Fleet's winter maneuvers. In January 1914 the brigade landed on the small Caribbean island of Culebra and repulsed a mock attack by an "enemy" landing force. Following the maneuver, Lejeune, recently promoted to colonel, received command of the brigade since its former commander, George Barnett,* had become major general commandant of the Marine Corps. Shortly afterward, Lejeune and the brigade landed at Vera Cruz in April 1914, as a result of the Tampico affair which had exacerbated American relations with the Huerta regime in Mexico. Reinforced by other units, Lejeune relinquished command of the brigade to a more senior colonel and reassumed command of his old regiment.

After his departure with the Marine forces from Mexico in December 1914, Lejeune's next assignment was in Washington as assistant to the commandant, in effect the headquarters chief of staff. During this eventful period (1915–1917), the Marine Corps became involved in both Haiti and the Dominican Republic and began planning for expansion as a result of the outbreak of war in Europe and the growing preparedness movement in the United States. In 1915 and 1916, Lejeune was a member of a personnel board headed by the assistant secretary of the Navy, Franklin D. Roosevelt. The recommendations of this board provided much of the basis for provisions of the Navy Act of 1916 which increased the

Marine Corps by five thousand men to a peacetime strength of nearly fifteen thousand men and created six Marine brigadier general slots. Lejeune became a brigadier general in January 1917. Following the U.S. entry into World War I in April 1917, a Marine regiment departed for France in May.

In September Lejeune took command of the Marine base at Quantico, Virginia, which had become the Marine Corps overseas training and staging center, and in May 1918 he departed for France. Although General John Joseph Pershing* rejected his plea for a Marine division in the American Expeditionary Force, Lejeune received command in June of the Army's 64th Brigade. In July Lejeune became the commanding general of the 2d Division, the first Marine officer to command an Army division. Under Lejeune, now a major general, the 2d Division, which included the Marine 4th Brigade as well as Army units, won a series of victories in the late summer and fall of 1918 including the battle of St. Mihiel, Blanc Mont Ridge, and the Meuse-Argonne. Following the Armistice in November, the 2d Division occupied the Coblenz sector of Germany east of the Rhine River. After his return from Europe with the 2d Division in August 1919, Lejeune again took over the Quantico base.

In June 1920 Secretary of the Navy Josephus Daniels,* in a controversial move, asked for the resignation of Major General Commandant George Barnett and selected Lejeune to fill the position. Lejeune served as commandant from 1920 to 1929, under three presidents (Woodrow Wilson, Warren Harding, and Calvin Coolidge). Lejeune voluntarily stepped down from the commandancy in 1929 and retired from the Marine Corps on November 12, 1929.

Upon his retirement, Lejeune assumed the superintendency of the Virginia Military Institute. He retired from his second career in 1937 at the age of seventy. He was promoted to lieutenant general in February 1942, under the provisions of new legislation, but he died of cancer in November of the same year in Baltimore. The large Marine base on the eastern coast in North Carolina, Camp Lejeune, was named after the general.

Lejeune was one of the architects of the modern Marine Corps. Although he attained national prominence as a wartime division commander in a land war in Europe, throughout his career Lejeune insisted on the Marine Corps' close relationship to the Navy. He saw the mission of the Marine Corps "to provide the Navy with an efficient expeditionary force habituated to ship life, accustomed to being governed by Navy laws, and regulations, and officered by a personnel whose members have been closely associated with the officers of the Navy officially and unofficially throughout their naval careers."

During the first decades of the twentieth century, Lejeune was closely associated with the Marine Corps Advance Base Force. Although the Advance Base Force was largely defensive, it was the predecessor of the modern Marine Expeditionary and Fleet Marine Force. As early as 1915, Lejeune defined the advance base mission in both defensive and offensive terms. In a presentation at the advance base school, he made the distinction between the Marine role in a war with a naval power and in a war with a land power. In a war with a naval power, the mission of the Marines would be traditional: to seize and defend a base for the fleet while awaiting the decisive naval engagement which would determine the course of the war. In a war with a nonnaval power, on the other hand, Lejeune foresaw a more aggressive role for the Marine Corps. He wrote: "Our duties if organized into regiments and brigades, would be that of the advance guard of an Army. The Marine Corps would be first to set foot on hostile soil in order to seize, fortify, and hold a port from which, as a base, the Army would prosecute its campaign."

Despite the above lecture, in which Lejeune acknowledged his debt to Marine Captain Earl H. Ellis,* Lejeune's strengths lay as a field commander and an administrator rather than as a military theorist. At Vera Cruz and especially in France, Lejeune proved to be an effective combat leader. As assistant to the commandant from 1915–1917, Lejeune pushed for congressional legislation to increase the size of the Corps and organized an informal staff at Headquarters, Marine Corps, that completed much of the prewar planning for the expansion of the Corps.

It was as commandant of the Marine Corps from 1920 to 1929 that Lejeune made his greatest contribution. His political adeptness permitted the Marines to maintain both a stable strength (approximately twenty-one thousand) and their share of the military budget during a period of retrenchments and cutbacks. Based on his association with the Army War College and his experience in France, Lejeune introduced several reforms. He instituted a modern staff system at headquarters, established the Marine Corps Schools (which provided a general program of officer education, extending from young lieutenants to senior field officers), and made Marine aviation an integral part of the Corps' organization. Despite the commitment of the Corps during his commandancy to various missions, from guarding the mails to intervening in Caribbean republics and China, Lejeune maintained the integrity of the Marine Expeditionary Force, which held landing maneuvers with the Fleet. Marine headquarters prepared various war plans, including the Ellis Micronesia plan which foreshadowed the Marine Central Pacific Campaign against Japan.

Lejeune prepared the pathway for the development of modern amphibious doctrine which took place at the Marine Corps Schools in the 1930s and came to fruition in the Pacific during World War II.

BIBLIOGRAPHY

Heinl, Robert D., Jr. *Soldiers of the Sea*. Annapolis, Md.: Naval Institute Press, 1962.
Lejeune, John A. *The Reminiscences of a Marine*. Philadelphia: Dorrance and Company, 1930.
Lewis, Charles L. *Famous American Marines*. Boston: L. C. Page and Company, 1950.

Millett, Allan R. *Semper Fidelis: The History of the U.S. Marine Corps*. New York: Free Press, 1980.

Simmons, Edwin H. *The United States Marines 1775–1975*. New York: Viking Press, 1976.

                                                        JACK SHULIMSON

LEMAY, Curtis Emerson (b. Columbus, Ohio, November 15, 1906), Air Force combat commander and chief of staff. LeMay is considered the architect of the Air Force's Strategic Air Command.

Curtis LeMay entered World War II as a promising young major with special knowledge in aerial navigation and bombardment. He emerged from that conflict as a highly successful combat commander and major general. General Carl A. Spaatz,* first Air Force chief of staff, described LeMay as the greatest air combat commander of the war. Often blunt in his manner, LeMay based his success on innovation, ability to lead men, and perseverance which he learned in his youth.

Curtis LeMay was born in Columbus, Ohio, the eldest child of Erving LeMay and Arizona Carpenter, descendants of Ohio farm families. The family moved frequently as LeMay's father worked on various railroad and construction jobs. After living in Pennsylvania, Montana, and California, young Curtis returned to Ohio, graduated from high school in Columbus, and began working his way through Ohio State University. He studied civil engineering and completed his Reserve Officers Training Corps (ROTC) training as an honor graduate. LeMay left college early, however, and joined the National Guard in order to secure a flight school appointment. After training at March and Kelly Fields, he received his pilot's wings on October 12, 1929. LeMay then joined the 27th Pursuit Squadron at Selfridge Field, Michigan.

While assigned to Selfridge, LeMay completed his college degree, worked with local Civilian Conservation Corps (CCC) camps, and participated in the controversial air mail operation of the Air Corps in 1934. In that year, he married Helen Maitland and soon transferred to Hawaii where he established a full-time navigation school designed to aid crew members flying over water. By late 1936 LeMay concluded that bombers would have a more decisive impact than fighters on the outcome of future war, and he requested transfer to a bombardment unit. In 1937 he joined the 305th Bombardment Group at Langley Field, Virginia, where he continued to develop aerial navigation techniques and trained others in the art of navigation. Acknowledged as the best navigator in the Air Corps, he participated in a number of exercises demonstrating the capability of aircraft to intercept ships at sea—first finding the USS *Utah* in 1937 and then locating the Italian liner *Rex* the following year under very well-publicized circumstances. While at Langley, LeMay was among the first to fly the new B–17s and navigated a flight of those bombers on a good-will tour to South America in 1937 and 1938. Shortly after, LeMay left his bomb group to attend the Air Corps Tactical

School at Maxwell Field, Alabama, and by the end of the 1930s his faith in the future of aerial bombardment was deeply rooted.

In late 1940 the Air Corps undertook a rapid expansion and from the 34th Bomb Group Captain LeMay received command of a squadron assigned to Westover Air Base, Massachusetts. He spent part of his time at Westover flying with Canadians and transporting personnel across the North Atlantic to England. Then in May 1942, as a new lieutenant colonel, LeMay was given command of the 305th Bomb Group and was sent to various Western bases where he began training his units for bombing operations against the Axis powers. Shortages of equipment and time made his task exceedingly difficult; still, he realized they would soon be entering combat, and he won the nickname ''Iron Ass'' for driving his men so hard. These experiences left an indelible mark on his mind—after the war he would strive above all else to insure that his airmen would be properly equipped, trained, and ready to enter combat. LeMay's 305th Bomb Group joined the American forces in England by the fall of 1942, and he quickly won a reputation as an innovative tactician. Before his arrival, aircrews flew evasive actions while trying to bomb their targets, and their accuracy suffered. Crew members believed that any aircraft holding the same heading for more than ten seconds in a combat zone would be shot down. LeMay disputed this contention with a mathematical analysis showing a bomber could fly straight and level for an extended period without additional losses. To prove his point, LeMay led a bombing attack in a new box formation and during the seven minutes preceding bomb release flew without evasive action. No aircraft was lost to ground fire, and the bombing scores improved dramatically. LeMay also instituted the practice of target study by his crew members before flying combat missions, and soon they doubled the number of bombs placed on target. In June 1943 Colonel LeMay became the commander of the 3d Bombardment Division based in England and in August led the famed shuttle bombing raid on Regensburg, Germany, landing in North Africa. He became a brigadier general a month later.

In August 1944 Major General LeMay was transferred to the China-Burma-India theater to head the 20th Bomber Command. After ''flying the Hump'' to support forward bases and bombing selected targets in China, LeMay was given command of the 21st Bomber Command based on Guam in January 1945. From the Marianas LeMay began his strategic bombing attack on Japan, once again using unconventional tactics. To reduce fuel requirements and thereby deliver heavier bomb loads against weak Japanese defenses, he stripped his B–29s of defensive armament and removed the guns, gunners, and ammunition. LeMay ordered his airmen to attack their targets singly, not in formation, and at low levels. Disbelieving crews found these techniques worked extremely well and without any additional aircraft losses. In March 1945 the 21st Bomber Command devastated four strategic cities in Japan before temporarily exhausting its supply of incendiary weapons. The end of the Pacific war came six months later after two B–29s from LeMay's command dropped atomic bombs on Japan.

Following V-J Day, LeMay temporarily left operational command and became deputy chief of staff for research and development. After launching an active R & D program for the Air Force, Lieutenant General LeMay assumed command of the U.S. Air Forces in Europe on October 1, 1947. The next spring, the Soviet Union blockaded Berlin, and LeMay played a key role in keeping the Western Allies in the city. Under his command, air transports supplied the military and civilian population, and to the surprise of friend and foe, the airlift was able to support the beleaguered city during the winter months. Within a year, the Soviets ended their blockade.

The Berlin crisis of mid–1948 uncovered serious weaknesses in the Strategic Air Command (SAC), the nation's strategic bombing force, and General Hoyt Sanford Vandenberg,* the Air Force chief of staff, ordered LeMay back to the United States in October 1948 to rebuild the command. LeMay immediately instituted realistic training and worked to expand the number of planes and men available to SAC. By the time the Korean War erupted in June 1950, the foundation for a modern deterrent force was established. While head of SAC, LeMay adopted the first jet bombers (B–47s and B–52s) and tankers (KC–135s) into his command and accomplished the preliminary work of incorporating intercontinental ballistic missiles into the deterrent force. In 1951 LeMay became the youngest four star general in American history since Ulysses Simpson Grant.*

After commanding SAC for nine years, LeMay became Air Force vice chief of staff under General Thomas White, and from 1961 to 1965, he served as chief of staff. At the Pentagon, he recommended a greater U.S. military role during the 1962 Cuban missile crisis and urged an expansion of strategic bombing against the North in the early years of the Vietnam War. Always concerned about American military strength and readiness, he frequently argued against the defense decisions of the Secretary of Defense, Robert Strange MacNamara.*

After his retirement on February 1, 1965, LeMay became an executive for an electronics manufacturing firm. Concerned that America was drifting toward socialism and hoping to stop the trend, he accepted the vice-presidential candidacy of the American Independent party led by Governor George Wallace of Alabama in 1968. In the presidential election, Wallace and LeMay garnered 13 percent of the popular vote and collected forty-six electoral votes.

Although LeMay made many important and lasting contributions to U.S. military aviation, his most important work occurred between 1948 and 1957 when he developed a strong strategic bombing force. The procedures and the state of preparedness he instituted in his organization set standards for other Air Force commands. In those years, American foreign policy increasingly depended upon the nuclear deterrent held by the Strategic Air Command LeMay had created.

LeMay's brilliance lay in his common sense approach to leadership. He could quickly analyze the critical elements of every problem and devise practical solutions. Journalists have typically depicted LeMay as a tough-minded, cigar chomping, no nonsense commander, but they usually have overlooked his ability to understand and to motivate men. LeMay realized, above all else, that a unit was only as good as its men; therefore, he always directed his first concerns toward people and as a commander operated on three principles. LeMay believed each man had to understand the importance of his job, however small. Next, he believed a commander needed to establish clear goals for his unit and, in order to maintain high morale, insure some progress was made toward reaching those objectives. Finally, he believed a commander must recognize and demonstrate sincere appreciation to those who accomplished their tasks. When commanders practiced these considerations, he argued, men would follow and perform beyond the call of duty. In large measure, these leadership principles justified the rich praise of General Spaatz and accounted for LeMay's continued success after World War II.

BIBLIOGRAPHY

Anders, Curt. *Fighting Airmen*. New York: Putnam, 1966.
Borowski, Harry R. "Capability and the Development of Strategic Air Command, 1946–1950." Unpublished Ph.D. dissertation, University of California, Santa Barbara, 1976.
LeMay, Curtis E. "U.S. Air Leadership in World War II." Proceedings, Eighth Military History Symposium, *Air Power and Warfare*. Edited by Alfred F. Hurley and Robert C. Ehrhart. Washington, D.C.: U.S. Government Printing Office, forthcoming.
——— (with MacKinlay Kantor). *Mission with LeMay*. Garden City, N.Y.: Doubleday and Company, 1965.
Sturm, Ted R. "The Man and the Strategist." *Airman* (February 1965).

                                                    HARRY R. BOROWSKI

LETTERMAN, Jonathan (b. Canonsburg, Pa., December 11, 1824; d. San Francisco, Calif., March 15, 1872), military surgeon and medical administrator. Letterman is considered to be the founder of modern military field treatment and evacuation of wounded.

Letterman's father, an eminent surgeon and practitioner, educated his son to follow him into his profession by hiring a private tutor for him until his entry into Jefferson College, a local school, in 1842. He was graduated three years later and attended Jefferson Medical College in Philadelphia, graduating in 1849. He immediately went before an Army Medical Board in New York City and, after passing the examination, was appointed an assistant surgeon on June 29, 1849. Letterman was assigned to duty in Florida with the forces campaigning against the Seminole Indians. In 1853 he was transferred to Fort Ripley, Minnesota, staying there for a year before accompanying troops marching from Fort Leavenworth, Kansas, to Fort Defiance, New Mexico. While there he took part in an expedition against the Gila Apaches. After taking a year's leave he reported to Fortress Monroe, Virginia, in 1859, for duty in the office of General Richard Satterlee, chief medical purveyor for the Army. The next year, he joined Major James Carleton's expedition against the Paiute Indians in California.

Shortly after the outbreak of war in 1861, Letterman accompanied California troops to New York and was assigned to duty with the Army of the Potomac, then appointed medical director of the Department of West Virginia. On June 19, 1862, he was transferred back to the Army of the Potomac as medical director, reporting to General George Brinton McClellan* on July 1. At this time the army was at Harrison's Landing following its retreat after being turned back from Richmond by Robert Edward Lee* during the Seven Days' battles. The army was exhaused in both body and spirit, with disease becoming epidemic and supplies of all types in short supply. Letterman took charge of a Medical Department that was deficient in medical supplies (which had been lost, abandoned, or exhausted) and medical officers, the majority of whom were broken down by fatigue.

Because of the proximity of the operations of the Army of the Potomac to Washington, its successes and failures were reported widely in the national press and the nation's level of morale depended, in great part, upon its performance. By dint of hard work and the support of Army Surgeon General William Alexander Hammond,* Letterman drastically improved the health of the Army and gave McClellan a superbly tuned fighting machine. By the end of October, he had put together a medical organization in the Army of the Potomac which would form the basis of subsequent field medical service worldwide and which is still in use today. October also marked his marriage to Mary Lee of Maryland, whose family was closely connected to the Lees of Maryland and Virginia. Three months later he asked to be relieved from duty, stating that the Army's Medical Department had been organized leaving only the ordinary routine of duty. His request was granted, and he was transferred to the Department of the Susquehanna as medical inspector of hospitals.

In December 1864 he resigned his commission and moved to San Francisco as superintendent of a commercial company, which did not prosper. He then resumed the practice of medicine and published, in 1866, *Medical Recollections of the Army of the Potomac*. The next year he was elected coroner of the city and county of San Francisco. In November of the same year his wife died. In 1868 he was commissioned surgeon general of California. The Regents of the University of California elected him to the university's Board of Medical Examiners in 1870.

On November 13, 1911, the Army General Hospital at the Presidio in San Francisco was named Letterman General Hospital as a memorial to one of the Army Medical Department's greatest members.

Letterman's most notable achievements occurred during a four-month period while serving with the Army of the Potomac, in 1862, when he revolutionized medical field service. After a strenuous retreat at the end of McClellan's campaign to capture Richmond, the Army of the Potomac was in an unfit condition for combat. Letterman's primary consideration at that time was to improve the health of the Army to ready it for further campaigning. To accomplish this he ordered vast amounts of medical supplies and equipment to replenish depleted stocks, sent north all sick and wounded who could not be expected to recover in a reasonable period of time, brought in medical officer replacements to provide a proper level of manpower, wrote strict regulations on sanitation and had them strictly enforced, gave instructions to the line officers on how best to preserve the strength of the men in drills and camp life, and attempted to establish a nutritious diet for the troops. In these actions he had the support of both Hammond and McClellan.

After accomplishing his first goal—improving the Army's health—Letterman proceeded to his plan to reorganize the Medical Department of the Army of the Potomac to relieve the suffering of the wounded and to return as many men to the line as rapidly as possible. In the first week of August, he established the Ambulance Corps, which was composed of officers specially selected from the Quartermaster Corps and men from the line to perform the sole job of evacuating wounded from the battlefield and transporting them and the sick from field hospitals to general hospitals. The Ambulance Corps was under the direct control of the Medical Department. In October he reorganized the medical supply system, reducing both the number of items and the quantity to be carried per regiment. This saved on transportation, cut down on waste, and assured the medical officers of a readily available stock of medicines and equipment.

Later in the same month (October 1862), Letterman established a system of mobile field hospitals and an evacuation plan to give prompt attention to casualties, sending to general hospitals all those needing long-term care. Furthermore, he set up a better triage system in which casualties were sorted into three categories—lightly wounded who were treated last, fatally wounded who received no treatment, and severely wounded who were treated first. At each step on the chain of evacuation, the less severely wounded were retained for quick return to the line, while those needing further, more extensive, treatment were evacuated to the rear, thus ending the practice of sending all wounded back north and losing them to the Army. This system formed the basis of most triage plans for the next one hundred years.

Letterman's integration of these four systems into a coherent whole coupled with his policies of strict sanitation produced results so favorable that all other Union armies adopted his methods. Indeed, their simplicity and utility were such that armies throughout the Western world adopted them.

BIBLIOGRAPHY

Adams, George W. *Doctors in Blue: The Medical History of the Union Army in the Civil War*. New York: Henry Schuman, 1952.

Clements, Bennett A. *Memoir of Jonathan Letterman, M.D.* Reprinted from *Journal of the Military Service Institution* (September 1883).

Kelly, Howard A., ed. *A Cyclopedia of American Medical Biography*. Vol. 2. Philadelphia: W. B. Saunders Company, 1912.

Letterman, Jonathan, *Medical Recollections of the Army of the Potomac*, New York: D. Appleton and Company, 1866.

Smith, Joseph T. "Review of the Life and Work of Jonathan Letterman, M.D." *Bulletin of the Johns Hopkins Hospital* 27, No. 306 (August 1916).

DWIGHT OLAND

LEWIS, Meriwether (b. Albemarle County, Va., August 18, 1774; d. Grinder's Stand, Tenn., October 11, 1809), explorer, territorial governor. Lewis was co-leader and official commander of the Lewis and Clark Expedition, the most important American exploration of the North American continent, and for a short time, governor of Louisiana Territory.

Meriwether Lewis was born on a plantation, called Locust Hill, at the foot of the Blue Ridge not far from "Monticello," the home of Thomas Jefferson. Lewis was of English and Welsh descent. His father, who died in 1779, was an officer in the American Revolution. In 1780 Lewis' mother married Captain John Marks, and following the Revolution the Marks family moved to Georgia, where Meriwether lived for several years. Returning to Albemarle County when he was thirteen years old, Lewis helped manage his father's plantation and was educated by a series of tutors.

In the summer of 1794 Lewis began his military career when he joined the Virginia militia as a private and participated in the march against the Whiskey Rebels in western Pennsylvania. Having been promoted to ensign, the following May Lewis joined the Second Sub-Legion of the Regular Army. He soon transferred to the Fourth Sub-Legion and then to the Chosen Rifle Company commanded by William Clark,* who was to become the co-leader of the Lewis and Clark Expedition. In November 1796 Lewis transferred to the 1st U.S. Infantry Regiment, and during much of the next four years he served on the Western frontier. In 1798 he was promoted to first lieutenant, and in December 1800 he was advanced to captain and appointed regimental paymaster.

In the spring of 1801 Lewis became President Thomas Jefferson's private secretary. Some time after that, Jefferson selected Lewis to command a military expedition to explore across the western half of the North American continent. Jefferson had been trying since 1783 to have such an expedition sent out, and in 1792 Lewis, then only eighteen years old, had volunteered for the assignment but had been considered too young and inexperienced to qualify. The project was formally launched with Jefferson's message to Congress of January 18, 1803, requesting authorization, and an appropriation of $2,500, to send a military expedition to explore up the Missouri River to its source in the Rocky Mountains and then down the nearest westward-flowing stream—presumably the Columbia—to the Pacific Ocean. Jefferson's two main purposes for the proposed mission were to prepare the way for the extension of the American fur trade and to advance geographical knowledge of the continent. Immediately following his appointment to command the expedition, Lewis began acquiring scientific instruction and arranging for necessary supplies and equipment and for the personnel of the party. With the president's concurrence, he invited William Clark, his old company commander, to join him in leading the expedition, and Clark accepted. Although the two officers were treated as equals on the expedition, Lewis was its official commander, Clark holding a commission as only a lieutenant.

Completing his preparations and receiving detailed instructions from the president in June, Lewis left Washington on July 5, 1803. He traveled overland to Pittsburgh and by keelboat from there to Wood River, Illinois, opposite the mouth of the Missouri, stopping en route at the Falls of the Ohio to pick up Clark and several young Kentucky recruits for the exploring party. The expedition remained at Camp Wood River from December 1803 until May 1804. During those five months, Lewis was mainly occupied in gathering additional supplies and equipment, as well as recruits, and in collecting information about the Missouri from traders and boatmen who had been some distance up the river. Clark was primarily in charge of the camp.

All preparations having been completed, on May 14, 1804, the expedition started up the Missouri. The permanent party consisted of the two officers, twenty-seven enlisted men, a halfbreed hunter and interpreter, and Clark's Negro body servant. In addition, there were six enlisted men and eight hired French boatmen who were to accompany the expedition for the first season's travel and then return with the party's journals and the scientific specimens that had been collected. Traveling at an average rate of about fifteen miles a day, by the end of October 1804 the expedition reached the Mandan Indian villages in present North Dakota and went into winter quarters nearby. On April 7, 1805, it resumed its journey up the Missouri. Although there were still only thirty-one persons in the exploring party, it now included a Frenchman and his young squaw, Sacajawea, the Shoshone birdwoman. Reaching the headwaters of the Missouri in the latter part of August, the explorers made a portage of the Rocky Mountains and then descended the Columbia River system to the Pacific, arriving there in the middle of November. After wintering near the ocean, on March 23, 1806, the expedition started for home and arrived back in St. Louis on September 23, 1806.

The Lewis and Clark Expedition had accomplished its mission with remarkable success. During an absence of a little more than twenty-eight months, it had covered more than eight thousand miles, much of it never before seen by white men. On that entire journey, only one man lost his life, and that was as a result of an ailment probably totally unrelated to the expedition. Although having met thousands of Indians, the explorers had only one violent encounter with them. It occurred while Lewis was high up the Marias River, near the Canadian border, and resulted in the death of two Indians. The total expense of the undertaking, including the special congressional appropriation of $2,500, was something less than $40,000. At this small cost, Lewis and Clark and their companions took the first giant step in opening the Trans-Mississippi West to the American people. Not only had they explored a great part of the Louisiana Territory, but they had also helped to lay the basis for the United States' claim to the Oregon Country.

Following Lewis' return from the Pacific, on March 3, 1807, President Jefferson appointed him governor of Louisiana Territory, in which capacity he was also *ex-officio* commander in chief of the territorial militia and superintendent of Indian affairs. Detained in the East by business related to the expedition and to the Burr Conspiracy, Lewis did not assume his post in St. Louis until March 8, 1808. There his main concern was with Indian affairs—keeping the tribes of the Missouri and the upper Mississippi at peace with each other and promoting the American fur trade with them, while seeking to minimize the influence among them of the Spanish to the west and the British to the north.

Unsuited by temperament and experience for the office, the governor quickly ran into difficulties. Strong-willed and lacking in political suppleness, he quarreled with Frederick Bates, the territorial secretary, and soon became unpopular with many of the inhabitants of the territory. Lewis communicated only infrequently with his superiors in Washington and failed to consult them on his policies and plans, especially with regard to the management of Indian affairs. Consequently, he fell under their severe criticisms and probably would not have been reappointed to a second term of office had he lived out the first.

Lewis actually served as governor of Louisiana for only about a year and a half. In September 1809 he left St. Louis for Washington, D.C., in order to explain some of his acts as chief executive and to renew his efforts to secure the publication of his and Clark's journals of the expedition. On the way, on October 11, while stopping overnight at a tavern, called Grinder's Stand, on the Natchez Trace about seventy miles southwest of Nashville, Tennessee, he died in a mysterious and violent manner. The evidence as to whether he was murdered or committed suicide is inconclusive.

Meriwether Lewis was one of the greatest explorers in American history. His background and training as a frontier youth and military officer prepared him superbly for command of the Lewis and Clark Expedition. His commitment to the enterprise was total. His steely determination and complete devotion to duty, coupled with his intrepid leadership, were undoubtedly essential to its success. Of the expedition's two leaders, Lewis had more formal education. The better trained scientifically and the more literate, he was the author of most of the scientific information contained in the journals. Essentially a rather moody and introspective loner, he was less skillful than Clark in dealing with people, both red and white.

Although his role as the official leader of the Lewis and Clark Expedition won him undying fame, Lewis' life after that historic event was largely one of frustrated hopes and unfulfilled expectations. His plans to publish his and Clark's journals of the expedition, so ardently desired by Jefferson, came to naught. His performance as governor of Louisiana Territory was very disappointing. A rather stiff and inflexible man of largely military background, he found it difficult, if not impossible, to compromise and engage in the give and take required in a political office. Consequently, he soon found himself at odds with many of his subordinates and with much of the public as a whole. Similarly, in his dealings with the Indians he showed a lack of humanity and understanding, cynically believing that the Indians could be managed only by appealing to their love of gain and their fear of punishment. When some of his acts as governor affecting the Indians were repudiated by his superiors, he was threatened with financial ruin. Thus, at only thirty-five years of age, Meriwether Lewis, facing rejection and failure, came to the end of his life. He was indeed a minor tragic hero of American history.

BIBLIOGRAPHY

Allen, Paul, ed. *The History of the Expedition Under the Command of Captains Lewis and Clark.* Philadelphia: Bradford and Inskeep, 1814.
Bakeless, John. *Lewis and Clark: Partners in Discovery.* New York: William Morrow and Company, 1947.
Cutright, Paul R. *Lewis and Clark: Pioneering Naturalists.* Urbana: University of Illinois Press, 1969.
Dillon, Richard. *Meriwether Lewis: A Biography.* New York: Coward and McCann, 1965.
Fisher, Vardis. *Suicide or Murder? The Strange Death of Governor Meriwether Lewis.* Denver: Alan Swallow, 1962.
Lamar, Howard R., ed. *The Reader's Encyclopedia of the American West.* New York: Thomas Y. Crowell, 1977.

JOHN L. LOOS

LIGGETT, Hunter (b. Reading, Pa., March 21, 1857; d. San Francisco, Calif., December 30, 1935), infantry officer. Liggett rose to command the First Army of the American Expeditionary Force during World War I.

Hunter Liggett was the son of James and Margaret (Hunter) Liggett. His father was a tailor by vocation but a politician by avocation; he served a brief term, 1879 to 1882, in the Pennsylvania legislature. Although there was no family pressure for him to pursue an Army career—his father was not even a Civil War veteran—Liggett entered the U.S. Military Academy in 1875. He graduated forty-first out of sixty-seven in the class of 1879. For the next thirteen years he served in Montana, Dakota, and Texas, commanding troops in garrison and the field. Although Liggett did not participate in any of the major Indian campaigns, he was involved in several smaller skirmishes that entitled him to the Indian Campaign Badge. One such incident in March 1880 consisted of a thirty-hour, 120-mile pursuit of an Indian band, culminated in a brief skirmish, and resulted in casualties on both sides. The regimental commander commended Liggett's leadership during the action.

From the time he was commissioned until the Spanish-American War, Liggett served with a single regiment, the 5th Infantry. As with most officers of this era, his promotions came slowly; he made first lieutenant in 1884 and captain in 1897. When the regiment left the frontier in 1892 Liggett became regimental adjutant, the unit's principal staff and administrative officer, stationed initially at St. Francis Barracks, Florida, then Fort McPherson, Georgia. It was his first assignment as a staff officer, the first time he was not directly in command of troops.

With the Spanish-American War came a promotion, diversified assignments, but also disappointments. Liggett accepted a volunteer commission as a major and assistant adjutant general. He was a division adjutant in Florida, Alabama, and Georgia from June 1898 to April 1899. But he missed the Santiago Campaign in 1898 and got to Cuba only briefly in 1899. Liggett began a period of service in the Philippines in December 1899. As a volunteer major he commanded a subdistrict on Mindanao for a year. In October 1901 he rejoined the 5th Infantry, at his permanent grade of captain, and commanded troops in Abra Province on Luzon. From the end of 1901 to mid-1902 he returned to a staff assignment as brigade adjutant at Dagupan.

Liggett received his promotion to major in May 1902, which necessitated a transfer from the 5th Infantry to the 21st Infantry and departure from the Philippines for Fort Snelling, Minnesota. He was with his new regiment at that post for one year before becoming the adjutant general of the Department of the Lakes with headquarters at Chicago. He held that staff position for the next four years until September 1907. In that month he again transferred, this time to become a battalion commander with the 13th Infantry at Fort Leavenworth, Kansas.

The next six years were crucial in the development of Liggett's career. Promotions came more rapidly: to lieutenant colonel in 1909, to colonel in 1912, and to brigadier general in 1913. He received instruction at the Army's most advanced schools. Although not officially a student, while at Fort Leavenworth Liggett participated in Staff College conferences, exercises, and wargames. During 1909–1910 he attended the Army War College. Important assignments in policymaking positions also came Liggett's way. After graduation from the War College, he stayed on as a director (1910–1913) and eventually president (1913–1914) of the institution. Concurrently, he served as chief of the War College Division, the principal planning agency of the War Department General Staff. In these posts, Liggett not only held positions of importance, but also made significant contributions to the Army as well. As a director and president of the War College, he helped reshape the curriculum, giving structure to the course and adding considerable work in military history, operational planning, and general staff duties. He also sought to improve the admission standards so that only officers well-prepared academically could attend the college. From his position on the General Staff, Liggett worked hard to improve the Army's entire system of educating officers, prepared war plans for interventions in Mexico and the Caribbean, and sought means to improve American defenses in the Philippines.

Upon promotion to brigadier general in 1913, Liggett left the War College and the General Staff to assume command of the Department of the Lakes. He remained in important command positions for the next eight years, until his retirement in 1921. From the Lakes command in Chicago he went next to Texas City, Texas, in 1914 to command the 4th Brigade of the 2d Division and then to the Philippines as a brigade commander. He remained there until early 1917, in April 1916 becoming commander of the Philippines Department (at the time the Army's largest overseas command). On March 4, 1917, he reached the pinnacle of military success when he was promoted to major general, only one of seven then in the Army. One month after America's entrance into World War I, Liggett returned to the United States as commander of the Western Department in San Francisco. He remained at that post until September when he assumed command of the 41st Division, composed largely of National Guard troops from Western states.

Liggett took the 41st Division to France in October 1917. Shortly after arriving overseas he toured the Western Front. The purpose was to observe the organization and operations of the French and British armies but also to be observed and assessed by the more experienced Allies. Liggett did not make a good first impression. He was portly, had been recently troubled by rheumatism, and at sixty was somewhat older than most Allied commanders. One English general reported that Liggett was "too old" and "not active enough" for an active field command. General John Joseph Pershing* disagreed. Upon completing his tour of the front in November 1917, Liggett returned to command the 41st Division. Two months later Pershing selected him as commander of the I American Army Corps. Liggett took command on January 20, 1918.

It was a signal honor for Liggett because the I Corps was to have tactical control of the first American divisions operating together in combat in France. Pershing recognized that despite physical limitations Liggett possessed command experience, professional knowledge, strong character, and a sense of proportion found in few other senior American officers. That Liggett was highly respected throughout the officer corps made Pershing's decision that much easier. The I Corps did not immediately become an active operational headquarters. During the winter and spring of 1918, American divisions entered the front piecemeal and participated only in limited actions. Liggett's headquarters did retain administrative control and supervised the training of the American divisions then in France. On July 4, 1918, the corps (consisting of the 2d and 26th U.S. Divisions and the 167th French) finally took over a portion of the Sixth French Army front. Liggett commanded those divisions in the defensive action near Chateau-Thierry where the German spring and summer offensive was finally halted.

Despite difficulties, Liggett's corps played an important role in the ensuing Aisne-Marne counteroffensive. Inexperienced American troops and commanders made mistakes, suffered unnecessary casualties, and sometimes failed to achieve assigned objectives. Liggett tolerated the mistakes made by the troops but was critical of some of his subordinate commanders. In hard fighting and constant pressure, the I Corps succeeded by early August in driving the Germans back twenty miles to behind the Ourcq and Vesle rivers. For the remainder of August and into September Liggett's corps was on the defensive, first in Champagne and then in Lorraine where it prepared for the first major American offensive of the war.

As one of the four corps in the newly formed First Army, the I Corps assisted in the rapid reduction of the St. Mihiel Salient, long an objective of American planners. Immediately following this operation, which lasted from September 12 to 16, the First Army began a second, more difficult offensive against determined German resistance. Liggett's leadership during the Meuse-Argonne Campaign (September 26-November 11) justified Pershing's faith in him. The I Corps anchored the Army's left flank, advancing north through the treacherous terrain in the Argonne Forest. Liggett pushed his assault divisions (the 77th, 28th, and 35th) relentlessly, but they made only slow progress. To break the stalemate Liggett and the operations section at First Army headquarters simultaneously conceived of an attack westward through the forest against the flank of the German defenders. Liggett assigned the task to the fresh 82d Division which attacked on October 7. By October 10 the Argonne was in American hands. Although Liggett's plan succeeded in clearing the forest, he was disappointed that many Germany troops escaped to establish another strong defensive position. But Liggett had little time to reflect on the attack.

On October 12, he relinquished command of I Corps to Joseph Theodore Dickman*; on October 16 Liggett replaced Pershing as First Army commander. Characteristically, he used the period from October 12 to 16 to visit various units, accumulate information, and assess the condition of his new command. After more than two weeks of sustained fighting and several major assaults, the condition of the First Army was not good. For the next two weeks Liggett "tightened up" the First Army. While there was a lull in the fighting, Liggett brought depleted divisions up to strength, talked with his commanders to improve tactical procedures, ensured better coordination within First Army headquarters by instituting daily meetings among the senior staff, and promoted a former protegé, George Catlett Marshall,* to be chief of operations. Meanwhile, Pershing had relieved several division commanders and one corps commander who had not performed adequately. When the First Army resumed the offensive with an all-out attack on November 1, the assault divisions were more experienced, the logistics support more substantive, and the immediate corps objectives more realistic than for the initial September 26 attack which began the Meuse-Argonne operation. The measures which Liggett instituted to improve the effectiveness of his army before the battle and his operational leadership during the battle contributed significantly to the success of the November 1 attack. That attack broke German defenses along most of the First Army front, permitting the most rapid American advance since the start of the Meuse-Argonne operation. The Armistice of November 11 halted Liggett's First Army.

Following the Armistice, Liggett continued as First Army commander until the unit disbanded on April 20, 1919. On May 2 he became commander of the Third Army, which then consisted of all American occupation forces in the Rhineland. When the Third Army disbanded on July 2, 1919, he returned to the

United States where he assumed command of the Western Department, the position he held just before going to France. On March 21, 1921, Liggett retired from the Army as a major general at age sixty-four. By act of Congress he advanced to the retired rank of lieutenant general in 1930. In retirement he wrote two books about his war experiences: *Commanding an American Army: Recollections of the World War* (1925) and *A.E.F.: Ten Years Ago in France* (1928). He died at San Francisco on December 30, 1935.

During World War I Hunter Liggett held perhaps the two most important operational commands in the American Expeditionary Force. As I Corps commander he trained and led the first divisions to fight under independent American command. As commander of the First Army, he led nearly one million men in the concluding offensive of the war. Liggett's managerial ability, tactical sense, and compassion for his troops (one of the few criticisms of his leadership was that on occasion he was "too much influenced by a kind heart") were important factors in the success of American arms in France. His wartime leadership was clearly his most significant contribution to the Army; yet his prewar career had an influence on the service as well. Liggett helped foster the professionalization of the officer corps by bridging the gap between older officers who were products of the Indian-fighting Army and younger, school-trained men who were often Staff College or War College graduates. He influenced the older generation to appreciate the need for a more systematic, intellectual approach in solving military problems. While he encouraged the professionalism of the younger officers, his concern for personal leadership and understanding of human nature tempered their often overintellectualization of the art of war. Liggett's style of leadership as well as his thoughtful, analytical approach epitomized the changing concept of military professionalism of this era.

BIBLIOGRAPHY

Coffman, Edward M. *The War to End All Wars: The American Military Experience in World War I*. New York: Oxford University Press, 1968.
Liddell-Hart, Basil H. *Reputations Ten Years After*. Boston: Little, Brown and Company, 1928.
Liggett, Hunter. *A.E.F.: Ten Years Ago in France*. New York: Dodd, Mead and Company, 1928.
———. *Commanding an American Army*. Boston: Houghton Mifflin Company, 1925.
Millett, Allan R. *The General: Robert L. Bullard and Officership in the United States Army, 1881–1925*. Westport, Conn.: Greenwood Press, 1975.
Pogue, Forrest C. *George C. Marshall: Education of a General, 1880–1939*. New York: Viking Press, 1963.

TIMOTHY K. NENNINGER

LINCOLN, Abraham (b. near Hodgenville, Ky., February 12, 1809; d. Washington, D.C., April 15, 1865), president of the United States. Lincoln was commander in chief of U.S. armies and navies during the Civil War.

Abraham Lincoln's father was a Virginia-born Kentucky frontiersman whose ancestor Samuel Lincoln had gone from England to Massachusetts in 1637. Abraham's mother, Nancy Hanks, about whose ancestry almost nothing is known, was also a Virginian by birth. When Abraham was seven, the family moved from a Kentucky farm to the wild forest of southern Indiana, where he grew to manhood. Both of his parents were illiterate, and his school attendance totaled no more than one year. When he was twenty-one, he accompanied his father and stepmother to Illinois.

The next year Lincoln left them and set out on his own. In New Salem, Illinois, he tried to make his way as a storekeeper, postmaster, and surveyor. Eventually he prepared himself for the law by independent study. In 1837 he took up residence in Springfield, the new state capital, to begin his law practice. By the 1850s, with the Illinois Central Railroad and other corporations as clients, he had made himself one of the most successful lawyers in the state. In 1842 Lincoln had married Mary Todd, a member of a socially prominent family of Lexington, Kentucky. To the Lincolns were born four sons, only one of whom survived to adulthood. This was Robert Todd Lincoln, who held the position of secretary of war under Presidents James A. Garfield and Chester A. Arthur.

As early as 1832 Lincoln had gone into politics, losing his contest for a seat in the Illinois legislature. Later (1834–1842), he won election to four successive two-year terms in the Illinois lower house, where he became a respected leader of the state's Whig party. He served one term (1847–1849) in the national House of Representatives. While there, he denounced President James K. Polk for starting the war with Mexico but voted for supplies for him to fight it. The political situation in Illinois was such that Lincoln could not expect a second congressional term, and after campaigning for the Whig Zachary Taylor,* he was disappointed when Taylor, as president, failed to reward him with an appointment as commissioner of the General Land Office.

Frustrated, Lincoln withdrew from active politics for a time but resumed political activity after the adoption of the Compromise of 1850 and, with still greater determination, after the passage of the Kansas-Nebraska Act in 1854. He now devoted himself to the cause of free soil. In vain, he sought a U.S. senatorship as a Whig in 1855 and as a Republican in 1858. His 1858 campaign against the well-known Stephen A. Douglas brought him national attention and made him available for the Republican presidential nomination in 1860. As the Republican candidate, he got a clear majority in the electoral college, though less than 40 percent of the popular vote.

Lincoln's election precipitated the secession of the lower South and the formation of the Confederate States of America. His call for state militia, after the Confederates' firing on Fort Sumter, induced four additional slave states to secede. Within six weeks of his inauguration he faced the War of the Rebellion, which remained the preoccupation of his presidency. Reelected in 1864, he had scarcely begun his second term when, just as the war was ending, he fell victim to an assassin's bullet. He died on the fourth anniversary of his original call for troops.

Lincoln entered the White House with practically no preparation for his role as commander in chief. He possessed no military experience except for his brief service as a captain of Illinois militia in the Black Hawk War when, according to his own later account, he saw no "live, fighting Indians" but had "many bloody struggles with the mosquitoes." He lacked administrative experience except for what he had received as the senior partner in a highly informal two-man law firm. His effectiveness as commander in chief has been the subject of much controversy. On balance, however, expert opinion holds that, despite his handicaps, he proved highly effective on the whole.

Lincoln personally made the most important decisions regarding Union strategy, and he made them without, or against, recommendations from his military advisors. The first big decision, which General in Chief Winfield Scott* opposed, was to send an expedition to Fort Sumter in April 1861. Lincoln announced in advance that the ships would attempt to provision the garrison and—unless this was resisted—would make no effort to reinforce it with munitions or men. When the Confederates nevertheless opened fire on the fort, they made themselves the aggressors in the eyes of most Northerners. The result was not only the beginning of war but also, to a considerable extent, the unification of the North.

The second big decision was to impose a blockade, which Lincoln proclaimed on April 19, 1861. This he did on his own initiative after consulting Secretary of State William H. Seward. General Scott in his "Anaconda Plan" proposed to bring about a gradual economic strangulation of the Confederacy by tightening the blockade and getting control of the Mississippi River. Lincoln approved of this but wished to supplement it with more direct and more active measures. With Scott's reluctant approval he made his next important decision; he ordered General Irvin McDowell* with the Army of the Potomac to advance into Virginia and seize the railroad junction of Manassas.

The resulting Union defeat in the First Battle of Manassas, or Bull Run (July 21, 1861), caused Lincoln to ponder the question of basic military policy. He summarized his conclusions in identical letters (January 13, 1862) to Generals Don Carlos Buell* and Henry Wager Halleck*: "I state my general idea of this war to be that we have the *greater* numbers, and the enemy has the *greater* facility of concentrating forces upon points of collision; that we must fail, unless we can find some way of making *our* advantage an over-match for *his*; and that this can only be done by menacing him with superior forces at *different* points, at the *same* time; so that we can safely attack, one, or both, if he makes no change; and if he *weakens* one to *strengthen* the other, forbear to attack the strengthened one, but seize, and hold the weakened one, gaining so much." In this, his fourth major decision, Lincoln rounded out, in essence, the strategy that was eventually to win the war.

There remained the twofold task of securing the soldiers and sailors and achieving the organization to put the plan fully into effect. George Brinton McClellan,* who briefly (1861–1862) replaced Scott as general in chief, refused to carry out Lincoln's idea of a direct, overland approach to Richmond, and he failed to show the aggressiveness that Lincoln considered necessary. Lincoln therefore demoted him, and the two were at cross purposes throughout the Peninsula Campaign. In appointing McClellan and other commanders of the Army of the Potomac—John Pope,* Ambrose Everett Burnside,* Joseph Hooker,* George Gordon Meade*—Lincoln took into account their military records. Each man had distinguished himself on some field, but at the head of the Army of the Potomac each demonstrated a lack of the qualities that Lincoln was looking for. Although Lincoln made occasional suggestions to these generals, he did not always provide them with clear and consistent direction. From July 1862 to March 1864 he kept Henry W. Halleck as general in chief, even though Halleck hesitated to assume responsibility. During that time Lincoln, Halleck, and Secretary of War Edwin McMasters Stanton* formed a kind of war council, and there was little unity of command.

During the last year of the war Lincoln finally arrived at an efficient command system. In March 1864 he brought his most consistently winning general, Ulysses Simpson Grant,* from the West and made him general in chief. Grant became a key member of the war-direction arrangement that Lincoln now worked out. Overseeing everything was Lincoln himself, the commander in chief. Taking charge of logistics was Stanton, the secretary of war. Serving as a presidential advisor and as a liaison with military men was Halleck, the chief of staff. And directing all the armies, while accompanying the Army of the Potomac, was Grant, the general in chief.

At last Lincoln was in a position to launch the kind of pressing, coordinated campaigns that he had long advocated. He kept a watchful eye on Grant but, as a rule, let him have his own way since his way was usually the same as Lincoln's. Lincoln had no occasion to overrule Grant as he had repeatedly overruled McClellan, because Grant was willing to fight the war along Lincolnian lines. Lincoln's strategy culminated in Grant's Wilderness Campaign; the siege of Richmond and Petersburg; the capture of Atlanta by William Tecumseh Sherman*; Sherman's march through Georgia and the Carolinas; and finally, Grant's victory at Appomattox.

Lincoln had taken a keen interest not only in the conduct but also in the tools of war. Inventors and promoters of new weapons often brought their drawings or models to him, and he arranged for tests, sometimes conducting them himself. He intervened with the Ordnance Bureau to bring about the adoption of breech-loading, repeating rifles and also machine guns, mortars, explosive bullets, and incendiary shells. Thus, he contributed to the development of military technology.

As commander in chief, Lincoln had come to believe that he possessed a special "war power." This, he thought, authorized the president to do things in wartime he could not constitutionally do in peacetime. Lincoln made the most extreme exercise of his supposed war power when he issued the Emancipation Proclamation. He justified the Proclamation as a war measure, one that would weaken the enemy by depriving him of slave labor. Lincoln, however, stretched executive authority much less than later war presidents were to do, justifying themselves on the basis of his Civil War example.

BIBLIOGRAPHY

Ballard, Colin R. *The Military Genius of Abraham Lincoln.* London: Oxford University Press, 1926.
Bruce, Robert V. *Lincoln and the Tools of War.* Indianapolis, Ind.: Bobbs-Merrill, 1956.
Randall, James G. *Lincoln the President.* 4 vols. New York: Dodd, Mead, 1945–1955.
Williams, Kenneth P. *Lincoln Finds a General: A Military Study of the Civil War.* 5 vols. New York: Macmillan Company, 1949–1959.
Williams, T. Harry. *Lincoln and His Generals.* New York: Alfred A. Knopf, 1952.

                                                                RICHARD N. CURRENT

LINCOLN, Benjamin (b. Hingham, Mass., January 24, 1733; d. Hingham, Mass., May 9, 1810), American commander of the Southern Department during the Revolutionary War.

Benjamin Lincoln was born into a family deeply rooted in the life and public affairs of Hingham, where his father, a farmer and maltster, was a leading citizen. The town also held the key to the younger Lincoln's career. Like his father and grandfather before him, Lincoln was elected town clerk; again like his father, he passed through various ranks in the local militia and succeeded his father as regimental commander.

An ardent Whig, Lincoln became progressively more involved in the Revolutionary movement, at both the town and colony level. When fighting erupted in 1775, he marched his recently reorganized 2d Suffolk Regiment—he had taken the initiative in throwing out Tory members—to Cambridge to assist in bottling up the British regulars in Boston.

Increasingly recognized as an influential, activist leader colony-wide by the Massachusetts Provincial Congress, Lincoln became muster master of the colony's forces and soon afterward accepted the presidency of the Provincial Congress itself. The year 1776 found him returning to the field as a major general of militia, cooperating with the American Continental commanders in driving the British from Massachusetts and in securing the withdrawal of George Washington's* army from New York City.

Washington admired Lincoln's dedication—his loyalty, hard work, and cooperation, and indeed they were factors in his military success, modest though it was compared to that of Nathanael Greene,* or Benedict Arnold,* or Daniel Morgan.* In calling him to the attention of the Continental Congress, Washington described him as "a Gentleman well worthy of Notice in the Military Line... having prov'd himself on all occasions an active, spirited, sensible Man."

Congress, also impressed by Lincoln and mindful that Massachusetts' support was essential, elevated the Bay State militia officer over the heads of Washington's brigadiers and appointed him a major general in the Continental Army. It was a most controversial step, but its impact may in time have been lessened by the friendly, easy-going Lincoln's very fine human qualities.

In 1777 Lincoln's appointment paid dividends, even though in April his troops at Bound Brook, New Jersey, were surprised and temporarily thrown back by a British raiding force under Lord Charles Cornwallis. More importantly, Lincoln, ever popular with his fellow New England soldiers, was sent by Washington to rally men from that region in behalf of the American Northern Army, which was then feebly opposing General John Burgoyne, who had recently captured Fort Ticonderoga. Washington accurately predicted that Lincoln would "have a degree of influence over the Militia, which cannot fail being very advantageous." And turn out they did, with Lincoln employing them to rally the inhabitants and to cut Burgoyne's lines of communication with Canada. Later, Lincoln joined Horatio Gates* and was his second-in-command during the climactic days of the Saratoga Campaign that witnessed the defeat and capture of Burgoyne's invading army.

Lincoln, who had received a musket ball in his right ankle near Saratoga, received from Washington "shoulder and sword knots" in recognition of his wounds and service. In September 1778 Congress gave Lincoln his first and only theater command: the Southern Department with headquarters at Charleston, South Carolina, where he arrived on December 4.

Lincoln's new duties coincided with Britain's decision to shift the brunt of the war to the American South. In December 1778 royal forces overran Georgia, and in the spring of the following year Lincoln repulsed General Augustine Prevost's drive toward Charleston. In September 1779 Lincoln's force, assisted by the Comte d'Estaing, besieged Prevost at Savannah, but the French admiral was less than fully cooperative, and a frontal assault on the city ended in failure, prompting d'Estaing to sail away with his fleet. Lincoln, ever laboring under shortages of men and equipment, saw his situation go from bad to worse when in February 1780 Sir Henry Clinton landed a superior army from New York and moved northward toward Charleston. Although Lincoln himself had grave doubts about his ability to withstand a siege, South Carolina officials insisted that he defend the capital. By April, with the city surrounded, escape was impossible, supplies ran low, and British shells rained down on the soldiers and inhabitants. Finally, on May 12, 1780, Lincoln surrendered the metropolis and its fifty-five hundred defenders, one of the severest losses through capitulation in American military history.

Even so, there was scarcely a word of criticism for Lincoln, who subsequently was exchanged and spent the next winter recruiting Continental troops in Massachusetts. The next year he played an active role in the Yorktown Campaign. Leading the army to Virginia, he then commanded the allied right wing during the siege. Because of his own humiliation at Charleston, Washington thoughtfully bestowed upon Lincoln the honor of receiving the British surrender on October 19, 1781.

Lincoln's military career was far from over since he received from the new Confederation government the first appointment as secretary of war, a post he occupied for two years. A strong nationalist, he favored beefing up congressional authority under the Articles of Confederation, and he advocated a more effective postwar military establishment than most of his countrymen at the time would support. In 1786 Governor James Bowdoin chose Lincoln to command the Massachusetts militia, partly at least because of his popularity in the western part of the state, where Shays' Rebellion had broken out. Lincoln moved into the disaffected region and with a mixture of leniency and measured force helped bring the rebels to heel. Later, Lincoln performed various services for President Washington's administration before retiring to Hingham and dying in the house of his birth.

Lincoln was a political general, not unlike many others who held commissions during America's wars from the Revolution through the Spanish-American War. Appointed because of his statewide influence, he and similar political generals were valuable for arousing support for the war effort, not because of their military talents. If some such appointees were disasters, such was not the case with Lincoln, who time and again in the Revolution was instrumental in mobilizing the manpower of Massachusetts and New England.

But his very virtues in New England—those of local prestige—hardly aided him in the South, where, though personally well liked, he was viewed as an outsider. He contrasted strikingly with the hotblooded Carolinians.

Pious in behavior, he eschewed profanity, practiced frugality, and rose early, being the very personification of Yankee morality and thrift. No better than an average soldier, he nonetheless was a valuable officer because of his loyalty to the cause and his effectiveness in New England. Physically obese, weighing over two hundred pounds, Lincoln was slow in movement as well as somewhat lethargic when it came to decision-making, as his unfortunate handling of the situation at Charleston in 1780 would indicate. Indeed, he was methodical in all he did.

BIBLIOGRAPHY

Alden, John R. *The South in the Revolution*. Baton Rouge: Louisiana State University Press, 1957.

Bowen, Francis. *Life of Benjamin Lincoln*. Boston: Gray and Bowen, 1864.

Lawrence, Alexander A. *Storm over Savannah*. Athens: University of Georgia Press, 1951.

Nickerson, Hoffman. *Turning Point of the Revolution*. Boston: Houghton Mifflin Company, 1928.

Shipton, Clifford K. "Benjamin Lincoln: Old Reliable." In *George Washington's Generals*. Edited by G. A. Billias. New York: William Morrow, 1964.
Uhlendorf, Bernard, ed. *Siege of Charleston*. Ann Arbor: University of Michigan Press, 1938.

R. DON HIGGINBOTHAM

LITTLE TURTLE (b. near Fort Wayne, Ind., ca. 1752; d. Fort Wayne, Ind., July 14, 1812), Miami chief. Little Turtle was one of the most important Indian warriors between Pontiac* and Tecumseh.*

Michikinikwa (Little Turtle's tribal name) was born on Eel River twenty miles northwest of Fort Wayne, the son of a Miami chief. Little is known of Little Turtle's early career. His close association with the British and their interests in the Great Lakes region began in the American Revolutionary War. Except for his participation in the massacre of the Illinois-French expedition of Augustin de la Balme in 1780, his exact role in the Western campaigns is unknown. He clearly associated the best interests of the Indians with those of the British at Detroit, and he learned the tactical significance of surprise and ambush. He became outspoken in his desire to secure the cooperation of all tribes in the Old Northwest in their efforts to repulse American settlement north of the Ohio River. While the tribes along the Maumee River (between modern Fort Wayne and Toledo) were determined in this goal, the Lake Indians of both Canada and the United States plus the Iroquois were reluctant to assist them. The result was a decided advantage to the Americans, provided they could destroy the Maumee Valley citadel where the warring tribes had their farms and villages.

By 1790 Little Turtle had emerged as the principal captain of the Miami. That September, Major General Josiah Harmar* marched out of Cincinnati with 1,450 troops, mostly militia. The force met virtually no opposition until it reached the vicinity of Little Turtle's village where two reconnaissance expeditions were ambushed by the Indians. Harmar lost 262 men, including 79 regulars, and withdrew.

After this victory, Little Turtle assumed military direction of the Maumee Valley tribes with the assistance of the Shawnee Chief Blue Jacket, the Delaware Chief Buckongahelas, and Alexander McKee, deputy Indian superintendent for the British, who had a trading post at the Maumee Rapids. Military necessity compelled the usually independent Miami, Shawnee, Delaware, and Wyandot to accept political unity. While sending raiding parties into the upper Ohio Valley, most of his efforts involved consolidation of tribal villages in the vicinity of modern Defiance, Ohio, and in husbanding his resources against the expected march of General Arthur St. Clair* into the tribal homelands.

St. Clair was unable to begin his advance until September 1791. Some twenty-three hundred raw regulars and three hundred Kentucky militia moved slowly northward building fortifications about a day's march apart up the Great Miami Valley toward the center of the Indian Confederacy. Constructing and garrisoning these posts plus desertion reduced his force to fourteen hundred when it encamped in modern Mercer County, Ohio, one hundred miles north of its starting point in Cincinnati. Since St. Clair was ill, principal responsibility for the operation fell upon Major General Richard Butler, an experienced veteran of the Revolution. Because there was little firm, cleared high ground in the marshy area, Butler divided the force into two sections, with the militia separated by 450 yards from the main encampment.

Little Turtle's force gained strength as St. Clair's lost it, so that the Indian commanded approximately fifteen hundred well-armed warriors. The advice of McKee and two British Army officers was supplemented by Tecumseh's intelligence reports which described in detail the Americans' strength, location, and disposition of forces. In one of the boldest moves in frontier history, Little Turtle positioned his forces around those of his antagonist and attacked at dawn on November 4, while the Americans were dispersed for breakfast. Never before had Indians assaulted an encamped white army. The total surprise and ferocity of the attack quickly forced the militia to flee their bivouac area for the main encampment. The whole American force was compressed into a small area, making easy targets for the Indians. Bayonet charges could not dislodge the Indians from the forest, and soon the senior American officers began to fall— including Butler and eight field grade officers. Slowly tightening his encirclement, Little Turtle seemed on the verge of annihilating his foe when St. Clair, roused from his sick bed, rallied his troops and directed a bayonet charge down the route of American advance that allowed nearly five hundred to escape.

Little Turtle failed to pursue; instead, the Indians looted the encampment and tortured the prisoners to death. He sent raiding parties into central Kentucky with Tecumseh leading some of the more daring attacks. Knowing the Americans would counterattack, Little Turtle continued his consolidation efforts and sought additional Indian and British support.

During August-October 1792 a grand Indian council of twenty-eight tribes assembled on the Auglaize River in modern Defiance County, Ohio, to reaffirm and enlarge the confederacy. Although the Iroquois were somewhat reluctant to join, their tribal lands in New York being particularly vulnerable to American attack, they agreed to renew the demand for an Ohio River boundary between the Americans and Indians and for British mediation of all disputes between the two peoples. Chief Joseph Brant* of the Iroquois delivered this message to American commissioners at Fort Niagara the next summer. It was an ultimatum the Americans would not accept. Brant tried to convince the Maumee tribes of the futility of their demands but failed. Meanwhile, Major General Anthony Wayne* with the newly formed Legion of the United States and Kentucky militia marched out of Cincinnati and established Fort Recovery at the site of St. Clair's defeat. To counter this threat the English reestablished Fort Miamis at the Maumee Rapids, thereby convincing many Indians of the authenticity of British support.

By mid-1794 Little Turtle had over two thousand braves on the Maumee. Many were too impatient to await Wayne's overextension of his supply lines, and Little Turtle faced logistical problems of supporting such a force over an extended time period. Dispersing his warriors to the south, the Miami chief sought to cut the American line of communications. He successfully destroyed a convoy within sight of Fort Recovery but could not restrain his enthusiastic followers from a foolhardy assault on the fort itself. Their bloody repulse cooled the Lake Indians' enthusiasm for the war and many drifted northward, thereby forcing the Maumee warriors to follow. Wayne's cautious advance with nightly entrenchments offered the Indian chief no opportunity to attack.

When Wayne advanced directly to the center of the Maumee villages at the juncture of the Auglaize and Maumee rivers, Little Turtle opened negotiations with the Americans while moving his people to the vicinity of Fort Miamis. British reinforcements to their post encouraged the Indians to interpose themselves between the fort and the Americans at the natural barrier of "fallen timbers," a two-mile wide belt of tornado-downed trees that portended great advantages to the Indians.

Little Turtle's thirteen hundred braves plus Loyalists and French couriers de bois awaited the attack, but Wayne refused battle for two days. Following a custom of fasting before combat, the Indians went without food during this period. Unable to fast any longer, many of the warriors returned to their lodges when Wayne suddenly attacked and routed the Indians, August 20, 1794.

Little Turtle lost his leadership role in the confederacy to Blue Jacket before the battle took place. This came because of his growing suspicion of the sincerity of British support for the Indian cause. A trip to Detroit in July convinced him that British assistance would stop short of direct military aid. His opening negotiations with Wayne on August 13 may have been a sincere effort rather than the delaying tactic it is usually described as being. There is some dispute as to whether Little Turtle and the Miami were engaged in the Fallen Timbers battle. Whatever the case, the Miami suffered few casualties. While Wayne's infantry coolly dislodged the braves from their positions, the British refused to admit the fleeing Indians into Fort Miamis. The disillusioned tribes fled northward, leaving their villages and cornfields to Wayne's systematic devastation.

Although the Indian losses at Fallen Timbers were minor (forty to fifty out of only four hundred engaged), the failure of British support combined with the humiliation of fleeing the scene of battle resulted in a decision of total Indian capitulation to U.S. sovereignty in the Old Northwest at the Treaty of Fort Greenville, August 3, 1795. Little Turtle was a principal Indian negotiator at this meeting. Thereafter, the Miami chief remained loyal to the United States.

He received special treatment from the American government, including an annuity of $50.00, a Negro slave, and a house. Although his prestige among many Indians fell sharply, he is credited with keeping the Miami out of Tecumseh's confederacy. He made several visits to Eastern cities, visiting with Presidents John Adams and Thomas Jefferson, and became sort of a folk hero to his former adversaries. His portrait hung in the national capitol until, ironically, the British burned it in 1814. Little Turtle was particularly outspoken against the introduction of alcohol among the Indians. He died at Fort Wayne, Indiana, near where he lived after the Greenville treaty.

Little Turtle mobilized and led the largest Indian force ever to confront the white advance into the Middle West. He excelled in ambush, in surprise, and in intelligence activities. His defeat of St. Clair constitutes the only known Indian attack on an encamped main force. It was the most disastrous defeat inflicted upon a white army in the northern woodlands, exceeding as a percentage of the command the casualties sustained by Edward Braddock* at Monongahela, Nicholas Herkimer of Oriskany, or Zebulon Butler at Wyoming Valley. "It was," writes Walter Havinghurst, "the worst disaster in U.S. military history until Custer's ambush on the Little Big Horn three generations later."

But the Miami chief suffered from the normal deficiencies of Indian leaders. His logistical support required that he live off the land, something much easier for raiding parties than the large numbers he needed to confront the American Army. Moreover, his command authority over the various tribes allied with him was minimal. Nowhere was this more apparent than during the Wayne Campaign. The attack on Fort Recovery best illustrates this problem. The fickleness of the Indians toward a single commander cost him direction of the Fallen Timbers battle. His defensive position in that engagement was excellently suited for his warriors' combat style. That Blue Jacket did not follow Little Turtle's tactics does not detract from Little Turtle's choice of a battlefield.

His genius was his tactical versatility to meet particular situations. Against Harmar he lured a reconnaissance force into an ambush. Against St. Clair he attacked an encamped foe. Against Wayne he sought first to destroy the American line of supply and then sought defensive combat in a location best suited to his forces and least adaptable to the tactics of the Legion of the United States. Probably the highest praise for Little Turtle came from the British commander at Detroit in 1794 who described him as "the most decent, modest, sensible Indian I have ever conversed with."

BIBLIOGRAPHY

Havighurst, Walter. *The Heartland: Ohio, Indiana, Illinois*. Revised edition. New York: Harper and Row, 1974.

Knopf, Richard C. " 'Cool Cat George' [Washington] and the Indian Wars in Ohio." *The Historic Indians in Ohio*. Ohio American Revolution Bicentennial Conference Series, Number 3. Columbus: Ohio Historical Society, 1976.

———. "Fort Miamis: The International Background." *Ohio State Archaeological and Historical Quarterly* 61 (April 1952): 146–66.

Van Every, Dale. *Ark of Empire: The American Frontier, 1784–1803*. New York: William
    Morrow, 1963.
Wilson, Frazer E. "St. Clair's Defeat." *Ohio State Archaeological and Historical Quar-
    terly* 2 (July 1902): 30–43.

DAVID CURTIS SKAGGS

LONG, Stephen Harriman (b. Hopkinton, N.H., December 30, 1784; d. Alton, Ill., September 4, 1864), Army officer; engineer, explorer, inventor.

Stephen H. Long was one of the thirteen children of Moses and Lucy Long,
settled, middle-class townspeople in Hopkinton. Not much is known about his
childhood and youth, but he probably attended whatever local schools served
the families of his town. By 1806 he was a student at Dartmouth College, and
he graduated from that institution in August 1809 at the age of twenty-five. For
several years he worked as a teacher and then as principal of a public school in
Germantown, Pennsylvania. By the time the War of 1812 began, he had become
known as a good mathematician and inventor. Through his acquaintance with
General Joseph Gardner Swift,* then chief of engineers in the U.S. Army, Long
received an appointment as second lieutenant in the Corps of Engineers. By the
time his commission arrived in early 1815, the war had ended, but he soon went
to West Point as an assistant professor of mathematics.

In the demobilization and reorganization of the Army that came after the war,
Long fared well. Because of close personal relations with General Swift, he
applied for and received an appointment in April 1816 as a member of the newly
established Topographical Engineers at the rank of brevet major. His first assignment as an engineer took him to St. Louis, then a raw frontier town. From
there he traveled north to examine Army garrisons in Illinois and Iowa, as well
as surveying the needs of that region for other forts. In 1817 the War Department
sent him north again, this time to examine the portage between the Fox and
Wisconsin rivers, and to choose sites for forts along the Mississippi. On this
expedition he picked a site at the junction of the Mississippi and Minnesota
rivers for what became Fort Snelling a few years later.

In 1818 Secretary of War John Caldwell Calhoun* approved Long's proposal
to build a steamboat and lead a team of scientists and explorers west. Long
designed and built the *Western Engineer*, the first sternwheel steamboat used in
the West. His trip became known as the Scientific Expedition of 1819, from
which federal officials expected much. The expedition included the first really
competent and experienced scientific explorers after Meriwether Lewis* and
William Clark.* In 1820 the expedition headed west along the Platte River.
They followed that stream until they reached the Front Range, and then they
turned south to the Arkansas River. There Long divided his command, sending
one part of it east along the Arkansas, while he led the others south searching
for the headwaters of the Red River. They mistook the Canadian for that stream
and turned east only to discover their mistake when it was much too late to

correct it. Despite much hardship and the loss of many of their scientific journals, these men gathered a wealth of data about the Missouri Valley, the Central Plains, and several of the streams that crossed them. Edwin James, the expedition botanist, geologist, and surgeon, recorded most of the explorers' findings in his multivolume *Account of an Expedition from Pittsburgh to the Rocky Mountains, Performed in the Years 1819 and '20*. In 1823, only a year after this project had been completed, Long led another group of scientists up the Mississippi to the Minnesota River. Then they followed that stream west to the Red River of the North and traveled along it north into Canada. After circumnavigating Lake Superior, they returned to the United States, having gathered considerably less valuable data than on the expedition of 1819–1820. This ended Long's duties as an explorer because once the report of this journey had been submitted, he received orders to help with river improvement work in the Ohio Valley.

A year later, in 1827, he was one of several Army engineers assigned to help plan the route of the Baltimore and Ohio Railroad. For a time he served as president of that railroad's Board of Engineers. By 1830 he had become recognized as one of the leading railroad planners in the nation. His theories for grades and curves as well as the engineering tables which he developed greatly reduced the time it took to survey potential routes for new lines of track. By 1830 he was involved in helping to plan the inclined planes needed to complete the Pennsylvania Portage Canal system in that state. Shortly after that he went south to participate in survey work in Kentucky and North Carolina. During the 1830s the War Department allowed its engineers frequent furloughs so that they could help with state and local internal improvement projects, and Stephen Long did as much of this work as anyone. He developed several mechanical improvements for railroad locomotives, carried out the Memphis Railroad survey, spent several years in New England as a surveyor and engineer, prepared a manual on bridge building, and for a time became the chief engineer for the state of Georgia while working on the Western and Atlantic Railroad.

In 1838 this civilian activity ended, and for the rest of his career, Long labored under War Department orders. Nearly all of his assignments revolved around the problems of river transportation. By 1839 he was busily trying to improve navigation on the Cumberland River. His orders repeatedly took him back to the great raft of the Red River, the largest natural obstruction to river navigation anywhere in the country. Just prior to the Mexican War he began directing the operations of government snag-boats on the Ohio and Mississippi rivers. During the war he supervised the construction of steamboats for the Army, and beginning in 1848 he began work on four large marine hospitals meant to serve the boat crews on the major inland waterways. As a result of his efforts, by the mid-1850s hospitals opened at Paducah and Louisville, Kentucky; Natchez, Mississippi; and Napoleon, Arkansas. During the 1850s Long served as superintendent of Western Rivers, working out of Louisville, and also as a member of the Board of Engineers for Lake Harbors and Western Rivers. In both capacities, he focused his attention on river and harbor improvements. He also worked at clearing more of the great raft of the Red River and for a time supervised efforts to dredge out major channels at the mouth of the Mississippi. When the Civil War began, Long was promoted to the rank of colonel and became the chief of topographical engineers stationed in Washington. Two years later the Corps of Engineers absorbed his command, and in June 1863, at the age of seventy-eight, Stephen Long retired. In September 1864 he died at his home in Alton, Illinois.

A competent, conscientious, and somewhat contentious person, Long served his country well. His career spanned the years 1815 to 1863, an era in which the republic grew from a small, technologically backward society into a large industrially sophisticated one. He is most often remembered for his activities as an explorer in the years immediately after the War of 1812 when he was the most active government-sponsored explorer on the frontier. His expedition across the Central Plains in 1820 received much negative attention, primarily because he described much of that region as a desert. Nevertheless, his assessment of the agricultural potential of the Plains proved accurate for much of the rest of the nineteenth century. Pioneer farmers rarely had the knowledge, skill, or equipment to farm the plains successfully at that time. Of more importance was the fact that his expeditions gathered and made available to the growing American scientific community vast amounts of new data on a broad range of scientific topics. His companions examined and recorded much information that moved directly into the main currents of scientific knowledge of that day.

Long's other activities proved of more long-range significance to American expansion and development than did his explorations. His work in planning the route for the Baltimore and Ohio Railroad in the late 1820s gave him data for several books he published on railroad surveying. By 1830 he developed a set of mathematical tables that could be used in computing curves and grades of track, and that were widely used and copied. That same year he published a pamphlet on bridge building in which he described a successful wooden frame railroad bridge. Perhaps his least satisfactory duties resulted from the continued need to clear the major Midwestern rivers of navigational obstructions. He repeatedly labored to complete wing dams, to improve snag boats that removed trees and other debris from the river channels, and to dredge sandbars. He supervised crews of engineers and laborers' efforts to improve navigation on the Red River in Arkansas and to keep open major channels of the Mississippi south of New Orleans. In these efforts his work was only partially successful because the frequent floods on these streams brought more snags and produced new sandbars and other obstructions almost annually.

Throughout his career as an Army engineer, Stephen Long never commanded troops in battle. Rather, he labored long and hard at routine tasks that eventually strengthened the nation. His explorations increased American knowledge of parts of the continent, while his railroad, survey, bridge building, and river dredging all served to improve transportation facilities. This helped strengthen the country and speeded national economic development.

BIBLIOGRAPHY

Fuller, Harlan M., and LeRoy R. Hafen, eds. *Journal of Captain John Bell, Official Journalist for the Stephen H. Long Expedition to the Rocky Mountains, 1820.* Vol. 20 (Far West and Rockies Series). Glendale, Calif.: Arthur Clark Company, 1957.

James, Edwin, comp. *Account of an Expedition from Pittsburgh to the Rocky Mountains Performed in the Years 1819 and '20, by Order of the Hon. J. C. Calhoun, Sec'y of War: Under the Command of Major Stephen H. Long.* Vols. 14–17 (Early Western Travels). Edited by Reuben G. Thwaites. Cleveland, Ohio: Arthur Clark Company, 1904–1907.

Keating, William H. *Narrative of an Expedition to the Source of St. Peter's River, Lake Winnepeek, Lake of the Woods, &c. Performed in the Year 1823, by Order of the Hon. J. C. Calhoun, Secretary of War, Under the Command of Stephen H. Long, U.S.T.E.* 2 vols. Philadelphia: 1824. Reprinted with an introduction by Roy P. Johnson. Minneapolis, Minn.: Ross and Haines, 1959.

Long, Stephen H. "Voyage in a Six-Oared Skiff to the Falls of St. Anthony in 1817." *Minnesota Historical Society Collections* 2. Minneapolis, 1860–1867.

Nichols, Roger L., and Patrick L. Halley. *Stephen H. Long and American Frontier Exploration.* Newark, Del.: University of Delaware Press, 1980.

Wood, Richard G. *Stephen Harriman Long, 1784–1864: Army Engineer, Explorer, Inventor.* Glendale, Calif.: Arthur Clark Company, 1966.

ROGER L. NICHOLS

LONGSTREET, James (b. Edgefield District, S.C., January 8, 1821; d. Gainesville, Ga., January 2, 1904), Army officer. Longstreet is considered one of the leading Confederate commanders of the Civil War.

The Longstreets, apparently of Netherlands stock, had been established in New Jersey until the general's grandfather moved to Georgia. James Longstreet's first years were spent on a plantation near Gainesville, and at an early age he was taken by his parents to the neighborhood of Augusta, Georgia. His father, also James, died in 1833. Longstreet's uncle, Augustus Baldwin Longstreet, a jurist, literary figure, minister, editor, politician, and educator, had a major role in James' upbringing. The family then moved to Somerset, Morgan County, Alabama.

In 1838 Longstreet was admitted to the U.S. Military Academy from the Huntsville area of Alabama. Attending West Point at the same time were William Tecumseh Sherman,* Richard Stoddert Ewell,* George Henry Thomas,* William Starke Rosecrans,* Ulysses Simpson Grant,* Henry Wager Halleck,* and many other future Civil War commanders. Academically, Longstreet was not a great success; he was graduated in 1842, fifty-fourth in a class of fifty-six.

Brevetted second lieutenant, Longstreet joined the 4th Infantry at Jefferson Barracks near St. Louis where he became an even better friend of Grant. He later served at Natchitoches, Louisiana, and with the 8th Infantry at St. Augustine, Florida.

During the Mexican War, Longstreet, under Zachary Taylor,* was at Palo Alto, Resaca de la Palma, and Monterrey. During the advance of Winfield Scott* to Mexico City, he was at Vera Cruz, Cerro Gordo, Churubusco, and Molino del Rey. He was brevetted captain after Churubusco and major after Molino del Rey. He was seriously wounded at Chapultepec.

Longstreet then served on the frontier, before becoming a major in the Paymaster's Department in 1858. There was no question where his loyalty lay during the secession crisis. His resignation from the U.S. Army was effective June 1, 1861. Owing to his sound reputation, he was commissioned a brigadier general in the Confederate forces from June 17, 1861.

Following his able handling of troops at First Bull Run (Manassas) in July 1861, Longstreet was promoted to major general in October. He commanded a division under Joseph Eggleston Johnston* in Virginia and was at Yorktown in April of 1862, before skillfully conducting the rearguard action at Williamsburg on May 5 during Johnston's retreat toward Richmond.

At Seven Pines (Fair Oaks) on May 31, he was charged with being slow and misinterpreting orders. He is credited with competent leadership in the Seven Days' battles near Richmond, June 25 to July 1, 1862. He was now under Robert Edward Lee,* who had taken over from the wounded Johnston. With over half of Lee's infantry, Longstreet followed Thomas Jonathan ("Stonewall") Jackson* north from Richmond and, with Lee and Jackson, was instrumental in defeating General John Pope* at Second Bull Run (Manassas) on August 30.

Continuing to advance with Lee's army into Maryland, Longstreet performed well at Antietam (Sharpsburg) in September. Recommended by Lee, he was promoted to lieutenant general on October 11, 1862, and was formally given command of the I Corps of the Army of Northern Virginia. On December 13 at the Battle of Fredericksburg, Longstreet's corps successfully held firm on the Confederate left in Lee's defensive victory. In Longstreet's first independent command he was detached from Lee and sent to the Suffolk area of Virginia. Thus, he and most of his troops were absent from the Battle of Chancellorsville in early May 1863.

With the death of Jackson following Chancellorsville, Longstreet was undoubtedly Lee's leading corps commander. Commanding the right flank of Lee's army on July 2 at Gettysburg, Longstreet led the famous assault on the Federal left, and men of his corps were also involved in the famed Charge of George Edward Pickett* on July 3. Gettysburg was the most controversial of Longstreet's battles.

After a masterful move by railroad to Georgia, Longstreet arrived just in time to have his corps play a major role under Braxton Bragg* in the Confederate victory at Chickamauga in September. Detached from Bragg, Longstreet was not successful in another independent command at Knoxville in the fall of 1863.

Moving with his men back to Virginia, Longstreet fought skillfully at the

Battle of the Wilderness, rallying the corps of Ambrose Powell Hill* on May 6, 1864. While leading troops in the forefront of the fight, Longstreet was gravely wounded by his own men. Returning to duty in November, he was involved in the later phases of the defenses of Richmond and the Appomattox Campaign of 1865.

Following the war, Longstreet headed an insurance agency and was a cotton merchant in New Orleans. Turning to the Republican party, which he joined, he held a series of political offices from 1869 to his death at Gainesville, Georgia, in 1904. He was surveyor of customs in New Orleans, postmaster of Gainesville, U.S. minister to Turkey, 1880–1881, U.S. marshal for Georgia, and U.S. railroad commissioner.

Longstreet wrote several articles which fueled the fires of controversy over his Civil War leadership, particularly in regard to Gettysburg. He followed these articles with a memoir, *From Manassas to Appomattox*, first published in 1896. He was married to Maria Louise Garland of Lynchburg, Virginia, in 1848, and after her death in 1889, he married Helen Dortch.

Longstreet became known, properly, as Lee's "old war horse." Despite a storm of criticism after the war, he still must be considered one of the most capable and effective Confederate generals. In recent years historians have generally taken his side in the several controversies and have restored his position as a major American military figure.

Somewhat more than six feet in height, Longstreet was a striking figure in his rough uniform. His endurance was considerable, and his perception remained keen in the face of physical demands. Generally amiable, he was known primarily as a stoic, taciturn, and dependable commander. However, his temper could be roused when someone disagreed with his firmly held, dogmatic opinions. Part of his sparseness in words may have been a result of his partial deafness.

Longstreet is often credited with being tactically a tenacious defensive fighter, and that aspect of his command abilities was superior. Furthermore, he was an excellent organizer. Looking over his entire career, however, one sees that Longstreet was an aggressive, well-prepared, and hard-striking offensive general as well, particularly at Second Manassas, Chickamauga, and the Wilderness. His soldiers had great respect and admiration for him and followed him wholeheartedly. Under adverse conditions he could evince self-reliance and poise and could transfer this attitude to his men, often leading them in person.

In assessing Longstreet and the adverse criticism of his actions, one has to try to determine how much of this attack was caused by the general's turning to the Republican party during Reconstruction, and, in addition, how much was defense of Lee. Longstreet was highly censured for his change in politics, and, on occasion, former friends and associates refused to talk with him. In his own behalf, he explained that the only way constitutional government could be reestablished was to comply with congressional legislation. While Longstreet had been critical of Lee at Gettysburg shortly after the battle, the real imbroglio of words began in 1873, after Longstreet turned Republican. He was attacked by General Fitzhugh Lee,* General Jubal Anderson Early,* and others. The primary criticism leveled against Longstreet is that he delayed carrying out Lee's orders to attack with his right flank on July 2, and that this delay to drive toward Little Round Top was a critical factor in the Confederate defeat. Furthermore, Longstreet is accused of not obeying orders on July 3. But the whole idea of Pickett's charge was undoubtedly a mistake. Several contemporary accounts blame Lee, and the commanding general accepted the blame.

Lee never uttered a word in criticism of Longstreet or anyone else for the defeat at Gettysburg. Throughout the war Lee continually called on Longstreet for advice or to carry out actions, and there seems to have been a close personal relationship between the two generals.

Longstreet was never reckless with the lives of his men, but when the necessity arose, he attacked or defended with an energy and drive that usually got the job done. While his position as a very high grade commander and strong tactical fighter now seems secure, most authorities do not credit him with being an outstanding strategist or an independent leader. His stubbornness and unlimited self-confidence in his own judgment may well have been too often expressed.

Any Army commander in history would have been blessed with an associate such as "Old Pete" Longstreet, truly a reliable general whose record will stand long in history.

BIBLIOGRAPHY

Codington, Edwin B. *The Gettysburg Campaign: A Study in Command.* New York: Charles S. Scribner's Sons, 1968.

Freeman, Douglas Southall. *Lee's Lieutenants.* 3 vols. New York: Charles S. Scribner's Sons, 1942–1944.

———. *R. E. Lee.* 4 vols. New York: Charles S. Scribner's Sons, 1934–1935.

Sanger, Donald B., and Thomas R. Hay. *James Longstreet.* Baton Rouge: Louisiana State University Press, 1952.

Tucker, Glenn. *Lee and Longstreet at Gettysburg.* Indianapolis, Ind.: Bobbs-Merrill Company, 1968.

E. B. LONG

LOOKING GLASS (b. Montana Territory, ca. 1832; d. Bear Paw Mountains, Montana Territory, October 5, 1877), Nez Perce Indian chief.

Looking Glass (Allalimya Takanin) was known as a fine warrior and buffalo hunter. In January 1863, Looking Glass, Sr., died, and his son took his father's small trade mirror, put it around his own neck, and took his father's name. Looking Glass, and his contemporaries Joseph,* White Bird, Toohoolhoolzote, and Big Thunder refused to sign the Nez Perce Treaty of 1863 which ceded 6,932,270 acres to the federal government. Thus, Looking Glass was a nontreaty Nez Perce who did not honor the agreement signed by the Christian Nez Perce chiefs, including Lawyer and Timothy.

By the 1870s the Nez Perce were facing many difficulties. White men were stealing their property and murdering their people. Looking Glass met with Joseph, White Bird, and Toohoolhoolzote to discuss the course to follow. In 1874 and 1875 Looking Glass joined Joseph and other chiefs who opposed war. He and other nontreaty Nez Perce leaders met with General Oliver Otis Howard* and Indian Agent John Monteith at Fort Lapwai, Idaho. Looking Glass was against the forced removal of the nontreaty Nez Perce to the reservation, but he had always supported his tribesmen who had refused to sign treaties, despite the fact that most of his own lands were within the boundaries of the reservation. Looking Glass agreed to remain on his own land on Clear Creek near the Middle Fork of the Clearwater River, above present-day Kooskia, Idaho.

Open warfare between the Army and the Nez Perce began on June 17, 1877, with the Battle of White Bird Canyon. Looking Glass was not involved, residing peaceably at his village on the reservation. Nevertheless, General Howard feared Looking Glass and sent an Army patrol to arrest him, thus forcing him to join the hostiles. Looking Glass united with the other nontreaty Nez Perce on the south fork of the Clearwater River where he fought against some Idaho volunteer troops. Following the Battle of the Clearwater, the principal Nez Perce leaders met at Weippe, Idaho, to discuss their course of action.

Looking Glass was a central figure in these discussions, for he argued convincingly that the nontreaty Nez Perce should cross the Lolo Trail, enter Montana, and join forces with the Crows. He reasoned that the whites in Montana were friendly and that the Nez Perce could leave their Idaho enemies behind by entering the Bitterroot Valley. At Weippe, Looking Glass offered the alternative of traveling to Canada if the whites in Montana proved hostile. On the strengths of these plans formulated by Looking Glass, the Nez Perce crossed the Bitterroot Mountains on the Lolo Trail. As Looking Glass and the Nez Perce descended into Montana, their scouts reported that soldiers and civilians were concentrating on Lolo Creek. Captain Charles C. Rawn commanded thirty-five soldiers from Missoula, Montana, as well as nearly two hundred volunteers. Looking Glass, Joseph, and White Bird rode to the barricade that Rawn had built to block the trail.

Looking Glass spoke for the Nez Perce, stating that the Indians did not want to fight, and he asked that the people be permitted to pass the barricade unmolested. Rawn declined to let them pass, and he met Looking Glass on two occasions to demand their surrender. Looking Glass refused and instead deployed his warriors into a screening line which gave the women, children, and wounded sufficient time to move unharmed into the Bitterroot Valley. Once safe from the soldiers, the Nez Perce met in council to discuss a proposal to head north into Flathead country and on into Canada. White Bird, Toohoolhoolzote, and Red Owl favored the plan, but Looking Glass convinced the warriors to follow him to the Big Hole Valley's buffalo country to live with the Crows.

Convinced that they had left Howard and the war behind, Looking Glass slowed the march and camped at the Big Hole. Looking Glass took few precautions, refusing to set up pickets or send out scouting parties. He was confident that his people were out of danger, and he feared that his young warriors might kill some whites which would trigger more hostilities. Meanwhile, Colonel John Gibbon* with 238 soldiers and volunteers surprised the Nez Perce on August 9, 1877. Although the Nez Perce forced Gibbon to retreat, the Indians suffered greatly, losing between sixty and ninety men, women, and children, including twelve of their best warriors. The people said nothing to Looking Glass after the battle, but all believed he was at fault. Looking Glass lost his role as the primary leader to Lean Elk (also called "Poker Joe").

From the Big Hole, the Nez Perce traveled south, back into Idaho, to Camas Meadows where Looking Glass participated in a brief battle with Howard's troops. The Nez Perce then entered Wyoming and rode through the center of Yellowstone Park. They began their northern march toward Canada, traveling down the Clark Fork River and reentering Montana. The journey was extremely difficult for the Indians who had suffered greatly for the past three months from want of rest and food. As the Nez Perce progressed north toward Canada, the leaders held another council. Looking Glass pointed out that the soldiers were far behind, and he urged the chiefs to travel more slowly for the benefit of the tired and wounded. Lean Elk was against a slower pace, fearing that the soldiers might yet attack before they crossed into Canada. Since Howard's soldiers were some distance behind the Nez Perce, the leaders agreed to slow down the march.

Unknown to the Indians, Howard had sent a message to Colonel Nelson Appleton Miles* at Fort Keogh asking for assistance. Miles led a force of 383 men west in order to intercept the Nez Perce before they crossed the border. On September 22, 1877, the Indians went into council, where Looking Glass insisted that Lean Elk was not a worthy leader because he was pushing the people too hard. Looking Glass then asserted that henceforth he would be leader again. Apparently there was little opposition, and Looking Glass assumed command. The chief ordered the people to move at a slower pace, and he urged his young men to hunt buffalo. By September 30 the Nez Perce were camped in the Bear Paws Mountains of Montana and were only about forty miles from the border when they were attacked by Miles. The Battle of Bear Paws, September 30 through October 5, was the last engagement of the Nez Perce War. While Joseph favored surrender, Looking Glass was opposed to the idea, stating that "I will never surrender to a deceitful white chief." Looking Glass decided to flee across the border to Canada and live with Sitting Bull's* Sioux. He never made it, for he became the last casualty of the battle. Looking Glass was struck in the forehead by a bullet fired by a Cheyenne scout.

Looking Glass is best known for his role in the Nez Perce War of 1877. Although he had supported the nontreaty Nez Perce and their claim to the land ceded by Chief Lawyer, he did not favor war against the whites. After being attacked by an Army patrol, Looking Glass reluctantly entered the fight. From July 1 through October 5, 1877, Looking Glass was one of the most important leaders of the hostile Nez Perce and at times the principal war chief. Looking

Glass provided the strategy of crossing the Lolo Trail, entering Montana, and resettling in the buffalo country. He successfully effectuated the crossing of the mountains and the entering of the people into Montana.

Looking Glass was responsible for remaining too long at the Big Hole, which gave Gibbon time to mount an attack. Looking Glass lost his status as principal war chief following the Battle of the Big Hole but regained it as the Nez Perce neared the Canadian border. Under his leadership, the Indians slowed their pace as they moved toward the "Grandmother Country," and Looking Glass insisted that the people camp and rest. This was a tactical mistake for the Nez Perce, and it was a fatal error for Looking Glass.

BIBLIOGRAPHY

Beal, Merrill D. *"I Will Fight No More Forever": Chief Joseph and the Nez Perce War.* Seattle: University of Washington Press, 1963.
Brown, Mark H. *The Flight of the Nez Perce.* New York: Putnam's, 1967.
Haines, Francis. *The Nez Perces: Tribesmen of the Columbia Plateau.* Norman: University of Oklahoma Press, 1955.
Josephy, Alvin M. *The Nez Perce Indians and the Opening of the Northwest.* New Haven, Conn.: Yale University Press, 1965.

CLIFFORD EARL TRAFZER

LOVELL, Joseph (b. Boston, Mass., December 22, 1788; d. Washington, D.C., October 17, 1836), military surgeon, first surgeon general of the U.S. Army Medical Department.

Joseph Lovell was a member of a prominent Boston family. His father served in the Continental Army, and his grandfather in the Continental Congress. He attended school in Boston and graduated from Harvard College in 1807. His professional education included both informal training as an apprentice to a Boston physician and formal medical studies at the Harvard Medical School, from which he received his M.D. degree in 1811.

In the spring of 1812 Lovell was appointed to the position of regimental surgeon in the U.S. Army, where his work called the attention of his superiors in the Medical Department to his "accurate and discriminating mind." Initially assigned to manage the new general hospital at Burlington, Vermont, he also served at a number of hospitals in the Northeast during the course of the War of 1812, including facilities along the Niagara frontier.

Lovell's considerable medical and administrative talents attracted favorable attention during the War of 1812, and when the wartime Medical Department was disestablished at the end of that conflict, he was retained in the Army. By 1817 he had risen to the position of medical director for the Northern Department, and in the spring of 1818, when he was not yet thirty years old, he was appointed the first surgeon general for the newly formed permanent Medical Department.

As surgeon general, Lovell faced a multitude of problems. The surgeons making up the new department were a motley crew, some too old or too poorly trained to perform the duties expected of them, and many so accustomed to working independently that it would prove difficult to bring them to accept the discipline necessary to the successful operation of the department. The large number of forts scattered across the expanding nation rendered the size of his staff inadequate. Furthermore, few post hospital facilities were adequate for the shelter of the sick. And the state of the art of medicine was such that physicians, civilian and military alike, were often powerless in the face of infection and disease.

Nevertheless, Lovell moved promptly to bring discipline and order to the Medical Department. One of his first acts was to require reports from each surgeon concerning the health of the men at his post and conditions that might affect their health and to insist that these reports be filed on time.

Although he never saw the size of his staff expanded to the point where each post had at least one surgeon and the largest or least healthy at least two, Lovell succeeded in changing the structure of his department so as to maximize its flexibility and thereby to minimize the efforts of understaffing. When necessary, he hired civilian physicians on contract to care for soldiers when no regular Army doctor was available.

Lovell was particularly anxious to improve the caliber of his staff. To achieve this goal, in 1832 he initiated the requirement that all doctors, regardless of their background or political connections, pass a rigorous examination in order to be accepted for service as Regular Army surgeons. In addition, from that time on, no medical officer would be retained longer than five years in the department without passing a second examination.

To attract able young physicians to the department, Lovell urged that the salary offered to its members be raised, and in 1834 he was finally successful in obtaining increases for all Army surgeons except, ironically, himself, and also in having automatic raises granted medical officers after five and ten years of service. He also attempted whenever possible to give the individual medical officer some choice as to his station.

Lovell encouraged the surgeons of the department to improve their professional skills. He sent them the latest medical books and journals, retaining an additional one or more copies of each item for his own office. Thus, he started a collection around which the modern National Library of Medicine was later formed. He encouraged his subordinates to conduct private practices, when this could be done without diminishing the quality of the care given military patients, in the belief that they would thereby add to their understanding of the diseases of the area in which they were stationed. With Lovell's aid and advice, William Beaumont* undertook his pioneering work in the field of human digestion while serving as a member of the Medical Department.

Fully aware of the importance of preventive medicine, Lovell encouraged his surgeons to vaccinate all men not immune to smallpox and urged line officers to be more concerned about the health of their commands. He suggested that the Army's rations include ample supplies of vegetables as well as meat and that care be taken to provide food of good quality. He pointed out that variety both in the foods offered and in their preparation was also desirable.

Well aware of the fact that the Army's sick were often denied the shelter of a good hospital, Lovell systematically gathered data from his surgeons concerning the condition of these institutions at the various posts. He reported on what he learned to his superiors, in the not-always-unfounded hope that money would be found to improve or rebuild those that were unsatisfactory and to start the construction of hospitals at posts where there was no housing set aside specifically for the use of the sick.

While Lovell was surgeon general, the Army was twice called upon to conduct a major campaign against the Indians. During the Black Hawk War of 1832, although few soldiers were wounded, many fell victim to cholera, a disease before whose onslaughts Army surgeons were helpless. In the first year of the Second Seminole War (1835–1842), malaria quickly proved to be a more formidable foe than the Indian. The nature of the war in Florida, which required that the Army operate in small units divided among many posts, placed a great strain upon the small Medical Department, but the organization that Lovell had created proved equal to the challenge.

Lovell did not live to see the end of the Seminole War, however. He was still a relatively young man when he died in 1836, his death reportedly hastened by that of his wife a few months earlier.

The challenge that faced Lovell as the first surgeon general of the newly formed Army Medical Department was great. Before 1818 a medical department was established only to meet the demands of war and was hastily disbanded once hostilities ceased. In peacetime, there was no central organization at the national level to direct and support the work of the Army's surgeons. Lovell's predecessors were never able to set long-range goals or to build upon past achievements. Lovell was well aware of the confusion that characterized the makeshift wartime departments, staffed by undisciplined surgeons who were unfamiliar with the demands of military medicine, and uncertainly supplied.

The quiet and unpretentious Lovell proved to be a talented administrator and a wise choice to lay the foundations of the new department. By the time of his tragically premature death, he had brought order and discipline to every aspect of the operations of the department. His staff was composed of career military surgeons, well trained and fully aware of what was expected of them. Supply centers were established at strategic locations, and all those who were involved in the purchase or use of supplies were held strictly accountable for them. The cost per man of medical care had dropped dramatically.

To Lovell's skill as an administrator, however, was joined his vision as a scientist. The Medical Department's collection of data on health and meteorological conditions throughout the country suggests that Lovell was aware of the unique potential for significant contributions to medical science possessed by a widespread and disciplined organization. Although the collecting of weather data would eventually be turned over to the Weather Bureau, the Medical Department would continue after Lovell's death to use its resources for the advancement of medical science.

BIBLIOGRAPHY

Ashburn, Percy Moreau. *A History of the Medical Department of the United States Army.* Boston: Houghton Mifflin Company, 1929.

Bayne-Jones, Stanhope. *The Evolution of Preventive Medicine in the United States Army, 1607–1939.* Washington, D.C.: Office of the Surgeon General, U.S. Department of the Army, 1968.

Brown, Harvey E. *The Medical Department of the United States Army from 1775 to 1873.* Washington, D.C.: Surgeon General's Office, 1873.

Mann, James. *Medical Sketches of the Campaigns of 1812, 13, 14.* Dedham, Mass.: H. Mann and Company, 1816.

Phalen, James M. *Chiefs of the Medical Department United States Army 1775–1940.* Carlisle Barracks, Pa.: Medical Field Service School, 1940.

Pilcher, J. E. *Surgeon Generals of the Army of the United States of America.* Carlisle, Pa.: Association of Military Surgeons, 1905.

MARY GILLETT

LUCAS, John Porter (b. Kearneysville, W. Va., January 14, 1890; d. Great Lakes Naval Hospital, Ill., December 24, 1949), military commander. Lucas was an expert in amphibious warfare.

Lucas received a Bachelor of Science degree upon graduation from the U.S. Military Academy in 1911 and the degree of Master of Science from the Colorado Agricultural College in 1917.

After being commissioned a second lieutenant of cavalry in 1911, Lucas started to move up the ladder of promotion. He was made first lieutenant in 1916, captain the next year, and major and then lieutenant colonel in 1918. However, after the war Lucas, as most officers, was reduced in grade, in his case to captain. On July 1, 1920, he was transferred to the field artillery and promoted to major, a rank he held until 1935, when he made lieutenant colonel. As the world crisis deepened, Lucas was promoted to colonel and then to brigadier general in 1940 and major general on August 5, 1941, a grade he was promoted to permanently on January 24, 1948, with date of rank from August 24, 1944.

Lucas' assignments sent him to all parts of the world. He served in the Philippine Islands from December 1911 until August 1914, when he was assigned to the 13th Cavalry Regiment at Columbus, New Mexico. Lucas was commanding the machine gun troop of the regiment that repulsed a Pancho Villa raid on Columbus on March 9, 1916. He then served with the Punitive Expedition into Mexico from March 1916 until February 1917, when he went to Camp Stewart at El Paso, Texas. He was aide de camp to Brigadier General George Bell, Jr., at El Paso until August 1917. He then became aide de camp to the 33d Division commander and commandant of the division's infantry school at

Camp Logan, Texas. In January 1918 he took command of the 108th Field Signal Battalion of the 33d Division.

In May 1918 Lucas went to Europe and was wounded in action near Amiens, France, in June. Following hospitalization in London, he returned to the United States for duty in the Washington, D.C., area, first at the Army War College and then with the Committee on Educational Special Training. In July 1919 he went to the University of Michigan at Ann Arbor to be professor of military science and tactics for one year. Following a four-month tour with the 3d Field Artillery at Camp Grant, Illinois, he attended the Field Artillery School at Fort Sill, Oklahoma, graduating in June 1921. For the next two years he was an instructor at the Field Artillery School and then attended the Command and General Staff School at Fort Leavenworth, Kansas, graduating in June 1924. He served as professor of military science and tactics at Colorado Agricultural College for five years, leaving in July 1929 to assume command of the 1st Battalion, 82d Field Artillery, at Fort Bliss, Texas. In June 1931 he was enrolled at the Army War College at Washington, D.C., graduating in June 1932. He stayed in the Washington area until June 1936, serving in the Personnel Division, G–1, War Department General Staff.

After a brief tour at Fort Sam Houston, Texas, Lucas took a refresher course at the Field Artillery School at Fort Sill, Oklahoma, and, in December 1936 he took command of the 4th Field Artillery at Fort Bragg, North Carolina. In December 1937 he was appointed a member of the Field Artillery Board. He assumed command of the 1st Field Artillery at Fort Sill in July 1940 and in October was named artillery commander of the 2d Division at Fort Sam Houston, Texas. In July 1941 he became commanding general of the 3d Infantry Division at Fort Lewis, Washington. The division conducted landing exercises in Puget Sound and at the mouth of the Columbia River. Lucas' reports of these exercises were important in trying to correct deficiencies in amphibious training. From April 1942 until May 1943, he served as commanding general of III Army Corps at Fort McPherson, Georgia.

In May 1943 Lucas returned to combat, serving as the personal representative of General Dwight David Eisenhower* in the North African and Sicily Campaigns. He briefly commanded the II Corps in Sicily and in September 1943 assumed command of VI Corps in Italy. Under him, the corps fought through southern Italy to the Venafro line on January 3, 1944. The corps then was chosen to mount a landing at Anzio to relieve the pressure on the Cassino front and perhaps make an end run around the Gustav Line through the Alban Hills to Rome. The landings on January 22, 1944, surprised the Germans, who had lightly defended the area because they believed an attack would more likely come nearer the mouth of the Tiber River. Thus, the landing was initially a success, but the invaders, instead of moving quickly to interior positions, stopped to consolidate their forces. The Germans, determined to maintain control of the Alban Hills, then tried to eliminate the Anzio forces by concentrating seventy thousand troops within two weeks. The Germans tied down the invaders but, through the tenacity of Lucas' troops and of naval fire, the invaders retained their hold. During the battle, Lucas was replaced in his command after complaints by the supreme allied commander in the Mediterranean, General Harold R.L.G. Alexander, that the VI Corps headquarters was negative and lacking in drive. In March 1944 Lucas returned to the United States as deputy commander and then commander of the Fourth Army at Fort Sam Houston, Texas. In June 1946 he left that command to go to Nanking, China, as chief of the Army Advisory Group. Leaving that command in January 1948, he returned to the United States to become deputy commanding general, Fifth Army, at Chicago, Illinois, on April 10, 1948.

General Lucas led his corps to impressive victories in Italy. He led his corps through roadless mountain passes to the key city of Avellino, to a rapid advance beyond the Colore River, and to a brilliantly executed crossing of the Volturno River despite severe opposition. The corps faced terrible weather conditions, inferior road networks, a determined enemy, and tenuous supply lines. Lucas then planned and coordinated the efforts of combined British and United States forces for an amphibious landing at Anzio in less than thirty days. His forces held the beachhead despite extremely adverse weather conditions, heavy artillery bombardment, and the constant threat of attack by aircraft. Lucas' personal example of courage to his corps was such that he received a Silver Star for his actions following an air raid and during an artillery bombardment of January 26, 1944. Yet his service in Italy ended in his being replaced while the Battle at Anzio was still in a critical phase.

Nearly all analysts of Anzio fault Lucas to some degree for his caution. Most disagree with Alexander that Lucas should have at once taken Alban Hills, a massive mountain terrain difficult to gain. Moreover, the German reinforcements would have feasted on an Allied line stretched from the hills to the beach. Instead, these same analysts argue, Lucas should immediately have moved in the northeast to take Cisterna and in the north to Aprilia-Campoleone. For his part, Lucas certainly heeded his American commander General Mark Wayne Clark's* advice to remember Salerno and not take reckless risks. For a time after the landing Lucas believed he was being pushed, not simply to take the two key points of Cisterna and Campoleone, but the Alban Hills themselves. Lucas thought, quite rightly, that he would have to wait for reinforcements to attain that objective. In the end, however, nearly all agree that there was a more fundamental reason for the stalemate at Anzio. That reason is summed up most succinctly by A. Russell Buchanan in *The United States and World War II*, Volume 1, p. 183: "In retrospect, Anzio appears to have been a case of attempting too much with too little." Even George Smith Patton, Jr.,* the offensive genius, would have had to contend with that.

BIBLIOGRAPHY

Blumenson, Martin. "General Lucas at Anzio." In *Command Decisions*. Edited by Kent Roberts Greenfield. Washington, D.C.: Office of the Chief of Military History, 1960.

————. *Salerno to Cassino. United States Army in World War II.* Edited by Stetson
    Conn. Washington, D.C.: Office of the Chief of Military History, U.S. Army,
    1969.
Buchanan, A. Russell. *The United States and World War II.* Vol. 1. New York: Harper
    and Row, 1964.
Clark, Mark W. *Calculated Risk.* New York: Harper and Brothers, 1950.
Hibbert, Christopher. *Anzio—The Bid for Rome.* New York: Ballantine Books, 1970.
Starr, Chester G. *From Salerno to the Alps.* Washington, D.C.: Infantry Journal Press,
    1948.

JOSEPH P. HOBBS

LUCE, Stephen Bleeker (b. Albany, N.Y., March 25, 1827; d. Newport, R.I.,
July 28, 1917), naval officer. Luce inspired several generations of American
naval officers who sought to modernize their service and was first president of
the Naval War College.

Luce was the second son of Vinal and Charlotte Bleeker Luce. His father's
family had come from England and settled in Martha's Vineyard, while his
mother's came from one of the old Dutch families of New York. When he was
six years old, the family moved to Washington, D.C., where his father, a former
druggist, became a clerk in the Treasury Department.

Stephen was appointed a midshipman in the Navy at the age of fourteen by
President Martin Van Buren in October 1841. Luce's first six years at sea were
spent in the 38-gun frigate *Congress* and the 74-gun ship-of-the-line *Columbus.*
The *Congress* served on both the Mediterranean and South American Stations,
while the *Columbus* took the young midshipman around the world and made the
first visit by an American warship to Japan in 1846. After spending two cruises
afloat, Luce attended the newly established Naval Academy, becoming a member
of the second class to be sent to Annapolis. After passing his examinations in
1849, he was assigned to the 18-gun sloop-of-war *Vandalia* on the Pacific Station
for a three-year tour of duty. Subsequently, he was assigned to various ships of
the Coastal Survey on the Atlantic Coast. During this period, he was married
on December 7, 1854, to a childhood friend, Elisa Henly, daughter of Commodore John C. Henly and a grandniece of Martha Washington. They had three
children. From 1857 to 1860, Luce served as lieutenant in the 20-gun sloop-of-
war *Jamestown* on the east coast of Central America. In these years, he gained
wide experience and began to reflect on the need to improve naval education,
organization, training, and administration, the task in which he would spend his
career.

Orders to the Naval Academy in 1860 as an instructor in seamanship and
gunnery provided Luce with his first opportunity to write and to publish. His
first major publications were revisions of textbooks in the subjects he taught.

When the Civil War broke out, Luce prepared to move north with the Academy
to the safety of Newport, Rhode Island. En route, he was ordered to report

immediately to the steam frigate *Wabash* in which he served until January 1862. In this ship, he participated in the early activities of the South Atlantic Blockading Squadron, the operations at Hatteras Inlet, and the Battle of Port Royal, South Carolina. Luce returned to his duties at the Naval Academy in 1862 and commanded the frigate *Macedonian* during her European midshipman's cruise in the summer of 1863. While in Europe, he carefully observed English and French naval training. Shortly after his return to Newport, Luce was ordered to command the monitor *Nantucket* on blockade duty off Charleston. During this period of quiet sea duty, Luce wrote and published his first series of articles on the need to improve naval training. In September 1864 he was ordered to command the gunboat *Pontiac* in which he served until the end of the war.

Returning to the Naval Academy at Annapolis in 1865, Luce continued his interest in naval training. Furthermore, he sought to encourage the establishment of nautical colleges for training merchant seamen. In 1868 he was ordered to command the *Mohongo* in the North Pacific Squadron. After a cruise in the Gulf of California, Luce took command of the steam sloop *Juniata* in Philadelphia. Ordered to the North Sea, he observed the French blockade of Germany during the Franco-Prussian War. From 1872 to 1875 he served as equipment officer at the Boston Navy Yard and devoted a great deal of effort to the reform of maritime training. He prepared a draft of the congressional bill which extended the Morill Land Grant College Act to nautical training, and he was instrumental in establishing what is now the State University of New York Maritime College at Fort Schuyler. From 1875 to 1877 he commanded the *Hartford* and turned to concentrate his energy on the reform of naval training. During this period, he came in contact with Colonel Emory Upton* who encouraged his line of thinking and Congressman W. C. Whitthorne of Tennessee, a leader of the naval reform movement in Congress. In command of the training ship *Minnesota* (1877–1881), Luce worked for the establishment of the Bailey Medal for outstanding naval apprentices and served on the board that selected Coaster's Harbor Island at Newport as a permanent base for naval training. Promoted to commodore in 1881, he took command of the newly formed Training Squadron, served on the board to investigate Navy yards, and began to work for the establishment of a college for advanced studies in naval warfare. Appointed acting rear admiral in July 1884, he took temporary command of the North Atlantic Station until September 1884, when he became the first president of the Naval War College. Commissioned rear admiral in 1886 (then the highest rank in the U.S. Navy), he was ordered to command the North Atlantic Station until his retirement in 1889. Luce used the squadron for tactical exercises and first applied practical tests of tactical theories developed in Naval War College wargames.

After his retirement, Luce retained a close relationship with the Naval War College and began an active and influential career writing on naval subjects. He served as president of the Naval Institute from 1887 to 1898. In 1901 he was returned to active duty on the Naval War College faculty. In 1909, Luce served on the Moody Commission which recommended administrative changes in the Navy Department. Luce was retired in 1910, and his active writing career ended following an illness in December 1911.

First and foremost, Stephen B. Luce was a naval officer and seaman, but as such he was a teacher, writer, organizer, administrator, and leader. During his career, he developed a perception of the Navy as a flexible tool for applying force. He believed that if a navy was to fulfill its function successfully, it must be efficiently controlled by men who were not only technically proficient, but who also understood the political limitations and implications of force. With this basic theme in mind, Luce worked for improvements in education and organization during a time of great technological innovation. He promoted standardized procedures throughout the service, established a basic training program for seamen, and the Naval War College for educating officers who would establish naval policy, develop strategy, and manage the Navy's functions. He was greatly influenced by the idea of the scientific study of history through the works of T. H. Buckle and J. K. Laughton, by the military theories of E. B. Hamley, Emory Upton, and Jomini as well as by the expansionist ideas of Theodore Roosevelt* and Henry Cabot Lodge.

Luce appreciated the technological revolution of his age, but he saw such innovation only as an additional reason to improve education and organization in order to use and to control technology properly. He was the acknowledged leader of naval intellectuals and influenced a number of rising officers such as Bradley Allen Fiske,* William Sowden Sims,* Henry Taylor, and Alfred Thayer Mahan.* Luce was not an original theorist, but a subjective thinker, the leader of a reform faction that was strongly opposed by the technicists within the Navy. In his own time, he served as a catalyst of new ideas which became the fundamental perceptions in the development of American naval education, organization, administration, and strategic theory in the twentieth century.

BIBLIOGRAPHY

Gleaves, Albert. *Life and Letters of Stephen B. Luce: Rear Admiral, U.S.N., Founder of the Naval War College*. New York: G. P. Putnam, 1925.
Hayes, John D., and John B. Hattendorf, eds. *The Writings of Stephen B. Luce*. Newport, R.I.: Naval War College, 1975, and Washington, D.C.: U.S. Government Printing Office, 1977.
Herrick, Walter R., Jr. *The American Naval Revolution*. Baton Rouge: Louisiana State University Press, 1966.
Spector, Ronald. *Professors of War: The Naval War College and the Development of the Naval Profession*. Newport, R.I.: Naval War College Press, 1977.

JOHN B. HATTENDORF

M

MAC ARTHUR, Arthur (b. Springfield, Mass., June 2, 1845; d. Milwaukee, Wis., September 5, 1912), Civil War hero, infantry officer, American commander in the Philippines, lieutenant general.

Arthur MacArthur was the older of the two sons of Arthur and Aurelia (Belcher) MacArthur. His mother was from a long-established Massachusetts family; his father, born in Scotland, immigrated to the United States in 1825 and settled in Massachusetts. Although the senior MacArthur had a successful law practice and was active in local politics, in 1849 the family moved to Wisconsin. There the father continued his legal and political interests, eventually serving as lieutenant governor, governor (for six days), and state circuit judge. Throughout his life the younger Arthur MacArthur retained his ties to Wisconsin. He spent most of his youth in that state, received his formal education in the Milwaukee public schools, served with the 24th Wisconsin Volunteer Infantry throughout the Civil War, and eventually retired there.

Rebuffed in attempts for an appointment to West Point, on August 4, 1862, Arthur volunteered his services and received a commission in the 24th Wisconsin. He first saw combat in October 1862 at Perryville, Kentucky. The seventeen-year-old regimental adjutant was cited for bravery in this action and brevetted to captain. It was the first of many battles and acts of bravery for the young officer. At Murfreesboro (December 30, 1862–January 3, 1863), when the regimental commander fell, MacArthur assumed command, issued timely orders, and generally held the 24th Wisconsin together. At Missionary Ridge (November 25, 1863) he led the unit's assault and planted the regimental colors on the crest of the ridge; eventually, he received the Medal of Honor for this feat. In recognition for his leadership, on January 25, 1864, MacArthur was promoted to major and given command of the regiment. While leading the 24th, he suffered wounds in battles at Kennesaw Mountain (June 27, 1864) and Franklin (November 30, 1864). The wounds sustained at Franklin ended his Civil War combat, although in March 1865 he was brevetted to lieutenant colonel. When the 24th

Wisconsin mustered out in June 1865, MacArthur left the service as an experienced regimental commander at age twenty.

As he returned to Milwaukee, MacArthur was uncertain about his future. After studying law for several months, he realized the appeal of military life. In February 1866 he received a commission in the Regular Army, but only as a second lieutenant in the 17th Infantry. By the end of 1866 he had transferred to the 36th Infantry and had been promoted to captain. But it was thirty years before he regained his wartime rank of lieutenant colonel.

Shortly before the end of 1866 MacArthur joined the 36th Infantry at Fort Kearney, Nebraska Territory, where he saw typical frontier duty—protecting travelers along the Oregon Trail, providing security for railroad construction crews and mining prospectors, and guarding Fort Bridger, the principal Army supply depot in Wyoming. But in 1869 a reduction in Army appropriations resulted in the consolidation of the 36th and 17th Infantries. As a junior captain MacArthur was left unassigned to await orders. He spent the next year on leave and then on recruiting duty in New York. Finally on July 5, 1870, the War Department assigned him to the 13th Infantry at Fort Rawlins, Utah Territory. Relief from the hardship and drudgery of the frontier came in October 1874 when the 13th Infantry was sent to Louisiana on occupation duty. For MacArthur, the South had its attractions. During the winter of 1874–1875 he met Mary Pinkney Hardy in New Orleans. In May 1875 they were married at her home in Virginia. The MacArthurs had three sons—Arthur III (b. 1876), Malcom (b. 1878, died of measles 1883), and Douglas* (b. 1880).

Following his wedding, Captain MacArthur had a brief respite from troop duty, serving for a year on examination and promotion boards in Washington. But he returned to Louisiana and the 13th Infantry in 1876 as a company commander. Routine company duty continued for another ten years. In 1877 it included quelling labor violence in Pennsylvania; in 1878 and 1879 it entailed frequent moves among small posts in Louisiana and Arkansas; and in 1880 it meant returning to the frontier, this time at Fort Wingate, New Mexico. In February 1884 the company transferred to Fort Seldon on the Mexican border where MacArthur took on additional duties as post commander. He received a campaign badge for the role his troops played in the 1885 campaign against Geronimo*; it was the only Indian War campaign medal MacArthur won despite his lengthy frontier service.

In 1886, when Indian troubles ceased along the border and the 13th Infantry was dispersed among a number of posts, Company K, commanded by MacArthur, went to Fort Leavenworth, Kansas, the site of the newly established Infantry and Cavalry School. The school commandant used MacArthur as a senior instructor in infantry tactics, as well as a company commander. In 1889 MacArthur finally received promotion to major and assignment as an assistant adjutant general at the War Department in Washington. There he helped formulate a policy requiring examinations for promotion of officers below the rank of colonel; at the time this was an important reform within the officer corps. In

1893 he returned to the West, to the headquarters of the Department of Texas, still as an assistant adjutant general. Finally promoted to lieutenant colonel in May 1896, he remained an assistant adjutant general but transferred to the Department of the Dakotas where he was when the war with Spain began in April 1898.

On May 27 MacArthur received a commission as a brigadier general of volunteers and was assigned as the adjutant general of III Corps. Before the corps embarked for Cuba, however, the War Department transferred him to San Francisco to command a brigade of volunteers destined for service in the Philippines. On August 13, 1898, MacArthur's brigade participated in the capture of Manila, including the firefight at Singalong, the only appreciable skirmish of the operation.

But defeat of the Spanish did not bring peace to the islands. In February 1899 Filipino insurgents attacked American troops near Manila. This marked the beginning of what came to be known as the Philippine Insurrection. Over the course of the next year MacArthur held a number of important tactical commands and was prominent in the military suppression of the *insurrectos*. As a major general of volunteers he led the 2d Division in repulsing the initial guerrilla attack. In the spring of 1899, commanding the Department of Northern Luzon, he conducted a campaign that cleared the insurgents from the southern part of the Central Luzon Plain. That fall MacArthur's troops cooperated in a three-pronged envelopment to capture the main enemy body and end the insurrection. The operation captured the *insurrecto* capital at Tarlac, freed the remainder of the Central Luzon Plain, and broke the resistance of the main enemy army. But Emilio Aguinaldo, the leader of the insurrection, escaped to continue an intense and protracted guerrilla campaign for another year and a half.

MacArthur continued to play a key role in the military operations against the guerrillas on Luzon. On May 6, 1900, he relieved Major General Elwell S. Otis, the commanding general of the Division of the Philippines and military governor of the islands. As overall military commander in the Philippines, MacArthur combined aggressive military operations against the guerrillas with humane civic action, including establishing a system of public education, instituting a tariff system, and revising the harsh Spanish civil law code. Despite these civic measures, MacArthur believed at least a decade of military occupation was needed before the islands would be pacified. His view clashed with that of William Howard Taft who arrived in June 1900 to oversee as rapid a transition to civil government as could be effected. MacArthur, the military governor, and Taft, the civil governor, never reconciled their differences on how best to govern the Philippines.

After returning from the Philippines in 1901, MacArthur commanded in succession the Departments of the Colorado, the Lakes, and the East, and the Division of the Pacific. In March 1905 the War Department sent him to Manchuria to observe the last stages of the Russo-Japanese War after which he served several months as a military attaché in Tokyo. From November 1905 to August 1906 MacArthur toured foreign military posts and observed armies and operations in Burma, Ceylon, China, India, Indochina, Malaya, and Siam. He returned to the United States and resumed his duties as commander of the Division of the Pacific.

Over a period of years MacArthur had become increasingly critical of some of the recent War Department reforms and openly resentful that officers once his subordinates had reached positions of responsibility greater than his (especially as chief of staff). As a result, his relations with President Theodore Roosevelt* and with Taft, who became secretary of war in 1904, were strained. Although promoted to lieutenant general in September 1906, the highest rank in the Army, MacArthur did not become the chief of staff. Frustrated and disappointed, he refused when offered the command of the Eastern Department and requested either an assignment suitable to his rank or retirement. In early 1906 the War Department ordered him to Milwaukee to await further instructions. When no additional orders came, on June 2, 1909, he retired. In retirement he became active in the Military Order of the Loyal Legion, a Civil War veterans' organization. On September 5, 1912, while addressing a reunion of veterans of the 24th Wisconsin, MacArthur was fatally stricken by an apoplectic attack. He was buried in Milwaukee.

Arthur MacArthur was of that generation of U.S. Army officers, which included Adna Romanza Chaffee, Jr.,* Nelson Appleton Miles,* William Rufus Shafter,* and Samuel Baldwin Marks Young,* that entered the service as volunteers during the Civil War, received Regular Army commissions after Appomattox, endured the hard campaigns and slow promotions of the postbellum Indian-fighting Army, and became the Army's leadership during and after the Spanish-American War as the United States emerged as a world power. While MacArthur shared a common experience with these officers, his own career was exemplary as well. As one of the outstanding combat leaders in the Civil War, he was arguably the best regimental commander in the Union Army. His postwar service was typical for a Regular Army infantry officer—hard campaigns on the frontier but little combat. Yet, he enhanced his reputation as an administrator and leader, eventually getting an important staff position in the War Department. MacArthur was one of those transitional figures in the growing professionalization of the late nineteenth-century officer corps. As Civil War combat commander and Indian War campaigner, his image was that of a heroic leader. But he was also active in the effort to establish professional standards and schools— as an instructor at the Infantry and Cavalry School, in preparing the order requiring promotion examinations, and in 1907 in helping to found the School of Musketry at the Presidio of Monterey. MacArthur's tactical leadership was an important ingredient in the successful military suppression of the Philippine Insurrection. Despite his differences with Taft, his performance as military governor significantly contributed to the overall pacification of the islands. Although denied his goal of becoming chief of staff, MacArthur was promoted to lieutenant general, the only officer of that rank in the Army at the time. The promotion culminated a forty-seven year military career which saw MacArthur rise from youthful combat veteran during the Civil War to become one of the Army's leadership elite during the era of the Spanish-American War.

BIBLIOGRAPHY

Gates, John Morgan. *Schoolbooks and Krags: The United States Army in the Philippines, 1898–1902.* Westport, Conn.: Greenwood Press, 1973.

James, D. Clayton. *The Years of MacArthur: Volume I, 1880–1941.* Boston: Houghton Mifflin Company, 1970.

Miller, Stuart C. *Benevolent Assimilation: The American Conquest of the Philippines, 1899–1903.* New Haven, Conn.: Yale University Press, 1982.

Wolff, Leon. *Little Brown Brother.* New York, Doubleday and Company, 1961.

TIMOTHY K. NENNINGER

MAC ARTHUR, Douglas (b. Little Rock, Ark., January 26, 1880; d. Washington, D.C., April 5, 1964), Army officer, Allied theater, occupation commander.

Douglas MacArthur was the third son of Arthur MacArthur,* who was a distinguished commander in the Civil War, Spanish-American War, and Philippine Insurrection and the Army's highest ranking officer in 1906–1909. Douglas graduated from West Point with highest honors in 1903 and was commissioned a second lieutenant of engineers. During the following decade he served as a junior engineering officer in the Philippines, the United States, and Panama; was an aide to his father and to President Theodore Roosevelt*; graduated from the Army Engineer School of Application; and worked in the office of the chief of engineers. He was a member of the War Department General Staff, 1913–1917, his more unusual assignments including an intelligence mission with the Vera Cruz Expedition and service as War Department censor.

Upon America's entry into World War I, he was soon promoted to colonel and became chief of staff of the 42d Division, sailing with it to France in fall 1917. He served with the 42d also as brigade and division commander in the Champagne-Marne, St. Mihiel, and Meuse-Argonne operations, rising in rank to brigadier general, earning numerous decorations for heroism, and receiving two wounds in action. After the Armistice he participated in the German occupation until April 1919.

That summer he began a three-year term as superintendent of the Military Academy, followed in the 1920s by two command assignments in the Philippines, command of two corps areas in the States, duty on the court-martial of Brigadier General William ("Billy") Mitchell,* and head of the American Olympic Committee in 1928. He was promoted to major general in 1925 and five years later to general when he was appointed chief of staff of the Army. Because of the Great Depression his efforts as the Army's military head, 1930–1935, were largely devoted to preserving the establishment's meager strength. In autumn 1935 he went to the Philippines as military advisor to the Commonwealth and spent the next six years organizing Filipino defense forces. In 1936 he was designated field marshal of the Philippine Army; he retired the next year from the U.S. Army.

He was recalled to active duty as a major general in July 1941 and was given command of U.S. Army Forces in the Far East. He was advanced shortly to lieutenant general and in December to general. After the war with Japan started, he commanded a stubborn defense of the Philippines against the Japanese invaders. Before the islands fell, he went to Australia in March and subsequently assumed command of the newly established Southwest Pacific Theater.

In the Papuan Campaign, August 1942–January 1943, his Australian and American forces thwarted a Japanese drive on Port Moresby and then undertook a counteroffensive that drove the enemy out of southeastern New Guinea. In a series of amphibious assaults, September 1943–August 1944, his American Sixth Army captured the rest of New Guinea's strategic coastal points while also seizing the Admiralties and western New Britain. From early 1944 onward he employed Australian units primarily to contain or eliminate bypassed enemy garrisons. His American forces struck north of the Equator in autumn 1944, invading Morotai in the Moluccas and Leyte and Mindoro in the Philippines.

MacArthur's largest campaign of the war began in January 1945 with the Sixth Army's invasion of Luzon; by July most of the island was secured. Meanwhile, he unleashed his Eighth Army to conquer the rest of the Philippines and sent his Australian forces to invade Borneo and Brunei. Promoted to general of the Army in December 1944, he was named commanding general of U.S. Army Forces in the Pacific in April 1945. With the capitulation of Japan he received the additional appointment of Supreme Commander for the Allied Powers to accept the formal Japanese surrender in Tokyo Bay and to command the ensuing Allied occupation of Japan.

Under his efficient, if sometimes autocratic, direction the Japanese occupation, 1945–1951, was marked by success in eliminating militarist, ultranationalist, and feudal vestiges and by vigorous, although not always productive, efforts to reform that nation's political system, economy, labor relations, society, public health and welfare programs, and educational structure. Among the noteworthy achievements were a liberal constitution, land reform, women's rights, and amicable relations between Japan and the United States. In early 1947 MacArthur was given the added responsibility of heading the Far East Command, which comprised all American forces in Japan, Korea (until 1949), the Ryukyus, the Philippines, the Marianas, and the Bonins.

Shortly after the Korean War began in June 1950, he was designated commander in chief of the United Nations Command, which ultimately included units of eighteen nations, although predominantly South Korean and American. After stopping the North Korean offensive along the Naktong River that summer, MacArthur's forces launched a counteroffensive in September, highlighted by a bold amphibious assault at Inchon, that soon produced a virtual disintegration of the North Korean Army. As his troops advanced toward the Yalu River in November, massive Communist Chinese field armies attacked his widely separated Eighth Army and X Corps, forcing their retreat south of the 38th Parallel. By early 1951, however, the United Nations units had returned to the offensive, driving into North Korea again. In April President Harry S. Truman relieved MacArthur of his commands because of serious differences over civil-military relations and strategic direction of the war.

Conservative Republican factions attempted in vain to get MacArthur nominated for the presidency in 1944, 1948, and 1952. He accepted the board chairmanship of Remington Rand (later Sperry Rand) in 1952 and, except for board duties and occasional speeches, retired in seclusion in New York City. His *Reminiscences* was published in 1964. During his long career he received a large number of American and foreign military decorations as well as honorary degrees and special recognition by Congress. He was honored by a state funeral in Washington, D.C., and was buried in Norfolk, Virginia.

It is unlikely that any biographer will probe fully the personality of MacArthur. His was an enormously complex blend of contradictory traits—egotistical yet modest, flamboyant but shy, austere and gracious, aloof but charming, decisive yet hesitant. Opinions of MacArthur the man vary greatly but usually depend on the degree of personal acquaintance with him: most of his staff officers were bound to him by charisma and intense loyalty, while his severest critics generally had little or no personal contact with him. For the researcher, analysis of his personality is complicated by the host of myths that grew about him, many of which have never been separated from reality, and by the paucity and unrevealing nature of his personal papers. Moreover, his elusiveness is compounded by his mastery of role-taking, whereby he could project, often with uncanny skill, the image he desired for a particular occasion or audience. His beliefs ranged from ultraconservative to liberal, depending on the issue. Thus, while gaining the admiration of American rightists for his militant anticommunism, he could also appeal to former New Dealers with his reforms in Japan.

MacArthur's genius showed most lucidly in his leadership as West Point superintendent, wartime theater commander in the Southwest Pacific, and occupation administrator in Japan. Among his most significant, if not best known, achievements were his pioneering reforms at the Military Academy, 1919–1922, that brought the school, then at its all-time ebb, a revitalized and more versatile curriculum, modernized teaching methods, and new standards of excellence. "If Sylvanus Thayer* was the Father of the Military Academy," one authority asserts, "then Douglas MacArthur was its savior."

While the formulation of strategy in the Pacific and Korean wars was undertaken primarily by the Joint Chiefs and their planners, MacArthur excelled at implementing strategic directives with imagination, shrewdness, and boldness, exploiting to the fullest the often minimal logistic support he received and achieving objectives with extraordinarily low casualty rates among his forces. British Field Marshals Alan Brooke and Bernard Montgomery, among other leaders of World War II, declared him to be the outstanding Allied commander of that conflict. His mastery at coordinating ground, naval, and air forces of several nations in well-executed amphibious assaults was demonstrated on scores of occasions in the war against Japan, but his most brilliant stroke in amphibious warfare, the Inchon Operation, was carried to success when he was seventy years old. For all his triumphs, however, he also bore the command responsibility for the defeats by Japan in the Philippines, 1941–1942, and by China in Korea in 1950.

Operating his general headquarters in Tokyo with an effectiveness seldom achieved in so large a bureaucratic structure, MacArthur presided over the vast network of occupation programs with dedication, idealism, empathy, and firm control, making his administration in Japan one of the most enlightened of any occupation in history. Indeed, his leadership in occupied Japan may be viewed by future authorities as the most important phase of his career.

To one who studies MacArthur's behavior over his five decades of military service it is unfortunate but predictable that a leader with such monumental gifts and flaws would face a climactic clash such as occurred in his controversy with Truman in 1950–1951. Although they were evident in episodes on a lesser scale previously, that collision made tragically apparent his more serious limitations, namely, an acute sensitivity to criticism, an inability to adjust to limited warfare or to considerations of global strategy, and an attitude of condescension toward superiors that bordered on insubordination.

BIBLIOGRAPHY

James, D. Clayton. *The Years of MacArthur*. 2 vols. to date. Boston: Houghton Mifflin Company, 1970–1975.
MacArthur, Douglas. *Reminiscences*. New York: McGraw-Hill, 1964.
Whan, Vorin E., Jr., ed. *A Soldier Speaks: Public Papers and Speeches of General of the Army Douglas MacArthur*. New York: Frederick A. Praeger, 1965.
Willoughby, Charles A., ed. *Reports of General MacArthur*. 4 vols. Washington, D.C.: U.S. Department of the Army, 1966.

                                                                    D. CLAYTON JAMES

MC CLELLAN, George Brinton (b. Philadelphia, Pa., December 3, 1826; d. Orange, N.J., October 29, 1885), Army officer. McClellan was the controversial Union Army general in chief in the Civil War, and moulder and early commander of the Army of the Potomac.

Of Connecticut ancestry, George B. McClellan was born in Philadelphia, the son of a prominent physician who founded Jefferson Medical College. Following education at the University of Pennsylvania Preparatory School, young McClellan, by special action, was permitted to enter the U.S. Military Academy at West Point two years before having attained the minimum age. A brilliant cadet, he graduated second in his class of fifty-nine in 1846, during the Mexican War, and was commissioned in the Corps of Engineers.

On the triumphant campaign for Mexico City led by Winfield Scott,* Mc-

Clellan won two brevets for courageous and exemplary conduct and refused a third as unmerited. This service was followed by a three-year instructorship at West Point, engineering duties that took him across the country on surveys for possible transcontinental railroad routes, and—by then a captain—membership in the American mission in the mid-1850s to observe the siege of Sevastopol in the Crimean War. After his tour, he remained in Europe to study the military practices, institutions, and equipment of a number of nations, which he reported in a lengthy and perspicacious volume published by the Congress. Also emanating from his recommendations was the famous "McClellan saddle," which he brought back to America and which was used by the cavalry as long as the Army had horses.

McClellan resigned from the Army in 1857 to become chief engineer of the Illinois Central Railroad and then vice president of that railway, one of whose lawyers was Abraham Lincoln.* McClellan was subsequently named president of the Ohio and Mississippi Railraod.

When the Civil War erupted, McClellan returned to the Federal service as major general of U.S. Volunteers in command of troops from Ohio, Indiana, and Illinois. In this capacity, on his own initiative, he launched a vigorous offensive into the mountains of northwestern Virginia, winning victories in the miniature but significant battles in June and July 1861 at Philippi, Rich Mountain, and Carrick's Ford. These accomplishments went far toward shaping the creation in 1863 of the new pro-Union state of West Virginia. McClellan received warm encomiums from General in Chief Scott, President Lincoln, and the cabinet for his "activity, valor, and . . . successes." Then, following the staggering Union defeat at First Bull Run on July 21, 1861, he was called to Washington, D.C., to assume command of what was soon known as the Army of the Potomac.

Though slightly under medium height, McClellan was a handsome, erect, muscular man with dark red hair, mustache, and touch of a goatee. He was a soldier of commanding presence. This able officer became one of the most popular—and controversial—generals ever to command American troops in war. He took the summer, autumn, and winter of 1861 to organize and build the truly superb Army of the Potomac which, under a number of inept future commanders, proved to be, first, the shield of the Union and, eventually, under George Gordon Meade* and Ulysses Simpson Grant,* the sword that would compel the surrender of the Confederate Army under Robert Edward Lee* in 1865. From November 1, 1861, to March 11, 1862, the thirty-five-year-old McClellan was general in chief of all the Union armies, and he was an imaginative chieftain who early saw the necessity of coordinated action by all the Federal field forces.

Slowed by a severe case of typhoid fever and occasionally by his own magnification of difficulties, McClellan delayed the advance of the Army of the Potomac against the Confederate capital of Richmond until the early spring of 1862. After protracted and at time heated debates with Lincoln and the hostile secretary of war, Edwin McMasters Stanton,* over the timing and route of movement, the general landed his army at Fortress Monroe and marched up the historic Peninsula between the York and James rivers through the heaviest rains known there in twenty years. Overly cautious, he laid siege to Yorktown, which fell on May 4, 1862, after a month's investment. When he reached a point some four miles from Richmond, McClellan was attacked by graycoats under Joseph Eggleston Johnston* on May 31 in the two-day Battle of Fair Oaks (Seven Pines), but, after an initial setback, the Federal commander repulsed the enemy assaults and inched closer to Richmond. With Lee now in command of the army of Northern Virginia, heavy Confederate attacks in the great Seven Days' Battle in the last week of June were—except at Gaines' Mill—repelled by McClellan, the fighting culminating in the massive and bloody repulse of the Southerners at Malvern Hill. The Union suffered more than fifteen thousand casualties in the Seven Days compared to more than twenty thousand casualties sustained by the Confederates.

When Lincoln visited the army at nearby Harrison's Landing, McClellan and all of the other generals but one urged that it be reinforced and allowed to continue the operation against Richmond. But, despite "Little Mac's" protestations, the president and the new general in chief, the inept Henry Wager Halleck,* ordered the Army of the Potomac back to Washington, thereby giving up the campaign. A number of its divisions served under the command of John Pope* in his disastrous Second Manassas Campaign in August 1862. With Pope badly defeated in that engagement and the demoralized army retreating in rout upon Washington, McClellan was again put at its head. It was one of the most trying assignments given a commander on either side during the war.

In a remarkable feat, McClellan reorganized his army while on the march northwestwardly from Washington to enable it to confront Lee and counter his first invasion of the North. Wresting the vital initiative from the hitherto victorious gray leader in the Battle of South Mountain on September 14, 1862, McClellan gained a triumph that impelled Lee to fight in a cramped defensive position along the Antietam Creek at Sharpsburg, Maryland. There, on September 17, in the bloodiest single-day's battle of the war, McClellan, in fourteen hours of desperate fighting, hurled a series of heavy attacks at the Confederates; but, owing chiefly to the procrastination of Ambrose Everett Burnside* on the Federal left, the resulting piecemeal blows, though winning much ground, were unable to smash or rout Lee's army. Although gaining little more than a tactical draw, McClellan had nonetheless won a strategic success of inestimable value; the battle of Antietam had blocked the threat of foreign intervention in the war. When McClellan failed to advance into Virginia as swiftly as the administration wished, and owing also to political factors, he was relieved of his command on November 5, 1862, to be replaced by the least effective of the Union corps commanders, Burnside.

McClellan ran unsuccessfully for the presidency in 1864 on the Democratic ticket. He had resigned from the Army on election day. In the years after Appomattox, Little Mac headed several large engineering enterprises, indulged his tastes in the arts, languages, literature, travel, and mountain climbing, and was an able and popular governor of New Jersey for two terms. McClellan died of heart trouble in 1885, one of the most beloved of Union Army generals. One of his pallbearers was his old Confederate opponent on the Peninsula, Joseph E. Johnston.*

McClellan's reputation as a major figure among Civil War generals is assured. It is based largely on his taking over command of the main Federal army in the East after it had suffered two terrible defeats at Manassas and shaping that massive host into a magnificent fighting machine. His Peninsula Campaign was well conceived and planned, and less direct involvement by the administration might have gone far toward making it more successful than it was. Too, his tactical handling of the Army of the Potomac in the Seven Days battle, culminating in one of Lee's worst defeats, at Malvern Hill, was impressive, as was his whipping of the Army into shape sufficient to gain the all-important initiative at South Mountain and, with heightened morale, to turn back Lee's invasion at Antietam at a time when Great Britain was close to recognizing Southern independence and intervening decisively in the war on behalf of the Confederacy.

On the minus side, McClellan was too much the perfectionist, ever hoping to plan operations down to the last detail without allowing for the inspiration of the moment to cope with imponderables that would inevitably arise. But many of his best efforts were hampered by the hostile and powerful Radical Republicans in Congress, by the belligerent Stanton and the ineffective Halleck, and occasionally by the well-meaning but initially inexperienced Lincoln.

Knowledgeable in the use of the combined arms of infantry, cavalry, and artillery, and possessing an encyclopedic and comprehensive grasp of military art and science, McClellan was flawed by his inability to mesh with the system of civil-military relations inherent in the American polity, a balance which he recognized but with which he found it difficult to accommodate himself. Yet, in the final analysis, his achievements—some of them masterful—outweighed his shortcomings, and the Union was fortunate that, in the early stages of the conflict, a lesser man was not at the helm of their main military effort in the East.

BIBLIOGRAPHY

Hassler, Warren W., Jr. *Commanders of the Army of the Potomac*. Baton Rouge: Louisiana State University Press, 1962.
————. *General George B. McClellan, Shield of the Union*. Baton Rouge: Louisiana State University Press, 1957.
McClellan, George B. *McClellan's Own Story: The War for the Union*. New York: C. L. Webster, 1887.
Myers, William S. *A Study in Personality: General George Brinton McClellan*. D. Appleton-Century, 1934.
Williams, T. Harry. *Lincoln and His Generals*. New York: Alfred A. Knopf, 1952.

WARREN W. HASSLER, JR.

MC CLERNAND, John Alexander (b. Hardinsburg, Ky., 1812; d. September 20, 1900, Springfield, Ill.), Army officer. McClernand was commander of the Union XIII Corps at Vicksburg.

McClernand, one of the more successful "political" generals of the Civil War, eventually lost his command and his military career because of intra-army politics. At an early age he moved with his widowed mother from Kentucky to Shawneetown, Illinois. There he grew up and, like many ambitious young men in Illinois, read law, opened a law office, and entered politics. He held a seat in the Illinois legislature (1836–1842) and between 1843 and 1861 served six terms as a representative to Congress. As a staunch Democrat, he figured prominently in the sectional struggles of the 1850s, and in 1860 he supported Stephen A. Douglas for the presidency. In the ensuing secession crisis, McClernand directed his considerable political and oratorical ability against the Republicans and the secessionists in equal proportion. His aim was to establish the northern Democrats as the great center, the conservative force in the nation.

When compromise failed and war came, McClernand entered the Union Army as a brigadier general of volunteers. In common with many Democrats, especially from the Northwest, he sympathized with the South in some respects, but not to the extent of accepting secession. No man from his section, he said, could stand by and see the Mississippi closed off by a foreign power. Though appointed by President Abraham Lincoln* for obvious political reasons (his standing with the Democrats and especially those of southern Illinois), McClernand became an effective troop commander. He led a division at Forts Henry and Donelson (February 1862), and at Shiloh (April 1862).

Following the Shiloh-Corinth Campaign, McClernand returned to Illinois, presumably at Governor Richard Yates' request, in order to assist in recruiting. At some point during the late summer of 1862, McClernand resolved to go to Washington, there to place before the president the idea of raising a large force in the Northwest, which the Illinois general would then lead in a grand campaign to open the Mississippi. Lincoln concurred (he knew that McClernand was a popular Democrat and a formidable recruiter), but the order from Secretary of War Edwin McMasters Stanton* that formalized the plan was hedged in terms that led to McClernand's eventual dismissal. Victor Hicken, the authority on McClernand's career, has written: "As clever as McClernand was, he did not understand at this stage that he was operating against three of the subtlest minds in the nation—those of the President, Stanton, and [Henry Wager] Halleck.*" The order read that McClernand would command only so far as the needs of the service, as interpreted by General in Chief Halleck, might demand. In short, the stage was set for McClernand to raise a large force, which could be taken under the overall command of Ulysses Simpson Grant.* McClernand took charge of Union forces at Millikens Bend, Mississippi, in late 1862, superseding a thoroughly disgruntled William Tecumseh Sherman.* McClernand's first project was the capture of Arkansas Post, which he effected in early January 1863. This success led Grant, at the behest of Sherman and James Birdseye McPherson,* to bring McClernand under his command for the movement against Vicksburg. McClernand was understandably chagrined, but the transfer was justified by the original orders signed by Stanton and now put into effect by Halleck.

McClernand, commanding the XIII Corps, played a significant role in the Vicksburg Campaign, as a troop leader and as the focus of a power play engineered by Grant, Sherman, and McPherson, and prompted by his own impolitic statements, private as well as public. While he handled his corps in a competent manner, he was so thoroughly out of favor with the West Pointers that it was only a matter of time until he faced removal.

Grant's opportunity came after the Union assault against Vicksburg on May 22. When the assault had practically bogged down, McClernand sent word to Grant that elements of his corps were inside the Confederate works and with support from Sherman or McPherson he could effect a general breach. Grant, reluctantly, ordered a renewal of the assault but without success and with significant additional casualties. McClernand was criticized for what seemed to be at least bad judgment, but the storm broke when, in his typical spread-eagle style, he issued a congratulatory order to his corps, giving it great credit for its work on May 22 and implying it had not been properly supported at a critical time. When this order appeared in the newspapers, Grant ordered McClernand's relief on the grounds that he had not cleared his public statement through the proper military channels.

McClernand returned to Springfield where he pursued his defense via a series of letters to the president. Unfortunately for McClernand, Grant took Vicksburg. As Lincoln put it, he could not return McClernand to the XIII Corps without in effect forcing Grant's resignation. In early 1864 McClernand did return to his command, in time for the Red River Expedition under Nathaniel Banks, but he fell seriously ill with malaria and once again returned to Illinois, out of the war for good. Following the war he served in minor political positions and attempted, unsuccessfully, to salvage his wartime reputation.

McClernand's place in the history of the Civil War has rested largely on his negative role as a foil for Grant and Grant's West Point associates in Mississippi. In short, McClernand was an obstacle to be overcome before Grant could fully emerge as the leader of *the* Union Army. This analysis is not necessarily an accurate portrayal of McClernand as a person and particularly not as a soldier. Indeed, he was an ambitious man; he was also given to public boasting and was personally irascible. He was jealous of his prerogatives and did not hesitate to use his political connections to further his military career. Of course, these lines could apply to practically every major military figure of the Union Army.

McClernand used his considerable political appeal to raise troops for the Union, even while promoting his own interests. He guarded his position with good reason; there were those in high places who were anxious to see him trimmed to size. His irascibility could be described in other contexts as frontier roughness of manner or admirable directness. As a troop leader, he was personally courageous, and from all accounts he was fully capable of commanding soldiers in the field, from the regimental to the corps levels. He received considerable praise (including that in Grant's reports) for his leadership at Fort Donelson and Shiloh, and while he ran afoul of Grant in 1863, his capture of Arkansas Post and his subsequent command of the XIII Corps suggest that he was capable of greater things. Whether he could have handled the Army of the Tennessee can only be a matter for conjecture. However, there is nothing in his career prior to his relief to suggest that he could not have. Certainly, when compared to other "political" generals who commanded armies—Benjamin Franklin Butler* and N. P. Banks— McClernand ranks well. Had he managed to defer more gracefully to Grant, he might have ascended to higher command; he was the senior corps commander.

McClernand's fellow Illinoisan and "political General" John A. Logan fell victim to a similar trade union mentality on the part of the West Pointers, when in 1864, Sherman would not name him commander of the Army of the Tennessee following McPherson's death. No doubt Logan was as fully capable as Oliver Otis Howard,* or most of the other corps commanders in Georgia. Logan's bitterness was fairly sublimated, but he later made the point that graduation from West Point did not necessarily determine the quality of the officer; that success in the field should also be considered. In this light, both he and McClernand were ill treated by the military and political establishment. These two political generals, at least, could not play the Army's political game as well as could their adversaries.

BIBLIOGRAPHY

Bearss, Edwin C. *Decision in Mississippi.* Jackson, Miss.: Mississippi Commission on the War between the States, 1962.
Catton, Bruce. *Grant Moves South.* Boston: Little, Brown and Company, 1960.
Hicken, Victor. *Illinois in the Civil War.* Urbana: University of Illinois Press, 1966.
Liddell Hart, B.H. *Sherman.* New York: Dodd, Mead and Company, 1929.

JOHN T. HUBBELL

MACDONOUGH, Thomas (b. New Castle County, Del., December 31, 1783; d. at sea, November 10, 1825), naval officer. Macdonough is known for his victory on Lake Champlain during the War of 1812.

Thomas Macdonough was the sixth of ten children of Major Thomas Macdonough, a wealthy physician who was a judge and served as speaker of the Delaware Council. Little is known of his early years. Shortly after the return of his brother James, who had lost a leg in the battle between the American frigate *Constellation* and the French frigate *Insurgente*, Thomas, then a clerk in Middletown, decided to enter the Navy. He received his midshipman's warrant on February 5, 1800, shipped for the West Indies aboard a 24-gun corvette the following May, and took part in the capture of three French vessels during the Quasi-War.

Macdonough had political connections who saved him from dismissal when the Navy was reduced in 1801 and procured his assignment to the 38-gun frigate *Constellation*, which was operating against Tripolitan pirates in the Mediterranean. In 1803 he was transferred to the 38-gun frigate *Philadelphia*. Later that year the pirates' capture of the *Philadelphia* led to his posting to the 12-gun schooner *Enterprise* commanded by Stephen Decatur.* With Decatur he took part in the burning of the *Philadelphia* (February 16, 1804) and an attack on Tripolitan gunboats. His courage in leading a boarding party led to his promotion, and during the following year Macdonough served as first lieutenant aboard the *Enterprise* and later aboard the 16-gun schooner *Syren*. Years later, he called these years in the Mediterranean and his service with Commodore Edward Preble* "the school where our navy received its first lessons."

In 1806 Macdonough was ordered to assist Isaac Hull* in constructing gunboats at Middletown, Connecticut. There he married Lucy Ann Shaler and received his permanent commission as a lieutenant (January 1806). He spent the years 1807 and 1808 aboard the 18-gun sloop-of-war *Wasp* on a voyage to England and the Mediterranean and in enforcing the Embargo along the Atlantic Coast. Since he had little chance for promotion, he obtained a furlough from the Navy and captained a merchant ship on a voyage to England and India. Such a leave of absence was a common practice among American naval officers of the time.

When war broke out with Britain in 1812, Macdonough returned to the Navy as first lieutenant of the *Constellation*, which was then fitting out in Washington. When active service did not appear imminent in that capacity, he sought and received orders transferring him to command of the gunboats defending Portland, Maine. From there he was ordered to Burlington, Vermont (October 1812), to take command of naval forces on Lake Champlain.

It was near the end of the operating season when Macdonough arrived, and he devoted the remainder of the year to fitting out the three sloops and two gunboats that comprised his squadron. Early the following spring one of his subordinates lost two of the sloops when he foolishly attacked the enemy at Isle aux Noix. Ascendancy then passed to the British, who, for the first time, ventured into American waters and captured some merchant vessels before approaching Burlington. Macdonough was working under severe handicaps throughout this period but soon was able to complete work on three sloops and four gunboats, and with these he forced the enemy to retreat into Canadian waters.

The spring of 1814 brought increased significance to the Lake Champlain region. Prior to this time, both the British and the Americans had focused their attention on the Great Lakes and the West, and Macdonough had been allocated few naval stores, seamen, or shipwrights. When the victory by Oliver Hazard Perry* on Lake Erie secured that area for the United States, Britain shifted its attention eastward to the Hudson River Valley. Control of Lake Champlain was essential to the success of operations in the area, and there ensued a naval building race in which neither side obtained a clear advantage.

In August British General Sir George Prevost began moving his fourteen thousand-man army southward. He was supported on his flank by Captain George Downie's squadron of sixteen vessels mounting ninety-two guns. Its flagship, the frigate *Confiance* (37 guns), was the largest ship on the lake and far superior to Macdonough's 26-gun corvette *Saratoga*. American General Alexander Macomb* had his forty-five hundred-man army, largely composed of raw militia, dug in at Plattsburgh, New York, on the western bank of the lake, but it was no match for Prevost's men who were veterans of Wellington's campaigns. Macdonough knew that his four ships and twelve galleys would be destroyed by the British in open water. He knew also that a victory by Prevost would allow the British to use their field artillery to force him out into the lake. Thus, he decided to anchor his ships off the town of Plattsburgh in such a position that he could support Macomb's right flank and at the same time deny the enemy the opportunity to bring his superior fleet to bear. Goaded by Prevost, Downie attacked the Americans on September 11, 1814, only to die in the opening minutes of the battle. In time, both flagships' broadsides were so shattered that neither could continue effective fire. Macdonough then used a preset kedge anchor to swing the *Saratoga* around to bring a fresh broadside to bear. The British failed in their attempt to execute the same maneuver, getting the *Confiance* only half way around and thus allowing the *Saratoga* to rake her. Macdonough's victory was complete. Every British vessel was near sinking; the American ships were in little better condition and unable to pursue the British Army when the naval loss rendered Prevost's position untenable and forced him to retire to Canada, leaving behind a large quantity of stores. The battle had been so fierce that a British veteran of Trafalgar described that fleet action as ''a mere flea bite in comparison with this.'' Macdonough received a congressional resolution of thanks and promotion from the rank of master commandant (which he had held since July 24, 1813) to that of captain, to date from the time of the battle.

Following the peace, Macdonough briefly commanded the *Fulton First*, the Navy's first steam vessel which was then under construction in New York. On July 1, 1815, he relieved Isaac Hull in command of the Portsmouth Navy Yard where he spent the next three years fitting out ships and planning shore facilities. During this period his health was in decline, and service in a milder climate seemed wise. In April 1818 he obtained command of the 44-gun frigate *Guerriere* and made a voyage to the Mediterranean. For the five succeeding years he was officially the commander of the 74-gun line-of-battle ship *Ohio*, which was then under construction in New York. He actually passed most of the time at his home in Delaware serving the Navy in various administrative capacities.

Macdonough repeatedly applied for service afloat and in 1824 obtained command of the 44-gun frigate *Constitution* setting sail for the Mediterranean in October. The warmer clime failed to repair his health, and a year later he boarded a merchant brig in Gibraltar to return home. Macdonough died en route on November 10, 1825. His remains were carried to New York City for an elaborate funeral and then to Middletown for burial beside his wife who had died three months earlier. Five of the couple's ten children survived them.

Macdonough's place in history is secured by his service on Lake Champlain from 1812 to 1815. At the least, his victory at Plattsburgh saved northern New York and Vermont from enemy occupation and deprived the British of grounds for territorial claims in the peace settlement. Had Macdonough been defeated, Prevost would almost certainly have successfully executed a plan much like John Burgoyne's of the Revolution. American peace negotiators used Macdonough's victory to obtain a treaty even before the outcome of the Battle of New Orleans was known. His battle with Downie has often been cited as a model of tactical preparation and execution. Carefully choosing his position and preparing for every possible contingency, Macdonough forced an enemy with superior power to engage him at a disadvantage. His victory is often considered the climactic battle of the war.

Throughout his career, Macdonough was a conscientious officer who was revered by his men, and he was always on close personal terms with his fellow officers. He was a good administrator and a man of trusted judgment who served on several courts-martial. His courage under fire, his sense of tactical timing, and his seamanship made him one of the best of "Preble's boys."

BIBLIOGRAPHY

Dean, Leon W. *Guns over Champlain*. New York: Rinehart, 1946.
Lewis, Charles L. *Famous American Naval Officers*. Boston: L. C. Page, 1942.
Mahan, Alfred T. *Sea Power in Its Relations to the War of 1812*. 2 vols. Boston: Little, Brown and Company, 1905.
Muller, Charles G. *The Proudest Day: Macdonough on Lake Champlain*. New York: John Day Company, 1960.

JAMES C. BRADFORD

MC DOUGALL, Alexander (b. 1732, Isle of Islay, Inner Hebrides, Scotland; d. New York City, June 10, 1786), Revolutionary War general.

McDougall's family moved to New York in 1738 as part of a large movement of Highland Scots looking for opportunity. Plans for frontier settlement in upstate New York fell through, and so his family lived in New York City where Alexander helped his father deliver milk to city customers. He served a short period as a tailor's apprentice at which time he learned the fundamentals of reading and writing.

McDougall became a sailor in his early teens, and at age nineteen he returned to his native Scotland to visit kinsmen. There he married a distant cousin, Ann Nancy McDougall. By age twenty-five he commanded an 8-gun sloop with a crew of sixty-two. In two years he commanded a 12-gun vessel with a crew of ninety and had a letter of marque to prey on French shipping signed by the governor of the Leeward Islands. As a result of privateering during the French and Indian War, he made a small fortune and settled in New York City. In 1763 his wife died, and he married Hannah Bostwick.

Before 1765 there is no indication McDougall took part in any political issues. He kept to his business matters. After 1765 he began to take an active part in politics. In 1768 an anonymous pamphlet entitled "A Son of Liberty to the Betrayed Inhabitants of the City and Colony of New York" was declared to be libel. The printer testified that McDougall was the author, and he was jailed in February 1770. He refused to post bail and gathered quite a reputation and following while he was in prison. He was released over a year later in March 1771 when he emerged as a popular leader and martyr for freedom. His popularity and that of other radical leaders declined steadily until April 1775 when battles took place at Lexington and Concord, Massachusetts.

On June 30, 1775, New York appointed four regimental colonels, one of whom was McDougall, who commanded the 1st New York Regiment. He was most successful in recruiting his unit from the slums and docks of the city, a fact commented upon by many who saw his soldiers.

General Philip Schuyler* ordered McDougall to fortify New York City, but he was only partially successful. He did gather most of the military stores in the city and shipped a large part to George Washington's* army, keeping the remainder from the British. By the end of July 1775, McDougall's regiment, led by Rudolphus Ritzema, became part of the Canadian Invasion while McDougall was ordered to remain in New York City recruiting and gathering supplies. He was criticized for staying behind, but John Jay and General Schuyler came to his defense. On May 1, 1776, McDougall's regiment was placed in the Continental Army, and in August 1776, in response to Washington's request for additional brigade commanders, McDougall was named brigadier general. His first action was on Long Island. Washington put McDougall in charge of the evacuation of Long Island because of his maritime background, and later his troops guarded Hell's Gate. The evacuation of Long Island was one of the noteworthy military movements of the war.

His first battle was in October at White Plains where he constructed fortifications on Chatterton's Hill. He also commanded the sixteen hundred men defending the hill. During a frontal attack his militia broke and forced his retreat. From all accounts American resistance to that point had been staunch. On McDougall's orders as the principal American commander the rest of his troops made an orderly withdrawal. As usual, British pursuit was short-lived, but his men did guard King's Bridge over the Croton River on the retreat route.

Since McDougall was in poor health, Washington assigned him to protect the Highlands which flank the Hudson River north of Westchester County. In this area there was much guerrilla-type warfare. He was responsible for laying the chain across the river and maintaining a spy network that operated into British-held New York City.

Washington called him south to participate in the Battle of Germantown on October 4, 1777. His troops performed well on Old School House Lane where his command and John Peter Muhlenberg's men drove to the center of town before they were stopped and almost encircled. They fought their way back to friendly forces and provided a rearguard element when the Army panicked.

On October 20, 1777, McDougall was promoted to major general, but his health forced him to take a leave of absence from the Army. In March 1778 he rejoined the Army and returned to the Hudson River to work on defenses. He spent the winter of 1779 at Fishkill but asked to be relieved of command at West Point in December because of failing health. In June 1780 he thought himself fit, and Washington ordered him to West Point. In October 1780 McDougall was elected as a New York delegate to the Continental Congress. Washington released him from service with the understanding that he would return to the Army if needed. He served in Congress from January to March 1781. He was elected secretary of the new Marine Department but did not wish to continue in the office because he would have to relinquish his major general rank.

In 1782 McDougall quarreled with his senior commander, Major General William Heath, and seven court-martial charges were drawn up against McDougall. His trial began at West Point in April 1782 where after several weeks he was acquitted on all charges except demeaning his commanding officer. His punishment was a reprimand from Washington.

McDougall acted as an intermediary negotiating for soldiers' pay and rewards with Congress. He was instrumental in founding the Society of Cincinnati and was its first treasurer-general. He was one of the select officers at Fraunces' Tavern where Washington made his farewell.

He served in the New York Senate from 1784 to 1786 and helped organize the Bank of New York and was elected its first president. By April 1786 his health failed completely, and he was confined to bed. On June 10 he died at the age of fifty-three.

One of the best commentaries on his career was made by McDougall himself: "Although my services have not been brilliant, yet neither the state of which I am subject nor the army of which I am a member have been disgraced by them." McDougall was clearly a secondary figure, but one of the many without whose efforts the war would not have been successful. He was a leader of men; he was ambitious and usually worked on the edge of authority. His life-style in New York City was considered gauche by some of the established families. Honor was paramount; however, after the death of his son in the Quebec Campaign he ignored several slights and remained in the service to his country as his health would allow. His promotion to brigadier general was based on political rather than military considerations, but he performed well in battle and his advance to major general was due to military merit.

McDougall was among a small group of senior officers who looked upon Washington as the essence of the war effort. Washington thought highly of him, as did the Marquis de Lafayette* and other principal generals. After Germantown, Washington recommended McDougall for promotion by saying, "from the time of his appointment as brigadier, from his abilities, military knowledge and approved bravery, (he) has every claim to promotion."

McDougall had unglamorous jobs such as ferrying troops on Long Island, acting as rearguard commander, dealing with spies and civilian problems, and defending the Highlands in an irregular type of warfare. He was a good drinking companion, honest, outspoken in his opinions, considerate of his men, and keen to defend the causes and friends he held dear. At the war's end he was the tenth ranking American general.

He received pay only twice during the war and depleted his wealth by outfitting four regiments during the course of the war. Toward the end of the conflict he was forced to decline several assignments because he was financially unable to appear as his rank dictated.

McDougall went from pirate to nouveau riche, to political dissenter to military organizer and combat leader, and then to bank president and senator. He used the period of social and political turmoil to better his position without compromising his principles. In other terms he went from a radical leader to an effective general to a conservative bank president. He was one of the few whose talents operated before, during, and after the war. If his health had been better, he might have been a primary national figure.

BIBLIOGRAPHY

Boatner, Mark M. *Dictionary of the American Revolution.* New York: David McKay, 1976.
Champagne, Roger J. *Alexander McDougall and the American Revolution in New York.* Schenectady, N.Y.: Union College Press, 1975.
McDougall, William L. *Biography of General Alexander McDougall.* Westport, Conn.: Greenwood Press, 1977.

LYNN L. SIMS

MC DOWELL, Irvin (b. Columbus, Ohio, October 15, 1818; d. San Francisco, Calif., May 4, 1885), Army officer. McDowell commanded the Union Army at the First Battle of Bull Run in the Civil War.

Irvin McDowell came of a good family with excellent background and connections. His early education was in France, but in 1834, at age sixteen, he received appointment to the U.S. Military Academy at West Point. He graduated four years later, ranking twenty-third in a class of forty-five. His first assignment was with the 1st Artillery Regiment along the Canadian border, but in 1841 he returned to West Point for a four-year posting as adjutant and instructor of tactics.

The War with Mexico sent McDowell south on the staff of General John Ellis Wool.* At Buena Vista, McDowell performed gallantly and won a brevet captaincy, but with the return of peace, he continued in his staff duties. He served in several bureaus of the War Department including the Adjutant General's Office, and in 1858–1859 he returned to the Continent to study military administration as an official observer.

McDowell was a major with more than twenty years' service when the Civil War began. Furthermore, he had high connections in the Army thanks to his years in Washington at headquarters. He was aide de camp to Lieutenant General Winfield Scott* and was certain to receive an important command in the coming war. McDowell enjoyed wide respect within the military establishment, although he suffered from personal traits that put off many with whom he needed to work. Gluttonous by nature, aloof, seemingly cold, and inattentive, unable to remember names, McDowell unintentionally alienated many about him. Thus, he began the war with serious handicaps, the more so since he began almost at the top.

Thanks to the backing of Scott, several cabinet members, and congressmen, McDowell received a brigadier generalcy and command of the Department of Northeastern Virginia. His task was to raise an army to defend the capital and put down the rebellious army in Virginia. McDowell moved with energy and ability in building his army and did so even against the opposition of Scott, who soon discovered that his protegé would not be manipulated. Thus, Scott and others joined those who had already been offended by McDowell's manner.

Yet no one could seriously fault McDowell's energy and results. By late June 1861 he had formed and trained a substantial army in the Washington-Alexandria area, and under constant pressure from President Abraham Lincoln* and others within the government, produced a plan for meeting and defeating the Confederate Army which was then forming around Centreville. Not even Scott could criticize his plan, which called for a move around the enemy right flank to cut off the Rebels from their capital in Richmond and their supply. With thirty-seven thousand Union troops to twenty thousand Confederates, McDowell should have been able to do it.

On July 16 McDowell's army began to march south toward Centreville and Bull Run, a small stream that flowed nearby. In the battle on July 21, McDowell and the Union suffered one of the most humiliating defeats in American military history, thanks chiefly to the ineptitude of General Robert Patterson,* who allowed major reinforcements to come to the Confederate Army facing McDowell. Nevertheless, the defeat effectively destroyed McDowell's further service in command of his army.

Shortly after the battle at Bull Run, McDowell lost his command to George Brinton McClellan,* and then took charge of the I Corps of McClellan's army. He did not perform well in the battles of the second Manassas Campaign, and afterward he took a leading role in the inglorious defamation and court-martial of General Fitz John Porter.* McDowell himself was under investigation, being charged with treason by many who could not forget his Bull Run disaster. Accused of being drunk—he was a teetotaler—and criminally incompetent at Second Manassas, McDowell won exoneration but his career was ruined.

Until May 1864 he performed minor administrative duty and then went into virtual exile in command of the Department of the Pacific. Yet he worked well in the difficult task of commanding a vast expanse of territory with only nine thousand soldiers. At war's end he remained in the Army, transferring from post to post and regaining much of his lost stature. In 1872 he replaced George Gordon Meade* as commander of the Division of the South but four years later returned to command the Pacific territory. He retired in 1882 and lived out his days in San Francisco, serving for a time as park commissioner.

McDowell deserved better both in his own time and afterwards. His strategic and tactical planning in his Bull Run Campaign was of a high order, particularly for that stage of the war. He showed a full appreciation of the limitations and capabilities of all branches of the service, excepting only an underestimation of the potential of cavalry. He realized the enormous impact that the railroad could have on the war, and he knew better than most that if Patterson failed to keep the small army of Joseph Eggleston Johnston* occupied in the Shenandoah Valley, Johnston could use the rail line to join Pierre Gustave Toutant Beauregard* and the Confederates in his front with great speed, which is exactly what happened. McDowell was flexible in the field, a trait not enjoyed by many better generals. When personal examination of the terrain around Bull Run showed that he could not turn the Confederate right flank as he had planned, he quickly adapted his plan to envelop the left flank instead.

In actual battle, McDowell performed with no more or less ability than did other generals—North and South—in the first days of the war. He wasted his command by allowing piecemeal attacks in regimental and brigade strength rather than taking advantage of his initial numerical superiority over the enemy. Furthermore, his use of staff did not allow him to remain fully informed of what transpired on all parts of the field, with the result that he never exercised real control over his whole army in the fight. At Bull Run he learned the same lessons that many other outstanding Federal commanders would learn in the war, but his was the misfortune to be the first to have to learn them, and at the cost of a defeat that became a national disgrace. And thanks to the defects in his own personality, McDowell unwittingly created an atmosphere in which many high-ranking officers and civilians were glad of an excuse to make him the scapegoat for what was really more a failure for the Union War Department than for McDowell the general. Asked to do too much too soon with too little cooperation, he had scant opportunity to succeed.

BIBLIOGRAPHY

Barnard, John G. *The C.S.A. and the Battle of Bull Run.* New York: Van Nostrand, 1862.
Beattie, Russell H. *Road to Manassas.* New York: Cooper Square, 1961.
Davis, William C. *Battle at Bull Run.* New York: Doubleday and Company, 1977.
Fry, James. B. *McDowell and Tyler and the Campaign of Bull Run.* New York: Van Nostrand, 1884.
Johnston, R. M. *Bull Run, Its Strategy and Tactics.* Boston: Houghton Mifflin Company, 1913.

WILLIAM C. DAVIS

MACKENZIE, Ranald Slidell (b. New York City, N.Y., July 27, 1840; d. New Brighton, Staten Island, N.Y., January 19, 1889), Army officer. Mackenzie is considered to be one of the finest cavalry commanders of the post-Civil War Indian campaigns.

Ranald Slidell Mackenzie was born into a military family. His father was

Commodore Alexander Slidell Mackenzie of the U.S. Navy. The commodore died soon after seeing service in the Mexican War, and the Mackenzie family moved to Morristown, New Jersey, where young Ranald spent much of his adolescence. At the age of fifteen Mackenzie entered Williams College, and in 1858 he was admitted to the U.S. Military Academy at West Point, New York. In 1862 he was graduated first in a class of twenty-eight and commissioned in the Corps of Engineers.

Mackenzie quickly saw action in the campaigns of the Army of the Potomac. He was wounded at the Second Battle of Bull Run and brevetted for gallant conduct. He saw further action at Chancellorsville and Gettysburg, earning brevet promotion to major. In November 1863 he received the permanent rank of captain. Mackenzie was promoted to colonel and in June 1864 was assigned to command the 2d Regiment, Connecticut Volunteers, a unit in the VI Corps. Mackenzie asserted his command vigorously and, according to one of his subordinates, "developed as to be a greater terror to both officers and men than Early's grape and canister." While leading the regiment into action at Petersburg and in the Shenandoah Valley, Mackenzie suffered a total of five wounds, including the loss of two fingers from his right hand, a disfigurement that later led the Indians to christen him "Bad Hand."

Mackenzie finished the war as commander of the 2d Brigade, 1st Division, VI Corps, holding the brevet rank of major general. He was twenty-four years old and, with six wounds and seven brevets, had attained more rank and honors than any other man in his West Point class. General Ulysses Simpson Grant* described him as "the most promising young officer in the army."

Mackenzie was reduced to his permanent grade of captain following the war and returned to the Corps of Engineers, but was soon appointed colonel of the newly organized 41st Infantry Regiment. His command was one of the first Negro units in the Regular Army and was viewed as a dubious experiment by many critics in both the Army and Congress. Mackenzie and his lieutenant colonel, William Rufus Shafter,* brought the new unit under a regime of strict discipline and thorough training, and it served well along the Rio Grande frontier in Texas (1867–1869). The 41st and 38th Infantry were consolidated to form the 24th Infantry in 1869, and Mackenzie assumed command of the newly created regiment.

On February 25, 1871, Mackenzie was transferred to command the 4th Cavalry at Fort Concho, Texas. Under his guidance the regiment soon earned the reputation of being one of the finest units in the Army. Throughout 1871–1872, Mackenzie, with his new headquarters at Fort Richardson, Texas, mounted long-range patrols and unflaggingly pursued the Comanches and Kiowas who left their Fort Sill reservation to raid south into Texas. Mackenzie's decisive victory over Chief Mow-way on the North Fork of the Red River in the summer of 1872 brought a year of comparative peace to the north Texas plains region.

In March 1873 Mackenzie and the 4th Cavalry were transferred south to Fort Clark, Texas, to quell the depredations of Kickapoo and Apache warriors who were striking the settlers from refuges in Mexico. With the covert approval of Secretary of War William Belknap, Mackenzie launched a surprise attack across the border on May 18, 1873. The grueling seventy-hour, 150-mile march resulted in the destruction of three Kickapoo and Apache villages near San Remolino, Mexico. Despite a pursuit mounted by Mexican cavalry, Mackenzie shepherded his troops and prisoners safely over the Rio Grande with the loss of only one killed and one wounded. While his violation of the border stirred up a minor diplomatic storm, his audacity in conceiving and executing the raid won him a reputation as a commander who got results.

Mackenzie saw repeated action in northwest Texas during the 1874 Red River War against the Comanches, Kiowas, and Southern Cheyennes. The climax of that campaign was Mackenzie's victory at Palo Duro Canyon on September 28. Leading his troops down a precipitous canyon trail in the predawn darkness, Mackenzie launched an attack that killed only four Indians but resulted in the capture of their accumulated food supplies and the bulk of their horse herd. Tons of clothing and food were burned, and more than one thousand horses were shot at his orders. The hostiles escaped from the canyon but were forced to return to the reservation or face starvation.

Subsequently, Mackenzie inveighed against government corruption on the Indian reservations, suppressed the outbreak by the Northern Cheyennes under Chief Dull Knife in Wyoming during the autumn of 1877, and served another tour of duty on the troubled Mexican border. In May 1880 he led the 4th Cavalry north to Colorado to put down a threatened uprising among the Utes at the White River Agency, and in August 1881 he supervised the transfer of more than fourteen hundred recalcitrant Utes to a new reservation in Utah.

On October 30, 1881, Mackenzie was appointed to command the District of New Mexico. Plagued by raids from Mexico staged by renegade Apaches, the inhabitants of the territory feared that the reservation tribes might be incited to take similar actions. The situation was restored with Mackenzie's typical efficiency, and he was promoted to brigadier general in recognition of the superb record he had compiled during his postwar service.

An assignment as commander of the Department of Texas accompanied his promotion, and Mackenzie arrived in San Antonio on October 30, 1883. It was there that the physical and mental toll exacted by his extensive field service and near-fanatical devotion to duty became apparent. The usually solitary and monastic officer began to court an army widow, and wedding plans were announced. At the same time his behavior became eccentric and irrational. Formerly an abstainer, Mackenzie engaged in drunken binges. He was bordering on a complete mental and physical collapse when he was relieved of command and committed to the Bloomingdale Asylum in New York.

Major General Winfield Scott Hancock* headed the examining board that subsequently visited the asylum and, over Mackenzie's anguished pleas, found him to be suffering from "general paralysis of the insane" as a result of "wounds received and exposure in the line of duty.'' Mackenzie was honorably retired on March 24, 1884. He died at his sister's home at New Brighton, Staten Island, on January 19, 1889 at the age of forty-eight.

Ranald S. Mackenzie's military reputation rests on his skill as a cavalry commander on the postwar frontier. Few other officers served over such a wide area of the frontier and enjoyed such consistent success in their operations.

The reasons for Mackenzie's success are easily discerned. He possessed both a keen grasp of the essentials of his profession and an understanding of the strategic realities of war in the Trans-Mississippi West. Tireless and aggressive, as well as a strict disciplinarian, Mackenzie demanded the utmost from both officers and men. Personally of an ascetic nature, he never required more from his subordinates than he was willing to give himself. A stickler for detail and procedure, he was not blind to the need for innovation in meeting the demands imposed by frontier warfare. At one point he petitioned to have his troops' single-shot Springfield carbines replaced with Winchester repeaters.

Mackenzie conducted operations that were not distinguished by a great deal of bloodshed. He recognized that killing Indians was the slowest and most expensive means of bringing peace to the frontier. The destruction of their camps and horse herds coupled with the effect produced by the knowledge that any hostile act would elicit swift and certain retribution upon the entire tribe forced Indians to choose the reservation in preference to a fugitive existence. He adopted the policy of never abandoning a pursuit once the trail had been found. After San Remolina and Palo Duro Canyon, every tribe on the Southern Plains knew that there was no longer any place of refuge secure from Mackenzie and the 4th Cavalry. His single-minded aggressiveness produced results, for as William Tecumseh Sherman* remarked, the Red River Campaign directed by Mackenzie ''was the most successful of any Indian campaign in this country since its settlement by the whites.'' A Texas journalist eulogized Mackenzie in pragmatic terms. ''He was always prompt in the saddle and never tangled his spurs in the maze of endless red tape.''

BIBLIOGRAPHY

Carter, Robert G. *On the Border with Mackenzie, or Winning West Texas from the Comanches*. New York: Antiquarian Press, 1961.

Haley, James L. *The Buffalo War*. New York: Doubleday and Company, 1976.

Utley, Robert M. *Frontier Regulars: The United States Army and the Indian, 1866–1890*. New York: Macmillan Publishing Company, 1973.

Wallace, Ernest. *Ranald S. Mackenzie on the Texas Frontier*. Lubbock: West Texas Museum Association, 1964.

WAYNE AUSTERMAN

MC NAIR, Lesley James (b. Verndale, Minn., May 25, 1883; d. St. Lô, France, July 25, 1944), military trainer. McNair trained the U.S. Army's ground forces in World War II.

Lesley McNair, son of a Scottish-born father, entered the U.S. Military Academy in August 1900, at the age of seventeen. He graduated four years later, eleventh in a class of 124 whose members included Joseph Warren Stilwell* and Innis Swift. Commissioned a second lieutenant of artillery, McNair reported to Fort Douglas, Utah, in September and remained there until June 1905, when he transferred to the Ordnance Department with duty station at the Sandy Hook Proving Ground, New Jersey. That year he married Clare Huster, whom he had met and courted while at the Academy. His subsequent Ordnance assignments were with the Office of the Chief in Washington and at Watertown Arsenal, Massachusetts. He was promoted to first lieutenant in 1905 and to captain in 1907.

McNair returned to his original branch in 1909, reporting to the 4th Field Artillery at Fort D. A. Russell, Wyoming. He remained with this unit for nine years with stations ranging from San Antonio, Texas, to Fort Sill, Oklahoma. During this time, McNair spent over seven months in France witnessing French artillery training (1913) and, with his regiment, participated in Frederick Funston's* Expedition to Vera Cruz, Mexico (1914), and the Punitive Expedition into Mexico (1916–1917).

McNair was promoted to major in May 1917 and shortly thereafter was detailed to the General Staff Corps. He went to France with the 1st Division, but he soon joined General Headquarters, American Expeditionary Forces (AEF), as a lieutenant colonel. John Joseph Pershing* liked this quiet, talented officer and promoted him twice—to colonel in June 1918 and brigadier general in the following October. At thirty-five, he was the youngest general in the AEF and recipient of the Distinguished Service Medal for his work as senior artillery officer of the General Staff's Training Section. The French appreciated him, too; McNair's award of Officer of the Legion of Honor came from the hands of Marshal Henri Pétain.

Immediately after the war, McNair reverted to his permanent rank of major and reported to Fort Leavenworth as instructor at the General Service School. Later, he had staff jobs in Hawaii and Washington, served as assistant commandant of the Field Artillery School and as professor of military science and tactics at Purdue University, graduated from the Army War College, and had a stint with the Civilian Conservation Corps. He got back his star in March 1937 as commander, 2d Field Artillery Brigade, Fort Sam Houston, Texas.

In 1939 McNair returned to Fort Leavenworth, this time as commandant of the Command and General Staff School. He remained there for less than a year, but his accomplishments were significant. He revitalized the peacetime curriculum and supervised a much needed revision of FM 101–5, the Staff Officer's Field manual. General George Catlett Marshall* was happy about this assignment, writing to McNair: "You at Leavenworth are one of the great satisfactions I have at the moment in visualizing the responsibilities of the next couple of years."

General Marshall called McNair to Washington to serve as Chief of Staff,

General Headquarters, better known as GHQ, activated on July 26, 1940. The war in Europe had caused Marshall concern over the preparedness of the U.S. Army. GHQ would oversee and speed up mobilization by directly supervising the organization and training of all field forces within the continental United States. McNair worked directly for Marshall who, as Army chief of staff, also served as commander of the field forces. Promotions came quickly—major general in September 1940, lieutenant general in June 1941.

A major Army reorganization in March 1942 saw the elimination of GHQ and the emergence of the Army Ground Forces, Army Air Forces, and Army Service Forces (originally, the Services of Supply). McNair, now almost fifty-nine, received command of Army Ground Forces (AGF). His record at GHQ had been auspicious. He had presided over initial mobilization of the ground Army and had played an equally important role in such sensitive matters as organization and doctrine. McNair's problems and accomplishments with AGF were to exceed those he had experienced with GHQ.

When McNair took over the Army Ground Forces, its strength was about 780,000 officers and men. By July 1943, it had reached a peak strength of 2.2 million. In addition to his headquarters at the Army War College, Washington, D.C. (now Fort McNair), General McNair oversaw a variety of schools, boards, replacement training centers, and special commands whose activities pertained to the combat arms. For part of the war, he also commanded the tactical armies and corps located in the continental United States.

McNair was no armchair general. He spent more than half his time in the field, traveling over two hundred thousand miles during his four years with GHQ and AGF. In 1943 he visited U.S. troops in North Africa and was severely wounded by an enemy shell fragment. The following year, McNair again spent a few hours observing troops on the battlefield, and this time he was killed. He had succeeded George Smith Patton, Jr.,* as *pro tem* commander of the 1st U.S. Army Group, the mythical force in England that was to confuse the enemy as to the true location of the principal cross-channel invasion. On July 25, 1944, he stood near St. Lô, Normandy, observing Eighth Air Force bombers prior to the VII Corps attack that was Operation COBRA. The bombs landed short, inflicting over six hundred American casualties, one of whom was Lesley McNair, the first U.S. Army three star general to die in combat. It was bitter irony that his only son, Colonel Douglas McNair, chief of staff of the 7th Infantry Division was killed on Guam by a Japanese bullet just twelve days later.

Lesley McNair was one of the most capable U.S. generals in World War II and certainly one of the least known. Although he was unquestionably admired by General Marshall, McNair's World War II decorations came only after death, when two oak leaf clusters were added to the Distinguished Service Medal he had won during World War I. He was posthumously promoted to general in July 1954, a gratuitous gesture that doubtless prompted a skeptical smile in some corner of Valhalla.

McNair's principal contributions to the U.S. Army were in the fields of training and doctrine. As an artillery officer in World War I, he was instrumental in improving the artillery support of the infantry, and he recognized the impact of changing combat conditions on military tactics. In the late 1930s he played an influential role in the tests that were to transform the bulky square division of two brigades, each with two regiments, into the streamlined triangular, three-regiment division.

Interspersed with these doctrinal activities were command assignments, most of which related to training—deputy commandant of the Field Artillery School and commandant of the Command and General Staff School. As chief of staff, General Headquarters, "he prepared and executed the training program of the ground forces of the Army during the early stage of the unprecedented mobilization of the armed forces of this country," to quote from his Distinguished Service Medal citation. And as commander of the Army Ground Forces he finished this momentous task, converting more than three million men into effective soldiers and thoroughly professional combat units.

At GHQ, McNair continued his campaign against wasteful and unwieldy organizations. Through his efforts, and in face of opposition, the strength of the 1943 infantry division tables of organization was reduced by 1,250. Inasmuch as sixty-six infantry divisions were mobilized, this reduction meant a savings of 82,500 men.

McNair carried out his duties without ostentation. He refused to move his headquarters to the Pentagon, preferring instead the quiet, military atmosphere of his Army War College location. His staff was lean, numbering 163 officers in March 1942 and growing to only 277 by the end of World War II. This figure represented only 3.6 percent of the total number of officers on duty in the War Department and at the headquarters of the three major commands.

General McNair stressed the promulgation of sound direction followed by personal supervision. He said that "Leadership is the first essential of good training, as of battle itself." He once told Lieutenant General Ben Lear that a commanding officer was not only the trainer of his unit, but also its builder. Toward that end, McNair instilled in individuals and units alike the feeling that they were members of the larger teams that eventually would be tested in combat. He stressed the importance of progressive unit and combined arms training until its culmination in realistic, large-scale maneuvers.

In the final analysis, Lesley McNair was the prime builder of the U.S. armies that contributed so greatly to Allied victory in World War II. And for this his place in history is secure.

BIBLIOGRAPHY

Greenfield, Kent Roberts, Robert R. Palmer, and Bell I. Wiley. *The Army Ground Forces, The Organization of Ground Combat Troops. United States Army in World War II*. Washington, D.C.: U.S. Government Printing Office, 1947.

Kahn, E. J., Jr. *McNair, Educator of an Army*. Washington, D.C.: The Infantry Journal, 1945.

Palmer, Robert R., Bell I. Wiley, and William R. Keast. *The Army Ground Forces, The Procurement and Training of Ground Combat Troops. United States Army in World War II*. Washington, D.C.: U.S. Government Printing Office, 1948.

Whitaker, John T. "Lieutenant General Lesley James McNair." In *These Are the Generals*. Foreword by Walter Millis. New York: Alfred A. Knopf, 1943.

BROOKS E. KLEBER

MC NAMARA, Robert Strange (b. San Francisco, Calif., June 9, 1916), secretary of defense, 1961–1968.

Robert S. McNamara, the son of Robert James McNamara, a businessman, and Clara Strange McNamara, displayed as a youth the drive and intellectual capacity that would mark his later career. He compiled a distinguished academic record in high school and at the University of California, Berkeley, where he majored in economics and was elected to Phi Beta Kappa. He went on to earn an MBA degree at Harvard in 1939 and, after working briefly as an accountant in San Francisco, returned to Cambridge as an assistant professor of business.

During World War II, McNamara achieved recognition for the application of management techniques to logistic problems. Rejected for military service because of poor eyesight, he designed and taught a course at Harvard to train Air Force officers in statistical analysis. Later commissioned in the Army, he played a key role in the B–17 and B–29 bomber programs, coordinating the intricate details of production, crew training, and supply. He also spent time in India and China, developing plans to expand air transport across "The Hump" and devising new methods for assessing B–29 bomber damage. By the end of the war, he had advanced to the rank of lieutenant colonel and was awarded the Legion of Merit.

During the next fifteen years, McNamara emerged as one of the top corporation executives in the United States. Originally planning to return to Harvard, he instead joined a group of former Air Force officers, the so-called Whiz Kids, to form a consulting service for major businesses. One of their clients was the Ford Motor Company, then in serious financial straits, and McNamara decided to remain with Ford after the consulting was completed. His rise within the corporation was meteoric, from controller in 1949 to a vice-presidency in 1957, and he helped rescue Ford from the near disaster that followed production of the Edsel by developing the compact Falcon and changing the Thunderbird to a luxury four-seater. In 1960, Ford was enjoying record sales, and McNamara was elected president of the corporation, the first person not a member of the family to hold that position. McNamara was frequently described as a "human computer" for his capacity to absorb and analyze great masses of data. His reputation as a managerial genius and as a liberal businessman attracted him to President-elect John F. Kennedy who named him secretary of defense.

McNamara initiated drastic changes in the Pentagon. Assuming control of an agency employing 2.5 million military personnel and 1.5 million civilians with a budget of over $40 billion, he brought in his own "Whiz Kids," a team of youthful civilian management experts, to apply systems analysis to Pentagon operations. More concerned with results than popularity and with scant regard for military tradition or political interests, he centralized control over intelligence and supply operations that had been scattered among the various services, streamlined budgetary procedures, and ruthlessly eliminated bases and weapons systems that did not meet his standards of cost-effectiveness. He imposed tighter civilian control over the military than any of his predecessors and to a large degree tamed the interservice rivalries that had raged since the end of World War II.

McNamara's principal task as secretary of defense was to develop military capabilities based on the concept of "flexible response." Persuaded that Dwight David Eisenhower's* reliance on nuclear weapons had left the United States muscle-bound in many crises, the Kennedy administration sought a rounded arsenal that would enable the nation to respond to threats at various levels. McNamara delayed production of the B–70 bomber and of an antiballistic missile (ABM) system on the grounds that they were too expensive and of unproven reliability, and would speed up the arms race without enhancing American security. To ensure a second-strike capability, however, he expanded the numbers and improved the quality of America's offensive missiles. He also worked tirelessly to build up conventional forces, enlarging the armed services by more than three hundred thousand men and developing an airlift capacity that permitted the dispatch of select units to any part of the world within a short time.

McNamara played a more important role in shaping American foreign policy than any of his predecessors as secretary of defense. He proposed and then oversaw implementation of the "quarantine" scheme during the Cuban missile crisis. Under Kennedy and then under Lyndon B. Johnson, he played a vital role in the expanding American commitment in Vietnam. His advice was instrumental in the decision to escalate the war in 1965. Over the vigorous opposition of the Joint Chiefs of Staff, he insisted that the conflict must be kept limited, and he maintained tight control over the bombing of North Vietnam. In all, he visited South Vietnam nine times to assay progress, and he became so closely identified with the conflict that for a time it was called "McNamara's War."

By 1967 McNamara's position had become untenable. A massive Soviet buildup of strategic weapons, including an ABM system, led to charges that the secretary of defense had left the United States vulnerable. Progress in Vietnam was at best slow, and McNamara was attacked by doves for waging a futile and immoral war and by hawks for preventing the military from securing victory. McNamara himself had become increasingly disenchanted by the war that bore his name. He was troubled by the rising toll of civilian casualties and by the bitter domestic opposition, brought home to him time and again when he had to shove his way through and shout down angry protestors. Most important, he concluded that the policy of gradual escalation had neither diminished North Vietnam's will to fight nor promoted stability in South Vietnam. As a consequence, he quietly pressed for changes in policy, advocating a partial or total stoppage of the bombing, a shift to a defensive ground strategy, and a scaling down of American political objectives to secure a negotiated settlement. Johnson was also frustrated by the lack of progress in Vietnam and was concerned by the domestic protest, but he regarded McNamara's proposals as thinly disguised surrender and rejected them. Relations between the two men became so strained in 1967 that they scarcely spoke to each other. In November McNamara agreed to leave the Defense Department to become president of the World Bank.

McNamara's management of the Defense Department provoked heated controversy. In his zeal to eliminate waste and duplication of effort, he stepped on vested interests in the military and in Congress, and his abrasiveness and lack of political finesse further antagonized his adversaries, sometimes needlessly. On occasion, his drive for efficiency produced major blunders, as in the case of the TFX aircraft, a multipurpose fighter-bomber designed to meet the needs of both the Air Force and the Navy. The questionable practicality of the project, bitter opposition from the military, and hints of political deals in awarding the contract set off an extended debate and eventually a congressional investigation. McNamara stubbornly stuck by his project, however, and refused to concede a mistake even when the aircraft performed poorly. Despite the flaws in his leadership, he brought long overdue reforms and much needed efficiency to a vast, seemingly uncontrollable bureaucracy. He established firm civilian control and ran the Defense Department longer and more effectively than any of his predecessors.

Charges that McNamara left the United States vulnerable to a steadily expanding nuclear power appear grossly overdrawn. The Soviet buildup was to a large degree beyond his control. Although he eliminated some weapons systems and refused to build others, defense spending increased significantly during his tenure and the United States maintained qualitative and in many cases quantitative superiority in missiles and nuclear warheads. His willingness to accept eventual parity in some form appears only realistic in retrospect, and the concept of mutual vulnerability, which he regarded as the most reliable basis for deterrence, became the framework for the strategic arms limitation agreements of the 1970s. His attempt to maintain an adequate defense capability without imposing excessive costs on the nation and intensifying the arms race remains one of the great challenges of modern times. That he failed reflects less the weakness of his approach than the inherent difficulties of the undertaking.

Without Vietnam, McNamara would probably be remembered as one of the great secretaries of defense, perhaps one of the great cabinet officers of recent American history. Responsibility for the debacle must be widely shared, but his role was clearly pivotal. Certain that the gradual application of American military power would force North Vietnam to acquiesce in an independent, non-Communist South Vietnam without provoking a wider war, he urged a major escalation in 1965, and his advice may have been decisive. The assumptions upon which his recommendations were based turned out to be badly flawed, however, and the United States could achieve no better than a bloody stalemate. Only belatedly did McNamara perceive the massive destruction and human costs his policies brought, and even after he saw them, he did not wage an effective campaign to change a policy he was certain was not working. His loyalty to the president is commendable, and the dilemma he faced in 1967 was most difficult. But the nation was not well served by his unwillingness to vigorously challenge a bankrupt policy.

After leaving office in 1968, McNamara worked quietly and effectively as president of the World Bank to persuade the advanced nations to share their wealth and technology to assist in the modernization of the less developed nations. He retired from the bank in 1982.

BIBLIOGRAPHY

Enthoven, Alain C., and K. Wayne Smith. *How Much Is Enough?* New York: Harper and Row, 1971.
Halberstam, David. *The Best and the Brightest.* New York: Random House, 1972.
Roherty, James M. *Decisions of Robert S. McNamara: A Study of the Role of the Secretary of Defense.* Miami, Fla.: University of Miami Press, 1970.
The Senator Gravel Edition: The Pentagon Papers. Boston: Beacon Press, 1971. Vols. 2, 3, 4.
Trewhitt, Henry L. *McNamara.* New York: Harper and Row, 1971.

GEORGE C. HERRING

MC NARNEY, Joseph Taggart (b. Emporium, Pa., August 28, 1893; d. La Jolla, Calif., February 1, 1972), Army officer, Air Force officer, deputy chief of staff of the U.S. Army during World War II and postwar commander of the American occupation of Germany.

Joseph T. McNarney was the son of James Pollard and Helen Taggart McNarney, a prosecuting attorney and a former teacher and dedicated temperance worker, respectively. He graduated from the U.S. Military Academy with the famed class of 1915, which eventually produced no fewer than sixty general officers. Commissioned into the infantry, McNarney in 1916 joined the aviation section of the Signal Corps and qualified as an Army pilot and observer at San Diego, California, where in 1917 he married Helen Wahrenberger, a schoolteacher. The union lasted until McNarney's death; the couple had one daughter.

Over the last fourteen months of World War I, McNarney served in various capacities with the American Expeditionary Force in France. Besides staff assignments, he commanded an air observation group. By May 1919 he was a temporary lieutenant colonel, although once back in the United States he reverted to a permanent captaincy. In July 1920 McNarney transferred officially from the infantry to the Air Service. Not until 1936 did the Army's single-list, seniority-based promotion system permit his elevation to permanent lieutenant colonel. Despite his comparatively low rank during the interwar years, McNarney was generally recognized within the service as an officer of exceptional promise. After five years as a student and instructor at the Air Corps Tactical School at

Langley Field, Virginia, he graduated with honors in 1926 from the Command and General Staff School at Fort Leavenworth. He attended the Army War College in Washington in 1929–1930 and taught there from 1933 to 1935. McNarney spent much time on General Staff duty, first with the Military Intelligence Division at the War Department in the late 1920s, and from 1935 to 1938 at General Headquarters, Air Force, at Langley Field. In the early 1930s he commanded a group, and subsequently a wing, of bombers.

McNarney won the confidence of Chief of Staff George Catlett Marshall* during the three years preceding American participation in World War II. In the War Department from 1939 he was successively a member of the War Plans Division, the Joint Army and Navy Planning Committee, and the Permanent Joint Defense Board for Canada and the United States. He attained the temporary ranks of full colonel in May 1940 and brigadier general the following April and then spent May to December of 1941 in London with the War Department's Special Observers Group. After Pearl Harbor he was a member of a special commission under Supreme Court Associate Justice Owen J. Roberts to determine the causes of that debacle. As a major general in January 1942, McNarney headed a special War Department panel to plan a long-needed overhaul of that ponderous bureaucracy. Once the agency was streamlined by a presidential executive order that took effect on March 9, 1942, McNarney took office as Marshall's deputy chief of staff, becoming a lieutenant general two months later. He was promoted to full general in 1945. As Marshall's deputy, McNarney assumed many of the chief's administrative burdens, oversaw the preparation of the Army's budget requests, and appeared frequently before congressional committees. During Marshall's numerous absences from Washington, McNarney was acting chief of staff. He was a leading Army spokesman in favor of a unified postwar department of defense. In October 1944 McNarney went to the Mediterranean to become deputy Allied supreme commander and U.S. theater commanding general. In November 1945 he replaced General of the Army Dwight David Eisenhower* in command of the U.S. forces in Europe and as military governor of the American occupation sector of Germany. From March 1947 until his retirement from the now-independent Air Force on January 31, 1952, McNarney was the American representative on the United Nations Military Staff Committee, then chief of the Materiel Command of the Air Force, and finally special advisor to the secretary of defense. Upon his retirement, he entered the aircraft industry as president of the Convair Division of General Dynamics and later as senior vice-president of the General Dynamics Corporation. He spent his last years in Alhambra, California.

Described as ''dour, taciturn, and officially ruthless'' by contemporaries, Joseph T. McNarney was the ideal agent of War Department reorganization in 1942. Marshall selected him because McNarney ''had been an outstanding member of the War Plans Division, was familiar with General Staff procedure and . . . with the Air Corps, had been close to active operations, . . . had seen British governmental machinery at work, [and] had been in Moscow'' with the 1941 mission of presidential confidant Harry L. Hopkins. More importantly, in the words of Marshall's biographer, McNarney was ''a tough hatchetman with a rhinoceros hide and the nerve to push through the reorganization in the face of rugged infighting'' by War Department bureaus opposed to their own reduction or elimination. The reorganization plan had first been outlined before Pearl Harbor by junior staff officers, but only a special war powers act made possible its implementation by executive order. McNarney's seniority and drive as head of the Soviet Committee, as some of its critics styled it, were essential to the quick adoption of the plan.

The reorganization shrank the General Staff from eight hundred to three hundred officers, with those enjoying direct access to the chief of staff being cut from sixty to six. The administrative responsibilities of the Army's combat arms and services were shifted from the General Staff to three nearly autonomous functional commands. The War Plans Division became the upgraded Operations Division, an agency which for the duration of the war served as Marshall's global command post. During this nearly three years as Marshall's deputy, McNarney kept the General Staff on a tight leash. He recalled with pride that the flood of routine papers that normally swamped Marshall's desk largely ceased as of March 9, 1942. Under Marshall and McNarney, the Army practiced the decentralized management characteristic of leading American business corporations.

The great bulk of the army had been shipped overseas before McNarney left for the Mediterranean. His successor in Washington, Lieutenant General Thomas T. Handy, had long headed the Operations Division and was better suited to collaborate with Marshall on strategic decisions. In the Mediterranean McNarney was inevitably overshadowed among Americans by Lieutenant General Ira Clarence Eaker,* who commanded all Allied air forces in the theater, and by Lieutenant General Mark Wayne Clark,* Allied commander on the Italian front from November 1944.

In the postwar occupation of Germany, McNarney was essentially a supernumerary over Lieutenant General Lucius DuBignon Clay,* who headed the Office of Military Government. Knowledgeable about Washington politics and blessed with the complete confidence of Secretary of State James F. Byrnes, Clay acted as a virtually independent proconsul over the defeated Germans. McNarney devoted most of his attention to the American occupation troops, who were in a state of lax discipline when he assumed command. McNarney's appointment of Major General Ernest N. Harmon to command a special military constabulary contributed to a general improvement of American discipline.

In August 1946 Lieutenant General Walter Bedell Smith* reported to Chief of Staff Eisenhower that Clay was unhappy under McNarney, who appeared to be ''doing a good job.'' But ''it simply is very difficult to like him personally.'' The State and War departments concluded that Clay was more essential in Germany than McNarney, and McNarney's transfer was quietly arranged. As one historian has commented, ''his going left scarcely a ripple.''

McNarney's wartime activities in Washington were unquestionably the high point of his service. Although he had begun his active career as a World War I aviator and was to conclude it as an aerospace business executive, his historical importance was that of a military manager rather than of an airman. McNarney's industriousness, personal honesty, capacity for objective thinking, and readiness to assume responsibility all prompted Marshall to say to Eisenhower in 1943, "Thank God for McNarney. He is a crutch that I lean on all the time." Before Eisenhower was sent to command the European Theater of Operations in 1942, he had recommended his 1915 West Point classmate for the assignment, and in 1944 he commended McNarney to Sir Henry Maitland Wilson as an officer whose "views will be his honest convictions and without any thought of their effect upon himself. I regard him as one of our finest. . . . He is tough but most sensible."

BIBLIOGRAPHY

Cline, Ray S. *Washington Command Post*. Washington, D.C.: U.S. Government Printing Office, 1953.

Hewes, James E., Jr. *From Root to McNamara*. Washington, D.C.: U.S. Government Printing Office, 1975.

Peterson, Edward N. *The American Occupation of Germany*, Detroit: Wayne State University Press, 1978.

Wittels, David G. "These Are the Generals—McNarney." *Saturday Evening Post*, February 13, 1943.

RICHARD G. STONE, JR.

MACOMB, Alexander (b. Detroit, Mich., April 3, 1782; d. Washington, D.C., June 25, 1841), veteran of War of 1812; commanding general of the U.S. Army, 1828–1841.

Alexander Macomb was the son of a highly successful Irish merchant who was associated with the John Jacob Astor fur business at Detroit and then moved to New York City and speculated in shipping and Western lands. Macomb was educated at an academy in Newark, New Jersey, and early displayed an interest in the military, enrolling at the age of sixteen in a New York City militia company. When war with France seemed imminent, Macomb through Alexander Hamilton secured a Regular Army commission on January 10, 1799, as cornet of light dragoons, and served briefly as an aide to Adjutant General William North. He was promoted to second lieutenant on March 2, 1799, and discharged on June 15, 1800.

Macomb reentered the Army on February 16, 1801, as a second lieutenant in the 2d Infantry, and was made secretary to General James Wilkinson's* commission to treat with Indian tribes in the Southeastern states. On October 12, 1802, Macomb was appointed a first lieutenant in the new Engineer Corps and entered the U.S. Military Academy. He and James Wilson of Pennsylvania were the first to complete a course of study there. Macomb remained at West Point until promoted to captain on June 11, 1805, and assigned new duties. From

1807 to 1812 he was chief engineer in charge of improving coastal fortifications in the Carolinas and Georgia. He attained the rank of major on February 23, 1808, and was promoted to lieutenant colonel on July 23, 1810.

With the declaration of war with Great Britain, Colonel Macomb served briefly as acting adjutant general in Washington, D.C., but quickly requested field duty. Commissioned a full colonel on July 6, 1812, he raised the 3d Artillery Regiment in New York and by winter was garrison commander at Sackets Harbor. Macomb was involved in the capture of Fort George on the Niagara River in May of 1813 and commanded the reserve force with Wilinson's ill-fated St. Lawrence Expedition that fall. Promoted on January 24, 1814, to brigadier general, Macomb in August assumed command at Plattsburgh, New York, and strengthened the fortifications there. In early September, with some forty-five hundred men he stalled a British force of fourteen thousand while Captain Thomas Macdonough* engaged and destroyed the enemy's supporting fleet on Lake Champlain. His vigorous defense in this critical battle brought special honors from Congress and the state of New York and promotion to brevet major general to date from September 11, 1814.

In 1815 Macomb served on the board of general officers that reduced the Army to peacetime status. The board divided the forces into two divisions (North and South), cut the number of enlisted men from sixty thousand to ten thousand, and pared the officer corps from 2,271 to 489 men. The postwar military establishment included eight artillery battalions, one light artillery regiment, eight infantry regiments, and one rifle regiment. Macomb briefly commanded the Third Department (lower New York and New Jersey) and then went to Detroit to take charge of the Fifth Department, which sprawled over Illinois and Michigan territories.

As instructed by his division commander, General Jacob Jennings Brown,* Macomb put most of his garrisons to work building roads and forts, assignments that created problems in administration and discipline. Macomb grumbled about inspection policies, clashed with regimental officers who questioned his authority, and stressed the need for a more centralized command system. When another Army reduction occurred in March 1821, Brown was appointed to the newly created position of general in chief, and Macomb was reduced in grade to colonel (June 1, 1821) and assigned to command the elite Engineer Corps.

Upon Brown's death in February 1828, Colonel Macomb, supported by the New York congressional delegation and profiting from bickering between Brigadier Generals Winfield Scott* and Edmund Pendleton Gaines* over seniority, was appointed to the rank of major general and made general in chief of the Army. Although a popular officer—and the Army's senior brigadier prior to his demotion in 1821—Macomb entered office amid controversy. For six months an insubordinate Scott refused to recognize Macomb's appointment and even called for his arrest!

Macomb sought to infuse vigor and prestige into his position. Whereas Brown, partially paralyzed for seven years, had acted primarily as a military advisor to the secretary of war and the president, Macomb moved to bring staff branches and bureaus under his personal control. To reroute Army channels he ordered an insubordinate Roger Jones, adjutant general, court-martialed in 1830, and the next year he forced the Corps of Engineers to submit to regular inspections. A clique of engineers—which included Andrew Talcott and Robert Edward Lee*— unsuccessfully sought support in Congress for Macomb's removal.

Macomb was responsive to the need for change in the Army. He discontinued the traditional whiskey ration, issued a revised set of Army regulations, and promoted modernization of the artillery and ordnance departments. He cooperated smoothly with the executive branch during the South Carolina nullification crisis, the Black Hawk War, the Florida campaigns, Indian removals from the South, and border problems during the Patriot War. Macomb died of apoplexy in Washington, D.C.

General Macomb was regarded by his contemporaries as a dignified, affable officer, a man of integrity and honor. From his earliest years in service he enjoyed influential contacts, gained a reputation for thoroughness in staff detail, and by 1815 had acquired a broad acquaintance with the military arms, serving successively in infantry, engineer, artillery, and command positions.

Assigned to the frontier after the War of 1812, Macomb became acutely aware of the problems generated by poor communication and a loose command structure. As general in chief of the Army, he made a concerted effort to define and enhance his position and authority. In the early years of his administration, he brought the adjutant general and the Engineer Corps to heel, and he handled Scott's insubordination with patience and tact. No crusader, Macomb leaned on trusted staff officers for advice and used his office to investigate needs and implement changes. Much credit is due Macomb for seeking to end abuses in the Army, for promoting modernization of the artillery, and for defining channels of command.

Macomb also was an author. As early as 1809 he compiled and published *A Treatise of Martial Law and Courts Martial*. In 1836 he edited a work by his son-in-law Samuel Cooper entitled *Tactics and Regulations for the Militia*, and four years later he published *The Practice of Courts Martial*.

As general in chief of the U.S. Army, Alexander Macomb mingled freely in Washington society, maintained good relations with the president and Congress, and articulated clearly the army's needs. His administration established patterns that not only enhanced the prestige of the Army but also brought it into closer step with other armies of the world.

BIBLIOGRAPHY

Memoir of Alexander Macomb, the Maj. Gen. Commanding the Army of the U.S., by Geo. H. Richards, Esq., Capt. of Macomb's Artillery in the Late War. New York: M'Elrath, Bangs and Company, 1833. Ann Arbor: University Microfilms.

Prucha, Francis P. *The Sword of the Republic: The U.S. Army on the Frontier, 1783–1846*. New York: Macmillan, 1969.

Skelton, William B. ''The United States Army, 1821–1837: American Institutional History.'' Ph.D. dissertation, Northwestern University, 1968.

HARWOOD P. HINTON

MC PHERSON, James Birdseye (b. November 14, 1828, near Clyde, Ohio; d. July 22, 1864, Atlanta, Ga.), Army officer. McPherson was commander of the Union Army of the Tennessee during the Civil War.

The son of a pioneer couple in Sandusky County, Ohio, McPherson went to West Point at the age of twenty. He was graduated in 1853 at the head of his class and remained at the Military Academy for another year as an instructor. After a period in New York City, he was assigned in 1857 to engineering duties at Alcatraz Island in San Francisco. There he became something of a social lion and became engaged to Emily Hoffman, of a prominent Baltimore family. As the strains of sectional conflict reached even the Pacific, the politically conservative McPherson tended to blame the abolitionists and Southern ''fire-eaters'' equally for the troubles. When the war came, McPherson, though saddened by the prospect of fighting against Southerners, some of whom were his personal friends, returned to the East.

As his first assignment, Captain McPherson had to raise a company of regulars. The difficulty of such a task led him to write to Major General Henry Wager Halleck,* whom he had known in California, with the request that Halleck use his influence to get McPherson into ''active service somewhere.'' Thus, on December 1, 1861, McPherson reported to Halleck in St. Louis as aide de camp with the rank of lieutenant colonel.

McPherson participated in campaigns under Ulysses Simpson Grant* against Forts Henry and Donelson as lieutenant colonel of engineers on Grant's staff. A collateral (and secret) duty was to report to Halleck on Grant's alleged propensity to drink. McPherson found the reports ill-founded and became one of Grant's greatest admirers and loyal supporters. As a staff officer at Shiloh, he defended Grant's conduct of the battle.

McPherson's rise was spectacular even by Civil War standards. He supervised military railroads in the upper Mississippi and upon Grant's recommendation received command of a division in time for the aftermath of the Corinth Campaign. In October 1862 he was named major general of volunteers and subsequently to the command of the XVII Corps. His handling of this corps during the Vicksburg Campaign greatly enhanced his reputation in the Army and gained for him the admiration of Grant and William Tecumseh Sherman.* When Grant was named general in chief and Sherman commander of the Department of the West, McPherson was given command of the redoubtable Army of the Tennessee.

Following a short tenure as military governor of Vicksburg, McPherson planned to take a furlough so that he might go to Baltimore and marry Emily Hoffman. However, Sherman called him to Chattanooga to assist in the preparations for the Georgia Campaign. The first major engagement of the campaign found McPherson involved in a situation that cast doubt upon his ability in independent command. This was the famous flanking movement around Joseph Eggleston Johnston* and his Army of the Tennessee, strongly placed at Dalton, Georgia. McPherson was to lead his force of some fifteen thousand to Johnston's left, through Snake Creek Gap, and to Resaca where he was to seize and hold the railroad. Sherman expected that this flanking movement would force Johnston to retreat.

McPherson did not seize Resaca, but after probing the works there withdrew to the safety of Snake Creek Gap. When Sherman followed McPherson with the bulk of his army (under George Henry Thomas*), Johnston retreated to Resaca and, after an inconclusive battle there, withdrew his army safely across the Oostenuala River. Sherman's disappointment in McPherson was manifest. But Sherman was lenient in his reports; at a crucial moment, he said, his young friend had been a "little timid."

In the advance on Atlanta, McPherson's command became the maneuver element of the Union Army, earning the sobriquet "Sherman's Whiplash." The flanking tactics forced Johnston finally into a grudging retreat into the fortifications of Atlanta, where, on July 18, 1864, he was replaced by John Bell Hood.* Hood, true to his reputation as an aggressive field commander, launched major assaults against Thomas on July 20 and then on July 22 against the Union left and the Army of the Tennessee. After hours of desperate fighting the Confederate attack was beaten back, but in the early stages of the fighting, McPherson rode into a line of Confederate skirmishers and was shot dead from the saddle.

Sherman wept for the loss of his friend and protegé. Later, in a touching letter to Emily Hoffman, he berated himself for not allowing McPherson to marry as planned. It would have been better, he said, for Miss Hoffman to be the "bride of McPherson dead than the wife of the richest merchant in Baltimore."

McPherson was a man of notable character and charm, intelligent and scholarly, compassionate and steadfast in his duties. He, of all the West Pointers in high command, seems to have gained the confidence and admiration of the volunteers, officers and men alike. But McPherson's outstanding record at the division and corps level was tarnished by his tenure as commander of the Army of the Tennessee. B. H. Liddell Hart has charged that his action, or inaction, at Resaca illustrated his lack of imagination and dash; that he did not grasp that Sherman's orders presumed aggressive leadership on his part; that his failure to seize Resaca and destroy the railroad bespoke a defect of character, a literal-mindedness all too common among Civil War officers, especially among West Pointers. In short, McPherson was overrated.

Yet others on the scene have defended McPherson. Joe Johnston, not a disinterested witness, argued that had McPherson established himself at Resaca, he (Johnston) would have detached sufficient troops to crush him while holding Sherman in check at Dalton. John McAllister Schofield,* who commanded the

Army of the Ohio during the Georgia Campaign, believed that the fault was
Sherman's for not assigning a larger force (presumably Thomas and the Army
of the Cumberland) to the flanking maneuver. According to one of McPherson's
staff officers, Brevet Major Rowland Cox, McPherson himself said that had he
attacked Resaca or remained in front of the Confederate works, Johnston would
have cut him off "as you cut off the end of a piece of tape with a pair of shears."
Cox further argued that "It is not, I think, too much to say that on that day, as
upon a subsequent occasion, he saved the Army of the Tennessee from utter
destruction."

That "subsequent occasion," of course, was July 22, 1864, when Mc-
Pherson's army fought what came to be called the Battle of Atlanta. The Army
of the Tennessee had approached the city from the east, along the railroad from
Decatur. When, on July 18, Hood replaced Johnston, McPherson, although he
had not seen Hood since their graduation from West Point, impressed upon his
staff that they must expect an attack at any time. At 4:00 A.M. on July 22,
McPherson received a message from Sherman that he was to move forward and
occupy the exterior lines of the Atlanta defenses. McPherson, as was his custom,
made a personal reconnaissance and to his staff declared "that he anticipated
during the day an engagement such as had not taken place during the campaign."
Accordingly, he ordered Grenville Dodge to move his XVI Corps to the left,
extending that flank toward Decatur. At about 7:00 A.M., he received a penciled
note from Sherman: "Instead of sending Dodge to your left, I wish you would
put his whole corps at work destroying the railroad back to and including Decatur." Sherman would then swing McPherson to the right on another of those
patented whiplash movements. Yet McPherson thought that Sherman's order
should be delayed; he was convinced that he would be attacked, and he expected
the attack to fall upon his left front. He sought out Sherman, who agreed that
Dodge should continue moving into position on the left, but if no general attack
had commenced by 1:00 P.M., at least one division of the XVI Corps should be
detached to destroy the railroad to Decatur.

At mid-day, McPherson instructed Dodge to detach a division and carry out
Sherman's orders. Scarcely had the order been dispatched than heavy firing
broke out on the left; it was the full-scale attack that McPherson had anticipated.
He rode to the firing and witnessed William Joseph Hardee's* first assaults
against Dodge's corps. McPherson's intelligent deployment of his forces had
averted a disaster. After some minutes, McPherson noted a gap between Dodge
and Frank Blair's XVII Corps, and sent a message to John A. Logan to fill that
gap with units from the XV Corps. Then, accompanied only by an aide, he rode
toward Blair's left. Unexpectedly, McPherson rode directly into grayclad skirmishers from Pat Cleburne's division. Ignoring a command to surrender, he
spurred his horse away; a shot through his upper body brought him down,
mortally wounded.

In Ohio a heroic statue marks the grave of the young general whose contributions to the Union cause, while great, were not fully realized.

BIBLIOGRAPHY

Bearss, Edwin C. *Decision in Mississippi*. Jackson, Miss.: Mississippi Commission on
the War between the States, 1962.
Catton, Bruce, *Grant Moves South*. Boston: Little, Brown and Company, 1960.
Lewis, Lloyd. *Sherman, Fighting Prophet*. New York: Harcourt, Brace and Company,
1932.
Liddell Hart, B. H. *Sherman*. New York: Dodd, Mead and Company, 1929.

JOHN T. HUBBELL

MAHAN, Alfred Thayer (b. West Point, N.Y., September 27, 1840; d. Washington, D.C., December 1, 1914), naval officer, historian, theoretician. Mahan has been called the philosopher of sea power by modern authorities.

Alfred Thayer Mahan was the eldest son of Dennis Hart Mahan,* professor of civil and military engineering at the U.S. Military Academy; his middle name was taken from Sylvanus Thayer,* whom his father admired. He entered Columbia College in New York City in 1854; two years later he transferred into the third (sophomore) class at the U.S. Naval Academy and was graduated in 1859, second in the class. During his first class year he earned the enmity of his classmates by putting several of them on report for minor infractions of discipline. They, in turn, "silenced" him.

This was the first of many bitter personal controversies that marked his naval and literary careers. Mahan was a man of enormous ego and temper; he was quick to take offense at real or imagined slights, slow to forgive criticism, unwilling to admit error. Indeed, he went through life with only one close personal friend. As his daughter remembered him, he was "The Cat That Walked By Himself."

From 1859 to 1885 Mahan's naval career was unremarkable and unexciting. He served ingloriously throughout the Civil War on blockade duty and obscurely in various billets ashore and afloat after the war. He was not a skillful seaman. Collisions, groundings, and other nautical mishaps marred his commands at sea. He feared the sea, was unnerved by the responsibility of command, sought assiduously to avoid assignments to sea duty, and was bored and frustrated by his profession. On several occasions he considered resigning his commission.

What Mahan discovered he could do, and do exceedingly well, was write naval history. In 1883, while serving at the Brooklyn Navy Yard, he wrote his first book, a competent account of U.S. naval operations during the Civil War. It caught the eye of Captain Stephen Bleeker Luce,* whose protegé he became. At this juncture in his naval career, Commander Mahan was neither an imperialist nor an enthusiast for the modern steam and steel "New Navy" that the nation was belatedly beginning to build. He was not concerned with the foreign policy implications of the New Navy or the technological problems it posed.

The major turning point in Mahan's service career, and in his isolationist view of American foreign policy, came in 1885 when Luce, founder and first president of the new Naval War College in Newport, Rhode Island, secured his assignment to the faculty of the experimental institution. He began teaching naval history at the college in 1886. In 1886–1888 and 1892–1893 he served as its president. Against great opposition from within the Navy, he fought to keep the institution from being absorbed into other naval training facilities, and he worked to install there a curriculum that emphasized consideration of the transcendent historical, theoretical, tactical, and strategical "principles" of naval warfare. He was less concerned that his officer-students study the engineering, ordnance, and architecture of the ships of the New Navy. Mahan's foresight in this regard made the War College the intellectual command center of the reemerging U.S. Navy and defined for it the scholarly mission it has since pursued.

During his first tour as lecturer-president of the War College, Captain Mahan researched and wrote his brilliant, seminal study, *The Influence of Sea Power Upon History, 1660–1783*. Published in 1890, the book was filled with newly discovered imperialist convictions derived from his reading of naval history. It brought its obscure author instant worldwide acclaim and fame. It also brought him into personal association with the leadership of the nascent imperialist movement in the United States, specifically with vigorous Republican party nationalists like Theordore Roosevelt,* Henry Cabot Lodge, and John M. Hay.

These men, and others, were urging the historical, geopolitical, and economic necessity of American commercial, ecclesiastical, and territorial expansion abroad—an expansion that would be sustained strategically and operationally by a revived U.S. Navy and would be effected in diplomatic concert with Great Britain, America's partner in the superior "Anglo-Saxon race" that was destined by God to uplift the world's "backward" peoples spiritually and materially. The new imperialists quickly seized upon Mahan's argument that nations had waxed or waned throughout history in direct relation to their effective acquisition, maintenance, and employment of great navies and merchant marines.

Mahan was seldom, if ever, consulted on major foreign policy decisions by the imperialist leadership of the Republican party in the turbulent years ahead; indeed, they often outdistanced and embarrassed him in the scope, ambition, and crudities of their expansionist activities. But they were as eager to enlist his persuasive pen in their cause as he was pleased and flattered to volunteer it. The more he wrote, the more flamboyantly expansionist he became. As their leading propagandist for American imperialism and navalism, the grateful Republicans protected and rewarded Mahan, whose ranks he formally joined in 1894.

They supported his curricular orientation at the War College, opposed his banishment to sea in 1893 by the anti-imperialist Cleveland administration (he had publicly recommended the annexation of Hawaii), quashed fitness reports critical of his command of the protected cruiser *Chicago* (1893–1895), eulogized him when he retired from the Navy in 1896, called him back to active duty in 1898 to serve on the Naval War Board during the Spanish-American War, placed him on the American delegation to the Hague Peace Conference in 1901, subsidized his writing by ordering him to detached duty at the War College when he needed additional income, and promoted him to rear admiral on the retired list in 1906.

The last two decades of his life were spent almost entirely in writing, a successful second career in which he made considerable amounts of money.

Mahan's lasting reputation rests primarily on his role in defining the cerebral mission of the Naval War College and in clearly explaining to Americans the relationship between naval power, diplomacy, and national security at a time when the competitive state system was girding itself for World War I. His argument from history that nations economically dependent on the sea will perish beneath it unless they marshal and maintain their sea power capability remains a powerful one. A devout Anglican, devoted Anglophile, and sympathetic historian of the Royal Navy and the British Empire, Mahan also contributed positively to the Anglo-American diplomatic rapprochement of 1897–1914.

But as a self-taught historian who became president of the American Historical Association (1902–1903), Mahan's current standing in Clio's retinue is not particularly high. The central idea in his *Influence of Sea Power Upon History,* and in similar books and articles that followed, was not original with him. He never claimed it was, although he did suggest that God had personally revealed the concept to him. Actually, the book was a skillful synthesis of the research and insights of others. Its persuasive influence, at home and abroad, stemmed from the fact that the sea power argument, with its capitalist, colonialist, racist, and militarist overtones, comported nicely with the imperialist urges and ambitions of the world's major industrial nations on the eve of World War I. On the other hand, the thought that the flow of history might have had upon it other influences than sea power made little impression on Mahan. And his conviction that God's mathematically ordered universe was filled with various historical "principles" and "laws" awaiting discovery by divinely inspired historians seems naive in retrospect.

Moreover, Mahan's philosophy of history, which principally sought to justify war as an inevitable and necessary historical phenomenon—glorious, uplifting, civilizing, productive of progress, and wholly Christian—was based largely on the ideas of his uncle, Milo Mahan (1819–1870), an Episcopal clergyman who wrote several books that sought to marry ancient Pythagorean numerology to fundamentalist Anglican theology. The conceptual offspring of this peculiar union was a volatile universe in which sinful mankind was moved toward perfection by the God-directed dialectical clashes of opposing historical forces (thesis, antithesis, synthesis) expressed in numerical terms.

Nor did Mahan's extensive comments on naval tactics, strategy, and technology appear to have much modern applicability. His contribution to the development of battlefleet tactics essentially repeated, in naval terms, Antoine Henri Jomini's (1779–1869) earlier observations on Napoleonic infantry and cavalry tactics which had affirmed the historical "law" that superior concentrated firepower brought skillfully to bear on a lesser segment of an enemy's force would invariably result in victory. Mahan's insistence on the additional historical axiom that a prudent nation must strategically concentrate its naval forces on the outbreak of war made good sense until 1945. Nuclear weaponry would render such concentration virtually suicidal today.

Furthermore, Mahan had little interest in the complex, ever-changing relationships between strategy, tactics, and technology, since he believed that certain immutable military principles (like that of "concentration") were inherent in the universe and that these wholly governed the "art" and "science" of warfare; technological developments, such as airplanes or submarines, had little influence on these larger cosmological determinants.

In fine, Mahan's influence was far greater in his own time than it is now. His insistence, however, that "command of the sea" is important to American security and prosperity, and to the nation's ability to choose peace or war as its overseas interests may require, seems as relevant today as when he wrote it.

BIBLIOGRAPHY

Livezey, William E. *Mahan on Sea Power*. Norman: University of Oklahoma Press, 1947.
Mahan, Alfred Thayer. *From Sail to Steam: Recollections of Naval Life*. New York: Da Capo Press Reprint Series, 1968. (1st ed., New York: Harper, 1907.)
———. *The Influence of Sea Power upon History, 1660–1783*. Boston: Little, Brown and Company, 1890.
Puleston, William D. *Mahan: The Life and Work of Captain Alfred Thayer Mahan, U.S.N.* New Haven, Conn.: Yale University Press, 1939.
Seager, Robert, II, *Alfred Thayer Mahan: The Man and His Letters*. Annapolis, Md.: Naval Institute Press, 1977.
———, and Doris D. Maguire, eds. *Letters and Papers of Alfred Thayer Mahan*. 3 vols. Annapolis, Md.: Naval Institute Press, 1975.

ROBERT SEAGER II

MAHAN, Dennis Hart (b. New York City, N.Y., April 2, 1802; d. by drowning in the Hudson River near West Point, N.Y., September 16, 1871), military educator. As professor of military and civil engineering, and of the science of war at the U.S. Military Academy, Mahan was the principal teacher of the military art to nearly all the West Point graduates who commanded in the Civil War.

The son of Irish immigrants, his father a carpenter, Mahan was a frail youth whose aspiration was to be an artist. He sought appointment to the Military Academy because drawing was a part of the heavily engineering curriculum under Sylvanus Thayer.* Entering West Point in 1820 from Virginia, whither his family had moved and where at Norfolk he had grown up, he discovered a fascination for military subjects. He also revealed a brilliance that immediately caught Thayer's attention. From his second year he was acting assistant professor of mathematics. He graduated first of thirty-two cadets in the class of 1824 and remained at the Academy for two years, first as assistant professor of mathematics, and then as principal assistant professor of engineering. In 1826 he was ordered to Europe to study both military instruction and civil engineering, with emphasis on waterways and roads. While carrying out these broad instructions, he completed a course at the French School of Application for Engineers and Artillery at Metz, probably the leading school in the world in those aspects of military study that West Point was to continue to emphasize. Returning to West Point, he resumed his career as assistant professor of engineering in 1830 and became professor two years later.

Mahan developed a fourth-year course that was the capstone of the Academy curriculum, with a growing quotient of tactics and strategy, entitled by 1843 "Engineering and the Science of War." In both engineering and military subjects, Mahan dealt largely with material about which little had been published in the United States or even in the English language. Therefore, he developed his own texts from his translations of French works, lithographing these versions of materials that often he had brought home with him from Europe on a small press that he had also brought from Europe. Out of his texts developed his published books: *Complete Treatise on Field Fortification* (1836); *Elementary Course of Civil Engineering* (1837); *Summary of the Course of Permanent Fortification and of the Attack and Defence of Permanent Works* (1850); *Industrial Drawing* (1852); *Descriptive Geometry as Applied to the Drawing of Fortification and Stereotomy* (1864); and *An Elementary Course of Military Engineering* (1867). The books on engineering became the foundation of engineering literature in the United States. Mahan's most important book in its impact on military history was *An Elementary Treatise on Advanced-Guard, Out-Post, and Detachment Service of Troops, and the Manner of Posting and Handling Them in Presence of an Enemy, With a Historical Sketch of the Rise and Progress of Tactics, &c., &c.* (1847, 1853, 1863). Its implausible title notwithstanding, this book, especially in its final edition, is a comprehensive survey of tactics and strategy. Along with *Elements of Military Art and Science ...*, written by Mahan's favorite pupil, Henry Wager Halleck,* and in its first edition antedating Mahan's book by a year, *Out-Post* (as it is commonly called) was the foundation of an American professional military literature.

Out-Post assumes a professional level of military officership and a similar competence among the soldiers. Its author not only contributed greatly to professional military study but also helped nurture the disdain of the professional for the military amateur so conspicuous in the attitudes of such a student of his as Emory Upton.* Nevertheless, the title page of *Out-Post* states that the book is "especially for the use of officers of militia and volunteers," and it was in fact widely used for militia and volunteer training before and during the Civil War. To the disgust of the stoutly Unionist author, pirated editions appeared in Richmond and New Orleans during the war. Meanwhile, before the war Mahan had also helped nourish the military tradition of the state from which he had been appointed as a cadet, by encouraging the founding of the Virginia Military

Institute, which used his texts and until 1860 called its summer encampment Camp Mahan.

Mahan was a formidable teacher when invoking the West Point system of frequent enforced recitations; the thought of being caught unprepared by him still terrified William Tecumseh Sherman* in the 1880s. Yet Mahan was also a most unmilitary figure, "the most particular, crabbed, exacting man I ever saw," according to Cadet Tully McCrea. "He is a little slim skeleton of a man and always nervous and cross." Having resigned his second lieutenant's commission on January 1, 1832, when he became a professor, he not only dressed as a civilian but also constantly carried an umbrella. His dedication to West Point was so complete that reaction against it may have helped turn his sons Alfred Thayer Mahan* and the second Dennis Hart Mahan away from the Army to the Navy (though a third son, Frederick A., graduated from West Point). His model of complete dedication to the military profession was also so thorough that it demanded an absolutely apolitical stance, and Mahan never voted. When in 1871 the academic board of the Military Academy decided that Mahan's age required his retirement from the faculty, he soon afterward fell from a boat into the Hudson River. Life without West Point may have lost its meaning for him.

Mahan was first an engineer, but his military teaching did not tie tactics and strategy to the supposedly inherent caution of the engineer. To Mahan, the fortifications erected by the military engineer were useful to the defensive as a temporary expedient, to help exhaust the enemy, and as points of departure and support for the attack. The spade is as important in war as the musket, but the offensive, nevertheless, was Mahan's preferred mode of war, and he instilled in his students the conviction that only the offensive was likely to bring victory in war. Even for the army on the strategic defensive, the attack is the most potent tactical weapon. "Vigor on the field and rapidity of pursuit should go hand in hand for great success." "Carrying the war into the heart of the assailant's country, or that of his allies, is the surest way of making him share its burdens and foiling his plans." "If Fortune is on the side of the heavy battalions, she also frequently grants her favors to superior activity and audacity."

Mahan was not fond of stressing the value of the heavy battalions. His military hero, his prime exemplar of sound strategy, was Napoleon. When faculty and students at West Point founded a Napoleon Club, Mahan was almost inevitably its president. Mahan's Napoleon was not the Napoleon of Carl von Clausewitz's interpretation but the Napoleon of Antoine Henri Jomini, whose writings strongly influenced Mahan and whose thinking was akin to Mahan's. Mahan favored the offensive not of the heavy battalions but of indirection and maneuver. His emphasis on deceptive maneuver accounts in turn for his emphasis, even in the title of his principal military book, on the activities of advanced guards, outposts, and reconnaissances that screen maneuver. To gain information about the enemy and deprive him of information in turn, Mahan recommended that one-fifth to one-third of any force be detailed as reconnaissance parties, advanced guards, and outposts. "There are no more important duties, which an officer may be called upon to perform, than those of collecting and arranging the information upon which the . . . operations of a campaign must be based."

For deceptive maneuver as the essence of the offensive, speed of movement is as important as adequate intelligence and screening. "In this one quality," speed, "reside all the advantages that a fortunate initiative may have procured." "No great success can be hoped for in war in which rapid movements do not enter as an element. Even the very elements of Nature seem to array themselves against the slow and over-prudent general."

Clearly, it was not Mahan's teaching at West Point that encouraged some of the generals of the Civil War to become slow and overprudent. On the other hand, too much of a positive influence should not be claimed for Mahan's teaching of the art of war to Civil War generals. Mahan's concepts of grand tactics and strategy were crammed mainly into a single fourth-year course, in the largely nonmilitary West Point curriculum. To speak either of Mahan's influence, or of Jomini's through Mahan and West Point, as conditioning Civil War generalship can readily make American soldiers of the 1860s appear much more bookish than they were, and far less the military improvisers confronted with new conditions that they had to be.

At the same time, Mahan's insistence on meticulous intelligence, screening, and reconnaissance and on rapid movements underline his call for a high degree of professional competence in officers and similar skill in soldiers. He remains, most centrally, a founder of military study as professional study. What makes the mastery of an occupation a profession is that its education be rooted in historical study, that a series of guiding principles be drawn from historical experience. Such was Mahan's approach to the study required for military officership: "No one can be said to have thoroughly mastered his art, who has neglected to make himself conversant with its early history. . . . It is in military history that we are to look for the source of all military science."

Above all, in military history the student should look to Napoleon. Interpreted by Mahan to a generation and more of West Point cadets, Napoleon left a profound impression upon the American approach to war. Mahan's Napoleon was par excellence the aggressive, offensive-minded commander, the general of swift maneuver against an enemy's exposed flank and rear, and the general who through such maneuver demonstrated "those grand features of the art [of war], by which an enemy is broken and utterly dispersed by one and the same blow."

BIBLIOGRAPHY

Ambrose, Stephen E. *Duty, Honor, Country: A History of West Point*. Baltimore: Johns Hopkins University Press, 1966.

Dupuy, R. Ernest. *Men of West Point: The First 150 Years of the United States Military Academy*. New York: Sloane, 1951.

———. *Where They Have Trod: The West Point Tradition in American Life*. Philadelphia: Lippincott, 1940.

Puleston, W. D. *Mahan: The Life and Work of Captain Alfred Thayer Mahan*. New Haven, Conn.: Yale Univesity Press, 1939.

Weigley, Russell F. *Towards an American Army: Military Thought from Washington to Marshall*. New York: Columbia University Press, 1962.

RUSSELL F. WEIGLEY

MALLORY, Stephen Russell (b. Trinidad, British West Indies, 1811; d. Pensacola, Fla., November 9, 1873), senator, cabinet officer. Mallory performed competently as Confederate secretary of the Navy during the Civil War (1861–1865).

The product of an American father and an Irish Catholic mother, Mallory moved with his family to Key West, Florida, in 1820. Two years later his father died of tuberculosis. Mallory helped his widowed mother operate a boarding house. His formal education was limited to a few months in a school at Mobile, Alabama, and three years in a Moravian boys' school at Nazareth, Pennsylvania. Returning to Florida, Mallory read law in the office of a local judge while serving as inspector of customs at Key West. As a volunteer aboard a small gunboat, he saw action in the Seminole War (1836–1838). Subsequently, Mallory practiced law, specializing in maritime cases, and gladly accepted President James Polk's appointment as collector of customs for Key West (1845–1849).

In 1851 the Florida legislature elected Mallory to the U.S. Senate, and two years later the Democratic leadership assigned him to chair the Senate Committee on Naval Affairs. During eight years on this committee, Mallory became one of the most knowledgeable civilians on naval matters in the South. He studied European naval developments, inspected U.S. Navy facilities, ships, and ordnance, encouraged the building of six Navy steam frigates, and advocated reinstituting flogging as a standard punishment (it had been outlawed in 1850). Mallory sponsored legislation creating the Naval Retiring Board to retire or furlough overage and inefficient officers. The board concluded that two hundred officers should be retired or discharged. The most notable of these was Matthew Fontaine Maury,* a brilliant, irascible, and lame officer. Maury successfully appealed the board's decision but never forgave Mallory for its action. In early 1861 Mallory was one of several Southerners who believed that secession could lead to war. Consequently, Mallory and other important Southerners—including Jefferson Davis,* John Slidell, and Judah P. Benjamin—signed a resolution advising caution in handling the crisis over Fort Pickens, the Federal fort at Pensacola, Florida. Mallory left his seat in the Senate in February 1861, when Florida seceded from the Union.

The part that Mallory played in the "Pickens episode" prompted members of the Provisional Congress at Montgomery, Alabama, to oppose his nomination as secretary of the navy, despite the fact that the others involved were prominent secessionists. Alternative choices for the navy portfolio might have included Matthew Maury; Lawrence Rousseau, a seventy-one-year-old Louisianian and former captain in the U.S. Navy; John Perkins, Jr., a graduate of Yale College and Harvard Law School, who was a cotton planter, lawyer, and former Louisiana congressman with no evident experience in naval matters; and Charles M. Conrad, a New Orleans lawyer who formerly had been U.S. senator from Louisiana and secretary of war under President Millard Fillmore (1850–1853). Conrad became chairman of the Committee on Naval Affairs and one of Mallory's leading detractors in the Confederate Congress.

Although Mallory had limited administrative experience, he was familiar with the Navy and many of its officers, and took his new post confidently. He quickly established a Navy Department—naturally patterned after the Federal model—and set his objectives for the Confederate States Navy: to send out commerce-raiding cruisers to destroy Northern shipping on the high seas; and to build or buy ironclad warships to break any blockade imposed by the Federal Navy. In the coming years, Confederate cruisers swept the oceans of Yankee merchantmen and whalers, forcing American ships to change to flags of convenience, but Mallory failed to create a squadron of armorclads to break the cordon formed by the Union's wooden-hulled blockaders.

Mallory worked industriously on a low budget with little cooperation from the War Department during the war. He sent agents to Europe to contract for ships—including the dreaded *Alabama*, developed rolling mills and supply shops necessary to support a navy, and finally decided to involve the Navy in blockade running. But he was up against the Union Navy, which had grown quickly from its well-established yards, converted dozens of vessels to military use, capitalized on the capabilities of Northern industries, and benefited from the excellent administration of Secretary of the Navy Gideon Welles* and Assistant Secretary Gustavus Vasa Fox.* On May 2, 1865, Mallory resigned his cabinet post as the Confederacy crumbled. He was captured and imprisoned for ten months at Fort Lafayette, New York.

Upon being released, Mallory established himself in a law practice in Pensacola. In newspaper editorials and public speeches he opposed the Radical Republican Reconstruction program. He died in Pensacola on November 9, 1873.

Stephen Mallory was a rotund, ruddy-faced man who loved to eat large meals and drink fine wines. He got along well with Jefferson Davis,* whom he had known in the U.S. Senate. President Davis, a West Pointer who concentrated on land warfare, took little notice of the Navy. Mallory was one of only two cabinet members who held their posts throughout the entire war; the other was John Reagan, postmaster general.

Within three months of the firing on Fort Sumter, Mallory had formulated his naval strategy for the war. That strategy—like the Confederacy itself—was a gamble. Mallory correctly recognized the need to break any Union blockade of the Southern coast. He decided to take the unproven method of building or buying a few ironclad warships similar to those in England and France rather than relying on numbers of conventional wooden men-of-war. This was a visionary policy, but for it to succeed Mallory needed modern technical facilities and a munificent budget. He had neither. The navy yard at Norfolk was soon captured, as were the docks at New Orleans; Confederates destroyed the navy yard at Pensacola when they reckoned that they could not hold the city. Consequently, Mallory had to look to other places, such as Memphis, Tennessee, for shipbuilding sites. The ironclad policy was risky, but Mallory saw no other way to proceed; the South had few wooden ships, and he correctly judged that it would be impossible to try to match the Union Navy ship-for-ship, by purchase (at home or abroad) or by construction. A few Southern ironclads, he dreamed, could devastate the Northern timberhulls and then go on to attack major Union ports, creating havoc and perhaps helping to bring the war to an early end. However, James D. Bulloch, Mallory's chief agent sent to Europe to contract for construction of warships, found it unexpectedly complicated to circumvent European laws regarding building vessels for military use. Moreover, it was terribly difficult to buy ships and munitions on suspect credit. In view of these hindrances, Bulloch did a splendid job, though sometimes he and other Southerners abroad unwittingly bid against one another for the same services or supplies.

The most striking products of the Confederate efforts in Europe were the commerce-raiding cruisers *Alabama* and *Florida*. The cruisers were not ironclads, but imitated the intentions of other nations with weak navies—to prey on unarmed merchant ships—and formed the second part of Mallory's naval strategy. The cruisers aimed to lay waste to Northern commercial shipping, and consequently try to weaken the blockade by drawing off Union ships from their coastal patrol. Mallory baited his hook and waited. The Union lost dozens of merchantmen and whalers to the *Alabama* and her sisters, but President Abraham Lincoln* and Secretary Welles did not snap at the hook. On the contrary, more Union ships were put on blockade duty as the war progressed, thus forcing Mallory to realize that the Confederate Navy should participate in blockade running.

To his credit, Mallory did everything his powers, budget, and imagination would allow to build ironclads within the Confederacy. Given the scattered resources and neophyte industrial plants he had, it was remarkable that fifty armorclads were laid down or planned, and twenty-two were commissioned. Unfortunately for the Confederacy, many of the ships Mallory had been depending upon to break the blockade (including the *Louisiana, Mississippi, Arkansas,* and *Virginia*) were blown up by their builders or crews to prevent them from falling into Northern hands. Taking such suicidal action emphasized the general military weaknesses of the Confederacy—its vulnerability to Union combined operations which Mallory did not have the coast artillery or manpower to prevent, and the glaring lack of cooperation between the "land-minded" War Department and the Navy Department. In fact, throughout the war the Navy Department was crippled because Mallory lacked the assertiveness to demand a fair percentage of Southern conscripts, and he never obtained from the president or his secretaries of war the logical concession that draftees with maritime experience—pilots, sailors, riverboatmen, mechanics, shipwrights, and the like—should automatically be sent to the Navy.

There is no doubt that Mallory was an enthusiastic worker. He encouraged the development of "torpedoes" (mines), and he tried to deal with the politicized problem of naval promotions by creating a separate ranking list called the Provisional Navy. But at times his enthusiasm led him to approve schemes that actually drained off valuable time, men, and munitions—such as trying to buy the French Navy's armorclad *Glorie*, planning a raid on Buffalo, New York, with a vessel purchased in Canada, starting a Confederate Naval Academy, or sending John Taylor Wood on numerous raids and cutting out adventures. Nevertheless, the exploits of Confederate naval officers such as Raphael Semmes* and John N. Maffit boosted Southern morale. And considering the unproven record of some of Mallory's "floating fortresses," the epidemic of "ram-fever" that infected many Union naval commanders was surprising indeed. The reluctance to challenge the *Tennessee*, one of the Confederate armorclads, probably delayed the attack on Mobile for several months.

It is ironic that as chairman of the U.S. Senate Committee on Naval Affairs Mallory did all he could to build up and improve the Federal Navy in the 1850s, publicizing the experiments of John Adolphus Bernard Dahlgren* and recommending the addition of new ships. However, in the Senate he had time to become acquainted at leisure with men, problems, and machines. Concentrating on building the *Virginia* and protecting Norfolk during the war, he could not attend personally to the many construction problems on the *Louisiana* and the *Mississippi* in New Orleans, and he could not see to the defense of that city. As a consequence, he lost them all. The South never recovered from these blows by an opponent capable of launching multiple attacks. The war would not wait for Mallory and his Confederates to make all of their visions into reality.

BIBLIOGRAPHY

Durkin, Joseph T. *Stephen R. Mallory: Confederate Navy Chief*. Chapel Hill: University of North Carolina Press, 1954.

Merli, Frank J. *Great Britain and the Confederate Navy*. Bloomington: Indiana University Press, 1970.

Patrick, Rembert W. *Jefferson Davis and His Cabinet*. Baton Rouge: Louisiana State University Press, 1944.

Still, William N., Jr. *Iron Afloat: The Story of the Confederate Armorclads*. Nashville, Tenn.: Vanderbilt University Press, 1971.

Vandiver, Frank E. *Rebel Brass: The Confederate Command System*. Baton Rouge: Louisiana State University Press, 1956.

Wells, Tom H. *The Confederate Navy: A Study in Organization*. Tuscaloosa: University of Alabama Press, 1971.

JOSEPH G. DAWSON III

MARCH, Peyton Conway (b. Easton, Pa., December 27, 1864; d. Washington, D.C., April 13, 1955), military leader and administrator; Army chief of staff, 1918–1921.

March was a member of a distinguished family. His father, Francis Andrew, was a famous philologist while his mother, Margaret Conway, was related to the great Virginia families. In his generation, four of the five sons were in *Who's Who in America*. After graduation from Lafayette College, March went to West Point where he graduated in 1888. For ten years his was the routine of an artillery officer in a peacetime army dominated by Civil War veterans.

In the Spanish-American War and Philippine Insurrection, March made a brilliant reputation. He completed the two-year course at the Artillery School in March 1898, just in time to take command of the Astor Battery. He led this privately financed unit of volunteers ranging from Ivy Leaguers to veterans of British colonial campaigns into action in the Philippines. His heroism at the Battle of Manila won him a recommendation for the Medal of Honor from Major General Arthur MacArthur.* Later, during the Insurrection, as MacArthur's aide and then as a major and lieutenant colonel in the 33d Volunteer Infantry, he received five more citations for gallantry. As a provincial governor and commissary general of prisoners, he also gained administrative experience. In 1901, General MacArthur wrote about him: "no officer has rendered more efficient or brilliant field service than he in the Island of Luzon."

March spent about half of the next sixteen years with troops, but his most noteworthy assignments were as a member of the first War Department General Staff and of the powerful Adjutant General's Department. The first also afforded him an opportunity to see the Russo-Japanese War as an observer with the Japanese. The second placed him in a position where he could learn thoroughly the intricacies of the Army bureaucracy and brought him to the attention of Secretary of War Newton Diehl Baker.*

When the United States intervened in World War I, March was a colonel in command of the 8th Field Artillery. Within a few months, he was a major general and the chief of artillery of the American Expeditionary Force (AEF). In France he supervised the planning and development of the artillery program until February 1918 when Secretary Baker called him back to Washington to be the chief of staff.

During the first eleven months of the war, Hugh Lenox Scott,* Tasker Howard Bliss,* and John Biddle attempted to cope as chiefs of staff with the problems of mobilizing and bringing to bear the military effort of the United States. While many of the delays, mistakes, and outright failures could be blamed on lack of proper organization and the necessity to compress the process of changing from peace to war footing in such a brief period, Baker and others saw the need of a more effective administrator in the position of chief of staff.

March took over as acting chief of staff on March 4, 1918. In May he became the chief of staff and received the temporary rank of full general. He saw that his basic task was to get enough men to France to win the war. When he came to power, there were fewer than 1.7 million men in the entire Army with some quarter of a million in the AEF. The measure of his success is in the statistics: the Army more than doubled in total strength, and the AEF expanded to some

2 million in the eight months prior to the Armistice. To achieve this result, March strove consistently for a more efficient and effective General Staff, War Department, and Army.

Within the War Department, he decisively established the primacy of the General Staff by ruthlessly clipping the power of the chiefs of the administrative bureaus and by placing the supply organizations under his assistant chief of staff, Major General George Washington Goethals.* In the Army, generally, he sought to increase efficiency by creating new branches which reflected technological innovations: Air Service, Tank Corps, Motor Transport Corps, and Chemical Warfare Service. He also abolished the distinctions between the National Army, National Guard, and Regular Army. His much criticized shortening of the West Point course to one year was perhaps due more to his long-term desire to reform the Military Academy than to the need for a relatively few more wartime lieutenants. As chief of staff, he attempted to eliminate outside political influence in the Army, and, through his institution of regular press conferences, he tried to make information more available. Behind all of these changes was the metamorphosis of the Office of Chief of Staff to a much more powerful position which he spelled out in General Order No. 80 as the "immediate adviser of the Secretary of War on all matters relating to the Military Establishment" with the rank and authority of the nation's senior soldier.

Although General John Joseph Pershing,* the commander of the AEF, was pleased with the primary result of March's actions—namely, the tremendous increase in the troops in the AEF—he was irritated by the fact that March did not subordinate himself as his predecessors in Washington had done. There was friction and one major dispute over the eventual strength of the AEF. Pershing expected March to put his 100 Division Plan into effect without giving full consideration to the domestic capability to sustain this program. Then he refused to accept a lesser strength plan. The surprisingly quick end of the war prevented the situation from getting out of hand.

After the Armistice, March remained in office until June 30, 1921. In this anticlimactic period he supervised the return of the AEF, the demobilization of the emergency Army, and the transition of the Regular Army to peacetime duties. Faced with opposition from Pershing and others as well as the simple fact that Congress and the people wanted to cut the Army to the bone, March failed to get the five hundred thousand strength he wanted. Nor was there a chance for the three-month universal training program which he supported.

In retirement, he lived in Europe, New York, and, finally, Washington and maintained interest in military matters. Deeply hurt by the lack of recognition which Pershing's memoirs gave him and the War Department for their wartime contributions, March responded in 1932 with *The Nation at War*. Not content to describe his and the War Department's activities, March severely criticized Pershing and gave the old controversy a thorough airing. He followed the events of World War II (in which two of his sons-in-law, Joseph M. Swing and John

Millikin, became generals) and the Korean War with great interest. Finally, in 1953, President Dwight David Eisenhower* presented him with the thanks of Congress—a tribute that curiously did not refer to his wartime achievements.

March's place in history rests on his role in the American victory in World War I. After the war, Secretary Baker succinctly stated what this soldier did and evaluated his contribution in two letters. In 1919 he explained to the chairman of the Senate Military Affairs Committee:

> The Chief of Staff was the head of the organization at home. His driving power, his high professional equipment, and his burning zeal imparted to our whole machine an impetus which never slackened . . . [as he] organized, expedited and stimulated our mobilization at home, and made effective that support and cooperation upon which, under modern war conditions, the success of the commander in the field depends.

Seventeen years later, in a letter to the former chief of staff, Baker emphatically summed up the importance of his work: "The war was won by days. Your energy and drive supplied the days necessary for our side to win."

A brilliant, decisive, hard man, March had little time for the amenities. This lack of tact and apparent insensitivity caused criticism, contributed to the animosity which many military and political leaders felt toward him, and unquestionably denied him some of the credit and honors his accomplishments deserved. As George Catlett Marshall* pointed out, this trait of antagonizing people was a great weakness; yet, General Marshall still considered March "a master administrator." Douglas MacArthur* was more complimentary: "He was that rare combination—a courageous leader and a skilled administrator. . . . A tremendous officer—a tremendous Chief of Staff." What honors could surpass that tribute?

BIBLIOGRAPHY

Coffman, Edward M. *The Hilt of the Sword: The Career of Peyton C. March.* Madison: University of Wisconsin Press, 1966.
———. *The War to End All Wars: The American Military Experience in World War I.* New York: Oxford University Press, 1968.
March, Peyton C. *The Nation at War.* Garden City, N.Y.: Doubleday, Doran and Company, 1932.

EDWARD M. COFFMAN

MARCY, Randolph Barnes (b. Greenwich, Mass., April 9, 1812; d. West Orange, N.J., November 22, 1887), Army officer and explorer.

Though a native son of the urbane and sophisticated Massachusetts environment, Randolph B. Marcy spent virtually his entire adult life in military service on the far western frontier. Receiving his commission upon graduation from West Point in 1832, the twenty-year-old brevet second lieutenant went immediately to Michigan and Wisconsin where he served for thirteen years, except for brief recruiting stints in the East.

Marcy's first chance to distinguish himself in combat came at Palo Alto and Resaca de la Palma, south Texas scenes of the opening battles of the Mexican War (1846–1848). In 1846 he was promoted to the rank of captain. During the succeeding twelve years he made his home at various military posts throughout Texas and Indian Territory. It was during this period that Marcy and elements of the 5th Infantry Regiment conducted a number of reconnaissances to locate sites for new forts. From his efforts emerged a line of posts and an important military road extending across the rolling plains of northwest Texas. These building projects, undertaken by the Army during the early 1850s, not only helped protect the surrounding region, but also helped facilitate civilian travel across the Southwest to the California gold fields.

Subsequently, Marcy participated in two military ventures at opposite ends of the country. The first of these occurred in southern Florida during 1857 when a renewed outbreak of Seminole hostilities forced the War Department to transfer some of its troops from the Western forts. Marcy's service in Florida abruptly ended when he received orders to join Colonel Albert Sidney Johnston* in an expedition to suppress an alleged Mormon rebellion in Utah. Mormon raids on Army livestock and destruction of military supply lines left the invading force in a precarious position and compelled Johnston to send Marcy on a dangerous mission across the Rocky Mountains back to supply stations in New Mexico. The winter march of 634 miles severely taxed the energies of Marcy's soldiers and left many with acute frostbite. But Marcy accomplished his mission and saw to it that the badly needed supplies were transported to Johnston's starving and immobilized army.

At the outset of the Civil War, Marcy had attained the rank of major and was recognized as one of the most notable explorers in the Army. His career continued to advance during the first two years of the war as he served as chief of staff to his son-in-law, General George Brinton McClellan,* commander of the Army of the Potomac. Although McClellan's military role gradually declined over the following three years, Marcy served for two years as brevet brigadier general of volunteers. In 1878 he was named inspector general of the Army and continued in that position until his retirement three years later. When he died of a heart attack on November 22, 1887, Marcy left behind not only a distinguished military career, but also three autobiographical works that were widely read by his contemporaries and later generations: *The Prairie Traveller* (1859), *Thirty Years of Army Life on the Border* (1866), and *Border Reminiscences* (1872).

Randolph B. Marcy's significance in American history rests upon his two lengthy reconnaissances of the Southern Plains during the midnineteenth century. The first of these occurred in 1849 when he escorted several hundred California-bound emigrants from Fort Smith, Arkansas, to Santa Fe, New Mexico. The

War Department had long wished to survey the area as a possible route for a future railroad, and thus Marcy was entrusted with both the welfare of the travelers and the responsibility of compiling a detailed report on the land and its resources. Following the meandering course of the Canadian River across Indian Territory and through the Texas Panhandle, Marcy made the first detailed maps of this *terra incognita*. Eighty-five days after leaving Fort Smith, the combined civilian-military party reached Sante Fe, where the two groups parted company.

While the civilians continued on to the gold fields, Marcy undertook the second part of his mission to map an overland route from Doña Ana, New Mexico, eastward across Texas to Preston Depot on the Red River. This southern course, more than three hundred miles shorter than the Canadian River trail, gained immediate public attention, and within three years it became a primary artery for overland migration. Furthermore, John Butterfield was so impressed with this winter-free Oxbow Route that he established his mail coach service along its course. By the 1870s the Texas and Pacific railroad had likewise negotiated its right-of-way along the same line and with it came the farmers and town-builders who had been so long delayed in their advance across west Texas.

Because of his laudable performance in the 1849 reconnaissance, Marcy received a similiar assignment three years later. The adjutant general ordered him to take Company D, 5th Infantry and explore the Red River to its headwaters. Until this time the origin point for the Red River had remained uncertain because the earlier expeditions of Zebulon Montgomery Pike* and Stephen Harriman Long* had confused its headwaters with those of the Rio Grande and Canadian River, respectively. In addition to tracing the Red River's course, the exploring party compiled detailed scientific reports, as well as procuring animal and plant specimens for eventual scholarly study. The explorers also met with leaders of the Wichitas to impress upon them the virtues of peace, but they were not successful in negotiating a similar understanding with the Comanche and Kiowa bands.

Upon completing the reconnaissance on July 28, 1852, Marcy and his second-in-command, Captain George B. McClellan, could take justifiable pride in the accomplishments of their mission. They had successfully followed the Red River to its source in the Texas Panhandle and had reported valuable topographical and scientific data. Moreover, they had carefully explored the Wichita Mountains and outlined a general plan for a future military post and Indian reservation to be located in the vicinity, leading eventually to the establishment of Fort Sill and the Comanche-Kiowa Reservation.

BIBLIOGRAPHY

Goetzmann, William H. *Army Exploration in the American West 1803–1863*. New Haven, Conn.: Yale University Press, 1959.

Hollon, W. Eugene. *Beyond the Cross Timbers: The Travels of Randolph B. Marcy, 1812–1887*. Norman: University of Oklahoma Press, 1955.
Wallace, Edward S. *The Great Reconnaissance*. Boston: Little, Brown and Company, 1955.

MICHAEL L. TATE

MARCY, William Learned (b. Sturbridge [now Southbridge], Mass., December 12, 1786; d. Ballston, N.Y., July 4, 1857), lawyer, statesman, secretary of war, secretary of state.

William L. Marcy traced his ancestry on both sides back to seventeenth-century Massachusetts. Graduating from Brown University in 1808, he settled in Troy, New York, where he read law and was admitted to the bar in 1811. He had become imbued with Jeffersonian doctrine while still a student and quickly became involved in local politics. Soon after his arrival in Troy, Marcy joined the Invincibles, a militia unit composed mainly of Republicans. He warmly supported the War of 1812 and served with his unit in several campaigns. He resumed his practice of law in Troy following the war and held various local political offices.

Marcy came to be associated with the political group known as the ''Albany Regency,'' which was then being developed under the leadership of Martin Van Buren and which would dominate New York Democratic politics for two decades before it split over a variety of issues in the 1840s. His political connections secured for him the post of state adjutant general in February 1821, from which he was often addressed thereafter as ''General'' Marcy. Two years later he accepted the state comptrollership of New York and moved to Albany, which would remain his home for the rest of his life. In the decade that followed, Marcy served successively as comptroller (1823–1829), associate justice of the state Supreme Court (1829–1831), and U.S. senator (1831–1833). Throughout he remained a staunch political ally of Van Buren. Marcy resigned from the Senate in January 1833 to become governor of New York, a post he held until 1839. While continuing as a party loyalist, he provided New York with sound government and began to display a growing conservatism that would later lead to his break with Van Buren in the division of the New York Democracy.

President Van Buren appointed Marcy as one of two commissioners to negotiate with a similar team from Mexico over claims of U.S. citizens upon that country in 1840. Marcy exercised good skill in the negotiations which yielded an agreement in the amount of nearly $2.4 million. This work occupied him through April 1842. In the intraparty struggles of the New York Democracy of the 1840s, Marcy sought to steer a middle ground but found himself increasingly thrown with the anti-Van Buren ''Hunker'' element because of his fiscal conservatism. President James K. Polk appointed him secretary of war in March 1845 as a compromise between the two emerging factions of the New York Democratic party, but the move did not please the Van Burenites.

Marcy inherited the War Department at a time when political and diplomatic intrigue threatened the United States with potential conflict on two fronts—Texas and Oregon. He brought to his task his experience in the militia in the War of 1812 and his service as adjutant general of New York. He also had a personal acquaintance with several of the high-ranking officers with whom he would have to work. In particular he had worked with General Winfield Scott* during the Canadian border troubles of the 1830s. The organization of the Army in 1845 was fairly simple. The secretary himself had a staff of nine clerks, two messengers, and a handyman, while the staffs of subordinate offices such as the adjutant general and quartermaster general were even smaller. The entire Army numbered but fourteen regiments (eight of infantry, four of artillery, and two of dragoons). The infantry still used the flintlock musket which Scott considered quite reliable while the artillery relied mainly on heavy guns used for coastal defense. Each of the artillery regiments had a company of well-trained "light" artillery to provide greater mobility. But all regiments of whatever branch were undermanned, with the companies averaging in the forties rather than the conventional one hundred. Maximum enlisted strength on the eve of the Mexican War numbered only 7,883, with actual enrollment probably about a thousand less because of various circumstances.

Marcy made no radical changes in his department. Despite his reputation as a spoilsman, he left both his internal staff and that of the Army at large virtually unchanged, even though both were decidedly Whiggish in flavor. He apparently had no desire to politicize the Army and saw no need to upset the internal working structure of the department as long as it functioned effectively. Beyond that, much of his time in the early months of the administration was absorbed with general patronage matters and various nonmilitary problems that came within his jurisdiction including Indian affairs, pensions, and mineral leases.

In the months that followed, Marcy generally supported the policies of President Polk with regard to both Mexico and Oregon, but his main efforts centered on Mexico. He ordered General Zachary Taylor* to the western Texas frontier on July 30, 1845. Although he did not anticipate war at that point, he agreed with Polk on the need for preparedness. With the Slidell negotiations getting nowhere early in 1846, he ordered Taylor to advance to the Rio Grande. Simultaneously, he pushed Congress, with little success, for an increase in the size of the regular companies to eighty and for authorization to call up fifty thousand volunteers as needed. He also asked for appropriate support monies. The lethargic Congress finally sprang into action when word came that Taylor's force had been attacked on the Rio Grande. One day after voting war, it authorized the volunteers while increasing company strength in the Regular Army to one hundred enlisted men each. Within a week it also sanctioned a regiment of mounted riflemen and a company of engineers.

The coming of war found the country ill prepared to fight a major conflict, and Marcy must bear his share of the responsibility. No overall war plans had been made. Much of the secretary's knowledge of Mexico had come through miscellaneous reading. The basic plan of operations was worked out in a lengthy evening conference between him, General Scott, and the president on May 14. It called simply for the seizure of northern Mexico including New Mexico and California. Twenty thousand volunteers were to be called for immediate service from the Southern and Midwestern states, with the additional thirty thousand mustered as a reserve.

Unfortunately, beyond this point the war effort fell victim to differences between Scott and the other two over timing and strategy, with the general delivering a caustic letter to Marcy on May 20 when the secretary sought to spur him on at the president's insistence. While Scott condemned Marcy as his enemy, the secretary in reality was his supporter, realizing that the general's military abilities outweighed his temperament. While General Taylor received the command in northern Mexico, Marcy ultimately secured Scott's appointment to lead the Vera Cruz Campaign which would presumably put a capstone to the war. At the same time he sought to improve the Regular Army. While defending the efforts of the volunteers, Marcy believed regulars better suited to fighting on foreign soil. Congress eventually went along with this, although it took more time than Marcy would have liked. In seeking to speed the flow of supplies, the secretary found himself bogged down in military bureaucracy and the inadequacy of the fledgling American industrial machine to quickly produce the necessary materials. Still the war moved forward to a successful conclusion. When Polk became involved with political appointments in connection with Scott's expedition, resulting in considerable friction at the front, the secretary again found himself caught between the two in a caustic crossfire that required the general's suspension and a court of inquiry. Marcy handled himself well in the interchange and again proved himself Scott's friend. At the same time he helped defuse any political use the general might have tried to make of the matter.

Following the Polk presidency, Marcy retired to private life while remaining active in politics. He actively supported the reunion of the New York Democracy following the Barnburner revolt of 1838. With the return of the Democrats to national power in 1852, President Franklin Pierce appointed him secretary of state, a position he served quite creditably.

Marcy was in the difficult position of serving as secretary of war under an activist president who was probably one of the hardest working chief executives in American history. While he, along with Polk, Scott, and the War Department staff, can be faulted for not having a war plan geared up when the conflict with Mexico broke out in May 1846, it must be remembered that all of them underestimated the seriousness of the crisis from the point of view of the Mexican psychology. Once war came, Marcy proved an able administrator within the difficulties of the logistics imposed on him from the outside by the times.

To his credit, Marcy realized that political differences should be kept to a minimum in gearing up and running a war machine—something Polk and Scott found difficult to do. Hence, Marcy played the unheralded role of mediator between the president and his top commander and indeed with General Taylor also, receiving condemnation but little appreciation from either side. Because of the strain on his health, he was forced to take periodic vacations which the workaholic Polk did not fully understand. For all of this he does not come off well in Polk's diary. But Polk's biographer, Charles G. Sellers, summed up the secretary well: "Marcy proved to be an industrious, thorough administrator, whose waspish tongue was a salutary stimulant to the drowsy bureaus of the War Department."

BIBLIOGRAPHY

Pletcher, David M. *The Diplomacy of Annexation: Texas, Oregon and the Mexican War.* Columbia: University of Missouri Press, 1973.

Sellers, Charles G. *James K. Polk, Continentalist, 1843–1846.* Princeton, N.J.: Princeton University Press, 1966.

Smith, Justin H. *The War with Mexico.* 2 vols. New York: Macmillan Company, 1919.

Spencer, Ivor Debenham. *The Victor and the Spoils: A Life of William L. Marcy.* Providence, R.I.: Brown University Press, 1959.

White, Leonard D. *The Jacksonians: A Study in Administrative History, 1829–1861.* New York: Macmillan Company, 1954.

                                                                    WILLIAM E. PARRISH

MARION, Francis (b. Berkeley County, S.C., 1732 (?); d. Berkeley County, S.C., February 27, 1795), partisan leader in the American Revolution.

Francis Marion, the engimatic partisan leader during the American Revolution, was born in 1732 in rural South Carolina rice country and reared at a plantation on Winyah Bay, near Georgetown. In these isolated surroundings, he received only a meager education. His one longing was for adventure at sea. At the earliest possible month, when he was fifteen, Marion enlisted on a schooner to the West Indies. The voyage was a disaster; the ship capsized, leaving Marion adrift for seven days before he was rescued. Chastened, Marion returned to his farm.

He still sought excitement, however, and in 1756, during the French and Indian War, he enlisted in the South Carolina militia as a lieutenant. Soon he was embroiled in fierce fighting against the Cherokees. In his initial encounter two-thirds of his company perished; the pugnacious young officer was characterized by his command as "an active, brave and hardy soldier."

At the age of forty-one Marion purchased his own estate, "Pond Bluff," four miles below Eutaw Springs, on the Santee River. The importunate political troubles with Great Britain gave Marion little opportunity to enjoy his farm. He was elected to his colony's Provincial Congress in 1775, and, when hostilities with the parent state flared, Marion enlisted as one of ten captains in an infantry regiment.

Marion spent the initial year of the War for Independence recruiting and training troops, securing installations in Charleston that Britain chose not to defend, and supervising the construction of new fortifications in and about the harbor of Charleston. In late June 1776 he played an active, though minor, role in aborting General Henry Clinton's attempt to invade the city. During this year

Marion was promoted first to the rank of major and then, following the action at Charleston, to lieutenant colonel.

Colonel Marion saw little action during the next thirty-six months. He spent most of the period in garrison duty in Charleston, training his men and earning a reputation as a priggish commander. Late in 1779, however, after British forces seized Savannah, Marion served in the Franco-American Expedition, led by General Benjamin Lincoln* and the Count d'Estaing, to retake the Georgia port. Marion's regiment spearheaded the attack of the South Carolina forces, a bloody foray that was repulsed with the loss of about 20 percent of the troops. With the collapse of the assault Marion was posted at remote Shelton, charged primarily with responsibility for tracking down deserters from the Savannah Campaign. He was recalled to Charleston in January 1780, when it became obvious that Britain again planned an assault on the city.

Marion played no role in the defense of Charleston, however. In March he suffered a broken ankle—the evidence indicates that the accident occurred at a raucous party—and General Lincoln ordered Marion and all other officers "unfit for duty" to evacuate the city. Until July the colonel remained in hiding from marauding Tories; then, his ankle partially mended, Marion joined General Horatio Gates'* Southern Army in North Carolina.

Colonel Marion soon was restive. Without an independent command and intrigued by the partisan activities of Thomas Sumter, Marion requested a leave to direct militia activities in the Williamsburg district, a Whig stronghold in eastern South Carolina. Gates consented, ordering Marion to disrupt the flow of supplies from Camden to General Charles Cornwallis' legions.

At age forty-eight, Marion commenced his guerrilla activities in August 1780. With congenitally malformed ankles and knees, a disability now exacerbated by his slowly healing broken ankle, Marion appeared to many to be incapable of enduring the rigors of a martial life. Contemporaries described him as short and lean, with a high forehead, an aquiline nose, and dark, piercing eyes. Henry ("Light-Horse Harry") Lee,* who twice acted in concert with Marion's force, thought the leader was taciturn and modest. He dressed sparsely, and during his two years of partisan strife he lived on an exiguous diet of lean beef, hominy, and potatoes. He disdained alcoholic beverages, preferring a concoction of vinegar and water with each meal. His force generally had no tents and few blankets; the men lived a Spartan existence, concealed in forests and swamps, often moving cryptically several miles each night from camp to camp.

Marion's band quickly became skilled practitioners of irregular warfare. They launched sporadic, rapier raids against the British lines of supply. They struck at British camps to rescue American prisoners, once liberating one hundred and fifty captives of the debacle at Camden. They engaged in the macabre business of stalking and plundering Tories. Frequently, they were ordered to seize supplies, boats, and even slaves for use by American forces. In the fall of 1780 Cornwallis even complained to Clinton that "Col. Marion had so wrought on the minds of the People . . . that there was scarce an Inhabitant between the

Santee and the Peedee that was not in arms against us.'' Banastre Tarleton, the implacable commander of Loyalist partisans, allegedly referred to Marion as a ''d—d *old fox*'' who could not be apprehended by Satan himself; the ''Swamp Fox'' nickname grew from the popularization of that acerbic comment.

Marion had hardly assumed command when Britain stepped up its campaign against southern Whigs. In August 1780 fifty-nine prominent Carolinians were dispatched into exile in Florida, and numerous estates were arrogated. The policy of harassment played into Marion's hands, however, giving him—for a brief, euphoric period—sufficient volunteers with which to work. Perceiving the danger, the British, in September, debouched a force through the Cheraws in northeastern South Carolina to extirpate Marion. His mobility limited by cumbersome field artillery pieces, Marion was nearly trapped. He escaped, of course, but he never again traveled with field pieces.

In December 1780 Nathanael Greene* supplanted Gates as commander of the Southern army. Realizing he was unlikely to receive adequate assistance from Congress, Greene turned to the partisans. Marion was placed in charge of the Carolina low country and Sumter of the high country, but Sumter was given overall command. Marion fumed, and at times he deliberately refused to cooperate, prompting Greene to excoriate the commander and to order him to ''Cooperate with [Sumter] in any manner he may direct.''

The next nine months were perhaps Marion's most active period. He and Lee took Fort Watson in April, reducing a force of one hundred and twenty British. Late in May he seized Georgetown, an important coastal town. Thereafter, the governor provided him with the names of specific Loyalists, and Marion was ordered to arrest the men and confiscate their property.

In September Greene commanded Marion to attach his force to the Southern army, and three days later he fought under Greene at the Battle of Eutaw Springs. Greene adopted the strategy that had been employed successfully by Daniel Morgan* at Cowpens. Militia forces under the command of Marion, Andrew Pickens,* and the Marquis Francis de Malmedy were placed in the frontline to take the first shock of the enemy assault; better disciplined Continental troops comprised the second line. After four hours of fierce fighting, during which time each side lost about five hundred men in killed and wounded, the British withdrew. Marion's men gave a good account of themselves, and Greene lauded their ''degree of Spirit and firmness'' that ''would have graced the soldiers of the King of Prussia.''

Within a month of this encounter Cornwallis' army surrendered at Yorktown, and the war began to wind down. Marion, however, remained active throughout 1782 hunting down Loyalists and endeavoring to prevent supplies from reaching the British troops holed up in Charleston. He also returned to politics and was elected to the State Senate. In December 1782 his brigade was officially disbanded.

Marion returned to ''Pond Bluff,'' which had been nearly extirpated through neglect and by war. His marriage, at age fifty-four, to Mary Videau, a wealthy forty-nine-year-old spinster, facilitated the restoration of the farm. He lived prosperously, though not happily, for the next dozen years. He continued to serve in the South Carolina Senate, and he was elected to the state's constitutional convention in 1790. Marion died on February 27, 1795.

Francis Marion played a substantive role in thwarting Britain's "Southern Strategy" during the Revolution. Imperial planners believed British armies could drive Continental forces from the region and that Loyalist partisans then would pacify each colony and restore civilian government. Marion's activities hindered and intimidated the Tories. In addition, his tactics of harassment had a pernicious effect on British forces, producing shortages of some supplies and delays in the receipt of other essentials.

Marion was not without fault. Jealous of his independence, he often sullenly refused to cooperate with the other partisan commanders. Yet, overall, this reserved, hirsute, bellicose man was an adroit leader, a commander who controlled his men with light reins. His failings arose more from manpower shortages and from lack of ammunition than from errors of command. His greatest talent was to grasp the real meaning of guerrilla warfare, to acknowledge that his purpose was to destroy and to disrupt his foes, not to seize and hold the territory over which he fought.

BIBLIOGRAPHY

Rankin, Hugh F. *Francis Marion: The Swamp Fox*. New York: Thomas Y. Crowell, 1973.
Simms, William Gilmore. *The Life of Francis Marion*. New York: George F. Cooledge and Brother, 1844.
Weigley, Russell F. *The Partisan War: The South Carolina Campaign of 1780–1782*. Columbia: University of South Carolina Press, 1970.

JOHN FERLING

MARSHALL, George Catlett (b. Uniontown, Pa., December 31, 1880; d. Washington, D.C., October 16, 1959), chief of staff of the Army, secretary of state, secretary of defense, Nobel Laureate.

Originally from Virginia, Marshall's forebears were for three generations residents of Kentucky. He was descended on his father's side from his great great grandfather, the Reverend William Marshall, brother of Chief Justice John Marshall's father. The future general attended private and public schools in Uniontown before entering the Virginia Military Institute in 1897. He graduated in 1901 holding the rank of first captain. He was commissioned as second lieutenant of infantry on February 3, 1902. He was married eight days later to Elizabeth Carter Coles, of Lexington, Virginia.

Marshall arrived in Manila just at the close of the Philippine Insurrection in 1902 and was assigned to duty with the 30th Infantry Regiment on the island of Mindoro. For several months he was the officer in charge of a part of a company in the southern part of the island. After serving for several months in

Manila, he returned to the United States in 1903 and was assigned to Fort Reno, Oklahoma, and then sent on a mapping detail in west Texas.

In 1906 he entered the Infantry and Cavalry School at Fort Leavenworth, Kansas, graduating first in his class and remaining for a second year at the Army Staff College. From 1908 to 1910 he was an instructor in the Fort Leavenworth schools. During summers he gained valuable experience by assignments to various maneuvers where he had an opportunity to perform staff duties far in excess of his rank. He became a first lieutenant only in 1907 and a captain in 1916.

He had a number of short assignments in the 1910–1913 period, the longest being to the Massachusetts militia as instructor and the second longest as a company commander in the 4th Infantry Regiment at Fort Logan Roots, Arkansas. He also took part in the Texas maneuvers as an officer in the maneuver division. From 1913 to 1916 he was again in the Philippines. Early in 1914 he won great acclaim for stepping in on a moment's notice to act as chief of staff of an invasion force in the Philippine maneuvers of that year. During this period he served as aide to Major General Hunter Liggett,* then head of the Philippine Department.

He returned to San Francisco in 1916 where he was aide to the commander of the Western Department, Major General James Franklin Bell,* former chief of staff of the Army, who had discovered Marshall at Fort Leavenworth and thereafter did much to push his military experience and education. When Bell moved to the Eastern Department, Governor's Island, New York, in 1917, he took Marshall with him and recommended him for an assignment overseas.

Marshall accompanied the 1st Division units overseas in June 1917 as training officer. Later, as operations officer, he helped to plan the first U.S. attack in France. In the summer of 1918 after rising to the rank of lieutenant colonel, he was assigned briefly to General Headquarters at Chaumont where he helped to plan operations in the St. Mihiel salient. Later as First Army chief of operations, he helped move hundreds of thousands of troops in and out of the Meuse-Argonne salient, winning the nickname of "Wizard" for his grasp of logistics.

Following the war, he worked on occupation plans for Germany as chief of staff of VIII Corps and was assigned in the spring of 1919 to General John Joseph Pershing* as aide. He traveled through Western Europe, taking part in numerous victory parades before returning to Washington in September 1919. For a number of months, he accompanied Pershing and other members of the staff on inspection trips to camps and munitions plants throughout the United States, getting excellent training for future chief of staff duties in wartime. He worked with Pershing on details of the National Defense Act and helped to present it to Congress. He also helped Pershing prepare his reports on World War I. Marshall remained as aide until 1924 when he was assigned to Tientsin, China, as executive officer of the 15th Infantry Regiment. In his three years there he learned something of Chinese language and culture and on two occasions as acting commander had the problem, which he dealt with successfully each time, of coping with marauding members of bands of warlords fighting for control of North China.

In 1927, Marshall was assigned to the staff of the Army War College and was just beginning his teaching when his wife died suddenly. Shortly afterward, he was reassigned as lieutenant colonel in charge of instruction at the Infantry School, Fort Benning, Georgia. In his five years there, he stressed study of World War I lessons and realism about possible future conflict. His staff included Omar Nelson Bradley,* Joseph Lawton Collins,* Joseph Warren Stilwell,* Matthew Bunker Ridgway,* and Walter Bedell Smith.* It is estimated that some 165 future generals attended classes or acted as staff members there in that period. While there, in 1930, he married for a second time, with Pershing acting as best man. His wife, Katherine Tupper Brown, widow of a Baltimore attorney, was the mother of three children (the younger son was later killed in the fighting at Anzio).

Marshall commanded a battalion of the 8th Infantry Regiment at Fort Screven, Georgia, in 1932–1933, and won promotion to colonel. He then commanded briefly the 8th Infantry Headquarters at Fort Moultrie, South Carolina. Much of his time in the two assignments was spent in developing Civilian Conservation Corps (CCC) camps in Florida and South Carolina. From 1933 to 1936 he was senior instructor of the Illinois National Guard. Promoted to brigadier general at the end of that service, he assumed command of the 5th Infantry Brigade at Vancouver Barracks, Washington. His duties also included supervision of Civilian Conservation Corps camps in that area. During this period he welcomed the first Soviet crew to make a transpolar flight from the Soviet Union to the United States. Bound for Oakland, California, a fuel shortage forced them to land on the parade ground almost in front of Marshall's quarters.

In the summer of 1938 Marshall was appointed to head the War Plans Division in Washington and later in the year to be deputy chief of staff of the Army. In the following spring, he was nominated for the post of chief of staff of the Army. He was sent almost at once on a special good-will tour to Brazil. From July 1 to September, Marshall acted as chief of staff while his predecessor, Malin Craig,* was on terminal leave. On September 1, shortly after Hitler attacked Poland, Marshall was sworn in as a permanent two star general and then as temporary four star.

During the next two years, Marshall labored to enlarge and train the Army and Army Air Forces, to increase munitions production, and to sell the Army's program to Congress and the public. Meanwhile, he was selecting officers for a possible conflict, injecting war realism into training, striving to get weapons to Britain, China, and the Soviet Union as well as to his own forces. This period saw the adoption and, then, extension of the Selective Service Act, large peacetime maneuvers, and talks with Great Britain about common action in case the United States entered the war. Raising the total Army and Army Air Forces strength to the authorized level of two hundred thousand, he started these services on the way to a wartime high of more than 8 million men and women. With the attack on Pearl Harbor, he reorganized the War Department staff on a wartime basis, establishing the Operations Division as a Washington command post. Marshall was to play a leading role in the various early war conferences as the leading proponent of the cross channel strategy. He was present at all the major meetings beginning with Argentina in the summer of 1941 and including the Washington meetings, two Quebec meetings, Cairo-Tehran, Malta and Yalta and Potsdam, as well as special missions he made to London in April and July 1942 to talk to Winston Churchill and in 1943 with Churchill to Algiers. He also went to the Normandy beaches with other chiefs of staff in June 1944. In late 1943 he flew to the Pacific to talk with Douglas MacArthur* and visited most of the U.S. divisions in the line in Europe in October 1944.

He retired on November 20, 1945, and within less than a week President Harry S. Truman asked him to go to China in an effort to bring peace between the Chinese Nationalists and Communists. After a year of patient effort, he gave up the mission as a failure and returned home to accept the task of secretary of state, succeeding James F. Byrnes.

As secretary of state, Marshall spent much of his time attending Council of Foreign Ministers' meetings in Moscow and London and a meeting of the U.N. General Assembly in Paris as well as U.N. meetings in New York. He also attended Latin American meetings in Brazil and Bogota. His secretaryship was marked by the proclamation of the Truman Doctrine, the recognition of Israel, preliminary negotiations for the treaties leading to the North Atlantic Treaty Organization, and the Berlin airlift. He is best known for the European Recovery Act which followed the address he gave during the Harvard Commencement of 1947. He indicated that various leaders shared the credit for the authorship but believed that his chief role lay in his strong nonpolitical stance which made it possible for him to work with both parties and in his series of speeches and appearances he made throughout the country and before Congress to sell the idea of aid to Europe. Marshall returned from the Paris meeting of the U.N. General Assembly meeting near the end of 1948 for the removal of a kidney. He resigned for reasons of ill-health in January 1949.

Within a few months, Marshall was back as head of the American Red Cross. Before the year had ended, Truman asked him to take over as secretary of defense in order to deal with problems raised by the Korean War. Special legislation was passed waiving, in his case only, the prohibition against a military man serving as head of defense. Agreeing to stay one year, Marshall worked to rebuild the manpower of the Army, to press for increased war production, and to push legislation for universal military service. He resigned in September 1951, terminating service that covered almost the first half of the century.

He had been involved in the recall of Douglas MacArthur earlier that year. Although he initially counseled delay in that action, he approved the president's action and, later, in hearings before a congressional committee, made a strong statement in behalf of strong civilian control over military affairs. Before the end of his secretaryship, he came under heavy attack by Senator Joseph Mc-Carthy, who charged him with being soft on communism. Marshall was defended by members of Congress of both parties but was to undergo several years of attacks for the Army's failure to protect Pearl Harbor, for the failure of his China policy, and for the recall of MacArthur. His alma mater proclaimed a special day in his honor and named one of the barracks arches (the other two are named for George Washington* and Thomas Jonathan ["Stonewall"] Jackson*) for him, and the governor of Virginia gave him Virginia's highest civilian award.

In December 1953 Marshall was invited to Oslo, Norway, to become the first professional soldier to receive the Nobel Prize for Peace. It was made clear that the award was given for his great contributions to the reconstruction of Europe. Marshall died at Walter Reed Hospital in Washington in 1959 and was buried at Arlington National Cemetery.

BIBLIOGRAPHY

Pogue, Forrest C. *George C. Marshall: The Making of a General, 1880–1939*. New York: Viking Press, 1963.
———. *George C. Marshall: Ordeal and Hope, 1939–1942*. New York: Viking Press, 1966.
———. *George C. Marshall: Organizer of Victory, 1943–1945*. New York: Viking Press, 1973.

                                                        FORREST C. POGUE

MARSHALL, Samuel Lyman Atwood (b. Catskill, N.Y., July 18, 1900; d. El Paso, Tex., December 17, 1977), military writer, journalist, Army officer. Marshall pioneered combat history techniques during World War II.

When "SLAM" Marshall was six, he awoke on a Christmas morning to hear his father reading from Arthur Conan Doyle's *The White Company*. "If such wonderful stuff came from books," he resolved, "they were what I would go after." So began Marshall's life-long affair with the "wonderful stuff" of books, and more particularly military books. Before his death he would write thirty.

Marshall was born in Catskill, New York, at the turn of the century, the son of an immigrant English brickmaker. Because of his father's trade, the boy lived a peripatetic life from the first. At age twelve, he found himself in Niles, California. There he worked as a child extra in the early "Bronco Billy" Western movies, then being filmed by the Western Essanay Studio. Before long, however, the Marshall family moved again, this time to El Paso, Texas. It was a place that in 1914, Marshall said, had a "fierce frontier flavor."

This was the El Paso of Fort Bliss, the cavalry, and—only a shot away—Revolutionary Mexico. Here the family came to rest, and young Marshall finished his formal schooling. He excelled in sports and read constantly but did poorly in school. "I was no good, and simply refused to study," Marshall wrote later. It was here, too, that he made his first acquaintance with the U.S. Army. His father's brickworks were next door to Camp Cotton, where the 16th Infantry was garrisoned.

Thus, Marshall enlisted after the declaration of war in 1917 with at least a passing knowledge of the military life. Eventually, he saw service with the 90th Infantry Division at Soissons, St. Mihiel, the Meuse-Argonne, and Ypres-Lys. He was an adept soldier and something of a teacher, spending a good deal of his time as an instructor in various small weapons and tactics. In 1919, still in France, he was commissioned a lieutenant of infantry. Thereafter, he often said he was the youngest officer in the American Expeditionary Forces.

The years after the war were uncertain ones for Marshall. He made a bad marriage and had difficulty adjusting to peace. He clearly had acquired a taste for the military life and remained in the National Guard until bad debts forced him to resign his commission. Finally, by 1922 he had found a spot as the sports editor and then the city editor for the El Paso *Herald*. This sort of work was much more to his liking, and he did well, traveling quite often into Mexico and Central and South America to report on the frequent upheavals of the region.

In 1927, Marshall took a position with the Detroit *News*, a paper he would stay with until 1967, with a few interruptions. In the years before World War II, Marshall developed into a first-class and peripatetic journalist, covering Latin America and the Spanish Civil War in 1936–1937. He also began to write humor columns for the *News* and became one of the country's better known writers on the sport of polo.

Marshall's interest in military affairs, meantime, had evolved beyond an addiction to reading. Sometime in the 1930s he opened a correspondence with J.F.C. Fuller, who then was regarded as the foremost writer on military affairs in the English-speaking world. With Fuller's encouragement and with his own recent observations in Spain, he began to try his hand at longer articles on military affairs. And although he occasionally drew on his own experiences, it was "through independent study as a member of the working press" that he developed his touch for things military.

Strongly influenced by Fuller's views on the future of mechanized war, his imagination overtaken by the war in Europe, Marshall wrote his first book in 1940. Entitled *Blitzkrieg*, it was perhaps the first such work on this subject to appear in the United States. While the book was elementary by comparison to the speculations already made by Fuller, B. H. Liddell Hart, and others across the Atlantic, its chief value was its timeliness. This work—as well as the one he published the following year, *Armies on Wheels*—brought him to the attention of the War Department just as America entered the war.

Secretary of War Henry Lewis Stimson* saw that Marshall was assigned as a major to the Office of War Information. Discontented there, Marshall soon joined the fledgling historical service which the Army was establishing in the General Staff. After suffering through several months of office work in Washington, Marshall contrived to be shipped out to the Pacific to help record the Army's campaigns.

Now a lieutenant colonel, Marshall arrived at the front in time to participate in the invasion of the Marshall and Gilbert Islands. After one firefight on the Island of Kwajalein, Marshall chanced to discuss the recent action with one of the combatants. Another soldier heard the discussion and joined in. To Marshall's surprise, the two soldiers disagreed on important facts about the action's progress. Marshall then began to understand just how little he, or even the participants in the battle, knew about what had happened to them. So it was that in an island jungle Marshall discovered the subject that was to dominate the rest of his life's work—the man in battle and the dynamics of battle itself. He turned his attention away from the war fought at headquarters to the war fought on the firing line. He began to move among the rifle platoons and heavy weapons squads more and more, interviewing soldiers individually. When the opportunity arose, he would assemble a recently fought company and interview the men en masse.

In 1944 Marshall returned briefly to Washington before being posted to the European Theater of Operations shortly before D-Day. He brought his views with him and attempted to suffuse historical operations in Europe with the same energy and daring that had characterized his work in the Pacific. He had only limited success. The mission of the historical service was to capture the entire military record of the war, not only the record of small-unit action, but Marshall was impatient with this approach. With a few other likeminded historical officers, Marshall nevertheless continued to work in his own way, often driving his more traditional and classically trained superiors to distraction. He made airborne operations his special province, although he formed a sympathetic attachment to several infantry battalions along the way. His work frequently took him to the battlelines, and some of these lines were often active. In the end, he may have spent more time under fire than many riflemen.

As the war drew to a close, Marshall was made chief historian of the European Theater of Operations, and he was therefore well placed to see that the records of the campaign—and those of his enemy—were preserved. He established an innovative program to interview the surviving members of the German High Command. These after-action interviews (Marshall would not have called them interrogations) survive today and constitute a valuable source for scholars of World War II.

Marshall returned to the United States and newspaper work in 1946, and began the book that is now his best known work, *Men Against Fire*. In this work, Marshall attempted to codify all that he had learned about men in combat during the war. His experiences had taught him that the soldier is ill prepared for what awaits him on the battlefield, despite the training he may have had. He concluded that the disjunctures between a soldier's training and the soldier's battle meant that fewer than 25 percent of all infantrymen ever fired their weapons in combat, a fact that he said his own observations had verified. The book was not well received by a war-weary public, but professional soldiers began an argument over its findings that has not yet subsided.

As the Korean War began in 1950, Marshall once more put on a uniform and rushed to the front, working as an operations analyst with both the Army and the Marine Corps. Using the techniques he had developed during World War II, Marshall roamed the frontlines, gathering data that could be put to immediate use by the people who counted most to him—the soldiers in combat. He produced technical reports on weapons and small-unit tactics that were rushed to the line from his typewriter. In one particular case, a Marshall report was the cause attributed to a drop in American casualties from Chinese machine gun tactics. These reports represented what Marshall meant when he spoke of "usable" military history. For his work in Korea, Marshall was promoted to brigadier general in the reserves.

In the years following the Korean War, Marshall never seemed to sit still. From his observations during the war, Marshall wrote two books, *The River and the Gauntlet* and *Pork Chop Hill*. Both works were in what had now become recognizable as a distinct Marshall style: an intense focus upon the human side of war, an exciting and realistic narrative in an anecdotal stream. By virtue of these and his other works, Marshall was becoming a favorite lecturer in military service schools and colleges and on public speaking circuits as well. His newspaper column with the *News* went into syndication, and in these pieces Marshall ranged far and wide on military questions and national defense policies. For a time, a Marshall article would appear somewhere on the average of once a month.

During the early 1950s, Marshall also developed a sympathy for the cause of Israel. He saw in that country a fighting spirit and a military effectiveness against overwhelming odds that naturally attracted him, given his now well-enunciated interests. Israeli military men also developed a fondness for the author of *Men Against Fire* and, with some reason, thought that Marshall's philosophies suited their army very well. Out of this mutual admiration issued two more Marshall books, *Sinai Victory* and *Swift Sword*, dealing with the wars of 1956 and 1967. Both were written in vintage Marshall style.

Although he had retired from the Army Reserve in 1960, Marshall could not sit by while many of his old friends in uniform (some of whom were now senior commanders) went to Vietnam. Despite his age and health (he had just recovered from a heart attack), Marshall went to Southeast Asia twice, in 1966 and 1968, to see the war and write about what he found. But it was a different war for Marshall, and while he wrote about it in the old style, he found himself increasingly at variance with the tastes of his fellow journalists and the reading public. Although he wrote four books about the war, they were among his least successful. Like the army he loved, Marshall was alienated from the public that sustained him.

In the early 1970s, Marshall returned to El Paso and retired. He continued to write and lecture, and he produced his last book, *Crimsoned Prairie*. He also began assembling his memoirs, which were published posthumously as *Bringing Up the Rear*. In his last years, Marshall tended his unmilitary hobbies of music and porcelain collecting and contemplated the fruits of a life of intellectual adventuring. He died in December 1977, survived by his third wife, Cate, one son, and three daughters.

When Marshall died, the military historian Lynn Montross wrote, "it may be doubted whether Stephen Crane or Ambrose Bierce have written with such sustained realism about combat." The comparison is apt, for Crane and Bierce were newspapermen with a penchant for the dramas of combat.

Marshall would never claim to be a military historian, though his library's shelves were stuffed with military history. He was alternatively sensitive and proud of his lack of academic training in the field. He was impatient with research and claimed never to have taken longer than six weeks to write any book. Facts were not immutable to him, and he was not above altering them for effect, or marshaling those congenial to his arguments and ignoring those that were not. And yet Marshall practiced a kind of history during an American generation that had few "professional military historians" to rely upon; and after all, the three leading military historians of the 1930s and 1940s—Douglas Southall Freeman, Allan Nevins, and Walter Millis—were all journalists.

For all that, the key to understanding Marshall's techniques and work is his journalistic upbringing. The method he discovered on Kwajalein was not substantially different from that he used first working for the El Paso *Herald*: find the focal point of the action, get to the scene as quickly as possible, interview individually and collectively all who had a part, withdraw, cast conflicting versions one against the other, and decide what to write. Too, he wrote as he might have in a city room: quickly, in clear, truncated sentences, with anecdotes for emphasis. For Marshall, writing was action, not contemplation. His life moved too fast for that.

Neither was Marshall's approach to military history particularly original. Although his concept of how battle worked was more orderly than Leo Tolstoy's famous battle piece in *War and Peace*, and more skeptical than Ardant du Picq's battle *qua* elan in *Studies in Combat*, Marshall's complaint was the same. Neither military history nor military theory had dealt satisfactorily with the central fact of war—the battle itself, and the man who found himself inside it. It was the "interior battle" that mattered most to Marshall and his intellectual forebears, and in pursuit of that battle all other pursuits mattered little. Like many whose works are inspired by a passion, Marshall was fond of overstatement. A friend once said of Marshall, "Sam could never leave a fact alone." Marshall perhaps would have replied that the facts of battle never left him alone.

BIBLIOGRAPHY

Marshall, Cate, ed. *Bringing Up the Rear*. San Rafael, Calif.: Presidio Press, 1980.

Marshall, S.L.A. *Island Victory*. Washington, D.C.: Infantry Journal Press, 1944.
————. *Men Against Fire*. New York: William Morrow Company, 1947.

ROGER J. SPILLER

MAURY, Matthew Fontaine (b. near Fredericksburg, Va., January 13, 1806;
d. Lexington, Va., February 1, 1873,) naval officer. Maury served in the Union
and Confederate navies, and is considered the father of oceanography.

After Maury's parents, of Huguenot stock, moved from Virginia to a farm
near Franklin, Tennessee, Matthew attended a country school until the age of
twelve, when he entered Harpeth Academy. Despite the death of an older brother
in the naval service, he decided to follow the sea and obtained a midshipman's
warrant in 1825. He then made three extended cruises covering nine years. In
no ship, he noted, was the schoolmaster able to organize the midshipmen into
a school. In 1834, while on leave of absence, Maury married Ann Hull Henderson, of Fredericksburg, where he established his residence.

In 1836, a text on navigation he had begun while last afloat appeared under
the title *A New Theoretical and Practical Treatise on Navigation*. The first
scientific book on navigation ever written by an American naval officer, it was
very favorably received both abroad and at home and won him assignment as
both astronomer and hydrographer in the Exploring Expedition that was to start
in 1837 for the South Seas. Disliking Charles Wilkes,* its commander, he asked
to be detached from it and in 1838 and 1839 engaged in a survey to find the
best site for a navy yard in the harbors of the southeastern United States.

That he believed much was wrong with the Navy was revealed in 1838 when,
under pseudonyms, he published twelve articles in a newspaper, the *Richmond
Whig and Public Advertiser*. After suffering a permanently injured right knee in
a stagecoach accident, under the name of Harry Bluff, he further criticized the
Navy, this time in the *Southern Literary Messenger*, wherein a sketch of him
revealed his identity. Forthrightly, he criticized the poor quality of the Navy's
civilian leadership, waste, and fraud in building and repairing ships, political
influence in officer promotion, the lack of a naval academy, the poor system of
rules and regulations, and the lack of attention being given to the Pacific coast,
where he saw a great future for America. Furthermore, he argued that Britain
should not be allowed to search even those American ships illegally engaged in
the African slave trade and that subsidies be provided to encourage the building
of steam packets to compete with those of Britain and France. Most of the
reforms he suggested were adopted within three years.

In 1842, when he was but thirty-six years old, Maury was appointed superintendent of the Depot of Charts and Instruments (later the U.S. Naval Observatory, separated from the Hydrographic Office). He thus entered into the study
of the atmosphere, a science heretofore neglected. From log books submitted
by naval ships—which others considered rubbish—he deduced the data that
appeared in *The Wind and Current Chart of the North Atlantic* (1847), which
he followed with *Explanations and Sailing Directions to Accompany the Wind*

and Current Charts (1851). At his request, all American ship captains were asked to fill in data on blank charts he provided, and at his suggestion an international congress on oceanography was held at Brussels in 1851. Soon America relied much less upon the charts and nautical almanac provided by the British Admiralty. Moreover, Maury was among the first to advocate the building of a canal across the Isthmus of Panama.

Simultaneously with his hydrographic work, Maury published the first volume of American astronomical observations (1846) and also undertook studies that resulted in what he deemed his "greatest work," *The Physical Geography of the Sea* (1858). Could a cable be laid across the Atlantic along "the telegraph plateau" from Newfoundland to Ireland he discerned from a bathymetrical profile he made of its bottom? Given the poor state of the art of making deep-sea soundings—he used a line and sixty-pound lead sinker—and of coring (driving a tube into the ocean floor to gather samples of it)—he made various errors, as particularly Lieutenant Otway H. Berryman, whom he had trained but used different machines and techniques, pointed out. The cable laid by Cyrus Field in 1858 soon failed, but a new line succeeded in 1866.

In 1855, Maury served on a naval board directed to "pluck" officers unfit for duty at sea. Ironically, although he was America's, if not the world's, foremost scientist of the sea, because of his bad knee he was placed on leave of absence; hence, he was subject to recall to duty but ineligible for promotion. In consequence of petitions from friends and various state legislatures, and a press crusade in his favor, however, in 1858 he was not only restored to duty but was also promoted to the grade of commander. Among other objectives, Maury sought to expand Southern commerce. To this end he was instrumental in having an expedition explore the Amazon River, 1851–1852, a task undertaken by his brother-in-law, William L. Herndon, who conceived the idea.

During the months before the irrepressible conflict between the North and South, he suggested conference and conciliation, but his sympathy clearly lay with his own section. On April 20, 1861, three days after Virginia seceded, he resigned from the Navy and then accepted a commission as a commander in the Navy of the Confederate States of America. As chief of the Confederate Naval Bureau of Coast, Harbor, and River Defense, Maury was developing an electric mine when he was sent to England to acquire warships and use his eloquence in favor of the Southern cause. Excluded from pardon in amnesty proclamations issued after the war, he served Emperor Maximilian of Mexico as commissioner of immigration, with the objective of colonizing former Confederate families. When the scheme failed, he declined an offer to head Mexico's national observatory and returned to England, where he wrote a series of school geographies.

In 1868 he returned to the United States and served as professor of meteorology at the Virginia Military Institute, at Lexington. He issued a preliminary report of surveys of the state in *Physical Survey of Virginia, No. 1* (1868) and was also instrumental in having an agricultural branch of the Institute founded—the

Virginia A&M College at Blacksburg. In addition, he lectured widely on the
need of establishing a land meteorology like that he had established for the sea
and for a telegraphic weather service for farmers. He died while on such a tour.

Largely self-educated, Maury was an indefatigable worker. His *Wind and
Current Chart of the Atlantic*, soon joined by similar charts of the Pacific and
Indian oceans—and by track charts, pilot charts, trade wind charts, thermal
charts, rain charts, storm charts, and even whale charts—greatly reduced sailing
times, hence transportation costs, and made sailing less dangerous. Use of his
basic chart cut ten to fifteen days from the New York to Rio de Janeiro run,
and fifty days from New York to San Francisco. He produced the first textbook
of modern oceanography, which he showed was a distinct branch of science and
also one with many practical uses. Had his work on electrical mines not been
interrupted during the Civil War, the course of the war might have been different,
for mines accounted for the sinking of more Union ships than any other single
cause.

Maury should be remembered as the first superintendent of the Naval Observatory and the first hydrographer; the precursor of the U.S. Weather Bureau;
founder of the science of oceanography and the World Meteorological Organization; the "pathfinder of the seas" as well as locator of the site for the first
transatlantic cable; champion of naval reform and reorganization in the Navy;
and inventor of the first wartime electrically controlled underwater mine.

BIBLIOGRAPHY

Cowen, Robert C. *Frontiers of the Sea: The Story of Oceanographic Exploration*. Garden
    City, N.Y.: Doubleday, 1960.
Hawthorne, Hildegarde. *Matthew Fontaine Maury: Trail Maker of the Sea*. New York:
    Longmans, Green and Company, 1943.
Jahns, Patricia. *Matthew Fontaine Maury and Joseph Henry: Scientists of the Civil War*.
    New York: Hastings House, 1961.
Latham, Jean L. *Matthew Fontaine Maury: Trail Blazer of the Sea*. Boston: Houghton
    Mifflin Company, 1956.
Williams, Frances L. *Matthew Fontaine Maury: Scientist of the Sea*. New Brunswick,
    N.J.: Rutgers University Press, 1963.

                                                              PAOLO E. COLETTA

MEADE, George Gordon (b. Cadiz, Spain, December 31, 1815; d. Phila-
delphia, Pa., November 6, 1872), Army officer. Meade was commander of the
Union Army of the Potomac in the Civil War, and the victor at the Battle of
Gettysburg.

George Gordon Meade was born in Cadiz, Spain, his father—an American
citizen—being a U.S. naval agent and, until ruined as a result of the Napoleonic
Wars, a wealthy businessman. Young Meade's early education was gained in
Philadelphia, Washington, and Baltimore. He was graduated from the U.S.
Military Academy at West Point in 1835, standing nineteenth in a class of fifty-

six. After a year's service in the Second Seminole War, Meade resigned from the Army in 1836 and for six years pursued a livelihood as a civil engineer. In 1840 he was married to Margaretta Sergeant, who bore him six children. Rejoining the Army in 1846, Meade won a brevet in the Mexican War at Monterey. This combat service was followed by routine assignments, including survey work along the Great Lakes and northern border. He was promoted to captain in 1856.

When the Civil War started in 1861, Meade was appointed brigadier general of volunteers and named to the command of one of the brigades in the famous Pennsylvania Reserves. In this capacity he served in the Peninsula Campaign, led by George Brinton McClellan,* in the spring and early summer of 1862. At Glendale Meade was severely wounded. But he returned in time to fight at Second Manassas in August under John Pope* and, as a division commander, with McClellan at South Mountain and Antietam in September. In November Meade was promoted to major general of volunteers. At Fredericksburg in December he commanded a division under Ambrose Everett Burnside*; Meade's troops temporarily broke through two Confederate defensive lines commanded by Thomas Jonathan ("Stonewall") Jackson.* At Chancellorsville, under Joseph Hooker,* in April-May 1863, he headed the V Corps, which was not heavily engaged.

In all of these operations, Meade had performed most capably as a combat leader of reliability and sagacity. He was tall and graceful, though slightly stooped, possessed an aquiline nose and quick-moving eyes, and his graying brown hair was thinning. He wore spectacles for nearsightedness, and his regulation army hat brim was pulled down all around. His commanding presence and steady mien were marred only by a sharp, violent temper which cascaded forth in moments of great stress. This made it difficult to approach him even with important matters in the heat of battle. None recognized this irascibility more than Meade himself, and he was swift to make amends. But on occasion he indulged in self-pity and self-deprecation, and he was thin-skinned to criticism.

But Meade's assets bulked large. He was adept at terrain analysis and in the use of the combined arms of infantry, cavalry, and artillery. Though cautious, he was an unrelenting combatant, and he was a man of the highest honor, character, and integrity. These talents and traits were to be fearfully tested within a few weeks after Chancellorsville.

With Robert Edward Lee* launching his second invasion of the North in early June 1863, President Abraham Lincoln* and General in Chief Henry Wager Halleck* named Meade to succeed Hooker in command of the Army of the Potomac. This was on June 28, just three days before the greatest battle ever fought in the Western Hemisphere erupted at Gettysburg on July 1—a combat that would rage for three bloody days.

On the first day, neither Meade nor Lee was on the field as portions of their armies collided unexpectedly west and north of Gettysburg. Relying upon such accomplished subordinates as John Buford, John F. Reynolds, Abner Doubleday, and Winfield Scott Hancock,* Meade's outnumbered forces held back the at-

tacking Confederates for over eight hours and then fell back in some disorder
to a strong position on Cemetery Ridge south of the town. Meade arrived on
the battlefield during the night, determined to stay and fight it out on the morrow,
and concentrated the rest of his army at Gettysburg. Lee did the same with his
grayclad legions, now somewhat outnumbered by the Federals.

On the second day of the battle—July 2—fighting commenced in the late
afternoon. After having spent most of the time securing his right wing, Meade,
upon hearing the engagement reopen with heavy attacks by James Longstreet*
upon the Union left at the Peach Orchard, Wheatfield, Devil's Den, and the key
Little Round Top, daringly exposed his right wing by rapidly shifting troops to
his threatened left, thereby checking the Southern assaults after they had scored
some initial gains. Meade's army repelled a blow against East Cemetery Hill,
although the Confederates managed to gain a lodgment on the evacuated lower
slopes of Culp's Hill on the extreme Federal right.

Meade called a night-time council of war of his top generals and concurred
in their recommendation to remain and fight it out on the defensive at Gettysburg.
The National commander grasped the initiative at 4:00 A.M. on July 3 when he
attacked the graycoats on Culp's Hill. In some seven hours of unrelenting combat
the Federals pushed the Confederates off the hill, thereby ending their threat to
the Union right.

Estimating that Lee would then attempt to overwhelm his center, Meade
deployed sufficient infantry and artillery forces to meet such a challenge. In
midafternoon, following the heaviest artillery cannonade of the war—lasting an
hour and fifty minutes—Lee hurled against the Union center some fifteen thousand Southern troops, under George Edward Pickett,* across nearly a mile of
open fields in what comprised one of the greatest infantry charges of history.
Despite the gallantry of the attackers, Meade's artillery fire, and then his musketry
volleys, tore apart the gray phalanx. A few hundred intrepid Confederates dented
the Federal line at ''The Angle'' of a stonewall near the copse-of-trees objective,
only to be enveloped by Meade's supporting infantrymen. The remnants of the
assaulting force fell back in confusion to their starting point on Seminary Ridge.

It was probably wise that Meade refrained from trying to mount a counterattack;
had he done so, it would most likely have suffered the same fate as Pickett's
charge. The National commander had sustained some twenty-three thousand
casualties out of about eighty-eight thousand engaged, as against Lee's losses
of approximately twenty-eight thousand out of some seventy-five thousand. In
Lee's retreat from Gettysburg, Meade pursued circumspectly and rejected the
gamble of assaulting the Army of Northern Virginia along the Potomac River
near Williamsport, Maryland. When sharply criticized by Lincoln for "permitting" Lee to retire safely into Virginia, Meade asked to be relieved of his
command—a proffer that was not accepted by the president. There was only
desultory, indecisive fighting between Meade and Lee in the remaining summer,
fall, and winter months of 1863, the operations being restricted largely to those

of maneuver. The two armies then went into winter quarters near the Rapidan River.

When Ulysses Simpson Grant* was named general in chief of all the Union armies in March 1864 and established his field headquarters with the Army of the Potomac—thus, in effect, reducing Meade to his executive officer—Meade took this occurrence in stride. Although the arrangement made for an awkward command relationship, both generals—so different in characteristics and personality—worked hard to get along together amicably. The major decisions in the costly 1864 battles of the Wilderness, Spotsylvania Court House, Cold Harbor, and Petersburg were made by Grant, and very few and limited successes were gained. At Cold Harbor Meade wisely prevailed upon Grant to desist from ordering further suicidal frontal attacks. And in the final Appomattox Campaign in April 1865, which led to Lee's capitulation on April 9, Meade showed to good advantage.

In the seven years of life remaining to him after the Civil War, Meade was given command of the Third Military District (Alabama, Georgia, and Florida), one of the five military occupation districts in the ex-Confederacy. He won the respect of most Southerners for his firm but fair dealings and policies. From 1869 until he died in 1872, he commanded the Military Division of the East, with headquarters in Philadelphia. On October 31, while taking his daily walk from the office with his wife, he was stricken with a terrible pain in his back, in the area of his old Glendale wound. Pneumonia set in and led to his death.

Posterity has not, perhaps, treated Meade fairly. He was, to a high degree, eclipsed by the very success he scored at Gettysburg, and, as General Francis A. Walker had declared, "There is probably no other battle of which men are so prone to think and speak without a conscious reference to the commanding general of the victorious party, as they are regarding Gettysburg." In addition to skillful tactical handling of his army at Gettysburg, Meade showed the marks of good military leadership when, without trying to handle too many details himself, he entrusted tasks of great importance to such accomplished subordinates as W. S. Hancock, John Reynolds, and Gouverneur K. Warren. For the first time in the Civil War in the Eastern Theater of Operations, the teamwork of the top generals of the Army of the Potomac was of a high order.

Having been in command only three days before the pivotal Gettysburg engagement, Meade approached many of the trying decisions gropingly at first; but, in the final analysis, almost all of his major actions and judgments proved to be unerringly correct. Lee thought that Meade, along with McClellan and Grant, were the most able generals he had faced during the war. In unhesitatingly accepting the command at a crucial moment and successfully meeting the stern challenge at Gettysburg, Meade, in the words of historian James G. Randall, "fulfilled a responsibility unexcelled, unless by Washington, in previous American history."

Despite some limitations, George G. Meade is perhaps entitled to more recognition than he has received as the victor over the redoubtable Robert E. Lee in one of the most critical and decisive battles in which the nation has ever been engaged. The rest of his life may also serve as a model for the professional soldier in a republic such as the United States.

BIBLIOGRAPHY

Cleaves, Freeman. *Meade of Gettysburg*. Norman: University of Oklahoma Press, 1960.
Coddington, Edwin B. *The Gettysburg Campaign: A Study in Command*. New York: Charles Scribner's Sons, 1968.
Hassler, Warren W., Jr. *Commanders of the Army of the Potomac*. Baton Rouge: Louisiana State University Press, 1962.
Meade, George. *The Life and Letters of George Gordon Meade*. 2 vols. New York: Charles Scribner's Sons, 1913.
Pennypacker, Isaac R. *General Meade*. New York: D. Appleton, 1901.

WARREN W. HASSLER, JR.

MEIGS, Montgomery (b. Augusta, Ga., May 3, 1816; d. Washington, D.C., January 2, 1892), Army officer. Meigs served as quartermaster general of the U.S. Army during the Civil War.

Montgomery Meigs came from one of the oldest and most talented of American families. Charles Meigs, his father, and a pioneer of modern obstetrical medicine, instilled in young Montgomery a strong sense of patriotism and service. This paternal persuasion, coupled with a family military tradition dating to the American Revolution and a strong personal inclination to mechanics, convinced young Meigs to enroll at the U.S. Military Academy to become an engineer. Accordingly, Meigs entered the West Point class of 1836. He excelled and was graduated fifth in a class of forty-nine.

After temporary duty with the field artillery, Meigs entered the Corps of Engineers, which was then the elite organization of the Army. He was assigned as a military engineer to the completion of Fort Mifflin near Philadelphia. Subsequently, he fulfilled important duties in the peacetime service with the engineers that would well prepare him for his later career. In collaboration with Lieutenant Robert Edward Lee,* Meigs contributed to the navigational improvements on the Mississippi River. Meigs' first important independent command occurred in 1838 when he was placed in charge of the disbursement of funds to construct fortifications on the Delaware River below Philadelphia. In this capacity he demonstrated an unbending morality and sense of duty that would be characteristic of all his commands. From 1839 to 1841 he served on the Board of Engineers for Atlantic Coast Defenses. During the next several years, Meigs served as the military engineer in charge of the construction of Fort Wayne at Detroit, Michigan, and then that of Fort Montgomery on Lake Champlain.

In 1852 came an appointment that, except for one short span of time, would begin Meigs' career in Washington, D.C., and make that city his permanent home. The Fillmore administration had ordered the Corps of Engineers to undertake a survey to determine the best method of supplying a safe, dependable water supply to the District of Columbia. Meigs received the assignment to conduct the survey from General Joseph G. Totten, chief of the Corps of Engineers. After several months of surveying the various possible routes, Meigs' recommendation of the construction of an aqueduct was accepted. In March 1863 Lieutenant Meigs was named superintendent of the construction of the Washington Aqueduct and was also ordered to supervise the addition to the Capitol.

Meigs displayed great enthusiasm and pushed the projects under his supervision at great speed. He also undertook to solve the engineering problem of erecting a new dome for the Capitol. All went well until the new administration of James Buchanan. Buchanan's secretary of war, John B. Floyd, was a political appointee who unnerved Meigs' sense of duty by insisting upon political appointees at the expense of efficiency in construction of the aqueduct. Meigs' continued appeal for remedy to Buchanan and criticism of Floyd resulted only in his virtual exile; he was placed in charge of completing the fortifications at Dry Tortugas in the Florida Keys. Appeals to powerful friends in Congress such as Jefferson Davis* and Robert Toombs could not prevent this banishment.

Duty on Dry Tortugas detained Meigs but a short while, and he was back in Washington in time for the inauguration of President Abraham Lincoln.* Once again Meigs was assigned to work on the aqueduct and the Capitol. As tension mounted between North and South, Secretary of State William Seward requested that Meigs advise Lincoln of the feasibility of holding Fort Pickens at Pensacola. He served as the chief engineer in the successful relief of that fortification.

Realizing that his talents lay not in field command, Meigs accepted with relief the appointment in May 1861 as quartermaster general of the U.S. Army. In 1864 he was brevetted major general of volunteers. He maintained his position as quartermaster until, under pressure to resign to permit promotion of other officers, he retired in 1882. Quartermaster General Meigs accomplished little in his department after 1865; in fact, the Quartermaster Department reflected the lethargy that seemed to seize the postwar Army.

In retirement, he continued an active life, designing, planning, and then supervising the construction of the U.S. Pension Office building in Washington.

Two remarkable accomplishments stand out in Meigs' record. One is the construction of the Washington Aqueduct, and the other, his service as quartermaster general of the Union Army.

Supervising the construction of the Washington Aqueduct served Meigs as a school in administration and Washington politics, invaluable for his years as quartermaster general. The aqueduct is an example of the peacetime role of the Corps of Engineers. Other officers could have supervised the aqueduct, but it is a matter of record that under Meigs the work proceeded with greater alacrity than usual for a public work, especially one so close in geographic proximity to Congress.

At the beginning of the Civil War, Meigs played an important part in convincing Lincoln that Fort Pickens could be held, but he was primarily important for his contributions as the quartermaster general of the U.S. Army. With the important exceptions of arms, food, and medicine, Meigs was responsible for supplying the armies of the Union with many items, including clothing, equipment and accouterments, tents, and horses. In addition, he had under his auspices wagon as well as rail and water transportation. During the course of the war, Meigs reorganized the Army's wagon transportation system, tremendously improving its efficiency. Furthermore, he issued numerous contracts to manufacturers. For example, the further mechanization of the shoe industry of the United States was encouraged through Meigs' influence because the demands of the Army were so great; the service used 3 million pairs of shoes each year during the war.

The accomplishments of Meigs during the Civil War were myriad. Issuing many contracts to manufacturers naturally meant that he handled huge sums of money; it is estimated that he spent $1 billion between 1861 and 1865, with all moneys accounted for. Of course, fraud and waste continued to be problems, but under Meigs' direction, the Quartermaster Department took strong action to contain dishonesty and tightened enforcement of regulations. In 1864 Meigs convinced Congress that it was necessary to reform the Quartermaster Department to make it more efficient. The principal reform was to divide the department into nine divisions of responsibilty and to promote certain officers in order to increase their authority.

Meigs also gave his attention to supplying troops in the field. The Gettysburg Campaign was an outstanding example of the efficiency of Meigs and the Quartermaster Department. As the Army of the Potomac under George Gordon Meade* moved rapidly northward to counter the advance of Lee's Confederate Army, Meigs and Herman Haupt,* chief of construction and transportation of the U.S. Military Railroad, adroitly shifted the line of supply to keep abreast of the Union Army. Subsequently, Meigs provided for supply bases at Fredericksburg and Belle Plain, which served the Union Army under Ulysses Simpson Grant.* Moreover, Meigs personally recommended establishing the principal part of the famous "cracker line" that supplied Chattanooga, besieged by Confederates under Braxton Bragg,* and arranged for supplying the troops of William Tecumseh Sherman* in Savannah in 1865.

Historian Allan Nevins concluded that Meigs was symbolic of a new United States emerging from the Civil War, better equipped to oversee vast business enterprises and to bring, as Meigs demonstrated, organization from chaos. In the end, Meigs' honesty and ability to deal with Congress and Secretary of War Edwin McMasters Stanton* gave shape to the Quartermaster Department. In effect, he acted as a one-man equivalent to the War Industries Board of World War I.

BIBLIOGRAPHY

Nevins, Allan. "A Major Result of the Civil War." *Civil War History* 5 (September 1959): 237–50.

Shannon, Fred A. *The Organization and Administration of the Union Army, 1861–1865*. Cleveland: Arthur H. Clark Company, 1928.

Weigley, Russell F. *Quartermaster General of the Union Army: A Biography of M. C. Meigs*. New York: Columbia University Press, 1959.

RONALD RIDGLEY

MELVILLE, George Wallace (b. New York City, N.Y., January 10, 1841; d. Philadelphia, Pa., March 17, 1912), naval officer, engineer. Melville is remembered as the engineer in chief who transformed the U.S. Navy through innovations in steam propulsion between 1887 and 1903.

George Wallace Melville was descended from a line of adventurous and doughty Scotsmen. His father, Alexander, was a chemist and an immigrant, but his mother, Sara Douther Wallace Melville, was a native New Yorker. During his primary education in the New York public schools, Melville showed an aptitude for mechanics and subsequently studied engineering at the Brooklyn Collegiate and Polytechnic Institute. Upon completion of his studies, he worked at the engineering firm of James Binns in Brooklyn until July 1861 when he joined the Union Navy, three months after the outbreak of the Civil War. He was nearing his twenty-first birthday.

As third assistant engineer, Melville quickly distinguished himself and soon commanded the attention of his superiors. He served briefly on the side-wheeler *Michigan* in the Great Lakes and for a longer period on the steamer *Dakotah* in the Atlantic. In this latter billet, Melville witnessed the destruction of the *Merrimack* off Norfolk Harbor, and the retreat of the army under General George Brinton McClellan* to Harrison's Landing in Virginia. He was with the *Dakotah* when it later ferried dispatches to Admiral David Glasgow Farragut* in the upper reaches of the Mississippi. Toward the end of this duty, Melville was felled by typhoid, which he had contracted while serving in Virginia, and was hospitalized at Key West, Florida.

A very resilient man, he soon recovered and briefly served on the *Santiago de Cuba,* the sloop *Wachusett*, and the *Tonaranda,* before returning to the *Wachusett*, Captain Napoleon Collins. While serving on this ship he was promoted to second assistant engineer in October 1863 and played a significant role in the ramming and capture of the Confederate cruiser, *Florida*, in Bahia Harbor, Brazil, in October 1864. Not only was it his idea to ram the *Florida*, but Melville also briefly inspected the cruiser in civilian clothes to determine the best approach. For the remainder of the war, Melville served in the fleet of Admiral David Dixon Porter,* played a part in the capture of Fort Fisher, and witnessed the destruction of Richmond, Virginia, while serving on the gunboat *Maumee*. He rose to the rank of first assistant engineer in 1865.

After the war, Melville saw service on the *Tacony* and was present at the French evacuation of Mexico in 1867. Between 1869 and 1871 he served on the South Atlantic Squadron's flagship *Lancaster* and subsequently served as chief engineer of the steamer *Tigress* which in April 1873 rescued the remnants of the crew of the Arctic explorer *Polaris* off Labrador. Much credit was given to Melville for the performance of this feat. Two years later, Melville joined the *Tennessee*, the flagship of the Asiatic Squadron, and again earned commendations for his engineering skill.

In 1879 he volunteered for service as chief engineer on the *Jeanette*, a ship designed for Arctic explorations under the command of Lieutenant George W. DeLong. Trapped in the ice only a month later, the *Jeanette* drifted west toward Siberia for twenty-one months before it was crushed and sank on June 11, 1881. During this ordeal Melville was promoted to chief engineer and commended by DeLong for extraordinary engineering skill in keeping the *Jeanette* together, and its crew in good spirits. Of the three boats that left the stricken ship, only the one commanded by Melville survived, and his heroic efforts to find DeLong were so admired and well known to contemporaries that it made him a hero. In response, Congress promoted him in 1882, the year he returned from the Arctic, and appropriately noted that his exploits had "invoked the admiration of the world."

Two years later, in May 1884, Melville ventured again into the Arctic to rescue the ill-fated party of Army Brigadier General Adolphus Washington Greely,* trapped at Lady Franklin Bay. Melville had proposed an attempt in September 1883, but the Navy rejected the proposal as too hazardous because of expected bad weather. Many of Greely's men died because of the delay, but the survivors were rescued by Melville aboard the *Thetis* on June 22, 1884.

The admirable service record of the man, culminating in these two dramatic exploits, earned Melville worldwide acclaim and led to his appointment in August 1887 as engineer in chief of the Navy by President Grover Cleveland. Forty-four senior officers were bypassed in favor of Melville, and Congress capped this singular honor in September 1890, with another promotion and the presentation of a special medal.

Melville served as engineer in chief for almost seventeen years, the longest tenure to that date of any bureau chief. His administration covered the era of the Spanish-American War and the development of the "New Navy." He rose to the rank of captain in 1899 and retired in 1903 in the grade of rear admiral.

His early deeds and later engineering innovations brought him many honors including the Knight of St. Stanislaus, First Class, from the czar of Russia, a doctor of science from the University of Pennsylvania, and a doctor of laws from Georgetown University. He was an active member of numerous scientific and engineering organizations, including the National Geographic Society, the Institution of Naval Architects of Great Britain, and he was also a past president of the American Society of Mechanical Engineers. He remained a commander in chief of the Military Order of the Loyal Legion until his death. He died on Sunday, March 17, 1912, at his home in Philadelphia at the age of seventy-one.

Melville's Arctic deeds gave him instant fame, but his reputation remains forever strong because of his innovative administration at the U.S. Navy's Bureau of Steam Engineering. R. H. Thurston, late professor of the U.S. Naval Academy, noted that Melville brought "all the modern scientific methods and all the resources of the applied sciences" to bear on the construction of the "New Navy," and was "responsible for the most extensive and vitally essential innovations" in the "machinery of propulsion."

This assessment is in all respects true, for it was Melville's design of the machinery for the much approved forty-one hundred ton protected cruiser *San Francisco* in 1887, which put an end to the Navy's practice of buying ship designs abroad. This earned him promotion to the post of engineer in chief. Not content with this significant contribution, Melville reversed the policy of placing the engines of fighting ships horizontally and below the waterline to provide more space for other departments. Instead, he installed vertical engines, notably on the first battleship *Maine*, thereby creating swifter and more efficient vessels.

The use of coil water-tube boilers on larger warships to replace the established cylindrical boilers was another Melville innovation. The success of these boilers, used first on the monitor *Monterey*, was so signal that many foreign navies quickly converted to their use.

Melville's most significant contribution was probably the introduction of the use of triple screws in U.S. Navy ships. This was not an invention of the engineer in chief, for the French had previously experimented with them, but Melville's use of triple screws on the protected cruisers *Columbia* and *Minneapolis* made these large ships the fastest in their class for almost a decade.

Melville was an enthusiast for speed in all warships and spent the last five years of his administration urging this policy. As a result, the new battleships *Maine, Missouri,* and *Ohio* were designed for eighteen rather than sixteen knots which was standard, but he was less successful in his advocacy of twenty-three knots for the armored cruisers *Washington* and *Tennessee*.

A restless and indefatigable man of ideas, Melville was successful in developing a refined method for testing the trial speeds and assessing the steaming radius of ships, as well as for determining the relative utility of coal and oil as fuel. Visionary in all things, he perceived the need for an engineering training program for naval officers and was successful in establishing the Post-Graduate School of Marine Engineering at the Naval Academy. In this he made a contribution that assumed greater significance with the years, for the "age of technology" had now dawned, and the "New Navy" would have to be commanded by men with increased technological knowledge if it was to compete with other emerging naval powers. The United States was fortunate in having George Wallace Melville set the example at such a pivotal time.

BIBLIOGRAPHY

Bennett, Frank M. *The Steam Navy of the United States.* Pittsburgh: Press of W. T. Nicholson, 1896.

Cathart, William L. "George Wallace Melville," *Journal of the American Society of Naval Engineers* 24 (May 1912): 477–511.

Ellsberg, Edward. *Hell on Ice: The Saga of the* Jeanette. New York: Dodd, Mead and Company, 1938.

Melville, George W. *In the Lena Delta*. Boston: Houghton Mifflin Company, 1885.

Thurston, R. H. "Rear-Admiral G. W. Melville, U.S.N., and Applied Science in Construction of the New Fleet." *Popular Science Monthly* (December 1903): 183–86.

JOHN C. WALTER

MENOHER, Charles Thomas (b. Johnstown, Pa., March 20, 1862; d. Washington, D.C., August 11, 1930), artillery reformer, combat commander, pioneer chief of the Army Air Service. Menoher was one of the key figures in the debate over an independent air force after World War I.

Of Scotch-Irish descent, the son of a Union soldier, Menoher graduated from West Point in 1886 and joined the 1st Artillery. American artillery regiments included both coast and field companies (batteries) and acted as administrative conveniences rather than tactical organizations. He preferred service with the technically backward field artillery because it promised active employment in war. Field companies consisted of slow firing guns which used black powder and recoiled out of battery with each shot. Direct—line-of-sight—fire over open sights constituted the preferred mode of action. The Army improvised all tactical organizations above the company in wartime. By 1910 a group of "artillery progressives" had completely reversed this situation. Modern, full-recoil, rapid-fire guns using smokeless powder, a tactical regiment, and the organization of divisional artillery used in World War I as outlined in the *Field Service Regulations of 1910*, the use of indirect fire, and the complete separation of the coast and field artillery into separate branches had become the norm. The reformers included a number of older officers, such as Brigadier General J. P. Story, Major General William P. Duvall, and many younger ones, such as Captain, later General, Peyton Conway March* and Menoher.

After graduating from the Artillery School at Fortress Monroe in 1894, Menoher became interested in "aerial navigation." At the time this meant the balloon with which the Signal Corps was experimenting. In an artillery context, using a balloon as an observation platform put Menoher on the side of the advocates of indirect fire. Apparently (the paper he wrote is no longer extant), Menoher was considering the proper tactical employment of balloons, the only officer at this time to do so. However, his most important contribution, at least in terms of immediate impact, lay in modernizing the mountain artillery—field artillery packed on the backs of mules rather than drawn by horses. He became the Army's acknowledged expert.

After service in the Spanish-American War and the Philippine American Wars in which he attracted the favorable attention of Brigadier General E. B. Williston and Brigadier General, later Major General, James Franklin Bell,* Menoher organized the Army's first modern mountain battery in 1901. Three years later he served on the board of officers which mandated indirect fire as the primary method of employing field artillery. In 1905 as a member of the General Staff, he prepared the report recommending a regimental organization for the field artillery. During these years, Menoher acquired the reputation of a tactful, professionally competent officer. By 1916 he was a colonel in command of a provisional field artillery brigade on the Mexican border. The following year he received his star and with it a posting to France where he commanded the School of Instruction, Field Artillery, until December 1917 when General John Joseph Pershing* appointed him to command the 42d, "the Rainbow," Division. As a temporary major general, Menoher led his division in the successful defense of Champagne against the last Ludendorff offensive, the Allied counterattack at Soissons, and the American offensives at St. Mihiel and in the Meuse-Argonne. On November 10, 1918, Pershing recognized his good work by appointing Menoher to command the VI Corps, but the war ended before Menoher had an opportunity to make an impression on his new organization.

On January 2, 1919, Menoher, a brigadier general in the Regular Army since November 1918, became the director (later redesignated chief) of the U.S. Army Air Service. As a division commander he had shown great interest in the air units attached to his organization, but in all other respects he lacked the technical background demanded by the new job. The very fact that he was an outsider, however, meant that his reputation was unaffected by the various deficiencies of the wartime Air Service. In the United States, Secretary of War Newton Diehl Baker* had unwisely allowed two coequal organizations to develop—one charged with procurement and production and the other with training and operations. Only toward the end of the war had the War Department combined the two into a single agency headed by a civilian, but the conflict had ended before the new arrangements could make any fundamental changes in a wasteful and inefficient operation. The leading military airman in the United States, Brigadier General William L. Kenly, had done a good job in a bad situation, but he was too closely identified with the old regime. In France the two leading pilots, Brigadier General Benjamin Delahaub Foulois* and Brigadier General William ("Billy") Mitchell,* had demonstrated administrative incompetence and engaged in an unseemly and debilitating feud. Their superior, Brigadier General Mason Matthew Patrick,* was perhaps too closely identified with Pershing, whose relations with March, the chief of staff, were somewhat strained. Menoher, known and trusted by Pershing, March, and Baker, became an obvious choice because of his loyalty, tact, and managerial abilities. In his new post Menoher faced four major tasks: (1) to demobilize the wartime organization; (2) to organize the Office of the Chief of the Air Service in a way that would permit coordination of all Air Service activities; (3) to secure congressional authorization of an Air Service separate from the Signal Corps in peacetime; and (4) to obtain regular commissions of appropriate rank for Air Service pilots, many of whom held only temporary wartime rank. Menoher's success in all these endeavors was overshadowed in the press by controversy with his chief assistant, "Billy" Mitchell.

In July 1919 the American Aircraft Commission, chaired by Assistant Secretary of War Benedict Crowell, reported in favor of a separate department of the air, a conclusion with which Mitchell, a convert to the potential of strategic bombing, agreed. Secretary Baker, however, did not. In August he appointed a board chaired by Menoher to reexamine the question. After hearings which Mitchell believed were biased in favor of the ground perspective, the board found in favor of an air arm organized as a separate branch within the Army equivalent to the infantry or cavalry. The board's conclusions became the basis for interwar air doctrine, but the findings only signaled the opening of a bitter fight for independent air power. Mitchell took his case to the members of the Air Service, the Congress, and the public. A man with real genius for publicity, he agitated for a public demonstration of the airplane's efficiency when pitted against battleships. The campaign culminated in the famous tests off the Virginia Cape in the summer of 1921 in which Air Service bombers sank a captured German battleship. By this point, the War Department considered the question of a separate air force settled in the negative. Continued public discussion of the issue by a serving officer constituted insubordination. Major Oscar Westover, Menoher's executive officer who later became a major general and chief of the Air Corps, believed that Mitchell was destroying all military discipline within the Air Service. Menoher, a major general in the Regular Army since March 1921, had already unsuccessfully attempted to persuade the secretary of war to relieve Mitchell from duty in Washington. When someone leaked Mitchell's confidential report on the bombing test which included a call for an independent air force, Menoher again requested Mitchell's relief. With Mitchell at the height of his popularity following the sinking of the battleship *Ostfriesland* (July 21, 1921), Secretary of War John L. Weeks refused. Menoher then submitted his resignation as chief of the Air Service which Weeks accepted to take effect on October 4, 1921. After commanding the Hawaiian Division, the Department of Hawaii, and the IX Corps Area with headquarters in San Francisco, Menoher retired in 1926 to Washington, D.C., where he died four years later.

Menoher's place in American military history rests on his contribution as chief of the Air Service. The programs he instituted between 1919 and 1921 established the basis for the organization that evolved into the modern U.S. Air Force. The reforms represented what Menoher accurately perceived to be the consensus among Army officers as to the proper role of the air arm in war. Observation had been the primary function of air on the Western Front; it had denied both coalitions strategic, but not tactical, surprise and served as the eyes of the greatest killer of the conflict, artillery. Pursuit acted to clear the air space for observation. Only infrequently did it intervene directly in the ground war in close air support or interdicting enemy communications. The primitive bombers more frequently participated in the latter. Strategic bombing—aside from the sustained German offensive against London—existed more in theory than in practice. One student of the period divides the contending parties in the independent air force controversy into "realists," represented by Menoher who wanted air doctrine and organization to reflect current technical and tactical capabilities, and "visionaries," such as Mitchell who stressed the potential of air power. Menoher, however, did not oppose a strategic bombing force as long as it existed within the Army. The idea that Menoher or the General Staff were hide-bound traditionalists opposed to innovation was a myth invented by Mitchell to unify the Air Service behind his leadership. In the fiscal year 1920 budget, Menoher proposed and the General Staff approved $85 million for the Air Service, of which he intended to devote $43 million to research and development. The opposition came from Congress, particularly the House, which cut the appropriation back to $25 million. The fact is that both Menoher and Mitchell miscalculated the degree of technological progress attainable under peacetime conditions. The difference between the two men went much deeper than the "realist" and "visionary" distinction implies. Menoher represented a wide-ranging reform impulse in the Army, the combined arms movement, that began in the 1880s. It emphasized the interrelationship and interdependence of all arms; success in battle would come only if infantry, cavalry, artillery, and the new arms armor and air worked together effectively. The ideal implied cross-training so that members of the various branches could better understand the capabilities and limitations of branches other than their own.

On the level of high policy the positions of Menoher and Mitchell carried certain important implications. Menoher saw the Air Service as part of the combined arms team, which meant that like the other branches of the army the air would remain small in peacetime and expand only if war threatened. This traditional mobilization policy, one variant of which John McAuley Palmer* was then giving eloquent expression, contrasted to Mitchell's position. Mitchell's proposals contained the implication of a relatively large regular force in peacetime capable of deterring war or, if deterrence failed, of winning it in the opening stages, a view historically associated with the writings of Brevet Major General Emory Upton.* After 1945 the Strategic Air Command became the institutional embodiment of the Mitchell position, while Menoher's found expression in the tactical air commands which supported the American armies in France and Germany in 1944 and 1945 and in the Fifth Air Force in Korea and the Seventh Air Force in Vietnam.

In 1919 the future was large enough to encompass both Menoher's and Mitchell's visions for the Air Service, but it was not large enough to permit the means by which Mitchell sought to achieve his ends. While Baker remained secretary of war and March remained chief of staff, Menoher received sufficient backing from his superiors to counteract the widespread press support Mitchell enjoyed. The change of administration and the promotion of Pershing to chief of staff, a post he graced mainly by his absence from the capital, allowed Mitchell to win the last confrontation with Menoher. It was ironic that Menoher suffered defeat defending civilian supremacy, a principle his civilian superior hesitated to embrace. The denouement meant more than just the blighting of the career of one excellent soldier. It contributed significantly to the lack of trust and cooperation between air and ground officers that would characterize the interwar years and hamper the American effort in the early months of World War II.

BIBLIOGRAPHY

Duffy, Francis P. *Father Duffy's Story*. New York: George H. Doran, 1919.
Futrell, Robert Frank. *Ideas, Concepts, Doctrine: A History of Basic Thinking in the United States Air Force, 1907–1964*. Maxwell Air Force Base, Ala.: Air University, 1974.
Greer, Thomas H. *The Development of Air Doctrine in the Army Air Arm, 1917–1941*. USAF Historical Study No. 89. Maxwell Air Force Base, Ala.: Office of Air Force History, 1953.
James, D. Clayton, *The Years of MacArthur: 1880–1941*. Boston: Houghton Mifflin Company, 1970.
U.S. War Department, Director of the Air Service. *Annual Report, 1919–1921*. Washington, D.C.: U.S. Government Printing Office, 1919–1921.

EDGAR F. RAINES

MERRITT, Wesley (b. New York City, N.Y., June 16, 1834; d. Natural Bridge, Va., December 3, 1910), Army officer. It was largely through Merritt's diplomacy and military tactics in the Philippine Islands in 1898 that the United States elected to annex the archipelago.

Wesley Merritt, seventh of eleven children born to an unsuccessful New York City attorney, spent his adult life in the U.S. Army and probably saw as much active combat as any soldier in the latter part of the nineteenth century. In 1837 his father, John W. Merritt, moved the family to Illinois, where he was in turn a farmer, editor, and politician. His son Wesley read law briefly under his father. In 1857 Merritt accepted an appointment to West Point, declined by his brother, and was graduated twenty-second of forty-one classmates in 1860.

Commissioned in the cavalry (dragoons), Merritt began a meteoric rise in rank that culminated with his having attained the rank of brevet major general of volunteers by the end of the Civil War. His advancement was due not only to exceptional leadership and tactical abilities but also to his service as aide de camp to General Philip St. George Cooke,* one of the officers who initially developed the heavy cavalry or dragoon concept for the United States. At the beginning of the Civil War, Cooke was considered among the best of the senior cavalrymen in the Army. Initially the commander of the cavalry of the Army of the Potomac, Cooke ensured that upon his relief, Merritt moved into a position of responsibility under his successor, General George Stoneman. By May 1863, Merritt as a captain in the 2d U.S. Cavalry was commanding a brigade at Chancellorsville. In June Merritt along with George Armstrong Custer,* was jumped over hundreds of senior officers to the rank of brevet brigadier general. After the Battle of Gettysburg, Merritt remained with the cavalry arm of the Army of the Potomac, developing a distinguished combat record. Following the Appomattox Campaign as deputy commander to General Philip Henry Sheridan,* Merritt was named one of three commissioners to accept the Confederate capitulation, an act that was carried out magnanimously and gracefully.

Merritt held several important commands in the West after the war. In the summer of 1865, he led the column of Union troops that occupied San Antonio, Texas, and assumed duties as chief of cavalry, Department of Texas. In 1866 he reverted to his regular rank as lieutenant colonel and was assigned to the 9th Cavalry, a black regiment, until his next promotion, to colonel, in 1876. He assumed command of the 5th U.S. Cavalry on July 5 just after Custer's defeat at the Little Big Horn. By virtue of a delay in joining other pursuing forces, Merritt drew the wrath of General George Crook,* and the Sioux escaped with minor losses to their pursuers. The 5th Cavalry, under Merritt, also participated in the latter stages of the Nez Perce Campaign in 1877 and was present when Chief Joseph* uttered his words of surrender to General Oliver Otis Howard* and Nelson Appleton Miles*: "I shall fight no more forever." Merritt also witnessed the evidence of the slaughter of the employees of the Indian Agency Station at Milk Creek, Utah, by the Utes in 1879 and was ordered out in pursuit until recalled by an order from Carl Schurz, then secretary of the interior. Merritt was nonplussed at the divergencies between two official agencies, particularly when his unit was required to spend an arduous winter encamped at Milk Creek. In the course of his post-Civil War service, he married Caroline Warren of Cincinnati, Ohio.

Merritt returned to his alma mater, West Point, as the twenty-first superintendent on September 1, 1882, remaining there until June 30, 1887. To his credit, he served in the rank of colonel following two generals, John McAllister Schofield* and Oliver O. Howard.* Following this period as an educator, he was again promoted to brigadier general, this time in the Regular Army, transferred to Fort Leavenworth, Kansas, and assumed command of the Department of the Missouri, then a rather quiescent theater in the last decade of the Indian Wars.

In 1895 Merritt was again promoted, and his headquarters transferred to Chicago with enlargement of the department. In 1897 he assumed command of the most prestigious Military Department, that of the East, headquartered on Governor's Island in New York Harbor. At this time he was one of the three senior major generals in the Army.

Upon the outbreak of the war with Spain in 1898, Merritt was selected by President William McKinley and Secretary of War Russell Alexander Alger* to head the first American "Army of Occupation" bound for the Philippine Islands. He arrived in Manila Bay in the third contingent of Regular Army and National Guard forces dispatched to the islands on July 25. This force of almost eleven thousand was designated the VIII Corps, and among its senior officers was General Arthur MacArthur.* At a time when the United States had not decided whether it would merely liberate the islands from Spain or annex them as American possessions, it was General Merritt who, in conjunction with Admiral George Dewey,* maneuvered Emilio Aguinaldo and the Filipino nationalist insurgents from military control. After passing his forces through Filipino lines to assault positions near Manila. Merritt and Dewey "stage-managed" an attack and surrender with the Spanish commander. The insurgents were excluded from these proceedings, giving the United States *de facto* control of the capital on August 13, 1898.

In September Merritt was ordered to Paris where he testified before the U.S. Commission to arrive at terms for a treaty with Spain. His testimony regarding permanent annexation was ambiguous. In the same year, in London, he married his second wife, Laura Williams of Chicago.

Upon his return to the United States, Merritt resumed command of the Department of the East until June 16, 1900. In an earlier writing he correctly predicted the anti-American insurgency which would rage throughout the islands until 1902 due to Filipino hatred on account of differences in "race and religion" and because the United States was "conquering a territory." He retired by statute on June 16, 1900, and assumed residence in Natural Bridge, Virginia, where he died in 1910.

Merritt's long, continuous, and exceptional service marked him as one of the best small-unit commanders in the cavalry arm of the Army of the Potomac. His courage, skill, and ability to assume increased responsibility on short notice were in large measure due to his rapid rise both during and following the Civil War. His service in the Indian Wars, if not brilliant, was steadfast and reliable, despite occasional brushes with superiors such as Crook and Miles. It is evident that Merritt, as did many other officers of the Indian campaigns such as Howard, developed a sympathy for their declining adversaries, but in the manner of professional soldiers believed that to fight and parlay were mutually disruptive endeavors.

It is also likely that after four hard years of fighting the most stern adversaries of the century, the Army of Northern Virginia, these same soldiers found that their enemies in the Western states, Cuba, and the Philippines were not enemies who merited the ruthless destructive tactics and strategies of total war demanded by war against the Confederacy. Merritt understood the implacable hatreds that could be aroused from the one-sided conflict in the name of greed and conquest that had been the Indian Wars. Thus, he was reluctant, it seems, to stand four square for the "manifest destiny" policies of Elihu Root,* Leonard Wood,* Theodore Roosevelt,* and other expansionists.

Merritt's contributions to the nation were entirely military and, unlike many other West Point graduates, there is no civil side to his service by which to gauge him. He appears always to have placed duty ahead of self and to have moved up in the ranks of the officers' corps by ability and not by political influence in an era when an officer's most valuable assets might be measured by the number of congressmen and governors whom he could count among his friends. One of his highest awards was made by Congress in 1902 at the conclusion of his military service: "Commission for Distinguished Services" (for gallant services). By the first centennial of the founding of West Point, only twenty-one Military Academy graduates had been so designated.

If it were necessary to list Merritt's most unique and lasting accomplishments to American national security, they would be (1) the military decision and actions to seize Manila in 1898, thus completing America's "political" conquest of the islands and assisting in resolving the controversy that raged over whether to turn the islands over to native insurgents or retain them as the western-most bastions of the country; and (2) Merritt's postretirement appearance before congressional committees at the request of Secretary of War Elihu Root in which Merritt and other distinguished senior officers such as John Schofield argued convincingly for the adoption of an Army General Staff system and the founding of the War College. These institutions have persevered to this time.

BIBLIOGRAPHY

Cosmas, Graham A. *An Army for Empire*. Columbia: University of Missouri Press, 1971.

Milller, Stuart C. *Benevolent Assimilation: The American Conquest of the Philippines, 1899–1903*. New Haven, Conn.: Yale University Press, 1982

Millis, Walter. *The Martial Spirit: A Study of Our War with Spain*. Boston: Houghton Mifflin Company, 1930.

Starr, Stephen Z. *The Union Cavalry in the Civil War*. 2 vols. Baton Rouge: Louisiana State University Press, 1979–.

Utley, Robert M. *Frontier Regulars: The United States Army and the Indian, 1866–1890*. New York: Macmillan Company, 1973.

Weigley, Russell A. *History of the United States Army*. New York: Macmillan Company, 1967.

Wolff, Leon. *Little Brown Brother*. New York: Doubleday and Company, 1961.

JAMES B. AGNEW

METACOMET (b. ca. 1642, Mount Hope Peninsula, R.I.; d. Squannakonk Swamp, August 12, 1676), Pokanoket [Wampanoag] Sachem, son of Osamequin [Massasoit]. Metacom is more commonly known as King Philip and as the putative leader of the New England Indian uprising that bears his name, "King Philip's War" (1675–1676).

King Philip's War signaled the end of Indian resistance in New England; yet even the simplest elements of the life of [Metacom, Pometacom] Metacomet are obscure. Nothing is known of his early years. The date of birth is based on a contemporary statement that in 1664 the Pokanoket Sachem was twenty-two. No written descriptions of his physical appearance exist; Paul Revere's engraving is patterned after woodcuts of John Verelst's paintings of the "Four Indian Kings" who visited England in 1710. Even Metacom's Christian name tantalizes. In June 1660 Wamsutta, Metacom's elder brother and then Sachem, asked the Plymouth General Court to confer English names on him and his brother. The court, drawing on classical tradition, renamed the Sachem "Alexander Pokanoket," and his brother "Philip." The title of "King Philip" came later and originally was a term of derision among Plymouth officials who disliked what they saw as Metacom's "ambitious and Haughty spirit."

What is known of Metacom is that his frustration at being unable to prevent Plymouth's encroachment on Pokanoket land and rights led him into war. Historians have identified several causes of King Philip's War. Of prime significance in creating tensions was the contempt Puritans and Pilgrims held for the Indian. Daniel Gookin voiced the general disdain, asserting that "These poor, brutish barbarians . . . are like unto the wild ass's colt, and not many degrees above beasts in matter of fact." This attitude lay behind Increase Mather's assertion that "the Lord God of our Fathers hath given to us for a rightful Possession" of New England, and Cotton Mather's later insistence that "The war was begun by a fierce nation of Indians, upon an honest, harmless, Christian generation of English."

Plymouth's rapid expansion also paved the road to war. By the mid-1660s all open land had been occupied. In 1667 Plymouth established the town of Swansea on Pokanoket Territory, in direct contradiction of previous promises not to buy more Indian land. As more settlers moved into the area, Indian complaints grew. English cattle and pigs wandered into Indian cornfields. Puritan missionary efforts undermined the stability of Pokanoket society by splitting up families and creating alternative leaders to the traditional sachems and shamans. English justice was yet another grievance, for the Pokanokets believed that "if 20 of there onest Indiand testified that a Englishman had dun them Rong, it was as nothing; and if but one of their worst Indians testified against any Indian or the King, when it pleased the English it was sufitiant." Above all, the Indians complained that the English defrauded them of their lands. By 1675 the Pokanokets told John Easton, the deputy governor of Rhode Island, that "they had no Hopes left to kepe ani Land."

Finally, Plymouth's growing fear after 1660 that Charles II would withdraw the colony's charter also contributed to Indian-white tensions. Plymouth sought to strengthen its claim of authority over the Pokanokets, especially with respect to the Indians' right to sell land to other than Plymouth settlers. If Plymouth could establish this claim, more land would be available for settlement and a precedent securing its charter would obtain. In 1664 Plymouth officials sent Major Josiah Winslow to bring Wamsutta in for questioning—by force if necessary—about a recent sale, and Wamsutta died shortly after being released. Then, in 1669 Plymouth claimed for itself the power to judge whether the Pokanokets had land to spare.

Metacom became Sachem upon the death of his brother, but it was not until 1671 that Indian-white animosities led the Pokanokets to act. In March they made a public show of force near Swansea. Plymouth ordered Metacom to Taunton in April where Metacom admitted that he had by "the Naughtiness of my Heart, violated and broken this Covenant with my friends," and that he would hand over his warrior's guns. When the other Pokanoket villages failed to comply, Plymouth threatened war. Metacom persuaded Massachusetts to come to his aid, but when the three parties met, Massachusetts sided with Plymouth and Metacom was forced to confess his guilt, pay a fine, subject himself to Plymouth, and agree to sell land only with the Plymouth Court's permission. In effect, Philip had become Sachem in name only.

The immediate cause of Metacom's war was the mysterious death of John

Sassamon, a Christian Indian, past secretary to Metacom, and English spy. In January 1675 Sassamon's body was discovered under the ice of Assawompsett pond. At first it was believed he had drowned accidentally, but later his body was found to have injuries that indicated murder. Not long thereafter a Christian Indian, claiming to be an eyewitness, charged three Pokanokets—including one of Metacom's counselors—with the crime. Plymouth conducted a hasty and questionable jury trial and the three were hanged, with the last reportedly confessing the crime when the first rope around his neck broke.

Metacom's position during this incident was a difficult one. Before his death Sassamon had implicated Metacom in a conspiracy to attack Plymouth and had also expressed fears for his life if the Pokanokets found him out. In March Metacom denied the charge, but by the opening of the trial his actions heightened Plymouth suspicions. By April Metacom's warriors had begun to arm themselves, and Pokanoket messengers had visited nearby Indian villages to enlist support against the English. Certainly Metacom's actions during the first six months of 1675 exposed the weakness of his position. Metacom reinforced Plymouth's suspicions by refusing to meet with English officials outside his own territory. Among the Pokanokets, Metacom's inability to protect his people diminished his status. As he himself noted a week before the war began, the trial of the three Pokanokets was performed without the presence of Indian leaders to insure a fair hearing.

Unable to halt the executions, and probably fearing for his own safety, Metacom acquiesced in the demands of his young warriors, thus opening the way to war. In June came reports of threatening Indian activity around Swansea and Rehoboth. By the middle of the month, Metacom prevented his men from killing a Plymouth official, but then "was forced to promise that on the next Lord's Day when the English were gone to meeting [that] they should rifle their houses." On June 23 English settlers killed an Indian looter, and the next day nine settlers were killed and two wounded in retaliation.

Metacom's role during the war that followed can only be suggested. Until December 1675 his warriors ambushed colonial forces or attacked outlying settlements, quickly withdrawing into nearby swamps for protection. During the winter Metacom appealed to the Mahican Indians for aid, but Edmund Andros, the governor of New York, enlisted the Mohawks to attack Metacom's forces, effectively breaking the Pokanokets' strength. Although aided on his return in January 1676 by Narragansett and Connecticut Indians (mostly Nipmucks) now involved in the expanded theater of war, Metacom could no longer maintain the momentum of the previous year. Short of powder, unable to plant crops, and constantly harassed by English forces now using Indian tactics and Indian scouts, the Pokanoket Sachem returned to Mount Hope urged on, as Douglas Leach put it, "by some great compelling sense of tragic drama." Shortly after the English captured his son and wife—an incident which, according to Indian prisoners "had almost broke his heart"—Metacom died on August 12 while attempting to escape an English ambush, shot by an Indian whose brother Metacom had killed for earlier suggesting peace. The war was effectively at an end when the English commander Benjamin Church* looked upon Metacom's body and described it as a "doleful, great, naked, dirty beast."

Assessments of Metacom have tended to extremes. Too often he has been portrayed either as a great patriot or as "the perfidious Caitiff." Such judgments tell more about the authors than Metacom, for these opinions follow the division between those who see the heroism of the Noble Savage and those who see only the cruelty of the Ignoble Savage. For a clearer understanding of Metacom, one must look more closely at two issues that have divided scholars: the goals of King Philip's War and Metacom's leadership.

At present, two general assessments hold the field. In 1958 Douglas Leach insisted that "the war was actually a struggle for survival between two mutually antagonistic civilizations" [p. 178]. More recently, Francis Jennings rejected that conclusion, arguing that the Indian "purpose was to salvage some measure of self-government and secure territory." Leach and Jennings also disagree on the scope of the war: for Leach, the war erupted out of a conspiracy among the Indian tribes of New England, whereas Jennings rejects this "conspiracy theory" because it rests on a too ready acceptance of contemporary English opinions, a view supported by ethnohistorical analysis.

Debate over the nature of King Philip's War has not expanded into a useful discussion of Metacom's leadership. Leach described Philip as "the supreme ruler of the Wampanoags" who was a "proud man embittered by the humiliations imposed upon him through superior strength." Metacom failed because, in Leach's words, "his war began prematurely, was poorly organized, and soon escaped from Philip's control. He had undertaken a project that was far too big for his strength and ability." Jennings does not analyze Metacom's abilities, for he focuses primarily on Puritan duplicity. Nevertheless, Leach's notion that Philip was out of his depth contains a measure of truth. It may be that Metacom's actions were those of a well-meaning but inadequate leader, faced with more powerful enemies, moved by circumstances and chance, seeking to preserve his people's freedom, yet without a vision of how to attain that end short of a war he could not win.

BIBLIOGRAPHY

Jennings, Francis. *The Invasion of America: Indians, Colonialism, and the Cant of Conquest*. Chapel Hill: University of North Carolina Press, 1975.
Langdon, George. *Pilgrim Colony: A History of New Plymouth, 1620–1691*. New Haven and London: Yale University Press, 1966.
Leach, Douglas Edward. *Flintlock and Tomahawk: New England in King Philip's War*. New York: Macmillan Company, 1958.

Lincoln, Charles H., ed. *Narratives of the Indian Wars, 1675–1699*. New York: Charles Scribner's Sons, 1913.
Vaughan, Alden. *The New England Frontier: Puritans and Indians*. Boston and Toronto: Little, Brown and Company, 1965.

RICHARD L. HAHN

MIDDLETON, Troy H. (b. near Georgetown, Miss., October 12, 1889; d. Baton Rouge, La., October 9, 1976), World War II Corps commander, educator.

Troy H. Middleton was born and grew up in rural Mississippi. His military career may be said to date from his education at Mississippi A & M. College, where he was the principal cadet officer in his graduating class of 1909. Middleton secured an alternate appointment to West Point, but as the principal appointees did not withdraw, he decided to enlist in the Army in March 1910. He did not regret this turn of fate inasmuch as he received his commission as second lieutenant in 1912, as opposed to the West Point Class of 1914.

Middleton served in Vera Cruz, Mexico, from April to November 1914. In the months following the United States' entry into World War I Captain Middleton took part in the training of new units, until his posting to Europe in the spring of 1918. Now a major, Middleton commanded the 1st Battalion, 47th Infantry, 4th Infantry Division, and went into combat near the River Ourcq in July 1918.

It was in the Meuse-Argonne in late September-October 1918 that Middleton began to display the fine tactical intuition and calmness under fire that were the hallmarks of his career. By mid-October he was a lieutenant colonel in command of the 39th Infantry and led an attack in the Bois de Forêt which was the furthest penetration of the German lines yet by the 4th Infantry Division, an action for which he received the Distinguished Service Medal. Promoted once again, Middleton was the youngest colonel in the American Expeditionary Force.

After the Armistice Middleton served in the occupation forces on the Rhine until July 1919, when he was ordered to Camp Benning as part of the first faculty of the new Infantry School, a further recognition of his outstanding talents as a combat commander. Reduced to the peacetime rank of captain, Middleton served on the Benning faculty until June 1921; he then entered the Benning Advanced Infantry course himself, graduating first in his class in June 1922. In the academic year 1923–1924 he attended the Command and General Staff School at Fort Leavenworth, along with classmate George Smith Patton, Jr.,* and stayed on again with the faculty through 1928. In 1928–1929 he attended the Army War College.

In need of duty with a civilian component of the Army, Major Middleton requested ROTC and was sent to Louisiana State University (LSU) as commandant of cadets in July 1930. It was the beginning of a professional association that lasted for the rest of his life. Middleton was at LSU for six years, followed by a brief tour in the Philippines. He returned to the United States in 1937 and retired from the Army, seeing little prospect for further promotion and also desirous of seeking greater financial security for his family. Middleton therefore accepted the position of dean of administration at LSU. When financial scandals rocked the university in 1939, Middleton took on the jobs of acting vice-president and comptroller. LSU was not back on sound footing until June 1941.

In January 1942 Middleton was recalled to active service as a lieutenant colonel, although he had twice offered his services before, once prior to and once immediately after Pearl Harbor. In the early wartime confusion he was shuttled from posting to posting until June 1942 when, as brigadier general, he arrived as assistant commander of the 45th Infantry Division, Fort Devens, Massachusetts. That summer Middleton received his second star and full command of the 45th.

A National Guard unit, the 45th entered combat at the invasion of Sicily on July 10, 1943, where it won high accolades as one of the best trained divisions in the Army, again a reflection of Middleton's abilities. In Sicily it was the 45th which bore the brunt of the decision by General Harold Alexander to give Bernard Montgomery an additional highway to aid his slowed advance. Accepting with customary grace, Middleton executed a complex maneuver to the west across the rear of the 1st Division in order to reenter the line. From there the 45th took part in the advance northward and succeeded in cutting Sicily in two. Once the division reached the northern coast it turned east, where it engaged in heavy fighting until its relief on July 31, 1943.

Middleton next led the 45th in the Salerno invasion. When the Germans counterattacked and threatened the Allied line and beachhead, Middleton reacted calmly throughout the crisis. Once the line was restored and the advance resumed, the 45th remained in combat for six weeks along the Volturno Valley and then went into reserve. Several weeks later Middleton returned to the United States for medical treatment for a recurrent knee injury. His future career was now doubtful, but Generals George Catlett Marshall* and Dwight David Eisenhower* both agreed that his talents as a combat leader were too valuable to waste. Middleton went to Britain in March 1944 to prepare to command the VIII Corps after D-Day; General Marshall also sent along a sergeant who was a physical therapist.

The VIII Corps was activated on June 12, 1944, and after the success of Operation COBRA it held open the exit from the Cotentin Peninsula. As part of the exploitation now under the command of General Patton and the Third Army, the VIII Corps entered Brittany. There the more cautious Middleton found himself caught between the more aggressive Patton above and his own eager armor subordinates below. Working in a sector virtually without front, flanks, or rear, Middleton experienced some difficulties reining in his armor units and feared they were spreading out too far. Patton, of course, pushed for an enthusiastic exploitation. Finally, while the major fighting moved quickly east, Middleton was left to clear Brittany, which included the lengthy siege and reduction of Brest. During this period Middleton's command was virtually autonomous.

By the end of 1944 the VIII Corps, now composed of largely untried or combat-weary divisions, rejoined the main line, holding eighty-eight miles of front with less than seventy thousand men in the Ardennes, a decision for which General Omar Nelson Bradley* took full responsibility. The VIII Corps caught the full brunt of the German attack on December 16, 1944, providing the supreme crisis and test in Middleton's career. Once again he reacted with admirable calm, withdrawing grudgingly, controlling his units carefully. Middleton was among the very first to recognize the importance of Bastogne as a hub of the road network, and it was his decision to hold the city with the 101st Airborne Division, an order that even Patton at first thought highly questionable. A large part of the credit for slowing and ultimately limiting the German attack at the Bulge deservedly went to Middleton.

The remainder of the war was almost anticlimactic. By V-E Day Middleton was a lieutenant general. Retiring once again, he returned to LSU, once again as comptroller. In December 1950 he was elected president of the university, taking office early the next year; he remained in that post until 1962. In addition, he also served on the Doolittle Board (Board to Investigate Officer-Enlisted Men Relationships, 1946); the Military Education Panel of the Service Academies Board (1949); a special committee to investigate cheating at West Point (1951); and as chairman of the Louisiana Commission on Human Relations, Rights and Responsibilities (1965–1970).

Troy Middleton stands out as one of the best U.S. combat commanders of the twentieth century. He displayed a keen ability to read developing situations correctly and to respond accordingly, always with a calm that was remarkable. This was noticeable during the early crisis at Salerno and throughout the confused days of the Bulge, where his control of the tactical situation seriously disrupted the German timetable. Moreover, Middleton was always counted on as a reliable subordinate, one who could take and execute even disagreeable orders, such as the transfer of the needed highway in Sicily. Generals Marshall, Eisenhower, and Bradley all had abundant faith in him, and even though he might bridle at Middleton's caution versus his own dash, Patton called him ''one of the easiest Corps Commanders to do business with I have ever known, and also one of the most efficient.''

Of equal importance was Middleton's role as an educator, both within the army during the important interwar years and later at LSU. There Middleton played a major role in saving a politicized and scandal-ridden university and helped make it a well-run educational institution.

BIBLIOGRAPHY

Blumenson, Martin. *Breakout and Pursuit*. Washington, D.C.: Office of the Chief of Military History, 1961.
———. *The Patton Papers, 1940–1945*. Vol. 2. Boston: Houghton Mifflin Company, 1974.
———. *Salerno to Cassino*. Washington, D.C.: Office of the Chief of Military History, 1969.

Bradley, Omar N. *A Soldier's Story*. New York: Holt, Rinehart and Winston, 1951.

Cole, Hugh M. *The Ardennes: Battle of the Bulge*. Washington, D.C.: Office of the Chief of Military History, 1965.

Eisenhower, John S. D. *The Bitter Woods*. New York: G. P. Putnam's Sons, 1969.

Garland, Albert N., et al. *Sicily and the Surrender of Italy*. Washington, D.C.: Office of the Chief of Military History, 1965.

Price, Frank James. *Troy H. Middleton: A Biography*. Baton Rouge: Louisiana State University Press, 1974.

MARK M. LOWENTHAL

MILES, Nelson Appleton (b. near Westminster, Mass., August 8, 1839; d. Washington, D.C., May 15, 1925), Army officer. Miles was one of the Army's premier Indian-fighters and the last commanding general of the Army (1895–1903).

Born to an established farming family in Massachusetts, Nelson Miles learned his letters and numbers at a nearby academy. He then went to Boston seeking a job and more schooling. Miles clerked in a crockery store and took classes at night to supplement his education. In 1860 he concluded that a civil war was likely and sought instruction from a retired French Army officer. After the firing on Fort Sumter, he borrowed money to raise a company of volunteers, but only gained a lieutenancy in the 22d Massachusetts Volunteer Infantry Regiment.

Miles fell to his military duties with an ardor that impressed senior officers. He became aide de camp to Brigadier General Oliver Otis Howard* and served on Howard's staff during the Peninsula Campaign with the Army of the Potomac under General George Brinton McClellan.* Miles was wounded at the Battle of Seven Pines. Subsequently, his rise up the ranks was rapid: lieutenant colonel of the 61st New York Volunteer Infantry at the Battle of Antietam (September 1862); colonel of the 61st New York at Fredericksburg (December 1862), where he was shot through the throat and praised in dispatches by his division commander, Major General Winfield Scott Hancock.* Severely wounded at Chancellorsville, Miles had to miss the Battle of Gettysburg. Promoted to brigadier general of volunteers (May 1864), he led a brigade and fought in the major actions from the Wilderness to Appomattox, earning his brevet as major general for actions at the Battle of Reams' Station (August 1864).

On the strength of his record, Miles sought a commission in the Regular Army. Meanwhile, he was given the controversial task of guarding Jefferson Davis.* He ordered that Davis be manacled in a dank cell at Fortress Monroe, Virginia. Miles was made colonel of the newly created 40th Infantry Regiment of black troops stationed in North Carolina. He evidently did not care either for an assignment with black troops or Reconstruction duty. In 1868 he wed Mary Sherman, niece of General William Tecumseh Sherman* and U.S. Senator John Sherman of Ohio, thus linking himself to one of the nation's influential families. In 1869 Miles obtained a transfer to the 5th Infantry and began his service in the Trans-Mississippi.

From 1869 to 1890, Miles led soldiers against the major Western tribes and built a reputation as America's most successful Indian-fighting Army officer. Under the strategic direction of Major General Philip Henry Sheridan,* he led one of four columns in the Red River War (1874–1875) against the Comanche, Kiowa, and Southern Cheyenne in Texas and Indian Territory (Oklahoma). Following the defeat of Lieutenant Colonel George Armstrong Custer* (1876), Miles commanded one of the columns that forced the Sioux and Northern Cheyenne into Canada or onto reservations. In 1877 he got the credit for defeating the Nez Perce under Looking Glass* and Chief Joseph,* although General Howard, his old mentor, arrived on the field before the tribe surrendered. Meanwhile, in the Department of Arizona, Major General George Crook* had been unable to defeat the Apaches. In 1886 Sheridan relieved Crook and posted Miles to Arizona. Miles defeated the Apaches and captured their charismatic leader Geronimo.* Miles was promoted to brigadier general (1880) and major general (1890). He was in command of the Military Division of the Missouri for the denouement of the Indian Wars—the tragedy at Wounded Knee (1890), where the Sioux, inspired by the Ghost Dance and their legendary leader Sitting Bull,* appeared on the verge of taking the warpath. Following an argument over a demand that the Indians surrender all weapons, the Army killed more than two hundred "hostiles"—including women and children.

In 1895, as the senior major general and upon the retirement of John McAllister Schofield,* Miles inherited the title and office of commanding general of the Army. Ulysses Simpson Grant* (1865–1869), Sherman (1869–1883), and Sheridan (1883–1888) had previously held the office, and all had found it difficult to function in a command with an ill-defined role vis-à-vis the Army bureau chiefs. Schofield had contented himself with giving advice to the secretary of war and the president. Miles wanted to make the postion one of genuine leadership rather than a ceremonial sinecure. For three years Miles thrashed about in official Washington, dealing abruptly with bureau chiefs who jealously guarded their independence. Matters were made worse by Miles' intense dislike for Secretary of War Russell Alexander Alger.* At the outbreak of war with Spain in 1898, Miles was fit, trim, and in very good health, quite capable of acting as either the senior field commander or a top presidential advisor and coordinator of Army training, assignments, and campaign plans, something analogous to a chief of staff. Miles wanted both and got neither. Because of personality conflicts with President William McKinley and Secretary Alger, Miles' effectiveness decreased steadily. The command of the field army in Cuba went to Major General William Rufus Shafter.* McKinley and Alger allowed Miles to plan and lead the successful invasion of the Spanish colony of Puerto Rico (July–August 1898).

After the Spanish war, apparently as a prelude to entering politics, Miles caused a controversy by accusing the War Department of supplying poisoned beef to the Army. He also criticized McKinley's policy of suppressing the Philippine *insurrectos*. Furthermore, Miles disagreed with plans proposed by

Secretary of War Elihu Root* to reorganize the American Army and create the position of chief of staff. President Theodore Roosevelt* was pleased to force Miles to retire in 1903 at the mandatory retirement age of sixty-four.

During his long retirement, Miles lived uneventfully in Washington, D.C. The general wrote two volumes of memoirs. He died in 1925.

Nelson Miles had a lengthy, distinguished, and controversial career. Commissioned to serve the Union in 1861, he rose from volunteer lieutenant to brevet major general, and subsequently fought against the major Western Indian tribes. He was awarded the Medal of Honor in 1892 for his Civil War exploits and became commanding general of the Army—all very heady for a former crockery clerk.

Miles' reputation rests on his record of accomplishment in the West. Miles developed into an outstanding regimental and independent field force commander. He earned a reputation as a vain, egotistical, ambitious, hard-driving, knowledgeable, skilled, determined, and aggressive officer. He got results. Although he joined the critics—including Sheridan—who disparaged Crook's use of Indians of one tribe to fight their own tribesmen, Miles often used scouts and auxiliaries, especially when he directed the campaign against the Apaches. Miles took pride in trimming his uniform with bear fur (which earned him the sobriquet "Old Bear Coat"), experimenting with the heliograph in the Southwest, and increasing the mobility of his infantrymen by mounting them on captured Indian horses. Miles followed Sheridan's example of destroying captured supplies and ponies to deprive the tribes of their logistic support. Miles deserves recognition for aggressively pursuing the Sioux and Nez Perce, but his victory over the Apaches was gained by use of false flags of truce and made absolute by exiling entire bands to prisons in Alabama and Florida. Grateful politicans pointed out that the removal of the Apaches opened up the Arizona Territory to settlement.

Unlike other prominent American military leaders, Miles did not crown his career with high elective office. His argumentative and sometimes offensive relations with Presidents McKinley and Roosevelt and Secretaries of War Alger and Root spoiled the end of his career. In 1899 Miles' public condemnation of the supply of tinned beef to the army by Secretary Alger and Commissary General Charles P. Eagan resulted in a great scandal and Eagan's and Alger's resignations, but no favorable results for Miles. If Miles had expected to gain the nomination of the Democratic party in 1900, he had badly miscalculated. The "embalmed beef" controversy poisoned the waters between the commanding general and the civilian administration, although McKinley did agree to approve Miles' promotion to lieutenant general in 1901.

Elihu Root replaced Alger in 1899 and designed a plan to revamp the U.S. Army along the lines of the German model. Initially, Root expected Miles to be the first chief of staff under the new system, but Miles, a stickler for tradition and apparently believing that the change was intended to degrade him, bitterly criticized the plan in public congressional hearings. General Schofield, Major

General Wesley Merritt,* and other officers favored the plan, which would give the chief of staff responsibility to supervise and coordinate the bureaus and field commands under the authority of the secretary of war. Rather than a step down, as Miles saw it, the position of chief of staff later became one of considerable power.

In his last months of active duty, Miles found other ways to aggravate the administration. He needlessly took the side of Admiral Winfield Scott Schley* against Admiral William Thomas Sampson* in their argument over each other's role in the Battle of Santiago. Miles deserved President Roosevelt's official and public censure for making statements detrimental to good conduct and discipline in the services. Furthermore, Miles used an inspection trip through Hawaii, Guam, and the Philippines to publicly condemn the Army's alleged mistreatment of Filipino prisoners and to meet with an *insurrecto* leader. These inopportune acts led Roosevelt to mark Miles' retirement with only a cold and pro forma announcement.

Miles' argumentativeness and use of newspapermen to promote his own image detracted from his contributions during the Spanish war. Among these were his calling attention to the dangers of a premature campaign into Cuba; recommending the need for strengthening Merritt's forces bound for the Philippines; inspecting the training camps in the United States, the port of embarkation at Tampa, Florida, and the frontline positions in Cuba; and masterminding the capture of Puerto Rico before the end of the war. Unfortunately, Miles could not let anyone, be it the secretary of war, the president, or a naval board of inquiry, have the last word if he disagreed with them. Miles was definitely a general of the nineteenth century and would have been completely out of his element trying to act as a coalition commander or senior officer of the American Expeditionary Force in a total war such as World War I.

BIBLIOGRAPHY

Cosmas, Graham A. *An Army for Empire: The United States Army in the Spanish-American War*. Columbia: University of Missouri Press, 1971.

Johnson, Virginia W. *The Unregimented General: A Biography of Nelson A. Miles*. Boston: Houghton Mifflin Company, 1962.

Miles, Nelson A. *Personal Recollections and Observations*. Chicago: Werner and Company, 1896.

———. *Serving the Republic*. New York: Harper, 1911.

Ranson, Edward. "Nelson A. Miles as Commanding General, 1896–1903." *Military Affairs* 29 (Winter 1965–1966): 179–200.

Utley, Robert M. *Frontier Regulars: The United States Army and the Indian, 1866–1890*. New York: Macmillan Company, 1973.

JOSEPH G. DAWSON III

MITCHELL, William (b. Nice, France, December 28, 1879; d. New York City, N.Y., February 19, 1936), U.S. Army officer and pilot. Mitchell was the first major publicist of air power in the United States and a founder of the U.S. Air Force.

William ("Billy") Mitchell, an eighteen-year-old scion of a politically active and once wealthy family in Wisconsin, quickly became a second lieutenant in the Signal Corps of the U.S. Army at the outbreak of the war with Spain in 1898. He was commissioned six weeks after he dropped out of Columbian College (later George Washington University) to enlist in a volunteer regiment. He would not complete his degree work at George Washington until 1919, because the challenges of occupation duty in Cuba and combat service in the Philippines stirred him to accept a career commission in 1901 as a first lieutenant in the Signal Corps. By 1904, Mitchell was a captain.

Assignments to communications work and two years of study (1907–1909) at the Army's School of the Line and its Staff College absorbed his time until 1912. In the next year, a prestigious appointment to the General Staff put him in recurring contact with aeronautics, one of the emerging missions of the Signal Corps. In 1916 Mitchell left the General Staff to direct Army aviation until Lieutenant Colonel George Owen Squier* could take charge. Internal squabbles in Army aviation, its failure in Mexico, and the deteriorating international situation were opening new opportunities in aeronautics for officers such as Mitchell. Now a major, he became Squier's deputy, and, at his own expense, he learned to fly in his off-duty hours at a civilian flying school.

The relationship between Squier and Mitchell did not go well. In January 1917 Squier supported Mitchell's transfer to France as an observer. Mitchell reached Paris four days after the United States entered the world war, unsuccessfully tried to take charge of American aeronautical planning in Europe, qualified himself to wear the wings of a U.S. Army pilot, and intensively studied the employment of aviation on the Western Front. After his rival, Brigadier General Benjamin Delahaub Foulois,* conceded Mitchell's tactical knowledge and made way for him, he assumed direction, as a colonel, of American Expeditionary Force (AEF) aviation at the front.

Under Mitchell, American airmen enjoyed marked success in supporting the AEF ground forces, most dramatically in striving for a massive use of air power at the Battle of St. Mihiel. When the war ended, Mitchell was a heavily decorated brigadier general, firmly established as the senior American air combat leader.

This wartime success put Mitchell at the head of a group of AEF fliers who campaigned through the press and in Congress for an air force on the model of Britain's Royal Air Force, independent from the Army and Royal Navy. He was undaunted when a separate service was denied the American airmen in 1920. As the assistant chief of the Army Air Service in Washington, D.C., he perceived that the coming of air power had thrown into question the role of a U.S. Navy built around the battleship as the nation's first line of defense. The sinking by Mitchell and his aircrews of the former German battleship *Ostfriesland* in the bombing tests of July 1921 brought him to the peak of his standing with the American people, but no organizational changes resulted.

His superior, Major General Mason Matthews Patrick,* tried to keep Mitchell out of further controversy by sending him on temporary assignments away from Washington. In 1924, with the inadequately funded Army air arm deteriorating and his personal commitment to build an air force that would be his monument unflagging, he launched a strident publicity campaign. After voicing exaggerated claims that damaged his credibility in Congress, he lost his Air Service post with its rank as a brigadier general and was transferred to San Antonio, Texas, in March 1925.

His intransigence worsened, and in September 1925 Mitchell deliberately invited a court–martial to focus public attention on his views. He publicly condemned the Navy and War departments for "almost treasonable" neglect of national defense. President Calvin Coolidge gave Mitchell his court-martial, but defused the associated issues with a comprehensive and speedy report from a board of leaders in American aviation, chaired by Dwight Morrow. The seemingly inevitable finding of "guilty" by Mitchell's judges and his sentence, modified by Coolidge to five years' suspension from the Army at half-pay, left him no choice but to resign from the service.

From his Virginia estate, Mitchell renewed his publicity campaigns, publishing some one hundred magazine and newspaper articles and two of his five books in the next decade. His central theme was America's increasing vulnerability to the onset of the air age. Future wars would be decided by strategic bombing attacks on a nation's vital centers, or its material and psychological means of resistance. He anticipated the resurgence of German militarism and believed a war between the United States and Japan was certain. The war would begin with a destructive air attack against an ineffectively defended Hawaiian Islands and could be best deterred by the threat of American bombardment of Japan's highly inflammable cities.

These ideas, Mitchell argued, demanded a reorganization of the nation's military system with a department of defense supervising the activities of coequal land, sea, and air services. He sought a prominent place in such a reorganization through his family ties with the Democratic party. The election of Franklin D. Roosevelt in 1932 raised his hopes, but he soon antagonized the president. The downturn in his fortunes accelerated when the public, beset by worries about the Depression, no longer seemed interested in his ideas. As disappointing as these setbacks must have been, Mitchell still persisted in his uncompromising attitudes until he suddenly died at only fifty-six years of age from influenza complicated by heart trouble.

Mitchell was not an original thinker; his military theories owed much to the ideas of his colleagues in the various Army air operations and those of his associates in the international community of airmen he joined in France during World War I. Rather, his contribution came through his imaginative trail blazing in preparing the American people to understand the implications of those ideas for national security.

His impact on the U.S. military services was far reaching. His leadership assured the Army of sufficient air protection in France in World War I to fight the German ground forces without serious hindrance from their own more experienced air force. The Navy moved more quickly into the air age to find answers to the questions he raised. His combat success in France, earned under extremely difficult circumstances, set an inspiring precedent for American airmen in subsequent wars and was an indispensable dimension to the self-image of the future U.S. Air Force. However many his shortcomings, Mitchell's leadership in the immediate postwar years gave his followers, such as Henry Harley Arnold* and Carl Andrew Spaatz,* a sense of purpose that helped to sustain them until they had attained key appointments just before World War II. Central to that sense of purpose were the ideas that Mitchell identified for them, ideas whose realization he spurred. Those ideas included the global potential of air power; its application to the defense of the United States and its territories, especially those in the Pacific region; the possibilities of strategic bombardment; and the necessity for an air force, a full partner to the Army and the Navy in a department of defense.

In 1946 Congress recognized the realization of nearly all those ideas and Mitchell's other contributions by voting him a special posthumous medal for his "outstanding pioneer service and foresight in the field of American military aviation."

BIBLIOGRAPHY

Davis, Burke. *The Billy Mitchell Affair*. New York: Random House, 1967.
Devine, Isaac Don. *Mitchell, Pioneer of Air Power*. Revised. New York: Duell, Sloan and Pearce, 1958.
Hurley, Alfred F. *Billy Mitchell: Crusader for Air Power*. New ed. Bloomington: Indiana University Press, 1975.
Mitchell, Ruth. *My Brother Bill*. New York: Harcourt Brace, 1953.

ALFRED F. HURLEY

MITSCHER, Marc Andrew (b. Hillsboro, Wisc., January 26, 1887; d. Norfolk, Va., February 3, 1947), naval officer. Mitscher is regarded as one of the premier leaders of American aircraft carriers during World War II.

Raised in Washington, D.C., Mitscher was appointed to the Naval Academy from Oklahoma, where his father had been an Indian agent. Marc was nicknamed "Oklahoma Pete"—later shortened to "Pete"—for his wild antics which got him into disciplinary difficulties. An average student, he graduated 108th in his 1910 class of 131 midshipmen.

Reporting to the Pacific Fleet, he served aboard two armored cruisers. Mitscher moved to the Caribbean in 1912 for consecutive service in the gunboats *Vicksburg* and *Annapolis*, and the armored cruiser *California* (renamed *San Diego*), and he participated in the Vera Cruz incident of 1914. After brief duty in two destroyers, he reported for aviation training aboard the armored cruiser *North Carolina* at Pensacola, Florida, in October 1915.

Upon graduation as Naval Aviator No. 33 in June 1916, Lieutenant, junior grade, Mitscher received advanced flight training at Pensacola, including balloon and catapult experiments aboard the armored cruiser *Huntington*, in which he sailed on convoy duty during the summer of 1917. His subsequent World War I service took place at three naval air stations, Montauk Point and Rockaway on Long Island and Miami, Florida, in command of the latter two. In early 1919 he joined the aviation section in the Office of the Chief of Naval Operations and participated in the trans-Atlantic flights of the NC flying boats. His NC–1, of which he was a pilot, came down short of the Azores, but the achievement of going even that far earned him the Navy Cross.

Mitscher's considerable skills as a pilot then took him to the Pacific Fleet aircraft tender *Aroostook* at San Diego where he also commanded the naval air station (1919–1922); to the Anacostia Naval Air Station, as station commander; and the plans division of the Bureau of Aeronautics, during which duty he led Navy teams in the International Air Races at Detroit (1922) and St. Louis (1923). Transferred to the Navy's first aircraft carrier, *Langley*, in 1926, he helped to fit out and head the air department of the carrier *Saratoga* (1926–1929). He served as executive officer in the *Langley* (1929–1930) and the *Saratoga* (1934–1935). He landed the first airplane on the *Saratoga* in June 1928.

A leader in the Navy's growing air arm, Commander Mitscher returned to the Aeronautics Bureau (1930–1933) and then to the West Coast as chief of staff to Rear Admiral A. W. Johnson, Base Force air commander. Mitscher commanded the aircraft tender *Wright* (1937–1938) after another tour of duty at the Aeronautics Bureau and then led Patrol Wing 1 at San Diego in the rank of captain. He was assistant chief of the Aeronautics Bureau (June 1939–July 1941), at which time he reported to Newport News, Virginia, as prospective commanding officer of the new carrier *Hornet*, commissioned in October 1941.

In the Atlantic when war with Japan broke out, Captain Mitscher took the *Hornet* into the Pacific to launch Army bombers under the command of Lieutenant Colonel James Harold "Jimmy" Doolittle* against Tokyo, which he did successfully in April 1942. Two months later he brilliantly led his ship in the Battle of Midway, where his planes helped to sink four Japanese carriers. Selected for rear admiral the previous December, Mitscher assumed that rank in July as commander, Patrol Wing 2 in Hawaii, shifting in December to Nouméa in the South Pacific, to command Fleet Air in the Guadalcanal Campaign. In April 1943 he commanded Allied air forces in the Solomon Islands Campaign until August, when he took over Fleet Air on the West Coast of the United States.

Rear Admiral Mitscher took command of the Fast Carrier Task Force, Pacific Fleet (Task Force 58), in January 1944 and covered the landings in the Marshall Islands, going on to destroy Japanese naval air forces at Truk in the Caroline Islands and in the Marianas Islands during February, his flag aboard the new carrier *Yorktown*. Promoted to vice admiral in March, he raided the Palau Islands, then supported the landings at Hollandia, New Guinea, and struck Truk again in April. While covering the landings in the Marianas in June, his force defeated the Japanese Fleet in the Battle of the Philippine Sea. His flag was in the new *Lexington*, which he commanded during additional operations in the Marianas and strikes on the Bonin Islands.

Redesignated commander of the 1st Fast Carrier Task Force and Task Force 38 in August 1944, Vice Admiral Mitscher participated in the Philippine Campaign through November, including the battle for Leyte Gulf. His task force (58) covered the Iwo Jima and Okinawa landings between January and May 1945, his planes striking the Japanese homeland and sinking the superbattleship *Yamato*. In battling the deadly kamikazes, Mitscher received damage to his flagships, the carriers *Bunker Hill* and *Enterprise*, and ended up on the carrier *Randolph*.

In July 1945 he reported as deputy chief of naval operations for air in Washington, D.C, where he remained until early the next year. Promoted to the four star rank of admiral in March 1946, Admiral Mitscher spent the rest of his career in the Atlantic. He commanded the Eighth Fleet until September 1946. He died of a heart attack while serving as commander in chief of the Atlantic Fleet.

Mitscher knew no equal in the wartime Pacific Fleet for the respect and love of his men. That he was the complete professional and a fearless leader in battle accounted for part of their loyalty, but an added factor was his well-known, extraordinary efforts to save the lives of his airmen when they were in trouble. The most notable of his lifesaving efforts occurred on the night of June 20, 1944. His pilots, most of whom were inexperienced in night landings, were returning, exhausted and low on fuel with damaged aircraft, after their distant strike against the Japanese fleet. Mitscher ordered that all ships' lights be illuminated so that the pilots could see the flight decks.

A small, slight man, Mitscher spoke in low, barely audible tones and with a strict economy of words. Superbly calm in battle, he nurtured a quiet sense of humor while developing revolutionary carrier tactics before and in the midst of combat. He avoided publicity throughout his career, preferring to let his actions speak for themselves. Prematurely bald since his twenties, save for a thin wisp of light hair, the clear complexion of his youth had turned leathery from years in the open-air cockpits of the Navy's early planes and on the bridges of carriers. Three aircraft crashes had not interrupted his career, but the grueling round-the-clock battles of 1945 took their toll on his health. In all likelihood, he suffered a mild heart attack during that spring, but simply stayed in his sea cabin while his staff continued the fight under the able direction of his chief of staff, Arleigh Albert Burke.*

No officer ever questioned Mitscher's judgment (nor has any historian for that matter), except for Admiral Raymond Ames Spruance* when he rejected Mitscher's plea to attack the enemy fleet earlier in the Marianas operation—which led to a controversy in which Mitscher himself absolutely refused to participate. He was happiest—and most successful—when operating at sea as an independent tactical commander. At the helm of Task Force 58/38, "Pete" Mitscher molded the Fast Carrier Task Force into the most deadly naval force in history to that time which destroyed the Japanese fleet and left the carrier arm as the nucleus of the U.S. Navy for the ensuing generation.

BIBLIOGRAPHY

Deurs, George van. *Wings for the Fleet*. Annapolis, Md.: Naval Institute Press, 1966.
Morison, Samuel Eliot. *New Guinea and the Marianas*. Boston: Little, Brown and Company, 1957.
Reynolds, Clark G. *The Fast Carriers: The Forging of an Air Navy*. Rev. ed. Huntington, N.Y.: Robert Krieger, 1978.
Smith, Richard K. *First Across! The U.S. Navy's Transatlantic Flight of 1919*. Annapolis, Md.: Naval Institute Press, 1973.
Taylor, Theodore. *The Magnificent Mitscher*. New York: W. W. Norton, 1954.

CLARK G. REYNOLDS

MONTGOMERY, Richard (b. Swards near Feltrim, County of Dublin, Ireland, December 2, 1736; d. December 31, 1775, Quebec, Canada), Revolutionary War general, gentleman farmer, delegate to First New York Provincial Congress.

Richard Montgomery was the third son of four children of Thomas Montgomery, member of Parliament (MP) for Lyford, Ireland, and Mary Franklin. An older brother, Alexander, who served with General James Wolfe* against the French under the Marquis de Montcalm during the Great War for Empire, 1756–1763, and known as "Black Montgomery" is sometimes confused with Richard. Alexander went on to serve as MP for Dragheda, County of Donegal, for over forty years. A second brother was a merchant in Lisbon, and his sister married an impoverished nobleman, Viscount Ranleagh.

Following the advice of his brother, Richard sought a commission in the British Army after completing his education at Trinity and St. Andrew's College, Dublin, on September 21, 1756. He was appointed ensign in the 17th Foot Regiment and was immediately dispatched to North America where he participated in the siege of Louisbourg, Cape Breton, in 1757. His service against the French on Lake Champlain in 1759 gained him promotion to lieutenant and the position of regimental adjutant under William Haviland. They engaged in operations at Crown Point and Ticonderoga before joining General Jeffrey Amherst* at Montreal. Montgomery was then transferred to British operations in the Caribbean where he participated in the siege of Martinique and the capture of Havana. Securing a captaincy for his efforts, Montgomery was ordered to New York from which he returned to England in 1763. While in that colony, he met Janet Livingston, daughter of Robert R. Livingston, judge of the King's Bench, influential landholder, and head of one of the most powerful families in American history.

With war at an end, Montgomery found his prospects for further military advancement limited and possibilities for economic success nil. He suffered a desultory decade during which he acquainted himself with the contemporary liberal political views of Charles James Fox, Edmund Burke, and Isaac Barré. Unhappy that friends could or would not help him, he sold his commission in 1772 with the intention of migrating to America where he felt his "pride and poverty would be much more at ease." With limited funds, he purchased a sixty-seven acre farm at King's Bridge (Kingsbridge), now a part of New York City. He then wrote immediately to Judge Livingston on May 20, 1773, requesting permission to marry his daughter Janet who was thirty years old. A positive reply on June 21 took him to "Clermont," Livingston's country estate on the Hudson River, on July 24, where he was married. He settled on his wife's property in Barrytown near Rhinebeck-on-the-Hudson, later called "Montgomery Place."

He built a mill and laid the foundation for the main house and settled down to indulge himself in the life of gentleman farmer. Modest, attractive, and well loved by his new family, Montgomery found that his future was secure. But his preparations to build an estate to be called "Grassmere" were halted by the rapid estrangement of the colonies from British domination. The Livingstons became both philosophically and materially involved in the dispute, and Montgomery was a physical expression of that involvement. He was gratified by his appointment as a delegate to New York's First Provincial Congress in April 1775. However, though pleased by the news of Bunker Hill, he was not enthusiastic over his appointment on June 22 as the second of eight brigadier generals in the new colonial Army. The only non-native of New England, he was placed second-in-command to Major General Philip Schuyler.* He worried in letters over Schuyler's "nerves" and the general disarray of the colonial troops. "New Englanders . . . are the worst stuff for soldiers," he moaned; and "the first regts of Yorkers is the sweepings of the York streets." His sentiments were echoed by Gouverneur Morris who declared the officers to be "vulgar for the most part" and the soldiers to be "not the cream of the earth but the scum." The proud Montgomery declared that he would never again "hazard" his reputation "at the head of such ragamuffins."

By late summer 1775 General Montgomery's fortunes took a distinct turn as Schuyler's nerves gave out and he removed himself from command in favor of the young brigadier. Confronted with the large mission of taking St. John's, Montreal, and to "pursue any other measures in Canada to further the American cause," Schuyler had become morose and despondent and incapacitated. Montgomery soon learned of American successes at Ticonderoga and Crown Point, and his enthusiasm quickened. He declared that he "had courted fortune and found her kind." Writing to his wife from the field, he asked that she "write no more whining letters" as morale was most important and he wanted nothing to lower his spirits.

He turned his energies to making an army of his hungry, ragged band of less than five hundred. Exhibiting great personal courage, he exhorted his men to sacrifice. Limited supplies and much desertion did not prevent him from taking both St. John's and Montreal between September and mid-November 1775. During this campaign, using captured ammunition, he stripped the British 7th Fusiliers of their regimental colors, the first to be captured by an American force in the Revolutionary War. The British, under General Guy Carleton, withdrew to plan for the defense of Quebec after learning of the approach of another American army under Benedict Arnold's* command. General Arnold arrived at Quebec after a very difficult march from Maine, to find the fortress already reinforced by Carleton. He withdrew from the Plains of Abraham down the St. Lawrence River to await Montgomery's force which was already on the river making its way toward the objective. The two generals joined to lay plans for the conquest of Canada. Montgomery's army consisted of some three hundred men, while Arnold contributed around eight hundred tired troops to the contingent.

In England, meanwhile, Montgomery's activities in particular were cited by critics of the war's progress. In Parliament, Burke contrasted the situation of the British troops bottled up in Boston with the example of Montgomery's "insuperable perseverance and contempt of danger and death," while Lord North could only comment that though he was "brave, able, humane, and generous," he was still a rebel. "Curse on his virtues! They've undone this country," he replied. But agitation against the government continued with Charles James Fox's rejoinder that to be a rebel is no disgrace, that "the great asserters of liberty, the saviors of their country, the benefactors of mankind in all ages have been called rebels." Fox's statement fitted well with Montgomery's own declaration upon accepting his commission that "the will of an oppressed people compelled to choose between liberty and slavery must be respected."

Montgomery spent the better part of December planning for the assault on the Quebec fortress, while the British regulars of more than two thousand professionals waited patiently. Now a major general, Montgomery laid out his plan to Arnold for a two-pronged attack on the lower town in the hope that threats against business property would compel wealthy citizens to pressure Carleton to surrender. At 4:00 A.M. on December 31, the attack began in a blinding snowstorm. Montgomery had discounted the leadership of General Carleton, feeling that he would collapse under pressure. However, the heavier British artillery opened fire on Arnold's column, which almost gained entry to the fort despite the loss of Arnold with a shattered leg. Daniel Morgan's* force awaited reinforcement from Montgomery's column which had moved along the river and sawed their way through two timbered barricades and had come within sight of the enemy cannon when the alarm sounded. The indomitable Montgomery leaped forward with the cry: "Push on brave boys; Quebec is ours!" A withering hail of canister and grape met his charge. He went down immediately, shot through the head and dead where he fell.

Confusion swept the Americans. Young Aaron Burr took his group to the fore to continue the attack while Mongtomery's second-in-command Lieutenant Colonel Campbell, bringing up the rear, ordered a retreat. The shocked British also panicked, deserting their positions for the center of the town. But when they learned that the Americans had foundered, they immediately returned to their guns. As daylight came, the British had turned the Americans to retreat completely, capturing four hundred and retrieving the frozen corpse of the heroic Montgomery. One eyewitness account has it that Captain Burr had attempted to recover the body during the initial phase but had been beaten off by musket fire. General Carleton learned of Montgomery's identity from one of Arnold's officers. He ordered burial within the walls of Quebec with full military honors, which included government officials and military officers of the garrison in attendance.

The Continental Congress responded to the news of Montgomery's tragic death by passing a resolution ordering that a marble memorial be erected in St. Paul's Episcopal Church in New York City. Benjamin Franklin was authorized to purchase the monument in Paris. In 1818 the U.S. Congress passed an "Act of Honor" which was communicated to Great Britain to gain permission for the return of General Montgomery's body to New York. Permission was granted, and the remains were taken with great ceremony down the Hudson River, past the Livingston estates, and interred beneath the monument. An inscription was carved in the rocks of Cape Diamond fronting Quebec to note the time and place of his death.

General Montgomery died without issue, leaving his widow who lived alone with the memory of "her soldier" as she called him, for fifty-three years. She died in 1828. In his will made at Crown Point on August 30, 1775, Montgomery had requested simply that his debts be paid and that his sister, Lady Ranleagh, receive his Kingsbridge property and all personal fortune in that her large family "want all I can spare" and that since his wife would succeed to an ample fortune, it was unnecessary for him to provide for her. He suggested also that his wife might perhaps take one of his sister's children to live with her. His widow remained close to the Ranleaghs until her death.

BIBLIOGRAPHY

Armstrong, John. "Life of Richard Montgomery." In *American Biography*. Edited by Jared Sparks. New York, 1902.
Dangerfield, George. *Chancellor Robert R. Livingston of New York, 1746–1813*. New York: 1960.
Hunt, Louise Livingston. "General Richard Montgomery." *Harper's New Monthly Magazine* (February 1885).
Smith, Justin H. *Our Struggle for the Fourteenth Colony: Canada and the American Revolution*. New York: Putnam's 1907.

JACK J. CARDOSO

MOORE, James (b. Ireland (?), date unknown; d. Charleston, S.C., 1706), governor of South Carolina (1700–1703). Moore traded with and enslaved Indians; he fought the Spanish and Spanish Indians and extended English power on the Southern frontier.

Little is known about Moore's origins. Apparently, he was born in Ireland and emigrated to Barbados whence, in the mid-1670s, he came to South Carolina where he married Margaret Yeamans, the stepdaughter of Sir John Yeamans, a former governor. Ambitious, avaricious, and none too scrupulous, Moore managed his wife's plantation, obtained grants for sixty-six hundred acres by 1694, and energetically provided for a large family. He farmed; he explored far into the backcountry searching for precious metals. His enemies, and he had many, said he traded with pirates, but his major interest was the Indian trade. In exchange for guns, ammunition, kettles, cloth, and the like, friendly Indians sold Moore and other traders furs, deer skins, and, what was most prized, men and women captured from rival tribes. The furs and skins were shipped to Europe; the humans were usually sent to the West Indies. Moore helped establish a pattern of Indian relations that survived long after his death: the Carolinians traded with a nearby tribe, encouraged it to capture slaves from other tribes, and used it as a buffer against the Spanish in Florida and the French on the lower Mississippi. With first the Westoes and then, in turn, the Yamassee, the Lower Creeks, and the Cherokee, the Carolinians formed symbiotic relationships that lasted until the whites and the client Indians disagreed over land, trade goods, and mutual obligations. In 1680 the provincial government commissioned Moore and another trader to avert war with the hitherto friendly Westoes. Moore's desire for peace is suspect because after the negotiations failed and war began, traders prospered by enslaving the defeated Westoes. In 1690 Moore initiated trade with the Cherokee who, after his death, became one of the tribes who served the Carolinians as trading partners and guardians of the frontier. Of South Carolina's Indian wars, Moore was involved in only the Westo War of 1680 and the Apalachee Campaign of 1704, but although the Yamassee War of 1715 and the Cherokee War of 1761 came after his lifetime, he must be regarded as a founder of the system that caused those wars.

Moore's economic interests required that he be politically active. He and Maurice Matthews were leaders of the "Goose Creek men," a group of former Barbadians, Anglican in religion, who settled in Berkeley County near the tributary of the Cooper River. In the 1680s and early 1690s the "Goose Creek men" opposed the Lord Proprietors' efforts to increase quit rents and control the Indian trade. Moore played such a vociferous role in tumults during the governorship of James Colleton (1686–1690) that later, when political tensions eased, Moore and his friend Robert Daniel were the only ones excluded from the Lord Proprietors' general pardon of rioters. However, Moore was eventually forgiven. Through the 1690s most Dissenters sided with the Proprietors against the Anglican "Goose Creek men," but a realignment occurred after 1700 when the Proprietors and the Anglicans leagued together against the Dissenters. In 1700, upon the death of Governor Joseph Blake, Moore, a member of the council, replaced him and served until 1703. Friends of Landgrave Joseph Morton, a Dissenter, thought he should have become governor; they resented the way in which Moore had secured the post and remained hostile throughout his administration.

Governor Moore was preoccupied with the danger that the Spanish in Florida would unite with the French recently established on the Gulf Coast and that the two Bourbon powers would monopolize the Indian trade. Moore, who was well acquainted with the practices of Indian traders, sought, but did not get, legislation to prevent traders from abusing friendly Indians and driving them into the receptive arms of the Bourbons. Upon the outbreak of Queen Anne's War in 1702, Moore persuaded the Commons House of Assembly to support an expedition against St. Augustine. Its capture would mean English control of the "debatable land." Although the expedition was Moore's idea, he accepted command of it only after the legislature insisted. Underwritten by a £2,000 appropriation, Moore recruited six hundred whites, some Indians, impressed more than a dozen ships, and sailed south in October 1702. Spanish missions between Amelia Island and the St. Johns River were easily overrun by the English. Half the attacking force, under Colonel Robert Daniel, was landed at the mouth of the St. Johns and marched overland from there to St. Augustine, while Moore and the others sailed along the coast. By November 10 Daniel's and Moore's contingents were reunited and in possession of the town of St. Augustine but not its fort. Governor Jose de Zúñiga y Cerda had gathered all the whites, blacks, and mission Indians, men, women, and children, a total of about fifteen hundred "eaters," inside Castillo de San Marcos. There the governor resolved to endure a siege while awaiting relief summoned from Havana. The high, thick stone walls of the fort withstood the few small cannon Moore had brought, and the besiegers were too few to prevent foragers from leaving the fort to collect hay for the garrison's cattle. Belatedly realizing that mortars were needed to lob shells over the walls, Moore sent Colonel Daniel to Jamaica for the essential weapons. On December 26, before Daniel could return, four small warships arrived off St. Augustine. To the delight of the defenders and the despair of Moore, they were Spanish and carried troops. Unwilling to risk a battle, Moore retreated on December 29, 1702. By destroying Spanish missions between Carolina and St. Augustine, Moore had pushed the Spanish frontier to the St. Johns River, but many Carolinians, especially Dissenters, reproached him for too hasty a retreat from the Spanish relief force. Moore was accused of keeping for himself and his favorites plunder that should have been shared with everyone. Only two whites and a few Indians died on the expedition, but the venture left a debt of £6,000. South Carolina was obliged to make its first issue of paper money, and Charlestonians acquired a distaste for Floridian adventures that James Edward Oglethorpe* found to be still lingering in 1740.

In the spring of 1703 Moore was replaced as governor, but he remained politically influential. To redeem his military reputation, to capture slaves, and to weaken Spanish influence among the Indians, in early 1704 Moore at his own expense led fifty whites and one thousand Lower Creeks on a raid against the Apalachee, a tribe living under Spanish tutelage between the present Georgia border and Apalache Bay. On January 14, 1704, the Apalachee at the Ayubale mission succumbed to Moore after a nine-hour battle. The next day Moore defeated thirty Spanish and four hundred Indians who had come too late to save Ayubale. After those two battles, Moore met little resistance in conquering the entire Apalache region. Many Apalachee were killed in battle; a few Indians and some Spanish were tortured to death by the Creeks; perhaps six hundred Apalachee were sold into slavery; and thirteen hundred were forced to move to the Savannah River where they were positioned between the Creeks and the Carolinians and safely separated from the Spanish. Where Moore had raided, Spanish power was totally broken for over a decade, but it did revive after the Yamassee War of 1715.

Moore died in Charles Town in 1706 from yellow fever.

In his career Moore exhibited the military skill, political guile, and shrewd trading that were to establish English mastery over the Indians and ascendancy over European rivals along the Atlantic seaboard. Yet, his failure to bring proper siege artillery to St. Augustine indicates that his talent for military planning was defective. Whether his retreat from St. Augustine without fighting was justifiable must remain an open question. His overwhelming success against the Apalachee in 1704, a campaign that had greater consequences than the St. Augustine Expedition with which his name is most often associated, was only possible because he had Indian allies. While acknowledging Moore's skillful Indian diplomacy, it must be remembered that the prime reason he and other Carolinians were more successful than the Spanish in obtaining Indian allies was because English trade goods were better and cheaper than Spanish or French goods.

BIBLIOGRAPHY

Arnade, Charles W. *The Siege of St. Augustine in 1702*. University of Florida Monographs: Social Sciences No. 3. Gainesville: University of Florida Press, 1959.
Crane, Verner W. *The Southern Frontier*. Ann Arbor: University of Michigan Press, 1929.
McCrady, Edward. *The History of South Carolina Under the Proprietary Government*. New York: Russell and Russell, 1969. (Reprint of 1897 edition.)
Sirmans, M. Eugene. *Colonial South Carolina: A Political History, 1663–1763*. Chapel Hill: University of North Carolina Press, 1966.
Wallace, David D. *The History of South Carolina*. Vol. 1. New York: American Historical Company, 1934.

JOSEPH A. DEVINE, JR.

MORDECAI, Alfred (b. Warrenton, N.C., January 3, 1804; d. Philadelphia, Pa., October 23, 1887), Army ordnance officer, engineer. Mordecai is best known for his contributions to the development and organization of pre-Civil War weapons systems.

Alfred Mordecai was the son of a merchant and educator, and received his early schooling at home and at the local academy founded and directed by his father. Appointed to the U.S. Military Academy he graduated first in his class in 1823 and was commissioned a second lieutenant of engineers. He served in this capacity for nine years, as an instructor at the Military Academy, as assistant enginer in the building of Fortress Monroe and Fort Calhoun at Hampton Roads, and as assistant to the chief of engineers. In 1832, as a result of an Army reorganization, Mordecai was appointed a captain of ordnance, many years before the time he would have attained that rank as an engineer.

During the more than a quarter of a century that he served in the Ordnance Department, Mordecai held many important positions, including command of the Frankford, Pennsylvania, Washington, D.C., and Watervliet, New York, arsenals. He took part in valuable missions abroad, authored a number of important technical works, and, in a period when promotions were painfully slow, rose to the rank of major. He carried out extensive research on weapons and ammunition, primarily at the Washington Arsenal, which he commanded for more than a decade and where, during the Mexican War, he was responsible for vital shipments of ordnance supplies. He was assistant to the secretary of war and to the chief of ordnance, as well as assistant inspector of arsenals. He published a handy and useful digest of American military laws, served on the West Point Board of Visitors, helped revise the Army regulations, and went to Mexico to investigate a large and, as it turned out, fraudulent war claim.

His most important work was as a key member of the Ordnance Board, on which he served from its establishment in 1839 until the eve of the Civil War. Created originally to standardize and systematize Army ordnance equipment, the board quickly developed a much broader role in the approval and development of all new Army weapons, ammunition, and related equipment. Through its close direction of testing, evaluation, and design, it became probably the most important single factor in the growth of American military research and development during this period.

Mordecai and his fellow members formulated the first complete system of artillery for the American Army. He himself played a vital part in collecting, analyzing, and organizing the great body of data studied by the board, including the responsibility for coordinating and writing the final report and drawing the plates for it. This report was published over his name in 1849 as *Artillery for the United States Land Service*. He also did most of the work on the first *Ordnance Manual* ever published by the American Army (1841), was solely responsible for its second edition (1850), and contributed to several editions of the published ordnance regulations.

In 1840 Secretary of War Joel R. Poinsett dispatched Mordecai and three others to Europe to study and report on the development and manufacture of weapons. Their observations—constituting probably the most important American military mission to Europe since the Revolution—were a valuable contribution to the work of the Ordnance Board in organizing and standardizing Army artillery. Fifteen years later Mordecai was again in Europe, this time sent with two fellow officers by Secretary of War Jefferson Davis* to observe the Crimean

War and study European military developments in general. The reports of the group—all published and widely read—and the material brought back from Europe were significant additions to American understanding of the tools and techniques of warfare. Mordecai's observations dealt largely with organization and weapons, and were primarily responsible for the Army's subsequent adaptation of the "Napoleon," the bronze smoothbore gun-howitzer (U.S. Model 1857) that became the most widely used and effective field artillery piece on both sides in the Civil War.

Complementing Mordecai's work on the Ordnance Board were his many years of research and experimentation with ballistics and gunpowder. He published his most important findings in an 1845 *Report on Experiments on Gunpowder*, with a second volume four years later. These works proved particularly valuable to the Ordnance Department, were distributed throughout the Army and to private powder manufacturers, scientific societies, and schools, were studied at West Point, and were translated into French and German. Well received in Europe, they became the basis of Mordecai's reputation abroad.

The outbreak of the Civil War in 1861 brought Mordecai face to face with a dilemma. Torn by conflicting ties to North and South, his loyalty to the Union balanced by his unwillingness to take arms against his family, subject to pressures from both sides, he deplored the coming war and finally made the only decision that conscience and logic would permit. In May 1861 he resigned his commission, determined to maintain a strict neutrality throughout the war. To this end, he declined an offer from Confederate President Jefferson Davis to head the South's Ordnance Department, as well as several others from individual Southern states. By the same token, he refused to accept any position that seemed to contribute to the Northern war effort. He spent the war years teaching mathematics in Philadelphia, the birthplace of his wife, even as his oldest son and namesake graduated from West Point and began a long and distinguished Army career. In 1865 Mordecai became assistant engineer on the Mexican Imperial Railway, but the collapse of Maximillian's government forced him to return to Philadelphia the following year. From then until his death he was treasurer and secretary of the Pennsylvania Canal Company, which ran the canals and coal companies of the Pennsylvania Railroad.

Mordecai's military career spanned a remarkable period in the growth of American military technology. The years between his admission to West Point and his resignation from the Army saw the introduction to the military art of new and careful methods of research and development. These provided more exact procedures for testing and experimentation, made sciences of metallurgy and ballistics, revolutionized production methods, and brought greater efficiency, uniformity, and durablility to the tools of war than had ever before been possible. Mordecai was an important part of this, although he shares with many others like him a relative anonymity when compared with those who won their fame on the battlefields.

His role was characterized by the application of a precise, disciplined methodology to the development and standardization of new or improved weapons, ammunition, and equipment. "My ability," he wrote at the close of his military career, "consists in a knowledge and love of order and system, and in the habit of patient labor in perfecting and arranging details; and my usefulness in the Army arises from the long continued application of these qualities to the specialties of my habitual business."

Within this framework, Mordecai made his contribution in many specific areas: in the systematization of American artillery and small arms, in endless experiments and tests of weapons and ammunition, in the adaptation of European advances to American military technology, in increasing the Army's knowledge of ballistics and metallurgy, and in countless other invaluable ways. These contributions, as one of his younger contemporaries wrote later, "came, not in the shape of a few large nuggets, but in a steady stream of gold dust sustained for many years and far outweighing the nuggets in the end." His work was valued for its accuracy, its precise and systematic nature, and its immediate applicability.

BIBLIOGRAPHY

Falk, Stanley L. "Soldier-Technologist: Major Alfred Mordecai and the Beginnings of Science in the United States Army." Ph.D. dissertation, Georgetown University, 1959.

Mordecai, Alfred. *Artillery for the United States Land Service, as Devised and Arranged by the Ordnance Board*. Washington, D.C.: J. and G. S. Gideon, 1849.

———. *A Digest of the Laws Relating to the Military Establishment of the United States*. Washington, D.C.: Thompson and Homans, 1833.

———. *Report of Experiments on Gunpowder, Made at Washington Arsenal, in 1843 and 1844*. Washington, D.C.: J. and G. S. Gideon, 1845.

———. *Second Report of Experiments on Gunpowder, Made at Washington Arsenal, in 1845, '47, and '48*. Washington, D.C.: J. and G. S. Gideon, 1849.

Padgett, James A. ed. "The Life of Alfred Mordecai as Related by Himself." *North Carolina Historical Review* 22, No. 1 (January 1945).

U.S. Congress, Senate. *Military Commission to Europe in 1855 and 1856: Report of Major Alfred Mordecai*. 36th Cong., 1st Sess., Ex. Doc. No. 60. Washington, D.C.: George W. Bowman, 1860.

STANLEY L. FALK

MORGAN, Daniel (b. probably in New Jersey, likely 1735; d. Winchester, Va., July 6, 1802), general in the War of American Independence.

Daniel Morgan, who always avoided any discussion of his early life, was a product of the Virginia frontier where he settled in 1753. A teamster with the Braddock Expedition in 1755, later, in the French and Indian War, he served in the Virginia rangers and suffered a wound in a now-unknown skirmish. As a militia officer, he also fought Indians in Lord Dunmore's War in 1774.

In 1775, the forty-year-old Morgan, a veteran frontier fighter, raised one of the companies of backwoods riflemen called for by the Continental Congress. After joining George Washington's* American Army at Cambridge, Massachusetts, Morgan and his company were included in Benedict Arnold's* expedition against British Canada. After an arduous march through the Maine wilderness, Arnold was wounded in the American attack on the city of Quebec, and Morgan took command, but eventually he and his men were captured.

Released from captivity the following year, Morgan received a promotion to colonel and gained from Washington a special corps of light infantry composed of picked Continentals from the western counties of Pennsylvania, Maryland, and Virginia. They were officially known as the Rangers but were more commonly called Morgan's Riflemen, a unit that put together a splendid combat record during its brief existence.

Morgan's rifle regiment played a crucial role in the campaign of 1777, especially after it was detached from Washington's immediate command in New Jersey and sent to upstate New York, where General Horatio Gates'* American Northern army was feebly contesting the southward advance from Canada of British General John Burgoyne. Morgan's frontiersman, dressed in hunting garb and skilled in Indian tactics, so terrorized Burgoyne's redskinned allies that they refused to continue their scouting activities. In the two major battles of the Saratoga Campaign, September 19 and October 7, 1777, Morgan's men pushed forward from Gates' entrenchments and began the action. They helped to throw the British off stride, and they took a heavy toll of the enemy, just as they subsequently led the American advance after the retreating Burgoyne, who later acknowledged the large part Morgan had played in his defeat and surrender.

A strong admirer of Washington, Morgan in the winter of 1777–1778 at Valley Forge spoke out angrily against the critics of the commander in chief, though it is doubtful whether Morgan and like-minded officers were correct in their view that a plot existed to remove Washington in the so-called Conway Cabal. By 1780, however, Morgan's relationship with Washington was strained. Most of Morgan's best rifle companies had been detached for Indian fighting, and afterward his regiment was disbanded. Disappointed because a new, large light infantry unit had been assigned to Anthony Wayne,* and because his promotion to brigadier general was not forthcoming, Morgan took his case to Congress. Although the lawmakers agreed that Morgan had been "Neglected," they felt that nothing could be done for him at the time. Contrary to what some historians have written, Morgan did not resign, accepting instead an "honorable furlough" until a promising assignment opened.

Ever loyal to the cause but nonetheless deeply disturbed, Morgan returned to his home near Winchester, Virginia, where he remained until the summer of 1780. Then he responded to a call from his Virginia neighbor and former commander, Horatio Gates,* now in charge of the American Southern army. Though in ill-health, he joined Gates in North Carolina, soon after Gates' defeat at Camden.

Morgan, now belatedly promoted to brigadier general, assisted Gates in reorganizing the Southern forces, but Gates was soon replaced by General Nathanael Greene,* who recognized that Morgan's talents lay in guerrilla warfare. Moreover, Greene lacked the resources to contest openly with his adversary, British General Cornwallis. Consequently, Greene divided his small command at Charlotte, North Carolina, sending Morgan into western South Carolina while Greene himself moved in a southeasterly direction. Morgan's success at arousing the country people prompted Cornwallis to send Banastre Tarleton's Tory Legion against the veteran frontiersman.

Morgan, falling back toward the border of the Carolinas, made a stand against Tarleton at the Cowpens on January 17, 1781. The location was an open slope with no protection for his flanks, and most of Morgan's men were militia, unaccustomed to formal combat. Even so, Morgan knew his troops, and he was a superb psychologist. Morgan's militia, placed in a long row in front of his regulars, were skilled marksmen who picked off many of Tarleton's men before filing off behind the regulars, according to Morgan's plan. Then, during the heavy exchange between Morgan's regulars and the Legion, Morgan hit the British flanks with his cavalry and reformed militia. The result was a double envelopment of the enemy, who immediately panicked and collapsed. Cowpens was the tactical masterpiece of the war. As Morgan said, he had "entirely Broke up Tarleton's Legion," the "flower" of Cornwallis' army.

After Morgan retreated into North Carolina and reunited with Greene, the American generals, with Cornwallis in close pursuit, retreated into Virginia. His health impaired by the arduous campaign, Morgan returned home and saw only limited service during the remainder of the war.

A farmer and grist mill operator in the postwar years, Morgan in the 1790s returned to public life. He commanded the militia forces that garrisoned Pittsburgh following the collapse of the Whiskey Rebellion in 1794, and he served one term as a Federalist member of the U.S House of Representatives. Convinced that the Jeffersonians were subverting the Constitution, "the envy and wonder of the surrounding world," the stormy old soldier once threatened to call out his Virginia militiamen against the Republicans, whom he denounced as egg-sucking chickens. Advancing age and crippling arthritis confined him to home during his final years.

Although Morgan was not a professional soldier in the modern sense, his life was bound up with things military, from his service in the colonial wars, through the War of Independence, and concluding with a lengthy, postwar career as a major general of Virginia militia, which included a campaign against the Whiskey Rebels. Moreover, though ill-educated, Morgan thought of himself as a military expert, as the Continental Army's leading authority on guerrilla or partisan tactics. His accumulative success with irregular tactics exceeded that of any other American leader, although Wayne, Andrew Pickens,* Thomas Sumter, and Francis Marion* also scored achievements with mobile, detached forces.

A splendid leader of men, Morgan—"the old wagoner"—was a warm, colorful leader who cared about his soldiers, and they in return responded to him, as, for example, when he persuaded untried militia to stand and fight at Cowpens. A contemporary correctly wrote of Morgan that no other officer "knew better how to gain the love and esteem of his men." His troops were mainly from frontier regions, where the rifle—with its great range and accuracy—was the preeminent weapon in hunting and Indian-fighting. Morgan, to be sure, would have been out of his element as a military administrator or as the commander of a division or an entire army. Fortunately for him, he was never assigned a post that exceeded his training or talents as were Israel Putnam,* Benjamin Lincoln,* and any number of other American Revolutionary generals.

Finally, Morgan's advance through the ranks, from humble beginnings to general officer, was unique by the standards of the eighteenth century when, especially in Europe, men of gentle birth and fortune dominated the officer corps. The American Revolution produced a democratic spirit in the land. Morgan, the outstanding combat officer in the Continental Army, symbolized that new day in America.

BIBLIOGRAPHY

Bass, Robert D. *The Green Dragoon: The Lives of Banastre Tarleton and Mary Robinson.* New York: Holt, 1957.
Callahan, North. *Daniel Morgan, Ranger of the Revolution.* New York: Holt, Rinehart and Winston, 1961.
Graham, James. *Life of General Daniel Morgan.* Cincinnati: Derby and Jackson, 1856.
Hart, Freeman H. *The Valley of Virginia in the American Revolution.* Chapel Hill: University of North Carolina Press, 1942.
Higginbotham, Don. *Daniel Morgan: Revolutionary Rifleman.* Chapel Hill: University of North Carolina Press, 1961.

R. DON HIGGINBOTHAM

MORISON, Samuel Eliot (b. Boston, Mass., July 9, 1887; d. Boston, Mass., May 15, 1976), historian. The leading historian of the American Navy, Morison wrote the 15-volume *History of U.S. Naval Operations in World War II.*

Reared in the comfortable environs of Boston, as were many generations of Eliots and Morisons before him, Samuel Eliot Morison enjoyed a traditional Brahmin upbringing. Educated in the classics at St. Paul's School in Concord, New Hampshire, Morison naturally matriculated at Harvard, enrolling with the class of 1908. As an undergraduate he took courses under a quartet of America's most distinguished historians, Frederick Jackson Turner, Albert Bushnell Hart, Edward Channing, and Charles Homer Haskins. After traveling in Europe and studying in France for a year, Morison returned to Harvard for graduate work in history, earning the Ph.D. in 1913. Following a sojourn in Europe and a brief stint at the University of California, Berkeley, Professor Morison reestablished himself at Harvard in 1915, eventually inheriting Channing's office in the Widener Library. Morison taught at Harvard for forty years and wrote *The Tercentennial History of Harvard University* (5 vols., 1929–1936).

Morison took as his exemplars Francis Parkman (1823–1893) and Thucydides (460–400 B.C.). Parkman visited many sites associated with the history in his books, which resounded with the clash of armies and empires. Parkman graphically related the stories of individual leaders—the death of General James Wolfe* on the Plains of Abraham, for instance. The classic *History of the Peloponnesian War* benefited from the fact that Thucydides had been present at many of the ancient battles he described. Morison often stressed that the heart of history was a well-written story of heroic men exploring new worlds, building colonies, establishing institutions, or fighting wars. Making no apologies for taking an avowedly traditional approach, he wrote narrative history for people to read, not sociological treatises or "scientific" analyses. Like Parkman, Morison depended heavily on diaries, letters, and other primary sources, and used thorough research to bring the hopes and fears, pain and pride, defeats and victories of the people of the past to modern readers. In his books Morison referred off-handedly to the works of poets, Shakespeare, and classical historians, assuming that his readers were familiar with such references.

Morison's writings and teachings were interrupted temporarily by the Great War. He served briefly as a private in the U.S. Army and remained in France after the Armistice as a research consultant to the American delegations at Versailles.

From 1913 on Morison produced a steady stream of books. In 1921 his *Maritime History of Massachusetts, 1783–1860* was published. Subsequently he wrote the books on Harvard and works on the Puritans and Massachusetts Bay Colony. One of Morison's major books dealing with maritime history, *Admiral of the Ocean Sea* (2 vols., 1942), a biography of Christopher Columbus, won the Pulitzer Prize for biography. The Columbus biography earned Morison an immediate favorable reputation with American naval officers and President Franklin D. Roosevelt.

After the Japanese attack on Pearl Harbor (December 7, 1941), arrangements were made by the U.S. Army for many historians to participate in chronicling the Army's battles and administration during World War II. Taking a different tack, Morison suggested to the president that he be authorized to write the complete story of the American Navy in the war. FDR agreed.

Given a small staff of research assistants, Morison set out to be a twentieth-century Thucydides. Holding the rank of lieutenant commander, U.S. Naval Reserve, he sailed on a dozen ships of war or lesser vessels—PT boats, destroyers, cruisers, battleships, and aircraft carriers. Morison observed battles, interviewed officers, sailors, and pilots, crisscrossing the Atlantic and the Pacific. The eventual result was the mammoth 15-volume *History of United States Naval Operations in World War II* (1947–1962). The series represented a sustained twenty-year effort that could have exhausted a committee of historians, no matter what their ages. Morison finished the last volume at age 75. While he had assistance over the years from many military officers and researchers, it was to a great extent the monumental achievement of one man—it was "Sam Morison's History."

In 1951, Morison retired from the Navy at the rank of rear admiral; and four years later he retired from the Harvard faculty, but he by no means retired from writing history. Remaining aloof from historical trends, he never veered to the "New Left," he rejected "psycho-history," and he was not captivated by quantification. He completed or revised many books during his "retirement," including *John Paul Jones: A Sailor's Biography* (1959), for which Morison won his second Pulitzer Prize; *The Two Ocean War: A Short History of the United States Navy in the Second World War* (1963); and *"Old Bruin": Commodore Matthew C. Perry, 1794–1858* (1967).

Morison was sole author of forty books and contributed essays or chapters to many collected works. A world traveler who relished reconnoitering locations that Columbus or Jones or Perry had visited, Morison used small airplanes and sailing craft to retrace the courses of explorers for his *European Discovery of America* (2 vols., 1971–1974). For most of his lifetime he called home the house in which he had been born—his grandfather Samuel Eliot's house at 44 Brimmer Street, Boston. Morison died in Boston on May 15, 1976.

Bernard Bailyn called Samuel Eliot Morison "the greatest American narrative historian since Francis Parkman." Morison's *History of U.S. Naval Operations in World War II* is Parkman-like in its sweep and scope. Sailors and navies of mighty nations clash with empires at stake. Morison definitely had his heroes—American Admiral Raymond Spruance,* best of the tactical commanders, in Morison's opinion, for his direction of the Battle of Midway, turning point in the Pacific war; and desk admirals such as Chester Nimitz* and Ernest King,* officers who had to implement strategy with the resources at hand. But Morison portrayed the antagonists fairly: German Admiral Karl Doenitz and Japanese Admiral Isoroku Yamamoto both have prominent places in the narrative.

Morison's *Naval Operations* differs remarkably from the multivolume projects of the Army (*U.S. Army in World War II*, 79 vols., 1946–19—), Air Force (*Army Air Force in World War II*, 7 vols., 1948–1954), and Marines (*History of U.S. Marine Corps Operations in World War II*, 5 vols., 1958–1971). The other services committed the efforts of large teams of researchers and historians. But none of those series has attained the widespread popular readership of "Sam Morison's History."

Morison relied on contacts within the Navy to get assigned to ships bound for action. He stood on the bridge of the cruiser *Brooklyn* at the North African landings in 1942; observed the ferocious night battles off Savo Island; sped along the coast of New Guinea's Papua peninsula in a PT boat; trod the French beaches shortly after D-Day; campaigned through the Gilberts, Marshalls, and Marianas; watched the battles off Samar and in Leyte Gulf; and cringed as *kamikases* crashed into ships near Okinawa. After a battle, Morison immediately wrote a rough draft of a chapter. For battles he did not see, he used interviews, read reports, and, after the war, filled out his narrative by consulting captured enemy documents. He later said that "the great value of being on a ship is getting the atmosphere of the battle, and personal interviews with the men. . . . " Morison shared the approach of interviewing participants after a battle with the Army's S. L. A. Marshall.* Although Marshall developed a more thorough interviewing technique than did Morison, the two historians discussed strategy, tactics, and historical research at various times during and after the war.

Morison conceived *Naval Operations* as basically a tactical story. Taking such an approach made strategic analysis a secondary matter, a point that several historians criticized. For instance, Robert Love contended that Morison "often errs when he moves from a discussion of particular actions to an analysis of their strategic rationale." Morison's brief foray into assessing high-level planning—*Strategy and Compromise* (1958)—did nothing to offset this shortcoming in the 15-volume series. Hanson W. Baldwin, military editor of the *New York Times*, graduate of the Naval Academy (Class of 1924), and perhaps Morsion's closest critic, hit the admiral hard for sacrificing explanations of strategy in favor of dramatic stories. Morison was "at his best," Baldwin found, "where he has been able to concentrate upon a well-defined, clearly articulated battle like Leyte Gulf." Moreover, Baldwin asserted that Morison "sometimes indulges in sweeping generalizations impossible to prove or disprove," and that his "Olympian prose" was wearing on the reader. As volume after volume of the *Operations* was published, the battles seemed to become repetititous. Morison countered that criticism (in volume five, *The Struggle for Guadalcanal*), writing that "if this tale has seemed repetitious with shock and gore, exploding magazines, burning and sinking ships, and plummeting planes—that is simply how it was." Morison was present at many of the war's important battles. Like Thucydides, using an aside or comment, Morison sometimes reminded readers that what he wrote was indeed based on personal observation. For example, in volume five Morison wrote, "For those of us who were there, Guadalcanal is not a name but an emotion." Such asides rankled some critics, who thought that they indicated a lack of objectivity. Academic critics were often complimentary, but fell on two sides, some citing Morison's "earnest striving for objectivity" and others viewing him as functioning "in every essential respect [as] . . . an official historian." But most of the comments were favorable: historians cited the volumes' "careful scholarship," "salty narrative," "vivid and human" stories, and their "general thoroughness, accuracy, and drama." Hanson Baldwin ultimately concluded that the series was "an indispensable description of the greatest Navy's battles in the greatest war in history."

Biographies of Christopher Columbus, John Paul Jones, and Matthew Perry and the fifteen-volume set on World War II built Morison's reputation as an expert on naval matters. He possessed voluminous knowledge and wrote award-winning books on naval history, including subjects from the 1490s to the 1940s.

No other American naval scholar could write or speak with such authority. Samuel Eliot Morison was the foremost American naval historian of the twentieth century.

BIBLIOGRAPHY

Bailyn, Bernard. "Morison: An Appreciation," *Proceedings of the Massachusetts Historical Society*, 89 (1977), 112–23.

Baldwin, Hanson W. "Sam Morison and the Navy," *Atlantic*, 186 (August 1950), 73–76.

————. "From Iwo Jima to Hiroshima," *New York Times Book Review* (November 6, 1960), 3.

Bargar, B. D. "Samuel Eliot Morison," in *Dictionary of Literary Biography*, volume 17, *Twentieth Century American Historians*. Detroit: Gale Research Company, 1983, 296–314.

Herold, David. "Samuel Eliot Morison, 1887–1976," in *American Writers: A Collection of Literary Biographies: 1979 Supplement*. New York: Scribners, 1979, 479–500.

Love, Robert W., Jr. "Fighting a Global War, 1941–1945," in Kenneth J. Hagan, ed., *In Peace and War: Interpretations of American Naval History, 1775–1978*. Westport: Greenwood Press, 1978, 263–89.

JOSEPH G. DAWSON, III

MURPHY, Audie (b. Hunt County, Tex., June 20, 1924; d. near Roanoke, Va., May 28, 1971), war hero, actor, author.

The baby-faced farmboy who was to become the most decorated American soldier of World War II was born the son of a sharecropper in northeastern Texas in 1924. Murphy's father "was not lazy, but he had a genius for not considering the future," and at the height of the Great Depression, he abandoned the family that then numbered nine children. Audie was a small boy, and this in combination with his poverty made him the butt of jokes at school. He was called "short-breeches" because his only pair of overalls shrank noticeably from repeated washings. He grew up combative, happiest when alone, and a dreamer. One adult seems to have made a good impression on him: a veteran of World War I with whom he worked in the cotton fields. Brought up on the veteran's tales of adventure, Murphy decided above all that he wanted to be a soldier.

Murphy's mother died when he was sixteen. His brothers and sisters were distributed among relatives or sent to an orphanage. War had just been declared, and Murphy set off to enlist in the Marines. Rejected by the Corps because of his size, he next tried the paratroops but failed again and finally settled, reluctantly, on the infantry. "The infantry was too commonplace for my ambition," he wrote later, but in the end it served his ambition well enough—he would never have to go back to the cotton fields.

After the usual training, where he acquired a new nickname—"baby"—he was assigned to the 15th Regiment, 3d Infantry Division, which was then in North Africa preparing for the invasion of Sicily. It was in Sicily in mid-1943 that Murphy first saw combat, a trade at which he became exceedingly adept. He was a proficient rifleman and came to understand the techniques of small-unit action, but he also developed the infantryman's fatalism so common to the line. He was not fearless and was both amazed and critical of comrades who were. Still, his feats in action set him apart from his fellow soldiers and marked him as a resolute and savage combatant. Always with Company B of the 15th Infantry Regiment, Murphy landed at Salerno, fought in the Volturno River Campaign, landed again at Anzio, and was part of the Allied force that fought its way to Rome. In the meantime, Murphy had advanced in rank by virtue of his skills and the attrition of his superiors during the hard campaigning. He had also won the first of his many decorations for gallantry. Following the capture of Rome, Murphy's unit was withdrawn to train for the Allied landings in southern France near Toulon and Marseilles, Operation ANVIL-DRAGOON.

At first, the campaign in southern France seemed hardly as bitter as the fighting he had witnessed in Italy, but as General Alexander McCarrell Patch's* Seventh Army began pressing through the Vosges Mountains on its way to the West Wall of Germany, enemy resistance became more resolute. During seven weeks of campaigning, Murphy's 3d Infantry Division alone lost forty-five hundred casualties. By now Murphy was one of the senior men in his old company as well as one of the most decorated, and during the early battles to reduce the Colmar Pocket he was given a battlefield commission. On January 26, 1945, just outside the village of Holtzwihr near Strasbourg, the Germans launched a local attack against Lieutenant Murphy's forward positions with six Panzers and 250 infantrymen. Ordering his own men to fall back to better defenses, Murphy remained behind on an abandoned tank destroyer to contest the enemy's advance. Using the tank destroyer's machine gun against the enemy's infantry, Murphy eventually killed enough (estimates run to about fifty) to break up the momentum of the German attack. Wounded in the leg during the melee, Murphy recalled his company and led them in a counterattack against the remaining Germans. For this accomplishment, Murphy was awarded the Congressional Medal of Honor, the United States' highest award for gallantry in action against the enemy.

By war's end, Audie Murphy was the nation's most decorated soldier, having won a staggering twenty-eight medals (by some counts, twenty-one), including one Belgian and three French decorations. He had spent an inordinate amount of time on the combat lines. He had just turned twenty-one, and his comrades still called him "baby."

After the war, Murphy was rightly celebrated by the country that thus far had given him little but youthful poverty and the horrors of the battlefield. After making the cover of *Life* magazine, Murphy was persuaded by James Cagney to attempt a career in motion pictures. Of his first effort, a bit part in *Beyond Glory* (1948), a courtroom drama set at West Point, Murphy said, "I had eight words in the script, seven more than I could handle." He also began work on his memoirs of the war, which he called *To Hell and Back* and had published to good reviews in 1949.

As time went by, Murphy worked steadily at his new trade. He always joked about his abilities before the cameras. When a director once admonished him for a mistake during a production, Murphy replied that the director had to remember he was working under a handicap. When the director asked what it was, Murphy answered, "no talent." Eventually, Murphy made some forty motion pictures, most of them B–grade Westerns in which he generally lived up to his own appraisal of his abilities. There were three notable exceptions, however. In 1951 he starred in John Huston's production of Stephen Crane's Civil War classic, *The Red Badge of Courage* (with a cast that included G.I. cartoonist Bill Mauldin), and four years later he played himself in the film version of *To Hell and Back*. In 1958, he starred with Michael Redgrave in the movie based on Graham Greene's *The Quiet American*.

Murphy's final years were difficult ones. Still living in southern California with his second wife (his first marriage in the early 1950s had been very brief) and a growing family, Murphy attempted to leave acting and move into the business world, but he apparently had much less talent for enterprise than for the movies. He was forced into bankruptcy in 1968. At the same time, his behavior took unusual turns. The early signs of the "drug culture" outraged Murphy, and he began cadging rides with police patrols in Los Angeles County. According to one account, Murphy also occasionally acted as an intelligence source on Mafia operations for the Los Angeles District Attorney's Office. Early in 1971, Murphy's reputation was sullied when he and a bartender friend were nearly charged with assault after an altercation with a man over the treatment of his dog. Only a few months later, while on a business trip, Murphy was killed in the crash of a private plane near Roanoke, Virginia. He was survived by a wife and two sons.

Toward the end of *To Hell and Back*, Murphy wrote, "I may be branded by war, but I will not be defeated by it." After the war, Murphy was plagued by nightmares and could not sleep without a loaded pistol beneath his pillow, but superficially it seemed for a time that his prediction would hold true. He made one film after another. His autobiography was successful, both commercially (seven printings) and as a piece of war literature. The book was a straightforward and illuminating view of that most mysterious of military subjects, the infantry-man's war. He was not interested in self-promotion; instead, he attempted to depict his life on the battlelines realistically. "The present tense was chosen for the book," Murphy wrote, "because in a combat man's life there is little left but the present tense. It was my purpose to tell the story as simply and honestly as I could, avoiding heroics because I do not believe in heroics." Murphy's war in *To Hell and Back* was hardly as literary as some of the trench literature of World War I, but in its realistic and often self-deprecating narrative, his book easily takes its place in the *guerre verité* tradition of literature that first appeared in the nineteenth century, when the plain soldier's voice began to be heard in war reminiscences.

Although Murphy's acting career was not distinguished, he nevertheless did three films in which he performed creditably and of which most actors would be proud. His work as Henry Flemming in "The Red Badge of Courage" was a role with which Murphy obviously had some sympathy and, guided by John Huston's directorial genius, was notable for its fidelity to Crane's original. In the film version of his autobiography, Murphy played himself with remarkable restraint and respect for the kind of war he and his comrades had fought. But it was in "The Quiet American" that Murphy was at his best, playing an earnest and naive young American of shadowy official purposes in the Saigon of 1958. It was perfect casting. The film now seems an eerie premonition of what would occur in Southeast Asia less than a decade later. Today, Murphy's films are hardly mentioned by film historians—in the last case, perhaps wrongly—but Murphy was an early type in Hollywood: the celebrity who, without formal training, makes his way into the film industry, there to be collected and employed until his celebrity fades.

That is what happened to Audie Murphy and at least partially explains his fall from the grace of heroism in the last decade of his life. In the most general terms, it is a process familiar to the story of all military heroes, for whom that single dramatic act is the apex of life, an act against which all other events compare so poorly. No doubt he knew this, even as he tried to escape its implications. While he gave away most of his medals to children, his later dalliances with civilian adventure were perhaps an attempt to regain the elemental honesty and exhilaration of his early battles with poverty and the enemy. Once asked how men survive war, Audie Murphy answered, "I don't think they ever do."

BIBLIOGRAPHY

Blumenson, Martin. *Salerno to Cassino: The U.S. Army In World War II*. Washington, D.C.: U.S. Government Printing Office, 1969.

Ellis, John. *The Sharp End: The Fighting Man in World War II*. New York: Charles Scribner's Sons, 1980.

Murphy, Audie. *To Hell and Back*. New York: Holt, Rinehart and Winston, 1949.

Simpson, Harold B. *Audie Murphy, American Soldier*. Hillsboro, Tex.: Hill Junior College Press, 1975.

U.S. Congress, Senate, Committee on Labor and Public Welfare, Subcommittee on Veterans Affairs. *Medal of Honor Recipients, 1863–1963*. 88th Cong., 2d sess. Washington, D.C.: U.S. Government Printing Office, 1964.

ROGER J. SPILLER

N

NIMITZ, Chester William (b. Fredericksburg, Tex., February 24, 1885; d. San Francisco, Calif., February 20, 1966), naval officer. Nimitz served in World War II as commander in chief, Pacific Fleet and Pacific Ocean Areas.

Karl Heinrich Nimitz was one of a group of German immigrants who arrived in Texas in 1846 and founded the town of Fredericksburg. His son Chester Bernard married Anna Henke, the local butcher's daughter. Five months later Anna was a widow and pregnant. The following February she gave birth to Chester William, the future fleet admiral. When Chester was five years old, Anna married his Uncle William, her late husband's younger brother, and the family moved to nearby Kerrville to manage a small hotel.

As he neared the end of his high school career, Chester, desiring further education but lacking the means, applied for an appointment to West Point. None being available, he gladly accepted an appointment to the U.S. Naval Academy and easily passed the entrance examination. Graduating in 1905, he stood seventh in overall achievement in a class of 114.

With the rank of passed midshipman, Nimitz was ordered to duty in the battleship *Ohio*, then the flagship of the U.S. Asiatic Fleet. In 1907, having passed the required examination, he was commissioned ensign and given command of a gunboat, in which he roved the Philippines. A war scare that year brought a number of laid-up warships back into service. Nimitz was ordered to Manila to get the destroyer *Decatur* back into commission and take command of her, an unprecedented responsibility for a twenty-two-year-old ensign. One night in mid-1908, Ensign Nimitz ran the *Decatur* aground, for which he was court-martialed and publicly reprimanded.

Here was a situation that could have ruined a young officer's career, but so flawless was Nimitz's record otherwise that within a few months he was promoted to lieutenant, completely skipping the rank of lieutenant, junior grade. Back in the United States he commanded a series of submarines and made himself an authority on diesel engines. At age twenty-six he became commander of a submarine division, and the following year he addressed the Naval War College on the subject of submarines. During this period, he married Catherine Freeman, who bore him a son and three daughters.

Sent to Europe by the Navy to study diesel engines, he returned to the United States and at the New York Navy Yard superintended the construction of diesel engines in the new oiler *Maumee*, of which he became executive officer and chief engineer. With her commanding officer he invented the system of underway refueling. Upon the entry of the United States into World War I, the *Maumee* proceeded to the mid-Atlantic to refuel U.S. warships en route to Europe.

Promoted to lieutenant commander, Nimitz in August 1917 reported as engineering aide to commander, Submarine Force, Atlantic Fleet, a duty that took him to the Mediterranean and the British Isles. Following the war, he served as senior member, Board of Submarine Design, and then executive officer of the battleship *South Carolina*. In 1920–1922 Nimitz met one of the most formidable challenges of his career by superintending the construction of the submarine base at Pearl Harbor, built mostly with salvaged war materials that he had collected, often without permission, from East Coast shipyards.

In 1922–1923 Nimitz was a student at the Naval War College at Newport, Rhode Island. Then, as tactical officer of the battle fleet, he introduced the circular formation, recently invented at the War College, and was instrumental in integrating the Navy's lone carrier, the *Langley*, into fleet maneuvers.

In 1926 Commander Nimitz was one of six naval officers selected to establish in American universities the first units of the Naval Reserve Officers' Training Corps. He set up, administered, and taught classes in the unit at the University of California at Berkeley. From 1933 to 1935 Captain Nimitz was commanding officer of the cruiser *Augusta*, flagship of the U.S. Asiatic Fleet. The following two years he served in the Navy Department as assistant to the chief of the Bureau of Navigation—as the Bureau of Naval Personnel was called until World War II. Then, attaining the rank of rear admiral, he went to sea again and briefly commanded Battleship Division One with his flag in the battleship *Arizona*. In mid-1939, back in Washington, Nimitz was chief of the Bureau of Navigation, training sailors and assigning them to duty in a navy expanding rapidly under threat of war.

Following the Japanese attack on Pearl Harbor, President Franklin D. Roosevelt relieved Admiral Husband Edward Kimmel* of command of the Pacific Fleet and appointed Nimitz to the post. On the last day of 1941, Nimitz became an admiral in assuming his duties as commander in chief, Pacific Fleet, which, because of the growing complexity of operations and communications, had become a land-based command. Nimitz made his headquarters at Pearl Harbor until 1945, when he transferred to Guam.

In March 1942 General Douglas MacArthur*, on presidential orders, flew from the Philippines to Australia, where he was given supreme command of the Southwest Pacific Area, which included Australia, New Guinea, the Philippines, and adjacent islands. At the same time Nimitz received an additional appointment as commander in chief, Pacific Ocean Areas, in which capacity he commanded all military and naval forces and operations, American and Allied, in the North, Central, and South Pacific Areas. He thus commanded the conquest of Guadalcanal and the drive across the Pacific via the Gilberts, the Marshalls, the Marianas, Iwo Jima, and Okinawa, and he commanded the Pacific Fleet at all times, even when it supported MacArthur's invasions of Hollandia and the Philippines.

Toward the end of 1944 Nimitz received his fifth star as fleet admiral. Following the defeat of Japan, at the surrender ceremony aboard the battleship *Missouri* in Tokyo Bay, September 2, 1945, Admiral Nimitz signed the instrument of surrender for the United States.

The following December, Fleet Admiral Nimitz began a two-year tour as chief of naval operations, succeeding Admiral Ernest Joseph King*. In 1949 Nimitz was engaged by the United Nations to supervise a plebiscite in Kashmir to decide whether it would join Pakistan or India. Prime Minister Nehru blocked the plebiscite, but Nimitz stayed with the United Nations until mid-1952, touring the United States and speaking as the United Nations good-will ambassador.

As fleet admiral, Nimitz theoretically remained on active duty the rest of his life, available for council to the Navy Department. In fact, however, he retired to "Longview," the home he had purchased in Berkeley, California. He refused many lucrative offers from business, preferring to maintain his image as naval commander and symbol of the Old Navy, but he did serve as a regent for the University of California.

Admiral Nimitz's fame, at least among the general public, derives almost exclusively from his command of the Pacific Fleet and Pacific Ocean Areas in World War II. In this capacity, as his biography notes, he "commanded thousands of ships and aircraft and millions of men, amounting to more military power than had been wielded by all the commanders in all previous wars." The British chiefs of staff left control of the Pacific War to the American Joint Chiefs of Staff, and these left operations in the Pacific Ocean Areas largely to Admiral Nimitz and to Admiral King, chief of naval operations and commander in chief of the U.S. Fleet. Nimitz and King, with their staffs, met at intervals in Washington, San Francisco, or Pearl Harbor to plan strategy. Thus, as area commander, Nimitz was not merely carrying out orders from above.

Besides the usual qualities of a successful commander in chief—leadership, judgment, organizational skill, ability to distinguish the essential from the trivial, decisiveness, and readiness to take calculated risks—Nimitz had other attributes that uniquely fitted him for his post. These included serenity, courtesy and consideration, unshakable integrity, and a rare perceptiveness in dealing with people. His famous serenity enabled him to think clearly and make the right decisions during the first four months of 1942, when it seemed that nothing could stop the Japanese advance; and during the Battle of Midway, when he could send out only three carriers and a few cruisers and destroyers to take on the whole Japanese Combined Fleet. All these qualities stood him in good stead in dealing with his fellow officers. Above him was the imperious, often caustic, Admiral King, who never hesitated to blast any officers, including Nimitz, when they failed to produce the results he expected. Below him were such stubborn, opinionated warriors as those whom the press aptly nicknamed "Bull" (William Frederick) Halsey, Jr.,* "Terrible" (Richmond Kelly) Turner,* and "Howlin' Mad" (Holland McTyeire) Smith.* On his own level was the brilliant but devious General MacArthur, who regarded Nimitz as his competitor for glory and strove to undermine his strategy. Nimitz treated all such officers with courtesy and fairness and with a calm command presence that won their respect and cooperation.

Admiral Nimitz was less well known to the public than were some of his subordinates, such as Admiral Halsey, or his fellow commanders in chief, Generals Dwight David Eisenhower* and MacArthur. His relative anonymity resulted in part from his shunning of publicity. But, in any case, he was not an attractive subject for journalism because there was nothing particularly striking about his appearance, his conduct, or his manner of expressing himself. He had no salient characteristics of appearance or personality. "He was," according to one observer, "impossible to caricature by word or line." Simplicity was his essence.

BIBLIOGRAPHY

Hoyt, Edwin P. *How They Won the War in the Pacific: Nimitz and His Admirals.* New York: Weybright and Talley, 1970.

Matloff, Maurice. *Strategic Planning for Coalition Warfare, 1943–1944.* Washington, D.C.: U.S. Government Printing Office, 1959.

———, and Edward M. Snell. *Strategic Planning for Coalition Warfare, 1941–1942.* Washington, D.C.: U.S. Government Printing Office, 1953.

Morison, Samuel Eliot. *History of United States Naval Operations in World War II.* 15 vols. Boston: Atlantic, Little, Brown, and Company, 1947-1962.

Morton, Louis. *Strategy and Command: The First Two Years.* Washington, D.C.: U.S. Government Printing Office, 1962.

Potter, E. B. *Nimitz.* Annapolis, Md.: Naval Institute Press, 1976.

E. B. POTTER

O

OGLETHORPE, James Edward (b. London, England, December 22, 1696; d. Cranham, Essex, England, June 30, 1785), military figure, politician, founder of the colony of Georgia in America.

The Oglethorpe family was a prominent one at the court of James II and followed the king into European exile. James Edward was the youngest child in a family of seven, including three sons. He spent much of his youth traveling between the European courts of the Stuarts, but even prior to Queen Anne's death he had made it clear that his loyalty belonged to the branch of the ruling house on the English throne. He therefore accepted the succession of George I with resignation, if not with enthusiasm. Although his mother, the former Eleanor Wall of Tipperary, and his sisters continued to agitate for the return of the Jacobites to England, James appears never to have been actively engaged in any of the plots that swirled about the female members of the family.

In 1713 he secured a commission as lieutenant in the 1st Regiment of Foot Guards, but in the following year Oglethorpe was a student at Corpus Christi College, Oxford. Corpus at that time was a hotbed of Jacobitism. James' youthful enthusiasms must have drawn him into the student political activities of the day, but there is no hard evidence to document this surmise. By 1716 he had resigned his commission, had gone to Paris, and in the following year joined Prince Eugene of Savoy as one of his aides de camp. He was present at the siege of Belgrade in that year and had an honorable, if not dramatic, role in the fighting there.

By 1718, as a result of the deaths of his elder brothers, he had returned to England in order to take over the responsibilities that now devolved upon the surviving son of a prominent, well-to-do, landed family. One of these responsibilities, he found, meant election to Parliament, where he followed his father as well as his brothers as member from Haslemere. James was first elected in 1722 and served that borough until his defeat in 1754.

In Parliament, Oglethorpe concentrated his considerable energies on such questions as imperial planning, impressment, the rights of individuals, prison conditions, and allied issues. He took his position very seriously and, as a result of his heavy workload and constant diligence, Oglethorpe made a name for himself. He was made chairman of an important committee in 1729 and was charged with investigating the conditions of the nation's jails. Out of his experiences with this committee grew his interest in American colonization.

In 1732 Oglethorpe and twenty other prominent men, who banded together as trustees, were given a charter by George II and were authorized to create a colony in the new world. Named for the monarch, Georgia was settled on February 1, 1733 (February 12, New Style) and was located at such a site where it would serve as a buffer zone protecting the vulnerable colony of South Carolina from incursions by the Spanish, French, or their Indian allies. Oglethorpe, who led the first shipload of colonists to America, emphasized the military nature of the province. Hence, the settlement pattern he imposed on the province from its inception was geared to the need for defense. Savannah's city plan, in fact, may have been inspired by Oglethorpe's recollections of army camps; land grants were restricted to tail male ownership and were generally only fifty acres in size. Oglethorpe courted the southern Indians assiduously and with considerable results; he established fortified places at strategic sites on the sea islands approaching Spanish Florida (particularly Fort Frederica on St. Simons Island); and he imposed British authority in the backcountry (Augusta) and closer to Savannah (the satellite towns of Hampstead, Highgate, Abercorn, and others). He assumed a particularly aggressive policy toward the Spaniards.

When news of the War of Jenkins' Ear reached Oglethorpe, he was on his way from Creek country where he had received the assurances of the natives that they would remain neutral in the event of an Anglo-Spanish conflict. Ever since 1733 Oglethorpe had been anxious to invade Florida and capture St. Augustine, and he bent his considerable energies to that end during the last months of 1739 and the early days of 1740. In May 1740 his full expedition—comprised in part of his own regiment, rangers from Georgia and Carolina, Highland Scots from Georgia, South Carolina volunteers, Indians, and assorted others—invaded Florida in force. Governor Manuel Montiano of Florida, however, had been forewarned and had received reinforcements at the Castel San Marcos in the form of additional troops and six half-galleys that protected the entrance to the town's harbor from the British squadron that lay off its mouth. With his plans for a joint land-sea assault thwarted, Oglethorpe instituted a siege, but a severe setback at Fort Mosa (or the Negro Fort) broke the spirit of his army. In addition, the Royal Navy became restless in its blockading position and feared the onset of the hurricane season perhaps even more than it did the Spanish. Oglethorpe reluctantly ordered the lifting of the siege on July 1, 1740.

The Spaniards under Montiano then invaded Georgia in the summer of 1742. Oglethorpe, who had been left to fend for himself by the Carolinians and the British squadron stationed in Charles Town, relied upon his own regiment as the heart of the force defending the British southern frontier, but he was aided in his fight by the hearty Highland Scots and a few loyal Indians. The decisive actions took place on St. Simons Island with a series of encounters up and down the military road connecting Fort Frederica with Fort St. Simons at the southern tip of the island. When Montiano found that he could neither dislodge nor intimidate Oglethorpe with his superior numbers, and having suffered setbacks along the military road, he ordered a retreat to Florida. By rebuffing Montiano, Oglethorpe showed considerable military skill in the handling of troops, and his own personal involvement in the action inspired confidence and admiration. In the following year Oglethorpe once again invaded Florida but lacked the proper forces to bring St. Augustine to its knees.

Also in 1743, he returned to England. In 1745 Oglethorpe's movements, when he and others were ordered to harry the defeated "Bonnie Prince Charlie," were considered by the duke of Cumberland to be so suspicious that Cumberland ordered him court-martialed. Although he was completely exonerated, Oglethorpe never held active command in the British Army again. It has come to light fairly recently that he went to Europe during the Seven Years' War and fought with Field Marshal James Keith against the French. His use of an assumed name and the lack of personal or official papers to cover his career during this period have thus far kept this aspect of his life in obscurity.

Oglethorpe lived on until June 30, 1785 and became one of the important figures on the periphery of the group led by Samuel Johnson. He sympathized with the American cause during the Revolution and lived to call upon—and converse with—the first U.S. ambassador to the Court of St. James, John Adams. When he died Oglethorpe was the senior general on the Army lists, but the title was basically an honorary one only.

Oglethorpe holds a secure place in American military history. Although tactical and logistical blunders cost him St. Augustine, it is generally conceded that by his inspired leadership during the Battle of St. Simons Island (traditionally known as the Battle of Bloody Marsh) Oglethorpe saved Georgia and, perhaps, the entire southern frontier of the British colonies from a potentially disastrous invasion by the Spanish.

BIBLIOGRAPHY

Coleman, Kenneth. *Colonial Georgia*. New York: Charles Scribner's Sons, 1976.

Ettinger, Amos Aschbach. *James Edward Oglethorpe, Imperial Idealist*. Oxford: Oxford University Press, 1936.

Ivers, Larry E. *British Drums on the Southern Frontier*. Chapel Hill: University of North Carolina Press, 1974.

McCain, James Ross. *Georgia as a Proprietary Province*. Boston: Richard G. Badger, 1917.

The St. Augustine Expedition of 1740, with an Introduction by John Tate Lanning. Columbia: South Carolina Archives Department, reprinted 1954.

Spalding, Phinizy. *Oglethorpe in America*. Chicago: University of Chicago Press, 1977.

PHINIZY SPALDING

OLDENDORF, Jesse Barrett (b. Riverside, Calif., February 16, 1887; d. Portsmouth, Va., April 27, 1974), naval officer. Oldendorf was the last admiral to cross the "T" of an enemy column, enfilading it with broadsides in a classic set piece battle among capital ships, at Surigao Strait in October, 1944 against the Japanese.

Jesse Barrett Oldendorf attended public schools in the town of his birth until his appointment to the U.S. Naval Academy from the Eighth District of California in 1905. He first went to sea during the summer midshipman cruise of 1906 in the small cruiser *Cleveland*; two summers later he completed his second practice cruise aboard the steam sloop *Hartford*, the Civil War flagship of Admiral David Glasgow Farragut.* Oldendorf graduated in 1909 as a passed midshipman; thereafter, he served two years at sea (then required by law) before being commissioned ensign, effective June 5, 1911. That tour of duty was in the 13,400-ton armored cruiser *California*.

By the time the United States entered World War I, Oldendorf had attained the regular rank of lieutenant (June 5, 1917) and had served consecutively in several U.S. ships, including the destroyer *Preble*, the 3,200-ton small cruiser *Denver*, the destroyer *Whipple*, and the armored cruiser *San Diego* (ex-*California*). During the American participation in the war, Oldendorf was in charge of the Armed Guard Unit attached to the U.S. Army transport *Saratoga*, later he was gunnery officer aboard the transport *President Lincoln*, and finally by August 1918 he was engineer officer in the armored cruiser *Seattle*. There he served until being transferred to the former German transport *Patricia* for a four-month assignment starting in March 1919. As lieutenant commander after the war, Oldendorf was assigned to a series of short billets: Pittsburgh Naval Recruiting Station (officer in charge), Baltimore Shipbuilding and Bethlehem Steel Company (naval inspector of machinery), and the Branch Hydrographic Office at Baltimore (officer in charge).

In the peacetime Navy of the 1920s, Oldendorf had his first command—the recently commissioned *Clemson* ("Flush Decker") Class destroyer *Decatur*, from May 1924 to May 1927. He also saw considerable staff duty during the decade: in 1921 as aide and flag secretary on the staff of the commander, Special Service Squadron, then operating in Central and South American waters; and in 1922 as aide to the commandant of the Mare Island Navy Yard in California. For a year after Oldendorf was detached from command of the *Decatur* in 1927, he was aide to the commandant of the Philadelphia Navy Yard. Holding the rank of commander, Oldendorf completed courses of instruction between June 1928 and July 1930 at the Naval War College as well as at the Army War College, then located in Washington, D.C. Afterwards he returned to sea as navigator of the *New York*, (a 27,000-ton battleship launched in 1914), in which he served until June 1932.

Oldendorf's career continued to mature during the remaining nine years before the attack at Pearl Harbor. He was an instructor in the U.S. Naval Academy's Department of Seamanship and Navigation for three years after leaving the *New York*. In June 1935 he returned to sea, this time for a two-year assignment as executive officer of the 32,500-ton battleship *West Virginia*. During his next tour of duty (officer in charge of the Naval Recruiting Section in the Bureau of Navigation), Oldendorf was promoted to the rank of captain, effective March 1, 1938. And shortly after war broke out on the European Continent in the autumn of 1939, he assumed command of the *Northampton* Class heavy cruiser *Houston*, a command he held until his transfer to the staff of the Naval War College not long before the Japanese attack at Pearl Harbor. Oldendorf was appointed rear admiral at fifty-five years of age early in World War II. The extensive experience of a sound thirty-year naval career made him destined for major wartime commands.

In the first half of 1942 he was commander of forces in the Aruba-Curaçao area, Netherlands West Indies, and until April 1943 he served as commander of the Naval Base, Trinidad. For the remainder of 1943 he commanded a task force of the Atlantic Fleet. In January 1944 he was assigned to the Pacific Fleet as commander of Cruiser Division Four, with his flag in the cruiser *Louisville*. By the end of that assignment in December 1944, Rear Admiral Oldendorf was promoted to vice admiral and designated commander, Battleship Squadron One, with additional duty in command of Battleship Division Two.

Not long after Japan surrendered, Oldendorf was ordered to duty in San Diego as commandant of the Eleventh Naval District and commander of the naval base. His last commands until retirement in 1948 were as commander of the Western Sea Frontier, with additional duty as commander of the Pacific Reserve Fleet. Oldendorf was advanced to the rank of admiral upon his retirement on September 1, 1948. At that time citations for exceptionally meritorious service were made by Secretary of the Navy John L. Sullivan and Admiral Louis E. Denfeld, chief of naval operations. These citations were added to many other decorations he received throughout a distinguished career, including the Distinguished Service Medal with two Gold Stars, the Legion of Merit with one Gold Star, the Navy Cross, and the Army Distinguished Service Medal.

Oldendorf was a linchpin in the four-phased naval battle for Leyte Gulf in October 1944, specifically in the Battle of Surigao Strait during the pre-dawn hours of October 25. Two of the four Japanese naval forces designed to repel the invading Allies steamed from the Sulu and Mindanao Seas for Leyte Gulf eastward and north through the narrow waters of Surigao Strait. The first Japanese force (two 30,600-ton battleships, a 9,000-ton heavy cruiser, and four destroyers) was under the command of Vice Admiral Nishimura Shōji. Some fifty miles behind Admiral Nishimura followed the units of Vice Admiral Shima Kiyohide: two 10,000-ton heavy cruisers, a 5,500-ton light cruiser, and four destroyers.

Oldendorf, then rear admiral, was well informed of these developments about twenty-four hours in advance. Thus, he anticipated night action with his force of six battleships, three heavy cruisers, five light cruisers, over a score of destroyers, and nearly two score of patrol-torpedo (PT) boats. He designed and executed a classic battle trap for the Japanese, the kind he had studied and plotted in maneuvers and Naval War College war games. The Japanese continued in the early morning hours of October 25 to plow doggedly toward the jaws of Oldendorf's carefully laid trap. The PT-boats, deployed the greatest distance down the strait, then the destroyers, launched successive waves of torpedo attacks. Soon the left and right flank cruisers fired their 8- and 6-inch guns, with the most northern battleships forming the battleline at the top of the "T" and arching their 16- and 14-inch shells over the cruisers. Much of the damage to the Japanese ships was inflicted by torpedoes—more than 130 were launched during the course of the battle. Effective torpedo action was an essential part of Oldendorf's plans, for his six battleships were old (five of them were veterans of the Pearl Harbor attack) and only three of them had up-to-date radar fire control equipment needed for fully effective night action. Moreover, none of the battleships had more than a small store of armor-piercing shells since originally bombardment was intended as their primary duty.

Oldendorf's plans worked ruinous damage on the Japanese vessels. All of Nishimura's ships were sunk or badly damaged by the time Admiral Shima's force started to enter Oldendorf's trap and run the gauntlet of PT-boat attacks. The Japanese light cruiser *Abukuma* was hit by a torpedo before Shima turned about behind a smoke screen and made good his escape from the narrow strait.

Admiral Oldendorf's opportunity was rare in the annals of naval history, and he took full advantage of the extremely hazardous tactical situation while running the minimum of risk to his own forces. It was his careful planning and leadership that greatly reduced the distinct likelihood that at some point during the huge night-time battle his own ships would be caught in a deadly cross-fire between Japanese and other Allied vessels. Or there was the danger that because of intricate battle maneuvers his own ships would be mistaken for the enemy. One Australian destroyer was almost fired upon in error, and one American destroyer was, in fact, the victim of "friendly fire," but Oldendorf quickly ordered all of his ships to cease fire before the silhouetted *Albert W. Grant* was damaged beyond all hope of survival. And after the Japanese were routed, Admiral Oldendorf did not succumb to the natural temptation to order an all-out pursuit to overtake and destroy the damaged Japanese ships. Daylight air attacks would be more effective, he reasoned. Evidence from the Japanese side in a postwar study revealed that in a hasty maneuver of pursuit Oldendorf's ships could well have fallen victim to Shima's destroyers ranging forth from a smoke screen. Two Japanese battleships and three destroyers were sunk within the strait; one badly damaged heavy and one light cruiser were easy marks for air attacks. In all, the Japanese lost about eighty-one thousand tons of ships and at least five thousand sailors; on the American side, thirty-nine sailors were killed and no vessels were sunk. The decisiveness with which Oldendorf defeated Nishimura's force helped to produce the rout of Shima's force. Moreover, news of Oldendorf's sweeping victory over Japanese forces in the Battle of Surigao Strait encouraged a certain amount of timidity among the Japanese a few hours later in the battle off Samar.

Oldendorf's prudence immediately after his initial victory ensured the availability of several units of his command for participation in another phase of the battle for Leyte Gulf. The June 3, 1945, issue of the *New York Times* carried the following summary:

> Oldendorf fought in the battle for Leyte Gulf the "kind of naval battle you dream about," and achieved overnight fame. He performed the classical naval maneuver of crossing the T on the enemy and virtually annihilated that portion of the Japanese Fleet which approached Leyte Gulf through Surigao Strait. "My theory," Oldendorf said, "was that of the old-time gambler—never give a sucker a chance."

And the naval historian Samuel Eliot Morison* wrote: "In the unearthly silence that followed the roar of Oldendorf's 14-inch and 16-inch guns in Surigao Strait, one could imagine the ghosts of all great admirals, from Raleigh and De Ruyter to Togo and Jellicoe, standing at attention to salute the passing of the kind of naval warfare that they all understood."

Three days after Admiral Oldendorf died in 1974, an editorial in the *Virginian-Pilot* eulogized him and observed that his place in history is all the more secure "now that the battleship has vanished." Perhaps so. Nevertheless, Admiral Oldendorf fully appreciated the important role that each type of vessel under his command played in the victory at the Battle of Surigao Strait; it was not inappropriate that on March 4, 1978, a *Spruance* Class destroyer was commissioned in his honor—the USS *Oldendorf* (DD–972).

BIBLIOGRAPHY

Dull, Paul S. *A Battle History of the Imperial Japanese Navy, 1941–1945*. Annapolis, Md.: Naval Institute Press, 1978.

Falk, Stanley L. *Decision at Leyte*. New York: W. W. Norton, 1966.

Morison, Samuel Eliot. *History of United States Naval Operations in World War II*. 15 vols. Boston: Atlantic, Little, Brown, 1947–1962.

U.S. Strategic Bombing Survey (Pacific). *Interrogations of Japanese Officials*. 2 vols. Washington, D.C.: U.S. Government Printing Office, 1946.

Woodward, C. Vann. *The Battle for Leyte Gulf*. New York: Macmillan Company, 1947.

CARL BOYD

OPECHANCANOUGH (b. location unknown, late 1540s?; d. Jamestown, Va., 1646), Pamunkey (Powhatan) chieftain and architect of the Indian uprisings of 1622 and 1644. Contemporary Virginia colonists considered Opechancanough to be the "Great generall of the Salvages."

As a member of a nonliterate Amerindian culture that was all but eradicated by seventeenth-century English colonization, Opechancanough is largely shrouded in mystery. Information about his activites after the arrival of the Jamestown colonists is, however, more accurate and complete than details concerning his origins and parentage.

Opechancanough was the classificatory kinsman or real "half-brother" of Powhatan, the supreme chieftain (*Mamanatowick*) of some twelve thousand Tidewater Virginia Algonquians in the early seventeenth century. Since the eighteenth century, some authorities have speculated that Opechancanough was not a Powhatan at all but "a Prince of a Foreign Nation" who emigrated to Virginia from some part of the Spanish West Indies or Mexico. One scholar even recently argued that Opechancanough was in fact Don Louis de Velasco, a Virginia Indian who was captured by the Spaniards in 1560, spent a decade abroad, led a party of Spanish Jesuits back to his homeland in 1570, and in 1571 renounced Catholicism and led his tribesmen in the slaughter of the missionaries. Such an intriguing but highly speculative interpretation is based more on the intense and verifiable animosity that Opechancanough *later* directed against the threatening intrusion of Englishmen than on solid evidence from an earlier era.

Opechancanough, the most talented and bellicose of all Powhatan leaders, was highly regarded within the tribal power structure when the English arrived in 1607. He was the chief, or *werowance*, of the strong, twelve hundred-member Pamunkey tribe that was headquartered in almost impregnable villages near present West Point, Virginia. Possessed of territory rich in maize, game, fish, and freshwater pearls, and controlling the headwaters of the York River, the Pamunkeys were the largest and most influential tribe in Powhatan's domain. Under Opechancanough, the Pamunkeys were regarded as the best, most disciplined of all Powhatan warriors, and he was reputedly able to mobilize one thousand bowmen for battle from his own and neighboring tribes.

In December 1607 Opechancanough and a large armed force captured Captain John Smith* and delivered him to Powhatan, and in November 1609 the Pamunkeys decimated a band of colonists who had invaded their villages to steal food. The mutual hostility generated by these and countless other incidents erupted into fierce fighting in the First Anglo-Powhatan War (1609–1614). Opechancanough's stronghold became the key in this struggle, and not until well-armed English musketeers inflicted defeat on the Pamunkeys in February 1614 did Indian resistance end.

The war had ravaged much of Powhatan's James River domain, and his authority was effectively shattered. In the midst of defeat and demoralization, Opechancanough emerged as the Powhatans' "chiefe Captaine," who, as reports of 1615 related, "hath already the commaund of all the people." When an aged Powhatan abdicated in 1617, Opechancanough assumed still more powers, and upon the *Mamanatowick*'s death the following year, he became the "great Kinge" of the Powhatans.

In retrospect, it appears that between 1614 and 1622 Opechancanough used his power and position to renew the fortunes and to revitalize the morale of his people. By 1622 he had achieved a greater military and political solidarity among some thirty tribes and several thousand tribesmen than had existed at the height of Powhatan's reign. Opechancanough's goal now more than ever was the elimination of all things English. While luring the colonists into complacency with pledges of peace, he was obtaining muskets for his men and spreading the belief that Powhatan warriors were immune to bullets.

The assassination of the charismatic and priestlike warrior-prophet Nemattanew ("Jack of the Feathers") was the spark in the powder that gave Opechancanough the perfect occasion to launch his fierce, famous, and near-fatal offensive against the hated white intruders. In the tactically brilliant Powhatan Uprising of March 22, 1622, over three hundred colonists, representing one-fourth of the total population, were killed in a single morning. The attack failed to achieve Opechancanough's goal of annihilation; instead, the uprising initiated a decade-long Indian war that would eventually extend beyond the borders of Virginia to involve tribes along the Potomac and Patuxent rivers.

The military highlight of this Second Anglo-Powhatan War was a rare two-day, open-field battle fought in autumn 1624 between an intertribal force of eight hundred warriors (dominated by Pamunkeys) and some sixty colonists. Opechancanough's men, fiercely adorned with red pigment, fox fur, and feathers, and armed with muskets, lethal four-foot arrows, and wooden clubs, faced the withering fire of English flintlocks to protect their vital maize fields and their equally precious reputation as brave fighters.

Heavy casualties among the Powhatans and a paucity of gunpowder among the English made combat less frequent and intense after this confrontation, but the conflict dragged on until 1632. Superior technology and constant reinforcement of the colonists eventually overcame Indian resistance in this first frontier war of attrition. However, Opechancanough's daring command of elusive and mobile forces earned him the title of "Great generall of the Salvages," and he himself avoided capture despite numerous English plots and the levy of a head bounty. It would be many years before English men and women, in Jamestown and in London, would forget the terror that the 1622 uprising and the succeeding decade instilled.

After a tenuous peace was concluded in 1632, the colony of Virginia grew stronger and expanded while the Powhatans declined. By the early 1640s, the English population and their extensive tobacco plantations threatened the very survival of Indian territory and culture. In response, an aged and blind, desperate but determined Opechancanough in 1644 led his warriors in yet another bloody uprising against the colony. On April 18, 1644, the Tidewater tribes killed some five hundred settlers, but they faced an even harsher retaliation than before from the eight thousand English then in Virginia.

This Third Anglo-Powhatan War ended in October 1646 after an English cavalry attack the previous summer had crushed the Pamunkeys. In that battle, Opechancanough, bedridden by infirmities, was finally captured. Carried to

Jamestown, he was humiliated by being placed on public display and died after being shot in the back. Opechancanough's death forever ended an era of inspired political and military leadership by a native population resisting subjugation and cultural destruction. With his passing, the defeated Pamunkeys were placed on a reservation north of the York River and became the tribute-paying allies of the English.

Over the centuries, Opechancanough's reputation as a leader and strategist has suffered both from romantic embellishment and prejudicial resentment. In 1705 the Virginia planter/historian Robert Beverley nostalgically described him as a "cunning and brave Prince," a "Man of large Stature, noble Presence, and extraordinary Parts" who, being "perfectly skill'd in the Art of Governing,...caused all the Indians far and near to dread his Name, and had them all entirely in Subjection." As late as the 1850s, the Indian scholar Henry Schoolcraft portrayed Opechancanough as a Native American "Solon"—a wise and courageous leader "inflexibly bent on preventing the progress of the Saxon race."

Most nineteenth-century appraisals, however, infected with the virulent racism that accompanied post-1860 warfare with the Plains Indians, either denounced or discounted the leadership of Opechancanough. White historians condemned him as a "barbarous" murderer of children, and in one of the only late nineteenth-century departures from this theme, a worse injustice was perpetrated: it was claimed that the "savage" mind of Opechancanough was incapable of having planned and executed the admittedly brilliant 1622 uprising and that the Spanish probably conceived the idea.

Only in the 1970s have there been renewed scholarly interest in, and less biased assessments of, Opechancanough and Anglo-Powhatan relations. Today it is becoming increasingly evident that, in mounting two massive, surprise attacks twenty years apart, and in fighting protracted guerrilla wars against overwhelming odds, Opechancanough deserved to rank with more famous Amerindian chieftains and dedicated opponents of colonial domination.

BIBLIOGRAPHY

Arber, Edward, and A. G. Bradley, eds. *Travels and Works of Captain John Smith*. 2 vols. Edinburgh: John Grant, 1910.
Barbour, Philip L., ed. *The Jamestown Voyages Under the First Charter, 1606–1609*. 2 vols., Cambridge: Cambridge University Press, 1969.
Beverley, Robert. *The History and Present State of Virginia*. Edited by Louis B. Wright. Charlottesville: University Press of Virginia, 1947. (Originally published London, 1705.)
Bridenbaugh, Carl. *Jamestown, 1607–1699*. New York: Oxford University Press, 1980.
Fausz, J. Frederick. "Opechancanough: Indian Resistance Leader." In *Struggle and Survival in Colonial America: Life Stories of Women and Men Who Coped*. Edited by Gary B. Nash and David G. Sweet. Berkeley: University of California Press, 1980.
———. "The Powhatan Uprising of 1622: A Historical Study of Ethnocentrism and

Cultural Conflict.'' Ph.D. dissertation, College of William and Mary, 1977. Ann Arbor, Mich.: University Microfilms, 1977.

J. FREDERICK FAUSZ

OSCEOLA (b. ca. 1804 near the Tallapoosa River, Ala.; d. January 30, 1838, on Sullivan's Island at Charleston, S.C.), Tallassee warrior. Osceola emerged as an Indian leader during the Second Seminole War.

Osceola (Billy Powell or Asi-Yahola) was born in about 1804 in the Upper Creek Towns on the Tallapoosa River in present-day Alabama. He belonged to the Tallassee tribe which had merged with the Creek Confederacy. His mother was a Creek woman of mixed-blood called Polly Copinger, and his father was William Powell, a Scottish-Creek mixed-blood Indian trader. Osceola developed into a frail boy with almost effeminate characteristics, including small feet and hands. During his youth, Indians knew Osceola as Billy Powell; in later life, he claimed to be a full-blooded Indian.

Following the War of 1812, Osceola's mother took him to Florida, an almost unpopulated area where many Upper Creeks fled after their defeat at the hands of Andrew Jackson* and the Lower Creeks. The Powells lived with refugee Indians and eventually joined the camp of Peter McQueen, a mixed-blood Creek who had been involved in the Fort Mims Massacre in 1813. After 1750, refugee Indians had settled in the Floridas and become known as "Seminoles" because, unlike the Creeks on the north, they lived more by hunting than by agriculture. The word was a corruption of Isty-Semole which meant "wild men." They lived a semi-sedentary life growing corn, beans, and melons while taking fish, turkeys, deer, and bears from the swamps. Late arrivals, like McQueen and Osceola, had no trouble settling among these largely Creek people.

Negroes found ready acceptance among the Seminoles who held blacks in a less restrictive form of slavery than existed in the United States or allowed them to live as free men in their own villages. Spanish and Seminole Florida became a haven for runaway slaves, and American slaveowners insisted that this nuisance be ended. In 1817 General Edmund Pendleton Gaines,* commanding troops on the Florida line, ordered soldiers across the international frontier to seize a Seminole chief who harbored runaways at Fowltown. After this attack, the Indians retaliated with raids. These hostilities brought on the First Seminole War (1817–1818).

Gaines and Andrew Jackson invaded Florida in March 1818 and, the following month, captured McQueen's village. Among the captives were Osceola and his mother. Released from captivity, the pair wandered to the Okefenokee Swamp, then south to Tampa Bay where McQueen had established a temporary camp. McQueen led his people to a new town site on Peas Creek and settled. Jackson took St. Marks and Pensacola, while John Q. Adams negotiated the Transcontinental Treaty with Spain under which the Floridas passed into American hands in 1821.

With the transfer of the Floridas to the United States, Alabamians and Georgians demanded that the government end the runaway slave problem. In 1823 U.S. commissioners made a treaty with Seminole chiefs at Moultrie Creek which confined the Indians to an inland reservation under the supervision of an agent and opened coastal areas to white settlement. The following year, many Indians moved onto the reservation as agreed. At this time, Osceola was a man of nineteen years who had grown into a warrior and hunter and the leader of a small group of Tallassees. In 1825 he moved his two wives, his children, and his band from the Peas Creek town onto the reservation where he became a minor chief under the Seminole principal chief, Micanopy. The treaty did not achieve peace. Starvation stalked the reservation people, and they wandered off their assigned lands to find food. Slavers attempted to take blacks from the Seminoles, and conflict continued between whites and Indians.

Following the passage of the Removal Bill of 1830 by Congress, the Jackson administration moved determinatively against the Indians of Florida. Secretary of War Lewis Cass sent James Gadsden to secure a removal treaty. Under highly questionable circumstances in which the treaty was altered after signing, some Seminoles agreed to move to the Indian Territory over the years 1833, 1834, and 1835 and to settle on lands granted to their former Lower Creek enemies. The Senate did not ratify the Treaty of Payne's Landing until April 1834, which negated the relocation scheme. Seminole opposition to removal grew, and Osceola leapt to a position of leadership due to his opposition to leaving Florida.

At a conference with Wiley Thompson, the U.S. Indian agent on the reservation, at Fort King in October 1834, Osceola and other Seminoles refused to go and demanded that the United States live up to the terms of the Camp Moultrie agreement. At a second conference held on April 23, 1835, Brevet Brigadier General Duncan Lamont Clinch* read a letter to the Indians from President Jackson and reinforced demands for removal. Under pressure, sixteen chiefs signed a treaty and agreed to assemble at Tampa on January 15, 1836, although Micanopy withdrew in defiance from the council. Osceola drew a knife and pinned the paper to the table stating that if it were Thompson's heart, he would know what to do with it. Later, Thompson arrested Osceola, and the leader signed under duress after five days' imprisonment.

Once out of Thompson's clutches, Osceola and other Seminole chiefs repudiated the accord and began to prepare for war. Seminole raids began, and, following a pact among the Seminole leaders to execute any Indian who complied with relocation, Osceola killed Emarthla, a pro-removal chief. The Seminoles withdrew to the interior of Florida and took refuge in the nearly inpenetrable, reptile-infested swamps. Osceola employed the age-old Indian tactic of hit-and-run to throw the enemy off balance. And, in December 1835, the Second Seminole War (1835–1842) was underway.

The Seminoles ambushed soldiers and raided plantations with devastating effects. Osceola led an attack on a military wagon train and repulsed its reinforcements after killing eight soldiers. On December 28, 1835, Osceola raided the reservation headquarters while three hundred Indians led by Micanopy, Jumper, and Alligator eliminated a one hundred-man military force commanded by Major Francis L. Dade east of Tampa. At the agency, five whites were killed, including Wiley Thompson. The Indians then withdrew to Wahoo Swamp near the Withlacoochee River pursued by General Clinch and eight hundred troops. In an engagement on December 31, the soldiers wounded Osceola, and the tribesmen faced obstacles as they fended for ammunition and food and confronted malaria in the swamps.

In early 1836 President Jackson gave overall command to Major General Winfield Scott,* and Major General Gaines marched into the field from New Orleans. The Indians responded and struck Scott's supply headquarters and even threatened St. Augustine. Due to an outbreak of hostility among the Creeks, the War Department sent Scott to Georgia, and Governor Richard K. Call assumed the Florida command. Through the summer of 1836, Call campaigned but could not bring the major Seminole bands to bay. Osceola kept his people in motion while avoiding a direct confrontation with the soldiers who suffered from malaria and heat. Since Call could not close the war, Thomas S. Jesup, the quartermaster general, took command and turned eight thousand regulars and volunteers against Osceola.

Jesup finally engaged a Seminole party in January 1837. Micanopy, Jumper, and Alligator fled into a swamp and concluded an armistice. In early March these Seminoles agreed to remove and to assemble all Seminoles at Tampa Bay in April. By May it appeared that the war was over when Osceola came into Fort Mellon on Lake Monroe. The chief looked haggard and unwell from the rigors of the conflict. However, news reached Osceola that Jesup was failing to protect the Indians and their property at Tampa, allowing slavers from the north to seize blacks and even Seminoles. Rumors also surfaced that the Indian leaders were marked for execution. Osceola fled on May 9, and, in June, he persuaded or forced Micanopy's and Jumper's people to escape back into the swamps.

Waiting until cooler weather, Jesup again entered the field in September 1837. Osceola had established a camp on the St. Johns River in northeast Florida, and Jesup moved from the west while Brigadier General Joseph M. Hernandez marched from St. Augustine on the east. The Indians proved exhausted, and surrenders took place in the face of the advancing troops. In October Osceola asked for a conference, and Jesup authorized Hernandez to meet and, if necessary, to capture Osceola. During a truce signaled by a white flag flying over Osceola's camp, Hernandez and two hundred troops seized Osceola when he refused to immigrate. The soldiers disarmed the Indians and conducted them to St. Augustine. Jesup confined Osceola at Fort Marion, but some Seminoles led by Coacoochee (Wild Cat) escaped. Jesup decided to send both Osceola and Micanopy to Fort Moultrie on Sullivan's Island at Charleston, South Carolina, to ensure that they would not flee. In captivity, Osceola's malaria caused his vitality to decline rapidly, and the Seminole leader refused to be treated by Dr. Frederick Weeden because the doctor was Wiley Thompson's brother-in-law. Osceola died a prisoner of the United States on January 30, 1838.

814

Osceola's military role among the Seminoles proved brief. He stood firm against removal and employed traditional Indian tactics against American commanders while making full use of the geography and environment of Florida which lent themselves admirably to Indian warfare. Small, mobile Seminole bands harassed much larger American forces for seven years during which the military reputations of many officers were besmirched. The Seminoles and especially their black allies inflicted heavy casualties on the Army and great cost on the government from 1835 to 1838. The war did not close until 1842 and represented the "bitterest episode in the annals of the frontier army." At that point, fewer than three thousand Seminoles had been transported to the Indian Territory at a minimum war cost of $20 million, which represented $6,600 for each Indian removed. For every two Seminoles located in the West, at least one soldier died. The government never overcame or removed a small band of determined Seminoles, and they did not make peace with the United States until well into the twentieth century.

BIBLIOGRAPHY

Foreman, Grant. *Indian Removal: The Emmigration of the Five Civilized Tribes of Indians*. Norman: University of Oklahoma Press, 1932.

Gibson, Arrell M. *Oklahoma: A History of Five Centuries*. Norman: Harlow Publishing Corporation, 1965.

Josephy, Alvin M., Jr. *The Patriot Chiefs: A Chronicle of American Indian Resistance*. Viking Compass Edition. New York: Viking Press, 1969.

McReynolds, Edwin C. *The Seminoles*. Norman: University of Oklahoma Press, 1957.

Mahon, John K. *History of the Second Seminole War, 1835–1842*. Gainesville: University of Florida Press, 1967.

Prucha, Francis P. *The Sword of the Republic: The United States Army on the Frontier, 1783–1846*. New York: Macmillan Company, 1969.

PETER M. WRIGHT

P

PALMER, John McAuley (b. Carlinville, Ill., April 23, 1870; d. Washington, D.C., October 26, 1955), infantry officer, military philosopher, historian. Palmer was an articulate advocate of a democratic army based on organized citizen-soldiers.

Inspired by his grandfather and namesake, a Civil War general, friend of Abraham Lincoln,* and significant figure in Illinois and national politics, John M. Palmer secured an appointment to the U.S. Military Academy, graduating with the class of 1892. Assigned to the 15th Infantry Regiment, then stationed at Fort Sheridan, Illinois, Palmer married Maude Laning of Springfield, whom he had known since childhood, in June 1893. His first taste of military action beyond garrison duty came in 1894 when his regiment had to deal with the riots that accompanied the great railroad strikes of that year. During two years at Fort Grant, Arizona, he experienced the last of the Old Army's frontier garrison life. In 1898 Palmer was detached from his regiment to take up an appointment as the first professor of military science and tactics at the University of Chicago. The coming of the war in Cuba cut short this assignment. Although Palmer reached Santiago after the hostilities ended, he did see action when his regiment participated in the relief expedition to China made necessary by the Boxer Rebellion in 1900.

From 1901 to 1906 Palmer served on the faculty at the U.S. Military Academy. Although he was an indifferent professor of chemistry, while at West Point he began writing in earnest and perfected his literary style, turning out a number of humorous articles with a serious "muckraker" purpose in *McClure's* magazine and elsewhere. In 1906 he went out to the Philippines where he was unexpectedly appointed civil governor of the Lanao District in Mindanao, then still occupied by unpacified warring Muslim chieftains. Palmer took great pride in the successes he achieved in his two years there in ending the practice of slavery and encouraging exports to sustain a prosperous community in peace.

Upon returning to the United States as a captain in 1908, Palmer attended the schools at Fort Leavenworth for two years before moving to the General Staff where he won favorable notice from Chief of Staff Leonard Wood* and Secretary of War Henry Lewis Stimson* with his plan for reconstituting the Army as tactical units instead of the prevailing company-sized posts that had characterized the garrisons of the Indian frontier. When Palmer rejoined his regiment it had moved to Tientsin, China, where it constituted a part of the international peace-keeping garrison. Upon his promotion to major, Palmer transferred to the 24th Infantry on duty at Corregidor in Manila Harbor. While there he drew up war plans for the defense of the Bataan Peninsula. In 1916 Palmer returned to the General Staff where he participated in formulating the Draft Act of 1917 and in drawing up the initial plans for the American Expeditionary Force (AEF) to be sent to France. In addition to his official duties, he actively assisted the private preparedness efforts of the Plattsburgh group and wrote for their journal, *National Service*.

When General John Joseph Pershing* assumed command of the AEF, he chose Palmer as his assistant chief of staff for operations. After arriving in France, Palmer drew up the master plan for the AEF effort against Germany. While recovering from a breakdown brought on by overwork, Palmer assisted in establishing the staff schools which were an important feature of the Pershing program. Later, he served on the mission sent to Italy to provide an American military presence there following the disastrous retreats of 1917. After a convalescent leave in the United States Palmer, by now a colonel, was given command of the 58th Infantry Brigade in the 29th Division, then serving with a French corps near Verdun. Palmer's brigade successfully breached the Hindenburg line not long before the Armistice. This performance by National Guard troops did much to confirm Palmer's faith in citizen-soldiers.

With the coming of peace, Pershing sent Palmer to Washington as his emissary in the anticipated postwar debate on how best to reorganize the army. When subsequently called to testify before the Senate subcommittee drafting such legislation, Palmer, in contrast to virtually all other witnesses, presented a comprehensive and coherent scheme of Army organization based upon a clearly articulated statement of principle. This performance, which probably marked the high point of his career, induced the senators to call for him to serve as a special advisor to the subcommittee. In this capacity he played a pivotal role in drafting the Defense Act of 1920 which was to be the organic statute of the Army for a generation. Although Congress rejected the provision for universal military training which Palmer advocated, many of his schemes for making the citizen components key elements in national defense were enacted. Unfortunately, the structure contemplated by the Defense Act was never fully implemented as successive budget cuts in the 1920s reduced the Army to a skeleton force. Even when Pershing as chief of staff made Palmer his special assistant, the leverage afforded by this position was insufficient to offset the severe reductions in appropriations. After brief service as a brigade commander in Panama, Palmer retired as a brigadier general in 1926.

Retirement by no means signaled the end of Palmer's career. At his summer retirement home in New Hampshire and his winter residence in Washington, he turned out numerous books and articles all aimed at convincing the public and his Army peers that they should regard building a strong organized reserve of citizen-soldiers, officers as well as enlisted men, as a primary concern of the regulars. When war broke out in Europe in 1939, he joined his friends from the Military Training Camps Association and others in a new effort that eventually helped secure passage of the Selective Service Act of 1940. Although Palmer was over seventy at the time, his broad knowledge of and manifest sympathy for citizen-soldiers led Chief of Staff George Catlett Marshall* to order him to active duty as a special advisor on the citizen components.

During most of the period from 1941 to 1946 Palmer assisted the Special Planning Division of the War Department in drafting plans and policies for the postwar Army. Despite his age, he proved to be a vigorous advocate, fending off efforts by his younger colleagues among the regulars to reduce the citizen-soldiers to a mere manpower pool, rank fillers in an expansible Regular Army; he favored territorially organized reserve units officered by reservists with virtually unlimited upward mobility as professionally and politically the most desirable form of citizen component in the total defense force. Although he helped persuade General Marshall to come out officially in favor of compulsory military training in peacetime as the source of manpower for the Army, this new effort to secure universal training was no more acceptable to Congress after the defeat of Germany and Japan than it had been after the Armistice in 1918.

Although John McAuley Palmer never enjoyed popular acclaim as a general, he was widely respected in the upper reaches of the military and national political communities. As George Marshall, his warm friend and associate of more than thirty-five years, put it, Palmer's role was that of "military elder statesman" for the Army. Perhaps more than any other Regular Army officer, he understood the need for devising an army, in his words, "commensurate with the democratic genius of our people." To this end, although himself a regular, he became the champion of the citizen-soldier. Not all Army officers by any means shared his convictions as to the role of the civilian components, but he did wield substantial influence, notably in his relations with George Marshall who was to shape the mightiest army the nation has ever raised and did so largely in the spirit of Palmer's thought. Palmer's major writings include *Statesmanship and War* (1927), *Washington, Lincoln and Wilson—Three War Statesmen* (1930), *General von Steuben* (1937), and *America in Arms* (1941 and 1943).

BIBLIOGRAPHY

Donaldson, W. H., ed. *Biographical Register of the Officers and Graduates of the U.S. Military Academy.* . . . Supplement 7, pp. 1892–93. Chicago: R. R. Donelly and Sons, 1930.
Holden, E. S., ed. *Biographical Register of the Officers and Graduates of the U.S.*

Military Academy....[Cullum]. Supplement 4, 1890–1900, pp. 535–36. Cambridge, Mass.: Riverside Press, 1901.

Holley, I. B., Jr. *General John M. Palmer, Citizen Soldiers, and the Army of a Democracy.* Westport, Conn.: Greenwood Press, 1981.

Register of Graduates and Former Cadets of the United States Military Academy. West Point, N.Y.: Alumni Foundation, 1970.

I. B. HOLLEY, JR.

PARKER, George Marshall, Jr. (b. Sac City, Iowa, April 17, 1889; d. Portland, Oregon, October 24, 1968), military commander. Parker commanded some of "The Battling Bastards of Bataan."

George Marshall Parker, Jr., as his father before him, fought for his country and was taken prisoner of war. George M., Sr., fought for the 21st Regiment Iowa Volunteer Infantry in the American Civil War and was captured and imprisoned for five months. Parker, Jr., would fight and be imprisoned in World War II.

Prior to World War II, Parker's career was fairly typical of the career officer. Graduating from Shattuck School in 1909, he was commissioned as a second lieutenant in the 21st Infantry Division in 1910. He saw service at various posts, camps, and stations in the United States and overseas, including tours in the Philippine Islands, along the Mexican border, and in the Panama Canal Zone. He graduated from the Command and General Staff School in 1923 and from the Army War College in 1925. By 1918 he had reached the grade of major but, as with most Army officers, he had to wait a long time for promotions in the years between World Wars I and II. It was 1934 before he received the silver oak leafs of the rank of lieutenant colonel. As World War II approached, he was promoted to colonel in 1939 and, in April 1941, to brigadier general. His second star, the rank of major general, would come less than two weeks after the United States formally entered World War II.

The outbreak of the war found Parker commanding the South Luzon Force on that main island of the Philippines. At the outbreak of war on December 7, 1941, Parker's force consisted of the 41st and 51st Philippine Army Divisions and a battery of U.S. field artillery. The force was charged with defense of the area generally south and east of Manila. Elements of the 51st were caught in the process of shifting units when the main Japanese landing in the sector began on December 24. By that time, General Douglas MacArthur,* commanding general, U.S. Army Forces Far East (USAFFE), had decided to abandon his plan of holding the beach area at all costs and instead withdraw to the Bataan Peninsula and hold it as a means to prevent full Japanese control of Luzon. Accordingly, Parker was placed in command of the Bataan Defense Force, which at first comprised only elements of the Philippine Division and supporting units, but which quickly included the 31st and 41st and then 51st Philippine Divisions. By January 7, 1942, USAFFE headquarters had moved to Bataan, and Parker's

II Corps forces were now defending the east coast of the peninsula while General Jonathan Mayhew Wainwright's* I Corps defended the west coast.

On January 9 the Japanese moved on Bataan. Giving ground grudgingly and taking advantage of terrain, by January 26 defending forces had nonetheless been pushed back to the line from Bagac on the west coast to Orion on the east coast which MacArthur had designated as the main line of resistance. But the defenders regrouped along this more narrow line and, aided by Japanese fatigue and disease, stopped the enemy. On February 8 the Japanese broke off the engagement to rest and reorganize. The morale of USAFFE's troops soared, but the victory was to be short-lived. On April 3, after a devastating air-artillery bombardment, the reinforced Japanese attacked the starving and disease-ridden defenders. Major General Edward P. King, Jr., who had only shortly before been placed in overall command of the forces on Luzon, surrendered unconditionally on April 9 to try to avert the slaughter of the remnants of his forces. Parker went into a captivity that would last over four years, moving from Luzon to Taiwan to Manchuria before being liberated in August 1945. On September 30, 1946, he retired in the rank of major general.

Students of military history have found much to criticize in their analysis of the loss of the Philippines to the Japanese during World War II. Most of the criticism, both strategic and tactical, centers on the dominating figure of MacArthur, but includes in its sweep many others. The United States came late and with little to the initial defense of the islands. Although MacArthur had been in the Philippines for some time, the maturing of the Philippine defense forces was slow in coming, for the Philippines to mid-1941 had been virtually written off as part of a general War Department Plan that called for maximum effort in Europe and minimal defensive containment in the Far East. As war with Japan loomed, American and Filipino forces were consolidated into a joint command under MacArthur, who then planned to repulse the Japanese at the beaches. MacArthur's target date for readiness was April 1942, but the Japanese struck in December 1941, while most of MacArthur's 120,000 Filipino and 13,500 ground troops were ill-equipped and ill-prepared, especially the Filipinos. Once war came, MacArthur tried to convince Washington that the Japanese were thinly spread and reinforcement was possible. But, although the Army urged relief, the Navy especially did not want to risk its small fleet trying to get through the Japanese blockade to try to relieve an area that did not have high priority in overall planning.

MacArthur and his command, USAFFE, also have been criticized. Planning was optimistic; troop shifting was uncertain and troop strength underreported; despite news of the attack at Pearl Harbor, the air force was largely surprised on the ground and destroyed; command structure at times made supervision and coordination less than desirable; dispersal of the troops on Bataan initially impaired contact between the two corps commanders and, later, placed the frontlines of the II Corps in exposed position along the Pilar-Bagac Road, the major means of lateral communication, as part of the deployment along the main line of resistance from Bagac to Orion.

Within this context, Parker and the other commanders operated. Each no doubt complained about tactical decisions, but, of course, each did so from the point of view of one commanding only part of the battle. The real problem for Parker and others was that, although on paper his forces outnumbered the invaders handsomely, his forces were underequipped and undertrained, and the Pacific Fleet, decimated at Pearl, could not relieve them. Starvation and disease, exacerbated by the lack of air and sea power, would ultimately overcome bravery and skill. Given the larger picture, defeat on Bataan was inevitable.

And yet, if ever the word "defeat" is used imperfectly, it is used imperfectly here, both for the battle and the man. The Japanese timetable called for Luzon to be conquered by the end of January and the rest of the islands two weeks later. Instead of a brief campaign of less than two months, the conquest took six months, with much of that due to the fierce resistance on Bataan. The defenders bought valuable time and showed the world that the Japanese could be withstood. General Parker exemplified this attitude. Although seriously ill when he entered captivity, he not only endured for four years, but he also kept his honor, his courage, and his commander's concern for his troops. On August 18, 1945, after the end of hostilities, General Parker assumed command of the prison camps and recommended that a brigadier general who had served under him be evacuated in his place on the first flight. Both the general and Parker were evacuated.

BIBLIOGRAPHY

Beck, John Jacob. *MacArthur and Wainwright*. Albuquerque: University of New Mexico Press, 1974.

Brougher, William E. *South to Bataan-North to Mukden*. Edited by D. Clayton James. Athens: University of Georgia Press, 1971.

James, D. Clayton. *The Years of MacArthur*. Vols. 1, 2. Boston: Houghton Mifflin Company, 1970, 1975.

Morton, Louis. *The War in the Pacific—The Fall of the Philippines. United States Army in World War II*. Edited by Kent Roberts Greenfield. Washington, D.C.: Office of the Chief of Military History, U.S. Department of the Army, 1953.

Rutherford, Ward. *Fall of the Philippines*. New York: Ballantine Books, 1971.

Wainwright, Jonathan M. *General Wainwright's Story: The Account of Four Years of Humiliating Defeat, Surrender, and Captivity*. Edited by Robert Considine. Garden City, N.Y.: Doubleday, 1946.

JOSEPH P. HOBBS

PARKER, Quanah (b. near Cedar Lake, Tex., ca. 1847; d. near Fort Sill, Okla., February 23, 1911), Nacone Comanche Indian leader.

Quanah Parker was already part of a legend at birth. His mother, Cynthia Ann Parker, was from one of the oldest white families in Texas. Captured at the age of nine, she was raised as a Comanche and married Nawkohnee or Peta Nacona, a Comanche chief. Quanah was one of several children to come of this union, and thus, became a character in one of the West's most tragic stories. In a raid commanded by Sul Ross, Texas Rangers recaptured Quanah's mother in 1860; subsequently, she starved herself to death when her white family denied her request to return to the Comanches. Quanah's father died shortly thereafter due to an infected wound.

Early in life, Quanah proved himself an intelligent and skilled warrior. While still relatively young, he distinguished himself in raids on local Mexican communities and in battles against the much-feared Texas Rangers. Because of his bravery and skill, he became chief of his own band in 1867. At that time, representatives from other Comanche bands joined with Kiowas, Apaches, Cheyennes, and Arapahoes in negotiations with officials of the U.S. government. The negotiations resulted in the Treaty of Medicine Lodge which ten chiefs signed under threat of severe punishment at the hands of the American Army. According to the treaty, these tribes had to move to small stretches of land in Indian Territory. Quanah was one of the Comanche chiefs who refused to acquiesce to the provisions of Medicine Lodge; by doing so, he found himself at war with the United States.

During the next seven years, Quanah led his Comanche warriors in repeated forays against the white settlers and soldiers in the Southwest. Quanah rarely involved his people in full-scale battle. Instead, Comanche warriors attacked suddenly and swiftly, killing a small number of soldiers and stealing horses whenever possible. Colonel Ranald Slidell Mackenzie* marveled at the unorthodox methods of Quanah and his Comanche band. Mackenzie, a brilliant cavalry commander, soon realized that conventional tactics such as those used in the Civil War could not succeed against the Plains Indians. Subsequently, American troops applied nearly constant pressure against Quanah and other Comanches. At the same time, the Comanches and other Plains tribes suffered from the loss of the buffalo primarily due to guns of white hunters. Inevitably, the tribes crumbled under this dual assault. In 1874 Quanah led a band of Comanche, Arapaho, Kiowa, and Cheyenne warriors in an attack against buffalo hunters encamped at Adobe Walls on the South Canadian River in the Texas Panhandle. The withering fire of the hunters' buffalo guns drove off the attacking Indians, and Quanah was slightly wounded in the battle. This fight initiated the Red River War. At the end of this war, in the spring of 1875, Quanah took his followers to Fort Sill, Oklahoma, where he surrendered to Mackenzie. Quanah was one of the last Comanche leaders to surrender his freedom for life on a reservation.

Peace brought many changes to one of the Comanche's fiercest war chiefs. Having stoutly resisted the white man's encroachment into Indian lands, Quanah now just as firmly supported peaceful adjustment to the tribe's new way of life. On learning the story of his mother's experiences, he assumed the name Parker and sought to contact her. He learned of her death and fought for the next thirty-five years to have her remains moved to Oklahoma; he succeeded only a year before his death.

Quite naturally, Quanah quickly became involved in tribal politics and the local administration of Comanche affairs. The young chief was careful to show the proper humility and respect for the older chiefs and soon became the Comanche's leading spokesman. Undoubtedly, the support of various military officers, especially Ranald Mackenzie, and agents of the Indian Bureau helped Quanah's political position. Like other Indian leaders, Quanah resented government interference in tribal affairs but he believed that the Comanches had to adapt to their new life or lose their identity. Thus, he helped track down Indians who ran away from the reservation and urged the return of whites taken prisoner during the years of war. Furthermore, Quanah rented tribal lands for $100,000 per year to white ranchers so that they could graze their cattle. Regarding tribal matters, he urged cooperation with agency officials, supported education for young Indians, and promoted agriculture as a means of achieving prosperity. He also defended the use of peyote in religious ceremonies, although Congress wanted to outlaw the drug.

During his years as peacetime leader, Quanah prospered both economically and personally. The Comanche chief had seven wives and eighteen children, and many considered him to be the wealthiest man in Indian Territory. He built a comfortable home west of Fort Sill and farmed a large tract of land there. Quanah traveled extensively; he visited Washington, D.C., several times to deliver speeches to Congress and to meet with federal officials in charge of Indian affairs. He also became friends with Theodore Roosevelt* and rode in the President's inaugural parade, as did the Apache Chief Geronimo.* In 1911 Quanah Parker died of natural causes and was buried next to his mother.

The historical significance of Quanah Parker can be found in the two major roles he played. He was a significant military leader during the wars fought between the Comanches and the whites, and then he became an important peacetime political leader during the thirty-six years following his surrender in 1875.

As a military commander Quanah was brilliant at guerrilla warfare. He successfully defended his people from the repeated forays of the U.S. Cavalry for several years. His hit-and-run tactics frequently caught cavalry commanders completely off guard. Unfortunately for Quanah, he only delayed the inevitable; the merciless, untiring pursuit of Mackenzie, the destruction of the wild horses and the buffalo, and the white man's superior weapons forced the tribes to surrender one by one. Tactically, Quanah remained unbeaten by his cavalry adversaries, but the Comanche's strategic position gradually deteriorated. Thus, his final choice was either the reservation or the destruction of the tribe, and Quanah chose the reservation.

For the remaining years of his life Quanah Parker fought a different kind of battle. After surrendering, the Comanches had to adjust to a new, settled style of life and try to accommodate themselves to white civilization. Neither goal was an easy task, and both required stable, practical leadership. Quanah filled this role in peace just as he had done during times of war. He consistently fostered programs, such as education and agricultural development, designed to benefit the tribe and ease the transition from the nomadic, fighting life-style of Indian tradition to the settled, peaceful existence required on the reservation. It required a special kind of realistic courage to manage this transition. Quanah Parker had that kind of courage.

BIBLIOGRAPHY

Edmunds, Dave R., ed. *American Indian Leaders*. Lincoln: University of Nebraska Press, 1980.
Fehrenback, T. R. *Comanches: The Destruction of a People*. New York: Alfred A. Knopf, 1974.
Tilghman, Zoe. *Quanah, Eagle of the Comanches*. Oklahoma City, Okla.: Harlow Publishing Company, 1938.
Wallace, Ernest, and E. Adamson Hoebel. *The Comanches: Lords of the South Plains*. Norman: University of Oklahoma Press, 1952.

JAMES WARE

PATCH, Alexander McCarrell (b. Fort Huachuca, Ariz., November 23, 1889; d. San Antonio, Tex., November 21, 1945), lieutenant general, U.S. Army; organizer of the Americal Division; corps and Army commander.

Alexander M. Patch was the son of Captain Alexander M. Patch. Although he was born in Arizona, young Alexander was raised in Lebanon County, Pennsylvania. He attended St. Luke's Preparatory School near Philadelphia and one year at Lehigh University before entering the U.S. Military Academy at West Point in 1909. Graduating from the Academy in 1913, he was commissioned a second lieutenant of infantry.

Patch was promoted to first lieutenant on July 1, 1916, and served that year with the 18th Infantry Regiment on the Mexican border. He was promoted to captain on May 15, 1917, and was sent to France during World War I with the 18th Infantry Regiment, 1st Division. While overseas, he attended the British Machine Gun School in England and then commanded the Machine Gun Battalion of the 1st Division. From April to October 1918 he was director of the Army Machine Gun School in France.

Returning to the 18th Infantry, he served in France and Germany with the regiment until February 1919, when he was reassigned to the Training Section, General Headquarters, American Expeditionary Force. His final assignment was with the chief athletic officer, Headquarters District of Paris during April and May 1919.

During his service in France, Patch was promoted to major on January 5, 1918, and to lieutenant colonel on October 31, 1918. He participated in the Aisne-Marne, St. Mihiel, and Meuse-Argonne campaigns.

Upon his return to the United States, Patch served for short periods at Camp Benning, Georgia, and with the Reserve Officers Training Corps Section of the

Committee on Education and Special Training, Washington, D.C. On March 15, 1920, he reverted to his permanent grade of captain but was promoted to major on July 1. In September he was reassigned as assistant professor of military science and tactics at Staunton Military Academy in Staunton, Virginia, remaining there until August 1924.

In June 1925 he was named the distinguished graduate of his class at the Command and General Staff College, Fort Leavenworth, Kansas. Following his graduation, Patch was assigned to Fort Eustis, Virginia, until August, when he returned to Staunton as professor of military science and tactics.

In August 1928 he was assigned to the 12th Infantry Regiment at Fort Washington, Maryland, where he remained until June 1931. He then became a student at the Army War College, graduated in June 1932, and returned once more to Staunton as professor of military science and tactics. While there, he was promoted on August 1, 1935, to lieutenant colonel.

In July 1936 he became a member of the Infantry Board, Fort Benning, Georgia, where he helped develop and test the three-regiment "triangular" division concept. He became an instructor of the Alabama National Guard in March 1939. The following August 6 Patch was promoted to the temporary grade of colonel and was given command of the 47th Infantry Regiment at Fort Bragg, North Carolina. In December he was ordered to training duty at that post.

Along with promotion to brigadier general, on August 4, 1941, Patch was assigned to command the Infantry Replacement Training Center, Camp Croft, South Carolina.

In early January 1942 he was summoned to Washington, D.C., and was told that he would take command of forces which were to be sent to New Caledonia, in the Pacific. His new command, designated Task Force 6814, included many units of the National Guard 26th and 33d Infantry Divisions which had been made surplus when those commands had reorganized into "triangular" divisions.

The Task Force sailed to the Pacific in late January. It was planned that General Patch should stay in Washington initially and then fly out to join the Task Force in Australia. However, he contracted pneumonia and did not join it until after the force had landed in New Caledonia in early March. He was promoted to the temporary grade of major general on March 10.

Other "surplus" commands joined the Task Force, until the War Department decided to form a division from these formations. Washington authorities suggested the division be named "Necal" (an early code word for the New Caledonia expedition). Patch suggested "Bush" Division. A private in one of the units offered "Americal"—American troops on New Caledonia. "Americal," it was, on May 27, 1942, and Major General Alexander M. Patch became its first commander. The newly formed division underwent intensive training under Patch's direction in order to prepare itself for active combat. He opened a special Officers' Candidate School in June so as to train and commission selected enlisted men from the division. Nearly 385 candidates were finally graduated from the course.

The Americal, under General Patch, relieved the 1st Marine Division on

Guadalcanal on December 9, 1942. He was given command of all troops on the island. He was named commander of the XIV Corps, embracing troops on Guadalcanal and neighboring islands, in January 1943 and remained in this assignment until April, when he was recalled to the United States.

That spring, he took command of the IV Corps area, headquartered at Camp Young, California, where he subsequently directed the training of some one hundred thousand men. He was sent to Sicily in March 1944 to command the Seventh Army.

In July Patch moved to Italy with the Seventh and on August 15, this army, along with five French divisions, invaded southern France in Operation DRAGON. On August 18, Patch was promoted to the temporary rank of lieutenant general. The Seventh Army, under his command, advanced rapidly through France, contacting George Smith Patton, Jr.'s* Third Army north of Dijon on September 11. Becoming part of the 6th Army Group, the Seventh advanced through the Vosges, Alsace, and seized Strasbourg in November. Patch's Seventh saw more hard fighting, as they defeated a heavy German attack in January 1945, closed the Colmar pocket in February, advanced through the Saar, was the first army to reach and cross the Rhine, captured Nuremberg and Munich, finally contacting General Mark Wayne Clarke's* Fifth Army at the Brenner Pass on May 4.

Recalled to the United States in June, General Patch was given command of the Fourth Army at Fort Sam Houston, Texas, on July 7. Again, he was training troops, a task in which he was considered a master.

This assignment was short-lived, however, because in October he was named to a special group to study and recommend what the Army's postwar organization and strength should be. The recommendations made by this group were interesting, sometimes imaginative—and controversial. One recommendation was the establishment of a separate air force. The study was barely completed when General Patch contracted pneumonia. He died on November 21, 1945, and was buried in the National Cemetery, West Point, New York, on November 24.

General Patch's decorations included the Distinguished Service Medal with two oak leaf clusters and the French Order of a Commander of the Legion.

Lieutenant General Alexander M. Patch, known as "Sandy," was noted as a disciplinarian with a "temper like the devil before dawn." He was not without a sense of humor, however, for he was also known for his deadpan wit. Less flamboyant than some other generals, he did, nevertheless, wear a scarf, upon which the map of France had been printed when his army invaded that country.

General Lesley James McNair* called Patch one of the finest corps commanders in the Army. General Dwight David Eisenhower* characterized him as "one of [America's] outstanding troop leaders." He seemed to have a special rapport with the troops he commanded. Although he was full of nervous energy, he was always mindful of his men and tried to spare them whenever possible. Perhaps he was influenced by his extensive knowledge of Rudyard Kipling's works. At any rate, he was able to chat easily with his men, often while rolling a cigarette from a sack of Bull Durham.

But perhaps the overriding characteristics of General Patch were his superior abilities as a leader and trainer of men. He alone was tasked with organizing and training a division overseas in World War II. The division he fathered—the Americal—earned many accolades later in the war. He alone was recalled to the United States twice during the war to take on the difficult, and vital, task of training large numbers of men for combat. He was one of the few senior officers who commanded large formations in both the Pacific and European theaters. From corps command in the Pacific, he rose to command the Seventh Army in Europe.

It is important to note that, in spite of the numerous reassignments he experienced during the war, he rose in rank and was, finally, entrusted with designing a formula for the postwar American Army.

His philosophy of leadership is aptly expressed in his article, which appeared in *Military Review*, December 1943, entitled "Some Thoughts on Leadership." The essence of this philosophy is that leadership is founded on character and that the greatest attributes of a leader are honesty, courage of purpose, and an unselfish attitude. Lieutenant General Alexander M. Patch epitomized these attributes in his own career.

BIBLIOGRAPHY

Cronin, Francis D. *Under the Southern Cross, The Saga of the Americal Division*. Washington, D.C.: Combat Forces Press, 1951.
Patch, Alexander M. "Some Thoughts on Leadership." *Military Review* 22, (December 1943).

                                                                    UZAL W. ENT

PATRICK, Mason Mathews (b. Lewisburg, W. Va., December 13, 1863; d. Washington, D.C., January 29, 1942), military engineer, Air Service leader.

The son of a Confederate surgeon, Mason Patrick attended public and private schools in Lewisburg. For two years after high school, the future soldier was a teacher in his hometown until he won a West Point appointment in 1882. Something of a scholar, the "Mountaineer" graduated in June 1886, ranking second in his seventy-seven-member class. Applause at his scholastic accomplishment and commissioning in the Corps of Engineers came from, among others, his friend and classmate John Joseph ("Black Jack") Pershing.*

The new officer served on Long Island for three years polishing his engineering skills. In June 1889 he was sent to Pennsylvania where he provided outstanding aid to the survivors of the disastrous Johnstown flood. Patrick's career advanced steadily on into the twentieth century. By 1916, he was Commander of the 1st Engineer Regiment in Texas, where General Pershing was chasing Pancho Villa. In April 1917 America entered World War I.

Colonel Patrick sailed for France in August 1917 with his 1st Engineers.

Shortly after stepping ashore, he was brevetted to the rank of brigadier general and placed in charge of lines of communications for the American Expeditionary Force (AEF). Later, he became director of construction and forestry operations and, as such, was effectively the U.S. Army's top engineer in Europe. But for a bit of internal bickering and poor management in another shop, it is probable that Patrick would have remained a road and bridge man for the remainder of the war.

Ever since the Army had purchased its first Wright Flyer in 1909, brass of that service had looked upon aviation as a stepchild peopled by eccentric young officers. For most of America's first year of the war, that view appeared correct; the Army aeronautical service was plagued with a variety of problems. Among the most serious was a failure on the part of American aircraft firms to produce good aircraft, the country's inability to help expand the good French program, lack of training for Yankee airmen, and feuding between the top Army air leaders in Europe.

In 1917-early 1918, the AEF Air Service was commanded by Brigadier General Benjamin Delahauf Foulois,* a pioneering aviator who had led Pershing's air effort against Pancho Villa. He had been appointed by Washington over the head of another flamboyant aeronaut, Colonel William ("Billy") Mitchell.* The latter, a friend of Pershing's, frequently complained to "Black Jack" about Foulois' "inefficiency." It was apparent that what was required was, in the words of historian James J. Hudson, a "square-jawed will and a strong hand able to apply discipline and see that the several units co-operated according to a given plan, on a given date, in a given way, and no other." Pershing, seeking a candidate with such qualities, soon called on his old West Virginia classmate, reasoning that this tough, crusty, mustachioed, nonflying officer could bring order out of confusion. In May 1918, Mason Patrick was named Air Service boss for the entire AEF.

With Patrick's appointment, the jockeying between Foulois and Mitchell died quickly, with Mitchell receiving command of operational units. Thanks largely to Patrick's managerial skill, the logistical and training difficulties facing the AEF Air Service were remedied in time for it to play a vital combat role in the fall 1918 St. Mihiel and Meuse-Argonne campaigns. By Armistice Day in November Patrick's air arm had grown to forty-five aircraft squadrons and twenty-three balloon companies, manned by some sixty thousand officers and men. In just over six months, he had turned a losing little service into a combat-winning organization.

Following the Great War, Patrick returned to the Engineer Corps for a two-year hitch. Then, once more, he was called to bring order to the Air Service. The hot-tempered youngsters, led by Mitchell, were on the warpath again, this time for an independent air force, and needed a restraining hand. In October 1921 Secretary of War John W. Weeks brought in the sixty-year-old to take charge.

On occasion, Patrick was portrayed as an old fogey by the air power enthusiasts of the Mitchell crowd. Such was definitely not the case; he was as dedicated to this service and its promotion as he had been to the Corps of Engineers. As one of his first acts to demonstrate this commitment, the white-haired major general learned to fly under the instruction of Major Herbert A. Dargue—a brave feat given his age and the state of aviation in 1922! During his six-year term, Patrick would, by working through channels, obtain important advances for Army aviation. These included the improvement of training and materiel, an experimental flight program, and much good-will through such public relations activities as the first flight around the world, accomplished by Army flyers in 1924, and the Schneider Cup Triumph of 1925, brought in by James Harold (Jimmy) Doolittle.*

Patrick and Mitchell, his deputy, seemed to fence personally for almost five years. When the new boss arrived at his office on that fall day in 1921, "Billy" was waiting to tell him how to run the service. Listening patiently, Patrick finally suggested that that chore be left to him. The younger man threatened to quit if his ideas were not purchased wholesale; the older man said fine. Mitchell, his bluff called, remained. There was a new understanding between the two.

The years 1921–1925 are often known as the Mitchell Years in the annals of U.S. military aviation. Recent research suggests that the West Virginian and his stormy lieutenant were not really at odds, but were mounting a two-pronged campaign for a more independent air force. Patrick, quietly and with great dignity, patiently testified before all the famous investigative boards of the early 1920s, urging the creation of an Air Corps similar to that of the U.S. Marines. Mitchell, taking the low road in articles, speeches, and in the famous battleship bombing demonstrations, called for an independent service, equal to both the Army and Navy. In different ways, both stressed the value of the airplane as a tool of American defense.

Were the two aviators in secret alliance, using different tactics to gain the same or similar end? We cannot say. It is known that on three occasions, Patrick sent Mitchell on "inspection tours" when the political heat was on. The chief and his deputy participated in many conferences, and as Mitchell's oratory got out of hand, Patrick did attempt to curb it while simultaneously protecting his associate from discipline further up the chain of command. In the end, neither was possible. Billy Mitchell, the "prophet of air power," was out in 1925, the result of America's most famous court-martial.

Though retired, Mitchell, aided by other aviation enthusiasts such as Will Rogers, kept the aviation publicity pressure on. Through skillful testimony from inside, Mason Patrick was able to achieve the Air Corps Act of 1926 which, while not bringing an independent service, is considered the first major step in the creation of the U.S. Air Force.

Major General Patrick retired from the Army in December 1927 after forty-one years of duty. He remained active in aeronautical circles producing a book, many articles, and well-received lectures. Afflicted with heart disease and cancer, he was forced to enter Walter Reed Hospital just before the attack on Pearl

Harbor. There, with his wife Grace and adopted son Bream at his bedside, he died on January 29, 1942, at the age of seventy-eight.

With appropriate ceremony, Patrick was laid to rest in Arlington National Cemetery in early February 1942. On August 26, 1950, the U.S. Air Force's long-range proving ground base at Cocoa, Florida, was named Patrick Air Force Base in honor of the old engineer who had given so much for the cause of American aviation.

Patrick's reputation rests primarily upon his service to U.S. Army aviation during its important early period. When Pershing was faced with Air Service difficulties in the spring of 1918, he reasoned, correctly, that the tough old engineer would be able to stand above the squabbles of the young air officers and bring order to a most confusing situation. Under Patrick's direction and supervision, the Air Service was able to make a useful contribution during the final Allied offensives of World War I.

During his six-year tenure as chief of Air Service, Patrick was able to institute several institutional reforms while demonstrating his promotional ability with international flights. Working behind the scenes, he met with a certain amount of success in dealing with his superiors, Mitchell and the younger air enthusiasts, and even the Congress. His crowning achievement, limited as it may have been, was the Air Corps Act of 1926, which laid a foundation for later Army Air Force-USAF advances.

When Patrick retired from the Army in 1927, he continued to support aviation in general and military aviation in particular. In addition to his 1928 book *The United States in the Air*, he wrote articles and gave many public lectures. Mason Patrick was fortunate in his lateral move from the Corps of Engineers to the Air Service at a time when army aviation was in its infancy. Unfortunately for him, the age which accompanied his years at the pinnacle of his adopted air service did not allow him to see the fulfillment of his visionary 1923 remark: "Undoubtedly, the next war will be decided in the air."

BIBLIOGRAPHY

Burlingame, Roger. *General Billy Mitchell, Champion of Air Defense*. New York: McGraw-Hill, 1952.
DuPre, Flint O. *US Air Force Biographical Dictionary*. New York: Watts, 1965.
Goldberg, Alfred. *A History of the United States Air Force, 1907–1957*. Princeton, N.J.: Princeton University Press, 1957. (Reprinted 1974.)
Hudson, James J. *Hostile Skies: A Combat History of the American Air Service in World War I*. Syracuse, N.Y.: Syracuse University Press, 1968.
Maurer, Maurer, ed. *The US Air Service in World War I*. 2 vols. Washington, D.C.: U.S. Government Printing Office, 1978.

MYRON SMITH

PATTERSON, Robert (b. Cappagh, County Tyrone, Ireland, January 12, 1792; d. Philadelphia, Pa., August 7, 1881), soldier, politician, manufacturer.

Robert Patterson was the son of Francis Patterson who, after being involved in the ill-fated Irish rebellion of 1798, emigrated with his family to Delaware County, Pennsylvania. Young Patterson's military career began in the War of 1812 when he served from October 1812 to April 1813 as captain, lieutenant colonel, and then colonel of the 2d Pennsylvania militia. Upon being transferred to the Regular Army in April 1813, Patterson was first lieutenant of the 22d and then the 32d U.S. Infantry before being promoted captain and deputy quartermaster general in June 1813. Patterson remained a captain with the 32d infantry until honorably discharged in June 1815.

At the termination of the War of 1812, Patterson began an extremely successful business career in Philadelphia. After establishing himself as a commission merchant, his business interests expanded to textile manufacturing. Financial success enhanced Patterson's political influence in the Pennsylvania Democratic party. He was a member of the convention that nominated Andrew Jackson* in 1824, served as Pennsylvania's commissioner of internal improvements in 1827, and was a presidential elector in 1836, casting his ballot for Martin Van Buren.

During these years, Patterson remained an officer in the Pennsylvania militia and devoted much of his time to improving its discipline and military preparedness. In the winter of 1838–1839 Patterson commanded the militia in the so-called Buckshot War that developed from the political disturbances surrounding the disputed governor's race. This experience enhanced his reputation as both a politician and a soldier.

In July 1846, shortly after the Mexican War began, Patterson was appointed major general of volunteers and placed in charge of organizing newly arrived recruits along the Rio Grande. Upon assuming command, Patterson found himself confronted by about eleven thousand troops, most of whom were devoid of discipline and many of whom were debilitated by disease. He demonstrated both energy and organization in implementing a rigid discipline and molding these men for active service.

Patterson's first major action was in Tamaulipas Province during the campaign against Tampico. Upon receiving orders, he marched from Matamoras through the interior to Victoria, and then to Tampico, where he linked up with General Winfield Scott.* Patterson accompanied Scott in the move to Vera Cruz and took part in the siege. Shortly thereafter, Patterson's greatest successes in the Mexican War came during the Battle of Cerro Gordo during which he commanded a division. When the Mexican forces fled the battle scene, Patterson led a cavalry pursuit that captured Jalapa. Although suspect with the professional soldiers because he owed his high rank to political influence, Patterson was mentioned favorably by General Scott in the official battle reports. When Scott began his move on Mexico City, Patterson remained in the Vera Cruz area, actively engaged in suppressing guerrilla bands and protecting supply lines.

Following the Mexican War, Patterson returned to his business interests and eventually became one of the nation's largest textile manufacturers. He also invested heavily in the South in sugar and cotton plantations, while promoting the improvement of both rail and steamship transportation out of Philadelphia.

Patterson's most controversial military service came at the beginning of the Civil War when he was sixty-nine years old. Three days after the firing on Fort Sumter, Patterson returned to the Army as a major general of volunteers on a three-month enlistment. He was placed in command of the Military Departments of Pennsylvania, Delaware, Maryland, and the District of Columbia with headquarters in the Hagerstown, Maryland, area. Most of his fourteen thousand troops were Pennsylvania militia. Patterson suggested immediate action to clear Confederate troops from the heights that dominated Harper's Ferry and then to invade the Shenandoah Valley as far south as Winchester to disperse Confederate troop concentrations. He was overruled in Washington, however, and shortly thereafter, General Scott, who feared hasty, unprepared action, weakened Patterson's force by removing the few Regular Army troops he possessed.

Once Patterson's army began to move on June 16, 1861, he easily took Harper's Ferry, forcing the Confederates under General Joseph Eggleston Johnston* to withdraw southward. This began a month of campaigning that proved extremely crucial for Patterson's military reputation. He was ordered by General Scott in vague and confusing language to hold Johnston in the Shenandoah Valley, preventing his movement to Manassas Junction, without risking defeat. Patterson, whose faulty intelligence greatly overestimated the size of Johnston's force, interpreted his instructions to mean that he should take no risks.

As Patterson cautiously led his army up the Shenandoah Valley toward Winchester, he was further perplexed by the generalship of his Confederate opponents, especially that of cavalry commander Captain James Ewell Brown Stuart.* Upon reaching Bunker Hill, north of Winchester, on July 15, Patterson began a series of erratic movements that doomed his campaign, and with it his military career. The next day, while expressing concern over the approaching expiration of his three-month enlistments, he resumed his march up the valley, talking in terms of attacking Johnston's troops at Winchester. But on July 17, Patterson, claiming the immediate need of reinforcements, withdrew to Charlestown, placing twenty miles between himself and his enemy. Screened by Captain Stuart's cavalry, Johnston, free from enemy pressure, began the movement of his troops to Manassas Junction where they proved to be crucial to Confederate success in the Battle of Bull Run. The result was that Patterson received much of the criticism for the Union failure in the first major battle of the Civil War.

Patterson's military career ended with the expiration of his enlistment on July 27, 1861. He returned to his business interests but spent the remainder of the Civil War attempting to vindicate his actions in the Shenandoah Valley. Patterson remained an officer in the Pennsylvania militia until 1867. Upon retirement he devoted his time to expanding philanthropic interests.

Most of Patterson's successes in the military came in the areas where his accomplishments in the business world provided experience. He was, for instance, a competent administrator in dealing with routine matters, and he emphasized accountability by enforcing strict discipline. His greatest battlefield success came during the Mexican War where he performed satisfactorily as a subordinate commander following specific orders. In both the Mexican War and the Civil War, however, Patterson demonstrated small ability at independent command. Overly cautious and unimaginative, Patterson was not an inspiring leader of men.

BIBLIOGRAPHY

Catton, Bruce. *The Centennial History of the Civil War: The Coming Fury.* Vol. 1. Garden City, N.Y.: Doubleday and Company, 1961.
General Scott and His Staff: Comprising Memoirs of Generals Scott, Twiggs, Smith, Quitman, Shields, Pillow, Lane, Cadwalader, Patterson and Pierce. Freeport, N.Y.: Books for Libraries Press, 1970. (First published in 1848.)
Henry, Robert Selph. *The Story of the Mexican War.* New York: Frederick Ungar Publishing Company, 1950.
Nevins, Allan. *The War for the Union: The Improvised War 1861–1862.* Vol 1. New York: Charles Scribner's Sons, 1959.

                                                            MARION LUCAS

PATTON, George Smith, Jr. (b. San Gabriel, Calif., November 11, 1885; d. Heidelberg, Germany, December 21, 1945), military commander. Patton, known for his relentlessly aggressive tactics, commanded the U.S. Third Army in World War II.

George Smith Patton, Jr., inherited a warrior's legacy from his father's family dating back to the American Revolution. His mother's family had amassed a considerable fortune in landholdings. Patton would love both war and the good life.

After attending Virginia Military Institute for one year, Patton won an appointment to the U.S. Military Academy. Because of a deficiency in mathematics, he graduated with the class of 1909, not 1908. He chose cavalry as his branch, serving at Fort Sheridan, Illinois, and Fort Myer, Virginia. In 1912 he became the first American to compete in the Olympics in the Modern Pentathlon, an event stressing horsemanship. In 1913 he went to the French Cavalry School to study saber methods and horsemanship. From 1913 to 1915 he attended and taught at the cavalry school at Fort Riley, Kansas. He next joined the 8th Cavalry at Fort Bliss and then Sierra Blanca, Texas. On March 13, 1916, he left 8th Cavalry to join the Punitive Expedition into Mexico as aide to General John Joseph Pershing.*

In Mexico Patton saw combat. He killed General Julio Cardenas and his orderly in a firefight. Promoted to captain on May 15, 1917, Patton again joined Pershing in the American Expeditionary Force. In November he became the first member of the Tank Corps and organized the first American tank training center at Langres, France. In August 1918 Patton saw combat as a tank commander. On September 23, during the Meuse-Argonne Offensive, he was wounded, receiving the Purple Heart and Distinguished Service Cross. He left Europe in 1919 as a colonel.

During the interwar years Patton lived well, but professionally he endured the consequences of being in an army reduced in size—he reverted to his rank of captain and did not achieve the rank of colonel again until 1938. He served in various units and attended the Army's advanced schools. He published more than a dozen articles in the *Cavalry Journal*.

As the Army prepared for World War II, Patton assumed greater responsibilities. In July 1940 he went to Fort Benning, Georgia, where he assumed command of the 2d Armored Brigade of the 2d Armored Division; then in April 1941 the division; and, in January 1942 the 1st Armored Corps. In March he organized the Desert Training Center near Indio, California. On the last day of July, he was ordered to Washington to prepare for the Invasion of Africa.

Patton entered combat in command of a thirty-two thousand man force landing on the west coast of Africa on November 8. In the wake of a near-disastrous battle at Kasserine Pass, General Dwight David Eisenhower* named Patton to rejuvenate the II Corps in March 1943. Within two weeks Patton transformed it into an effective unit. He received his third star and in mid-April was pulled out of combat to command the Seventh Army in the invasion of Sicily. He was to provide flank protection for the drive up the north coast to Messina by Montgomery's Eighth Army. Patton chafed at his role, and, from the moment he first went ashore on July 11, 1943, he assumed a more active role. Reacting to Montgomery's stalemate, he got permission to drive toward Palermo. Obtaining that goal on July 22, he wheeled east and captured Messina before the Eighth Army.

Patton's dash brought problems. His forces stalled at Troina for a time, and during this period, he slapped two soldiers in hospitals in separate incidents, contending that they were fit for combat. The controversy resulted in Patton's being left in Sicily in occupation duty, missing any role in the Italian Campaign and losing any possible chance to be the American ground commander in the cross channel invasion of Europe scheduled for mid-1944.

Patton's exile ended in January 1944 when he was brought to England. He went to France on July 6, 1944, a month after D-Day. He initially commanded a corps and then, on August 1, assumed command of the Third Army. Once the breakthrough was made at Avranches, Patton's forces exploited it. Within a week, much of Brittany had been reduced and the Third Army headed east across France for the Lorraine and Saar campaigns, as prelude to driving up the Palatinate corridor and crossing the Rhine between Mainz and Mannheim. But the weather and heavy fortifications, especially at Metz, forced Patton to halt in late November at the Saar. While he prepared for a fresh offensive, the Germans on December 16 attacked in the Ardennes.

Patton correctly anticipated that his Third Army would shift from its Saar bridgehead to the Ardennes front. This wheeling of men and vehicles in winter was a crucial part in the relief of Bastogne and the defeat of the Germans in the

Battle of the Bulge. He made Bastogne more important to the Germans by driving from it into the German flank, forcing the Germans to shift forces to meet that threat. By late January 1945 the Allies returned to the offensive. Patton's role was to be active defense in the area of the Siegfried Line through the Eifel hills past Trier and on down to the Saar. His defense was particularly active, and, despite rough terrain and stiff opposition, his forces captured Trier on March 1. Patton then received orders to move on Koblenz. His armored column struck out, and by March 8 elements of the First and Third had linked up a few miles west of the Rhine. Patton then crossed the Moselle, deep into the Saar. The Third Army then closed the Rhine from Koblenz south to Mannheim. On March 22 Patton's forces crossed the Rhine and began a dash across Germany to clear the Frankfurt Corridor in the direction of Kassel. The Third Army, comprising nearly five hundred thousand men at times, advanced thirty miles a day.

During this campaign, Patton dispatched a tank force sixty miles inside enemy territory to Hammelburg, where his son-in-law was being held. The raid was a complete failure. Patton's final disappointment occurred when he was forbidden to take Prague because of agreements with the Russians.

In September Patton lost his beloved Third Army because of his publicized reluctance to ban former members of the Nazi party from administrative jobs. He was given command of a paper army, the Fifteenth. On December 9, he received a broken neck in a highway accident, and, on December 21, 1945, in a German hospital in Heidelberg, he died in his sleep.

Patton was as complex as he was controversial, both as a person and as a commander. He was the unstable, arrogant, ambitious, detested man of action who loved war. He was also a man who, although proudly believing that he had been many times a warrior, loved beautiful things and was torn by self-doubt. But whatever the mix that made Patton what he was as a person, all these contradictions came together to form one of America's foremost commanders.

Whatever the controversies over Patton as commander, overall and in specific engagements, certain things remain clear. No commander was more audacious, yet Patton never blundered into a major disaster. He at times faced limited opposition, bogged down and fought vainglorious battles, but, commanding more daringly than any other, his forces suffered relatively small losses while gaining great amounts of territory and inflicting substantial losses. Unable to discipline himself, he made his men into martinets and he even inexcusably slapped two of them, but he also molded them into disciplined, effective fighting units. These men mocked and cursed him behind his back and complained, "Our blood, your guts," but they also said they would follow him into Hell. He forced subordinate commanders and men to extend themselves in a way that they might not otherwise have done and to attain the resultant sense of pride and satisfaction. Surely, one of the reasons for this was his personal courage. To the end he remained the commander who personally participated in the battle—anachronistic, perhaps, in a way of war increasingly demanding preparation at a desk, but if so, he was indeed quite a "magnificent anachronism."

Other characteristics of Patton in command reflected this personal touch. He tried hard to ignore limiting orders, often reconnoitering in such a way that his rock soup was started whereby one starts with a rock but the other ingredients change the nature of the soup from the original orders. Thus, he always probed for the lucky break and did not function easily as part of an integrated whole. He, therefore, preferred and was at his best in lightning armored attack. Clearly, few could be indifferent to such a commander, and perhaps that is a prime accolade for leadership.

Through all the controversy, the warrior remained a cavalryman—charge with horse, or charge with tanks, but charge!

BIBLIOGRAPHY

Blumenson, Martin. *The Many Faces of George S. Patton, Jr.* Colorado Springs, Colo.: U.S. Air Force Academy, 1972.
———. *The Patton Papers, 1885–1940* and *1940–1945*. 2 vols. Boston: Houghton Mifflin Company, 1972, 1974.
Codman, Charles R. *Drive.* Boston and Toronto: Litte, Brown and Company, 1957.
Essame, Hubert. *Patton: A Study in Command.* New York: Charles Scribner's Sons, 1974.
Farago, Ladislas. *Patton: Ordeal and Triumph.* New York and Toronto: Ivan Oblensky and George J. McLeod, 1963.

JOSEPH P. HOBBS

PENDLETON, Joseph Henry (b. Rochester, Pa., June 2, 1860; d. San Diego, Calif., February 4, 1942), Marine Corps officer. Pendleton is best known for his exploits in Nicaragua and his handling of the Military Government of Santo Domingo, 1916–1918.

Joseph Pendleton was born the son of a whaling ship officer in Pennsylvania. He was appointed as a cadet to the Naval Academy in 1878. After graduating from the Academy in 1882, he spent two years in the Navy as a cadet engineer. On July 1, 1884, Pendleton transferred to the Marine Corps and was commissioned a second lieutenant.

His first tours as a marine included shore duty at the Marine Barracks in Brooklyn, New York, Portsmouth, New Hampshire, and Mare Island, California, as well as brief sea duty aboard the sloop *Pensacola*. In 1892 he received his first command as officer in charge of the Marine Barracks at Sitka, Alaska. Two years later Pendleton became an instructor at the newly opened Marine School of Application at the Washington, D.C., Marine Barracks. During the Spanish-American War, he saw only brief service aboard the *Yankee* performing Cuban blockade duty.

In the years following the end of the Spanish-American War, Pendleton fulfilled various assignments, mostly in Alaska and the Pacific. In 1899 he was promoted to captain and returned to Alaska to command the Sitka Marine Barracks. In addition, he received high praise from the Navy's Bureau of Equipment for successfully supervising the construction of a new coal depot on Japonsky Island near Sitka. From 1904 to 1906 Pendleton served at various posts in Guam and the Philippines. In the summer of 1906, he was transferred and assigned to command the Marine Barracks at the Puget Sound Navy Yard in Bremerton, Washington. During his three years at Puget Sound, Pendleton ably assisted in construction of various naval facilities there. From 1909 to 1912 he was back in the Philippines, commanding the 1st Marine Brigade in Manila and at times the 2d Regiment at the Marine Post in Olongapo. Pendleton made good use of his leaves of absence to travel throughout China, Indochina, and the Philippines.

Pendleton's career subsequently took a new direction, and most of his remaining service was in the Caribbean and at San Diego, California. Pendleton set off for Nicaragua in September 1912 aboard the cruiser *California* to command the 1st Provisional Regiment. He assumed charge of all Marines in Nicaragua and soon proved his mettle by a victory at the Battle of Coyotepe. This battle, according to Secretary of the Navy Josephus Daniels,* resulted in "entirely crushing the revolution and restoring peace to Nicaragua." In 1913 Pendleton was dispatched to command the 2d Regiment at Guantanamo Bay, Cuba. In April 1914 he took command at San Diego of the reactivated 4th Regiment to meet the threat to American lives and property posed by revolutionaries in Mexico. He put the 4th Regiment in a high state of readiness, but no landings were made on Mexico's west coast.

In July 1914 Pendleton and his men were ordered back to North Island, San Diego. It was evident that Pendleton liked San Diego, and he saw great potential for a Marine training facility there. In fact, he spent much of his last ten years of active service campaigning for the establishment of the Marine Corps Base and Recruit Depot in the area of San Diego known as the Dutch Flats. In 1915 Pendleton devoted his energies to refurbishing the Marine facilities at North Island.

On June 4, 1916, Pendleton and his 4th Regiment received instructions to proceed to the strife-torn Dominican Republic (Santo Domingo). Within the brief span of a month, Pendleton's troops had not only landed but had also triumphantly carried the day in two major battles at Las Trencheras and at Guayacanas. "Uncle Joe," as he was fondly referred to by his men, was promoted to brigadier general in August and was soon detailed to command the 2d Provisional Brigade, which was made up of all the Marine units in the Dominican Republic. Upon creation of Admiral Harry S. Knapp's Military Government of Santo Domingo, Pendleton was ordered to assume the duties of secretary of war, navy, interior, and police, and he organized a new national police force. At two points during his stay in that country, Pendleton operated as the military governor. Although he was denied his ambition of fighting with Marine units in France, Major General George Barnett,* then commandant, saw to it that Pendleton received the Navy Cross for his meritorious work in the Dominican Republic from 1916 to 1918.

Except for brief stints at Parris Island, South Carolina, in 1919 and in the headquarters of the Department of the Pacific at San Francisco in 1924, Pendleton spent the rest of his active duty in San Diego. He presided over the new barracks there in 1921 and commanded the 2d Advance Base Force and the newly formed 5th Brigade.

Upon retirement as a major general on June 2, 1924, Pendleton became even more active in San Diego's civic affairs. He served both on the San Diego School Board and as mayor for the nearby community of Coronado. He was also director of the San Diego Centennial Exposition of 1934–1935.

Pendleton's leadership roles in both Nicaragua and Santo Domingo won him both the undying respect of his Marines and considerable official recognition. His greatest contribution, however, lay in his building up of a West Coast expeditionary force at San Diego which clearly foreshadowed the Fleet Marine Force of the 1930s and 1940s. The organization of the 4th Regiment as an expeditionary force in 1914 contributed directly to the practice and technique of Marine amphibious warfare. Pendleton prepared the regiment for possible landings in western Mexico that never developed, but he was able to exhibit the fine fighting qualities of the regiment in 1916 when called upon to make swift landings in the Dominican Republic. His expert handling of the fighting against rebels in Santo Domingo in the summer of 1916 showed that he also understood the basic concepts of land warfare. At both Las Trencheras and Guayacanas, he was able to dislodge rebel forces from strongly held positions in a relatively short period of time. Simultaneously, he impressed upon his men the need for patience and restraint in dealing with Dominican civilians, which paid off handsomely in excellent cooperation between American forces and the local populace.

Pendleton also applied his qualities of firmness, dedication, and patience to his goal of improving Marine facilities and instructional training at San Diego. His devotion to this goal bore fruit in the San Diego Marine Base. In addition, the Corps acquired and developed a huge Marine training center in World War II at a nearby site, which was named Camp Pendleton in the general's honor.

BIBLIOGRAPHY

Heinl, Robert D., Jr. *Soldiers of the Sea: The United States Marine Corps, 1775-1962.* Annapolis, Md.: Naval Institute Press, 1962.

Lewis, Charles L. *Famous American Marines.* Boston: L. C. Page and Company.

Moskin, J. Robert. *The U.S. Marine Corps Story.* New York: McGraw-Hill Book Company, 1977.

Schuon, Karl. *U.S. Marine Biographical Dictionary.* New York: Franklin Watts, 1963.

GIBSON BELL SMITH

PEPPERRELL, Sir William (b. Kittery, Maine, June 27, 1696; d. Kittery, Maine, July 6, 1759), merchant, political leader, general. Pepperrell commanded the colonial Army during the Louisbourg Expedition of 1745–1746.

William Pepperrell was the son of a former Devonshire seaman who prospered after moving to New England. By the time of William's birth, the elder Pepperrell owned a thriving mercantile establishment and land in southern Maine, which then was part of Massachusetts. As a young man, Pepperrell assisted his father in various commercial ventures and, at age twenty-one, became a full business partner.

Pepperrell's fortune grew rapidly through trade, shipbuilding investments, and land speculation. He traveled widely, forming important friendships with members of the colonial elite. In 1723, Pepperrell married Mary Hirst, Judge Samuel Sewall's grand-daughter. They had four children.

Kittery voters first sent Pepperrell to the general court in 1726; the community returned him to Boston as its representative for over twenty years. Governor Belcher, a close friend, appointed Pepperrell to the Council in 1727 and chief justice of the court of common pleas for York County three years later. Pepperrell also joined the militia, served several years as a junior officer, and, from 1726, commanded the Maine regiment. By the early 1740s Pepperrell was a prominent political leader and one of New England's wealthiest men.

When word of renewed war between England and France reached Boston late in 1744, Pepperrell was president of the Governor's Council. Attacks on Canso and Annapolis Royal prompted Governor William Shirley* to call for an expedition against Louisbourg, the great French fortress on Cape Breton Island. Pepperrell, who believed the reduction of Louisbourg was vital to regional security, helped Shirley win legislative approval of the audacious scheme. New Hampshire and Connecticut promised troops and authorized Shirley to appoint a single field commander.

Shirley sought to unite the colonies by offering the position to Pepperrell, who was respected and popular throughout the region. Pepperrell hesitated at first (he pleaded a lack of military experience), but, after appeals from family and friends, he accepted.

Lieutenant General Pepperrell and approximately four thousand volunteers, escorted by a small colonial navy, arrived off Canso, Nova Scotia, on April 4, 1745. Three men-of-war under Commodore (later Admiral) Peter Warren, sent by the Admiralty at Shirley's request, joined them on April 23. Warren assumed command of all armed vessels; Pepperrell retained control of the Army. After delays caused by ice and fog, Pepperrell's troops landed near Louisbourg on April 30 and quickly placed the city under siege.

With Warren's ships blockading the outer harbor, the siege continued irregularly through May and early June. Pepperrell was quite reluctant to risk a direct assault, but pressured by Warren, he finally prepared to storm the city. Before the attack could be delivered, however, the garrison capitulated. The French commander DuChambon, his troops demoralized and supplies low, agreed to terms on June 16. Pepperrell led his men into Louisbourg the following day.

For his services, Pepperrell was created baronet (the first man born in America so honored), commissioned colonel in the English Army, and authorized to raise a regiment, in America, on the regular establishment. Pepperrell retired from business soon after returning to Boston in 1746, but he remained active, devoting time to provincial politics and the affairs of his new regiment.

Pepperrell never again led troops in battle, although he was appointed temporary commander of all forces in New England and major general in the Royal Army in 1755. On February 20, 1759, he was promoted to lieutenant general. Pepperrell died at his Kittery estate in July of that year.

Pepperrell's reputation rests on his contributions to the success of the Louisbourg Campaign, arguably the greatest colonial military triumph. Despite the enthusiastic tributes of friends in New England, Pepperrell was not a brilliant field commander. He had not directed an army in combat prior to 1745 and, not surprisingly, displayed few strategic or tactical skills during the offensive. Fortunately for Pepperrell, English naval superiority, French weaknesses, and the physical endurance of farmers, artisans, and merchants made up for his most obvious shortcomings.

Pepperrell knew nothing of siege warfare, possessed no coherent plan, and grew increasingly indecisive—almost, it seems, to the point of inertia—after DuChambon refused to give up the fortress early in May. Unsure of his own ability, Pepperrell granted considerable freedom to inexperienced, but more aggressive subordinates. Such significant accomplishments as the occupation of the Grand Battery and the advance of colonial artillery to positions perilously close to the city's walls (where the small pieces could reach both the West Gate and the Citadel) owed more to the initiative of junior officers than to Pepperrell's generalship.

While Pepperrell's virtual abdication of operational control may have paid some unexpected dividends, his withdrawal prolonged the campaign and increased its price in money and lives. The disastrous assault on the Island Battery, for example, resulted largely from the absence of centralized planning and supervision.

Until very recently, most historians emphasized Pepperrell's passivity throughout the seige and accorded him a small part in the victory. Their narratives, with few exceptions, underestimated his valuable, if unspectacular, contributions to the conquest of Louisbourg. A capable spokesman for the project in the Massachusetts legislature, Pepperrell was equally effective at securing money, supplies, and volunteers throughout New England. His diplomacy improved relations between several colonial leaders (notably Shirley and New Hampshire's imperious Benning Wentworth) when it appeared that personal animosity would ruin the venture before any shots were fired.

Pepperrell also promoted cohesion within the Army, which was originally a loose collection of local units. Tact, patience, and personal charm enabled him to curb factionalism within the officer corps and to win the devotion of most soldiers, albeit at the expense of order and discipline. Aware that divided authority could endanger the expedition, Pepperrell moved quickly to create a harmonious partnership with Commodore Warren. The two officers became good friends, conflict between soldiers and sailors occurred infrequently, and cooperation at all levels characterized the period of active operations.

William Pepperrell, an experienced politician, deftly applied lessons learned in Kittery and in the general court to the problems of eighteenth-century coalition warfare. Under his guidance, diverse and often contentious groups united temporarily to wage a complex offensive. In light of the tumultuous history of numerous contemporary alliances, Pepperrell's mastery of the politics of command remains a remarkable achievement.

BIBLIOGRAPHY

Fairchild, Byron. *Messrs. William Pepperrell: Merchants at Piscataqua.* Ithaca, N.Y.: Cornell University Press, 1954.
Leach, Douglas Edward. *Arms for Empire: A Military History of the British Colonies in North America, 1607–1763.* New York: Macmillan Company, 1973.
Osgood, Herbert L. *The American Colonies in the Eighteenth Century.* Vol. 3. New York: Columbia University Press, 1924.
Parkman, Francis. *A Half-Century of Conflict.* Vol. 2. Part 6 of *France and England in North America.* Boston: Little, Brown and Company, 1910.
Pepperrell, Sir William. *The Pepperrell Papers. Collections of the Massachusetts Historical Society.* Sixth Series. Vol. 10. Boston: Massachusetts Historical Society, 1899.
Rawlyk, G. A. *Yankees at Louisbourg.* Orono: University of Maine Press, 1967.
Schutz, John A. *William Shirley: King's Governor of Massachusetts.* Chapel Hill: University of North Carolina Press, 1961.

ROBERT F. PIERCE

PERRY, Matthew Calbraith (b. Newport, R.I., April 10, 1794; d. New York City, N.Y., March 4, 1858), naval officer. Perry is famed as the naval commander and diplomat who led the naval expedition that secured the first treaty between the United States and Japan.

Matthew Calbraith Perry was a member of the distinguished New England family whose Quaker forbears settled in Massachusetts in 1639. Perry's father, Christopher, broke with Quaker pacifism to fight in the Revolution and to sire four sons who served in the Navy, one of whom was Matthew Calbraith's famed elder brother, Oliver Hazard Perry,* the victor on Lake Erie. By his wife, Jane Slidell, Matthew Calbraith Perry had three sons who served in the Navy and the Marines. And the Perry family was joined in marriage to the equally prestigious Rodgers family to form the Perry-Rodgers clan that has given sons to the Navy throughout its history.

After serving a year as midshipman on the 12-gun schooner *Revenge* under Oliver Hazard Perry, the younger Perry in 1810 joined the crack 44-gun frigate *President* as aide to Commodore John Rodgers.* Rodgers was a stern disciplinarian whom Perry held as a model in abiding affection. It was with Perry aboard that in 1811 the *President* engaged the British schooner *Little Belt* (22-guns) and in 1812 the frigate *Belvidera* (36-guns) at the outbreak of the War of 1812. After a cruise on the *President* to Norwegian waters, Perry was commissioned lieutenant (1813) and ordered to the 44-gun frigate *United States*, the flagship of Commodore Stephen Decatur,* which was confined to New Haven by the British blockade until almost the close of the war. After the war, Perry sailed as first lieutenant on the 16-gun brig *Chippewa* with the squadron of Commodore William Bainbridge* that forced peace on the Barbary pirates. He subsequently commanded one or more merchant ships belonging to his brother-in-law, John Slidell.

After Congress had declared that the slave trade was piracy, Perry in 1820 shipped as first lieutenant on the 18-gun corvette *Cyane* on her cruise to the African coast in search of slave traders and to assist with the establishment of a black settlement by the American Colonization Society. Next year, in command of the 12-gun schooner *Shark*, Perry helped move the colonists to the site of the present Monrovia, the capital of Liberia. From Africa in 1822 Perry transferred on the *Shark* to the newly organized West Indies Squadron to patrol against pirates. As first lieutenant and sometime commander of the 74-gun ship-of-the-line *North Carolina* (1825–1826), John Rodgers' flagship in the Mediterranean Squadron, Perry heroically led a landing party to extinguish a serious conflagration on the Smyrna waterfront and cordially assisted the Turkish Capudan Pasha preliminary to the conclusion of the first treaty between the United States and Turkey. Perry's promotion to master commandant came in 1826.

During a decade of shore duty as second officer and eventually as commandant of the New York Navy Yard (1833–1843), Perry distinguished himself as an innovator in the areas of steam propulsion, ordnance, education, and lighthouses. A strong promoter of steam propulsion, Perry supervised construction of the second steamer *Fulton* and demonstrated its effectiveness on the Potomac to the satisfaction of President John Tyler and other dignitaries. This led to the building of the superb steam frigates *Mississippi* and *Missouri* following Perry's designs. In 1839 he established the first naval gunnery center at Sandy Hook for testing shells, shot, and guns. Dedicated to the improvement of naval education, Perry in 1837 won congressional approval of an apprentice system for training youths as sailors, which was abruptly halted by the tragic mutiny on the brig *Somers* (1842). For the enlightenment of officers, Perry was instrumental in founding the Naval Lyceum at the New York Navy Yard and active in the short-lived *Naval Magazine*, the earliest professional American naval journal. He also advised the Navy Department on the Charles Wilkes* Exploring Expedition (1838–1842) and subsequently helped Secretary of the Navy George Bancroft* devise the first curriculum for the U.S. Naval Academy in 1845.

During the initial phases of the Mexican War (1846–1848), Perry served with energy and valor as second-in-command of the large squadron assembled under Commodore David Conner* to blockade the east coast of Mexico. After Perry relieved Conner in 1847, naval forces under his command assisted the army under General Winfield Scott* to capture Vera Cruz, independently captured a number of other Mexican coastal points, and encouraged a secessionist movement in Yucatan. At the war's end, Perry was ordered ashore as general superintending agent of mail steamers, in which capacity he supervised construction of government-subsidized fast mail steamers convertible to warships, among them the luxury liners of the ill-fated Collins Line.

The climax of Perry's distinguished career was his command of the expedition to reopen Japan to foreign intercourse. Although Perry wanted command of the prestigious Mediterranean Squadron, he accepted the assignment to Japan when assured that the administration would provide him with a squadron sufficiently powerful to impress the Japanese with the seriousness of his mission. Perry was instructed to seek assurances from the Japanese that Americans stranded on Japanese shores would be repatriated expeditiously and to obtain permission for American vessels to call at Japanese ports for coal, water, and other supplies as well as limited trade. Throughout his negotiations in Japan, Perry sought with firmness, dignity, and courtesy to impress upon the Japanese the power and determination of the United States. During his first visit to Edo (Tokyo) Bay in July 1854 with two steam frigates and two sloops, Perry presented his credentials and a letter from President Millard Fillmore to the Japanese emperor urging the Japanese to abandon their traditional "closed country" policy. After spending the winter on the China Coast, Perry returned to Japan the following spring with a far larger squadron to press for a treaty and to present gifts representing the material achievements of the West, such as a small steam train, a telegraph, and a printing press. The Japanese responded by agreeing in the Treaty of Kanagawa (March 31, 1854) to open two ports (Shimoda and Hakodate) to American ships seeking supplies and limited trade, to allow an American consul at Shimoda, to treat shipwrecked Americans humanely, and to extend most favored nation treatment to the United States. In the course of the expedition, Perry also secured a similar treaty of limited intercourse with the Kingdom of Ryukyu and purchased a fifty-acre tract for a coaling station at Port Lloyd in the Bonins. Upon his return to the United States, Perry was attached to the Naval Efficiency Board, but his final years were largely devoted to working with Francis Lister Hawks on the three monumental volumes of the *Narrative* of the expedition.

Fondly nicknamed by his subordinates "Old Bruin" and "Old Mat," Perry was a stern, taciturn, and impressive officer whose dedication, energy, and sense of responsibility perhaps commanded more respect than love. Although not endowed with the charisma of his dashing elder brother, the Perry of Lake Erie, Matthew Calbraith Perry possessed qualities of vision and judgment that eventually won for him first place among the officers of his generation as a diplomat, as a reformer, and as a naval commander. In his leadership of the Japan Expedition, the most spectacular achievement in nineteenth-century American naval diplomacy, Perry employed the diplomatic skills perfected in his dealings with Africans, Latin Americans, and others. The Japan Expedition, however, was far more than a simple mission to open relations between two countries, since it was the catalyst that released the forces within the island empire leading to its emergence as one of the great powers of the modern world. Although Perry's treaty did not complete the opening of Japan, it was a judicious first step on the path by which Japan eventually entered the modern world without experiencing the disastrous wars and humiliations suffered by neighboring China.

Perry's statesmanship has unfortunately overshadowed his important achievements as a progressive within the Navy. His support of technological progress, education for officers and enlisted men, and improved conditions on shipboard all mark Perry as an officer in the vanguard of his generation. As a fighting commander during the Mexican War, Perry displayed extraordinary energy, valor, and leadership in enforcing the blockade, but he also exercised superb administrative skills in the management of the largest squadron assembled by the Navy prior to the twentieth century. Both as naval commander and as naval diplomat, Perry was the expression of the spirit of Manifest Destiny that inspired Americans in the nineteenth century to bridge the continent and to carry their trade, their religion, and their flag across the seas to the world's most distant shores.

BIBLIOGRAPHY

Barrows, Edward M. *The Great Commodore: The Exploits of Matthew Calbraith Perry*. Indianapolis, Ind.: Bobbs-Merrill Company, 1935.
Morison, Samuel Eliot. *"Old Bruin": Commodore Matthew Calbraith Perry, 1794–1858*. Boston: Little, Brown and Company, 1967.
Pineau, Roger, ed. *The Japan Expedition: The Personal Journal of Commodore Matthew Calbraith Perry*. Washington, D.C.: Smithsonian Institution Press, 1968.
Walworth, Arthur C. *Black Ships off Japan: The Story of the Japan Expedition*. New York: Alfred A. Knopf, 1946.

WILLIAM R. BRAISTED

PERRY, Oliver Hazard (b. South Kingston, R.I., August 23, 1785; d. near Port of Spain, Trinidad, August 23, 1819), naval officer. Perry is considered the hero of the Battle of Lake Erie, September 10, 1813.

Oliver Hazard Perry was born in the Perry family homestead near Kingston, Rhode Island. His grandfather, Freeman Perry, held prominent judicial rank in the province, owing in part to his marriage into the aristocratic family of Oliver Hazard, and was a Quaker. Perry's father, Christopher R. Perry, with his five brothers, followed the sea as his vocation, thus leaving Perry's schooling largely to his mother, Sarah Wallace Perry, an intelligent woman of Scotch descent. The family made its home in Newport while Oliver was still young, and at the age of fourteen, in 1798, he signed on the 28-gun frigate *General Greene* as a midshipman under the command of his father. Perry reached the rank of lieutenant in 1802 during service on board the 28-gun frigate *Adams* in the Mediterranean. Following a respite back in the United States, Perry accepted appointment to the crew of the 38-gun frigate *Constellation* which sailed for Tripoli in July of 1803. While blockading the Tripolitan coast, Perry was given the captaincy of the 12-gun schooner *Nautilus* within the squadron of Commodore John Rodgers* and continued service at various Mediterranean ports. In 1805 Rodgers transferred Perry to the 44-gun frigate *Constitution*, and in 1806 they returned home.

Back in Rhode Island and Connecticut between 1807 and 1809, Perry directed construction of President Thomas Jefferson's gunboats and commanded several gunboat squadrons at New York and other ports to enforce the Embargo Act. Perry held command of the 12-gun schooner *Revenge*, patrolling the southern Atlantic coast. In 1811, back in Newport on a mission to survey that harbor, the *Revenge* ran aground. Following an investigation that found the pilot at fault, Perry was acquitted of the charge of negligence in the loss of the sunken vessel. The incident kept him on shore, and on May 5, 1811, he was married to Elizabeth Champlin Mason in Newport.

When war broke out in June 1812, Perry had command of a gunboat flotilla stationed at Newport. In mid-February of 1813 he received orders to report to Lake Erie for service under Commodore Isaac Chauncey.* He arrived at Presque Isle, the present site of Erie, Pennsylvania, in March, only to find that no American fleet existed to deter the British from controlling the Lake. Master Commandant Perry spent the spring building vessels. By summer he had ten vessels but lacked officers and men enough to encounter the British force of Captain Robert H. Barclay known to be patrolling in the Lake. When Commodore Chauncey finally sent a crew, which Perry considered a motley bunch, the commander proceeded to the difficult task of getting the vessels over the sandbar at the harbor. This was considered the more dangerous as Barclay's force had been patrolling the area diligently, but, to Perry's surprise, the British force was absent from its post during the American endeavor which took place between August 1 and 4. The task was a tricky as well as a physically difficult one of getting the two 20-gun brigs—*Lawrence* and *Niagara*—and the gunboats over the shallow sandbar at the harbor entrance. The trick was managed by securing "camels" to the frigates' hulls, pumping out the water, and floating the vessels across at a less than normal hull depth. On August 8 Perry received a contingent of eighty-nine men, led by Lieutenant Jesse Elliot, whom Perry placed in command of the second brig, the *Niagara*. By August 12 the fleet was on its way up the Lake in search of Barclay's force. At Seneca Perry conferred with General William Henry Harrison* who was having to hold up the movement of his army until the lake was cleared of British forces. At the British land base at Malden, up the Detroit River, Perry found Barclay's fleet at anchor on August 25. The confrontation of fleets was delayed by strong and uncertain winds, the outfitting of the British flagship, the corvette *Detroit* (20-guns) which was just built and launched, and the illness of Perry and much of his crew. Further manpower arrived at the end of August when General Harrison sent Perry about one hundred reinforcements to man the vessels. Perry's fleet was anchored in Put in Bay. On September 1 Perry returned to Malden where he learned that the *Detroit* was fitted out but that Barclay was still not ready for battle. Perry considered a direct attack on Malden to be too risky to undertake. Ten days later Barclay's fleet approached, and Perry sailed to meet it in the Lake. There, on September 10,

1813, the two fleets joined in battle. Perry's flagship *Lawrence* fought until shattered, whereupon Perry, having proclaimed "Don't give up the ship," transferred his command to the *Niagara* from which he proceeded to devastate the *Detroit* and much of the rest of the British fleet. The laggardness of the *Niagara* prior to Perry's boarding of it led to a bitter dispute between its commander, Jesse Elliott, and Perry, with Elliott claiming he had been treated unfairly in Perry's reports of the battle.

Perry went on shore to join Harrison's army in pursuit of the British Army. He assisted in the Battle of the Thames on October 5, another defeat for the British, and rejoined his fleet at Detroit. By mid-November he was home in Newport.

Perry resigned his command, accepted prize money from Congress, and assisted in defense preparations for coastal towns. In 1814 he assisted in the defense of Baltimore, having been promised command of the 44-gun frigate *Java* under construction there. In command of the *Java* Perry sailed for the Mediterranean in 1816.

During his duty there he struck Marine Captain John Heath in a burst of passion concerning the captain's conduct. This led to a court-martial at which Perry received only a reprimand. Back in Newport in 1818 the dispute with Elliott, which had been festering, worsened to the point that each party asked for a Navy court-martial. Meanwhile (in May 1819), Perry accepted President James Monroe's request that he undertake a diplomatic mission to Venezuela.

In command of the 28-gun frigate *John Adams* and the schooner *Nonsuch*, he sailed to the Orinoco River. Finding its mouth after much expenditure of time and difficulty, Perry was able to take only the smaller vessel up the river the several hundred miles to Angostura, the seat of the new republic. Simón Bolívar was away, but his vice-president received Perry warmly. The mission—to secure Venezuelan payment for captured American vessels—resulted in their agreement to the American demands on August 11. In the meantime, general sickness, probably yellow fever, had broken out among Perry's crew. Eager to leave, Perry nevertheless stayed three days following the agreement out of diplomatic courtesy. During the return journey down the river Perry contracted the fever. He died on board the *Nonsuch* at sea just prior to reaching the *John Adams* which was awaiting his return at Port of Spain, Trinidad. Perry was buried on Trinidad, escorted with British military honors. In 1826 his body was brought back to Newport on board the sloop-of-war *Lexington*.

Perry's reputation rests on his victory on September 10, 1813, at the Battle of Lake Erie. By the time of his death at the age of thirty-four, he had shown qualities of industriousness and perseverance that might have led him to even more noteworthy achievements. His victory on Lake Erie allowed the army of General Harrison to pursue and defeat the British army of General Henry Procter and thus secure the Northwest Territory to the United States. This ended all British plans for superiority over the Great Lakes area.

When Perry first arrived at Presque Isle, there was no fleet to command. Within days he had established both construction operations and command procedures. Once the vessels were ready, the commandant persevered in getting them over the bar, a feat many thought to be impossible. Once engaged in combat he fought as long as he had weapons and men: the victory appears to be justly attributed to Perry.

He went unhesitatingly on land where he took a leadership role in the military Battle of the Thames. The Battle of Lake Erie and the Battle of the Thames crushed forever British efforts to dominate the Northwest region. Perry's comment upon the Battle of Lake Erie—"We have met the enemy and they are ours"—might have been repeated in similar form after his successful mission to Venezuela.

The two blurs on Perry's career—the cases of Jesse Elliott and John Heath—do not appear to have diminished his public luster. The record indicates that Elliott did in fact fail to bring the *Niagara* to Perry's aid in the *Lawrence* during the heat of battle and that, therefore, Perry's censure was justified. In the case of the strike at Heath, Perry appears to have been in the wrong, perhaps temperamentally overwrought by inactivity or a complex of problems.

BIBLIOGRAPHY

Dutton, Charles J. *Oliver Hazard Perry*. New York: Longmans, Green and Company, 1935.
Forester, C. S. *The Age of Fighting Sail: The Story of the Naval War of 1812*. Garden City, N.Y.: Doubleday, 1956.
Guttridge, Leonard F., and Jad D. Smith. *The Commodores: The U.S. Navy in the Age of Sail*. New York: Harper, 1969.
Mahon, John K. *The War of 1812*. Gainesville: University of Florida Press, 1972.

                                                                        FRANK C. MEVERS

PERSHING, John Joseph (b. Laclede, Mo., September[?] 13, 1860; d. Washington, D.C., July 15, 1948), General of the Armies; commander of the American Expeditionary Force (AEF) in World War I.

Shaving a few months off his age so as to qualify for entrance, Pershing entered the U.S. Military Academy in 1882. He was a middling student but a natural leader, being elected president of his class and first captain of cadets. After a stint on the frontier in New Mexico and South Dakota, Pershing served as professor of military science at the University of Nebraska from 1891 to 1895. While there, he had outstanding success with a drill team (the Varsity Rifles), which, when he left in 1895, voted to change its name in his honor, becoming the Pershing Rifles, the first of scores of military companies in America to bear that name.

Pershing returned to West Point as a tactical officer in 1897, where his excessive sternness earned him the nickname "Nigger Jack" or "Black Jack"—a name derived from his service with Negro troops on the frontier. In the Spanish-

American War he did exceedingly well; one officer described him as "cool as a bowl of cracked ice" under fire. He served three tours in the Philippines (1899–1903, 1907–1908, 1909–1913), mostly in Mindanao among the fierce, war-like Moros, where he had considerable success in imposing American authority with a minimum of bloodshed.

In 1905 he married Helen Frances Warren, daughter of Senator Francis E. Warren, chairman of the Senate Military Affairs Committee. The following year he was suddenly promoted from captain to brigadier general, leapfrogging 862 other officers and leading to charges that he had been promoted because of senatorial "pull." Hoping to block confirmation of his promotion, some disgruntled colonels circulated rumors that he had fathered illegitimate children in the Philippines during his first tour. Pershing denied the charges, and the Senate confirmed the promotion, Senator Warren helping to ease the matter through committee. Apart from the senator's influence, Pershing's record was such that he undoubtedly would have become a general anyway, although perhaps not as soon.

Because of trouble on the Mexican border, Pershing served there from 1914 to 1916. While absent from home, his wife and three daughters were killed in a fire at the Presidio in San Francisco in 1915. Although his name was connected romantically with many women thereafter, he never remarried.

With his field experience in commanding the Punitive Expedition in Mexico from 1916 to 1917, Pershing was the logical choice for command of the American Expeditionary Force in Europe when America entered World War I. His only possible rival, Leonard Wood,* was never seriously considered.

The American buildup in Europe was agonizingly slow. Not until May 28, 1918, over a year after declaring war, did American troops engage in any offensive and that was only on a regimental level, at Cantigny. Because of what the Allies considered America's maddeningly slow participation in the war, and because Russia's exit would soon give the Germans manpower superiority on the Western Front, the Allies pressed vigorously for temporary amalgamation of American troops into French and British units. They contended that American staffs and commanders lacked sufficient experience, and by the time they gained it the war might well be lost. The Allies had well-trained staffs and commanders for divisions, corps, and field armies, but lacked the men to fill them. Hence, they argued, America should furnish the necessary manpower—at least during the spring and summer of 1918 when the enemy outnumbered them—to tide them over in the crisis.

The crisis was very severe, as the Germans manhandled Allied armies in five successive offensives (March, April, May, June, and July 1918). But Pershing, maintaining that the crisis was not as great as the Allies contended, steadfastly refused all Allied attempts at amalgamation. His objections were the loss of national identity, the difficulty of reclaiming American contingents without disrupting Allied divisions, language difficulties with the French, recriminations should Allied generals heap up American casualties, and differences in training methods. Specifically, Pershing objected to what he considered an undue Allied emphasis on training for trench warfare as opposed to open warfare.

The American contribution to victory, although late, was substantial. Highlights were the morale lifter at Cantigny, previously mentioned, the action of the 2d and 3d Divisions in blocking the road to Paris against a German breakthrough in May 1918, the 1st and 2d Divisions' spearhead of the Allied attack against the Marne salient on July 18, the subsequent elimination of that salient during late July and early August (the Aisne-Marne Offensive) involving three hundred thousand American troops, the attack on the St. Mihiel salient in September with five hundred thousand American troops, and the final forty-seven-day Meuse-Argonne Offensive which began on September 26 and broke through on November 1, employing an army of over 1 million men.

In addition, there was the moral contribution: the hope given the Allies by the ever-increasing number of American reinforcements and the discouragement caused Germany by the realization that the manpower ratio would grow steadily worse.

After the war Pershing served as chief of staff from 1921 to 1924, when he retired. His later years were devoted to work as chairman of the American Battle Monuments Commission, which supervised American memorials and cemeteries in Europe, and to his memoirs, *My Experiences in the World War* (1931), which won a Pulitzer Prize.

During the war Pershing had some serious disagreements with Peyton Conway March,* the Army chief of staff in Washington. They differed over promotions, over the number of divisions the Americans should have in Europe in 1919 (Pershing wanted far more than March believed possible), and over whether overseas officers should wear the Sam Browne belt. The most serious disagreement, however, concerned which of the two was supreme in the Army. March contended that, as Army chief of staff, he took "rank and precedence" over every other officer, including Pershing. Pershing looked on the Army chief of staff as merely a messenger boy delivering orders from Pershing's civilian superior, the secretary of war. Pershing considered March's contention that he was supreme as similar to a telegraph wire taking on airs simply because it carried an important message.

Part of the difficulty was due to Secretary of War Newton Diehl Baker's* confusion concerning General Staff principles and organization. Although it was quite clear in World War II that Army Chief of Staff George Catlett Marshall* was supreme over the European field commander, Dwight David Eisenhower,* World War I was the first war fought since the creation of the General Staff under Elihu Root* in 1903. It was not that clear which officer was supreme in World War I. Since three chiefs of staff had quickly come and gone before General March took office, and since, during that time, Secretary Baker had increasingly deferred to his overseas commander, Pershing, whom he greatly admired and desired to become America's great war hero, it was hard for March to assert his military supremacy. In actual practice, Secretary Baker permitted March to raise himself only to coordinate authority with Pershing, not superior.

As commander of the AEF, Pershing played an important role in the victory. A careful rather than a brilliant commander, he worked hard in planning an army on a scale sufficient to tip the balance. It was largely the tremendous American influx that converted an Allied rifleman deficit of 324,000 on March 21, 1918, to a 627,000 superiority by Armistice Day.

Captain B. H. Liddell Hart wrote in *Reputations Ten Years After*: "It is sufficient to say that there was perhaps no other man who would or could have built the structure of the American army on the scale he planned. And without that army the war could hardly have been saved and could not have been won."

In the amalgamation controversy, he took great risks, for if the Germans had broken through and won in 1918 the name "Pershing" would have gone down in history as a synonym for a man who made grandiose plans for a magnificent future which never came about because of failure to recognize an immediate crisis. Nonetheless, he did guess correctly in estimating that the successive Allied crises in 1918, especially the German breakthroughs in March and May, were not as severe as the Allies represented them and that they could in fact hold without Americans being amalgamated into their units.

For all of Pershing's talk about the advantage of open-warfare training and his indictment of the Allies for their defensive mentality and stress on trench warfare, the fact remains that during the last five months of the war, when the Germans were pushed back all along the front, the British advanced farther and faster than the Americans. In addition, they captured twice as many guns and almost four times as many prisoners.

Confronted with this fact, Pershing would later argue that his Americans were pushing against the most sensitive part of the German line, the pivot which the enemy had to hold lest he lose vital rail communication to his armies in the northwest, compelling him to withdraw all along the front. Since Field Marshal Paul von Hindenburg called the Meuse-Argonne "our most sensitive point" and said that "the American infantry in the Argonne won the war," there is something to be said for this.

Actually, it is questionable how much the AEF engaged in open warfare, so much lauded by Pershing, especially during the Meuse-Argonne Campaign. Day after day, the American First Army butted its head against stubborn German resisitance, inching its way ahead from September 26 until November 1, 1918, when it finally broke through. Had the war ended on October 31, instead of November 11, 1918, Pershing's reputation would have been considerably diminished. One has only to look at a war map dated October 31 to see how little the American First Army had advanced under his leadership in comparison with its Allies. The First Army breakthrough on November 1, under Major General Hunter Liggett,* provided a happy ending to the AEF experience, producing a euphoria similar to that caused by Andrew Jackson's* victory at New Orleans at the end of the War of 1812. People forgot the earlier failures and concentrated on the final success.

Pershing felt the Armistice was a mistake. "We shouldn't have done it," he said. "If they had given us another ten days we would have rounded up the entire German army, captured it, humiliated it.... The German troops today are marching back into Germany announcing that they have never been defeated.... What I dread is that Germany doesn't know that she was licked. Had they given us another week, we'd have *taught* them." He was correct about the German attitude. On Armistice Day, General Karl von Einem, commander of a German army, told his troops, "Firing has ceased. *Undefeated* [italics mine]...you are terminating the war in enemy country." A decade later Adolph Hitler was preaching the same error.

BIBLIOGRAPHY

Bullard, Robert L. *Personalities and Reminiscences of the War.* Garden City, N.Y.: Doubleday, Page, and Company, 1925.
Coffman, Edward M. *The Hilt of the Sword: The Career of Peyton C. March.* Madison: University of Wisconsin Press, 1966.
————. *The War to End All Wars: The American Military Experience in World War I.* New York: Oxford University Press, 1968.
Smythe, Donald. *Guerrilla Warrior: The Early Life of John J. Pershing.* New York: Charles Scribner's Sons, 1973.
Vandiver, Frank E. *Black Jack: The Life and Times of John J. Pershing.* 2 vols. College Station: Texas A & M Press, 1977.

DONALD SMYTHE

PHIPS, Sir William (b. Pemaquid, Maine, February 2, 1651; d. London, February 18, 1695), ship's captain, treasure hunter, commander of colonial forces, and first royal governor of Massachusetts.

William Phips was born into a large family struggling to eke out an existence in the frontier areas of Maine. Tending sheep for his widowed mother, Phips acquired the physical strength and emotional self-confidence that would be a trademark throughout his career. Dissatisfied with the restrictions of rural life, he became an apprentice to a ship's carpenter. After he mastered the trade, he moved to Boston where he hoped to improve his station in life.

As a young man in Boston, Phips demonstrated both his capacity for hard work and his boundless energy for self-promotion. Starting as a ship's carpenter, he was soon involved in the ship industry as a building contractor and as the commander of a small coastal vessel. His advancement was aided by an advantageous marriage to Mary Spencer Hull, the widow of a prominent merchant. Phips' rise in business and his marriage brought him valuable contacts but did not result in the social acceptance that he desperately desired.

Unsatisfied with the slow returns in shipbuilding, Phips sought a quicker route to wealth and social prominence. He plunged into the lucrative but risky and highly competitive business of treasure hunting. A 1683 voyage on the *Rose*, partially financed by Charles II, found no treasure but did demonstrate Phips' ability to lead men through sheer force of personality. On more than one occasion Phips had to face down attempted mutinies by his undisciplined crew. In 1686 he sailed again with private financing arranged by the duke of Albemarle and a royal patent to raise Spanish treasure. This time, through a combination of luck, skillful sailing, and outrageous bravado, Phips succeeded in locating and salvaging a Spanish wreck off the coast of Hispaniola.

In 1687 Phips returned to England with a huge fortune and was knighted by a grateful James II. Still longing for social acceptance at home, Phips purchased a position as provost marshal-general in the Dominion of New England and sailed for Boston. Ignored by Governor Edmund Andros and the other officials of the Dominion government, Phips fell into an alliance with the old Puritan leadership opposed to Andros. Returning again to England, Phips cooperated with Increase Mather in trying to restore the old charter and then sailed back to Boston in 1689 to find that his fellow citizens had already rebelled against the Andros government.

In March 1690 Phips officially allied with the old ruling elite. He joined the Mathers' church, became a freeman of the colony, and volunteered to lead an expedition against Port Royal. Massachusetts had long desired to lessen the French threat to the New England coast, and this seemed to be the perfect opportunity. As major general and commander in chief of the colonial forces, Phips made maximum use of his qualities of daring and bravado. Phips' fleet sailed from Boston in mid-April, caught Port Royal by surprise, and cowed the French garrison into surrender by the end of May.

Buoyed by this success, leaders of the New England colonies and New York now decided on a bold stroke to capture French Canada. Fitz-John Winthrop* was chosen to lead an army north to capture Montreal while Phips was to conquer Quebec with a combined army and naval force. Unfortunately, this time bluster was not enough, and the expedition was hindered by problems from the beginning. Departing late in the season, poorly provisioned, with inexperienced sailors, and lacking proper pilots, the expedition had little chance of success. Only Phips' leadership and grim determination enabled the fleet to reach Quebec at all. Because Winthrop's army had already abandoned the invasion, Louis de Buade, Count Frontenac, was able to concentrate his defenses at Quebec. When Phips saw that his bluffs had no effect on the French defenders, he had no choice but to order a return to Boston.

Convinced that the conquest of Canada was the key to New England's defense, Phips immediately sailed for England to seek royal support for a new expedition. There he found King William ready to confirm a new charter for Massachusetts. In accepting the new compromise charter, Increase Mather had asked for and received the privilege of selecting the first royal governor. Mather named Sir William Phips.

As governor of Massachusetts Phips continued to lobby for the conquest of Canada, but his personality problems continually frustrated attempts to bring it about. Although authorized as commander of all New England militia, Phips' high-handed attitude destroyed any effective intercolonial cooperation. As a result, control of the Connecticut militia was eventually transferred to the governor of New York. For this reason and others Phips refused to cooperate with Fletcher, thereby eliminating any chance for a combined effort against Canada. Phips continued to push for a royal fleet to attack Quebec, but when Sir Francis Wheler arrived in 1693 with orders to organize just such an expedition, Phips sulked over his inferior appointment as commander of New England Volunteers and Wheler had to abandon the project.

Phips' enemies lost no opportunity to report his failings in London. Although apparently popular with the ordinary townspeople in Boston, Phips had no real power either in the colony or England. In November 1694 he sailed for England in order to defend himself before the king. He died in London in February 1695.

Sir William Phips was not a military commander in the true meaning of the term. He was a strong, energetic, and ambitious colonist who through sheer determination and force of personality rose from apprentice carpenter to royal governor. His treasure hunting expeditions demonstrated his ability to command men as well as his ambitious disregard for higher authority. To achieve his goals Phips flaunted the representatives of England, Spain, and Massachusetts Bay. He showed little understanding of diplomacy in his dealings with fellow ship captains. Yet all these weaknesses could be overlooked as long as he continued to be successful in his pursuits.

The year 1690 brought Phips to his greatest opportunity. The well-executed expedition against Port Royal brought Phips the public acclaim necessary to be effective as a leader of New England militia forces. With a little luck Phips might have succeeded in taking Quebec in 1690 with untold consequences to colonial history.

Although the failure to take Quebec in 1690 cannot be laid too much to Phips' account, he does deserve a healthy share of the blame for subsequent failures. As governor of Massachusetts Bay he missed a golden opportunity to bring to fruition the defense consolidation begun under Andros and the unpopular Dominion government. While Phips pursued personal goals and nursed his wounded ego, intercolonial unity disintegrated.

As a military commander Sir William Phips was best in situations that required forceful action rather than skillful planning. He could command a ship full of cutthroats on a treasure hunt or bluff a surprised French fort into surrender. Yet, even though he understood the general strategy of a Canadian invasion, he lacked the patience or skill to provide the tactical and logistic support necessary to the success of such an invasion. Perhaps he would have acquired these skills had the governorship not brought along political complications and distraction.

BIBLIOGRAPHY

Barnes, V. F. "Phippius Maximus." *New England Quarterly* 1 (1928): 531–53.
———. "The Rise of William Phips." *New England Quarterly* 1 (1928): 271–94.

Mather, Cotton. *The Life of Sir William Phips*. New York: AMS Press, 1971. (Reprint of 1929 edition by Mark Van Doren.)
Thayer, Henry Otis. *Sir William Phips*. Portland, Maine, 1911.

DALE J. SCHMITT

PICKENS, Andrew (b. Paxton Township, Pa., September 19, 1739; d. Tamassee Plantation, present Oconee County, S.C., August 11, 1817), Army officer. Pickens was probably the most capable non-Continental officer to serve America during the War for Independence.

Of Scotch-Irish and French Huguenot ancestry, Pickens was the son of a pioneer who followed the classic migration route from Pennsylvania to Virginia (early 1740s) to the Waxhaw area (present Lancaster County) of South Carolina (early 1750s). Left fatherless at seventeen, Pickens was soon attracted by the adventure of the Cherokee War. He served as an officer in the South Carolina provincial regiment on James Grant's expedition in 1761 and formed his first acquaintance with such eminent men of the low country as Henry Laurens. In 1763 or 1764 he moved to the Long Canes area (modern Abbeville County) and established close ties to the important Calhoun clan by marrying Rebecca, cousin of John Caldwell Calhoun.* A justice of the peace by 1769, Pickens was a moderately well-to-do planter of Whig persuasion, acquainted with both the lowland aristocracy and the frontier leaders, on the eve of hostilities with Great Britain.

A militia captain like his father before him, Pickens took the side of the revolutionary Provincial Congress in the fall of 1775. When the Loyalist militia companies attempted to seize the backcountry, he opposed them in the Battle of Savage Old Fields and was probably involved in the ultimate dispersion of the Tories on Cherokee lands in December. After the Cherokee attacked the backcountry in July 1776, Pickens served with the Ninety-Six District's regiment on the punitive expedition that essentially eliminated that tribe as a military factor in the Revolution. By the fall of 1776 Pickens and militiamen like him had crippled the Loyalists and Indians, two auxiliaries the British would count on when they turned to their "Southern Strategy" in late 1778.

Pickens was promoted to major during the campaign against the Cherokee, the learning ground for his famous partisan or guerrilla tactics. He served in the abortive Florida Campaign of 1778 which saw elements of his regiment involved in active compaigning from April until November, marathon duty for citizen-soldiers. Promoted to colonel of the Upper Ninety-Six Regiment following the elevation of Andrew Williamson to brigadier general, Pickens thwarted the move by Lieutenant Colonel Archibald Campbell to establish control of the Augusta area in early 1779. With about four hundred men Pickens virtually annihilated a Tory force of seven hundred at Kettle Creek on February 14 and dispersed the Creek auxiliaries who attempted to join the British in March. Pickens led his regiment in the assault on Stone Ferry, covered the retreat of the main Continental force, and rushed to the backcountry to participate in the devastation of the Cherokee Valley Settlements in August and September.

After the fall of Charleston in May 1780, which was followed by the occupation of South Carolina, Andrew Pickens accepted British protection. Ironically, the suspected treason of Williamson after capitulation elevated Pickens to leadership of the backcountry patriots, but he remained scrupulously neutral until a Tory force plundered his plantation. Formally renouncing protection in November, Pickens joined Daniel Morgan* the following month, and together they destroyed Banastre Tarleton's force at the Cowpens. Governor John Rutledge promoted Pickens to brigadier general; Congress awarded him a sword for his role at Cowpens. During the race for the Dan River, Major General Nathanael Greene* named him to raise and command the North Carolina militia behind Lord Cornwallis' invading army. Pickens' success against the North Carolina Loyalists, particularly his defeat of Colonel John Pyle (February 24, 1781), prevented Cornwallis from establishing control in the North State and abetted Greene's buildup for the confrontation at Guilford Court House.

Returning to South Carolina in March, Pickens activated the dormant Ninety-Six Brigade and cooperated closely with Greene in the reconquest of the state. Pickens soon isolated the interior garrisons at Forts Ninety-Six and Augusta from the main British army, and he captured Augusta on June 5. He then attempted to restore order in the interior and resume protection of the frontier. Nevertheless, Pickens joined Greene in the low country and led his brigade into the sanguinary Battle of Eutaw Springs where he was wounded. The remainder of the war he spent in pursuit of Tory bands and in three effective campaigns against those Cherokee still assisting the British cause.

Prestige earned in war elevated Pickens to a part-time career as a legislator. Serving six terms in the South Carolina Assembly, one in the state Senate, and one term in Congress, Pickens utilized his knowledge of the backcountry on many committees studying Indian affairs, frontier defense, and border controversies. He helped negotiate the Beaufort Convention (1787) that settled the boundary with Georgia and, incidentally, provided for South Carolina's ownership of the Keowee Forks, an area in which he attained great landholdings. He participated in drafting most of the legislation pertinent to laying out the counties, actually surveyed the new jurisdictions, and helped establish a judicial system for the backcountry.

Building on his prestige as a warrior against the Indians, who called him Skyagunsta, Pickens in 1784 established Andrew Pickens and Company for trade with the Southern Indian nations. Trade and fairmindedness toward his recent foes earned their respect and led to his appointment as federal commissioner to negotiate with the Indians. Committed to the idea that lands could be obtained ''only through the medium of Congress, and then only by Treaty or Conquest,'' Pickens fought against efforts by individual states to coerce lands from the Indians. He helped negotiate the three peace treaties of Hopewell (1785–1786) with the Cherokee, Choctaw, and Chickasaw—each had sided with Britain during the Revolution. He failed to make peace with the Creek during the Confederation period, but he was the key figure behind the ultimately successful negotiation with that tribe in 1790. A legalist with regard to the rule of law, Pickens advised President George Washington* to make war on the Creek in 1793 after they violated terms of the Treaty of New York. Soon realizing that whites were more responsible than the red men for renewed hostilities, Pickens helped negotiate the Treaty of Coleraine (1796) which finally brought peace between the Creek and the United States. In collaboration with Benjamin Hawkins, Pickens in 1797 surveyed and marked much of the boundary between the United States and Indian Territory. The last negotiations in which Pickens was involved took place under President Thomas Jefferson. Pickens was satisfied with the treaties of Chickasaw Bluffs and Fort Adams (1801) with the Chickasaw and Choctaw. However, the Treaty of Fort Wilkinson (1802) with the Creek, in which a land cession was coerced, disillusioned him, and Pickens refused to serve again in negotiations with his red friends.

In about 1805 Pickens moved to Tamassee, his lands that abutted the Cherokee boundary. He lived in retirement until the renewed threat of war with Britain brought a last election to the South Carolina Assembly. Heading off a move to make him governor, Pickens worked fruitlessly in 1812–1813 to prepare his state for hostilities. He died peacefully and suddenly at Tamassee in 1817.

Despite the fame that has become attached to the guerrilla resistance to British occupation (1780–1782) in which Pickens played such a major role, he probably should be first remembered as a symbol of the function of the Southern militia-man. By the time the British adopted their Southern Strategy in 1778, the assistance of Loyalist and Indian auxiliaries was vital for success. In the early years of the war, long before the British seized Savannah, the patriot militiamen gave deathblows to those potential allies. Pickens continued to wage war against the Loyalists throughout the Revolution. Without the assistance of Colonel Boyd's Tories, Campbell could not hold interior Georgia in 1779. Without the rising of North Carolina Loyalists, Cornwallis was in an untenable situation at Hillsboro in 1781. In both cases Pickens perceived and struck where the British officers were most vulnerable—their dependence on Loyalist support.

Pickens was also the most successful South Carolina militia leader against the other potential ally, the red man. In fact, most of his guerrilla tactics he learned from those masters of ambush, the Cherokee. Campaigning against them on horseback, he learned the invaluable lesson of coordinating his partisan strokes with the main body; he always planned his movements to support those of Greene's Continentals during the reconquest. Some would consider keeping militiamen in siege lines for two weeks at Augusta as Pickens' greatest accomplishment. Although Henry Lee* hailed him as an innovator for his use of swords and horsemen against Indians during the campaigns of 1782, Pickens should be known best for his success in leading militiamen against both British allies in the critical opening years of the Revolution in the South.

BIBLIOGRAPHY

Ferguson, Clyde R. "Carolina and Georgia Patriot and Loyalist Militia in Action, 1778–
    1783." In *The Southern Experience in the American Revolution*. Edited by Jeffrey
    J. Crow and Larry E. Tise. Chapel Hill: University of North Carolina Press, 1978.
———. "Functions of the Partisan-Militia in the South During the American Revolu-
    tion." In *The Revolutionary War in the South*. Edited by W. Robert Higgins.
    Durham, N.C.: Duke University Press, 1979.
———. "General Andrew Pickens." Ph.D. dissertation, Duke University, 1960.
Hennig, Helen Kohn. *Great South Carolinians*. Chapel Hill: University of North Carolina
    Press, 1940.
Pickens, Andrew Lee. *Skyagunsta: The Border Wizard Owl, Major-General Andrew
    Pickens (1739–1817)*. Greenville, S.C.: Observer Printing Company, 1934.
Waring, Alice Noble. *The Fighting Elder: Andrew Pickens (1739–1817)*. Columbia:
    University of South Carolina Press, 1962.

CLYDE R. FERGUSON

PICKETT, George Edward (b. Richmond, Va., February 28, 1825; d. Norfolk, Va., July 30, 1875), Confederate general. Pickett lent his name to the
Confederate charge at the Battle of Gettysburg.

George E. Pickett, the eldest son of Robert Pickett, a prosperous planter of
Henrico county, Virginia, enjoyed all the advantages accruing to members of
the Tidewater aristocracy, not the least of which was an extended family of
influential relatives. After completing his early education at Richmond Academy,
Pickett read law in the office of one of these relatives, an uncle, Andrew Johnson
of Quincy, Illinois; it was from this state and through his uncle's influence that
Pickett was appointed to West Point in 1842.

Graduating at the very bottom of a fifty-nine member class in 1846, Pickett
was commissioned into the infantry. As a lieutenant during the Mexican War,
he participated in every important engagement of the campaign led by Winfield
Scott* to capture Mexico City, from the siege of Vera Cruz to the storming of
Chapultepec. He was twice brevetted: to first lieutenant for gallantry at Contreras
and Churubusco in August, and to captain for similar conduct at Chapultepec
on September 13, 1847.

After the war Pickett served at a variety of frontier posts in Texas until 1856,
when he was transferred to the Far Northwest to fight Indians. By now a captain,
Pickett achieved the modest pinnacle of his pre-Civil War fame in this remote
corner of the nation, not against the Indians but against the British in Puget
Sound. In 1859 in response to pleas from American settlers on San Juan Island,
who feared both a British invasion and further outrages by the Indians, Pickett
was ordered to occupy the island. This he did with sixty soldiers, and he continued
to hold his ground even when confronted by British threats and the guns of three
warships anchored broadside of his camp. Diplomacy later engineered a joint
British-American occupation of the island, but for his prompt and firm actions
Captain Pickett received both the commendation of his commanding officer and

the thanks of the Washington territorial legislature. Pickett continued in command of the American force on San Juan until June of 1861 when he resigned his commission to enter the Confederate Army.

Upon arriving in Virginia, Pickett was commissioned a colonel and assigned to duty on the lower Rappahannock River. There he won the good-will of Brigadier General T. H. Holmes, through whose influence he probably owed his promotion to brigadier general in February 1862. Pickett's command, the "Gamecock Brigade," fought with elan at Seven Pines, Gaines' Mill, and Williamsburg during the Peninsula Campaign. Having sustained a serious shoulder wound at Gaines Mill, Pickett missed the Maryland Campaign, but in October 1862 he was promoted to major general and assigned command of a division in the corps of James Longstreet.* His division saw little action at Fredericksburg. It was detached from the army of Robert Edward Lee* and participated creditably in the Suffolk Campaign during the Battle of Chancellorsville in early May 1863.

Elements of Pickett's division won everlasting, albeit dubious, fame for themselves and their commander on July 3, 1863, at the Battle of Gettysburg. Although most of the troops that assaulted the center of the Union line that day were not Pickett's, the heroic, fruitless, and bloody attack was immortalized as "Pickett's charge." The three brigades of Pickett's division suffered casualties of over 62 percent in the attack.

On September 23, 1863, Pickett was given command of the Department of Virginia and North Carolina. His attempt to capture New Berne, North Carolina, in February 1864 miscarried. He was ordered to Richmond and turned his command over to General Pierre Gustauve Toutant Beauregard* in late April. Before Beauregard's arrival, Pickett directed a sturdy makeshift defense against a Union force under Benjamin Franklin Butler,* on the Bermuda Hundred line. Pickett then returned to his old division at Cold Harbor and remained with the Army of Northern Virginia until its surrender. On April 1, 1865, his advance position at Five Forks on the far right of Lee's line at Petersburg was overrun by Union forces under the command of General Philip Henry Sheridan.* Five thousand Confederate troops, essentially all that was left of Pickett's command, were forced to surrender.

After the war Pickett was offered a brigadier general's commission by the Khedive of Egypt, but he refused foreign service because his wife could not accompany him. Thereafter he made a barely tolerable living as the Virginia agent of a New York life insurance company. In January 1851 Pickett had married Sally Minge of Richmond, who died shortly thereafter. He took a second wife in 1863, LaSalle Corbell, a woman he loved with passionate intensity, and had two children by her.

Unfortunately for his reputation as a soldier, it was Pickett's unhappy fate to have presided over two of the worst disasters ever to befall Confederate arms in the eastern theater, the charge at Gettysburg and the crushing defeat at Five

Forks. For the first disaster Pickett bears little responsibility but most of the glory. The assault that bears his name was planned by Lee and was carried out by a force that included three of Pickett's brigades plus elements of two other divisions. Although hardly responsible for the ensuing debacle, Pickett, in a report later suppressed by Lee, attempted to blame the attack's failure on lack of support.

Gettysburg not only shattered Pickett's command, but also appears to have permanently shaken Pickett himself. Prior to this time, Pickett had proven himself a capable, if hardly above average, subordinate commander. During the Seven Days' battles, and especially at Seven Pines, Pickett directed his brigade with energy and dispatch. Even so, as a subordinate he left much to be desired. He performed best only under the closest supervision. Longstreet liked him but was always careful to allow him little latitude. Quick thinking—much less imaginative action—was never Pickett's forte.

Moreover, a whimsical streak in his nature asserted itself often enough to make Pickett unreliable or quixotic under pressure. While in departmental command in North Carolina, for example, he ordered the court-martial and execution of twenty-two Carolina unionists, all of whom were serving in the Federal Army, for ''(constructive) desertion.'' During the Suffolk Campaign he absented himself from his division without orders so as to visit his fiancee. Such ''knight-errant doings in the field,'' commented one of his staff officers, were hardly inspiring to the division.

Five Forks was Pickett's most conspicuous failure. Charged with guarding this crucial crossroads along Lee's escape route from Petersburg and astride the southern approach to a vital rail line, Pickett allowed his force of almost ten thousand to be flanked and overrun. When the surprise blow fell, Pickett was two miles in the rear of his line—enjoying a shad-bake dinner. Barely averting capture, he gallantly attempted to rally his troops, but by the time he reached the field the damage had been done. He had not bothered to inform his subordinate commanders of his absence.

His complete culpability for the defeat is open to question, but his lack of judgment is not. And for it he incurred Lee's wrath: he was relieved of his command, or the pitiful remnant thereof, on April 8, 1865, just one day before Lee surrendered. But even then the luster of the heroic charge at Gettysburg surrounded him. And that luster, which only grew brighter with the passage of time, has often obscured the shortcomings of this dashing figure with the long, perfumed tresses. An average brigadier, George Pickett lacked both the stamina and the ability to handle a larger command.

BIBLIOGRAPHY

Coddington, Edward. *The Gettysburg Campaign: A Study in Command.* New York: Charles Scribner's, 1968.
Freeman, Douglas S. *Lee's Lieutenants: A Study in Command.* 3 vols. New York: Charles Scribner's Sons, 1942–1944.

Stewart, George R. *Pickett's Charge: A Microhistory of the Final Attack at Gettysburg, July 3, 1863*. Boston: Houghton Mifflin Company, 1959.

Tucker, Glenn. *High Tide at Gettysburg*. Indianapolis, Ind.: Bobbs-Merrill, 1958.

                                                              THOMAS E. SCHOTT

PIKE, Zebulon Montgomery (b. Lamberton, N.J., January 5, 1779; d. York (now Toronto), Canada, April 27, 1813), Army officer, explorer.

Zebulon Montgomery Pike was born into a family with a celebrated military tradition. His father had participated in the American Revolution and afterwards served as an officer in the U.S. Army. Young Zebulon joined his father's command as a cadet in 1794 and served at a variety of Western posts until receiving his commission as first lieutenant at age twenty. Prospects of only slow promotion through the ranks compelled Pike to seek difficult assignments and to improve his limited education. He taught himself Latin, French, mathematics, and elementary science, as well as familiarized himself with contemporary European military tactics. These skills advanced the young lieutenant beyond fellow officers and enhanced his prospects for leading future exploring parties into the uncharted interior regions of America.

While stationed at Kaskaskia, Illinois, Lieutenant Pike received the opportunity he had been awaiting. General James Wilkinson,* commander of the U.S. Army, ordered him to reconnoiter the upper Mississippi River, consult with the Indian tribes, and counter the British presence in the area. This expedition was necessitated by the Louisiana Purchase in 1803 and the need to extend American power into the northern limits of this newly acquired territory.

On August 9, 1805, Pike departed from a temporary camp near St. Louis and began his ascent of the Mississippi River with twenty men and four months of supplies loaded aboard a keelboat. The party stopped at convenient points along the way to exchange promises of friendship with representatives of the Sac, Fox, Santee Sioux, and Iowa tribes. By September 23, they had reached a Sioux village near the mouth of the Minnesota River, and there Pike secured a tract of about one hundred thousand acres for a future military post to safeguard American interests in the region. Pike continued upriver, first utilizing canoes and then constructing sleds to traverse the frozen river. Pike reached Leech Lake on February 1, 1806, pronounced it to be the ultimate source of the Mississippi River, and thus officially accomplished the main goal of his quest.

The explorers' arrival at St. Louis on April 30 marked the end of an arduous trip that had consumed nine months and had covered more than five thousand miles. Pike, who believed that the mission had been entirely successful, looked forward to an immediate promotion and a brief furlough, but neither was granted because General Wilkinson wanted him to undertake a lengthier investigation of the lands stretching westward to the Rocky Mountains.

Even before the second expedition began, however, some observers concluded that the Mississippi River Expedition had not been entirely satisfactory. Few Indian leaders traveled to St. Louis as they had promised, the Senate refused to ratify Pike's treaty with the Sioux, and the British traders did not terminate their political intrigues with the various tribes. Furthermore, Pike's maps were poorly drawn, and his journals contained numerous errors. Moreover, years later it became apparent that the expedition had mistakenly identified Leech Lake as the origin point for the Mississippi River, when in fact the true origin was the nearby Lake Itasca. These shortcomings detracted from the overall effectiveness of the expedition, but Pike's strengthening of American claims to the Northwest just prior to the War of 1812 aided the United States in postwar boundary settlements.

During his years of service in Western exploration, Pike continued to rise through the ranks. His 1801 marriage to Clarissa Brown, daughter of General John Brown of Kentucky, enhanced his career and allowed him to move within powerful military circles. By April 1813 he had advanced to the rank of brigadier general after engaging in several battles against the British at the beginning of the War of 1812. While leading his troops in a victorious assault on York (now Toronto), Canada, Pike was killed in the explosion of a British powder magazine. He was only thirty-four years old.

Zebulon Montgomery Pike's significance in American history depends upon his controversial journey from St. Louis to the southern Rocky Mountains in 1806–1807, and the impact it had upon U.S. relations with Spanish Mexico. Acting on orders from General Wilkinson, Pike departed St. Louis on July 15, 1806, at the head of a group numbering twenty-one soldiers, an interpreter, and a civilian surgeon, Dr. John H. Robinson. The expedition moved across Kansas to some Pawnee encampments where Pike had hoped to secure agreements of peace and intermediaries to effect contact with the Comanches. The undertaking was not a great success, but Pike did not press the matter because he was more concerned with Wilkinson's order to locate the source of the Red River. Following the Arkansas River to its headwaters, the party moved into Spanish territory and became hopelessly lost, due to the crude nature of Alexander von Humboldt's map which Pike consulted daily. An unsuccessful attempt to climb the mountain (Pike's Peak) which now bears his name and a general reconnaissance of the Royal Gorge area consumed vital time and put the expedition no closer to the headwaters of Red River which lay two hundred miles to the southeast.

Winter came with an uncompromising ferocity, and frostbite and fatigue took their toll on the men of the command. Short of supplies and immobilized by the deep snow, they constructed a small stockade for the ill near the present town of Canon City, Colorado. Pike and the remainder of his group continued shouthward until they reached the Rio Conejos which they mistakenly concluded with the object of their long search. There they built a larger stockade and sent word for their companions to join them.

The Spaniards were not idle in their search for the uninvited Americans. Pike knew that Lieutenant Don Facundo Malgares had orders to intercept him and that smaller scouting parties lay between his stockade and the New Mexico settlements. In his efforts to make contact with the Spaniards, Pike allowed Dr. Robinson to go to Santa Fe. The doctor talked openly with Governor Joaquin del Real Alencaster and told him where the exploring party was quartered. On February 26, 1807, one hundred Spanish soldiers arrived at the Conejos stockade and demanded its surrender. Pike offered no resistance and agreed to meet with officials in Santa Fe.

Pike's meeting with Governor Alencaster was most amiable, but the governor remained convinced that the Americans were on a spying mission. Alencaster's suspicions were borne out by the discovery of several documents, including a hand-drawn map showing a possible invasion route from the U.S. border to New Mexico; a letter from Pike to General Wilkinson stating that he personally would lead an army from St. Louis into Mexico; and a second letter to Wilkinson hinting that Pike would pretend to be lost so that he might scout the Spanish positions.

What to do with the Americans became a question of paramount importance for the Spanish officials. President Thomas Jefferson now demanded freedom for its members, and the release was granted to avoid diplomatic conflict. After a journey of two months across Spanish Texas, the men reached the U.S. military post at Natchitoches, Louisiana, on June 30, 1807.

Upon reaching the safety of American territory, Pike did not receive the public praise he had envisioned. Instead, he found his name associated with the recently discovered conspiracy involving Aaron Burr and General Wilkinson to establish a private empire in the Southwest. A military hearing authorized by Secretary of War Henry Dearborn* cleared the young officer of any complicity in the Burr plot, but most historians conclude that Pike was spying for the United States even though he was unaware of Wilkinson's personal intrigues. The publication of his journals in 1810 gave Americans their first view of the Southwest and created an early interest in the Santa Fe trade which would materialize a decade later.

BIBLIOGRAPHY

Coues, Elliott, ed. *The Expedition of Zebulon Montgomery Pike*. Minneapolis, Minn.: Ross and Haines, 1965.

Goetzmann, William H. *Army Exploration in the American West, 1803-1863*. New Haven, Conn.: Yale University Press, 1959.

Hollon, W. Eugene. *The Lost Pathfinder: Zebulon Montgomery Pike*. Norman: University of Oklahoma Press, 1949.

Jackson, Donald, ed. *Journals of Zebulon Montgomery Pike*. Norman: University of Oklahoma Press, 1966.

MICHAEL L. TATE

PILLOW, Gideon Johnson (b. Williamson County, Tenn., June 8, 1806; d. near Helena, Ark., October 8, 1878), lawyer, soldier. Pillow was a Confederate general of questionable talent.

Gideon Pillow graduated from the University of Nashville in 1827 and practiced law in Columbia, Tennessee. His association with James Knox Polk, later president of the United States, led to Pillow's appointment as brigadier general and, later, major general of volunteers during the Mexican War. He lacked both military training and experience but served under Zachary Taylor* on the Rio Grande and under Winfield Scott* in the Mexico City Campaign, receiving several wounds. Pillow represented himself as Polk's special envoy in the eyes of brother officers, and he maintained private correspondence with the president. This fact, plus publicity surrounding an anonymous letter (the famous "Leonidas Letter") in a New Orleans newspaper derogatory to Scott, embroiled the ambitious Pillow with the Army commander. Two successive courts of inquiry and an able defense by John C. Breckinridge exonerated Pillow, whom Polk considered "a gallant and highly meritorious officer" who was "highly persecuted" by Polk's potential political rival, General Scott.

Pillow enjoyed little political prominence, although he was influential in numerous political machinations involving the presidency in this period. He pursued the vice-presidency unsuccessfully in 1852 and 1856. He remained a conservative concerning Southern secession, opposed lower South extremists in the two Nashville conventions of 1850, and was a Douglas Democrat in 1860. He refused to view Republican victory that year as justification for disunion. But Pillow followed his native state out of the Union and became senior major general in Tennessee's provisional army in 1861. He enthusiastically helped build this army into a fighting force before it passed to Confederate control. He subsequently became a brigadier general in the Provisional Army of the Confederacy.

Great notoriety attended Pillow's Confederate career. He fought the Battle of Belmont, Missouri, November 7, 1861, and chafed at service under Major General (né Episcopal bishop) Leonidas Polk,* whom he considered unqualified to be his military superior. He was second-in-command under Brigadier General John Buchanan Floyd at Fort Donelson, February 12–16, 1862. During that ill-fated siege, Pillow refused to assume command for purposes of surrender, preferring to effect a breakout by the surrounded Confederate Army. Floyd passed the command to Pillow who in turn gave it to the next in command, Brigadier General Simon Bolivar Buckner. Floyd and Pillow escaped prior to Buckner's surrender of the work and approximately fifteen thousand soldiers to the Union forces of Brigadier General Ulysses Simpson Grant.* Pillow was relieved of duty from March through August 1862, pending an official inquiry into the disaster. Confederate Secretary of War George Wythe Randolph held him guilty of "grave errors of judgment in the military operations which resulted in the surrender of the army," but admitted no reason "to question his courage and loyalty." Pillow then engaged in bitter correspondence to regain command, repeatedly threatened resignation, but he never received assignment to field duty thereafter. He briefly served in temporary command of a brigade in Major General Breckinridge's division at the Battle of Murfreesboro, December 31, 1862, to January 2, 1863, due largely to his fortuitous presence at Army headquarters.

Pillow's patriotism and enthusiasm led to two further assignments for the Confederacy. General Joseph Eggleston Johnston* charged him with responsibilities for the new Volunteer and Conscript Bureau of the Army of the Tennessee in January 1863. His overly zealous performance of this duty led to repeated conflicts with the central Conscript Bureau in Richmond. Pillow later succeeded Brigadier General John Henry Winder as commissary general of prisoners in February 1865. Disliked by President Jefferson Davis* and scored for the Donelson failure, Pillow found himself penniless at the end of the war. He unsuccessfully attempted to rebuild his antebellum properties in Tennessee and Arkansas, and finally gravitated to Memphis, where in 1868, he formed a law partnership with former Tennessee governor Isham Green Harris. His postwar legal career was overshadowed by insurmountable personal debts from the wartime period, and he died with a reputation blemished by military failure and malcontent.

Controversy will ever attend the name of Gideon Johnson Pillow as an American military figure. Historians have generally followed the contemporary portrait of a quarrelsome, incompetent amateur, due in part to Pillow's own proclivity for bombastic writing, his adolescent search for attention and adulation, and his distinctly flamboyant inconsistency in the military sector. Of course, Pillow's role in the inglorious "opéra bouffe" surrender deliberations at Fort Donelson will always provide a touch of infamy. Controversy marked Pillow's civilian and military careers, and his peers either liked or despised the Tennessean with little feeling in between.

Like so many Americans of his era, Pillow was an opportunist. He sought to parlay every chance into personal advantage and economic, political, or military gain. His fame came not from brilliance of mind, but from crafty manipulation, boundless energy and enthusiasm, and the power of friendship—all ingredients of a frontier environment of which both Pillow and prewar, rural Tennessee were a part. A shrewd criminal lawyer, he turned courtroom success into local squiredom and vast estates. Then, searching for new outlets, he saw the Mexican War as a way to gain notice and possible political office, all the while espousing typical American noblesse oblige in the guise of patriotism. In this manner, Pillow reflected the classic tenets of the American citizen-soldier.

Yet, this citizen-soldier tradition found itself abutting a growing military professionalism as America matured in the middle years of the nineteenth century. Citizen amateurs like Pillow faced competition from either ancient and venerable warriors such as Scott and Taylor, or the younger generation of West Point-trained leaders. The stakes were similar for both groups—battlefield glory translated into career enhancement, status, rank, and fame. But the methods of the two groups differed somewhat, and Pillow's Mexican War record of conflict with his commander, flaunting of the military chain of command, and staged press releases to snatch glory at the expense of others hardly meshed with the teamwork, camaraderie, loyalty, and selflessness demanded of the professional soldier.

So again was the case when it came to the Civil War. Pillow now prided himself as a veteran, experienced soldier. He quickly became embroiled with others who were placed in positions superior to his own. As in the political and private sector, he sought rewards for his contributions which he magnified through word and action. His smouldering squabbles with Polk, Braxton Bragg,* Breckinridge, and the Confederate War Department dimmed his combat contributions. He proved incapable of the teamwork demanded by the exigencies of the modern battlefield. Most tragic, for example, was the little known or at least appreciated feud between Pillow and Buckner dating to one of Pillow's typical prewar political peccadilloes in which he campaigned for U.S. senator on a public rebuking of Winfield Scott's Mexican War record. Buckner, a loyal West Pointer and veteran of Scott's campaign, took exception in a strongly worded Louisville newspaper article. Neither man ever forgave the other. Apparently, the Confederate high command overlooked this point when both generals were sent to Fort Donelson. Yet, as early as 1857, the seeds of that disaster were sown via a typical American penchant: the use of criticism of military personalities and actions in a political campaign for public office. And Pillow was the culprit.

Still, Pillow, not Buckner, might have emerged from Fort Donelson as a hero. It was Pillow, not Buckner or even Floyd, who consistently advocated a breakout from Grant's encirclement rather than surrender. It was Pillow, not the others, who continually displayed dash and pluck in the eyes of the Confederate fighting men engaged in that four-day battle. On the other hand, it was also Pillow who contributed to the fog of battle and divided command by boastful telegrams to theater headquarters creating a false illusion of victory. It was Pillow whose garbling of the breakout directive led to an impasse at arms and eventual capitulation. And it was also Pillow who displayed wanton lack of military honor by fleeing his command and abandoning his men at the end of the conflict. From this one event alone, Gideon Pillow's reputation as a battlefield leader was shattered.

Unfortunately for both Pillow and the Confederacy, his more positive contributions as a soldier passed virtually unnoticed. Pillow successfully helped build a military machine for his native state in the early days of the conflict. As senior military member of Governor Harris's administration at Nashville, Pillow seemed undaunted by the immense task of self-defense. Yet, here was the ideal matrix of politics and war for which amateurs such as Pillow were well suited. The end result was a tool which Pillow and Harris passed to the Confederacy. The Tennessee army became not only the bulwark of Confederate defense in the West in 1861 and early 1862, but the genesis for the Army of the Tennessee, the principal field force in that theater for the duration of the war. Somewhat tragically, Pillow's own thirst for combat glory led to ultimate destruction of the very machine he helped to create, although he was but one of the factors in its demise.

Creation of the Tennessee army was merely a stepping stone to greater things in Pillow's planning. His parochial goals foundered on the needs of the Confederacy, for the central government needed to accommodate other Southerners and other priorities. To Pillow's discredit he reverted to his customary carping criticism and inflated claims for sympathy and redress. His later contributions to the conscript and prisoner of war activities became enshrouded by his vociferous desire to be reinstated in field command. He could never comprehend that shrill explanations for actions at Fort Donelson, compounded by personality quirks, and a spotty record for insubordination and quarreling simply made him unwelcome to serious Confederate soldiers overwhelmed with the more pressing tasks of the Confederacy's life and death struggle by 1864 and 1865.

The magnitude of personal sacrifice seemed to virtually overcome Pillow by this point. His private correspondence and official communiques with Richmond authorities all display despair and demoralization only thinly veneered by patriotism and enthusiasm for further service. The loss of his vast estates swept away by Union invasion, personal debts incurred while building the Tennessee army and now irredeemable due to the unmarketability of his cotton, and the refugee status of his family all preyed upon his neurotic personality. Nagged by an inability to successfully refute what he termed "misunderstanding" of his role at Fort Donelson, he emerged from the war as much a victim as a product of the eclipsed military dreams of the Confederacy.

Gideon Johnson Pillow typifies to some degree one aspect of the American military tradition. This tradition, bifurcated between citizen amateur volunteers and trained professional regulars, may be in need of some reanalysis. The citizen-soldier—however varied in personality, politics, class, and ethnic background—has continually played the preeminent role in American military history. Such reanalysis of this role, however, may not be aided by enigmatic figures such as Gideon Pillow. Yet, Pillow aptly reflects the intrigues and intricacies, the strengths and weaknesses, the stability, and the inconsistencies in our military tradition. Pillow certainly represented many of the hallmarks of the citizen-soldier. Vainglorious but brave, patriotic but ruggedly individualistic, testy but energetic, Pillow personified the "Minuteman" tradition, confronted in the nineteenth century by a new style of soldiering required by a modern style of warfare no longer entirely tolerant of honest but bumbling amateurism.

BIBLIOGRAPHY

Bell, Patricia. "Gideon Pillow." *Civil War Times Illustrated* 6 (October 1967): 13–19.
Connelly, Thomas L. *Army of the Heartland*. Baton Rouge: Louisiana State University Press, 1967.
———. *Autumn of Glory*. Baton Rouge: Louisiana State University Press, 1971.
Cunliffe, Marcus. *Soldiers and Civilians*. Boston: Little, Brown, 1968.
Stonesifer, Roy P., Jr. "Gideon J. Pillow: A Study in Egotism." *Tennessee Historical Quarterly* 25 (Winter 1966): 340–49.

BENJAMIN FRANKLIN COOLING

POLK, Leonidas (b. Raleigh, N.C., April 10, 1806; d. Pine Mountain, Ga., June 14, 1864), Army officer. Polk, known as the "Fighting Bishop," figured prominently in several Western campaigns of the Civil War.

A member of a prominent North Carolina family, Leonidas Polk was a cousin of President James K. Polk. His father was one of the founders of the University of North Carolina, which Leonidas attended from 1821 to 1823. Polk left the university to enter the U.S. Military Academy at West Point. While at the Academy, Polk became a close friend of Jefferson Davis,* a relationship that would later play an important part in Polk's career. In his senior year at the Military Academy, Polk experienced a religious conversion under the guidance of the post chaplain. Polk graduated eighth out of thirty-eight in the class of 1827 and received a commission in the artillery. Six months after graduation, Polk resigned his commission to study for the ministry.

Polk attended Virginia Theological Seminary and was ordained in the Episcopal Church in 1830. In 1831 he became a priest in the church. Ill-health prevented Polk from actively engaging in the ministry until 1838. At that time he assumed the duties of missionary bishop of the Southwest. In 1841 Polk was selected as the first bishop of the state of Louisiana. There he ran a large sugar plantation in Lafourche Parish in addition to his religious duties. Polk collected contributions of money and a grant of land for the establishment of the University of the South at Sewanee, Tennessee. He laid the cornerstone for the school in October 1860, but classes did not start until after the Civil War.

When the Civil War began, Jefferson Davis offered Polk a commission in the Confederate Army. Although hesitant at first Polk gave in to Davis' request and on June 25, 1861, was appointed a major general. He assumed command of Department No. 2 (Western Department) on July 13, 1861, with the responsibility of fortifying and defending the Mississippi River. On September 4, 1861, Polk ordered his Confederate troops to occupy Columbus, Kentucky, which threw Kentucky over to the Union cause. General Albert Sidney Johnston,* Polk's West Point roommate, assumed command of Department No. 2 on September 15, 1861, relieving Polk, who then became commander of the 1st Division of the department.

In November 1861 Polk submitted his resignation to Davis. Polk believed that he had accomplished his mission of fortifying the Mississippi and that the area was in Johnston's capable hands. Davis and Confederate Treasury Secretary Christopher G. Memminger urged Polk to remain in service. In part their requests were based on their desire to prevent Polk's highest ranking subordinate, Brigadier General Gideon Johnson Pillow,* from succeeding to Polk's command. Polk eventually gave in to these requests and withdrew his resignation.

Polk's first experience commanding troops in combat occurred on November 7, 1861, in an engagement at Belmont, Missouri. He conducted a counterattack against a Federal force commanded by Brigadier General Ulysses Simpson Grant* and defeated Grant following that general's assault on the camp of Pillow's troops. Following the fall of Fort Henry and Fort Donelson and the collapse of the Confederate defenses in Kentucky and central Tennessee, Polk led his troops to Corinth, Mississippi, to concentrate with the remainder of Sidney Johnston's command. At Corinth Polk's troops became the I Corps, Army of the Mississippi.

Polk commanded his corps at Shiloh, April 6–7, 1862, assuming command of the Confederate right wing during the course of the battle. During the invasion of Kentucky led by General Braxton Bragg,* Polk commanded the Right Wing, Army of the Mississippi, and on September 28, 1862, assumed temporary command of the Army. Polk was second-in-command to Bragg at the Battle of Perryville, October 8, 1862. For his services in this battle, Polk received a promotion to lieutenant general to date from October 10.

During the retreat from Kentucky, Polk temporarily commanded Department No. 2. When Bragg reorganized his army and renamed it the Army of the Tennessee, Polk resumed command of his old corps. He led his corps at the Battle of Murfreesboro, Tennessee, December 31, 1862-January 3, 1863, and in the Tullahoma Campaign in June 1863. Following the Battle of Chickamauga, Georgia, September 21–22, 1863, Bragg removed Polk from command because Polk had disobeyed an order to attack during the battle and because he had been critical of Bragg's handling of the Army. Bragg wanted Polk court-martialed, but Davis reinstated him and ordered him to report to General Joseph Eggleston Johnston* in Mississippi to replace Lieutenant General William Joseph Hardee.* Polk assumed command of the Army of the Mississippi on October 23, 1863.

Polk succeeded to command of the Department of Mississippi and East Louisiana on December 23, 1863, when Johnston left to take command of the Army of the Tennessee. On January 28, 1864, Polk's command was expanded and named the Department of Alabama, Mississippi, and East Louisiana. His troops opposed the Union's Meridian Expedition under Major General William Tecumseh Sherman* (February 3-March 5, 1864). Polk took three infantry divisions of his command to reinforce Joe Johnston at Resaca, Georgia, on May 4, 1864. This detachment was known as the Army of the Mississippi or Polk's Corps and participated in the opening stages of the Atlanta Campaign. Polk was killed by a cannon shell at Pine Mountain, near Marietta, while observing the movements of Union troops.

Although certainly one of the Civil War's most noted figures, Polk was not one of the war's better generals. Possessed of an impressive appearance and a commanding personality, he was very popular with his troops. His personal courage was unquestioned, as he demonstrated bravery under fire on several occasions. Yet, with one exception, Polk's performance in command was largely negative. His greatest service came in May 1864 when he personally led his infantry divisions from Mississippi to Resaca to aid Joe Johnston. Johnston had not requested so large a reinforcement, but Polk recognized the danger and probably saved Johnston's army by his quick action. On at least two occasions Polk put forward strategic plans that might have benefited the Confederacy if they had been implemented. He urged a unified command in the West following the Kentucky Campaign so that the war effort there would be more coordinated. Later, Polk suggested realistic operations involving coordinated attacks by the

Army of the Tennessee and the army in Mississippi to drive the Federals out of central Tennessee. The high command in Richmond did not heed his suggestion.

In the long run, Polk must be judged on the basis of the numerous negative aspects of his Civil War service. He was stubborn and sometimes childish. He quarreled frequently with equals, subordinates, and superiors. His most prominent feud was that with Braxton Bragg, whom he constantly tried to undermine. Polk used his friendship with Davis to attack Bragg both openly and in secret, much to the detriment of the war effort in the West. Even when his conduct bordered on insubordination, Polk evaded blame and reprimand. Polk had never learned how to be a good subordinate and to obey orders.

A good case might be made for the conclusion that Polk singlehandedly wrecked the Confederate defense of the West during the first year of the war. When placed in command of Department No. 2, Polk neglected all areas except the Mississippi River, thus leaving the equally vital central South largely undefended. This established a pattern which Sidney Johnston continued to follow after he superseded Polk. Regardless of the strength of Polk's Mississippi River line, these forts could always be flanked and taken from the rear by enemy forces moving down the Tennessee River. Polk's occupation of Columbus, Kentucky, was a serious mistake. Besides the fact that the action caused Kentucky to declare for the Union, Columbus was not even a good defensive position. Following the Federal attack at Belmont, Polk became immobilized at Columbus because he feared other attacks. This fear caused Polk to refuse to send troops to aid Fort Henry and Fort Donelson when those positions were attacked.

Because of his troublemaking, his quarreling with other generals, and his disastrous policies early in the war, the Confederacy might have been better off if Davis had accepted Polk's resignation in late 1861.

BIBLIOGRAPHY

Connelly, Thomas L. *Army of the Heartland: The Army of Tennessee, 1861–1862*. Baton Rouge: Louisiana State University Press, 1967.
———. *Autumn of Glory: The Army of Tennessee, 1862–1865*. Baton Rouge: Louisiana State University Press, 1971.
———, and Archer Jones. *The Politics of Command: Factions and Ideas in Confederate Strategy*. Baton Rouge: Louisiana State University Press, 1973.
Parks, Joseph H. *General Leonidas Polk, C.S.A.—The Fighting Bishop*. Baton Rouge: Louisiana State University Press, 1962.
Polk, William H. *Leonidas Polk: Bishop and General*. 2 vols. New York: Longmans, Green and Company, 1915.

                                                                   ARTHUR W. BERGERON, JR.

PONTIAC (b. probably on the Detroit River ca. 1720; d. Cahokia, Ill., April 20, 1769), Ottawa war chief.

Pontiac was perhaps not a full-blooded Ottawa, and nothing is known of his youth. He claimed to have been an active warrior on the French side in 1746 during King George's War. After assisting the French again in the French and

Indian War from 1755 to 1759, Pontiac and some neighboring chiefs went to Fort Pitt in 1760 to learn what kind of treatment they could expect from a British victory in the war. They were assured by Indian Agent George Croghan that trade would be resumed to their advantage and their land would not be taken. Fort Detroit passed into English hands on November 29, 1760, after the surrender of Canada.

But life under British rule was not what the Lakes Indians expected. Powder was no longer furnished as a gift to improve their hunting. Prices of trade goods were high. The English made no proffers of tobacco or rum out of friendship. Soldiers were not allowed to fraternize, and the Indians were not welcome in the fort. The French in Illinois (part of Louisiana and not included in the capitulation of Canada) and some of those at Detroit promoted Indian disappointment and unrest.

In 1762 Pontiac, one of the most dissatisfied, heard the Delaware Prophet preach in the Ohio Valley. The Prophet was exhorting the Indians to get rid of the white man by throwing off his culture and living self-sufficiently, as their ancestors had. The Prophet's authority was the divine Master of Life. Pontiac recognized an appeal that would unite the tribes in forcing out the British. He did not intend to oust the French, too, but to restore them as benign traders who would keep the Indians supplied with essentials they could not make and would not give up.

When the Detroit River tribes came in from their winter's hunt in 1763, Pontiac called for a general council of local Ottawa, Huron, and Pottawatomi on the Ecorse River, about ten miles below the fort, on April 27. There he delivered his own version of the Delaware Prophet's message and urged warfare, declaring he would enter the fort on May 1 with some of his braves to assess the strength of the garrison and the supplies of the traders, for plunder was a powerful incentive. This visit occurred, and Pontiac told Major Henry Gladwin he would return in a few days with many of his people for a formal visit.

Pontiac called a second war council at the Pottawatomi village on May 5 and meanwhile sent off messages to the Chippewa of Saginaw Bay, the Ottawa of northern Michigan, and the Mississaugi in Ontario to join him. But impatient to begin hostilities, Pontiac announced at the council his plan for a surprise attack on May 7. Gladwin knew of the plot by the next night and thwarted it. A second attempt to enter the fort with a large war party on May 9 was rebuffed. To prevent loss of face among his tribesmen, Pontiac decided to begin the uprising without the advantage of initial surprise. He ordered his village to move across the river a couple of miles above the fort, dispatched war parties to kill any English found outside the fort, and started firing on the stockade.

Pontiac might have used burning arrows to set fire to the buildings, but he did not want to burn any trade goods he hoped to seize. In addition, he might have broken into the fort by storming the stockade, but such an assault would have meant certain death for a few braves, and Indians lacked the discipline to sacrifice a few for the sake of the many. Instead, Pontiac tried to export his revolt by sending two war parties to other forts. He levied assessments of food on the French to feed his warriors and sent a French and Indian delegation to the French commandant in Illinois asking for help. Pontiac was joined by 120 Mississaugi, but the Huron were losing heart.

Fort Sandusky (Ohio) fell on May 16 to a force of Ottawa from Detroit and local Huron. Fort St. Joseph (Niles, Michigan) was captured by Pottawatomi on May 25. The couriers bound for Illinois aroused the Miami to seize Fort Miamis (Fort Wayne, Indiana) on May 27. Farther along they persuaded the Wea, Kickapoo, and Mascouten to capture Fort Ouiatenon (near Lafayette, Indiana) on June 1. The next day the Chippewa in northern Michigan by a ruse during an exhibition game of lacrosse got into Fort Michilimackinac (Mackinaw City), where they killed twenty-one and seized the two highest ranking officers. As a repercussion of this victory, the fort at Green Bay, Wisconsin, was abandoned.

The only British fort left in the West was Detroit. A shipment of provisions to it under an escort of ninety-seven men was captured on the north shore of Lake Erie by a detachment from Pontiac, and over half the escort was killed or taken. Pontiac then sent a war party of two hundred Ottawa eastward. At Fort Presqu'Isle (Erie, Pennsylvania) they were joined by Seneca from western New York who had just taken Fort Venango and Fort Le Boeuf. The combined force easily took Fort Presqu'Isle on June 22. Delaware, Shawnee, and Mingo laid siege to Fort Pitt and struck at Fort Ligonier.

The siege of Fort Detroit was a standoff. Pontiac could not prevent food and ammunition from reaching Gladwin by sailing ships. Gladwin dared not leave the fort to attack the Indians. Chippewa from Saginaw Bay and Pottawatomi from St. Joseph joined Pontiac and raised his strength to 870 warriors. He tried to stop a sailing vessel coming up the river, but it carried a reinforcement of fifty-five that easily beat off a canoe attack. On the night of July 9 he sent a fire raft downstream to bump against the two anchored ships and set them afire. The captains slipped their cables and swung around in the current as the blazing raft passed. Before the end of the month, the couriers to Illinois returned with two messages from the commandant. He told the French to take no part in the war, and he informed Pontiac he could offer no aid because he had heard that a peace treaty between France and England would be signed. Then on July 29 Gladwin was heavily reinforced by 260 redcoats under Captain James Dalyell in twenty-two batteaux which appeared out of the morning mist and tied up at the fort's water gate.

The ambitious captain was eager to punish the Indians, and reluctantly Gladwin let him take 247 men at dawn on July 31 to surprise Pontiac's village. Fully informed of the move, Pontiac prepared a surprise reception on the far side of Parent's Creek. As the British crossed the narrow bridge, the Indians in front opened fire, which rippled around along the extended flank of the marching column. Dalyell soon ordered a retreat, and Major Robert Rogers* used his rangers to prevent the Indians from closing in. Dalyell was killed, and his second-in-command was badly wounded. Protecting squads withdrew as the retreating column passed. By the time it regained the fort, twenty were dead, thirty-seven wounded, and a few had been taken prisoner—about 27 percent casualties. Signal as his victory was, Pontiac had not improved his long-term military position.

Marching west to relieve Fort Pitt, Colonel Henry Bouquet* was attacked near Bushy Run, twenty-six miles east of the fort, on August 5 and won a resounding victory despite 115 casualties. The Indian threat to western Pennsylvania collapsed. In order to stop supplies from reaching Detroit, the Seneca attacked the source: the portage road around Niagara Falls. They laid an ambush on September 14 at a spot called Devil's Hole. A convoy of wagons was struck and overwhelmed. When two companies (about eighty men) from Fort Niagara rushed to their rescue, they were cut down in a withering fire. A frenzied General Jeffery Amherst* in New York ordered the killing of Indian prisoners, the sending of small pox-infected blankets among the tribes, and a reward of £200 to the man who should kill Pontiac. He also promoted Gladwin.

The supply schooner reached the Detroit River on September 2 with a crew of only twelve. Anchored for the night off Turkey Island, it was attacked by 340 Ottawa and Chippewa in canoes. The desperate crew fought them off, losing the captain and one sailor, and four others wounded. The Pottawatomi now gave up the war and were followed by the Mississaugi; the Chippewa were discouraged; and a faction of Ottawa disowned Pontiac's leadership. Yet the chief held on, encouraged by a lying Frenchman from Illinois who told him that a detachment of French troops with packhorses of powder was coming. Pontiac called a council on October 20 but aroused no new determination for war. On October 29 a hard frost at Detroit was followed by four inches of snow. That night a French officer from Illinois brought official word of the treaty between France and England and strong advice to make peace. Pontiac's dream was over. Next day he dictated a note to Gladwin, asking him to "forget the bad things that have taken place." Gladwin replied that he could not make peace, only the general could. Before the middle of November, Pontiac departed with some faithful Ottawa families who camped on the Maumee River.

In April 1764 Pontiac visited Fort de Chartres and stirred up the Illinois Confederation to resist the coming of an English garrison. In July 1765 he met George Croghan at Fort Quiatenon and reluctantly agreed to make peace. He was sent to Sir William Johnson* in New York for formal ceremonies in July 1766, when he was shown great honors. Yet he spent the next three years in relative obscurity on the Maumee. On a visit to Cahokia (across the Mississippi from St. Louis), Pontiac was stabbed by a Peoria and killed. The motive for assassination is not known. Pontiac was buried in Saint Louis at an unknown location.

Pontiac inspired the greatest resistance to British dominion ever faced. He revealed astonishing perseverance in maintaining a siege of six months, contrary to Indian temperament. Yet he was doomed by lack of discipline in his followers and by striking too late to overcome the British. He did not conspire in advance with more than two other tribes; several others joined the uprising after he started it. White casualties during the war amounted to about four hundred and fifty soldiers plus a few hundred civilians in frontier raids.

BIBLIOGRAPHY

Hough, Franklin B. ed. *Diary of the Siege of Detroit*. Albany: Munsell, 1860.
Navarre, Robert. *Journal of Pontiac's Conspiracy 1763*. Translated by R. Clyde Ford. Detroit: C. M. Burton, 1912.
Parkman, Francis. *History of the Conspiracy of Pontiac*. Boston: Little and Brown, 1851.
Peckham, Howard H. *Pontiac and the Indian Uprising*. Princeton, N.J.: Princeton University Press, 1947; New York: Russell and Russell, 1970.

HOWARD PECKHAM

POPE, John (b. Louisville, Ky., March 16, 1822; d. Sandusky, Ohio, September 23, 1892), Army officer. Pope held Federal important commands in the Civil War and the Indian Wars.

John Pope came from a pioneer Illinois family. His father Nathaniel had been one of the organizers of that territory, serving both as territorial secretary and the first territorial delegate to Congress before being promoted to federal district judge in 1819, a post he continued to hold until his death in 1850. Abraham Lincoln* regularly practiced in his court and knew the Pope family well.

Graduated seventeenth of fifty-six in the West Point class of 1842, John Pope was assigned to the topographical engineers and saw duty in Florida and along the northeastern boundary over the next four years. He served with General Zachary Taylor* during the Mexican War and moved rapidly to the brevet rank of captain. Pope spent most of the following decade in the Southwest doing survey work. This experience provided him with valuable knowledge for his later posts as departmental commander during the Indian Wars. While on duty in Cincinnati in 1859 Pope met and married Clara Pomeroy Horton, whose father would serve as a Radical congressman from Ohio from 1861 to 1863.

Taking advantage of his father's friendship with Lincoln, Pope wrote the president-elect in January 1861 giving his views on the coming crisis. He was chosen as one of four military representatives to accompany Lincoln from Springfield to Washington and later offered his services as a personal aide to the president. But with the opening of hostilities, Governor Richard Yates asked Pope to organize the Illinois recruits, and he received the rank of brigadier general of volunteers on May 17.

Two months later Pope was ordered to Missouri under the command of John Charles Frémont.* Guerrilla warfare was already beginning in that beleaguered state, and Pope's efforts were directed toward keeping it under control. He did as good a job as anyone could have under the difficult circumstances. Pope was among the group that highly criticized Frémont and helped secure his removal.

Henry Wager Halleck,* who succeeded Frémont, called Pope to St. Louis in mid-February 1862 and gave him the command of the Army of the Mississippi which would form the central prong of a coordinated effort to drive the Confederates down the river and clear out the states on both sides of it. Pope moved against New Madrid and Island No. 10 which commanded a large reverse bend in the river. He surprised the Confederates at New Madrid by an overland march through the swamps and forced its abandonment on March 14. He then cut a canal at the head of the "Madrid Bend" to allow his transports to circumvent the batteries of Island No. 10 below. Crossing the river below that installation, Pope forced the Confederates to evacuate the adjoining shoreline and finally surrender the island itself on April 7 without bloodshed. During the campaign Pope gained promotion to major general of volunteers on March 21. These operations opened the Mississippi almost to Memphis, and Pope was prepared to continue his advance when recalled with his army to join the forces under Halleck advancing on Corinth in the wake of the Battle of Shiloh. He commanded the left wing throughout the entire campaign, and it was his army that occupied the city when the Confederates pulled out on May 29 following the siege.

Having gained a considerable reputation as a result of his efforts in the West, in part through his manipulation of the press which accompanied him and his unceasing correspondence with Washington officials, Pope was called east in June and given command of the forces protecting the capital, which were renamed the Army of Virginia. He issued a bombastic announcement that out west the Army always turned its face and not its back to the enemy. The key to success was to attack and win—a kind of rhetoric that did little to endear him to his subordinates.

With the withdrawal of George Brinton McClellan* from the Peninsula, Pope now faced the full brunt of the Army of Northern Virginia under Robert Edward Lee.* The number of Lee's troops slightly exceeded his own. Thomas Jonathan ("Stonewall") Jackson* struck the Union advance at Cedar Mountain on August 9 in what amounted to a standoff. As Pope's army retired north of the Rappahannock in the hopes of reinforcement from McClellan, Lee boldly sent Jackson and James Ewell Brown Stuart* on a wide flanking movement to the Union right to get astride its line of communications. Lee kept up a diversionary movement in Pope's front and then followed Jackson north on August 26. Discerning Lee's plan, Pope moved his forces against Jackson in the hope of preventing the reunion of the Confederates. But his plan of operations was faulty and marked by confusion. The campaign culminated in the second Battle of Bull Run on August 29 and 30, climaxed by a surprise flank attack from James Longstreet* on Pope's left on the afternoon of the second day, which gave the fight to the Confederates. Pope then ordered a general withdrawal, leaving the field to Lee.

Pope sought scapegoats and blamed McClellan, whom he accused of failing to reinforce him adequately, and various subordinates for his defeat. Among the latter was Fitz-John Porter,* who was court-martialed and dismissed from the Army for supposedly failing to obey orders on August 29 to hit Jackson's right flank and thereby prevent Longstreet's move of the following day. Porter spent the next twenty years seeking vindication and finally receiving it. The bitter feud between him and Pope had repercussions throughout the postwar army.

Although Lincoln generally accepted Pope's version of what went wrong, he, too, needed a scapegoat with Lee standing poised at the gates of Washington. Having reluctantly determined to restore McClellan to at least temporary command, the president exiled Pope to Minnesota where the Santee Sioux had just gone on the warpath. Though possessing limited manpower, Pope launched several expeditions that brought the situation under control.

In the process Pope came to the realization that the Army and the agents of the Bureau of Indian Affairs frequently worked at cross-purposes. Rather than sign treaties, which would only be broken in the future, and hand out annuities, Pope favored outright military control of tribes settled on lands that could adequately support them. The federal government would then provide subsidies for such things as buildings, tools, and subsistence. This would prevent exploitation of the Indians, and, with the help of missionary teachers, move them toward assimilation into American society. He constantly reiterated various versions of this program in communications with his superiors over the next twenty years.

Recognizing his administrative abilities, Lincoln appointed Pope to head the newly created Division of the Missouri in January 1865. With the exception of his supervision of the Third Military District (Georgia, Alabama, and Florida) in the postwar South (1867), and a tour with the Department of the Lakes (1868–1870), Pope would command the Department of the Missouri for most of the rest of his career (1870–1883). During that period he directed numerous campaigns against the tribes of the Southern Plains and the Southwest while also trying to protect their interests against unscrupulous white traders and "boomers." He completed his service commanding the Division of the Pacific (1883–1886). He retired to St. Louis but shortly before his death moved to the Ohio Soldiers' and Sailors' Home at Sandusky.

Pope rather tragically has been associated in the popular mind with the unfortunate 1862 campaign in northern Virginia culminating in the Second Battle of Bull Run. This episode engendered controversy from the moment it occurred as to whether Pope was the victim of his own ineptitude or of lack of support from McClellan and his supporters. There is truth on both sides. Few would dispute Pope's aggressiveness on the battlefield. Unfortunately, that same characteristic marked his interpersonal relationships and brought him enemies in its wake. Lincoln did him no favor in advancing him so rapidly without consulting his military subordinates. It was a campaign of miscues on the parts of all involved.

Generally overlooked is the role Pope played in the development of the West, first as a topographical engineer in the 1850s and later as a departmental commander during the Indian Wars. Few had the broad knowledge of this vast area that he had acquired from long first-hand experience. Although his arrogance and brusque manner sometimes got him in trouble, Pope had a vision of the needs of the Indians which may have been more realistic than that of either the many exploiters or the reformers of his era. Of those involved in the Indian Wars he probably handled his responsibilities more evenhandedly than most.

BIBLIOGRAPHY

Ellis, Richard N. *General Pope and U.S. Indian Policy*. Albuquerque: University of New Mexico Press, 1970.

Parrish, William E. *Turbulent Partnership: Missouri and the Union, 1861–1865*. Columbia: University of Missouri Press, 1963.

Utley, Robert M. *Frontier Regulars: The United States Army and the Indian, 1866–1891*. New York: Macmillan Company, 1973.

Williams, Kenneth P. *Lincoln Finds a General: A Military Study of the Civil War*. Vol. 1. New York: Macmillan Company, 1949.

Williams, T. Harry. *Lincoln and His Generals*. New York: Alfred A. Knopf, 1952.

WILLIAM E. PARRISH

PORTER, David (b. Boston, Mass., February 1, 1780; d. Pera, near Constantinople, Turkey, March 3, 1843), Naval Officer; Porter was a controversial example of the aggressive, quick-tempered pre-Annapolis American naval officer.

David Porter was the third of five generations of his family to serve the United States Navy with extraordinary distinction. His grandfather had commanded merchantmen out of Boston, and his father, David, and an uncle, Samuel, commanded a number of gunships during the Revolutionary War. Porter's father died in New Orleans in 1808 while serving as a sailing master. He had been nursed by the mother of young James G. Farragut. Farragut's mother died soon thereafter and was buried the same day as the elder Porter. The son offered to take one of the three Farragut boys into his large family, and Farragut's father accepted the offer from the family of his old friend. Taking the given name of his adoptive father, Farragut went on to lend additional glory to the Porter heritage. As a teenager, David Porter had turned naturally to the sea, sailing first with his father on voyages to the West Indies and later on his own during which he was twice impressed by the British Navy. He escaped both times, working his passage back home.

On January 16, 1798, he was made midshipman aboard the 38-gun frigate *Constellation*, under Captain Thomas Truxton,* which clashed with the French warship *Insurgente* (36-guns) the following February. For gallantry in action, Porter received command of his first prize in this battle. He was made lieutenant on October 9, 1799. Subsequently ordered to the Mediterranean in command of the 12-gun schooner *Enterprise*, he proceeded to capture the French schooner, *Diane*, and then off Malta, a Tripolitan cruiser, both heavily armed. In the Tripolitan War Porter next saw service in the 38-gun frigate *New York*. In 1803, he was captured off the 38-gun frigate *Philadelphia*, which had run aground under Captain William Bainbridge.* Porter remained in prison until peace was proclaimed. He progressed from the rank of master commandant in 1806 to captain on July 2, 1812.

With the declaration of war in 1812, he sailed from New York commanding the 32-gun frigate *Essex* and bearing a banner that read ''Free Trade and Sailors' Rights.'' He captured several British merchantmen as well as a transport carrying troops to Halifax. On August 13, 1812, he was attacked by the British sloop-of-war *Alert* (16-guns) and defeated it in eight minutes, the first British war vessel captured in the conflict. On December 11, he also caught the British packet *Nocton* with $50,000 aboard. Porter continued his cruise in the South Atlantic and the coastal waters off Brazil until January 1813 when he determined to proceed to the Pacific to destroy British whalers. Porter menaced the British whaling industry in the Pacific for ten months, causing an estimated $2,500,000 in losses. However, in February, 1814, two British warships brought Porter to battle off the Chilean coast and defeated *Essex*.

After the War of 1812, Porter served as a member of the Board of Navy Commissioners (1815–1823), and then took command of the Mosquito Squadron hunting pirates in the West Indies. A controversial incident involving an attack on a Spanish out-post in Puerto Rico prompted Porter's court-martial in 1825. Proud and defiant, he resigned his commission in 1826.

Porter arranged to take command of the navy of the Republic of Mexico (1826–1829), but that proved to be a difficult and bitter challenge. He returned to the United States in 1829 and sought an appointment in the foreign service. He held overseas appointments until his death in 1843.

David Porter was a fine example of the fighting officer of the early American Navy. Operating against the British whaling industry in the War of 1812, he captured some four hundred vessels, one of which, the *Atlantic*, he converted into a vessel of war, renaming it *Essex Junior*. The enraged British Admiralty sent out Captain John Hillyer with a picked crew and two powerful warships to destroy Porter. Meanwhile, Porter took temporary possession of the Marquesas Islands, placing him first among the innovative imperialistic American naval commanders of the nineteenth century. On February 3, 1814, he arrived in Valparaiso, Chile, accompanied by *Essex Junior*, and found Hillyer waiting with his *Phoebe* (38-guns) and its escort, *Cherub* (20-guns). The *Essex Junior* was so lightly armed that Porter ordered it to stay in the harbor. The *Phoebe* attacked Porter's stern while the *Cherub* moved in from the starboard side. Within half an hour the *Essex* had forced the *Phoebe* to leave the fight for repairs. Later, however, the longer range of the British guns proved too much for Porter as Hillyer backed off beyond the effective range of the *Essex*'s carronades and pounded the smaller ship. Aboard the helpless *Essex Junior*, Porter's foster son David Glasgow Farragut* watched as his intrepid stepfather tried to close with the *Phoebe*. Wind, tide, shattered masts, and broken navigational gear prevented the maneuver. With but seventy-five men left out of a crew of 255 and only one officer left standing to help him, Porter decided to surrender the hulk of the *Essex* after a fight that lasted more than two hours. With characteristic under-statement, Porter dispatched a statement to the American government: ''We have been unfortunate, but not disgraced.'' Later, Porter returned to the United States aboard the *Essex Junior* and was voted the thanks of Congress for his heroism.

When he sailed as commander of the Mosquito Squadron, Porter took with him his eleven-year-old son David Dixon Porter,* who like Farragut earlier would have the opportunity to see the compelling seamaster at his aggressive best. Using the 28-gun frigate *John Adams* as a flagship, he dispatched a companion vessel, *Beagle*, to investigate possible stores of pirate goods at Fajardo, Puerto Rico. The Spanish greeted the expedition with hostilty, and imprisoned the expedition's commanding officer. Consequently, Porter stormed the port with two hundred sailors and demanded an apology, which he immediately received. Completing his search for pirate stores and finding nothing, Porter and his men returned to their ships to continue their cruise. The Spanish, however, quickly registered a protest against Porter's belligerent actions, and following an investigation by the U.S. Navy Department, Porter was ordered to answer charges. Porter did not help his cause during the trial by publishing letters to American senior government officials relating his caustic views of the charges against him. He was convicted for taking unauthorized actions against a friendly nation, and given a light punishment of suspension from duty for six months. He resigned his commission in protest.

Still tied to the sea, Porter arranged to accept the appointment as commander in chief of the Mexican Navy. He received a $12,000 annual salary, a tract of land, and complete control of the service. It was difficult duty, however, as he found himself a victim of internal political struggles and the target of two assassination attempts.

The election of President Andrew Jackson* encouraged Porter to return to the United States in 1829, and his final years were devoted to useful diplomatic services. Porter turned to the new president for an assignment, and was made consul general for the Barbary States, stationed in Algiers. In 1831 he accepted an appointment as *chargé d'affaires* and then U.S. minister-resident at Constantinople where he served until 1843, when a combination of an enduring bout with yellow fever and a congenital heart problem proved too much for his small frame. After initial burial at San Stefano, his body was later taken to Philadelphia where it was buried in Woodland Cemetery near the Naval Asylum.

Porter's seamanship and fighting spirit served as examples to his son David Dixon Porter and his step-son David Glasgow Farragut. Porter had married the former Evelina Anderson on March 10, 1808. The couple had ten children, of whom two attained the rank of admiral and one the rank of commander in the U.S Navy, while another died as an officer in the Army during the Mexican War. Two other sons served as officers with the Confederacy.

BIBLIOGRAPHY

Lewis, Charles L. *David Glasgow Farragut: Admiral in the Making*. Annapolis: Naval Institute Press, 1941.

Long, David F. *Nothing Too Daring: A Biography of Commodore David Porter, 1780–1843*. Annapolis: Naval Institute Press, 1970.

Mahan, Alfred T. *Admiral Farragut*. New York: Appleton, 1892.
Porter, David. *Journal of a Cruise Made to the Pacific Ocean...in the U.S. Frigate "Essex."*... 2 vols. New York: Wiley & Halstead, 1815.
West, Richard S., Jr. *The Second Admiral: A Life of David Dixon Porter*. New York: Coward-McCann, 1937.

JACK J. CARDOSO

PORTER, David Dixon (b. Chester, Pa., June 8, 1813; d. Washington, D.C., February 13, 1891), naval officer. Porter is recognized as one of the most important Union naval officers of the Civil War.

Admiral David Dixon Porter was the third of ten children of the famous Commodore David Porter* and the former Evelina Anderson of Chester, Pennsylvania. Of the ten children, two became full admirals (David Dixon and the adopted son, David Glasgow Farragut*) and another became a commodore in the U.S. Navy. David Dixon Porter and his adopted brother, David G. Farragut, became virtual reproductions of the daring, controversial, fiercely nationalistic old commodore.

David Dixon Porter received a minimal education, some of it at Columbia College, a preparatory school in Washington, D.C. In 1824, at the age of eleven, he accompanied his father on the 28-gun frigate *John Adams* on a mission to suppress piracy in the West Indies. Two years later, when his father was commander in chief of the Navy of the Republic of Mexico, Porter was appointed a midshipman in the U.S. Navy. His first twelve years were spent cruising the Mediterranean and serving with the U.S. Coast Survey. Passed as midshipman in 1835, he was made lieutenant in 1841 and assigned to the warship *Congress* in which he sailed both the Mediterranean and Brazilian waters. Returning again to Washington, he worked on hydrographic surveys until 1846 when he was dispatched to the Dominican Republic on an observation mission for the State Department.

While on his first cruise in the Mediterranean, he met his future wife, George Ann Patterson, who was also aboard as guest of her father, Commodore Daniel T. Patterson, who had aided Andrew Jackson* at the Battle of New Orleans. The duty was one of the most pleasurable in Porter's long career. Upon his return to Washington, the couple was married on March 10, 1839. The marriage lasted nearly fifty-two years and produced eight children, three of whom became military officers, one each in the Army, Navy, and Marine Corps.

But the years immediately following the wedding were not the best. After a tour of duty with the Coast Survey, Porter applied for a combat command in the War with Mexico (1846–1848). He was assigned to the recruiting office in New Orleans for a year and then in 1847 was given a first lieutenancy on the war steamer *Spitfire*. After an initial frustration in attacking the Mexican city of Tabasco, he led a seventy-man landing party and captured the main fort. He was commended for his actions by Commodore Matthew Calbraith Perry* and given command of the *Spitfire*. But he was then reassigned to duties at the Coast

Survey and the Naval Observatory. Desperate for sea duty, Porter took a long furlough from the Navy to become captain of the merchant steamer, *Panama*, on a voyage through the Straits of Magellan and on to the Pacific coast. Service as captain of the mail steamer *Georgia* followed for the next two years. He then accepted the Australian Steamship Company offer to be captain of the merchant ship *Golden Age*, then reputed to be the fastest steamer afloat.

Porter decided to give the Navy another chance, however, and in 1855 he returned to take command of the steamship *Supply*; in her he went to North Africa to pick up camels for experimental use by the U.S. Army in the desert Southwest. While in the Mediterranean, he saw some of the war in the Crimea first hand. Porter was then given duty at the Portsmouth Navy Yard (1857–1860). Again disenchanted with the turn his career had taken, he began negotiating for a command position with the Pacific Steamship Company, and in 1861 he took a naval reassignment to the Pacific Coast Survey as a prelude to working for the commercial fleet. He was forty-eight years old with thirty-two years of service in the Navy, twenty of them at the rank of lieutenant.

With the coming of the Civil War, however, all of Porter's years of service proved worthwhile. Porter was involved in the relief expedition to Fort Pickens, Florida, and the attacks on the Confederate forts below New Orleans. In command of river gunboats on the Mississippi River, he fought in support of his foster brother, David Glasgow Farragut. Eventually, Porter took charge of blockade duty on the Atlantic coast and led an assault on Fort Fisher, North Carolina. He was the second naval officer to be promoted to the rank of admiral; Farragut was the first.

After the war, Porter was superintendent of the Naval Academy at Annapolis and head of the Board of Inspection. He wrote several works of naval history. After being stricken by a heart attack in Newport, Rhode Island, he died in Washington, D.C., in 1891.

Like his father, David Dixon Porter was a short man at five feet-six inches, with a spare, muscular frame and possessed of an imaginative wit, a vibrant personality, and a reputation for being generous to subordinates and critical of superiors. But fortune favored the prepared in April 1861, when the Navy Department chose Porter to command the *Powhatan* on a relief expedition to Fort Pickens at Pensacola, Florida, then under Confederate siege. The audacious Porter wrote his own orders, assigning an old friend, Samuel Barron, as chief of the Bureau of Detail. Unknown to Porter, Barron had joined the Confederate forces five days before. Secretary of the Navy Gideon Wells* notified President Abraham Lincoln* of his concern for Porter's loyalty to the Union. Lincoln canceled the Barron appointment and ordered Secretary of State William Seward to take Porter off the *Powhatan*. Porter received Seward's telegram as he prepared to sail, but used Lincoln's earlier creation of the relief mission as having precedence and immediately pushed off. He tried to take Pensacola, but the Army refused to cooperate and ordered him to desist. Porter remained on blockade duty for six weeks in the Gulf of Mexico. In August he cruised the West Indies and South American waters searching for the Confederate commerce destroyer, *Sumter*. Porter was promoted to commander and was sounded out on the feasibility of a naval expedition to take New Orleans.

At the request of the Navy Department, Porter consulted with Farragut about the New Orleans venture. Farragut was not enthusiastic about Porter's plan to have a mortar flotilla accompany the expedition but accepted it if Porter would join him. Guarding the approaches to the city some seventy miles below New Orleans were Forts Jackson and St. Philip, on either side of the Mississippi River. Porter's flotilla laid off the forts and pounded them ineffectively for six days (April 18–23, 1862). The bombardment apparently did little damage to the forts, and Farragut chose to run by them at night, one of the greatest exploits in American naval history. The equally indomitable Porter shelled the shore batteries from his flagship *Harriet Lane* and forced their capitulation on April 27. With New Orleans now in the hands of an army under Major General Benjamin Franklin Butler,* Porter continued up the river to support Farragut at Vicksburg, Mississippi. His flotilla was detached, and Porter was made commander of the Mississippi Squadron. He was promoted to acting rear admiral over eighty senior officers. His promotion was laid to his influence with Assistant Secretary of the Navy Gustavus Vasa Fox,* but Secretary Welles approved the promotion, despite his definition of Porter as a "boastful, ambitious" man "given to cliquism."

Admiral Porter's organizational talent came to the fore as he established control over three thousand miles of water, developed a shipbuilding yard at Cairo, Illinois, and supervised eighty fighting vessels. He joined Generals Ulysses Simpson Grant* and William Tecumseh Sherman* at Vicksburg in the campaign to take that city, with the aim of controlling the Mississippi River line. For his help in the campaign, Porter received the thanks of the generals,and was voted the thanks of Congress. By then a permanent rear admiral, he was unique in having never served in the navy ranks of captain or commodore.

For a time Porter commanded gunboats on the ill-fated Red River Expedition (March-May 1864) in Louisiana under Major General Nathaniel P. Banks. Porter narrowly avoided disaster and the loss of most of his gunboats to the Confederates. But his service was needed on the Atlantic coast, first as commander of the North Atlantic Blockading Squadron and then to conduct operations against Fort Fisher, guarding the important Confederate harbor at Wilmington, North Carolina. Assembling an armada of 120 vessels organized into four divisions— the largest naval contingent in U.S. history to that time—he bombarded the fort for three days. When the Confederates did not return the fire, he called on General Butler to begin the assault. Butler chose to make a reconnaissance, determined that Confederate resistance still existed, and retired with his troops to Hampton Roads, Virginia. Porter insisted on bringing in a new army and gained one of eight thousand soldiers under General Alfred H. Terry.* In a combined operation, during which Porter's ships conducted a terrific shelling of the Confederate works, the last great Atlantic Confederate coastal fortress fell on January 15, 1865. By early April 1865 Porter led a fleet of gunboats up the James River and commenced a bombardment that caused the Confederate commander, Raphael Semmes,* to scuttle his squadron. Triumphant, Porter received President Lincoln aboard his flagship. In recognition of his brilliant record, Admiral Porter received an unprecedented three votes of thanks by Congress.

For more than three years (1865–1869) Porter served as superintendent of the Naval Academy. In 1866 he and Farragut were promoted to vice admiral and admiral, respectively. Upon Farragut's death in 1870, Porter was raised to the rank of admiral, the highest rated officer in the Navy. President Grant made him advisor to the secretary of the Navy. Porter created the Board of Inspection, established requirements for the repair of all vessels, and laid out provisions for auxiliary sails on all steam-propelled ships. He became head of the Board of Inspection in 1877, a post he held for the rest of his life.

In his later years, Porter busied himself with historical writing. His works included the *Memoir of Commodore David Porter* (Albany, 1875), which recounted his father's career; a collection entitled *Incidents and Anecdotes of the Civil War* (New York, 1885); and his own opinionated *Naval History of the Civil War* (New York, 1886). Admiral Porter was one of the two most important naval leaders to come out of the Civil War era—the other, of course, being David G. Farragut.

BIBLIOGRAPHY

Anderson, Bern. *By Sea and By River: The Naval History of the Civil War.* New York: Alfred A. Knopf, 1961.
Milligan, John D. *Gunboats Down the Mississippi.* Annapolis, Md.: Naval Institute Press, 1965.
Reed, Rowena. *Combined Operations in the Civil War.* Annapolis, Md.: Naval Institute Press, 1978.
Soley, James. *Admiral Porter.* New York: D. Appleton and Company, 1903.
West, Richard S., Jr. *The Second Admiral: A Life of David Dixon Porter.* New York: Coward-McCann, 1937.

JACK J. CARDOSO

PORTER, Fitz-John (b. Portsmouth, N.H., August 31, 1822; d. Morristown, N.J., May 21, 1901), Army officer. Porter served as a corps commander in the Army of the Potomac during the Civil War, and his actions inspired a long-standing controversy.

As a professional soldier Fitz-John Porter boasted an impressive lineage. His grandfather served as a gunboat captain in the American Revolution. His father, John Porter, was a career naval officer, as was his uncle, Commodore David Porter.* Among his first cousins Fitz-John numbered five professional military men, including Admiral David Dixon Porter* of Civil War renown.

After a stint at Phillips Academy in Exeter, New Hampshire, and a preparatory course of studies at a private school in Massachusetts, Porter entered West Point in 1841, graduating in 1845, eighth in a class of forty-one. Assigned to the 4th Artillery, he spent several months as an instructor at Fortress Monroe before the Mexican War. During that conflict, in which he was twice brevetted for gallantry and once wounded, Porter saw action in northern Mexico with Zachary Taylor* and in all the important engagements during the drive on Mexico City led by Winfield Scott.* In 1849 Porter returned to West Point, serving successively as a cavalry and artillery instructor and, in 1853, as adjutant to the superintendent, Robert Edward Lee.* Duties as assistant adjutant general in the Department of the West at Fort Leavenworth and to Albert Sidney Johnston* during the Utah Campaign of 1857 and afterwards rounded out his pre-Civil War career.

In early 1861 Porter successfully carried out a secret mission to evacuate federal troops from the lower Texas coast. After the outbreak of hostilities Porter advanced rapidly. On May 14, 1861, he was promoted to colonel of the 15th Infantry Regiment in the Regular Army and to brigadier general of volunteers three days later. From late April to late July he served as chief of staff in the Department of Pennsylvania, charged with training and putting thirty regiments of soldiers into the field. Then, after serving for a month on the staff of General Robert Patterson's* Shenandoah army, General George Brinton McClellan* put Porter in charge of training troops around Washington, troops that would become the Army of the Potomac. Porter and McClellan soon became fast friends.

Porter achieved his most conspicuous accomplishments as a soldier during the Peninsula Campaign. As a division commander in General Samuel P. Heintzelman's III Corps, he directed the Yorktown siege and carried out an aggressive reconnaissance in force at Hanover Court House. On May 18, 1862, he succeeded to command of the V Corps. Isolated north of the Chickahominy from the rest of McClellan's army, Porter's corps withstood the brunt of Lee's attack at Mechanicsville on June 26. On the following day, from a new defensive position at Gaines' Mill along Boatswain's Swamp, Porter's force again stood fast until about an hour before dark when his line was breeched by an all-out Confederate attack. Porter's withdrawal to the south side of the river was orderly, however, and his corps led the Army of the Potomac on its march to the James. Porter was in tactical command of the Federal forces at the ensuing Battle of Malvern Hill on July 1, the last of the Seven Days' battles and a convincing Union victory. For his services during the campaign Porter was promoted on July 4, 1862, to major general of volunteers and brevet brigadier in the regulars.

On August 26, 1862, the V Corps became part of the short-lived Army of Virginia under General John Pope.* Porter's actions during the Battle of Second Manassas (August 29–30, 1862) have been the subject of controversy ever since. Stationed on the extreme left of Pope's line, separated from the main force by more than two miles, Porter's corps took no part in the first day's fighting. Convinced that he faced only the troops of Thomas ("Stonewall") Jackson,* late in the day Pope ordered Porter to attack Jackson's right flank and rear. Porter declined to obey the order since the assault would have carried him across the front of thirty thousand Confederate soldiers under General James Longstreet.*

On the second day of the battle Porter's troops, this time in the main line, shared the severe mauling received by the rest of the army.

Charged by Pope with disobedience, disloyalty, and misconduct in the face of the enemy, Porter was relieved of his command on September 5, 1862. McClellan reinstated him, and Porter's corps was present but did not participate in the Battle of Sharpsburg. Again relieved of his command on November 17, 1862, Porter was brought to trial by court-martial on Pope's charges, found guilty, and cashiered on January 21, 1863.

Not until 1886, when President Grover Cleveland signed a bill restoring his rank (but making no provisions for back pay), was Porter vindicated. During his long and agonizing struggle to clear his name Porter held a variety of business and political positions: mining surveyor and manager in Colorado, superintendent of construction for the Morristown insane asylum, public works and police commissioner in New York City, and assistant receiver for the New Jersey Central Railroad. In 1869 he declined an offer of command of the Egyptian Army. Porter retired from public life in 1897, having served his last years as fire department commissioner and post office cashier in New York City.

A discernible thread of arrogance skeined its way all through the life of Fitz-John Porter. Arrogance is not a particularly unusual quality in proud men, but in wise ones it is usually tempered with prudence. Not so in Porter's case. Whatever the merits of the charges that brought about his disgrace in 1863—and most modern writers dismiss them—Porter himself was at least partially responsible. Not only was his devotion to McClellan blind; it was also reckless. Not only was his disdain for Pope monumental—he was an "ass," in Porter's opinion—it was also public. Given these facts, along with a climate in Washington in late 1862 that put a premium on political orthodoxy, it is small wonder that Porter came to grief.

Unfortunately, the Army lost a fine soldier. Porter was an excellent administrator, without peer in the demanding task of training and organizing large bodies of troops for battle. His superiors in Pennsylvania recognized this early in the war, as did McClellan later on, and both made full use of his talents. Porter also had audacity of the sort that makes for fame. Not satisfied by merely following his orders to get Federal troops out of Texas in 1861, he also improvised a way to spirit out five batteries of guns. Two months later, while he was employed on the adjutant general's staff in Washington, Porter ordered reinforcements to St. Louis on his own authority and thereafter saw to it that Brigadier General Nathaniel Lyon (whose promotion he had championed) received the men and materiel he needed. Tenacious and all but immovable in defensive positions—his exploits on the Peninsula, which have been characterized as "some of the finest defensive fighting of the war," merited a justifiable acclaim—Porter appraised terrain with the eye of a born artillerist.

All of these excellent qualities were forgotten at his trial. Convicted on three of six charges of violating or ignoring the orders of his superior, Porter was ruined. It is difficult to escape the conclusion that he had been made a scapegoat for Pope. The seven-member court was stacked; some testimony was perjured; maps of the battlefield were grossly inaccurate. But most telling was the plain truth (openly stated in a series of telegrams to General Ambrose Everett Burnside*) that Porter was a favorite of the administration radicals and had nothing but contempt for Pope and by implication an overfondness for McClellan— factors that apparently weighed heavily on President Abraham Lincoln* when he approved the sentence of the court-martial.

As political factors had brought about his ruin, so too did they delay Porter's exoneration. His case was not reopened until 1878. The Schofield Board of Inquiry (composed of three general officers and chaired by John McAllister Schofield*), reporting in 1879, not only vindicated Porter's judgment at Second Manassas, but conclusively demonstrated—via accurate maps and testimony of former Confederate commanders—Pope's utter ignorance of actual conditions on the field. Although President Chestur Arthur pardoned Porter in May 1882 and remitted part of his sentence, partisan politics in Congress delayed his restoration to the Army for several more years.

From a strictly military point of view, Porter's conduct had been blameless. To have obeyed Pope's order to attack on August 29 would have been suicidal, as it was based on the erroneous assumption that a substantial enemy force had not yet arrived on the field. Even so, Porter had been prepared to carry out the order until dissuaded by one of his division commanders. According to the Schofield Board, Porter's conduct "saved the Union army from defeat...that day." Both of the other orders Porter allegedly disobeyed were also shown to be subject to interpretation. One charge—that he did not hew strictly to marching orders on August 27—was not only frivolous, but also based on an order impossible to carry out. The other charge concerned a joint order issued to General Irvin McDowell* and Porter earlier on August 29, a directive so garbled and murky that little sense can be made of it even today. Given the situation in 1862, it made even less sense then.

Ultimately, what felled Porter at the height of his career was not willful misconduct, but imputations of willful disloyalty. And though guilty of neither, Porter's indiscretion in expressing his opinions clearly marked him as dispensable, especially after McClellan's departure. Under such circumstances a complaint court, beholden to top officials in the War Department, could easily torture the evidence available to it. Certain of his innocence, unaware of the implications of his ill-advised communications with Burnside, and blind to the ruthlessness of his enemies, Porter refused the help of friends at his trial and refused to challenge the composition of the court, two final lapses of judgment that cost him dearly.

No one general could have possibly saved Pope's army at Manassas, much less his reputation afterwards. At the time, however, Fitz-John Porter, a capable and above-average officer, made an eminently suitable sacrifice. His fate illustrates a maxim that shrewder, more circumspect leaders have always known: A nation in the midst of war is often apt to forget that loyalty to its cause is not necessarily synonymous with loyalty to an individual leader. And a soldier who confuses the two treads a treacherous path indeed.

BIBLIOGRAPHY

Cox, Jacob D. *Second Battle of Bull Run as Connected with the Fitz-John Porter Case.* Cincinnati: P. G. Thompson, 1882.

Eisenschimel, Otto. *The Celebrated Case of Fitz John Porter: An American Dreyfus Affair.* Indianapolis and New York: Bobbs-Merrill Company, 1950.

Porter, Fitz John. *General Fitz John Porter's Statement of the Services of the Fifth Army Corps, in 1862, in Northern Virginia.* New York: Evening Post Steam Presses, 1878.

Ropes, John C. *The Army Under Pope.* New York: Charles Scribner's Sons, 1881.

Williams, Kenneth P. *Lincoln Finds a General.* Vol. 2. New York: Macmillan Company, 1951.

THOMAS E. SCHOTT

PREBLE, Edward (b. Falmouth [now Portland], Maine, August 15, 1761; d. Portland, Maine, August 25, 1807), naval officer. Preble commanded the U.S. Mediterranean Squadron, 1803–1804, during the Tripolitanan War.

Edward Preble was the ninth child and seventh son of Jedidiah Preble, a prominent provincial military officer, merchant, and political figure in the District of Maine. Educated at local schools in Falmouth and at Dummer School in Byfield, Massachusetts, the latter of which he attended during the early years of the American Revolution, Preble entered the Massachusetts state navy in April 1780 as a midshipman in the frigate *Protector*. Midshipman Preble made two cruises in the *Protector*: during the first of them he participated in the bloody battle between the *Protector* and the privateer *Admiral Duff*; the second ended in the capture of the *Protector* by two British frigates, and Preble was, for a few weeks, held prisoner at New York. Early the following year, 1782, he was appointed first lieutenant of the Massachusetts state sloop *Winthrop*, and served in her till the close of maritime hostilities in April 1783. *Winthrop* was primarily employed in protecting the Maine coasting trade against raiders operating out of the British-controlled Penobscot Bay area. Preble's most famous exploit while serving in the *Winthrop*, and the conspicuous deed that first established his public reputation, was the daring capture—with the aid of only fourteen men—of the Loyalist privateer *Merriam* under the guns of Fort George at Bagaduce (now Castine), Maine.

From 1785 until 1798 Preble served, with excellent reputation but without spectacular financial success, as master or supercargo of merchant vessels sailing from North Carolina and Massachusetts ports and trading to Europe, the West Indies, and Africa, as well as along the North American coast. In 1794, when Congress first enacted legislation authorizing a Federal navy, he immediately sought an appointment in the new organization, but he did not obtain one until after the outbreak of the Quasi-War with France in 1798, when he was commissioned lieutenant (April 9, 1798). After making one cruise in the West Indies as commander of the brig *Pickering*, Preble was promoted to the rank of captain, May 15, 1799, and took command of the 32-gun frigate *Essex* for an eleven-month voyage (January-November 1800) to Batavia (now Jakarta), Java. This cruise, undertaken to convoy valuable American merchantmen home from the East Indies, was notable both as the longest voyage yet attempted by a ship of the U.S. Navy and as the first time an American naval vessel had showed the flag beyond the Cape of Good Hope.

In the spring of 1803 President Thomas Jefferson selected Edward Preble as the commander of the third U.S. squadron sent to the Mediterranean during the 1801–1805 war with Tripoli. It is on his activities during the twelve months from September 1803 till September 1804 that Preble's reputation as a military commander principally stands. Commodore Richard V. Morris, Preble's pred-ecessor in the Mediterranean command, had proved unequal to the multiple military and diplomatic demands to which the commander of the U.S. Medi-terranean Squadron was subject, and was recalled and subsequently dismissed from the Navy. Preble's vigor and decisiveness were in notable contrast to Morris' inactivity and bewilderment, and immediately won him government approval and widespread public attention.

On his arrival at Gibraltar in the 44-gun frigate *Constitution* on September 12, 1803, Preble found Morocco at war with the United States. Mobilizing the ships of the returning United States Squadron as well as his own, Preble massed such overwhelming force along the coasts of Morocco that the sultan was forced by mid-October to reaffirm the highly favorable 1786 treaty between Morocco and the United States. But scarcely was the Moroccan problem solved, when the only other frigate of Preble's squadron, *Philadelphia*, Captain William Bain-bridge,* ran aground near Tripoli and was captured. Determined that the *Phil-adelphia* should never be of any use to the enemy, Preble planned and Lieutenant Stephen Decatur* executed a brilliant surprise raid in which the former American frigate was burned at her moorings in Tripoli Harbor during the night of February 16–17, 1804.

Because the small vessels of his own squadron (three brigs and three schooners) were not suitable for attacking the maritime defenses of the city of Tripoli, Preble—acting largely on his own initiative—borrowed from the Kingdom of the Two Sicilies six gunboats and two bomb ketches to supplement his own force, the only vessel of which capable of silencing the Tripolitan fortifications was the *Constitution*. Between August 3 and September 3, 1804, Preble launched a series of six attacks on the city of Tripoli and the shipping in its harbor. Of these, the first—resulting in the capture of three Tripolitan gunboats—was the most successful. Thereafter, the commanders of the enemy gunboats avoided close-range combat, and the firepower available to Preble was unequal to that of the Tripolitan fortifications. Concurrent attempts to end the war by negotiation failed because of Preble's distrust of the French mediator, Bonaventure Beaus-sier, as well as the American commander's lack of sensitivity to the internal political situation at Tripoli. The arrival of a larger U.S. squadron, sent out as a result of the loss of the *Philadelphia* and unavoidably commanded by a senior officer, terminated Preble's Mediterranean command on September 9, 1804.

Following his return to the United States, Preble was employed in superintending gunboat construction and as a trusted professional advisor to Secretary of the Navy Robert Smith. Although instinctively conservative politically and in earlier years identified with the Federalist party, Preble had gradually and inconspicuously shifted his political loyalties to the Jeffersonian Republicans and was the naval officer to whom President Jefferson turned to command a proposed—but never executed—naval expedition to counter the supposed treasonable designs of Aaron Burr in the Mississippi Valley. Preble died as a result of a chronic stomach or intestinal disorder that had undermined his health since the year 1800.

In the process by which the United States developed, more or less out of nothing, a professional naval officer corps during the years between 1798 and 1812, Edward Preble's place is that of one of the most important role-models for younger career officers. Fortunately, the apogee of Edward Preble's professional life coincided with the tenure in office (1801–1809) of Secretary of the Navy Robert Smith, the civilian official most responsible for, and interested in, the development of that professional officer corps.

A man of violent and ill-controlled temper, and a harsh disciplinarian, Preble earned first the grudging and then the enthusiastic admiration of his subordinates by his decisiveness and vigor, by his unhesitating use of prudent discretion and initiative, by his willingness to delegate important and responsible assignments to promising young men, by his fervent defense of what he held to be the national interests and national honor of the United States, and—most of all—by his refusal to give up in the face of great reverses and depressing odds in the enemy's favor.

Preble was a committed believer in the crucial role of force in the maintenance of international order. At the same time, his sixteen years in the merchant service and his close family and social ties to leading mercantile figures of Massachusetts made him sensitive to the economic needs of the U.S. merchant marine, which the Navy was established to assist and protect. Despite these years of merchant marine experience, Preble thought of himself as a professional naval officer: that is, as he would have expressed the idea, a person whose formative years had been spent in learning to be a military man; who had risen by demonstrated competence through each of the ranks from midshipman to captain; and who, by preference and conscious choice, devoted his mature years to service to his country. By temperament Edward Preble was an administrator and man of action rather than a military intellectual, consumed by an intense desire to leave a famous name; he sought that fame through self-sacrifice in his country's cause.

BIBLIOGRAPHY

McKee, Christopher. *Edward Preble: A Naval Biography, 1761–1807*. Annapolis, Md.:
    Naval Institute Press, 1972.
Pratt, Fletcher. *Preble's Boys: Commodore Preble and the Birth of American Sea Power*.
    New York: Sloane, 1950.

                                                          CHRISTOPHER McKEE

PULLER, Lewis Burwell (b. West Point, Va., June 26, 1898; d. Hampton,
Va., October 11, 1971), Marine Corps officer. Puller is considered to be an
outstanding tactical combat leader and was perhaps the most decorated marine
of all time.

Lewis "Chesty" Puller was born into one of the old families of Virginia, the
family's presence in that state dating from the middle of the seventeenth century.
His grandfather died fighting for the South in the Civil War. Growing up steeped
in the lore of the Civil War, Puller also was an avid reader of Julius Ceasar's
Gallic Wars. He enrolled at the Virginia Military Institute in 1917, but growing
impatient to enter the World War, he dropped out in 1918 to enlist in the U.S.
Marine Corps.

Puller was disappointed to learn that he was among several enlisted men chosen
to help train recruits in boot camp at the Marine Barracks, Parris Island, South
Carolina. After the war, he was sent to Officers' Training School and was
commissioned a second lieutenant in the Marine Corps Reserve in 1919. He was
almost immediately placed on the inactive list due to postwar cutbacks in the
Marine Corps.

Marine Captain William Rupertus talked Puller into returning to the Marine
Corps as a corporal, serving in Haiti as an officer of the *Gendarmerie d'Haiti*.
The *Gendarmerie* was a combined army and police established by a Haitian
treaty with the United States. Most of its officers were enlisted or commissioned
U.S. Marines, while its enlisted personnel were Haitians. Puller arrived in Haiti
in 1919 and stayed for five years. He used this tour to learn small-unit tactics
and participated in frequent action against the Cacos. In his first assignment he
exhibited the drive that marked his entire career. Puller had to take a pack train
of ammunition twenty-five miles from Port-au-Prince to Mirebalais and part of
the supplies an additional sixteen miles to Los Cohobos. At that time Puller did
not speak Spanish, and neither his twenty-five men nor their sergeant spoke
English. Not wanting to spend the night on the trail, Puller hurried his men
along. At one place, the *Gendarmerie* column rode into an equally surprised
column of Cacos. Puller instinctively had his men and pack animals charge.
Amidst the thunder and the dust the Cacos retreated. Puller arrived in Mirebalais
that night and then pushed on early the next morning for Los Cohobos. He
completed that mission so quickly that his department commander doubted at
first that Puller had actually gone to Los Cohobos. Thus, in 1919 Puller demonstrated the emphasis on fast marching and aggressive attacks that were to
become two of his characteristics. Furthermore, in Haiti he learned the impor-

tance of marksmanship and of not only leading his men from the front but also of caring for them in camp. Those concerns also became his life-long hallmarks. The Haitian govenment awarded Puller the *Medaille Militaire* for his services in action after he had been in the country only eight months. That was the first of his many combat decorations.

Puller returned to the United States in early 1924 as a new second lieutenant in the U.S. Marine Corps. During the next two years he served at the Marine Barracks, Norfolk, Virginia, completed the Basic School, required of all Marine lieutenants, and was assigned to the 10th Marine Regiment at Quantico, Virginia. In 1926 Puller became a student naval aviator at Pensacola, Florida. He did not succeed in earning pilot's wings, however. After a two-year tour at Marine Barracks, Pearl Harbor, he spent six months at San Diego before a combat tour in Nicaragua.

In December 1928 Lieutenant Puller was assigned to duty with the Nicaraguan *Guardia Nacional*, serving above his Marine Corps rank, as a captain. In 1930, Puller earned the first of his five Navy Crosses. (Puller was the only marine to earn five of them.) Puller had fought five actions against rebel forces between February and August 1930, routing the rebels each time without casualties to his own forces. In addition, he captured impressive amounts of enemy dispatches, munitions, animals, and food. In 1931, he went to the United States to attend the company officers' course at the Army Infantry School, Fort Benning, Georgia. Puller returned to Nicaragua in July 1932 to be greeted with the news that a price had been placed on his head by the leader of the rebels, Augusto Sandino. That September Puller led his company on a ten-day march of more than one hundred and fifty miles during which he fought four engagements and killed at least thirty rebels. Puller received a second Navy Cross for his aggressive exploits during that patrol.

In January 1933 Puller left Nicaragua for China where, in addition to other duties with the marine detachment guarding the American Legation at Peiping, he commanded the famous "Horse Marines," the mounted detachment that guarded American residences and outlying areas. While in China, he studied the Japanese and Chinese armies and acquired a respect for their endurance, marching, and fighting capabilities. He next commanded the marine detachment aboard the cruiser *Augusta* of the Asiatic Fleet, Captain Chester William Nimitz,* commanding.

In June 1936 Puller returned to the United States to teach at the Basic School in Philadelphia. On November 13, 1937, he married his Virginia sweetheart, Virginia Montague Evans. They eventually had three children. After returning to the command of the *Augusta*'s marine detachment, Puller served as a battalion executive officer and commanding officer with the 4th Marine Regiment at Shanghai, China. He returned to Camp Lejeune, North Carolina, in August 1941 to take command of the 1st Battalion, 7th Marine Regiment, 1st Marine Division.

In September 1942 the 7th Marines went in to reinforce the 1st Marine Division on Guadalcanal. There Puller won his third Navy Cross when his battalion stopped a regiment of veteran Japanese soldiers from seizing the vital Henderson Airfield. His half-strength unit killed more than fourteen hundred enemy on the night of October 24–25, 1942. In the wake of this outstanding action, General George Catlett Marshall* asked Puller to be one of a number of officers to return to the United States to give talks to raise morale and to explain the war effort. Puller, always in inspirational leader, was a success on this tour.

In January 1944 Puller won his fourth Navy Cross as executive officer of the 7th Marines. At Cape Gloucester, New Britain, he took command of two battalions when their commanding officers were wounded. Puller moved through heavy machine gun and mortar fire to reorganize the battalions and led them in taking a strongly fortified enemy position.

He commanded the 1st Marine Regiment during the fight for Peleliu in September and October 1944. He returned to the United States in November 1944 to train recruits. His abilities to lead and his interest in the welfare of the enlisted marine made him a natural officer for the position. He was famous for insisting that enlisted men ate before noncommissioned officers and they in turn ate before officers.

At the outbreak of the Korean War in 1950, Puller bombarded Marine Corps Headquarters with requests for a combat command. He was soon given the 1st Marines, his old regiment, which was then being reactivated at Camp Pendleton, California. He landed with his regiment at Inchon, Korea, that September. Later, he earned his fifth Navy Cross inspiring and directing the actions of his men during the bloody "attack in a different direction," as the Marines fought their way through the Chinese Communist forces to the coast during the withdrawal from the Chosin Reservoir. Puller also received the Army's Distinguished Service Cross for that action. In January 1951 he was promoted to brigadier general and was made assistant division commander of the 1st Marine Division.

Puller returned to Camp Pendleton to command the 3d Marine Brigade in May 1951. While training reinforcements, he continued to preach and practice his principles of physical fitness. To paraphrase his policy: if the enemy marches twenty miles a day, Marines have to march twenty-five. Puller was promoted to major general in 1953. In July 1954 he assumed command of the 2d Marine Division at Camp Lejeune and then served as deputy camp commander until he retired due to ill-health on November 1, 1955. He was promoted to lieutenant general at that time.

Puller served as a Marine officer and enlisted man for thirty-seven years. He held the Navy Cross with Gold Stars in lieu of four additional awards; the Army Distinguished Service Cross; the Army Silver Star Medal; the Legion of Merit with combat "V" and Gold Star; the Bronze Star Medal with combat "V"; the Air Medal with two Gold Stars; the Purple Heart Medal; the Presidential Unit Citation Ribbon with four bronze stars; the Marine Corps good conduct medal with one bronze star; and nineteen other U.S. decorations and seven foreign awards.

"Chesty" Puller's Marine Corps nickname came from the kind of stiffness with which he stood with his barrel chest thrown out. His reputation rests on his combat leadership and on his "Pullerisms." He often said that he owed his successes to his enlisted men and his junior officers. He carried his own pack, ate what his men ate, and walked when they walked. His presence rallied his men in combat, and, as he told them, "You don't hurt 'em if you don't hit 'em." As he was fond of telling the chain of command, the press, and any available audience, "Paperwork will ruin any military force." Upon his return to a combat unit in April 1943, Puller wrote the commandant of the Marine Corps, "It is respectfully requested that my present assignment to a combat unit be extended until the downfall of the Japanese government." His statement to the effect that ice cream and refreshment centers ("canteens") were making American fighting men soft, and his remarks about fighting men who drank whiskey and beer brought down the wrath of the temperance forces on him. But his reputation helped the Marine Corps through a peacetime crisis as well as its wartime needs when he came to the defense of the Corps at the trial in 1956 of Marine Staff Sergeant Matthew McKeon who was being tried for the death of six recruits during a night training march. At the court-martial Puller testified on the importance of rugged training for the marine's ability to survive in combat. His testimony had a strong impact on the court. His reputation at his death was such that the commandant of the Marine Corps and twenty generals came to his funeral in his parish church yard.

BIBLIOGRAPHY

Davis, Burke. *Marine! The Life of General Lewis B. (Chesty) Puller, USMC (Ret.).* Boston: Little, Brown and Company, 1962.

Montross, Lynn, et al. *U.S. Marine Operations in Korea.* 5 vols. Washington, D.C.: U.S. Government Printing Office, 1954–1972.

Schuon, Karl. *U.S. Marine Corps Biographical Dictionary.* New York: Franklin Watts, 1963.

Shaw, Henry I., Jr., et al. *History of U.S. Marine Corps Operations in World War II.* 5 vols. Washington, D.C.: U.S. Government Printing Office, 1958–1971.

MARTIN K. GORDON

PUTNAM, Israel (b. Salem Village, now Danvers, Mass., January 7, 1718; d. Brooklyn, Conn., May 29, 1790), senior major general in the Continental Army.

Israel Putnam was born to a prosperous farming family in colonial Massachusetts. In 1740 at the age of twenty-one he moved with his new bride, Hannah Pope, from land-short Salem Village to a frontier area of Connecticut that would later become part of the town of Pomfret and settled down to the life of a yeoman and local leader for fifteen years.

In the summer of 1755, Putnam, now a father of five children, volunteered to serve with Connecticut troops in the Seven Years' War and was sent to Albany, New York, as part of an intercolonial force that was to assault Crown Point.

His first battle at Lake George on September 8, 1755, occurred a few days after the Connecticut General Assembly had named him a second lieutenant, but his commission had not yet arrived and he fought the battle as a private. Shortly after, he joined a handpicked group of soldiers known as "Roger's Rangers" (under Robert Rogers*) who reconnoitered enemy territory in the northern Hudson and Champlain areas and were instructed to "distress the French and their allies, by sacking, burning, and destroying their houses, barns, and barracks." As one of these Rangers, Putnam became known as a man of unusual personal bravery and he became skilled in guerrilla warfare and scouting techniques. Given a special citation for his "extraordinary services and good conduct" by the Connecticut General Assembly, he was promoted to captain by the assembly in June 1756 and to major in March 1758. Putnam was captured by Indians near Lake George in August 1758 and, after enduring great physical hardships, was imprisoned at Fort Ticonderoga and at Montreal before being released in a prisoner exchange in the fall.

Putnam received his first experience in large-scale command as lieutenant colonel of the 4th Connecticut Regiment in an expedition commanded by Lord Jeffery Amherst* that successfully attacked Fort Ticonderoga in July 1759. After being part of several other northern campaigns led by Amherst in 1760 and 1761, Putnam was named acting colonel for the 1st Connecticut Regiment in an expeditionary force of about five thousand troops from Connecticut, New York, and New Jersey that attacked Cuba in the spring of 1762. Although the campaign was successful from a military standpoint and resulted in capturing Havana, Putnam and his men did not fare well; between shipwreck, battle wounds, and disease, nearly four hundred of the twelve hundred men under Putnam's command died. In the fall of 1762 Putnam returned to his family at Pomfret and except for an eight-month campaign in 1764 against the Indians in Pontiac's* Conspiracy, he remained at home in Pomfret until 1772, resuming the life of a farmer.

Putnam joined the Sons of Liberty of eastern Connecticut and was active enough speaking in various towns to be brought to the attention of the British Regular Army. Several times in the interwar years he served as a town selectman, deputy to the General Assembly, and church officer, and between January and August of 1773 Putnam led a small group of men on an exploring trip up the Mississippi to survey tracts of land to be given as rewards to colonial veterans of the Seven Years' War. Despite being caused some embarrassment at having raised troops on his own volition when he accepted at face value false reports of a battle between British regulars and Massachusetts militiamen in August 1774, Putnam was named a brigadier general by the Connecticut General Assembly shortly after the Battle of Lexington and was then the third-ranking officer in the colony. His abilities and leadership potential were suffuciently known to the British that their commander in the colonies, Thomas Gage, a friend of Putnam's from the Seven Years' War, offered him the rank of major general in the British Army if he would desert the rebel cause. Putnam refused the offer and distinguished himself in several skirmishes around Boston, leading the Continental Congress in June 1775 to appoint him a major general in the Continental Army. Instrumental in planning the Battle of Bunker Hill, Putnam was the ranking field officer for part of the battle and reputedly uttered the words that have become such an important part of the popular literature of the Revolution—"Don't one of you fire until you see the white of their eyes."

After wintering with the Continental Army in Cambridge, Massachusetts, Putnam was named by George Washington* to organize the defense of New York City, and he commanded the troops there from April 4, 1776, to April 13 when Washington arrived. In the subsequent Battle of Long Island of August 27, 1776, in which the Continental Army suffered a serious defeat, Putnam was the field commander of over half the troops. Many historians have laid the blame for the American loss upon his shoulders; others have laid the blame on his co-commander in the field, Brigadier General John Sullivan,* and still others have insisted that Washington as overall commander was responsible.

Washington certainly did not blame Putnam, for he put him in command of the defenses of Philadelphia in the winter of 1776–1777 and of the troops in the Hudson Highlands north of New York City in the winter of 1777–1778. Subsequently, however, Putnam did anger Washington by failing to comply with the orders Washington sent with his aide de camp, Alexander Hamilton, during the campaign in northern New Jersey and the Hudson Highlands. In addition, complaints reached Washington from local citizens that Putnam was too lenient in granting applications for passports to Loyalists and that he delayed unnecessarily in constructing fortifications for West Point. When Putnam's wife died and he requested leave to travel to Connecticut to attend to family matters, Washington willingly replaced him in March 1778 with Major General Alexander McDougall.* Putnam never reassumed this command, but a court of inquiry exonerated him of any malfeasance.

When Putnam applied for reassignment, Washington found himself in a quandry inasmuch as he had developed reservations over Putnam's abilities as a commander and strategist. But when Charles Lee* was removed in disgrace from his position as senior major general with the main Continental Army at White Plains, New York, Washington, however reluctantly, appointed Putnam to take Lee's place. When the Army split up for the winter, Washington assigned Putnam the command of the brigades that were posted to the vicinity of Danbury, Connecticut, and in the spring he was assigned command of the right wing of the Continental Army which consisted of troops from Virginia, Maryland, and Pennsylvania. Little of major consequence happened to his wing in the campaigns of 1779, and Putnam took a leave of absence in November to return briefly to his home. In December, on his way back from leave, he suffered a stroke which partially paralyzed him and ended his military career. He lived until May 1790 and was a much revered figure and famed storyteller in retirement.

Despite his very real contribution to the Seven Years' War as a scout and ranger, his high rank in the Continental Army, his close association with many of the leading military figures of the Revolution, and his involvement in several crucial Revolutionary campaigns, Putnam's fame rests primarily on his personal virtues rather than his brilliance or importance as a military strategist and commander. Aside from Washington, no other general in the Revolutionary War figures as prominently in the folk culture as Putnam. Known variously as "Old Put," "Old Wolf Put," and "The Plowman of the Revolution," he achieved this legendary status because he was extraordinarily brave, possessed a strong sense of integrity, displayed a rare compassion for both friend and foe, and more than any other high-ranking officer in the Revolution, personified the simple yeoman so enshrined in Revolutionary mythology. These attributes made Putnam a natural subject for popular glorification both in his own lifetime and since. Untrained formally in warfare and unlettered to the point that some of his communications are nearly indecipherable because of spelling and grammatical errors, Putnam was able to inspire both men who fought under his command and the succeeding generations of patriots.

BIBLIOGRAPHY

Alden, John. *The American Revolution, 1775–1783*. New York: Harper and Row, 1954.
Callahan, North. *Connecticut's Revolutionary War Leaders*. Chester, Conn.: Pequot Press, 1973.
Larned, Ellen D. *History of Windham County, Connecticut*. 2 vols. Worcester: Privately by the Author, 1874–1880.
Livingston, William Farrand. *Israel Putnam: Pioneer, Ranger, and Major-General, 1718–1790*. New York and London: G. P. Putnam's Sons, 1905.
Putnam, Eben. *History of Putnam Family in England and America*. Salem, Mass.: Salem Press Publishing and Printing Company, 1891.
Wallace, Willard. *Appeal to Arms: A Military History of the American Revolution*. New York: Harper and Bros., 1951.

                                                                            BRUCE DANIELS